Lecture Notes in Computer Science   **11155**

Commenced Publication in 1973
Founding and Former Series Editors:
Gerhard Goos, Juris Hartmanis, and Jan van Leeuwen

More information about this series at http://www.springer.com/series/7409

Aldo Gangemi · Anna Lisa Gentile
Andrea Giovanni Nuzzolese · Sebastian Rudolph
Maria Maleshkova · Heiko Paulheim
Jeff Z. Pan · Mehwish Alam (Eds.)

The Semantic Web: ESWC 2018 Satellite Events

ESWC 2018 Satellite Events
Heraklion, Crete, Greece, June 3–7, 2018
Revised Selected Papers

 Springer

Editors
Aldo Gangemi (iD)
University of Bologna
Bologna
Italy

Maria Maleshkova
Karlsruhe Institute of Technology
Karlsruhe
Germany

Anna Lisa Gentile
IBM Research - Almaden
San Jose, CA
USA

Heiko Paulheim (iD)
University of Mannheim
Mannheim
Germany

Andrea Giovanni Nuzzolese (iD)
CNR-ISTC
Rome
Italy

Jeff Z. Pan
University of Aberdeen
Aberdeen
UK

Sebastian Rudolph (iD)
Technische Universität Dresden
Dresden
Germany

Mehwish Alam (iD)
CNR-ISTC
Rome
Italy

ISSN 0302-9743   ISSN 1611-3349   (electronic)
Lecture Notes in Computer Science
ISBN 978-3-319-98191-8   ISBN 978-3-319-98192-5   (eBook)
https://doi.org/10.1007/978-3-319-98192-5

Library of Congress Control Number: 2018950531

LNCS Sublibrary: SL3 – Information Systems and Applications, incl. Internet/Web, and HCI

This Springer imprint is published by the registered company Springer Nature Switzerland AG
The registered company address is: Gewerbestrasse 11, 6330 Cham, Switzerland

Preface

The 15th edition of ESWC took place in Heraklion, Crete (Greece), during June 3–7, 2018. The program included three keynotes by Milan Stankovic (Sépage, Paris, France), Ioana Manolescu (Inria, Paris-Saclay, Paris, France), and Sebastian Rudolph (University of Dresden, Germany). The main scientific program of the conference comprised 48 papers: 31 research, nine resource papers, eight in-use papers, selected out of 179 reviewed submissions, which corresponds to an acceptance rate of 23.5% for the research papers submitted, 41% for the resource papers, and 32% for the in-use papers. The proceedings were published by Springer as LNCS volume 10843.

This volume includes the accepted contributions to the demonstration and poster track as well as the contributions to the PhD Symposium. During the poster and demo session, the researchers had the chance to present their latest results in the form of face-to-face presentations. In all, 41 contributions, were selected out of a total of 53 submissions and 28 of the accepted ones included live demos. In addition, the PhD Symposium program included nine contributions, selected out of 17 submissions.

Nine workshops and three tutorials were held as satellite events of the conference. The three tutorials were:

- Executing Knowledge Graph Initiatives in Organizations – A Field Guide
- Music Knowledge Graph and Deep-Learning Based Recommender Systems
- How to Build a Question-Answering System Overnight

The nine workshops were:

- Second Workshop on Semantic Web Solutions for Large-Scale Biomedical Data Analytics (SeWeBMeDA)
- 4th International Workshop at ESWC on Sentic Computing, Sentiment Analysis, Opinion Mining, and Emotion Detection
- 4th International Workshop on Social Media World Sensors
- Managing the Evolution and Preservation of the Data Web – MEPDaW 2018
- Workshop on Deep Learning for Knowledge Graphs and Semantic Technologies
- Second Workshop on Querying the Web of Data – QuWeDa 2018
- Third International Workshop on Semantic Web for Cultural Heritage – SW4CH 2018
- Third Geospatial Linked Data Workshop
- Semantic Web of Things for Industry 4.0 – SWeTI

While each of the workshops had a high-quality program of its own, the organizers were asked to nominate the best papers to be included in this volume. Finally, 11 papers were selected to be included in this book. The authors improved and extended these papers based on the reviewers' feedback as well as the discussions at the workshop.

As general chair, poster and demo chairs, PhD symposium chairs and workshop chairs, we would like to thank everybody who was involved in the organization of ESWC 2018. Special thanks go to the Poster and Demo Program Committee, PhD Symposium Program Committee and to all the workshop organizers and their respective Program Committees who contributed to making the ESWC 2018 workshops a real success. We would also like to thank the Organizing Committee and especially the local organizers and the program chairs for supporting the day-to-day operation and execution of the workshops.

A special thanks also to our proceedings chair, Mehwish Alam, who did an excellent job in preparing this volume with the kind support of Springer.

June 2018

Aldo Gangemi
Anna Lisa Gentile
Andrea Giovanni Nuzzolese
Sebastian Rudolph
Maria Maleshkova
Heiko Paulheim
Jeff Z. Pan

Organization

Program Committee

Maribel Acosta	Karlsruhe Institute of Technology, Germany
Nitish Aggarwal	IBM
Asan Agibetov	Medical University of Vienna, Austria
Henning Agt-Rickauer	HPI
Mehwish Alam	Semantic Technology Lab, CNR, Italy
Céline Alec	Université Caen-Normandie, France
Intizar Ali	Insight Centre for Data Analytics, NUI, Galway, Ireland
Vito Walter Anelli	Politecnico di Bari, Italy
Grigoris Antoniou	University of Huddersfield, UK
Mihael Arcan	Insight Centre for Data Analytics NUI Galway, Ireland
Luigi Asprino	University of Bologna and STLab (ISTC-CNR), Italy
Judie Attard	Trinity College Dublin, Ireland
Martin Atzmueller	Tilburg University, The Netherlands
Sören Auer	Leibniz Information Center Science and Technology and University of Hannover, Germany
Michele Barbera	SpazioDati SRL
Payam Barnaghi	University of Surrey, UK
Caroline Barriere	CRIM
Pierpaolo Basile	University of Bari, Italy
Valerio Basile	University of Turin, Italy
Hannah Bast	University of Freiburg, Germany
Martin Becker	University of Würzburg, Germany
Wouter Beek	Vrije Universiteit Amsterdam, The Netherlands
Khalid Belhajjame	PSL, Université Paris-Dauphine, LAMSADE, France
Vito Bellini	Politecnico di Bari, Italy
Eva Blomqvist	Linköping University, Sweden
Carlos Bobed	University of Rennes 1, France
Shawn Bowers	Gonzaga University, USA
Loris Bozzato	Fondazione Bruno Kessler, Italy
Christopher Brewster	TNO
Carlos Buil Aranda	Universidad Técnica Federico Santa María, Chile
Paul Buitelaar	Insight Centre for Data Analytics, NUI Galway, Ireland
Davide Buscaldi	LIPN, Université Paris 13, Sorbonne Paris Cité, France
Elena Cabrio	Université Côte d'Azur, CNRS, Inria, I3S, France
Jean-Paul Calbimonte	University of Applied Sciences and Arts Western Switzerland HES-SO, Switzerland
Diego Calvanese	Free University of Bozen-Bolzano, Italy

Mario Cannataro	University Magna Graecia of Catanzaro, Italy
Caterina Caracciolo	Food and Agriculture Organization of the United Nations
Irene Celino	CEFRIEL, Italy
Davide Ceolin	Vrije Universiteit Amsterdam, The Netherlands
Miguel Ceriani	Queen Mary University of London, UK
Michelle Cheatham	Wright State University, USA
Christian Chiarcos	Universität Frankfurt am Main, Germany
Key-Sun Choi	Korea Advanced Institute of Science and Technology, South Korea
Diego Collarana	Enterprise Information System (EIS)
Pieter Colpaert	Ghent University, Belgium
Andrea Conte	Reply, Italy
Oscar Corcho	Universidad Politécnica de Madrid, Spain
Francesco Corcoglioniti	University of Trento, Italy
Melanie Courtot	European Bioinformatics Institute (EMBL-EBI)
Francisco Couto	University of Lisbon, Portugal
Roberta Cuel	University of Trento, Italy
Edward Curry	Insight Centre for Data Analytics, NUI Galway, Ireland
Claudia d'Amato	University of Bari, Italy
Mathieu D'Aquin	Insight Centre for Data Analytics, NUI Galway, Ireland
Aba-Sah Dadzie	The Open University
Laura M. Daniele	TNO, Netherlands Organization for Applied Scientific Research, The Netherlands
Brian Davis	Insight Centre for Data Analytics, NUI Galway, Ireland
Victor de Boer	Vrije Universiteit Amsterdam, The Netherlands
Ernesto William De Luca	Georg Eckert Institute, Leibniz Institute for International Textbook Research, Germany
Jeremy Debattista	Trinity College Dublin, Ireland
Daniele Dell'Aglio	University of Zurich, Switzerland
Emanuele Dellavalle	Politecnico di Milano, Italy
Gianluca Demartini	The University of Queensland, Australia
Tommaso Di Noia	Politecnico di Bari, Italy
Dennis Diefenbach	Jean Monet University, France
Stefan Dietze	L3S Research Center, Germany
Anastasia Dimou	Ghent University, Belgium
Christian Dirschl	Wolters Kluwer, Germany
Dejing Dou	University of Oregon, USA
Mauro Dragoni	Fondazione Bruno Kessler, Italy
Alistair Duke	BT
Anca Dumitrache	Vrije Universiteit Amsterdam, The Netherlands
Michel Dumontier	Maastricht University, The Netherlands
Floriana Esposito	Aldo Moro Bari, Italy
Ralph Ewerth	Leibniz Information Centre for Science and Technology, Germany
Nicola Fanizzi	Università degli studi di Bari Aldo Moro, Italy

Stefano Faralli	University of Mannheim, Germany
Daniel Faria	Instituto Gulbenkian de Ciência, Portugal
Catherine Faron Zucker	Université Nice Sophia Antipolis, France
Anna Fensel	Semantic Technology Institute (STI) Innsbruck, University of Innsbruck, Austria
Miriam Fernandez	Knowledge Media Institute
Javier D. Fernández	Vienna University of Economics and Business, Austria
Agata Filipowska	Poznan University of Economics, Poland
Valeria Fionda	University of Calabria, Italy
George H. L. Fletcher	Eindhoven University of Technology, The Netherlands
Giorgos Flouris	FORTH-ICS
Flavius Frasincar	Erasmus University Rotterdam
Irini Fundulaki	ICS-FORTH
Luis Galárraga	Aalborg University, Denmark
Aldo Gangemi	Università di Bologna and CNR-ISTC
Daniel Garijo	Information Sciences Institute
Anna Lisa Gentile	IBM
Alain Giboin	Inria, France
Martin Giese	University of Oslo, Norway
Rafael S. Gonçalves	Stanford University, USA
Jorge Gracia	University of Zaragoza, Spain
Irlan Grangel	University of Bonn, Germany
Michael Granitzer	University of Passau, Germany
Alasdair Gray	Heriot-Watt University, UK
Dagmar Gromann	TU Dresden, Germany
Paul Groth	Elsevier Labs
Giovanna Guerrini	University of Genova
Alessio Gugliotta	Innova
Giancarlo Guizzardi	Federal University of Espirito Santo (UFES), Brazil
Christophe Guéret	Accenture
Amelie Gyrard	Kno.e.sis, Ohio Center of Excellence in Knowledge-enabled Computing, USA
Peter Haase	metaphacts
Lavdim Halilaj	Fraunhofer
Siegfried Handschuh	University of Passau, Germany
Andreas Harth	University of Erlangen-Nuremberg, Germany
Olaf Hartig	Linköping University, Sweden
Oktie Hassanzadeh	IBM
Jörn Hees	TU Kaiserslautern and DFKI
Sven Hertling	Uni Mannheim
Daniel Hienert	Leibniz Institute for the Social Sciences, Germany
Pascal Hitzler	Wright State University, USA
Robert Hoehndorf	King Abdullah University of Science and Technology, Suadi Arabia
Rinke Hoekstra	University of Amsterdam, The Netherlands
Aidan Hogan	DCC, Universidad de Chile, Chile

Laura Hollink	CWI
Anett Hoppe	Leibniz Information Centre for Science and Technology, Germany
Matthew Horridge	Stanford University, USA
Tomas Horvath	Eötvös Loránd University, Hungary
Katja Hose	Aalborg University, Denmark
Andreas Hotho	University of Würzburg, Germany
Zhisheng Huang	Vrije Universiteit Amsterdam, The Netherlands
Antoine Isaac	Europeana and VU University Amsterdam, The Netherlands
Ashutosh Jadhav	IBM
Valentina Janev	The Mihajlo Pupin Institute, Serbia
Krzysztof Janowicz	University of California, Santa Barbara, USA
Ernesto Jimenez-Ruiz	The Alan Turing Institute
Anna Jordanous	University of Kent, UK
Simon Jupp	European Bioinformatics Institute
Martin Kaltenböck	Semantic Web Company
Naouel Karam	Fraunhofer
Anna Kaspzik	Technische Informationsbibliothek
Tomi Kauppinen	Aalto University School of Science, Finland
Takahiro Kawamura	Japan Science and Technology Agency, Japan
Ali Khalili	Vrije Universiteit Amsterdam, The Netherlands
Evgeny Kharlamov	University of Oxford, UK
Sabrina Kirrane	Vienna University of Economics and Business, Austria
Tomas Kliegr	University of Economics, Prague, Czech Republic
Roman Kontchakov	Birkbeck, University of London, UK
Maria Koutraki	FIZ Karlsruhe, KIT, Germany
Kouji Kozaki	Osaka University, Germany
Adila A. Krisnadhi	Wright State University and Universitas Indonesia
Sebastian Köhler	Institut für Medizinische Genetik, Charite Universitätsmedizin Berlin, Germany
Christoph Lange	University of Bonn and Fraunhofer IAIS, Germany
Mike Lauruhn	Elsevier
Agnieszka Lawrynowicz	Poznan University of Technology, Poland
Danh Le Phuoc	TU Berlin, Germany
Maxime Lefrançois	MINES Saint-Etienne, France
Jens Lehmann	University of Bonn, Germany
Steffen Lohmann	Fraunhofer
Vanessa Lopez	IBM
Phillip Lord	Newcastle University, UK
Ismini Lourentzou	University of Illinois at Urbana - Champaign, USA
Bertram Ludaescher	University of Illinois at Urbana-Champaign, USA
Ioanna Lytra	Enterprise Information Systems, Applied Computer Science, University of Bonn, Germany
Valentina Maccatrozzo	Vrije Universiteit Amsterdam, The Netherlands
Christian Mader	Fraunhofer

Veronique Malaise	Elsevier BV
Maria Maleshkova	Karlsruhe Institute of Technology, Germany
Alessandro Margara	Politecnico di Milano, Italy
Nicolas Matentzoglu	EMBL-EBI
Diana Maynard	The University of Sheffield, UK
John P. McCrae	National University of Ireland, Galway, Ireland
Fiona McNeill	Heriot Watt University, UK
Edgar Meij	Bloomberg L.P.
Albert Meroño-Peñuela	Vrije Universiteit Amsterdam, The Netherlands
Aditya Mogadala	Karlsruhe Institute of Technology, Germany
Pascal Molli	University of Nantes, LS2N, France
Stefano Montanelli	University of Milan, Italy
Steven Moran	University of Zurich, Switzerland
Till Mossakowski	University of Magdeburg, Germany
Andreas Mueller	Schaeffler Technologies AG
Raghava Mutharaju	GE Global Research
Roberto Navigli	Sapienza University of Rome, Italy
Axel-Cyrille Ngonga Ngomo	Paderborn University, Germany
Vinh Nguyen	National Library of Medicine, NIH, USA
Andriy Nikolov	metaphacts GmbH
Lyndon Nixon	MODUL Technology GmbH
Vit Novacek	DERI, National University of Ireland, Galway, Ireland
Andrea Giovanni Nuzzolese	University of Bologna, Italy
Leo Obrst	MITRE
Fabrizio Orlandi	University of Bonn, Germany
Francesco Osborne	The Open University
Petya Osenova	Sofia University and IICT-BAS, Bulgaria
Guillermo Palma	Universidad Simón Bolívar, Venezuela
Matteo Palmonari	University of Milano-Bicocca, Italy
Themis Palpanas	Paris Descartes University, France
Jeff Z. Pan	University of Aberdeen, UK
Adrian Paschke	Freie Universität Berlin, Germany
Michele Pasin	Nature Publishing Group
Tommaso Pasini	Sapienza University of Rome, Italy
Pankesh Patel	Frauenhofer CESE, USA
Heiko Paulheim	University of Mannheim, Germany
Tassilo Pellegrini	University of Applied Sciences St. Pölten
Silvio Peroni	University of Bologna, Italy
Catia Pesquita	Universidade de Lisboa, Portugal
Rafael Peñaloza	Free University of Bozen-Bolzano, Italy
Hsofia Pinto	Algos, INESC-ID/IST, Portugal
Giuseppe Pirrò	Institute for High Performance Computing and Networking (ICAR-CNR), Italy
Antonella Poggi	Sapienza University of Rome, Italy
Axel Polleres	Vienna University of Economics and Business, Austria

Jedrzej Potoniec	Poznan University of Technology, Poland
María Poveda-Villalón	Universidad Politécnica de Madrid, Spain
Valentina Presutti	CNR, Institute of Cognitive Sciences and Technologies, Italy
Freddy Priyatna	Universidad Politécnica de Madrid, Spain
Gustavo Publio	AKSW/KILT, Universität Leipzig, Germany
Dharmen Punjani	National and Kapodistrian University of Athens, Greece
Guilin Qi	Southeast University
Steffen Remus	University of Hamburg, Germany
Achim Rettinge	Karlsruhe Institute of Technology, Germany
Martin Rezk	Rakuten
Martin Riedl	University of Stuttgart, Germany
Petar Ristoski	IBM Research-Almaden
Carlos R. Rivero	Rochester Institute of Technology, USA
Giuseppe Rizzo	ISMB
Víctor Rodríguez Doncel	Universidad Politécnica de Madrid, Spain
Mariano Rodríguez Muro	IBM
Francesco Ronzano	Universitat Pompeu Fabra, Barcelona
Ana Roxin	University of Burgundy, UMR CNRS 6306, France
Edna Ruckhaus	Universidad Politécnica de Madrid, Spain
Sebastian Rudolph	TU Dresden, Germany
Anisa Rula	University of Milano-Bicocca, Italy
Alessandro Russo	STLab, ISTC-CNR
Michele Ruta	Politecnico di Bari, Italy
Harald Sack	FIZ Karlsruhe, Leibniz Institute for Information Infrastructure and KIT Karlsruhe, Germany
Satya Sahoo	Case Western Reserve University, USA
Idafen Santana-Pérez	Universidad Politécnica de Madrid, Spain
Cristina Sarasua	University of Zurich, Switzerland
Felix Sasaki	Lambdawerk
Kai-Uwe Sattler	TU Ilmenau, Germany
Marco Luca Sbodio	IBM
Ralf Schenkel	Trier University, Germany
Stefan Schlobach	Vrije Universiteit Amsterdam, The Netherlands
Michael Schmidt	Amazon
Jodi Schneider	University of Illinois Urbana Champaign, USA
Juan F. Sequeda	Capsenta Labs
Barış Sertkaya	Frankfurt University of Applied Sciences, Germany
Nicolas Seydoux	LAAS-CNRS/IRIT
Hamed Shariat Yazdi	University of Bonn, Germany
Chaitanya Shivade	IBM
Pavel Shvaiko	Informatica Trentina
Mantas Simkus	Vienna University of Technology, Austria
Kuldeep Singh	Fraunhofer
Hala Skaf	Nantes University, France

Jennifer Sleeman	University of Maryland Baltimore County, USA
Monika Solanki	University of Oxford, UK
Steffen Staab	Institut WeST, University Koblenz-Landau, Germany; WAIS, University of Southampton, UK
Timo Stegemann	University of Duisburg-Essen, Germany
Thomas Steiner	Google
Armando Stellato	University of Rome Tor Vergata, Italy
Daria Stepanova	Max Planck Institute for Informatics, Germany
Sandra Stincic Clarke	BT Technology, Service and Operations
Markus Stocker	German National Library of Science and Technology, Germany
Umberto Straccia	ISTI-CNR
Olga Streibel	Bayer
York Sure-Vetter	Karlsruhe Institute of Technology, Germany
Mari Carmen Suárez-Figueroa	Universidad Politécnica de Madrid, Spain
Vojtěch Svátek	University of Economics, Prague, Czech Republic
Danai Symeonidou	INRA
Ruben Taelman	Ghent University, Belgium
Hideaki Takeda	National Institute of Informatics, Japan
Harsh Thakkar	University of Bonn, Germany
Krishnaprasad Thirunarayan	Wright State University, USA
Steffen Thoma	Karlsruhe Institute of Technology, Germany
Ilaria Tiddi	The Open University
Tabea Tietz	FIZ Karlsruhe, Germany
Riccardo Tommasini	Politecnico di Milano, Italy
Anna Tordai	Elsevier
Ignacio Traverso-Rebon	Karlsruhe Institute of Technology, Germany
Cassia Trojahn	UT2J and IRIT
Raphaël Troncy	EURECOM
Jürgen Umbrich	Vienna University of Economy and Business (WU), Austria
Ricardo Usbeck	Paderborn University, Germany
Astrid van Aggelen	CWI, The Netherlands
Marieke van Erp	KNAW Humanities Cluster
Jacco van Ossenbruggen	CWI and VU University Amsterdam, The Netherlands
Ruben Verborgh	Ghent University, Belgium
Maria Esther Vidal	Universidad Simon Bolivar, Venezuela
Maria-Esther Vidal	Leibniz Information Centre, Germany
Serena Villata	CNRS, Laboratoire d'Informatique, Signaux et Systèmes de Sophia-Antipolis, France
Simon Walk	Graz University of Technology, Austria
Sebastian Walter	Semalytix GmbH
Haofen Wang	Shenzhen Gowild Robotics Co. Ltd
Kewen Wang	Griffith University, Australia
Krzysztof Wecel	Poznan University of Economics, Poland

Trish Whetzel	EMBL-EBI/T2 Labs
Josiane Xavier Parreira	Siemens AG Österreich, Austria
Guohui Xiao	KRDB Research Centre, Free University of Bozen-Bolzano, Italy
Chenyan Xiong	Carnegie Mellon University, USA
Takahira Yamaguchi	Keio University, Japan
Ondřej Zamazal	University of Economics, Prague, Czech Republic
Amrapali Zaveri	Maastricht University, The Netherlands
Lei Zhang	Karlsruhe Institute of Technology, Germany
Ziqi Zhang	Sheffield University, UK
Jun Zhao	University of Oxford, UK
Antoine Zimmermann	École des Mines de Saint-Étienne, France
Daniel Zoller	University of Würzburg, Germany

Additional Reviewers

Agapito, Giuseppe
Arcan, Mihael
Bader, Sebastian
Bakkelund, Daniel
Barros, Márcia
Basile, Pierpaolo
Bin, Simon
Brosius, Dominik
Calabrese, Barbara
Chakravarthi, Bharathi Raja
Corman, Julien
d'Amato, Claudia
de Graaf, Klaas Andries
Ding, Linfang
Elias, Mirette
Fafalios, Pavlos
Ferreira, João
Fischl, Wolfgang
Gaignard, Alban
Galliani, Pietro
Galárraga, Luis
Ghiasnezhadomran, Pouya
Güzel, Elem
Ibrahim, Yusra
Idrissou, Al
Janke, Daniel
Jurgovsky, Johannes
Karlsen, Leif Harald

Klungre, Vidar
Lamurias, Andre
Lohr, Matthias
Malone, James
Matentzoglu, Nicolas
Milano, Marianna
Mireles, Victor
Monti, Diego
Montoya, Gabriela
Moodley, Kody
Mousavi Nejad, Najmeh
Müller-Budack, Eric
Nayyeri, Mojtaba
Neuhaus, Fabian
Nooralahzadeh, Farhad
Pandit, Harshvardhan Jitendra
Paudel, Bibek
Peñaloza, Rafael
Potoniec, Jedrzej
Revenko, Artem
Ringsquandl, Martin
Rizzo, Giuseppe
Rula, Anisa
Sadeghi, Afshin
Saha Roy, Rishiraj
Savkovic, Ognjen
Schlötterer, Jörg
Schmelzeisen, Lukas

Skjæveland, Martin G.
Sousa, Diana
Spahiu, Blerina
Springstein, Matthias
Steinmetz, Nadine
Sun, Chang
van Soest, Johan
Weller, Tobias

Westphal, Patrick
Wilke, Adrian
Zayed, Omnia
Zhou, Lu
Zhou, Qianru
Zhu, Rui
Zucco, Chiara

Contents

3rd Workshop on Geospatial Linked Data

**4th Workshop on Sentic Computing, Sentiment Analysis,
Opinion Mining, and Emotion Detection**

2nd Workshop on Querying the Web of Data

4th Workshop on Social Media World Sensors

Poster and Demo Papers

Finding Unexplainable Triples
in an RDF Graph

Jedrzej Potoniec[(⊠)]

Faculty of Computing, Poznan University of Technology,
ul. Piotrowo 3, 60-965 Poznan, Poland
Jedrzej.Potoniec@cs.put.poznan.pl

Abstract. We consider how to select a subgraph of an RDF graph in an ontology learning problem in order to avoid learning redundant axioms. We propose to address this by selecting RDF triples that can not be inferred using a reasoner and we present an algorithm to find them.

Keywords: Ontology learning · Explanation · RDF · OWL 2 RL

1   Introduction

Consider the following ontology learning problem: given an RDF graph and an ontology describing it, extend the ontology with new axioms, that inductively follow from the data. One of the possible pitfalls of an algorithm solving this problem is generating variants of an axiom already present in the ontology. If such a variant does not deductively follow the ontology, then the user must deal with the resulting redundancy. We postulate that the ontology in the ontology learning problem is a hypothesis, as understood in inductive reasoning, and so we expect it to explain some parts of the graph. It follows that to extend the ontology, one must concentrate on the triples that are not explained. We thus consider the following problem: how to select a subset of triples from the graph that are not explained by the ontology and thus provide new knowledge, which can be generalized and represented as new axioms in the ontology.

The contributions of the paper are as follows: (i) we introduce the notions of unexplained and unexplainable triples; (ii) we propose two algorithms to identify unexplainable triples. We use the following notation conventions: RDF triples are presented in Turtle syntax [2], while OWL axioms are expressed in Manchester syntax [4]. We use $\models$ to denote deductive inference, i.e. $\mathcal{O} \models \{t\}$ means that a triple t deductively follows from an ontology $\mathcal{O}$.

2   Unexplained and Unexplainable Triples

Consider an RDF graph consisting of the following two triples (expressed in Turtle syntax): {:rex a :Dog, :Animal.} and an ontology consisting of a single axiom {:Dog SubClassOf: :Animal}. We observe that the triple :rex a

© Springer Nature Switzerland AG 2018
A. Gangemi et al. (Eds.): ESWC 2018 Satellite Events, LNCS 11155, pp. 3–7, 2018.
https://doi.org/10.1007/978-3-319-98192-5_1

:`Animal`. in the sample graph is explained by the ontology, i.e., even if removed from the graph it can be restored using deductive inference. Conversely, the other triple could not be restored if removed, and thus represents new knowledge.

Definition 1. *Given an RDF graph $\mathcal{G}$ and an ontology $\mathcal{O}$, an* unexplained part *$\mathcal{G}_{\bar{\varepsilon}}$ is a subgraph of $\mathcal{G}$ such that: (i) it is sufficient to restore the rest of the graph: $\mathcal{O} \cup \mathcal{G}_{\bar{\varepsilon}} \models \mathcal{G}\backslash\mathcal{G}_{\bar{\varepsilon}}$; (ii) no triple from it can be restored if removed: $\forall t \in \mathcal{G}_{\bar{\varepsilon}}: \mathcal{O} \cup \mathcal{G}\backslash\mathcal{G}_{\bar{\varepsilon}} \not\models \{t\}$; (iii) it is subset-minimal, i.e., none of its proper subset has both properties. We call the remaining part of the graph an* explained part *and denote by $\mathcal{G}_{\varepsilon} = \mathcal{G}\backslash\mathcal{G}_{\bar{\varepsilon}}$.*

It is easy to observe that there may be multiple unexplained parts in a single graph. Consider $\mathcal{G} = \{: \mathtt{rex\ a}\ : \mathtt{Dog},\ : \mathtt{MansBestFriend}.\}$ and $\mathcal{O} = \{: \mathtt{Dog}$ EQUIVALENTTO: $:\mathtt{MansBestFriend}\}$. There exists two different unexplained parts: $\mathcal{G}_{\bar{\varepsilon}}^{(1)} = \{: \mathtt{rex\ a}\ : \mathtt{Dog}.\}$ and $\mathcal{G}_{\bar{\varepsilon}}^{(2)} = \{: \mathtt{rex\ a}\ : \mathtt{MansBestFriend}.\}$. Due to this, for the ontology learning problem, the usability of a single unexplained part is of limited use. Instead, we propose to consider a set of unexplainable triples, as defined below.

Definition 2. *Given an ontology $\mathcal{O}$ and an RDF graph $\mathcal{G}$, the set of* unexplainable triples *is the intersection of all possible sets of unexplained triples: $\bigcap_i \mathcal{G}_{\bar{\varepsilon}}^{(i)}$, where i iterates over all possible unexplained parts of the graph.*

These triples are the most interesting triples for learning new axioms, as they necessarily contain new knowledge, which is not explained by the ontology.

Theorem 1. *A triple t is unexplainable if, and only if, once removed from a graph it can not be restored using deductive inference.*

$$\forall t \in \mathcal{G}: \left(\mathcal{O} \cup \mathcal{G}\backslash\{t\} \not\models \{t\} \iff t \in \bigcap_i \mathcal{G}_{\bar{\varepsilon}}^{(i)} \right)$$

Proof. Assume there exists a triple t such that $\mathcal{O} \cup \mathcal{G}\backslash\{t\} \not\models \{t\}$, but $t \notin \bigcap_i \mathcal{G}_{\bar{\varepsilon}}^{(i)}$. It follows that there exists j such that $t \notin \mathcal{G}_{\bar{\varepsilon}}^{(j)}$ and from Definition 1 we get $\mathcal{O} \cup \mathcal{G}_{\bar{\varepsilon}}^{(j)} \models \{t\}$. As $\mathcal{G}_{\bar{\varepsilon}}^{(j)} \subseteq \mathcal{G}\backslash\{t\}$, from the monotonicity of reasoning, we conclude that $\mathcal{O} \cup \mathcal{G}\backslash\{t\} \models \{t\}$, contradicting the assumption.

Now assume that there exists a triple t such that $t \in \bigcap_i \mathcal{G}_{\bar{\varepsilon}}^{(i)}$, but $\mathcal{O} \cup \mathcal{G}\backslash\{t\} \models \{t\}$. From Definition 1 it follows that there exists j such that $t \in \mathcal{G}_{\varepsilon}^{(j)}$ and $t \notin \mathcal{G}_{\bar{\varepsilon}}^{(j)}$, but this contradicts the assumption.

Using Theorem 1, we can construct a naïve algorithm for computing the set of unexplainable triples by iterating over the graph, and for each triple checking whether the left-hand side of the theorem holds. While correct, such an algorithm is impractical due to its complexity and so we consider a special case of OWL 2 RL to construct a more practical algorithm.

3   Unexplainable Triples in OWL 2 RL

Using De Morgan's laws it follows from Theorem 1 that a triple can be restored iff it belongs to at least one set of explained triples: $\forall t \in \mathcal{G}: (\mathcal{O} \cup \mathcal{G}\backslash\{t\} \models \{t\}$ $\Longleftrightarrow t \in \bigcup_i \mathcal{G}_\varepsilon^{(i)})$ We can use this to construct an algorithm suitable for OWL 2 RL [6]. Assume that $\mathcal{O}$ is a consistent OWL 2 RL ontology and $\mathcal{G}$ is an RDF graph closed w.r.t. logical conclusions following from the ontology and the graph, i.e., there is no such triple t that $t \notin \mathcal{G}$, but $\mathcal{O} \cup \mathcal{G} \models \{t\}$. As deductive inference in OWL 2 RL can be realized using a set of rules, it follows that a triple t can be restored if, and only if, there exists a rule $P \to C$ such that for some assignment σ of RDF nodes to the variables of the rule: (i) all its premises and conclusions are present in the graph: $\sigma(P) \subseteq \mathcal{G}, \sigma(C) \subseteq \mathcal{G}$; (ii) t is in the conclusions: $t \in \sigma(C)$; (iii) t is not in the premises: $t \notin \sigma(P)$. By rewriting all the rules as SPARQL SELECT queries and answering them over the graph, we obtain all the triples that can be restored, and by subtracting them from the graph, we arrive at the set of unexplainable triples.

Consider $\mathcal{G} = \{: \texttt{rex a : Dog.}\}$ and $\mathcal{O} = \{:\texttt{Dog} \text{ SUBCLASSOF}: :\texttt{Animal}\}$, and let $\mathcal{G}' = \{t: \mathcal{O} \cup \mathcal{G} \models \{t\}\}$ be the graph closed w.r.t. the ontology. Consider the rule $cax\text{-}sco^1$: If T(?c1, rdfs:subClassOf, ?c2) *and* T(?x, rdf:type, ?c1) *then* T(?x, rdf:type, ?c2). Each of the literals in the rule corresponds to a SPARQL triple pattern, so the corresponding query can be written as follows: SELECT (?x AS ?subject) (rdf:type AS ?predicate) (?c2 AS ?object) WHERE {?c1 rdfs:subClassOf ?c2. ?x a ?c1, ?c2. FILTER(?c1!=?c2)} The answer to the query w.r.t. $\mathcal{G}'$ contains the triple :rex a :Animal. Should there be no filter clause in the query, it would also contain the triple :rex a :Dog., making the triple self-explanatory.

Some additional consideration must be given to the rules that require checking a variable number of premises, i.e., *prp-spo2*, *prp-key*, *cls-int1*. For them, we must make an assumption about the maximal length of the premises, e.g. by analyzing the axioms in the ontology and generating an appropriate queries in the run-time. Algorithm 1 presents a complete algorithm for computing the set of unexplainable triples. A proof of concept implementation is available at https://github.com/jpotoniec/UnexplainedTriples.

4   Related Work

The considered problem is rooted in the research on ontology learning. Multiple setups of the problem were considered, e.g. Lehmann et al. proposed a supervised learning framework DL-Learner and adapted it for ontology engineering [7]; Potoniec et al. developed Swift Linked Data Miner (SLDM) suitable for mining OWL 2 EL class hierarchy from a SPARQL endpoint [8].

The problem at hand is also closely related to the problem of providing a justification for an entailment, i.e. a minimal subset of axioms for the entailment

---

[1] The rules and their names from [6], Sect. 4.3.

Algorithm 1: Computing the set of unexplained triples given a OWL 2 RL ontology $\mathcal{O}$ and an RDF graph $\mathcal{G}$ closed w.r.t. the ontology. $Q_{\mathcal{O}}$ is the set of all SPARQL SELECT queries corresponding to the inference rules of OWL 2 RL w.r.t. the ontology $\mathcal{O}$ and $ANS(q, \mathcal{G})$ is the set of answers to the query q w.r.t. the graph $\mathcal{G}$.

$T \leftarrow \emptyset$
forall the $q \in Q_{\mathcal{O}}$ **do**
$\quad | \quad T \leftarrow T \cup ANS(q; \mathcal{G})$
end
return $\mathcal{G} \backslash T$

to hold, as considered by Horridge et al. [5]. In this work we are interested rather in detecting the parts of a graph that lack any justification. The problem can be also seen as a ontology modularization/segmentation problem, discussed e.g. by Seidenberg and Rector [9] or d'Aquin et al. [3]. It can also be seen as an inverse of the ontology completion problem, as defined by Baader et al. [1].

5   Conclusions

In this paper we introduced the notion of explained and unexplained triples, as a problem arising from selecting an appropriate subgraph of an RDF graph for ontology learning. We then used it to construct the set of unexplained triples for a given graph and demonstrated how such a set can be computed. Finally, we provide a proof of concept implementation of the presented algorithm. In the future, we plan to integrate the results with SLDM to measure their impact on the actual learning problem.

Acknowledgement. We acknowledge the support from the grant 09/91/DSPB/0627.

References

1. Baader, F., et al.: Completing description logic knowledge bases using formal concept analysis. In: Veloso, M.M. (ed.) IJCAI 2007, Proceedings of the 20th International Joint Conference on AI, pp. 230–235 (2007). http://ijcai.org/Proceedings/07/Papers/035.pdf
2. Carothers, G., Prud'hommeaux, E.: RDF 1.1 turtle. W3C recommendation, W3C, February 2014. http://www.w3.org/TR/2014/REC-turtle-20140225/
3. d'Aquin, M., et al.: Modularization: a key for the dynamic selection of relevant knowledge components. In: Haase, P., et al. (eds.) Proceedings of WoMO 2006, vol. 232. CEUR-WS.org (2006). http://ceur-ws.org/Vol-232/paper2.pdf
4. Horridge, M., Patel-Schneider, P.: OWL 2 web ontology language manchester syntax, 2nd edn. W3C note, W3C, December 2012. http://www.w3.org/TR/2012/NOTE-owl2-manchester-syntax-20121211/
5. Horridge, M., et al.: Toward cognitive support for OWL justifications. Knowl.-Based Syst. **53**, 66–79 (2013). https://doi.org/10.1016/j.knosys.2013.08.021
6. Horrocks, I., et al.: OWL 2 web ontology language profiles, 2nd edn. W3C recommendation, W3C, December 2012. http://www.w3.org/TR/2012/REC-owl2-profiles-20121211/

7. Lehmann, J., et al.: Class expression learning for ontology engineering. J. Web Sem. **9**(1), 71–81 (2011). https://doi.org/10.1016/j.websem.2011.01.001
8. Potoniec, J., et al.: Swift linked data miner: mining OWL 2 EL class expressions directly from online RDF datasets. J. Web Sem. **46**, 31–50 (2017). https://doi.org/10.1016/j.websem.2017.08.001
9. Seidenberg, J., Rector, A.L.: Web ontology segmentation: analysis, classification and use. In: Carr, L., et al. (eds.) Proceedings of WWW 2006, pp. 13–22. ACM (2006). http://doi.acm.org/10.1145/1135777.1135785

ATU-DSS: Knowledge-Driven Data Integration and Reasoning for Sustainable Subsurface Inter-asset Management

Lijun Wei[1(✉)], Heshan Du[1,2], Quratul-ain Mahesar[1], Barry Clarke[3], Derek R. Magee[1], Vania Dimitrova[1], David Gunn[4], David Entwisle[4], Helen Reeves[4], and Anthony G. Cohn[1]

[1] School of Computing, University of Leeds, Leeds, UK
l.j.wei@leeds.ac.uk
[2] School of Computer Science, University of Nottingham Ningbo China, Ningbo, China
[3] School of Civil Engineering, University of Leeds, Leeds, UK
[4] British Geological Survey, Nottingham, UK

Abstract. Urban infrastructure assets perform critical functions to the health and well-being of the society. In this paper, we present a prototype decision support system for sustainable subsurface inter-asset management. To the best of the authors' knowledge, this work is the first on assessing the underground space by considering the inter-asset dependencies using semantic technologies. Based on a family of interlinked city infrastructure asset ontologies describing the ground, roads and buried utilities (e.g. water pipes), various datasets are integrated and logical rules are developed to describe the intra-asset and inter-asset relationships. An inference engine is employed to exploit the knowledge and data for assessing the potential impact of an event. This system can be beneficial to a wide range of stakeholders (e.g. utility incident managers) for quickly gathering of the localised contextual data and identifying potential consequences from what may appear as an insignificant trigger. A video demonstrating the prototype is available at: http://bit.ly/2mdyIY4.

Keywords: Semantic technologies · Ontologies
Decision support system · Subsurface infrastructure
Sustainable streetworks

1 Introduction

The Assessing The Underworld (ATU) project[1] is a large interdisciplinary UK research programme that aims to address the challenges in sustainable management and maintenance of city infrastructure assets, especially how to reduce the

---

Quratul-ain Mahesar is now at the University of Aberdeen; her contribution to this paper was performed whilst employed at the University of Leeds.

[1] http://assessingtheunderworld.org/.

© Springer Nature Switzerland AG 2018
A. Gangemi et al. (Eds.): ESWC 2018 Satellite Events, LNCS 11155, pp. 8–13, 2018.
https://doi.org/10.1007/978-3-319-98192-5_2

economic, social and environmental costs/impact of streetworks. It is estimated that the direct costs of streetworks to local authorities are about £50M/year in the UK[2]. A consultation meeting with stakeholders (local authorities, utility companies of water/gas/electricity/sewage/communications, asset managers, traffic managers, consultants, contractors, ground engineers, testing houses) was organized at the start of the ATU project and several key challenges to sustainable streetworks in practice were identified: urban infrastructure assets, such as roads, ground and subsurface utilities are maintained by different stakeholders who plan and conduct streetworks independently; relevant infrastructure data is held by different owners and difficult to gather in a short period of time; moreover, lack of the knowledge of dependencies between different infrastructure assets makes it difficult for decision makers from one sector to consider the impact/damage of their actions on other nearby infrastructure assets [1]. For example, breaking up or opening a road can damage the ground and the buried utilities [6]. A leaking water pipe can erode the surrounding ground, leading to loss of support to the overlying road and eventually causing road collapse [1].

In order to address these challenges, we present a prototype decision support system (**A**ssessing **T**he **U**nderworld **D**ecision **S**upport **S**ystem or **ATU-DSS**) for subsurface inter-asset management using semantic technologies. It can assist practitioners (e.g. junior engineers) in making decisions about the impact of a trigger (e.g. planned works, loss of water pressure) with respect to its localised contextual data and its influence on different infrastructure assets. While semantic approaches have been used to manage infrastructure in several projects[3], this paper gives insights into the exploitation of semantic technologies in a new domain with high economic and societal importance - the underground world.

In the following sections, we first describe the system architecture of the ATU-DSS (Sect. 2). We then provide a general description of the demo from a user's perspective (Sect. 3).

2 System Components of the ATU-DSS

At the heart of the ATU-DSS is an integrated knowledge model of urban infrastructure assets, which was developed by consulting with domain experts (e.g. civil engineers, geotechnical engineers, geophysicists) in the project and extensively reviewing literature. This knowledge model consists of several interlinked modular ontologies which are referred to as *ATU ontologies*. The *ATU City Infrastructure Asset Ontologies* [2,3] define the properties and processes of the ground, roads and buried utilities (publicly available at https://doi.org/10.5518/190). The *ATU Trigger Ontology* defines the categories and properties of events (e.g. *WaterPipeObservation_LossOfPressure*) that require some decisions to be made in subsurface infrastructure asset management [1]. The *ATU Investigation*

---

[2] Asphalt Industry Alliance (2017) Annual Local Authority Road Maintenance.

[3] *INTERLINK*: https://roadotl.geosolutions.nl/; *Coinsweb* (Construction Objects and the INtegration of Processes and Systems): http://www.coinsweb.nl/.

Ontology encodes the knowledge of the available geophysical techniques for measuring different asset properties in shallow (0–5 m depth) streetworks surveys. The *ATU Environment Ontology* models the environment factors (e.g. rainfall, drought) affecting or being affected by the infrastructure assets based on several existing external ontologies (e.g. NASA's SWEET Ontology[4], the Environment Ontology[5], Ordnance Survey's Buildings and Places Ontology[6]). The ATU ontologies provide a common vocabulary for defining inference rules and integrating various datasets such that heterogeneous data can be used together in automated reasoning. For example, a rule *"Heavy and Long rainfall will infiltrate the road if the road crack penetrates the road surface."* is defined referring to the concepts in the *Environment Ontology* and the *Road Ontology* (see Fig. 2a), written as: *"EnvironmentRainfallIntensity (Heavy) + EnvironmentRainfallDuration (Long) + RoadCrackingDepth (High)* $\xrightarrow{(definite)}$ *RoadWaterInfiltration (Active)"*. Three scenarios have been considered when defining rules: rainfall with road cracking, pipe leakage and traffic overloading. The rule engine *Jess*[7] is used for rule development and reasoning, due to scalability reasons, since the reasoning performance of *Jess* depends not much on the number of rules/facts but on the number of partial matches generated by *Jess*. The ATU-DSS is designed using three-tier architecture consisting of a data layer, an application layer and an interface layer. The data layer consists of the ATU ontologies and real-world datasets. Informed by the ATU ontologies, several datasets were sourced from different data owners, including the historic meteorological data (e.g. rainfall, temperature.)[8], the road and historic traffic data[9], the information of buried utilities (e.g. pipe location, age)[10], the ground condition data from British Geological Survey (BGS) and local councils, as well as the information of sensitive population and services (e.g. hospitals, schools) from OpenStreetMap (OSM). Data on the local server is managed by a PostgreSQL database for its advanced support to geo-spatial calculation with PostGIS. OSM data is fetched on-demand with an API. The data layers are mapped to corresponding ontology concepts based on a predefined correspondence table. Some of them can be mapped directly, for example, the "BGS Depth to Groundwater Dataset" is mapped directly to the *GroundWaterTableDepth* concept in the *Ground Ontology*. Other data layers need preprocessing before being linked to ontology concepts. For example, rainfall duration is calculated based on the historical data from nearby weather stations and then mapped to the *EnvironmentRainfallDuration* concept. Currently, all these correspondences are manually defined to guarantee their correctness.

---

[4] https://sweet.jpl.nasa.gov/.

[5] http://environmentontology.org/.

[6] http://bit.ly/2Fq5u0F.

[7] http://www.jessrules.com/jess/docs/71/.

[8] Met Office Integrated Data Archive System (MIDAS) Land and Marine Surface Stations Data (1853-current). For a trigger, the 30-day weather data up to the occurrence day of this trigger is retrieved, displayed and used for analysis.

[9] UK Department for Transport (DfT) Traffic Statistics (updated annually).

[10] Data in testing regions were sourced from different utility companies.

We are also working towards automating the matching process by employing existing ontology matching techniques [4].

The application layer is built on the data layer and could suggest potential impacts of a trigger through automated reasoning. The user interface layer is accessible through a standard web browser, which allows decision makers to interact with the DSS such as reporting new triggers, viewing retrieved localised data and examining the inferencing results. The web framework is written with *Python Django (HTML/CSS/Javascript)* and *Geoserver* is used to provide web mapping services.

3   Demonstration of the ATU-DSS

This section will demonstrate how to use the ATU-DSS step by step. A video demonstrating the prototype is available at: http://bit.ly/2mdyIY4, using real data from a sinkhole happened in Manchester (UK) which caused a major disruption. As shown in Fig. 1a, the working procedure of ATU-DSS starts with a report of triggers (defined in the *ATU Trigger Ontology*) through the web interface. Each trigger is attached with a spatial geometry and should be provided by users. Then, the localised contextual data of a reported trigger is automatically retrieved based on its occurrence location and time. The retrieved data is displayed on the user interface and fed into the rule engine for automated reasoning of potential consequences. The uncertainty of facts and rules are also propagated during the reasoning process [5]. Once this process finishes, potential consequences are identified from the inferred facts and presented to users according to their estimated severity and likelihood. The system also gives explanations of potential consequences in the form of text and diagram[11] (e.g. Fig. 2b).

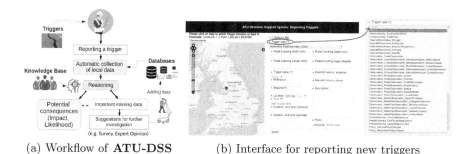

(a) Workflow of **ATU-DSS**   (b) Interface for reporting new triggers

Fig. 1. Workflow of the **ATU-DSS** (left); the interface for reporting triggers (©OSM)

By explaining and visualizing to users the reasoning process of arriving at a particular consequence, the system can help users make a more reasonable and informed decision. In the ATU-DSS, in cases where real data is missing

---

[11] The diagrams are automatically generated with a python package of Graphviz.

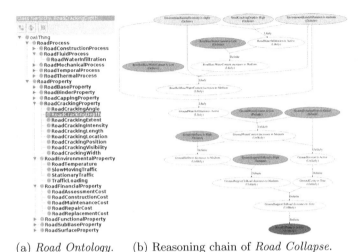

(a) *Road Ontology.*   (b) Reasoning chain of *Road Collapse.*

Fig. 2. Road ontology and graphic view of the reasoning chain of *RoadCollapse.*

(i.e. default values under worst case assumption are used) in the reasoning process [5], the system will not only remind users of the missing data but also suggest suitable investigation techniques to get the missing data (based on the *ATU Investigation Ontology*). Users can choose to accept the default value or add/update data after some investigation. When new data is added/updated, the whole reasoning process automatically re-activates. The system records which user makes a modification so that the provenance of all data is recorded. The justifications and the ability for users to see how modifying assumptions lead to different consequences can again help users make a more reasonable decision.

4   Conclusion and Future Work

In this work, we presented a prototype of a knowledge-driven decision support system for sustainable subsurface inter-asset management based on a family of urban infrastructure asset ontologies. The prototype includes an integrated geospatial database and an inference engine for assessing of the impact of triggers based on ATU ontologies. As future work, we will continue increasing the rule base by considering more scenarios; we also plan to do more evaluation of the system with more users and historic cases.

Acknowledgments. Financial support from EPSRC for the Assessing the Underworld (ATU) grant (EP/K021699/1) is gratefully acknowledged. Heshan Du is supported by NSFC with a project code 61703218. We thank all our colleagues in the ATU project for useful discussions. The contribution of all the industry partners and stakeholders involved in the research is gratefully acknowledged.

References

1. Clarke, B., Dimitrova, D., et al.: A decision support system to proactively manage subsurface utilities. In: International Symposium for Next Generation Infrastructure, Institution of Civil Engineers, London, 11–13 September 2017
2. Du, H., et al.: An ontology of soil properties and processes. In: Proceedings of the 15th International Semantic Web Conference (ISWC), pp. 30–37 (2016)
3. Du, H., Clarke, B., Entwisle, D., et al.: Ontologies for describing Properties and Processes of City Infrastructure Assets: the Ground, Roads and Pipes. University of Leeds. [Dataset] (2017). https://doi.org/10.5518/190
4. Euzenat, J., Shvaiko, P.: Ontology matching, 2nd edn. Springer, Heidelberg (2013). https://doi.org/10.1007/978-3-642-38721-0
5. Mahesar, Q., Dimitrova, V., Magee, D., Cohn, A.G.: Uncertainty management for rule-based decision support systems. In: IEEE International Conference on Tools with Artificial Intelligence (ICTAI), 06–08 November 2017, Boston, USA (2017)
6. Rogers, C.D.F., Hao, T., et al.: Condition assessment of the surface and buried infrastructure - a proposal for integration. Tunn. Undergr. Space Technol. **28**, 202–211 (2012)

Deep Learning and Sentiment Analysis for Human-Robot Interaction

Mattia Atzeni$^{(\boxtimes)}$ and Diego Reforgiato Recupero

Department of Mathematics and Computer Science,
Università degli Studi di Cagliari, Via Ospedale 72, 09124 Cagliari, Italy
m.atzeni38@studenti.unica.it, diego.reforgiato@unica.it

Abstract. In this paper we present an ongoing work showing to what extent semantic technologies, deep learning and natural language processing can be applied within the field of Human-Robot Interaction. The project has been developed for Zora, a completely programmable and autonomous humanoid robot, and it aims at allowing Zora to interact with humans using natural language. The robot is capable of talking to the user and understanding sentiments by leveraging our external services, such as a Sentiment Analysis engine and a Generative Conversational Agent, which is responsible for generating Zora's answers to open-dialog natural language utterances.

Keywords: Deep learning · Sentiment analysis
Human-robot interaction · Word embeddings
Natural language processing · LSTM

1 Introduction

Recent advances in automation and robotics are currently allowing humans to effectively cooperate with robots in several environments where the ultimate effectiveness of the interaction only depends on the actual success of accomplished tasks. This kind of scenarios is widespread in industrial settings and often requires a low degree of autonomy, thereby turning into a low-level and non-intuitive human-robot interaction, which cannot be fulfilled by inexperienced or untrained operators.

On the other hand, nowadays robots are starting to play important roles also in human environments, where a higher degree of autonomy, as well as a richer and more complex level of human-robot interaction, is required [4]. This gives rise to some main challenges and research opportunities, as robots should be able to cooperate with humans using natural language. Current research is mainly focusing towards supervised and unsupervised approaches for the semantic parsing of natural language commands into formal meaning representations [1]. In this context, human-robot interaction also involves natural language processing, knowledge representation and commonsense reasoning. Recently, Semantic Web

© Springer Nature Switzerland AG 2018
A. Gangemi et al. (Eds.): ESWC 2018 Satellite Events, LNCS 11155, pp. 14–18, 2018.
https://doi.org/10.1007/978-3-319-98192-5_3

technologies have also been applied to efficiently perform fine-grained sentiment analysis, resolving holders and topics on Linked Data [12].

Hence, in this paper, we present a use case and an ongoing work which shows how effectively sentiment analysis and deep learning can be used for human-robot interaction. The work has been accomplished using Zora[1], an interactive and programmable humanoid robot built on top of NAO by Zorabot[2]. The robot is capable of interacting with humans using natural language, by leveraging our external services, which allow *(i)* to generate the robot reply to a natural language question and *(ii)* to perform sentiment analysis on the given textual input.

2 System Architecture

The Zora robot is completely programmable and the Choregraphe suite[3] allows to *(i)* combine and create different behaviors using a visual programming app-roach, *(ii)* create animations by means of an intuitive and dedicated user interface and *(iii)* test behaviors and animations on simulated virtual robots, or directly on the real one. The system has been designed so that all the heavy computations run on a server, while the robot is only responsible for the interaction with the final user. Figure 1 shows the high-level architecture of the system.

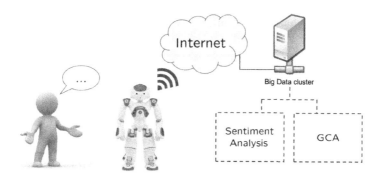

Fig. 1. High-level architecture of the system.

The robot is equipped with four microphones: two at the front of the head, and two at the back. Hence, the robot can easily record the human voice, which is contextually analyzed and turned into text by a speech recognition module powered by Nuance[4]. However, to improve performances, we are currently relying on cloud computing also for speech recognition. This allows us to pre-process

---

[1] http://zorarobotics.be/index.php/en/who-am-i.

[2] http://zorarobotics.be/index.php/en/.

[3] http://doc.aldebaran.com/1-14/software/choregraphe/index.html.

[4] https://www.nuance.com.

the sound recorded by the robot, in order to remove fan noise, which is quite disturbing for converting the human voice into written text. The resulting audio file is then sent to *IBM Watson Speech to Text*[5], to perform speech recognition.

Zora's reply to the natural language input can either be *(i)* an action triggered by a simple command from the user, such as "sit down" or "move your hand", or *(ii)* a natural language answer to the question asked by the user.

Hence, the result given by the speech recognition module is analyzed by means of *QiChat*[6], a language specifically designed to handle dialogs between the robot and humans. This allows checking whether the user input matches some simple command aimed at triggering an action corresponding to predefined behaviors which can be directly accomplished by the robot. In this case, Zora starts a new behavior to satisfy the user request.

If the user input does not match any predefined action, then it is sent to our RESTful web services, where the text is analyzed by a Sentiment Analysis engine and by a Generative Conversational Agent (GCA). This allows the robot to answer any question asked by the user and to understand sentiments hidden in the text. The following sections dig into more details about the Sentiment Analysis module and the GCA.

3   Sentiment Analysis

The sentiment analysis system has been implemented following our previous work in [2,5], but it has been significantly redesigned and improved to achieve better performances. The system has been implemented in Java and makes use of Stanford CoreNLP [8] for standard preprocessing tasks, such as sentence detection, tokenization, POS tagging and stop-words removal. On the other hand, feature extraction and classification have been implemented using Deeplearning4j[7]. Classification relies on recurrent neural networks (RNNs) and, more precisely, LSTM (Long Short-Term Memory), while feature extraction is achieved using neural word embeddings, obtained by applying the global log-bilinear regression model GloVe [10], trained on Wikipedia 2014 and Gigaword 5, for a total of 6 billion tokens and resulting in 300-dimensional word vectors.

The system has been trained for both polarity detection and subjectivity detection. Polarity detection has been achieved by training the model on the union of two datasets: *(i)* the *Large Movie Review Dataset*[8], introduced in [7], a balanced dataset consisting of 50000 highly polarized movie reviews extracted from IMDb[9], and *(ii)* a dataset containing one million reviews extracted from Amazon. This dataset is balanced as well, and it has been introduced in [11], within the Semantic Sentiment Analysis Challenge at ESWC2017.

---

[5] https://www.ibm.com/watson/services/speech-to-text/.

[6] http://doc.aldebaran.com/2-4/naoqi/interaction/dialog/aldialog_syntax_toc.html.

[7] https://deeplearning4j.org/.

[8] http://ai.stanford.edu/~amaas/data/sentiment/.

[9] http://www.imdb.com/.

The system has also been trained for subjectivity detection on a dataset which contains 5000 objective sentences and 5000 subjective sentences [9]. The performances of the system have been measured using 10-fold cross-validation, achieving an accuracy of 0.88 for polarity detection and 0.90 for subjectivity detection. Such results show a considerable improvement with respect to our previous work in [2], which was already ranked first at ESWC 2017 Challenge on Semantic Sentiment Analysis [11].

4   Generative Conversational Agent

The Generative Conversational Agent (GCA) allows the robot to perform open-domain dialog generation, that is creating meaningful and coherent responses given the dialog history. The implementation of the GCA is based on previous work in [6] and relies on sequence to sequence (seq2seq) modeling, thereby being language independent and capable of implicitly learning both semantics and syntax. Figure 2 shows the GCA model.

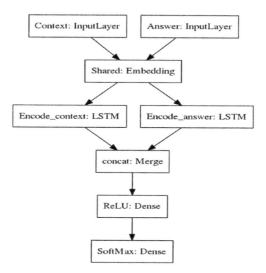

Fig. 2. The Generative Conversational Agent model.

The GCA architecture assumes the same distributions for input and output words, and, subsequently, an embedding layer, based on GloVe word embeddings, is shared between the encoding and decoding processes. The model makes use of two LSTM networks to process respectively the dialog context and the incomplete answer generated up to the current token. The resulting vectors are concatenated and provided to dense layers that predict the current token of the answer. The GCA has been trained on the *Cornell Movie Dialogs Corpus* [3], which includes more than 300000 natural language utterances.

5   Conclusion and Demo Showcase

In this paper, we have introduced a project aimed at making the Zora robot capable of *(i)* talking with humans using natural language, *(ii)* executing specific actions triggered by natural language commands and *(iii)* understanding sentiments by leveraging an external RESTful web service. The robot, along with how it is possible to effectively and easily use the Choregraphe suite and visual programming techniques to create new behaviors, will be showcased during the demo. A video showing an example of a basic interaction with Zora is available at: https://youtu.be/hoJYHLecZMs.

References

1. Atzeni, M., Atzori, M.: Towards semantic approaches for general-purpose end-user development. In: 2018 Second IEEE International Conference on Robotic Computing, pp. 369–376 (2018)
2. Atzeni, M., Dridi, A., Reforgiato Recupero, D.: Fine-grained sentiment analysis on financial microblogs and news headlines. In: Dragoni, M., Solanki, M., Blomqvist, E. (eds.) SemWebEval 2017. CCIS, vol. 769, pp. 124–128. Springer, Cham (2017). https://doi.org/10.1007/978-3-319-69146-6_11
3. Danescu-Niculescu-Mizil, C., Lee, L.: Chameleons in imagined conversations: a new approach to understanding coordination of linguistic style in dialogs. In: Workshop on Cognitive Modeling and Computational Linguistics. ACL (2011)
4. Dautenhahn, K.: Roles and functions of robots in human society: implications from research in autism therapy. Robotica **21**(4), 443–452 (2003)
5. Dridi, A., Atzeni, M., Reforgiato Recupero, D.: FineNews: fine-grained semantic sentiment analysis on financial microblogs and news. Int. J. Mach. Learn. Cybern. (2018). https://doi.org/10.1007/s13042-018-0805-x
6. Ludwig, O.: End-to-end adversarial learning for generative conversational agents. CoRR abs/1711.10122 (2017). http://arxiv.org/abs/1711.10122
7. Maas, A.L., Daly, R.E., Pham, P.T., Huang, D., Ng, A.Y., Potts, C.: Learning word vectors for sentiment analysis. In: Proceedings of the 49th Annual Meeting of the ACL: Human Language Technologies, pp. 142–150, June 2011
8. Manning, C.D., Surdeanu, M., Bauer, J., Finkel, J., Bethard, S.J., McClosky, D.: The Stanford CoreNLP natural language processing toolkit. In: Association for Computational Linguistics (ACL) System Demonstrations, pp. 55–60 (2014)
9. Pang, B., Lee, L.: A sentimental education: Sentiment analysis using subjectivity summarization based on minimum cuts. In: Proceedings of the ACL (2004)
10. Pennington, J., Socher, R., Manning, C.D.: Glove: global vectors for word representation. In: Empirical Methods in Natural Language Processing (EMNLP), pp. 1532–1543 (2014). http://www.aclweb.org/anthology/D14-1162
11. Reforgiato Recupero, D., Cambria, E., Di Rosa, E.: Semantic sentiment analysis challenge at ESWC2017. In: Dragoni, M., Solanki, M., Blomqvist, E. (eds.) SemWebEval 2017. CCIS, vol. 769, pp. 109–123. Springer, Cham (2017). https://doi.org/10.1007/978-3-319-69146-6_10
12. Recupero, D.R., Consoli, S., Gangemi, A., Nuzzolese, A.G., Spampinato, D.: A semantic web based core engine to efficiently perform sentiment analysis. In: Presutti, V., Blomqvist, E., Troncy, R., Sack, H., Papadakis, I., Tordai, A. (eds.) ESWC 2014. LNCS, vol. 8798, pp. 245–248. Springer, Cham (2014). https://doi.org/10.1007/978-3-319-11955-7_28

Pseudo-Random ALC Syntax Generation

Aaron Eberhart[✉], Michelle Cheatham, and Pascal Hitzler

DaSe Lab, Wright State University, Dayton, OH 45435, USA
aaron.eberhart@gmail.com, {michelle.cheatham,pascal.hitzler}@wright.edu

Abstract. We discuss a tool capable of rapidly generating pseudo-random syntactically valid ALC expression trees [1]. The program is meant to allow a researcher to create large sets of independently valid expressions with a minimum of personal bias for experimentation.

Manually providing sufficient unique expressions for testing in the development of a semantic reasoning application is both very time-consuming and potentially unscientific. For this reason, we have developed an integrated generator for creating syntactically correct ALC expressions. The random nature of this process precludes the possibility of generating any meaningful semantic information. However, expressions obtained from our tool are more than sufficient to serve as test cases necessary to validate the basic functionality of a reasoning application. In this paper we will describe the problem that the application is designed to solve, briefly touching on some of the logics. Next we discuss some of the features unique to our implementation and the design trade-offs involved. Finally, we will contextualize our work within current and possible future developments, then close with relevant technical information.

Problem. Usually the end goal of a reasoning application is to produce a system with semantic capabilities. The testing required to validate such a system is, however, mostly a response to purely syntactical questions. Does the application recognize and handle correct and incorrect forms of input? How do we define a valid input? Is there any significant potential for human-error affecting the results? These are problems that this project address. Devised as a solution to the first question, the expression generator is a way to bypass potential pitfalls in an intricate reasoning process by artificially creating only correct inputs. By restricting our domain to ALC we are able to explicitly define the sorts of expressions that will be allowed in our application. This also provides us with the basic logical framework for how the generator should run and the types of expressions it produces. If the application works properly, it should always only generate valid ALC expressions to feed into the reasoner. It is similarly important that, in addition to soundness, the generator be functionally complete over the set of all valid ALC expressions. In an empirical setting this is often the more difficult test, so we have endeavored to allow an output range as broad or specific as an experiment requires. Though there is always some degree of human-error in any study, it would be insufficiently rigorous for a researcher to enter in their

© Springer Nature Switzerland AG 2018
A. Gangemi et al. (Eds.): ESWC 2018 Satellite Events, LNCS 11155, pp. 19–22, 2018.
https://doi.org/10.1007/978-3-319-98192-5_4

own formulas. The tool we present should rapidly generate many random correct expressions and help reduce the researcher's own bias when making test cases.

Logic. The expression generator for this project is capable of building two distinct types of expression trees: one type for the TBox and one type for the ABox. Any TBox expression tree is created by first making an atom and then randomly choosing to expand the expression or end it. Expanding the expression tree involves either conjunction, disjunction, negation, or quantification. Ending a TBox expression creates either a subset or an equivalence with an unused Concept to avoid generation of expressions that directly reference themselves.

TBox expressions	
Operation	Result
New Expression	C, $\exists R.C$, or $\forall R.C$
Negation	$\neg$ {Original}
Conjunction	{Original} $\sqcap$ {New Sub-Expression}
Disjunction	{Original} $\sqcup$ {New Sub-Expression}
For All	$\forall R.${Original}
Exists	$\exists R.${Original}
Subclass	$C_{(new)} \sqsubseteq$ {Original}
Equivalent	$C_{(new)} \equiv$ {Original}

For an ABox expression, either a ground atom is produced and the generator finishes, or a TBox style expression is created and then eventually ground so that it becomes an ABox expression. The ABox generator will not return an expression that is not ground. All predicate and constant variable names are

ABox expressions	
Operation	Result
New Expression	$C(a)$, $R(a, b)$, or {New TBox Expression}
Negation	$\neg$ {Original}
Conjunction	{Original} $\sqcap$ {New Sub-Expression}
Disjunction	{Original} $\sqcup$ {New Sub-Expression}
For All	$\forall R.${Original}
Exists	$\exists R.${Original}
For All Ground	$\forall R.${Original} : a
Exists Ground	$\exists R.${Original} : a

randomly assigned except for the TBox finalizations; a, b, C, and R are only used here for convenience.

Solution. A unique specialization of our program is that it separates the expression generation from any normalization concerns. This allows for extremely rapid expression generation as well as the creation of more natural statements. We have included methods that normalize ALC expression trees into NNF so that a normalized copy can be obtained by someone using the program. A new random number generator was also integrated into the program due to the Java Random class' tendency to create very uniform expressions. Another feature of our program is that it contains constants that limit the types of expressions that can be created and can be tuned for a specific experiment. These control, for each expression created, the number of times the generator is allowed to make a sub-expression, the maximum quantification depth, and the maximum expression size. If their values are set very high or removed there is a possibility that the generator will get lost in subtree creation and take much longer than desired while building massive expressions. Some fine-tuning may be necessary to obtain the types of expressions needed for a given experiment. Additionally we have included a parameter that sets an upper bound on the number of arbitrary names the generator can use for individuals, and another for Roles and Concepts. This parameter has no effect on the overall structure of the expressions generated, though certain ranges may be valuable for comparison to semantically generated ontologies. Methods are provided that render expressions and complete knowledge bases into OWL functional syntax and description logic style strings for external evaluation.

Context. Our generator is similar to other methods [2,3] that create expressions of greater expressivity. However, these strategies require much stronger requirements on the types of formulas produced through artificial structural limitations that produce CNF expressions. By restricting our generator to ALC we are able create a wider range of expressions that we feel is more appropriate for reasoner experimentation, while still operating at high efficiency. Our program has no specific known obstacles to expansion so that it can generate more expressive statements, if that became necessary in the future.

Technical Information. This project was written in Java 1.8 with Eclipse Oxygen.1 4.7.1 build 20170914-1200. Testing was primarily performed on an Acer Aspire R5-471T computer with Windows 10 x64 and an Intel Core i5-6200U CPU running at 2.3 GHz and 8 GB of RAM. Current source code can be found at https://github.com/aaronEberhart/Reason.er.

The generator we describe can be useful in the development and testing of semantic reasoner experiments because it:

- Allows for relatively unbiased expression generation.
- Is optimized for the generation of ALC expressions.
- Enables quick creation of large numbers of formulas in an experiment.
- Creates only valid expressions, ensuring that tests run without problems.
- Produces syntactically diverse statements that enable thorough testing.

References

1. Baader, F., Horrocks, I., Lutz, C., Sattler, U.: Introduction to Description Logic. Cambridge University Press, Cambridge (2017)
2. Hladik, J.: A generator for description logic formulas. In: Horrocks, I., Sattler, U., Wolter, F. (eds.) Proceedings of DL 2005. CEUR-WS (2005). ceur-ws.org
3. Patel-Schneider, P.F., Sebastiani, R.: A new general method to generate random modal formulae for testing decision procedures. CoRR abs/1106.5261 (2011). http://arxiv.org/abs/1106.5261

A Protégé Plug-In for Annotating OWL Ontologies with OPLa

Cogan Shimizu$^{(\boxtimes)}$, Quinn Hirt, and Pascal Hitzler

Data Semantics Laboratory, Wright State University, Dayton, OH, USA
shimizu.5@wright.edu

Abstract. The Ontology Engineering community has recognized needs for both a simple, exstensible representation language for patterns and tools that support such workflows. In this demonstration, we describe a Protégé plugin that guides a user in documenting the loaded OWL ontology and its entities with annotations from the Ontology Design Pattern Representation Language (OPLa).

1 Motivation

The use of ontology design patterns (ODP) has established itself as an ontology engineering paradigm [3]. There are, however, a number of open challenges to be considered by researchers concerning the future of ODPs and modular ontology engineering. In this demonstration, we are particularly interested in both recognizing the substantial need for a robust pattern representation language and increasing the availability of easy-to-use, supporting tools. For a more thorough examination of these challenges and others, please see [2].

Utilizing a pattern representation language is an important piece for improving the development process, as it begins to address a perennial challenge in the Semantic Web community: ontology sharing and reuse; and as it applies to the ontology engineer: *ontology design pattern* sharing and reuse. A commonly used pattern representation language is immediately impactful by allowing the ontology engineer to more explicitly express

- how to use a pattern (e.g. what are natural "hooks" into the ODP)
- which other ODPs have been adapted or reused to create the pattern
- from where an ontology module was derived

Together, these examples can enable a so-called "smart" repository. Such a repository will allow an ontology engineer to more easily navigate and explore patterns and modules, thus realizing a centralized mechanism for the sharing, reuse, or adaptation of ODPs. As such, it is in the best interest of the community to utilize the pattern language.

As a first step in addressing this challenge, [4] presented the Ontology Design Pattern Representation Language (OPLa). OPLa annotations are fully compatible with OWL and its semantics are formally described. For each of our motivating examples we provide some concrete examples that illustrate exactly how OPLa can be used to formally describing those relationships.

© Springer Nature Switzerland AG 2018
A. Gangemi et al. (Eds.): ESWC 2018 Satellite Events, LNCS 11155, pp. 23–27, 2018.
https://doi.org/10.1007/978-3-319-98192-5_5

The MicroblogEntry pattern may contain the following triples:

```
mbe:Location   opla:ofExternalType          opla:externalClass .
mbe:Media      opla:reusesPatternAsTemplate nre:Media .
```

The first triple indicates that the Location is a "hook" for other engineers to use. The second triple indicates that the MicroblogEntry pattern has adapted the Media class from another ODP, in this case the NewsReportingEvent ODP [5,7]. Additionally, the ModifiedHazardousSituation ODP may contain the triple

```
mhs:     opla:derivedFromPattern    hs: .
```

which states that ModifiedHazardousSituation is derived from the HazardousSituation ODP [1,6]. Figure 1 provides a graphical overview for the other OPLa annotations.

However, like many forms of documentation, it is a tedious task to exhaustively perform. The key to adding complexity to any engineering process is making the change trivial to the end-user. As such, sufficient, easy-to-use tooling is necessary for facilitating process adoption. To address this, we have developed a Protégé plug-in that has been optimized for walking an ontology engineer through annotating their ontology, module, or pattern with the correct OPLa annotations.

2   Implementation

Our plugin, the OPLaTab (Fig. 2), is implemented for Protégé 5. At the time of this writing, plugin registration through the Protégéwiki[1] is ongoing. We provide a portal online[2] for a more detailed examination of the plugin's source code and .JAR file, and closer view of the interface and its use and installation.

The purpose of the OPLaTab plugin is to guide the user through the construction of a valid OPLa annotation. As such, it is optimized for annotating the ontology itself and its entities with only those annotations explicitly outlined in Fig. 1 and [4]. Thus, the interface is purposefully minimalist and restricted: it condenses all annotation functionality to a single screen and reduces the number of choices a user needs to make in order to insert an annotation into the ontology.

The tab's only silent behavior is to add the OPLa namespace to the ontology.[3] All other changes to the ontology are done via the "Save" and "Remove" buttons.

The interface is separated into three parts: navigation, construction, and view/remove. The plugin currently supports the annotation of the Ontology, Classes, Individuals, Object Properties, Data Properties, Datatypes and Annotations. By selecting one of these options, the construction area will be populated with the appropriate entities. Further, the list of annotation properties will update to display only those properties that are valid for the selected entity.

---

[1] https://protegewiki.stanford.edu/wiki/Main_Page.
[2] http://dase.cs.wright.edu/content/oplatab.
[3] http://ontologydesignpatterns.org/opla/.

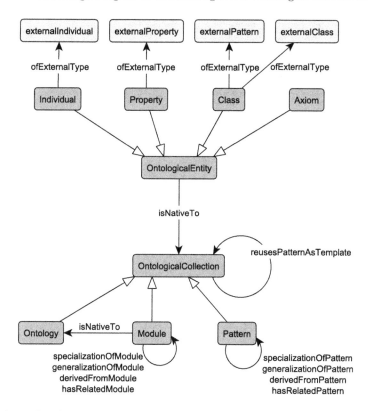

Fig. 1. A graphical overview of the Ontology Design Pattter Representation Language (OPLa) [4].

Finally, the view/remove area will display only OPLa annotations so that it is easy to identify which entities have yet to be annotated.

Currently, the annotation value for the annotation is user-dependent, in the absence of a standardized controlled vocabulary or repository. We briefly describe a sample workflow:

1. Select the ontology itself or an ontological entity.
2. Select the appropriate annotation property.
3. Enter the annotation value.
4. Save the annotation.

At this time, the bottom portion of the screen will update with the new annotation. The annotation may be removed by selecting the appropriate button.

3   Conclusions, Future Work, and Demonstration

OPLaTab is a useful tool for constructing OPLa annotations. There is currently an ongiong intention to develop a comprehensive tool suite for modular ontology

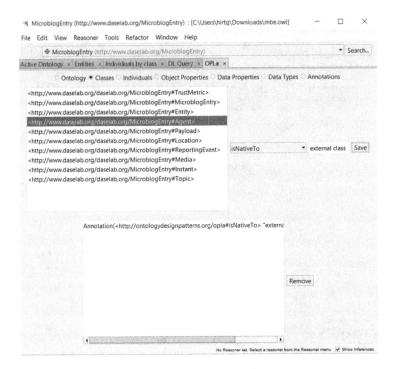

Fig. 2. A view of OPLaTab's interface. This view shows an example annotation be added to the loaded ontology.

engineering. We see OPLa becoming a central component of this tool suite. From visualization and interactive browsing to a smart repository, each will need some way of communicating to a user exactly how ontologies and ODPs relate to each other. As we provide more sophisticated tools in this realm, there are several foreseeable next steps.

While some of these next steps will require extensions to OPLA, OPLa was purposefully developed to be easily extendable. For example, it may be possible to embed visualization information into annotations, allowing software to determine which properties are visible at different levels of granularity. The same principle can be extended for interactive browsing. Perhaps most importantly, however, is the ability to connect to a machine-readable repository of ontology design patterns and modules. This "smart" repository can act as a dynamically updated controlled vocabulary of namespaces, thus allowing an ontology engineer to select the appropriate namespace when constructing their OPLa annotations.

Additionally, we will work to improve the user experience and look to more appropriately match the Protégé workspace.

Demonstration

The demonstration will consist of a live walkthrough of annotating a loaded ontology. In the interest of space, we have outlined in more detail a step-by-step walkthrough in our online portal.[4]

Acknowledgement. Cogan Shimizu acknowledges support by the Dayton Area Graduate Studies Institute (DAGSI).

References

1. Cheatham, M., Ferguson, H., Vardeman, C., Shimizu, C.: A modification to the hazardous situation ODP to support risk assessment and mitigation. In: Hammar, K., Hitzler, P., Krisnadhi, A., Lawrynowicz, A., Nuzzolese, A.G., Solanki, M., (eds.) Advances in Ontology Design and Patterns, vol. 32. Studies on the Semantic Web, pp. 97–104. IOS Press (2017)
2. Hammar, K.: Collected research questions concerning ontology design patterns. In: Hitzler, P., Gangemi, A., Janowicz, K., Krisnadhi, A., Presutti, V. (eds.) Ontology Engineering with Ontology Design Patterns - Foundations and Applications, vol. 25. Studies on the Semantic Web, pp. 189–198. IOS Press (2016)
3. Hitzler, P., Gangemi, A., Janowicz, K., Krisnadhi, A., Presutti, V. (eds.): Ontology Engineering with Ontology Design Patterns - Foundations and Applications, vol. 25. Studies on the Semantic Web. IOS Press (2016)
4. Hitzler, P., Gangemi, A., Janowicz, K., Krisnadhi, A.A., Presutti, V.: Towards a simple but useful ontology design pattern representation language. In: Blomqvist, E., Corcho, Ó., Horridge, M., Carral, D., Hoekstra, R. (eds.) Proceedings of the 8th Workshop on Ontology Design and Patterns (WOP 2017) co-located with the 16th International Semantic Web Conference (ISWC 2017), Vienna, Austria, 21 October 2017, vol. 2043. CEUR Workshop Proceedings (2017). CEUR-WS.org
5. Kowalczuk, E., Lawrynowicz, A.: The reporting event ODP and it's extension to report news events. In: Hammar, K., Hitzler, P., Krisnadhi, A., Lawrynowicz, A., Nuzzolese, A.G., Solanki, M. (eds.) Advances in Ontology Design and Patterns, vol. 32. Studies on the Semantic Web, pp. 105–117. IOS Press (2017)
6. Lawrynowicz, A., Lawniczak, I.: The hazardous situation ontology design pattern. In: Blomqvist, E., Hitzler, P., Krisnadhi, A., Narock, T., Solanki, M. (eds.) Proceedings of the 6th Workshop on Ontology and Semantic Web Patterns (WOP 2015) co-located with the 14th International Semantic Web Conference (ISWC 2015), Bethlehem, Pensylvania, USA, 11 October 2015, vol. 1461. CEUR Workshop Proceedings (2015). CEUR-WS.org
7. Shimizu, C., Cheatham, M.: An ontology design pattern for microblog entries. In: Blomqvist, E., Corcho, Ó., Horridge, M., Carral, D., Hoekstra, R. (eds.) Proceedings of the 8th Workshop on Ontology Design and Patterns (WOP 2017) Co-located with the 16th International Semantic Web Conference (ISWC 2017), Vienna, Austria, 21 October 2017, vol. 2043. CEUR Workshop Proceedings (2017). CEUR-WS.org

---

[4] http://dase.cs.wright.edu/content/oplatab.

An Editor that Uses a Block Metaphor for Representing Semantic Mappings in Linked Data

Ademar Crotti Junior[(⊠)], Christophe Debruyne,
and Declan O'Sullivan

ADAPT Centre, Trinity College Dublin, Dublin 2, Ireland
{ademar.crotti, christophe.debruyne,
declan.osullivan}@adaptcentre.ie

Abstract. The Linked Open Data cloud contains several knowledge bases with overlapping concepts. In order to reduce heterogeneity and enable greater interoperability, semantic mappings between resources can be established. These mappings are usually represented using mapping languages, where visual representations are often used to support user involvement. In prior work, we have proposed a visual representation based on the block metaphor, called Juma, and applied it to uplift mappings. In this paper, we extend its applicability and propose the use of this visual representation for semantic mappings that automatically generate executable mappings between knowledge bases. We also demonstrate the viability of our approach, in the representation of real mappings, through a use case.

Keywords: Linked data · Visual representation · Semantic mappings

1 Introduction

The Linked Open Data cloud[1] contains several knowledge bases with billions of triples, many of which have overlapping concepts. In order to reduce data heterogeneity and improve interoperability between these knowledge bases one can avail of semantic mappings [3]. Semantic mappings are represented using mapping languages, which can be complex and not as intuitive as one would like [1]. In such cases, visual representations can be used to support user engagement with the mapping task [4].

In previous work [5], we have proposed a visual representation for mappings, called Juma, **J**igsaw p**u**zzles for **ma**ppings. We have applied this representation for uplift mappings and showed how it can automatically generate mappings that can be exported to R2RML or SML representations, two syntactically distinct mapping languages [6, 7]. Juma is based on the block (or jigsaw) metaphor that has become popular with visual programming languages – where it is called the block paradigm – such as Scratch[2]. This metaphor allows one to focus on the logic instead of the language's syntax, targeting different types of stakeholders, especially non-experts.

---

[1] http://lod-cloud.net/ .
[2] https://scratch.mit.edu/ .

© Springer Nature Switzerland AG 2018
A. Gangemi et al. (Eds.): ESWC 2018 Satellite Events, LNCS 11155, pp. 28–33, 2018.
https://doi.org/10.1007/978-3-319-98192-5_6

In this paper, we employ the Juma method in representing semantic mappings that generate executable mappings. Executable mappings encode an interpretation of a semantic mapping in a given query language [11]. In this implementation, Juma will generate SPARQL CONSTRUCT queries from the visual representation of the semantic mappings. The main contributions of this paper are: the use of the block metaphor for semantic mappings that automatically generate executable mappings and a demonstration through a use case.

The remainder of this paper is structured as follows: Sect. 2 reviews the related work. Section 3 presents our visual representation applied to semantic mappings. A demonstration is presented in Sect. 4. Section 5 concludes the paper.

2   Related Work

In this section, we briefly discuss the state of the art in visual representations for semantic mappings. A survey [4] defined the main types of representations as tree and graph ones. **Tree representations.** These systems show ontologies as trees, usually side by side. Mappings are represented as lines that connect concepts between the trees. SAMBO [9] is an example of such system. AlignmentVis [1] combines a tree representation of mappings with statistical plots. **Graph representations.** The main visualization in these systems is a graph one. Most systems analyzed combine a graph representation with others. The system VOAR [12] combine graph and tree visualizations. RepOSE [8] only shows mappings as graphs. AgreementMakerLight [10] applies a different approach where ontologies and mappings are shown in a subgraph centered on a selected mapping.

The block metaphor combines a tree representation with visual elements, such as colors and shape, which show users how blocks are related to each other. In this paper, we apply the block metaphor in the representation of semantic mappings that automatically generate executable mappings. To the best of our knowledge, no other work combines a visual representation for semantic mappings and automatic query generation as executable mappings.

3   Using a Block Metaphor in the Representation of Semantic Mappings

In this work, we propose a new implementation of the Juma[3] method applied to semantic mappings[4]. As mentioned before, semantic mappings relate source and target elements from different ontologies, in order to reduce data heterogeneity and improve data interoperability.

---

[3] https://www.scss.tcd.ie/~crottija/juma/.

[4] A video is available at https://youtu.be/23RhrKbeM50.

We use Google's Blockly API[5] in this implementation. The main interface has menu options on the left-hand side and a workspace on the right-hand side. The menu options provide users with all blocks that can be used in the creation or editing of mappings within our visual representation. The workspace represents the current version of the mapping. The visual representation also uses colors to identity the type of structure that is being created.

In the tool, we make the distinction between simple and complex semantic mappings. Simple mappings relate one entity to another (one-to-one); complex mappings describe relationships between multiple entities (one-to-many, many-to-one, and many-to-many) [3]. Simple mappings have a specific block defining source and target entities with a relation block. This relation can be used to define class equivalence, property equivalence, sub-class, amongst others. Complex mappings rely on a different block that defines source and target elements. The source element defines how to select the attributes that are going to be used in the target element. In this implementation, source and target elements are defined in a similar way. One block is used to define the subject. Then, this block can be associated with predicate/object blocks. Which are used to define the triple patterns found in SPARQL.

Each function has a specific block. For example, to transform minutes in seconds, a block that represents such function would be available in the visual representation. This block is responsible to generate the SPARQL query code needed for such transformation. The same is true for any other function that would use filters or the aggregation of values, for example. We note that all functions within the current implementation of the visual representation have a similar design (with a name, parameters and optional values); and that it is possible to extend it to support other functions. There are also specific blocks for defining blank nodes and classes (see an example of a complex mapping in Sect. 4). It is also possible to add comments to the blocks in the representation, which can be used to explain matching results coming from the many matching algorithms available. The visual representation also supports zooming in and out, enabling and disabling parts of the mappings - disabled blocks are still visible but not used in the generation of the executable mapping.

The visual representation automatically generates executable mappings in the form of SPARQL CONSTRUCT queries. The reason for using SPARQL being that it has been shown to be able to represent a wide variety of mappings [13]. Furthermore, SPARQL is a W3C recommendation, widely used with many implementations.

Figure 1 shows an example of a simple class mapping. In this mapping the class dbpedia:MusicalArtist is mapped to mo:MusicArtist from the Music Ontology[6].

---

[5] https://developers.google.com/blockly/ .

[6] http://musicontology.com/specification/ .

Fig. 1. Visual representation of a simple mapping

4   Demonstration

The dataset used in the demonstration is based on the work published in [2] and consists of mappings between DBpedia and 11 other data sources. These are real use case mappings, designed independently of this research. The mappings were devised by the R2R Framework research [2] (52 simple mappings and 20 complex ones)[7]. We note that the current implementation has the built-in functions needed to represent these mappings. In order to evaluate our approach, we represented all mappings using Juma, generated executable mappings, and validated that the executed mappings produced the expected results. Figure 2 shows an example of a complex mapping from the dataset.

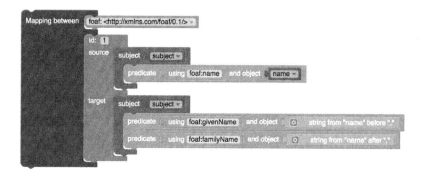

Fig. 2. Visual representation of a complex mapping

In this mapping, the property `foaf:name` is mapped to `foaf:givenName` and `foaf:familyName`. The property `foaf:givenName` uses the function string before. The property `foaf:familyName` uses the function string after. The parameters of the function are defined by clicking on the property icon. The generated executable mapping from in Fig. 2 is presented in Listing 1.

---

[7] The mappings are available as SPARQL CONSTRUCT queries at https://www.scss.tcd.ie/ ~ crottija/ juma/eswc2018/.

```
prefix foaf: <http://xmlns.com/foaf/0.1/>
#Id1
CONSTRUCT {
        ?subject   foaf:givenName    ?result1 .
        ?subject   foaf:familyName    ?result2 .      }
WHERE {
        ?subject   foaf:name    ?name .
        BIND (STRBEFORE(?name, ",") AS ?result1)
        BIND (STRAFTER(?name, ",") AS ?result2)      }
```

Listing 1: SPARQL CONSTRUCT query generated from a complex mapping

5   Conclusions and Future Work

In this paper, we propose the use of a block metaphor in the representation of semantic mappings. We have demonstrated our approach's expressiveness by applying it to real use case mappings from the R2R framework. By being able to express such mappings, we are encouraged that the approach can cope with simple and complex mappings, but further validation is needed to be conclusive.

In addition, previous work had shown us that this representation was useful, especially for non-experts, in the representation of uplift mappings [6]. Our intuition is that such a visual representation can also be beneficial to different types of users in the representation of semantic mappings. We believe that the combination of our visual representation with others might facilitate the creation, editing and understanding of semantic mappings by experts and non-experts alike.

Future work includes improving the visual representation by making it more intuitive and extending it to support other executable mapping representations. Moreover, the current implementation requires users to type in the concepts being mapped, with no integration with datasets during mapping creation/editing. Therefore, future work will also focus on minimizing the typing needed, validating it against the ontologies being mapped, and showing the ontologies together with mappings.

Acknowledgements. This paper was supported by CNPQ, National Counsel of Technological and Scientific Development – Brazil and by the Science Foundation Ireland (Grant 13/RC/2106) as part of the ADAPT Centre for Digital Content Technology (http://www.adaptcentre.ie/) at Trinity College Dublin.

References

1. Aurisano, J., Nanavaty, A., Cruz, I.F.: Visual analytics for ontology matching using multi-linked views. In: Proceedings of the International Workshop on Visualizations and User Interfaces for Ontologies and Linked Data (VOILA@ISWC 2015) (2015)
2. Bizer, C., Schultz, A.: The R2R framework: publishing and discovering mappings on the web. In: Proceedings of the First International Workshop on Consuming Linked Data (COLD@ISWC 2010) (2010)
3. Euzenat, J., Shvaiko, P.: Ontology Matching, vol. 18. Springer, Heidelberg (2007). https://doi.org/10.1007/978-3-642-38721-0

4. Granitzer, M., Sabol, V., Onn, K.W., Lukose, D., Tochtermann, K.: Ontology alignment - a survey with focus on visually supported semi-automatic techniques. Future Internet **2**, 238–258 (2010)
5. Junior, A.C., Debruyne, C., O'Sullivan, D.: Juma: an editor that uses a block metaphor to facilitate the creation and editing of R2RML mappings. In: The Semantic Web: ESWC 2017 Satellite Events (ESWC 2017) (2017)
6. Junior, A.C., Debruyne, C., O'Sullivan, D.: Using a block metaphor for representing R2RML mappings. In: Proceedings of the 3rd International Workshop on Visualization and Interaction for Ontologies and Linked Data (VOILA@ISWC 2017) (2017)
7. Junior, A.C., Debruyne, C., O'Sullivan, D.: Juma uplift: using a block metaphor for representing uplift mappings. In: 12th IEEE International Conference on Semantic Computing (ICSC 2018) (2018)
8. Lambrix, P., Ivanova, V.: A unified approach for debugging is-a structure and mappings in networked taxonomies. J. Biomed. Semant. **4**, 10 (2013)
9. Lambrix, P., Kaliyaperumal, R.: A session-based approach for aligning large ontologies. In: The Semantic Web (ESWC 2013) (2013)
10. Pesquita, C., Faria, D., Santos, E., Neefs, J., Couto, F.M.: Towards visualizing the alignment of large biomedical ontologies. In: Data Integration in the Life Sciences (DILS 2014) (2014)
11. Rivero, C.R., Hernandez, I., Ruiz, D., Corchuelo, R.: Generating SPARQL executable mappings to integrate ontologies. In: Conceptual Modelling - ER 2011, 30th International Conference (ER 2011) (2011)
12. Severo, B., Trojahn, C., Vieira, R.: VOAR 3.0: a configurable environment for manipulating multiple ontology alignments. In: Proceedings of the ISWC 2017 Posters & Demonstrations and Industry Tracks (ISWC 2017) (2017)
13. Thieblin, E., Amarger, F., Haemmerle, O., Hernandez, N., dos Santos, C.T.: Rewriting SELECT SPARQL queries from 1:n complex correspondences. In: Proceedings of the 11th International Workshop on Ontology Matching (OM@ISWC 2016) (2016)

A Diagrammatic Approach
for Visual Question Answering
over Knowledge Graphs

Dmitry Mouromtsev[1], Gerhard Wohlgenannt[1(✉)], Peter Haase[2],
Dmitry Pavlov[3], Yury Emelyanov[3], and Alexey Morozov[1]

[1] Intern. Laboratory of Information Science and Semantic Technologies,
ITMO University, St. Petersburg, Russia
`mouromtsev@mail.ifmo.ru, gwohlg@corp.ifmo.ru`
[2] metaphacts GmbH, Walldorf, Germany
`ph@metaphacts.com`
[3] Vismart Ltd., St. Petersburg, Russia

Abstract. In this demo we present a tool for visual question answering
(QA) over the Wikidata knowledge graph based on diagrammatic representation and reasoning. The demo is built on top of the metaphacts
platform with the Ontodia library embedded. In a user study, we demonstrate and evaluate the approach of diagrammatic question answering
using questions from the QALD7 (Question Answering over Linked Data)
benchmark for Wikidata. The effectiveness and limitations of the proposed approach are discussed in the evaluation and conclusions sections.
In the demo session at ESWC, we plan to present our tool for visual QA
and show its QA capabilities using incremental creation of diagrams.

Keywords: Visual data exploration · Knowledge graphs
Diagrammatic question answering · Wikidata

1 Introduction

One key challenge in the Semantic Web area is providing easy user access to the
plethora of data hidden in Linked Data repositories. Direct access to the data
requires an understanding of semantic query languages and the specific datasets.
One way of abstracting users from the datamodels are natural language interfaces
to Linked Data, which translate natural language queries into SPARQL and
thereby hide the complexity [2]. In many cases, however, visual access to data
is more intuitive. Many tools exist for browsing linked data, but they are not
designed specifically for QA.

In this demo[1] we present a tool for visual QA over Linked Data, which uses a
diagrammatic approach. The tool helps a user to navigate over knowledge graphs
(KG) and to find answers to questions by visual means only; we use the term

---

[1] http://wikidata.metaphacts.com.

© Springer Nature Switzerland AG 2018
A. Gangemi et al. (Eds.): ESWC 2018 Satellite Events, LNCS 11155, pp. 34–39, 2018.
https://doi.org/10.1007/978-3-319-98192-5_7

Diagrammatic Question Answering (DQA) to refer to the process. The benefits of visual exploration in data navigation include the quick detection of the most relevant properties and an easy understanding of the dataset characteristics. We use diagrammatic representations as an enabler of visual interaction with data and diagrammatic reasoning as way of data exploration. Diagrammatic representation and reasoning were suggested in visual language theory, which studies the cognitive and comprehensive features of this approach [5]. The tool is based on the Ontodia library[2], which was originally used for diagram-based collaborative ontology development [4].

We consider visual data exploration an information retrieval task, and evaluate our approach on the QA dataset from the QALD7[3] challenge. In the experiments, we apply an exploratory diagramming system that uses Wikidata as KG, metaphactory[4] as a KG platform and the Ontodia library as visual tool for data interaction.

2   System Description

The initial idea behind Ontodia was to enable a user to explore an unknown dataset. The graph nature of Linked Data inspired an incremental approach to visual exploration and a diagram-like semantic data representation. A user starts from a node of interest, and then uses the context menu to explore node properties and thereby the KG. By default all entity properties are listed alphabetically. A user can search for a specific property or topic of interest, then properties are sorted according to the query, with literal matches shown first, followed by the other properties ordered by similarity to the query. E.g., if a user is interested in the *family* relations of entity "Wolfgang Amadeus Mozart", they can start the investigation from the diagram shown in Fig. 1. For detecting properties similar to a query, we employ Fasttext word embeddings [1] to represent Wikidata properties and user queries, for details see Wohlgenannt et al. [6].

In a nutshell, our solution for step-by-step data exploration is realized via context menus of entities. The user connects additional relations and entities to the diagram until the query is answered. The context menu displays all the object properties or connections that a chosen node has in the dataset, whereas the datatype properties are visible by clicking on the expansion icon located below the node.

The system is executed in a browser/JavaScript environment and consists of two main parts: the Ontodia library and metaphactory platform. Ontodia is responsible for most of the user experience tasks of DQA, including diagrammatic representation and diagrammatic reasoning. It is embedded into the metaphactory platform, which serves as entry point to the DQA solution – with rich search functionality and as a foundation for building Semantic Web applications.

---

[2] www.ontodia.org.

[3] https://project-hobbit.eu/challenges/qald2017.

[4] http://www.metaphacts.com/product.

Fig. 1. Searching properties related to "family" of entity *Wolfgang Amadeus Mozart*

The demo application can be found at: http://wikidata.metaphacts.com. The basic QA process is exemplified by the following simple scenario:

1. Launch the demo application and enter the keyword that stands for the subject of the question.
2. Select a graph entity from the drop-down menu which best fits the subject.
3. Switch to diagrammatic representation clicking the "Show Diagram" icon.
4. Start data navigation from the root node by selecting the most relevant property in the context menu.
5. Build the graph incrementally, until arriving to the answer. Ontodia applies visual templates depending on the entity type (person, organization, location, etc.) to raise the expressivity of the diagram. Those visual templates can be freely configured by the user if needed.
6. Optionally, open the datatype properties of the selected node by clicking the expansion icon located below the node, which triggers the drown-down box.

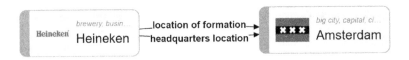

Fig. 2. Answering the question: *In what city is the Heineken brewery?*

Figure 2 shows a simple example diagram answering a query from the QALD7 challenge. The created diagram can also be saved and shared with other users.

3   Evaluation

In the evaluation, we address the research question whether diagrammatic representation and reasoning efficiently assist a user in QA and understanding knowledge from a large knowledge base.

3.1 Evaluation Setup

For the evaluation we reuse the QALD Benchmark, specifically task 4 "QA over Wikidata". QALD was originally developed for systems that interpret natural language queries. We adopted the benchmark to evaluate our approach of DQA, where the answers are not produced by a system, but through data exploration performed by human users. We designed four unique questionnaires with nine questions each[5].

The questions are grouped to the principles of question classification in QA [3]. Table 1 presents the main dimensions for classification, the question and answer type, and examples. We selected an equal number of questions for each type.

Table 1. Examples of test questions, and their classification.

Question type	Answer type	Example
WHO	Person	Who was the doctoral supervisor of Albert Einstein?
WHICH	Location	In what city is the Heineken brewery?
WHAT	Location	What is the capital of Cameroon?
NAME	Title	Show me all books in Asimov's Foundation series
HOW	Number	How many people live in Poland?

20 persons, from 8 countries, participated in the evaluation. Each participant obtained a questionnaire and an instruction sheet by email. 131 diagrams (of 140 expected) were returned by the users.

3.2 Evaluation Results and Discussion

Participants were instructed to go through the questions and to build diagrams containing the answers, if possible. We measured both precision and recall – as ratio of correct answers to given answers, and correct answers to expected gold standard answers, respectively. Some question types like WHAT and WHICH provide best results, with an F1 around 90%, for WHO and HOW questions we measure an F1 of about 75%. Only for NAME questions F1 is rather low (38%). As in the example in Table 1, this type of question usually involves the listing of many results items.

From the conducted user study we learned that the three the most common types of diagrams are: (i) two connected nodes, (ii) a complex diagram with multiple nodes and (iii) a diagram containing one node with drop-down datatype property box shown. The first type is rather simple and easy to understand. The diagram for the second type is more complex the interpret, it reflects the process

---

[5] https://github.com/ontodia-org/DQA/wiki/Questionnaries2.

of diagrammatic reasoning. In principle, the third type is the most simple, it contains only one node. E.g., for the question "How many people live in Poland?" a user only has to find the datatype property "population" in the drop-down box. However, many participants tried to solve such tasks only with object property connections, and failed to provide a result. In future work, we will take this finding into account to improve the user interface.

In general, the results are promising, but there are cases where it is difficult to find a correct answer with DQA, for example when the answer can be obtained only with joins of queries, or when it is hard to find the initial starting concept related to question focus.

4   Conclusions

The demo presents a tool developed for visual question answering using a diagrammatic approach (DQA). We evaluate the tool with questions from the QALD7 benchmark, specifically for QA over the Wikidata. For most types of questions, DQA provides promising results, and supports users in understanding the context of an answer and the characteristics of the knowledge graph itself.

The contributions of this work include: (i) a model for diagrammatic representation of semantic data, (ii) an exploratory diagramming system which integrates the metaphactory KG platform with Ontodia, and (iii) an evaluation of the diagrammatic approach with a user-study.

In future work we plan to solve the listed restrictions, eg. developing a more advanced property search box with embedded facet filtering to tackle more complex queries, or more powerful linguistic algorithms to address the problem of finding a suitable starting concept.

Acknowledgments. This work was supported by the Government of the Russian Federation (Grant 074-U01) through the ITMO Fellowship and Professorship Program.

References

1. Bojanowski, P., Grave, E., Joulin, A., Mikolov, T.: Enriching word vectors with subword information. arXiv preprint arXiv:1607.04606 (2016)
2. López, V., Unger, C., Cimiano, P., Motta, E.: Evaluating question answering over linked data. J. Web Sem. **21**, 3–13 (2013)
3. Moldovan, D., et al.: The structure and performance of an open-domain question answering system. In: Proceedings of the 38th Annual Meeting of ACL, ACL 2000, pp. 563–570 (2000)
4. Mouromtsev, D., Pavlov, D., Emelyanov, Y., Morozov, A., Razdyakonov, D., Parkhimovich, O.: Workflow supporting toolset for diagram-based collaborative ontology development implemented in the open budget domain. In: Sack, H., Rizzo, G., Steinmetz, N., Mladenić, D., Auer, S., Lange, C. (eds.) ESWC 2016. LNCS, vol. 9989, pp. 178–182. Springer, Cham (2016). https://doi.org/10.1007/978-3-319-47602-5_35

5. Narayanan, N.H., Hübscher, R.: Visual language theory: towards a human-computer interaction perspective. In: Marriott, K., Meyer, B. (eds.) Visual Language Theory, pp. 87–128. Springer, New York (1998)
6. Wohlgenannt, G., Klimov, N., Mouromtsev, D., Razdyakonov, D., Pavlov, D., Emelyanov, Y.: Using word embeddings for visual data exploration with Ontodia and Wikidata. In: BLINK/NLIWoD3@ISWC, International Semantic Web Conference (ISWC), vol. 1932 (2017). CEUR-WS.org

Simplified SPARQL REST API
CRUD on JSON Object Graphs via URI Paths

Markus Schröder[1]([⊠]), Jörn Hees[1], Ansgar Bernardi[1], Daniel Ewert[2],
Peter Klotz[2], and Steffen Stadtmüller[2]

[1] German Research Center for Artificial Intelligence GmbH (DFKI),
Kaiserslautern, Germany
{markus.schroeder,joern.hees,ansgar.bernardi}@dfki.de
[2] Robert Bosch GmbH, Stuttgart, Germany
{daniel.ewert,peter.klotz,steffen.stadtmueller}@de.bosch.com

Abstract. Within the Semantic Web community, SPARQL is one of the
predominant languages to query and update RDF knowledge. However,
the complexity of SPARQL, the underlying graph structure and various
encodings are common sources of confusion for Semantic Web novices.

In this paper we present a general purpose approach to convert any
given SPARQL endpoint into a simple to use REST API. To lower the
initial hurdle, we represent the underlying graph as an interlinked view
of nested JSON objects that can be traversed by the API path.

Keywords: SPARQL · REST API · URI · JSON · CRUD · Query
Update

1 Introduction

Nowadays, the majority of developers already know how to use web technologies such as REST APIs and JSON. However, in order to use Semantic Web technologies, they typically still need extensive additional training. Before being able to perform simplistic CRUD (create, read, update, delete) workflows, they first need to learn about RDF basics, URIs, Literals, BNodes and how they're used to model knowledge as a graph of triples (as opposed to more often used JSON representations). Further, in the process newcomers are overwhelmed with a multitude of encodings, serialization and result formats, before finally being able to interact with a triple store via SPARQL Update (and to understand what they are doing).

In this paper, we present an approach that aims to reduce this initial hurdle to use semantic technologies: We would like to allow Semantic Web newcomers to interact with a SPARQL endpoint without requiring them to go through extensive training first. To reach this goal, our approach transforms and simplifies a given SPARQL endpoint into a generic path based JSON REST API. During the design, we focused on simple CRUD workflows. To reduce complexity, we decided against attempting to cover all SPARQL capabilities, but instead provide

© Springer Nature Switzerland AG 2018
A. Gangemi et al. (Eds.): ESWC 2018 Satellite Events, LNCS 11155, pp. 40–45, 2018.
https://doi.org/10.1007/978-3-319-98192-5_8

Fig. 1. Illustration of basic REST API usage. Shown are excerpts of the JSON results for the different paths. Returned ids can conveniently be chained to walk the graph.

a trade-off between simplicity and expressivity. We use an easy to understand path metaphor to translate REST calls into corresponding SPARQL queries. Users can conveniently follow connections between the returned object views by iteratively extending the path of their requests. The resulting SPARQL response is translated back into an easy to understand and possibly nested JSON format.

A simple example can be found in Fig. 1. To get a list of all countries, users can access /class/dbo:Country. Chaining one of the returned ids, they can then access /class/dbo:Country/dbr:Germany and subsequently /class/dbo:Country/dbr:Germany/dbo:capital to arrive at /class/dbo:Country/dbr:Germany/dbo:capital/dbr:Berlin (or alternatively /resource/dbr:Berlin). An online demo can be found at http://purl.com/sparql-rest-api.

2   Related Work

Similarly to Battle and Benson [1] our approach offers simple access based on class and resource entry points. However, our approach significantly extends the expressiveness by allowing arbitrary length paths to walk the graph and using wildcards and property paths. Further our serialization format consequently abstracts away from triples, as will be detailed in the following section. Anticipating SPARQL Update, Wilde and Hausenblas [7] discuss application of REST to SPARQL, but users would still have to master SPARQL and write RDF statements. The BASILar approach [2] builds Web APIs on top of SPARQL endpoints by generating predefined REST resources. Similarly, grlc [6] builds Web APIs from SPARQL queries stored on GitHub. [3] describes a mapping approach from CRUD HTTP requests to SPARQL queries while [4] maps predefined REST calls to SPARQL queries, too. However, to work, these approaches need manual, up front definitions of mappings or SPARQL queries. Our API path to SPARQL mapping can be compared with RDF Path languages[1].

Summarizing, in contrast to the mentioned works our approach provides a zero-configuration REST to SPARQL conversion (evaluated during runtime) and uses easily understandable JSON objects (instead of triples).

3   Approach

As mentioned in the introduction, our approach aims to reduce complexity for Semantic Web newcomers by providing a simple to use, generic path based JSON REST API interface for a given SPARQL endpoint[2]. To achieve this, we (bidirectionally) translate[3] between the RDF predominant way of modelling knowledge in graph form and object oriented knowledge representations. The latter allows an easy to understand, nested serialization as JSON, which plays well together with our path walking metaphor.

Entry Points and Path Structure. Focusing on common use-cases, our API interface provides two entry points: /class and /resource. The former is used to browse instances of a known class, while the latter queries a resource by its known CURIE. An excerpt of the API's path grammar is shown in Listing 1.1. We allow arbitrary length traversal of the underlying graph by using the easy to understand folder metaphor: By alternating resources (RES) and properties (PROP) using the PATH rule we permit users to navigate the graph.

Listing 1.1. Excerpt of the API Path Grammar

```
API_PATH = "/api" (CLASS | RESOURCE)
CLASS =    "/class" RES PATH RQL?
RESOURCE = "/resource" PATH RQL?
PATH =     ("/" RES "/" PROP)* ("/" RES)?
```

Resulting JSON Syntax. As result format, we refrain from using JSON-LD, as it is an RDF (triple) serialization format driven by RDF specifics and often confuses novices expecting a simple, nested, object oriented format. Instead, we use simple JSON objects, which are modeled along the outgoing edges of a node x (so all triples of the form x ?p ?o). We refer to nodes as "ids" using their CURIEs, to stress that users are not required to actually know that these are CURIEs or URIs (to them it is just an identifier). In simple use-cases the JSON object response contains one of two JSON array fields (ids or values) or a JSON object id-map, as can be seen in Fig. 1. For consistency reasons, single id or value results are represented as arrays as well.

Resources are listed in ids using their CURIEs. This reduces the need for escaping in paths, and generates more readable paths allowing easy manual entry.

---

[1] https://www.w3.org/wiki/RdfPath.

[2] Our prototype only needs the endpoint's URI and a list of predefined namespaces.

[3] Transforming the API path to SPARQL and the result sets back to our JSON format.

Literals are listed in `values`. To allow correct round-tripping, each of them is represented as object containing its value, language and datatype, inspired by the SPARQL JSON result representation. `id-maps` are used to map ids (resources or properties) to further components, for example to list a resource's properties. As we allow unbounded nested results, `id-map` naturally contain `ids`, `values`, `id-map` and `value-map` (see further below).

HTTP CRUD Methods. Besides GET, our API supports POST, PUT and DELETE requests. The payload of POST and PUT is expected to be of the same structure as the GET results, allowing seamless round-trips. In general, all modifying requests extend information from the body with that encoded in the path (e.g., `/class/X/x` implicitly adds the triple `x a X.`). POST requests create a new resource and generate (and return) a new random identifier for the object specified in the body, while PUT requests create or update an object identified by the path. Depending on the path depth, DELETE requests delete a full resource (depth: 1, all in- and outgoing edges), the specified outgoing properties (depth: 2) or one specific triple (depth: 3).

Extended Expressiveness: Wildcards, Property Paths & RQL. Apart from these basic features, we extended our API with a couple of noteworthy features that seamlessly integrate into the path metaphor. A very powerful feature is the well known Bash wildcard ∗, which we allow in any RES and PROP position in the path. The asterisk is interpreted in an "all of them" way, introducing an additional nesting level for each asterisk in the resulting JSON. It allows to quickly create a partial view of nested objects, as can be seen in Fig. 2.

```
/resource/*/dbo:capital/*/(rdfs:label|skos:prefLabel)
         ①              ②                          ③
{
  ①"id-map": {
     "dbr:Germany": {
       ②"id-map": {
          "dbr:Berlin": {
             ③"values": [
               {"value": "Berlin", "datatype": "rdf:langString", "language": "en"},
               {"value": "Berlin", "datatype": "rdf:langString", "language": "de"},
               ...
]}}}, ... }}
```

Fig. 2. Example of path extensions using wildcards and a property path: The example lists all object ids with an outgoing `dbo:capital` edge, their corresponding linked object ids and their corresponding `rdfs:label` or `skos:prefLabel` as values. As can be seen each ∗ introduces an extra nesting level, while property paths (as in SPARQL) are transparently collapsed in the result.

As also shown in Fig. 2, we additionally permit the use of SPARQL property paths[4] in every PROP position by using surrounding brackets (e.g.

---

[4] https://www.w3.org/TR/sparql11-query/#propertypaths.

`/:x/(foaf:name|rdfs:label)/`). Reminding of regular expressions, this enables queries containing alternatives, inverse directions and multiple hops. Similarly to SPARQL, the followed property path is not shown in the result (collapsed).

Combining wildcards and inverse property paths also allows us to step over literals: For example, `/resource/*/foaf:name/*/(^rdfs:label)` will list all object ids that link to values via `foaf:name`, the corresponding Literals, and (other) object ids which use the same literal as `rdfs:label`. As Literals are complex objects they cannot appear as keys in JSON syntax. Hence, we introduce a last additional keyword to our JSON result format: `value-map`, which represents mappings of values to further components as a list of pairs.

Apart from wildcards and property paths, we allow the API paths to be extended with Resource Query Language (RQL)[5] methods, such as `regex`, `sort`, `limit` and aggregations like `count`, `sum` and `avg`.

Further Features: Batch & BNode Handling. We additionally implemented batch processing in order to bundle many similar requests into one and to reduce connection overhead. To avoid URI length restrictions and because processing a batch usually is a procedure, we implement it via JSON-RPC[6]. Moreover, a `/namespace` entry point can be used to to resolve prefixes, e.g. `/namespace/rdfs,owl`. Our API handles BNodes via their fixed (skolem) URIs as mentioned in [5] and supported by many triplestores (e.g., CURIE `_:b1` ⇔ URI `<_:b1>`)). This allows users to use and traverse BNodes like normal URIs.

4   Conclusion and Outlook

In this paper we presented an approach to turn any given SPARQL endpoint into a simple to use JSON REST API. To achieve this, our approach translates between CRUD API requests and SPARQL (Update) queries. The API paths allow users to simply navigate the underlying graph to their point of interest. The paths further allows wildcards and SPARQL property path components, seamlessly integrated in the API as deeper nestings of the resulting JSON.

While the development of our approach already embeds a lot of user feedback, in the future we would like to enhance our approach by adding further ideas. Apart from improvements in the areas of error messages and content negotiation, we especially would like to focus on supporting named graphs, introducing path based permissions and easy to use CRUD for simplistic TBox management.

A live demo showing various examples and their corresponding generated SPARQL queries, the source code, API docs and further information are available online: `http://purl.com/sparql-rest-api`.

---

[5] `https://github.com/persvr/rql`.
[6] `http://www.jsonrpc.org/specification`.

References

1. Battle, R., Benson, E.: Bridging the semantic Web and Web 2.0 with Representational State Transfer (REST): semantic Web and Web 2.0. Web Semant. Sci. Serv. Agents World Wide Web **6**, 61–69 (2008)
2. Daga, E., Panziera, L., Pedrinaci, C.: A BASILar approach for building web APIs on top of SPARQL endpoints. In: CEUR Workshop Proceedings, vol. 1359, pp. 22–32 (2015)
3. Garrote, A., García, M.N.: RESTful writable APIs for the web of linked data using relational storage solutions. In: CEUR Workshop Proceedings, vol. 813 (2011)
4. Hopkinson, I., Maude, S., Rospocher, M.: A simple API to the KnowledgeStore. In: CEUR Workshop Proceedings, vol. 1268, pp. 7–12 (2014)
5. Mallea, A., Arenas, M., Hogan, A., Polleres, A.: On blank nodes. In: Aroyo, L., et al. (eds.) ISWC 2011. LNCS, vol. 7031, pp. 421–437. Springer, Heidelberg (2011). https://doi.org/10.1007/978-3-642-25073-6_27
6. Meroño-Peñuela, A., Hoekstra, R.: grlc makes GitHub taste like linked data APIs. In: Sack, H., Rizzo, G., Steinmetz, N., Mladenić, D., Auer, S., Lange, C. (eds.) ESWC 2016. LNCS, vol. 9989, pp. 342–353. Springer, Cham (2016). https://doi.org/10.1007/978-3-319-47602-5_48
7. Wilde, E., Hausenblas, M.: RESTful SPARQL? You name it! – aligning SPARQL with REST and resource orientation. In: WEWST 2009, pp. 39–43 (2009)

Hate Speech Detection on Twitter: Feature Engineering v.s. Feature Selection

David Robinson[1], Ziqi Zhang[2(✉)], and Jonathan Tepper[1]

[1] Nottingham Trent University, Nottingham, UK
david.robinson2015@my.ntu.ac.uk, jonathan.tepper@ntu.ac.uk
[2] University of Sheffield, Sheffield, UK
ziqi.zhang@sheffield.ac.uk

Abstract. The increasing presence of hate speech on social media has drawn significant investment from governments, companies, and empirical research. Existing methods typically use a supervised text classification approach that depends on carefully engineered features. However, it is unclear if these features contribute equally to the performance of such methods. We conduct a feature selection analysis in such a task using Twitter as a case study, and show findings that challenge conventional perception of the importance of manual feature engineering: automatic feature selection can drastically reduce the carefully engineered features by over 90% and selects predominantly generic features often used by many other language related tasks; nevertheless, the resulting models perform better using automatically selected features than carefully crafted task-specific features.

1 Introduction

In recent years, social media has been increasingly exploited for the propagation of hate speech and the organisation of hate based activities [1]. Although social media companies are spending millions of euros every year on manually reviewing online contents and deleting offensive materials [3,7], they are still criticised for not doing enough and facing increasing pressure to address this issue.

The pressing situation has attracted increasing research using semantic content analysis techniques based on Natural Language Processing (NLP) and Machine Learning (ML) [1–4,8] to develop scalable, automated methods of hate speech detection. Substantial effort has been spent on developing novel, effective features (**feature engineering**) that better capture hate speech on the social media [1,2,6,7]. However, little work is done to understand how these distinctive features have - or not - contributed to the task and whether a **feature selection** process can further enhance the performance of such methods. This work fills this gap by analysing the effect of automatic feature selection on state-of-the-art ML based methods for hate speech detection using Twitter as a case study. We show surprising insights that challenge our existing perception of the importance of feature engineering. We prove that on this specific task, the automatic feature

© Springer Nature Switzerland AG 2018
A. Gangemi et al. (Eds.): ESWC 2018 Satellite Events, LNCS 11155, pp. 46–49, 2018.
https://doi.org/10.1007/978-3-319-98192-5_9

selection algorithm drastically reduces the carefully engineered feature space by over 90%, but improves ML algorithms to perform better using automatically selected features that are predominantly generic and used by many other tasks.

We structure the remainder of this work as follows: related work in Sect. 2, methodology in Sect. 3, experiments and conclusion in Sects. 4 and 5.

2   Related Work

State-of-the-art typically cast hate speech detection as a supervised text classification task [5]. These can be either **classic methods** that rely on manually engineered features consumed by ML algorithms such as SVM [1,2,6,7]; or **deep neural networks (DNN)** based methods that automatically learn multi-layers of abstract features from raw data [3,4,8]. While our earlier work [8] looked at DNN based methods, here we study the effects of feature engineering in classic methods.

Feature engineering is the process of analysing and designing predicative features for classifying hate speech. A wide range of features have been summarised in [5]. In short, these can include *simple surface features* such as word n-grams; *word generalisation* using, e.g., word clusters; *lexical resources* such as lists of abusive words; *linguistic features* such as Part of Speech (PoS) and dependency relations; *knowledge-based features* such as stereotypical concepts in a knowledge base; and *multimodal information* such as image captions. However, it is unclear how these different types of features contribute to the performance of the classifier. Most methods simply 'use them all', which creates high-dimensional, sparse feature vectors - particularly for short texts such as Tweets - that are prone to over-fitting.

3   Methodology

Our method is based on a state-of-the-art linear SVM based hate speech classifier introduced in [2]. It uses a number of different types of features, which are: (1) *surface* features, including word unigrams, bigrams and trigrams each weighted by TF-IDF, and filtered by a minimum frequency of 5; number of mentions (**#mentions**), and hashtags (**#hashtags**); number of characters, and words; (2) *linguistic* features, including Part-of-Speech tag unigrams, bigrams (i.e., two consecutive PoS tags), and trigrams, also weighted and filtered the same way as above; number of syllables; Flesch-Kincaid Grade Level (**FKGL**) and Flesch Reading Ease (**FRE**) scores to measure the 'readability' of a document; and (3) *sentiment* feature in terms of sentiment polarity scores of the tweet.

Extending this, we add additional surface based features as follows: the ratio between the number of misspelled words and the number of all words in the tweet; the number of emoji's (based on regular expressions); the number of special punctuations such as question and exclamation marks as they can be used as an expletive; the percentage of capitalised characters; and the lowercase hashtags from tweets.

We use **SVM** to denote the model using the **Original** feature set, and **SVM+** to denote that using both the original and extended feature sets (**enhanced**). Next, we use a state-of-the-art feature selection process based on Logistic Regression with L1-regularization as the estimator on the training data[1]. This calculates a 'feature importance' score for each feature, which is discarded if its score is below the default threshold. We use SVM_{fs} and $SVM_{fs}+$ to denote the SVM and SVM+ model with feature selection respectively.

4   Experiment

We use a total of 7 **public datasets** compiled in [8]. Briefly, **WZ-L** contains over 16k Tweets annotated for 'sexism', 'racism', and 'neither' [7], **WZ-S.amt** and **WZ-S.exp** contain the same set of some 6k Tweets annotated for the same classes by different groups of people [6]; **WZ-S.gb** merges WZ-S.amt and WZ-S.exp [3]; **WZ-LS** merges WZ-L and WZ-S.exp [4]; **DT** [2] and **RM** [8] each contains some 24k and 2k Tweets classified into hate or non-hate. We also use the CNN+GRU deep learning model described in [8] as state-of-the-art reference. For each dataset, we split it into 75:25 to use 75% for parameter tuning using 5-fold cross-validation experiments, and test the optimised model on the 25% held-out data. We report our results using in micro F1 in Table 1.

Table 1. Comparing micro-F1 on the different models (best figures in **bold**). The shaded columns show the percentage of features retained after feature selection

Dataset	SVM	SVM_{fs}	%Features	SVM+	$SVM_{fs}+$	%Features	CNN+GRU [8]
WZ-L	0.74	0.81	5.1%	0.74	0.81	5.1%	**0.82**
WZ-S.amt	0.86	0.87	3.4%	0.91	0.90	3.1%	**0.92**
WZ-S.exp	0.89	0.90	3.9%	0.90	0.91	3.9%	**0.92**
WZ-S.gb	0.86	0.91	3.4%	0.87	0.90	3.2%	**0.93**
WZ-LS	0.72	0.81	4.4%	0.73	0.81	4.0%	**0.82**
DT	0.87	0.89	4.4%	0.86	0.90	3.8%	**0.94**
RM	0.86	0.89	0.7%	0.88	0.89	0.6%	**0.92**

Table 1 shows that, comparing **SVM_{fs}** against SVM, or **$SVM_{fs}+$** against SVM+, clearly feature selection can further enhance the performance of the linear SVM classifier on this task. Sometimes the improvement due to feature selection can be quite significant (e.g., WZ-LS). Although none of the SVM based classifiers can outperform the CNN+GRU model, on the WZ-L, WZ-S.exp and WZ-LS datasets, the feature selected models can get very close to state-of-the-art performance. Table 1 also shows that after applying feature selection, the majority of both the Original and Enhanced features are discarded. In some

---

[1] http://scikit-learn.org/stable/modules/generated/sklearn.feature_selection. SelectFromModel.html.

cases (e.g., RM), the reduction is quite extreme. This has however, improved classification accuracy. Further analysis shows that, out of the Original feature set, features such as #mentions, #hashtags, FRE, and FKGL are completely discarded on all datasets. Word and PoS n-grams are the most predictive features as they are selected on all datasets. Other feature types appear to be only useful on isolated cases (i.e., 1 or 2 datasets). Similar situation is found for the Enhanced feature set, with only 2 out of the 5 **added** feature types selected for at least one dataset. This raises a controversial question that is whether the practice of feature engineering found to be fundamental to classic methods is really worthwhile. As it appears that with generic features such as word and PoS n-grams combined with feature selection, the systems can even outperform using a sophisticated sets of unselected features.

5   Conclusion

This work studied the effect of feature selection on the task of hate speech detection from Twitter. We have shown feature selection to be a very powerful technique as it is able to select a very small set of the most predictive features that are often generic and widely used in many other language-related tasks, to achieve much better results than models using carefully engineered features. In future, we will analyse the effect of feature selection in other tasks.

References

1. Burnap, P., Williams, M.L.: Cyber hate speech on Twitter: an application of machine classification and statistical modeling for policy and decision making. Policy Internet 7(2), 223–242 (2015)
2. Davidson, T., Warmsley, D., Macy, M., Weber, I.: Automated hate speech detection and the problem of offensive language. In: Proceedings of ICWSM 2017 (2017)
3. Gambäck, B., Sikdar, U.K.: Using convolutional neural networks to classify hate-speech. In: Proceedings of the Workshop on Abusive Language Online, pp. 85–90 (2017)
4. Park, J.H., Fung, P.: One-step and two-step classification for abusive language detection on Twitter. In: ALW1: 1st Workshop on Abusive Language Online (2017)
5. Schmidt, A., Wiegand, M.: A survey on hate speech detection using natural language processing. In: Proceedings of the Workshop on Natural Language Processing for Social Media, pp. 1–10. Association for Computational Linguistics (2017)
6. Waseem, Z.: Are you a racist or am i seeing things? Annotator influence on hate speech detection on Twitter. In: Proceedings of the Workshop on NLP and Computational Social Science, pp. 138–142. Association for Computational Linguistics (2016)
7. Waseem, Z., Hovy, D.: Hateful symbols or hateful people? Predictive features for hate speech detection on Twitter. In: Proceedings of the NAACL Student Research Workshop, pp. 88–93. Association for Computational Linguistics (2016)
8. Zhang, Z., Robinson, D., Tepper, J.: Detecting hate speech on Twitter using a convolution-GRU based deep neural network. In: Proceedings of ESWC 2018 (2018)

Incremental Data Partitioning of RDF Data in SPARK

Giannis Agathangelos[1], Georgia Troullinou[1], Haridimos Kondylakis[1(✉)], Kostas Stefanidis[2], and Dimitris Plexousakis[1]

[1] FORTH-ICS, Heraklion, Greece
{jagathan,troulin,kondylak,dp}@ics.forth.gr
[2] University of Tampere, Tampere, Finland
kostas.stefanidis@uta.fi

Abstract. Significant efforts have been dedicated recently to the development of architectures for storing and querying RDF data in distributed environments. Several approaches focus on data partitioning, which are able to answer queries efficiently, by using a small number of computational nodes. However, such approaches provide static data partitions. Given the increase on the continuous and rapid flow of data, nowadays there is a clear need to deal with streaming data. In this work, we propose a framework for incremental data partitioning by exploiting machine learning techniques. Specifically, we present a method to learn the structure of a partitioned database, and we employ two machine learning algorithms, namely Logistic Regression and Random Forest, to classify new streaming data.

1 Introduction

The recent explosion of the Data Web and the associated Linked Open Data (LOD) initiative have led to an enormous amount of widely available RDF datasets [2,4,5]. To efficiently store, manage and query these ever increasing RDF data, new clustered RDF database systems are constantly developed and produced [1], whereas when focusing on streaming data, incremental partitioning approaches are of crucial importance. A common way of incremental partitioning is to follow hash partitioning. For example, [8] adopts hash partitioning on triples subjects using MapReduce. [9] applies a graph partitioning approach for streaming RDF data. Query driven partitioning [3] leverages query knowledge to partition data so as to answer queries by single node computations.

Our approach combines the classical predicate and subject based partitioning along with the query workload knowledge. With this combination, we maximize the intra node execution when it comes to the chosen queries, but also other similar queries that contain combinations of predicate and subject categories we have seen so far. We manage and partition the incoming data incrementally, using machine learning techniques. Specifically, we demonstrate a method to learn the structure of a partitioned knowledge base eliciting its properties, and

© Springer Nature Switzerland AG 2018
A. Gangemi et al. (Eds.): ESWC 2018 Satellite Events, LNCS 11155, pp. 50–54, 2018.
https://doi.org/10.1007/978-3-319-98192-5_10

then classify the new streaming data to the appropriate computational nodes. We performed preliminary experiments using Logistic Regression and Random Forest for classification, and show the effectiveness of these algorithms in the incremental partition procedure.

2   Incremental Partitioning

Data partitioning is thorny issue in distributed RDF data storage. A step further, the classification of new incoming data to a distributed database should also follow the same policy in order to maintain the efficiency of the computational environment. Our goal is to extract the properties of partitioned data and learn from this structure in order to classify effectively streaming data respecting the existing distribution. The architecture of our incremental partitioning framework consists of two major components:

Data Manager: This component manages the distributed environment that consists of a set of computational nodes that interact to issue queries on existing data. As an RDF dataset is a collection of triples, usually in distributed environments, triples are partitioned across a cluster of machines and at querying, graph patterns are queried in parallel. Existing approaches try to minimize inter-machine communication during querying processing e.g. via vertical partitioning, partitioning triples based on their subject, or by combining different parts of the triples [6]. These techniques guarantee that all triples sharing a common property, i.e. a predicate, are stored on the same machine. We assume in our environment, the partitioning is performed using a combination of subject and predicate. Thus, the triples that contain the same combination of predicate and the corresponding instances of the domain classes can be accessed locally.

Incremental Partitioner: This component deals with incremental incoming data, selecting the appropriate computational node to store the corresponding triples. The functionality offered, is based on a machine learning classifier that assimilates the structure of the distributed database and assigns effectively the new triples to partitions.

Dataset Creation. A basic goal of a distributed database is to answer queries using a small number of computational nodes. Thus, triples found in same queries should be stored in the same machine. Based on this idea, we construct the dataset for training a classifier. The interesting part of this procedure is how to transform data and queries to samples, features and categories. Since efficient and effective query answering is the main goal of the partitioning process, queries should guide data distribution as well. As such, we select the user queries to represent the features of our dataset. In turn, the triples of our knowledge base will be the samples. Specifically, each sample is represented by a vector of binary values that corresponds to the existence of the specific sample/triple in each particular feature/query. Figure 1 depicts the stages for the construction of the final dataset for the classifier. Parsing each user query, we collect subjects

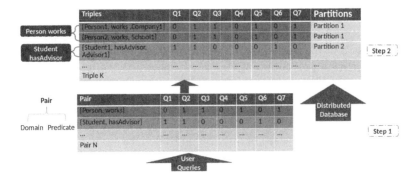

Fig. 1. Dataset construction.

and predicates that appear in each triple pattern and create the corresponding matrix. Each entry represents a pair (of a predicate and the corresponding
domain class) that its instances are identified within the queries. In case that
one subject or a predicate uses a variable, we generalize to every possible combination of the corresponding subject class with all predicates that have this
class as a domain and vice versa. Thus, we use the produced pairs (of query
predicates/domains) to create the first form of our dataset. However, we are
interesting in creating a set of samples derived from the (instance) triples and
the associated label/category for each triple. So, in a second step, all triples that
have the predicate and the instances of its domain classes are represented by the
corresponding feature vector of their domain-predicate pair. Then, each sample
is assigned to the computational node to which the corresponding triple belongs.

Classification. Next, we train the classifier and estimate its expected performance. Since the train procedure is crucial for the performance of the predictor,
we have to select the qualified parameters of the classifier that maximize its accuracy. This selection was done with the procedure of k-Fold Cross-Validation [7].

3   Preliminary Evaluation and Conclusion

To evaluate our approach, we used a part of the 3.8 version of DBpedia. To
create our vector space, we exploited the query logs from the corresponding
DBpedia endpoints and got access to more than $50\,\mathrm{K}$ user queries (features)
for a specific period of time. Specifically, our dataset consists of $1.9\,\mathrm{M}$ triples
derived from the triples contained in the corresponding DBpedia user queries.
We initially distributed data to computational nodes, using k-means, the most
widely adopted clustering algorithm. Euclidean distance was used as a distance
metric for k-means to assign each triple to one of 16 computational nodes based
on the existing features. In this part we do not intend to evaluate the performance
of the partitioning algorithm, but the correct categorization of the new incoming
triples. Thus our approach can be adapted to any partitioning algorithm.

We implemented our system in Apache Spark. Spark has been set up in a clustered environment of 4 computational nodes, each of them equipped with 230 GB of memory and a 38 core processor. For evaluation, we consider accuracy, precision and recall.

Algorithms: To model our problem as a classification task, we used two well-established classifiers, Random Forest and Logistic Regression. Both algorithms can handle the large number of features that we are dealing with. To find the best parameters for our algorithms, we implemented a 5-Fold Cross Validation[1].

Preliminary Results: Our dataset, by its nature, contains large number of duplicates, since large number of triples are instantiated under the same predicate-domain combination. This condition offers an efficient categorization of triples in different machines; correlated triples are placed in the same node. Nevertheless, due to the many duplicates, a classifier may not be able to classify efficiently new data. In our evaluation, we used as test samples data that in their majority has already been seen in the training procedure (Case I), while in a different scenario, we dealt with data unknown for the classifier (Case II). The dataset used in Case I contains the 20% of the original dataset, while in Case II we have a much smaller subset since we need samples that do not overlap with the train part. In Case I (Table 1), clearly both classifiers predict accurately, as they give an accuracy of 0.99. Due to the fact that a model classifies accurately the data instantiated to the majority of predicate-domain pairs, the classifier succeeds in categorizing data commonly queried by users. This is a crucial component of data partitioning. In Case II, we examine triples unknown to the classifier and we observe that the resulting metrics are as good as the first case for both classifiers. Thus, new incoming triples can be partitioned effectively in the distributed environment. Examining further Logistic Regression results, we observe that in Case I there is a small False Positive Rate since we can find samples that do not belong in their actual class. In the second case we do not observe the same result since the smaller sample size, results in statistically less plausible False Positives.

Table 1. Algorithms evaluation.

	Case I		Case II	
	Random Forest	Logistic Regression	Random Forest	Logistic Regression
Precision	0.937	0.999	0.897	1.0
Recall	0.932	0.999	0.90	1.0
Accuracy	0.998	0.999	0.985	1.0

---

[1] The best selected parameters for the final training are, for Random Forest, Max Depth: 10 and Number of Trees: 60, and for Logistic Regression, Regularization: 0.01, Max Iterations: 30 and Elastic Net Parameter: L2.

To conclude, in this paper, we propose an approach that combines machine learning algorithms and data partitioning techniques to classify data incrementally, and show the feasibility of our solution. As future work, we plan to deploy our work in a real clustered environment and measure the actual improvement on query execution times, comparing our solution with other competitive approaches.

References

1. Agathangelos, G., Troullinou, G., Kondylakis, H., Stefanidis, K., Plexousakis, D.: RDF query answering using apache Spark: Review and assessment. In: IEEE ICDE (2018)
2. Christophides, V., Efthymiou, V., Stefanidis, K.: Entity resolution in the web of data. Synth. Lect. Semant. Web Theory Technol. **5**(3), 1–122 (2015)
3. Hose, K., Schenkel, R.: WARP: workload-aware replication and partitioning for RDF. In: IEEE ICDE (2013)
4. Kondylakis, H., Plexousakis, D.: Ontology evolution in data integration: query rewriting to the rescue. In: ER (2011)
5. Kondylakis, H., Plexousakis, D.: Ontology evolution: assisting query migration. In: ER (2012)
6. Neumann, T., Weikum, G.: The RDF-3X engine for scalable management of RDF data. VLDB J. **19**(1), 91–113 (2010)
7. Refaeilzadeh, P., Tang, L., Liu, H.: Cross-validation. In: Liu, L., Özsu, M.T. (eds.) Encyclopedia of Database Systems, pp. 532–538. Springer, Boston (2009). https://doi.org/10.1007/978-0-387-39940-9_565
8. Rohloff, K., Schantz, R.E.: High-performance, massively scalable distributed systems using the mapreduce software framework: the SHARD triple-store. In: SPLASH (2010)
9. Wang, R., Chiu, K.: A stream partitioning approach to processing large scale distributed graph datasets. In: IEEE Big Data (2013)

Developing an Ontology
for Curriculum and Syllabus

Evangelos Katis[1], Haridimos Kondylakis[2(✉)],
Giannis Agathangelos[2], and Kostas Vassilakis[1]

[1] Department of Informatics Engineering, TEI Crete, Heraklion, Greece
evskg@sch.gr, kostas@cs.teicrete.gr
[2] FORTH-ICS, Heraklion, Greece
{kondylak,jagathan}@ics.forth.gr

Abstract. Semantic Web and ontology engineering can play significant role in the area of education. In this paper we focus on the conceptualization of educational knowledge structures in an academic setting. More specifically, we present the methodology and the development process of an educational ontology. That can be reused and applied to any type of course in different institutions and contribute to several curriculum tasks and course activities.

1 Introduction

The application of semantic web and ontological technology in education offer powerful benefits and will change the current education mode. Previous research [1–3] has already identified the importance of developing rich ontologies in the field, however, yet no current ontology conceptualizes educational entities within curriculum and syllabus with sufficiency and richness in order to support rich services on top is available. Curriculum management and development can be improved using ontologies in curriculum tasks like aligning, comparing, and matching between universities, educational systems or relevant disciplines. Having an ontology available, syllabus items can be effectively described and annotated enabling intelligent systems to support teaching and learning by offering automated services like syllabus semantic searching, matching and interlinking [6, 7], syllabus recommendation and evolution [5], etc.

The purpose of this work is the identification and conceptualization of the entities and procedures within an academic institution, aiming to model the core concepts of a higher education curriculum (Curriculum, Course, and Syllabus). The developed ontology aims to be highly transferable and reusable to other schools and universities.

2 Ontology Development

The design and the development of an ontology usually encompasses several tasks. In our approach we combined two widely used methodologies [8, 9] resulting in four main phases: (1) Domain and Purpose definition, (2) Ontology building, (3) Evaluation, (4) Documentation. Bellow we provide more details for each phase.

© Springer Nature Switzerland AG 2018
A. Gangemi et al. (Eds.): ESWC 2018 Satellite Events, LNCS 11155, pp. 55–59, 2018.
https://doi.org/10.1007/978-3-319-98192-5_11

(1) Domain and Purpose Definition. The purpose of this work is the identification of concepts and entities that play important role in a third-level curriculum, aiming to provide a semantic model for the main teaching and learning concepts within an academic environment. The developed ontology conceptualizes academic knowledge structures such as curriculum, course, syllabus, event, topic, etc. The definition of competency questions outlines the expectations that the designed ontology should fulfill - used in the evaluation process as well. Example competent questions include: (i) Which are the core Courses in a study program? (ii) Which degrees does a Person have? etc. (see [4] for the complete list).

(2) Ontology Building. Building a domain ontology requires deep understanding of the domain of interest. The necessary knowledge was acquired from domain experts, textbooks and existing ontologies. In addition to the educational ontologies found in the literature, search engines (*Google, Swoogle, OntoSearch, SemSearch*) and ontology repositories (DAML Ontology Library, *Ontolingua, SHOE*) were used to identify relevant ontologies. We identified five partly relevant ontologies. *Bowlogna* ontology [2] focuses mainly on study tracking and student mobility, and *BBC Curriculum* describes curricula in a broader view (www.bbc.co.uk/ontologies/curriculum). AIISO (vocab.org/aiiso/schema) has a different focus, targeting the structure of an organization while University Ontology (www.cs.umd.edu/projects/plus/SHOE/onts/univ1.0. html) does not include essential concepts (e.g. Syllabus, Event). A closely related ontology is also available only through a relevant paper [1]. Compared to these approaches, our ontology is more extensive and rich, modeling important concepts in Curriculum and Syllabus, supporting rich services on top. **Enumerate important terms**. In this phase, we made a complete list of all possible terms we would like either to describe or to make statements about. We inspected carefully existing related ontologies and analyzed a variety of textual syllabuses whereas templates and curriculum guides were also considered (such as www.adip.gr/en/accreditation-docs.php). The result was a comprehensive list of the important terms of the domain, shown in Table 1. **Define classes and class hierarchy**. We followed a top-down development process to organize concepts, starting from the "Whole" to the "Part". The most important terms are considered to be the top-level classes in our ontology with the remainder to be sub-classes or standalone classes. Finally, we ended up with 41 classes, as shown in Fig. 1. It must be noted, that some classes, i.e. *AdministrativeStaff*, *TechnicalStaff*, *Lecturer* and *Researcher*, are included mainly for classification reasons as well as for future use and extension of the ontology. In addition, ontology mappings have been established with relevant terms in other interconnected ontologies and vocabularies (such as Schema.Org and Dublin Core), in order to enable alignment and easier discovery by other organizations and search engines. **Describe the properties of classes**. In this step, we defined 54 *object properties* that describe relationships between individuals (instances of classes), 42 of which are participating in 21 pairs of inverse object properties. We also defined 76 *data properties* in order to attach rich information about individuals. Considering the class inheritance, each property is attached to the most general class. **Attaching facets to Properties**. Each *data property* has an appropriate value type, cardinality, and allowed values. For each object property we set the allowed values which are instances of other related classes, using the corresponding *domain* and the *range* definitions. It must be noted that, as a course might be taught by several instructors each year (corresponding to individual Syllabus) some properties related to Course (such as *instructorOf*, *supervisorOf*, *assistsInCourse*) have *Syllabus* as a range. **Create instances**. Finally, our ontology is enriched with a large number of individuals, since they are playing important role in evaluation process. We added a total of 549 individuals, most of them in classes that participate in the competency questions. Adding individuals allowed us also to test the completeness of the available domain terms and properties in modelling domain knwoledge.

Table 1. List of important terms within the subjects of Curriculum, Course and Syllabus

Curriculum	Syllabus
Curriculum	Syllabus
Educational organization	Topic
Discipline	Learning outcome
ProgramofStudy (Academic degree)	Teaching method
Person	Instructor (Professor)
Course	Student
Publication	Event

(3) Ontology Evaluation. We followed an internal technical evaluation approach. After the end of each phase, the author and relevant domain experts evaluated the available definitions. Special attention has been paid to the consistency, completeness and conciseness of the ontology. The final technical evaluation included, except manual examination and a software tool (oops.linkeddata.es/) that offers automate test against the most common errors and pitfalls in ontology development. Finally, the set of competency questions had been enriched, resulting in 27 questions in total. Those questions when then used to evaluate the ontology in corresponding usage scenarios with SPARQL queries.

(4) Ontology Documentation. Considering that effective knowledge sharing and reuse, requires adequate documentation, we have provided internal and external doc-umentation with various pieces of information. Internal documentation includes information annotated in ontology elements as metadata, written in two languages (English and Greek) giving to ontology bilingual character. External documentation includes an extended document that describes in details step-by-step the whole ontology development process, including, among others, purpose, class definitions, description of class properties, and evaluation.

Overview of the Ontology. Our ontology comprises of 41 concepts in a taxonomy, 9 of which are the top-level concepts of the ontology, namely the *FieldofStudy*, *Edu-cationalOrganization*, *Person*, *ProgramofStudy*, *Course*, *Syllabus*, *Event*, *Topic* and *Resource* (Fig. 1). It also includes 54 objects properties for establishing relations between concepts and 76 data properties for describing concepts characteristics in detail. All entities are enriched with additional annotation information. The generated ontology is also available online (http://xworks.gr/ontologies).

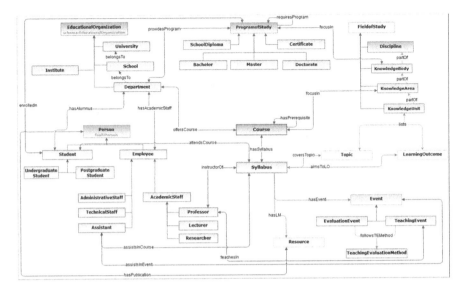

Fig. 1. Classes, class hierarchy and their relations of CCSO

3 Conclusion

In education, curriculum and syllabus offer important information to instructors and students. This paper presents an educational ontology for the semantic modeling of curriculum and syllabus in higher education with the methodology and development process briefly analyzed. The developed ontology has the potential to be reused and sharable among institutions and to contribute to information sharing and reuse.

References

1. Chung, H., Kim, J.: An ontological approach for semantic modeling of curriculum and syllabus in higher education. Int. J. Inf. Educ. Technol. **6**(5), 365–369 (2016)
2. Demartini, G., Enchev, I., Gapany, J., Cudre-Mauroux, P.: The Bowlogna ontology: fostering open curricula and agile knowledge bases for Europe's higher education landscape. Semant. Web **4**(1), 1–11 (2012)
3. Dicheva, D., Sosnovsky, S., Tatiana, G., Brusilovsky, P.: Ontological web portal for educational ontologies. In: AIED, pp. 19–27 (2005)
4. Katis, E.: Semantic modelling of educational curriculum & syllabus. TEI of Crete (2018)
5. Kondylakis, H., Despoina, M., Glykokokalos, G., et al.: EvoRDF: a framework for exploring ontology evolution. In: ESWC, pp. 104–108 (2017)
6. Marketakis, Y., Minadakis, N., Kondylakis, H., et al.: X3ML mapping framework for information integration in cultural heritage and beyond. IJDL **18**(4), 301–319 (2017)
7. Minadakis, N., Marketakis, Y., Kondylakis, H., et al.: X3ML framework: an effective suite for supporting data mappings. In: EMF-CRM, TPDL (2015)

8. Noy, N.F., McGuinness, D.L.: Ontology Development 101 : A Guide to Creating Your First Ontology. Stanford (2000)
9. Uschold, M., King, M.: Towards a Methodology for building ontologies. In: Workshop on Basic Ontological Issues in Knowledge Sharing, p. 15 (1995)

Computer-Assisted Ontology Construction System: Focus on Bootstrapping Capabilities

Omar Qawasmeh[1(✉)], Maxime Lefranois[2], Antoine Zimmermann[2], and Pierre Maret[1]

[1] Univ. Lyon, CNRS, Lab. Hubert Curien UMR 5516, 42023 Saint-Étienne, France
{omar.alqawasmeh,pierre.maret}@univ-st-etienne.fr
[2] Mines Saint-Etienne, Univ. Lyon, Univ. Jean Monnet, IOGS, CNRS, UMR 5516, LHC, Institute Henri Fayol, 42023 Saint-Étienne, France
{maxime.lefranois,antoine.zimmermann}@emse.fr

Abstract. In this research, we investigate the problem of ontology construction in both automatic and semi-automatic approaches. There are two key issues for the ontology construction process: the cold start problem (i.e. starting the development of an ontology from a blank page) and the lack of availability of domain experts. We describe a functionality for ontology construction based on the bootstrapping feature. For this feature, we take advantage of large public knowledge bases. We report on a comparative study between our system and the existing ones on the wine ontology.

Keywords: Ontology construction · Knowledge base

1 Introduction

Ontologies play nowadays an important role in organizing and categorizing data in information systems and on the web. This leads to a better understanding, sharing and analyzing of knowledge in a specific domain. As mentioned in [1], the development process of an ontology in a fully manual way can be a very complex task to achieve. This motivates the design and development of semi-automatic or fully-automatic tools to assist the knowledge engineer in the ontology development process. The process of ontology development is facing two main problems: the initiation of the extraction phase (cold start, blank page problem) [2], and the large number of micro-contributions that the domain experts must do. These problem are addressed by automatic or semi-automatic ontology development systems, that help in avoiding the cold start, and in minimizing the time spent by the domain experts. In this paper we propose the design of a new functionality focusing on the bootstrapping and combined with interactions with the knowledge engineer. Our functionality takes advantage of three large public knowledge bases: (a) DBpedia [3], (b) Wikidata [4] and (c) NELL (Never

© Springer Nature Switzerland AG 2018
A. Gangemi et al. (Eds.): ESWC 2018 Satellite Events, LNCS 11155, pp. 60–65, 2018.
https://doi.org/10.1007/978-3-319-98192-5_12

Ending Language Learner) [5]. We report on the evaluation of our functionality compared with other approaches, using the ontology for wine. The rest of this paper is organized as follows: Sect. 2 presents a short-state of the art in the field, Sect. 3 depicts our designed system, Sect. 4 reports on the results of experiments for evaluation, and Sect. 5 concludes the paper.

2 Automatic Ontology Development: A State of the Art

Bedini et al. [6] define four categories to classify the approaches for automatic ontology development: 1. Conversion or translation, 2. Mining based, 3. External knowledge based, and 4. Frameworks. We shortly present here a set of approaches that are related to our approach technique (External knowledge based). Kong et al. [7] use WordNet [8] as a general ontology to extract a set of concepts to build a domain specific ontology. Their system queries WordNet based on a set of keywords to extend the ontology by adding the list of new concepts. They compare their results to the wine ontology[1] developed by W3C. Table 1 shows their results comparing to the wine ontology. Kietz et al. [9] propose an approach that uses three knowledge bases to construct ontologies. They used a generic ontology to generate the main structure, a dictionary containing generic terms close to the required domain, and a textual corpus specific to the required domain to enhance and clean the ontology from unrelated concepts. The result is an ontology composed of 381 terms (200 new terms) and 184 relations (42 new relations). Cahyani and Wasito [10] propose an automatic system to build an ontology for the Alzheimers disease. Their system consists of the following steps: 1. a term relation extraction to match the extracted relations to Alzheimer glossary [2]. 2. matching with ontology design patterns. 3. builds and evaluate the ontology. To evaluate their system they use a list of 125 papers on Alzheimer disease. Their system is able to retrieve 1,995 correct terms with 42 relations. We propose in the next section an original functionality for semi-automatic ontology development tools.

3 A Semi-automatic Approach for Bootstrapping Ontology

As shown from the literature review, most of the approaches considering external knowledge bases make use of predefined dictionaries (e.g. list of concepts) or lexicons (e.g. WordNet), or they use specialized glossaries (e.g. Alzheimer glossary). Several limits can be listed regarding these resources: the existence and availability of such dictionary or glossary for a given domain, the limited richness of the vocabulary, and the supported languages (generally limited to English). In order to improve current automatic ontology construction, we propose a functionality

---

[1] https://www.w3.org/TR/owl-guide/wine.rdf.

[2] https://www.alz.org/care/alzheimers-dementia-glossary.asp.

using publicly available knowledge bases: DBpedia, Wikidata and NELL[3]. The pros of using these knowledge bases are that they are structured, very large, include rich relations, evolving in time, machine understandable and multilingual.

We follow a semi-automatic bootstrapping technique, where the user enters a set of keywords related to a specific domain (e.g. wine, grapes, and wine color, for the wine domain). Then by issuing a series of queries to the external knowledge bases, several classes and relations are extracted. Then the generated list is shown to the user for selection(see Fig. 1). After that, the set of classes is used to extract the instances from the NELL knowledge base. Our process is described in Algorithm 1. In the following subsections we present different phases implemented.

Algorithm 1: The General Algorithm Implemented by our System

```
 1  ConstructInitialOntology(keywords);
    Input     : keywords, a list of keywords given by the domain expert
    Output    : ⟨classes, relations, instances⟩ lists of terms.
 2  ⟨classes, relations, instances⟩ ← ⟨∅, ∅, ∅⟩
 3  foreach keyword in keywords do
 4      ⟨abstract, labels, uri⟩ ← queryDBPedia(keyword);              // see section 3.1
 5      ⟨classes, relations⟩ ← queryWikiData(keyword);               // see section 3.2
 6      instances ← queryNELL(keyword) ;                             // see section 3.3
 7      ⟨classes', relations', instances'⟩ ← pick(abstract, labels, uri, classes, relations, instances);
        // user picks
 8      classes ← classes ∪ classes';
 9      relations ← relations ∪ relations';
10      instances ← instances ∪ instances';
11  return ⟨classes, relations, instances⟩ ;
```

3.1 Extract General Information (DBpedia)

DBpedia knowledge base [3] contains structured information from Wikipedia that is accessible via a SPARQL endpoint [11]. In this phase, the set of keywords are used to perform queries over the DBpedia knowledge base to get some information that will help the user to choose clearly among the related terms that can be retrieved. For example, the output for the keyword "wine" is: the abstract from wine's Wikipedia page[4], the label in DBpedia in any supported language, and the different types from DBpedia (e.g. beverage, food).

3.2 Extract Classes and Relations (Wikidata)

Wikidata [4] is a collaborative, multilingual, structured knowledge base that can be read and modified by both humans and machines. The information on Wikidata is accessible by querying services. An initial query to Wikidata returns us the IDs of the users' keywords. Then, using these IDs, we perform different queries over the Wikidata to retrieve a set of classes and the relations. We use

---

[3] An executable jar file of our algorithm can be found here https://goo.gl/vCj3rU.
[4] https://en.wikipedia.org/wiki/Wine Last visit Jan-2018.

Results

Label: Wine@en Abstract: Wine (from Latin vinum) is an alcoholic beverage made from fermented grapes, generally Vitis vinifera or its hybrids with Vitis labrusca or Vitis rupestris. Grapes ferment without the addition of sugars, acids, enzymes, water, or other nutrients, as yeast consumes the sugar in the grapes and converts it to ethanol and carbon dioxide. Different varieties of grapes and strains of yeasts produce different styles of wine. These variations result from the complex interactions between the biochemical development of the grape, the reactions involved in fermentation, the terroir (the special characteristics imparted by geography, geology, climate, viticultural methods and plant genetics), and the production process...Type: http://dbpedia.org/ontology/Food

Validate

Class	Choose
red wine	☑
white wine	☐
rosé	☐
Organic wine	☐

Relations	URI	Used	Choose
instance of@en	http://www.wikidata.org/entity/P31	2209	☐
subclass of@en	http://www.wikidata.org/entity/P279	119	☑
depicts@en	http://www.wikidata.org/entity/P180	47	☐

Fig. 1. A subset of the classes and relations that are extracted for the keyword wine.

three different queries to have the following output: 1. Classes, with the parent-child relationship. For instance, the query was able to retrieve 80 different classes for the keyword "wine". 2. The most connected relations for each class. A list of relations that are connected to a specific class is retrieved along with the number of instances that are using this relation. For instance, the query with"wine" retrieves 6 different relations and their number of use. 3. Classes, along with their top-level high classes. A list of relations that are connected to two different classes are retrieved along with the number of instances that are using this relation. For example for the class wine and the class alcoholic beverage the query was able to retrieve 7 different subclasses.

3.3   Extract Instances (NELL)

Since January 2010, a computer system called NELL (Never-Ending Language Learner) [5] has been running continuously, in order to learn over time from the World Wide Web. NELL currently has more than 50 millions beliefs[5], which are attached to different levels of confidence, and features. We use three main files to access NELL: 1. Relations: contains 460 relations that were extracted manually. 2. Categories: contains 291 categories that were extracted manually. 3. Instances: contains 2,971,069 instances. In this phase, we use the NELL knowledge base in order to build a candidate list of instances that are related to the given set of keywords. NELL is queried based on a set of features such as domain, range, and confidence values. The next section discusses the initial experiments we use to validate our functionality.

---

[5] Based on: http://rtw.ml.cmu.edu/rtw/ Last visit: Oct-2017.

4   Evaluation and Demonstration

In order to validate our approach, we compare our results to those published in [7](See section 2). We therefore lead a similar experiment to evaluate our system, and we compare our results to the baseline ontology [6] and to the results in [7]. Authors in [7] use keyword "wine" to perform a query over WordNet. So that the comparison is fair, we used the same keyword "wine" as an input to our system. The raw results of our experiment, i.e., the full lists of classes, relations, and instances, our system suggests to the user, are made available in a Google sheet online[7]. Table 1 gives an overview of these results are compare them to the W3C's wine ontology and to the results of [7]. Out of the 80 classes our system extracted, 11 were already part of the W3C's wine ontology. We judge the remaining 69 relevant for a Wine ontology, so they could be used to extend this existing ontology. Our system also extracted 6 relations as listed in Table 2, apart from instanceOf and subClassOf, all of them are relevant for a wine ontology but not in the set of relations the W3C's wine ontology declares. As for the instances, we extracted 500 instances from NELL using a confidence threshold of 0.94 to filter NELL's beliefs. This experiment shows that our system performs better than [7] while proposing only relevant concepts, which allows us to assert it would be a good fit for the bootstrapping phase of ontology development. As for the demonstration experiments, a set of tasks could be done such as: let the users to choose a specific domain to test the functionality of the system, or to regenerate the experiments we already did on the wine domain.

Table 1. Comparison of the Number of Classes, Relations, and Instances between our proposed approach, [7]'s approach and the W3C's wine ontology

Approach	W3C's wine ontology	[7]'s wine ontology	Our approach
Class number	74	62	**80**
Property number	**13**	7	6
Instance number	161	98	**500**

Table 2. Set of RDF-Relations Extracted for the keyword wine

Relation	Count	URI of the relation
Instance of	2254	http://www.wikidata.org/entity/P31
Subclass of	96	http://www.wikidata.org/entity/P279
Depicts	35	http://www.wikidata.org/entity/P180
Main subject	8	http://www.wikidata.org/entity/P921
Has part	6	http://www.wikidata.org/entity/P527
Material used	6	http://www.wikidata.org/entity/P186

---

[6] https://www.w3.org/TR/owl-guide/wine.rdf.

[7] "wine" experiment: full lists of terms our System outputs http://bit.ly/2EEKItn.

5 Conclusion and Future Work

In this paper we propose an original approach for ontology bootstrapping based on the use of three external knowledge bases: DBpedia, WikiData, an NELL. Preliminary results shows that our system performs better than [7] that is based on WordNet. This allows us to assert it would be a good fit for the bootstrapping phase of ontology development, and could even be reused as a first step before applying other techniques. As for future work, we plan to extend the number of external knowledge bases that we query, to support the collaborative functionalities between the different parties, and to provide a web service for the functionality.

References

1. Blomqvist, E.: Pattern ranking for semi-automatic ontology construction. In: Proceedings of the 2008 ACM Symposium on Applied Computing, Brazil (2008)
2. Zhang, Y., Tudorache, T., Horridge, M., Musen, M.A.: Helping users bootstrap ontologies: an empirical investigation. In: Proceedings of the 33rd Annual ACM Conf. on Human Factors in Computing Systems, Seoul, Republic of Korea (2015)
3. Auer, S., Bizer, C., Kobilarov, G., Lehmann, J., Cyganiak, R., Ives, Z.: DBpedia: a nucleus for a web of open data. In: Aberer, K., et al. (eds.) ASWC/ISWC -2007. LNCS, vol. 4825, pp. 722–735. Springer, Heidelberg (2007). https://doi.org/10.1007/978-3-540-76298-0_52
4. Vrandecic, D., Krötzsch, M.: Wikidata: a free collaborative knowledgebase. Commun. ACM **57**(10), 78–85 (2014)
5. Carlson, A., Betteridge, J., Kisiel, B., Settles, B., Hruschka Jr., R.H., Mitchell, T.M.: Toward an architecture for never-ending language learning. In: Proceedings of the Twenty-Fourth AAAI Conference on Artificial Intelligence, USA (2010)
6. Bedini, I., Nguyen, B.: Automatic ontology generation: state of the art. PRiSM Laboratory Technical report. University of Versailles (2007)
7. Kong, H., Hwang, M., Kim, P.: Design of the automatic ontology building system about the specific domain knowledge. In: The 8th International Conference on Advanced Communication Technology, ICACT 2006. IEEE (2006)
8. Miller, G.A.: WordNet: a lexical database for English. Commun. ACM **38**(11), 39–41 (1995)
9. Kietz, J.-U., Maedche, A., Volz, R.: A method for semi-automatic ontology acquisition from a corporate intranet. In: EKAW-2000 Workshop Ontologies and Text, Juan-Les-Pins, France (2000)
10. Cahyani, G.A., Wasito, I.: Automatic ontology construction using text corpora and ontology design patterns (odps) in alzheimers disease. Jurnal Ilmu Komputer dan Informasi (2017)
11. Harris, S., Seaborne, A., Prudhommeaux, E.: Sparql 1.1 query language. W3C recommendation, vol. 21, no. 10 (2013)

Matching Offerings and Queries on an Internet of Things Marketplace

Victor Charpenay[1($\boxtimes$)], Hoan Nguyen[2], Mohamad Ibrahim[3], Achille Zappa[2], and Arne Bröring[1]

[1] Siemens AG — Corporate Technology, Munich, Germany
victor.charpenay@siemens.com
[2] Insight Centre for Data Analytics, National University of Ireland, Galway, Ireland
[3] Technical University of Clausthal, Clausthal-Zellerfeld, Germany

Abstract. A marketplace for the Internet of Things acts as the corner stone of an IoT ecosystem, by matching the offer (i.e., data or functionalities) with the demand coming from IoT applications (e.g. analytics). In this paper, we present the semantic matching implemented on the public BIG IoT marketplace, accessible at https://market.big-iot.org/.

Today, many Internet of Things (IoT) platforms have come up and provide data and functionalities of *things*, e.g., ThingWorx, Xively or Siemens MindSphere. In order to enable a vibrant and collaborative IoT ecosystem across these platforms, *marketplaces* are needed to enable *providers* to monetize the access to their platforms by *consumers* (e.g., applications or services). The BIG IoT project [1] offers such a marketplace and enables providers to register their IoT resources as *offerings* and consumers to formulate *queries* to discover these offerings. Once offerings and queries are registered on the BIG IoT marketplace, it is crucial to effectively support the matching between offerings and queries, so that consumers are reported which offerings suit their needs in near real-time.

1 Offering Model

The basis for our matching approach is a lightweight ontological model for IoT offerings and queries, which we illustrate in Fig. 1. Platform providers must register their offerings in the form of RDF documents we call *offering descriptions* (ODs), which describe in detail the offered platform resources as per our ontology. The OD is based on the *thing description* from the W3C's Web of Things working group [2].

At the core of our model are the two classes `Offering` and `OfferingQuery`. They respectively extend schema.org's classes `Offer` and `Demand`. A direct benefit of aligning with the well-known schema.org vocabulary is that BIG IoT offerings and queries could be crawled by search engines as an alternative to being registered on a marketplace. Every offering has a mandatory endpoint definition that specifies an IRI as well as the communication protocol and message type

© Springer Nature Switzerland AG 2018
A. Gangemi et al. (Eds.): ESWC 2018 Satellite Events, LNCS 11155, pp. 66–71, 2018.
https://doi.org/10.1007/978-3-319-98192-5_13

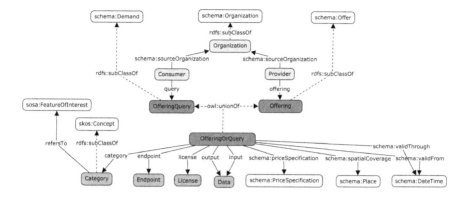

Fig. 1. Overview of the BIG IoT core ontology (http://schema.big-iot.org/core/).

used to access the resource (e.g. HTTP POST or CoAP GET). Queries may also define restrictions on the endpoint. To allow for large-scale data exchange, offerings and queries must provide input and output data definitions (inspired by JSON schema). These definitions are used both for matching and at access time to validate a consumer's input and the provider's output. Queries and offerings can also define a category, which is modeled as a SKOS concept in BIG IoT. Although categories are to be thought of as free-text tags defined by users (eventually becoming a folksonomy managed by the IoT community), we provide an initial category tree for the domains of mobility and environmental monitoring. Finally, queries and offerings can define non-functional properties such as spatial and temporal extent as well as price and license to refine the offering matching process [3].

RDF annotations in data definitions, as well as offering categories, are crucial for offering matching. In parallel to its core ontology, the BIG IoT marketplace also provides other cross-domain or domain-dependent ontologies, aligned both with schema.org and the widespread W3C SOSA ontology, designed to capture the semantics of IoT systems [4]. In particular, these ontologies extend the concept of `FeatureOfInterest`, e.g. by defining classes for concepts such as parking lot, traffic, or air pollution in a given area, which are used as a basis for the automatic derivation of a category tree for BIG IoT offerings.

2   Offering Matching

An important requirement that drives our approach is that results must remain intuitive to the various stakeholders of the BIG IoT marketplace. We therefore implemented a straightforward multi-modal boolean search algorithm, where for each aspect of the offering model presented above, the evaluation against an offering returns *true* or *false*. In practice, a SPARQL graph pattern is generated for each of these aspects from an offering query, the conjunction of which is evaluated against an RDF graph that includes all offerings. Figure 2 provides an example of a SPARQL query generated for matching. We review all six aspects of matching in the following.

IoT data points are typically associated to a precise geographical location. The spatial extent of an offering represents either the actual location of a sensor or a bounding box for a set of data points. An offering matches as soon as the bounding boxes of an offering intersect with that of a query (1). Similarly, IoT data is located in time (temporal extent). An offering can provide historical data or live data. A query that includes a time range will match offerings with historical data that overlap with this range. If no temporal extent is given, offerings with live data only will match (2).

Offerings can also match against a category (3). Our model currently includes 38 categories, defined hierarchically[1]. Subsumption reasoning is performed at registration time to add parent categories to an offering. For instance, ParkingCategory should also match offerings tagged with ParkingSiteCategory or ParkingSpaceCategory.

As mentioned in the previous section, offerings include data definitions annotated with

```
SELECT DISTINCT ?id
WHERE {
  ?offering a :Offering;
    :offeringId ?id;
    :isActivated "true"^^xsd:boolean.
```

```
1
  ?offering a :Offering;
    schema:spatialCoverage ?area.
  ?area wgs84:geometry ?geo.
  FILTER(bif:st_intersects(?geo, "...")).
```

```
2
  ?offering schema:validFrom ?validFrom;
    schema:validThrough ?validThrough.
  FILTER (?validFrom <= "1520812"^^xsd:long
    && ?validThrough >= "1518393"^^xsd:long)
```

```
3
  ?offering schema:category
    <urn:big-iot:ParkingCategory>.
```

```
4
  ?offering :input ?in;
    :output ?out.
  ?in :rdfAnnotation schema:GeoShape.
  ?out :rdfAnnotation mobility:ParkingSpace.
```

```
5
  ?offering schema:priceSpecification ?spec.
  ?spec :pricingModel ?pModel;
    schema:priceCurrency "EUR"^^xsd:string;
    schema:price ?amount.
  FILTER(?amount <=0.02).
  VALUES ?pModel {
    :per_access_price
    :free_price
  }
```

```
6
  ?offering :license ?license.
  ?license :licenseType :open_data_license.
}
```

Fig. 2. SPARQL query example

RDF. For matching, we discard structural information and only keep the set of RDF terms (4). Matching occurs when the set of terms in an offering fully contains that of a query (for both input and output). As for categories, reasoning is performed at registration time to expand the set of terms with those found in schema.org, SOSA and our own ontologies (which include 64 classes and 74 properties so far). Super-classes and domain and range classes are added to the set of terms, as per RDFS semantics. Here, offerings annotated with

---

[1] See http://big-iot.github.io/categories.

`GeoCircle` (subclass of `GeoShape`) and `distanceFromParkingSpace` (whose domain includes `ParkingSpace`) will match.

Finally, offerings can also be matched against a price or a license. Our BIG IoT core model includes several pricing models: subscription, per access payment, etc. and prices given in a query are interpreted as *maximum* amounts (5). As for pricing models, our model includes several licenses in use on various Open Data platforms: Creative Commons, Open Government License, any commercial license and public domain. Offering licenses must be an exact match (6).

3   Related Work

In information science, matching supply with demand within a market has been extensively studied, especially in the context of Web services. In particular, many works have been conducted to allow for the matchmaking between user needs and services at a semantic level, as the development of ontological frameworks such as OWL-S [5] and WSMO [6] shows. The general idea behind semantic matchmaking is to find a subsumption relation between supply and demand (modeled as RDF classes) using automated reasoning [7].

One limitation to pure semantic matchmaking is the potentially high heterogeneity between the various semantic models used across service providers, as well as a potential mismatch in the semantics used by providers and consumers. To address this, ontology matching techniques exist (either based on syntactic, structural or semantic features) to align semantic models with each other [8]. However, most of these techniques require human input, which, in the case of an IoT marketplace, would hardly scale.

The offering model we present in Sect. 1 accounts for a lightweight alternative to OWL-S and WSMO suited for IoT data by integrating spatio-temporal extents, as well as license and price. In the three large-scale pilots in which BIG IoT has been deployed (Barcelona, Piedmont and northern Germany), we could observe a very high heterogeneity across platforms with respect to data modeling, which led us to implement a matching algorithm that does not rely on pure semantic matchmaking, while still leveraging semantic models.

4   Demonstration and Conclusion

Our demonstration consists of a walk through the public BIG IoT marketplace, available at https://market.big-iot.org/ (see also Fig. 3). It currently contains 56 offering providers, providing 142 offerings, as well as 28 consumers. The number of offerings is still growing, as the project goes on. The data being offered on this marketplace is fairly diverse but offerings are mainly categorized in three domains: `EnvironmentalIndicatorCategory` (38), `MobilityFeatureCategory` (77) and `WeatherIndicatorCategory` (27). There are 12 offerings with the category `ParkingCategory` and charging less than 0.02€ per access, these two criteria being a subset of what is presented in Fig. 2. If we add the spatial and temporal extents, only 4 offerings remain.

Our demonstration should illustrate how our pragmatic approach towards semantic matchmaking already enables intelligent matching between offerings and queries of existing IoT platforms. This matching mostly exploits ontological models based on schema.org and SOSA that we developed for the domains of mobility and environmental monitoring.

In the coming months, the BIG IoT Marketplace and its APIs will be released as open source[2] and developers are encouraged to take part in this IoT ecosystem[3]. Further improvement of the matching algorithm is possible by leveraging structural information of data type definitions, which we plan in a future deployment of our marketplace. In parallel, we will further develop our domain models and plan to eventually contribute them to schema.org[4].

Fig. 3. Parking query

Acknowledgements. This work is supported by the project 'Bridging the Interoperability Gap of the Internet of Things' BIG IoT funded by the European Commission's Horizon 2020 program (Grant No. 688038).

References

1. Bröring, A., Schmid, S., Schindhelm, C.K., Khelil, A., Käbisch, S., Kramer, D., Phuoc, D.L., Mitic, J., Anicic, D., Teniente, E.: Enabling IoT ecosystems through platform interoperability. IEEE Softw. **34**(1), 54–61 (2017). https://doi.org/10.1109/MS.2017.2
2. Käbisch, S., Kamiya, T.: Web of Things (WoT) thing description. https://www.w3.org/TR/wot-thing-description/
3. Bröring, A., Ziller, A., Charpenay, V., Schmid, S., Thuluva, A., Anicic, D., Zappa, A., Linares, M., Mikkelsen, L., Seidel, C.: The BIG IoT API: Semantically Enabling Interoperability in IoT Ecosystems. IEEE Pervasive Computing, PCSI-2018-01-0008.R2 manuscript type: Special Issue - IoT Deployments (October/December 2018)
4. Haller, A., Janowicz, K., Cox, S., Le Phuoc, D., Taylor, K., Lefrançois, M.: Semantic sensor network ontology. https://www.w3.org/TR/vocab-ssn/
5. Martin, D., Burstein, M., Hobbs, J., Lassila, O., McDermott, D., McIlraith, S., Narayanan, S., Paolucci, M., Parsia, B., Payne, T., Sirin, E., Srinivasan, N., Sycara, K.: OWL-S: semantic markup for web services. http://www.w3.org/Submission/OWL-S/

---

[2] See https://projects.eclipse.org/proposals/eclipse-bridge.iot.

[3] See our developer guide at https://big-iot.github.io.

[4] See the http://iot.schema.org extension.

6. Roman, D., Keller, U., Lausen, H., De Bruijn, J., Lara, R., Stollberg, M., Polleres, A., Feier, C., Bussler, C., Fensel, D.: Web service modeling ontology. Appl. Ontol. **1**(1), 77–106 (2005)
7. Noia, T.D., Sciascio, E.D., Donini, F.M.: Semantic matchmaking as non-monotonic reasoning: a description logic approach. J. Artif. Intell. Res. **29**, 269–307 (2007)
8. Euzenat, J., Shvaiko, P.: Ontology Matching. Springer, Heidelberg (2007). https://doi.org/10.1007/978-3-540-49612-0

Exploiting Equivalence to Infer Type Subsumption in Linked Graphs

Russa Biswas[1,2](✉), Maria Koutraki[1,2], and Harald Sack[1,2]

[1] FIZ Karlsruhe – Leibniz Institute for Information Infrastructure,
Karlsruhe, Germany
[2] Institute AIFB, Karlsruhe Institute of Technology, Karlsruhe, Germany
{russa.biswas,maria.koutraki,harald.sack}@kit.edu

Abstract. Open Knowledge Graphs (KGs) such as DBpedia and Wikidata have been recognized as the foundations for diverse applications in the field of data mining and information retrieval. Each of these KGs follows a different knowledge organization as well as is based on differently structured ontologies. Moreover, it has been observed that type information are often noisy, incomplete or even incorrect. In general, there is a need for well defined and comparable type information for the entities of the KGs. In this paper, we propose an isomorphism-based approach to infer subsumption relations to RDF type information in Wikidata by exploiting the RDF type information from DBpedia.

Keywords: Knowledge graph · RDF · Wikidata · DBpedia

1 Introduction

Since the introduction of the Linked Open Data (LOD) cloud, the general purpose KGs like DBpedia, YAGO, Wikidata have been the focal point of research in the field of data mining and information retrieval. Hence, the correctness and completeness of such KGs is of great importance. However, many studies show that information in these KGs often can be noisy, incorrect and incomplete [3,6,7,9]. One way to account for the incompleteness of information in a KG is to harness the complementary information from different KGs.

Nevertheless, the different KGs are following different knowledge organization approaches [2,4,8] and use different underlying ontologies to represent knowledge, where explicit alignments amongst the different ontologies are not always available [5]. Therefore, a direct comparison of the KGs in the content level is a challenging task. For example, in Wikidata, the property wdt:P31 (instance of)[1] defines what we know as rdf:type. However, based on our observations, wdt:P31 follows different semantics and it differs in its use when compared to rdf:type in DBpedia. Thus, by relying only on wdt:P31 it is not possible to have a direct content-based comparison of the classes of the two KGs.

---

[1] https://www.wikidata.org/wiki/Property:P31.

© Springer Nature Switzerland AG 2018
A. Gangemi et al. (Eds.): ESWC 2018 Satellite Events, LNCS 11155, pp. 72–76, 2018.
https://doi.org/10.1007/978-3-319-98192-5_14

In this paper, we propose a light-weight isomorphism-based schema matching approach to harmonize two KGs having different underlying schema structure. For this study, we have used the two most popular KGs: DBpedia (English language) and Wikidata. The main aim of this work is to infer type subsumption relations in Wikidata by leveraging the existing equivalence relations between Wikidata and DBpedia. To this purpose we establish *conditional subsumption relations* between Wikidata properties and `rdf:type`.

2   Type Subsumption

Problem Description - We consider two RDFS[2] KGs, a source K_S and a target K_T, consisting of set of triples $K \subseteq E \times R \times (E \cup L)$, where E is a set of resources referred to as entities, L a set of literals, and R a set of relations. $\{C_{S_i}\}$ and $\{C_{T_j}\}$ is the set of classes in the source and target KG respectively. We assume that the classes and the entities of K_S and K_T are aligned i.e. K_S stores the statement $<C_{S_n}, \texttt{owl:equivalentClass}, C_{T_m}>$ and $<e_S, \texttt{owl:sameAs}, e_T>$.

In this work, we aim for a *conditional subsumption relation alignment*, as the schemas used for KGs vary heavily. Thus only *equivalence* alignments that have merely similar semantics or subsume one another are not enough to map the relations. Following the *relation subsumption* definition in [5] the goal is:

Goal. For two KGs, a source $K_S \subseteq E_S \times R_S \times (E_S \cup L_S)$ and a target $K_T \subseteq E_T \times R_T \times (E_T \cup L_T)$, and a relation $\textbf{rdf:type} \in R_S$, find relations $r_T \in R_T$ s.t. $r_T \subseteq \textbf{rdf:type}$. The *equivalence* relation between r_S and r_T, can also be expressed as a two-way subsumption relation: $r_S \equiv r_T$, iff $r_S \subseteq r_T$ and $r_T \subseteq r_S$.

Methodology - The aforementioned goal is achieved by exploiting the equivalence relations of classes and instances between the two KGs. The method is described with the help of the illustration in Fig. 1.

Step 1: For each class C_{S_i} in DBpedia, we determine the entities e_S of the class via `rdf:type` relation. Formally: $\forall C_{S_i} \in K_S : <e_S, \texttt{rdf:type}, C_{S_i}>$

Step 2: From the entities e_S, find those with `owl:sameAs` link(s) to corresponding e_T entities in Wikidata. Formally: $\forall e_S \in C_{S_i}, \exists e_T \in K_T : <e_S, \texttt{owl:sameAs}, e_T>$

Step 3: Determine the class C_{T_j} in Wikidata equivalent to DBpedia class, C_{S_i} via the `owl:equivalentClass` relation.
Formally: $\forall C_{S_i} \in K_S, \exists C_{T_j} \in K_T : <C_{S_i}, \texttt{owl:equivalentClass}, C_{T_j}>$5

Step 4: For each entity e_{T_j}, check if there is any relation (or relations) r_{T_j}, which connects to C_{T_j}. Formally: $\forall e_T, \exists r_{T_j} \in K_T : <e_T, r_{T_j}, C_{T_j}>$

3   Experimental Evaluation

This section discusses the results of the approach of inferring type subsumption relations in Wikidata leveraging existing mappings to DBpedia. Due to lack of space the full set of results can be found here [1].

---

[2] https://www.w3.org/RDFS/.

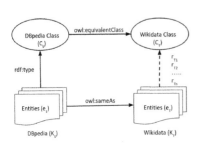

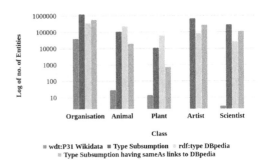

Fig. 1. Isomorphic approach to infer type subsumption relations in Wikidata with the help of DBpedia

Fig. 2. Comparison of the KGs (best viewed with color print) [1]

For this work, all the experiments were carried out on DBpedia 2016-10 version and Wikidata as of January 11, 2018. Out of the *524* interlinked classes between DBpedia and Wikidata, we conducted experiments on *327* classes, the instances of which are linked via `owl:sameAs`.

Results - The experiments establish the fact that the type information in Wikidata is often implicitly defined and 41 properties, including `wdt:P31` (instance of), hold a subsumption relation with `rdf:type` in DBpedia. Interestingly only the members of about 38% of these Wikidata classes can be accessed via `wdt:P31`. Furthermore, only 58% of the aforementioned 38% of Wikidata classes are using the property `wdt:P31` exclusively to denote the membership in a class. Table 1 shows some Wikidata classes and the properties serving as `rdf:type` ordered by the percentage of the class members which were retrieved via them.

Additionally, it is also interesting to notice that similar classes have similar type subsumption relations. For instance, for the classes in Wikidata denoting different kinds of professions such as, *Artist, Scientist* the property *occupation* (`wdt:P106`) defines the members of the class.

Figure 2 illustrates a comparison between DBpedia and Wikidata for 5 classes. It is interesting to notice that the number of instances retrieved from Wikidata via the new type subsumption relations (red bar) is much higher than via only `wdt:P31` (blue bar). Hence, more members of the classes can be retrieved using the subsumption relations leading to a strong foundation for the content level comparison of the KGs.

Furthermore, the green bar in the Fig. 2 represents the number of instances of the corresponding Wikidata classes using the type subsumption relations of Table 1, which also have `owl:sameAs` links to DBpedia. For all these classes, it has been observed that the height of the red bar (count of instances with new type subsumption relations) is higher than the green bar (count of instances with new type subsumption relations and `owl:sameAs` links to DBpedia), which reflects that Wikidata potentially contains more information than DBpedia for these classes. Also, it can be inferred that some of these entities in Wikidata are

Table 1. Type subsumption properties for Wikidata classes [1]

Class	Conditional $r_T \equiv$ `rdf:type`
Organisation	Instance of (P31) (99.7%), is a list of (P360) (0.2997%), has part (P527) (0.0003%)
Animal	Found in taxon(P703) (87%), instance of (P31) (8%), depicts (P180) (3.6%), category combines topics (P971) (1.04%), parent taxon (P171) (0.09%), is a list of (P360) (0.07%), part of (P361) (0.3%)
Artist	Occupation (P106) (98.3%), depicts (P180) (1.1%), instance of (P31) (0.4%), is a list of (P360) (0.2%)
Scientist	Occupation (P106) (99.99%), instance of (P31) (0.01%)

also present in DBpedia but are assigned to some other classes in DBpedia. This however can lead to further research on the correctness of the KG content.

Last, for the classes `dbo:Animal` and `dbo:Plant`, the number of instances in DBpedia (yellow) is higher than the number of instances that possess `owl:sameAs` links (green). Thus, some of the instances of these two classes in DBpedia are not instances of the corresponding `owl:equivalentClass` in Wikidata.

4 Conclusion and Future Work

This paper presented an isomorphic approach to infer type subsumption relations in Wikidata with the help of DBpedia. This approach can be extended to any two arbitrary KGs sharing equivalent classes and some equivalent instances. The results obtained in this study can be used as a starting point of further research on discovering potential errors or violations in the content of KGs. Next, we will explore the implicit type information stored in these KGs and contribute towards their completeness by predicting the type information using structural embeddings.

References

1. Directory with all achieved results. https://github.com/ISE-AIFB/Wiki_DB
2. Färber, M., Bartscherer, F., Menne, C., Rettinger, A.: Linked data quality of DBpedia, Freebase, Opencyc, Wikidata, and YAGO. Semant. Web **9**(1), 77–129 (2018)
3. Fleischhacker, D., Paulheim, H., Bryl, V., Völker, J., Bizer, C.: Detecting errors in numerical linked data using cross-checked outlier detection. In: Mika, P., et al. (eds.) ISWC 2014. LNCS, vol. 8796, pp. 357–372. Springer, Cham (2014). https://doi.org/10.1007/978-3-319-11964-9_23
4. Ismayilov, A., Kontokostas, D., Auer, S., Lehmann, J., Hellmann, S.: Wikidata through the Eyes of DBpedia. CoRR abs/1507.04180 (2015)
5. Koutraki, M., Preda, N., Vodislav, D.: Online relation alignment for linked datasets. In: Blomqvist, E., Maynard, D., Gangemi, A., Hoekstra, R., Hitzler, P., Hartig, O. (eds.) ESWC 2017. LNCS, vol. 10249, pp. 152–168. Springer, Cham (2017). https://doi.org/10.1007/978-3-319-58068-5_10

6. Melo, A., Paulheim, H., Völker, J.: Type prediction in RDF knowledge bases using hierarchical multilabel classification. In: WIMS, p. 14 (2016)
7. Paulheim, H., Bizer, C.: Type inference on noisy RDF data. In: Alani, H., et al. (eds.) ISWC 2013. LNCS, vol. 8218, pp. 510–525. Springer, Heidelberg (2013). https:// doi.org/10.1007/978-3-642-41335-3_32
8. Ringler, D., Paulheim, H.: One knowledge graph to rule them all? Analyzing the differences between DBpedia, YAGO, Wikidata & co. In: Kern-Isberner, G., Fürnkranz, J., Thimm, M. (eds.) KI 2017. LNCS, vol. 10505, pp. 366–372. Springer, Cham (2017). https://doi.org/10.1007/978-3-319-67190-1_33
9. Wienand, D., Paulheim, H.: Detecting incorrect numerical data in DBpedia. In: Presutti, V., d'Amato, C., Gandon, F., d'Aquin, M., Staab, S., Tordai, A. (eds.) ESWC 2014. LNCS, vol. 8465, pp. 504–518. Springer, Cham (2014). https://doi. org/10.1007/978-3-319-07443-6_34

Speleothem - An Information System for Caves Based on Semantic Web Technologies

Nikolaos Fanourakis[1,2] and Panagiotis Papadakos[2]([✉])

[1] Computer Science Department, University of Crete, Crete, Greece
[2] Institute of Computer Science, FORTH-ICS, Crete, Greece
`{fanourakis,papadako}@ics.forth.gr`

Abstract. Humans have used caves throughout history for a wide variety of needs, showcasing the importance of caves in human evolution. Nowadays, speleological clubs organize expeditions around and under the globe in an effort to understand, study and record the still unexplored and complex network of caves that lies underneath. Unfortunately, a common vocabulary for recording information related to caves and caving activities does not exist and most speleologists use adhoc and even non-digital forms to store it. This demo showcases the `Speleothem` system, an open-source information system for the domain of caves that exploits semantic web technologies and is built on top of a proposed vocabulary for caves and caving activities. `Speleothem` is designed in collaboration with a Greek speleological club, where it is planned to become operational in the near future.

1 Introduction

Caves have been used by humans throughout history for a wide variety of needs and purposes, and are highly interlinked with human evolution and civilization. They have been considered sacred places, decorated with parietal cave paintings by the first human artists (e.g. caves of Lascaux[1] and Altamira), and appear frequently in mythological and folklore stories. During bad weather conditions or war times, caverns have provided shelter for humans and livestocks and have been used for storing and mining resources (e.g. dairy products, water, minerals). Caves narrate the history of earth, and due to their isolation and remoteness they preserve important facts of the human history and host alien and fragile closed ecosystems. As a result they are considered sensitive information islands for a lot of scientific and academic disciplines, including but not limited to geology, anthropology, archeology, paleontology, biology, hydrology, seismology and folkloristics, and as such they are protected by local and international legislations.

Currently, a lot of people are visiting horizontal caves for their beautiful decorations or historical importance, and vertical ones for athletic and

---

[1] http://archeologie.culture.fr/lascaux/en.

© Springer Nature Switzerland AG 2018
A. Gangemi et al. (Eds.): ESWC 2018 Satellite Events, LNCS 11155, pp. 77–82, 2018.
https://doi.org/10.1007/978-3-319-98192-5_15

exploration reasons. Unfortunately, public or restricted access to cave related information is limited to either general information offered by local or global touristic portals (e.g. tripadvisor) or hard to find scientific publications and books that use complex terminologies. In addition, a lot of precious, delicate and difficult to extract information from previous expeditions is stored by local cave clubs in adhoc digital or non-digital forms. Consequently, the preservation, retrieval, validation, integration, and dissemination of information about caves, and the related human activities and their impact on them, is a rather cumbersome task. Addressing the above issues will not only provide a useful entry point to such information, but can also raise the awareness of the public opinion about the importance, sensitivity and particularities of this unseen underworld.

In this demo we present the `Speleothem` system, an open-source[2] web based system for storing and retrieving information about caves and cave related activities. It is based on semantic web technologies and introduces the `speleothem` vocabulary, especially designed for modeling cave related information. A SPARQL endpoint and a REST API for easy access to the data are also provided. The `Speleothem` system is designed in collaboration with the Speleological Club of Crete[3] where it is planned to become operational in the near future. Our aim is to offer a reference caving information system, on top of a domain specific knowledge base that stores information that can be used and linked by other external resources, for the general public, speleologists, speleological clubs and organizations.

2　Related Work

Software for caving has been limited to cave surveying, where by using specific electronic devices (or not) the software can create 2D or 3D representation of a cave (e.g. [1] and survex[4]), recording of locations, entrances and other cave related information over a map[5], or for showcasing the importance and fragility of caves (iCavern app [3]). Currently important cave related information is stored locally in cave clubs using adhoc digital or non-digital forms and vocabularies. Unfortunately, well-known ontologies (e.g. DBpedia) model only general information about caves[6] and miss other important entities and information, while others are too restrictive (e.g. the ontology described in [4] for mining equipment). In this work we propose the `speleothem` vocabulary, especially designed for modeling information about caves and cave related activities, that is at the core of the demonstrated `Speleothem` system.

---

[2] https://bitbucket.org/speleothem/speleothem.
[3] http://caves-crete.gr/.
[4] https://survex.com/.
[5] https://github.com/apgeo/silexgis, a relevant work based on a relational DB.
[6] http://dbpedia.org/ontology/Cave.

3   `speleothem` Vocabulary for Caves and Caving Activities

The current version of the proposed `speleothem` vocabulary consists of 50 classes, 25 object properties and 40 data properties. Using this vocabulary we can store information about the physical properties of the cave, such as the type and the size of the cavern, its location and entrances[7], the map of the cave (either in textual representations that can be used by other software like therion, or as sketches/images), collections of images of the cave itself and the outside environment, information related to the contained rooms and the natural or human created speleothems that it contains, along with their images. Each cave can be associated with climate data, living organisms, folklore stories or historical data. Regarding the caving activities, the vocabulary uses the foaf[8] vocabulary to store user profiles and caving clubs, and associates the profiles with caving equipment, special abilities of cavers (e.g. rescue training) and access policies to information. Furthermore, the vocabulary is able to hold important data about cave expeditions. `sameAs` connections with classes of other ontologies like from DBpedia[9] are also provided. A screenshot of the vocabulary using the Web-VOWL tool[10] (a web application for the interactive visualization of ontologies) is shown in Fig. 1. The current version of the `speleothem` vocabulary is online[11] but is not considered stable yet. We expect to make further refinements based on feedback from the SPOK club (where it is planned to become operational), and publish it using the best practices and the five stars policy described in [2].

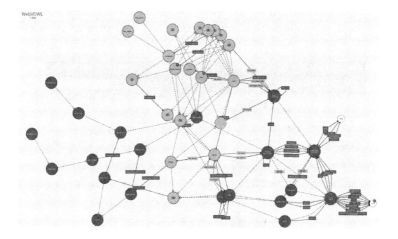

Fig. 1. The `speleothem` vocabulary as visualized by WebOWL

---

[7] http://www.geonames.org.
[8] http://xmlns.com/foaf/spec/.
[9] http://wiki.dbpedia.org.
[10] http://www.visualdataweb.de/webvowl/.
[11] http://www.speleothem.org/vocabulary/alpha.

4   Architecture and Implementation

The architecture of the `Speleothem` system is given in Fig. 2. The backend is implemented using Java technologies while the front-end is based on common web technologies and libraries (e.g. bootstrap, Google Maps API). The client sends AJAX requests to a REST service[12] that is implemented using spark-Java[13], which exploits the SPARQL endpoint[14]. We use RDF4J[15] for storing and querying the `Speleothem` knowledge base.

Fig. 2. The `Speleothem` architecture

5   Demo Scenarios

In the current demonstration we plan to showcase the following scenarios for different user roles (i.e. unregistered, registered and administrator):

Tour of a Cave: Public data like physical properties and position, cave climate, biological and historical data, and images (Fig. 3 shows the search screen). Moreover, registered users have access to detailed cave and rigging maps, past expeditions, and any information about rooms and speleothems (check Fig. 4).

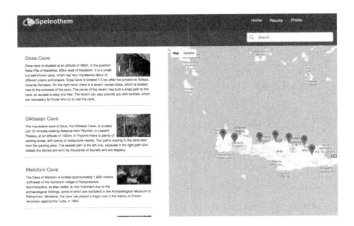

Fig. 3. Search results screen

---

[12] http://www.speleothem.org/rest.
[13] http://sparkjava.com/.
[14] http://www.speleothem.org/sparql.
[15] http://rdf4j.org/.

Fig. 4. Cave profile (Missions)

Fig. 5. Caving club profile

Expedition Overview: General information about a cave expedition, its aims, the participating cavers and clubs, previous related expeditions, a calendar and a report of the results, and possible revisions of cave data due to this mission.

Caving Club Overview: General club information, participated missions, members, general/rigging equipment and photos/sketches (check Fig. 5).

Caver Personal Information & Log book: User profiles of cavers, including caving clubs that they are members of, their personal equipment, important skills like knowledge of cave rescue and first aid techniques, participation in cave rescue exercises, and personal log book.

Cave Rescue: Organization and data logging during a cave rescue event.

References

1. Budaj, M., Mudrák, S.: Therion-digital cave maps therion-cartographie souterraine digitale. In: Presented on the 4th European Speleological Congress, Banska Bystrica, Slovakia (2008)
2. Janowicz, K., Hitzler, P., Adams, B., Kolas, D., Vardeman, I.I.: Five stars of linked data vocabulary use. Semant. Web **5**(3), 173–176 (2014)
3. Joop, S.D.: iCaverns: Interpretation, there's an app for that! (2013)
4. Liu, Z.H., Zeng, Q.L., Wang, C.L., Li, Y.S.: Research of equipment selection and matching expert system in fully mechanized caving face based on ontology. Key Eng. Mater. **419**, 117–120 (2010)

M-CREAM: A Tool for Creative Modelling of Emergency Scenarios in Smart Cities

Antonio De Nicola[1], Michele Melchiori[2], and Maria Luisa Villani[1(✉)]

[1] Computing and Technological Infrastructure Lab, ENEA, Rome, Italy
{antonio.denicola,marialuisa.villani}@enea.it
[2] Dip. di Ingegneria per l'Informazione, University of Brescia,
via Branze, 38, 25123 Brescia, Italy
michele.melchiori@unibs.it

Abstract. We present M-CREAM (eMergency-CREAtivity Machine), a novel tool for model-based elicitation of emergency management scenarios by city planners. M-CREAM suggests creative insights on new emergency situations to users, in the form of ontology-based conceptual models named mini-stories. Search and ranking techniques allow users to explore the mini-stories space, by leveraging semantic and computational creativity methods. A demonstration scenario focused on an Italian city illustrates the main features of the tool.

Keywords: Emergency management · Domain ontology
Contextual rules · Design pattern · Computational creativity

1 Introduction

A smart city aims at providing high quality of life to people living and visiting it. However, smart city ecosystems are threatened by several types of hazards, possibly hard to foresee, as natural disasters, terrorism, cyber attacks and cascading failures, due to the complexity of infrastructure interconnections. Thus, preparation to manage emergencies in this context is a relevant issue.[1]

We present M-CREAM[2], a new tool for emergency preparedness through scenarios elicitation and information sharing among different institutional operators who have a role in emergency management processes. Based on the architecture described in [3], the tool aims at easing human imagination and creativity to foresight emergency scenarios, by means of automatic creation of (parts of) emergency management (EM) scenario models, named *mini-stories*, by relying on formalized knowledge of the problem domain. In addition to [3], mini-stories are the basis for more detailed user descriptions of EM situations realizing scenario analysis models by means of a storytelling approach.

---

[1] https://www.smartresilient.com/emergency-preparedness.
[2] Demo video at https://youtu.be/HVuHxCttnss.

© Springer Nature Switzerland AG 2018
A. Gangemi et al. (Eds.): ESWC 2018 Satellite Events, LNCS 11155, pp. 83–88, 2018.
https://doi.org/10.1007/978-3-319-98192-5_16

The distinguishing features of the tool are: a domain ontology to describe the smart city ecosystem, the roles operating in it, and the types of hazards, which is used both to represent known emergency situations and search for new possible ones by means of semantic reasoning and computational creativity [2] techniques; a library of design patterns for EM scenario models; an engine for automatic generation of mini-stories based on design patterns and rules; intelligent search functions for exploring the mini-stories repository; automatic building the textual description of the full EM scenario from a pre-defined structure following a storytelling-type approach.

As far as we know, this tool is original in both aim and semantics-based EM scenarios modelling method. Previous works by some of the authors, e.g., [1], present a CREAM application to risk analysis of critical infrastructures, whereas a different creativity support to safety assessment in industry is proposed in [4].

Section 2 of the paper presents the M-CREAM architecture and modelling functions. The actual usage of the tool is described in Sect. 3 by means of a demonstration scenario involving typical users in EM.

2   M-CREAM for Scenario Modelling

The M-CREAM architecture, shown in Fig. 1, consists of a knowledge base and a set of modules to support creative scenario modelling through a web interface. Our approach, enhancing [3], requires some configuration activities on the knowledge base to adapt it to a specific city. These are performed by knowledge engineers through general purpose tools, like Protégé[3] and XML editors. The knowledge base components are the following.

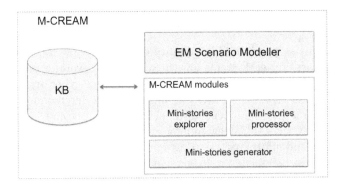

Fig. 1. M-CREAM architecture

EM smart city ontology and design patterns. The ontology integrates knowledge on hazards, critical infrastructures, (smart) services for companies and

---

[3] https://protege.stanford.edu.

citizens, emergency services, and users. These categories are linked by means of an upper level ontology based on the CEML metamodel, a SysML profile to model emergency management in socio-technical systems. CEML concepts include: *External Event, Service, Human Service, (Human) Resource*, and *User*[4]. Mini-stories are generated by means of CEML-based design patterns.

Scenario structure, representing a trace for user scenarios at run-time. A scenario is a composition of mini-stories. Similarly to games, it has a target state (e.g., recovery of people or extinguishing a fire), and an initial state, i.e., available resources and involved actors. Following this view, a scenario is associated with three stages: *opening, exploring* and *closing*. The first stage defines the initial role of actors involved in the scenario and the initial events. The second stage is when the actors explore the scenario and new situations could arise. In the third stage actors move towards the target state through actions and decisions.

Scenario context and relevance metrics. The scenario context refers to the actual city, with geographical and political characteristics. Space-time contextual rules, such as presence of infrastructure services (e.g., Rome does not have wind power plants) and current regulations on emergency management (e.g., the army does not intervene in case of clashes), are defined. These rules complete the formal requirements for the mini-stories generation by M-CREAM. Metrics such as on the economic impact of a damage, and their evaluation over the concepts of the ontology, allow to estimate the overall relevance of generated mini-stories.

The EM scenario modelling activities are performed by city planners through the web GUI of the *Scenario Modeller* component, shown in Fig. 2. A user selects a design pattern from a pre-defined list at the left-hand side of the GUI. Thus, the *Mini-stories generator* component produces a set of mini-stories based on that pattern, shown in the lower part of the GUI. The central part of the GUI shows a CEML diagram of a mini-story automatically generated from a design pattern. This represents the following situation. *The **Salt water intrusion** external event impacts on the **Water distribution network** service providing **drinking water** to users. The **Police** human service sends **policemen** to help in the emergency.* A textual description of the design pattern is reported over the diagram. The mini-stories generation process works as follows. Once a pattern is selected from the list, a SPARQL query is constructed by accounting for the CEML concepts and relationships used in that pattern to retrieve all of their specializations from the domain ontology. Structural and contextual rules provide filter statements for that query, which is implemented through the Apache Jena framework[5]. The *Mini-stories explorer* implements search methods to help users in the identification of scenario contents. These follow computational creativity techniques [2] according to which a new design can result from *transformation* of aspects of some known design and/or by *analogy* thinking. In particular, search functions use mini-stories ranking by relevance and semantic similarity elaborated by the *Mini-stories processor*. The toolbar of the central

---

[4] The OWL version of the ontology can be visualized by the WebProtégé tool at the address https://tinyurl.com/crisismng4-0.

[5] https://jena.apache.org.

panel of the GUI provides two means to automatically suggest a mini-story: a *Hint!* button shows a randomly chosen mini-story; a *Change* button modifies all or parts of a given mini-story *A* with concepts that are either semantically very distant or very similar to their correspondent in *A*. The toolbar of the lower panel provides mini-story filter functions and ranking by relevance (last column). User described mini-stories, as shown in the editing window of Fig. 2, associated with the three stages of scenario definition, can be selected from the list at the right panel, and combined to provide the full EM scenario description.

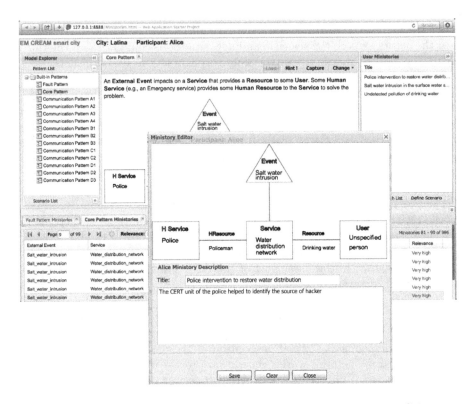

Fig. 2. M-CREAM GUI: patterns, mini-stories and user mini-story editing

3   Demonstration on a Case Study

M-CREAM has been positively evaluated at some Italian public institutions having an official role in emergency management. We report a narrative on how the tool was used during one experiment and the resulting relevant scenario[6].

The Civil Protection intends to prepare for facing emergencies caused by increasing seasonal temperatures in Italy in the last years. Various governmental

---

[6] Details are shown in the video at https://youtu.be/HVuHxCttnss.

institutions contribute to the activity of EM scenarios foresight from their own perspective, so employers of an environmental agency located in Latina use M-CREAM, which had been previously configured as follows.

A EM scenario will consist of one or two *start* (i.e., related to the opening stage) mini-stories based on the *Fault Pattern* (see the patterns list on the left side of Fig. 2), referring to services impacted by some events. Then a couple of subsequent mini-stories, based on *Communication Patterns*, represent how the information about the emergency is propagated. Finally, an *end* mini-story, based on the *Core Pattern*, describes intervention from emergency services.

The scenarios are located in Latina, a seaside city, and the environmental agency is mainly interested in water related hazards impacting on infrastructure services. Filter rules on events and infrastructures, such as absence of metro, are defined accordingly to restrict the scope of the mini-stories generation process.

Silvana, an employee of the agency, first focuses on the *highest relevant* mini-stories to describe the emergency of her scenario. While doing so, she considers a risk following a drought, based on two proposed mini-stories: one representing *salt water intrusion* interfering with *drinking water* from a *water distribution network*, and a second one showing the same event impacting on the *drought monitoring* service, which sends *information about critical situation* to an *enterprise*. So, she edits the following piece of scenario by describing those mini-stories. *A drought at Latina leading to an increased groundwater abstraction, caused salt water intrusion from the nearby sea. This event, once captured by the drought monitoring unit, is communicated to the water distribution company.* For the development of the scenario with unusual situations, Silvana decides to use the *Hint!* function on the Communication Patterns. After some tries, and usage of the *Change* function on the proposed mini-stories, she describes and connects three other mini-stories suggesting an interesting sequel that is so synthesized: *An hacker-type vandalism at the water company had caused the water quality alarm being undetected internally. An employee informs the city mayor of the possible water contamination and of the service interruption. The intervention of the police cybercrime unit at the water network allows to restore the service.*

Acknowledgements. This work is partially funded by Accordo di Programma Ministero dello Sviluppo Economico - ENEA, Ricerca di Sistema Elettrico. The authors kindly acknowledge the Environmental Pressure Department of ARPALAZIO.

References

1. Coletti, A., De Nicola, A., Villani, M.L.: Enhancing creativity in risk assessment of complex sociotechnical systems. In: Gervasi, O., et al. (eds.) ICCSA 2017. LNCS, vol. 10405, pp. 294–309. Springer, Cham (2017). https://doi.org/10.1007/978-3-319-62395-5_21
2. Colton, S., Wiggins, G.A.: Computational creativity: the final frontier? In: Proceedings of the 20th European Conference on Artificial Intelligence, pp. 21–26. IOS Press (2012)

3. De Nicola, A., Melchiori, M., Villani, M.L.: A lateral thinking framework for semantic modelling of emergencies in smart cities. In: Decker, H., Lhotská, L., Link, S., Spies, M., Wagner, R.R. (eds.) DEXA 2014. LNCS, vol. 8645, pp. 334–348. Springer, Cham (2014). https://doi.org/10.1007/978-3-319-10085-2_31
4. Maiden, N., Zachos, K., Lockerbie, J., Hoddy, S., Camargo, K.: Establishing digital creativity support in non-creative work environments. In: Proceedings of the 11th ACM Creativity and Cognition Conference. ACM (2017)

Context Spaces as the Cornerstone of a Near-Transparent and Self-reorganizing Semantic Desktop

Christian Jilek[1,2(✉)], Markus Schröder[1,2], Sven Schwarz[1], Heiko Maus[1],
and Andreas Dengel[1,2]

[1] Smart Data and Knowledge Services Department, DFKI GmbH,
Kaiserslautern, Germany
{christian.jilek,markus.schroeder,sven.schwarz,heiko.maus,
andreas.dengel}@dfki.de
[2] Computer Science Department, TU Kaiserslautern, Kaiserslautern, Germany

Abstract. Existing Semantic Desktops are still reproached for being too complicated to use or not scaling well. Besides, a real "killer app" is still missing. In this paper, we present a new prototype inspired by NEPO-MUK and its successors having a semantic graph and ontologies as its basis. In addition, we introduce the idea of context spaces that users can directly interact with and work on. To make them available in all applications without further ado, the system is transparently integrated using mostly standard protocols complemented by a sidebar for advanced features. By exploiting collected context information and applying Managed Forgetting features (like hiding, condensation or deletion), the system is able to dynamically reorganize itself, which also includes a kind of tidy-up-itself functionality. We therefore expect it to be more scalable while providing new levels of user support. An early prototype has been implemented and is presented in this demo.

Keywords: Semantic desktop · Context · Transparent integration
Self-reorganization · Managed forgetting

1 Introduction

After its hype finally receded about half a decade ago, rather few advances in Semantic Desktop (SemDesk) research have been reported. An overview of (modern) SemDesks can be found in [1]: Existing implementations are, for example, reproached for being rather complicated to use, not scaling well (thus draining lots of system resources), and there is still no real "killer app" available. Concerning SemDesk applications, two categories could be observed: newly created semantic applications and plug-ins to enhance traditional, non-semantic ones [1].

© Springer Nature Switzerland AG 2018
A. Gangemi et al. (Eds.): ESWC 2018 Satellite Events, LNCS 11155, pp. 89–94, 2018.
https://doi.org/10.1007/978-3-319-98192-5_17

As a successor to the *NEPOMUK Semantic Desktop*[1], DFKI's Smart Data & Knowledge Services department developed its own prototype[2] [5] making SemDesk technology ready for 24/7 usage in practice, covering private and corporate scenarios. After lessons learned in various projects, we now propose *Context Spaces* as an extension of this prototype addressing the issues mentioned before.

2   Approach

Context Spaces. One of SemDesk's cornerstones is the Personal Information Model (PIMO) [7], which tries to represent a user's mental model as well as possible (especially in a machine understandable way). Information items (files, mails, bookmarks, ...) that are related to each other in a person's mind, but are separated on their computer (file system, mail client, web browser, ...), can thus be interlinked. With *Context Spaces* (or *cSpaces* for short) we extend this idea by explicitly (and additionally) associating items with contexts of the user (see lower left of Fig. 1). This is based on the intuition that every activity is performed in a certain context. Hence, each information item stored on a person's computing device can be associated with one or more contexts (association strength may vary depending on the user's current context awareness). We therefore assume that users are explicitly aware of the concept of context [2] and that they are also aware of their current context (at least most of the time). Examples of such contexts are: *Spain holiday 2017*, *prepare ESWC18 paper*, or *my childhood memories*. We do not enforce a certain definition of context: users should be able to stick to their own conceptualization as much as possible. However, we do assume

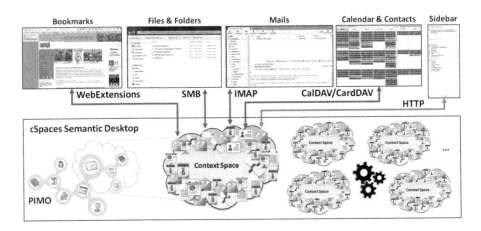

Fig. 1. Conceptual overview of the cSpaces Semantic Desktop

---

[1] www.semanticdesktop.org.
[2] This prototype is permanently used in the department since 2012, currently having a group knowledge graph of approx. 2.6 million triple statements.

that contexts express a certain relatedness of its elements. Besides being a kind of container for things, they may also be strongly related to (calendar) events or tasks. Our context model extends [9], e.g. by introducing context hierarchies or forgetting aspects. Instead of just having context as passive metadata, we in addition see it as an accessible element users can interact with (create new (sub)contexts, split or merge them, add/remove elements, etc.).

SemDesk user studies [8] revealed that people omitted rather specific relations in favor of basic ones (like *isRelatedTo* or *isPartOf*), whereas the system is formal where possible, e.g. representing calendar events or address book contacts. This matches our idea of providing a low effort opportunity to keep things a bit more tidied up when simply associating them with a certain context (or multiple contexts). Additionally, some of these associations may also be inferred by the system reducing manual effort even more, e.g. a received email reply can automatically be associated with the original mail's context. More advanced features supporting the user will be discussed in the section after next.

Transparent Integration. Using contexts as an explicit interaction element only makes sense if applications also respect them. Like illustrated in Fig. 1, we therefore integrate cSpaces into the rest of the system using standard protocols like *Server Message Block (SMB)* for files, *IMAP* for mails, *CalDAV* for calendar entries and tasks, and *CardDAV* for contacts. For web browsers, we use *Web-Extensions*[3], which provide cross-browser functionality and an integration level similar to having an underlying protocol. Thanks to these well-supported standards, we are able to inject our own file/mail/bookmark/calendar system deep into the surrounding system without modifying its code. Applications then operate on information items, which are actually parts of the knowledge graph (PIMO) transparently provided to them by the cSpaces app. Especially in corporate scenarios, it is very convenient if users may just work with the resources in their contexts without caring whether they are actually spread across various sources like intranet shares, for example.

Utilizing only standard protocols has certain limitations due to their rather basic, low-level character. Some activities, like writing a note or comment about a resource, can become inconvenient or non-intuitive. To avoid this, we provide an additional sidebar as a single interaction point for using advanced features. Users therefore do not need to learn a new (plugged-in) interface for each of their applications. They can just keep using them the usual way having only the sidebar as a new UI to become familiar with. From the development point of view, the effort of creating and maintaining plug-ins needed for higher level functionality is comparatively low to that of earlier SemDesks. They can be realized as *headless plug-ins* having very little functionality, often just the capability of *sending out* in-app events to the sidebar (that is why we also shortly call them "plug-outs"). In addition, their corresponding UI elements and logic are located

---

[3] https://wiki.mozilla.org/WebExtensions.

in the sidebar, where they can be easily reused. Plug-outs for different mail clients could, for example, share the same tagging UI.

Self-reorganization. Features discussed so far primarily aim at our system's ease of use. The other aspects mentioned in the beginning (scalability, missing "killer app") will be addressed using *Managed Forgetting*, by which we understand an escalating set of measures: temporal hiding, condensation, adaptive synchronization, archiving and deletion of resources and parts of the knowledge graph [6]. By having users work on cSpaces, we gather rich contextual information about all of their resources, which allows the system to semi-automatically help them in organizing their stuff. Thus, cSpaces are continuously spawned, retracted, merged, condensed, or forgotten. Some evidence for this is collected automatically (plug-outs, protocol logs), other hints are explicitly given by the user (create/modify cSpaces, tagging, etc.). As an example, let us assume we do a consulting job for company XY. The contract involves five meetings about different topics. Our system could represent this by having an overall cSpace containing general information about XY, e.g. contact and contract information. For each meeting, there could be an individual sub-cSpace about its respective topic. Several months after the job has been completed, the system starts to remove details, e.g. train schedule to get to the meeting or auxiliary material for doing the presentation. After some years have passed, the sub-cSpaces could be merged with their parent, since the separation into different meetings is not relevant anymore. Only the most important items, e.g. individual reports or an overall final report, are kept. All other items are either condensed, moved to an archive or deleted completely (which can be adjusted by the user on a general level). An item's current and estimated future value for the user are therefore continuously assessed resulting in different forgetting measures like temporal hiding (e.g. some items during one of the meetings), deletion, etc. This especially means that the system is able to reorganize itself to a certain extent, which especially includes a kind of tidying-up-itself functionality. Some of the described features have already been implemented and successfully used in our research and industry prototypes [3,4], however most of them are still under heavy development.

Demo. In an early proof-of-concept implementation based on [5], we already realized some of the file system, browser and calendar parts. The screenshots in Fig. 2 show a typical feature of our system: the user selects a different context using the sidebar. As a consequence, the *current context*, available as a folder in the file system as well as the browser, is dynamically reorganized by our app. Note that the system tries to present meaningful views on the current context in each app: e.g., the view in the browser only contains web links. To really get an impression of how the interaction with the system looks like, we kindly refer the reader to our demo video[4], which also shows some additional features.

---

[4] find this paper's demo website at https://pimo.opendfki.de/cSpaces/.

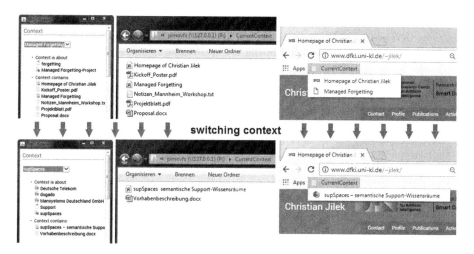

Fig. 2. Screenshot of sidebar, file explorer and browser before (top) and after a context switch (bottom), illustrating the effects of a dynamic reorganization of the system.

3   Conclusion and Outlook

In this paper, we presented a new SemDesk prototype based context spaces that users directly interact with and work on. The system is transparently integrated using mostly standard protocols complemented by a sidebar for advanced features. Users may thus stick to their favorite applications which should strongly contribute to the overall ease of use. Learning efforts are presumably low due to the sidebar being the only new UI that is introduced. By exploiting its collected context information and applying features of Managed Forgetting, the system is able to dynamically reorganize itself which also includes a kind of tidying-up-itself functionality. We therefore expect it to be more scalable than its predecessors while providing new levels of user support. Nevertheless, a lot of functionality still needs to be fully implemented and evaluated. We plan to do extensive user studies once the system matures.

Acknowledgements. This work was funded by the Deutsche Forschungsgemeinschaft (DFG, German Research Foundation) – DE 420/19-1.

References

1. Drăgan, L., Decker, S.: Knowledge management on the desktop. In: ten Teije, A., et al. (eds.) EKAW 2012. LNCS (LNAI), vol. 7603, pp. 373–382. Springer, Heidelberg (2012). https://doi.org/10.1007/978-3-642-33876-2_33
2. Gomez-Perez, J.M., Grobelnik, M., Ruiz, C., Tilly, M., Warren, P.: Using task context to achieve effective information delivery. In: 1st Workshop on Context, Information and Ontologies, CIAO 2009, pp. 3:1–3:6. ACM (2009)

3. Jilek, C., Maus, H., Schwarz, S., Dengel, A.: Diary generation from personal information models to support contextual remembering and reminiscence. In: 2015 IEEE International Conference on Multimedia & Expo Workshops, ICMEW 2015, pp. 1–6 (2015)

4. Jilek, C., Schwarz, S., Maus, H., Dengel, A.: Managed forgetting, data condensation & preservation in application. In: 2016 ACM International Joint Conference on Pervasive and Ubiquitous Computing: Adjunct, UbiComp 2016, pp. 1046–1053. ACM (2016)

5. Maus, H., Schwarz, S., Dengel, A.: Weaving personal knowledge spaces into office applications. In: Fathi, M. (ed.) Integration of Practice-Oriented Knowledge Technology: Trends and Prospectives, pp. 71–82. Springer, Heidelberg (2013)

6. Maus, H., Jilek, C., Schwarz, S.: Remembering and forgetting for personal preservation. In: Mezaris, V., Niederée, C., Logie, R.H. (eds.) Personal Multimedia Preservation: Remembering or Forgetting Images and Video, pp. 233–277. Springer, Heidelberg (2018). https://doi.org/10.1007/978-3-319-73465-1_7

7. Sauermann, L., van Elst, L., Dengel, A.: PIMO - a framework for representing personal information models. I-Semantics **7**, 270–277 (2007)

8. Sauermann, L., Heim, D.: Evaluating long-term use of the gnowsis semantic desktop for PIM. In: Sheth, A., et al. (eds.) ISWC 2008. LNCS, vol. 5318, pp. 467–482. Springer, Heidelberg (2008). https://doi.org/10.1007/978-3-540-88564-1_30

9. Schwarz, S.: A context model for personal knowledge management applications. In: Roth-Berghofer, T.R., Schulz, S., Leake, D.B. (eds.) MRC 2005. LNCS (LNAI), vol. 3946, pp. 18–33. Springer, Heidelberg (2006). https://doi.org/10.1007/11740674_2

SeGoFlow: A Semantic Governance Workflow Tool

Sven Lieber[(✉)] , Anastasia Dimou , and Ruben Verborgh

IDLab, Department of Electronics and Information Systems,
Ghent University – imec, Ghent, Belgium
{sven.lieber,anastasia.dimou,ruben.verborgh}@ugent.be

Abstract. Data management increasingly demands transparency with respect to data processing. Various stakeholders need information tailored to their needs, e.g. data management plans (DMP) for funding agencies or privacy policies for the public. DMPs and privacy policies are just two examples of documents describing aspects of data processing. Dedicated tools to create both already exist. However, creating each of them manually or semi-automatically remains a repetitive and cognitively challenging task. We propose a data-driven approach that semantically represents the data processing itself as workflows and serves as a base for different kinds of result-sets, generated with SPARQL, i.e. DMPs. Our approach is threefold: (i) users with domain knowledge semantically represent workflow components; (ii) other users can reuse these components to describe their data processing via semantically enhanced workflows; and, based on the semantic workflows, (iii) result-sets are automatically generated on-demand with SPARQL queries. This paper demonstrates our tool that implements the proposed approach, based on a use-case of a researcher who needs to provide a DMP to a funding agency to approve a proposed research project.

Keywords: Provenance · Workflow · Governance · Data management

1 Introduction

Funding agencies and other institutions require data management plans (DMPs) before research proposals can be approved, see e.g. H2020[1], FWO[2], NWO[3]. These DMPs are questionnaires asking questions like *What data will you collect or create?*, or *How will you ensure that stored data are secure?*. The aim of these plans is to assess if the performed data processing complies to FAIR[4] principles and force the creator to reflect over the planned data usage within a project. A DMP is only one example of a document describing data processing in a project.

---

[1] H2020 Programme Guidelines on FAIR Data Management in Horizon 2020, Europe.
[2] Fonds Wetenschappelijk Onderzoek – Vlaanderen, Belgium.
[3] Nederlandse Organisatie voor Wetenschappelijk Onderzoek, The Netherlands.
[4] Findable, Accessible, Interoperable, Re-usable.

© Springer Nature Switzerland AG 2018
A. Gangemi et al. (Eds.): ESWC 2018 Satellite Events, LNCS 11155, pp. 95–99, 2018.
https://doi.org/10.1007/978-3-319-98192-5_18

Another example are privacy policies. When the study includes the collection and processing of personal data, the consent of the participants is needed. Therefore, a privacy policy needs to be written and handed out to the participants.

Even though DMPs and privacy policies are different documents, yet both aim to describe certain aspects of data processing. However, information of multiple domains is needed to create a DMP or a privacy policy, For instance the legal domain, *which data are considered as personally identifiable information?* Or the technical domain, *are used data stores accessible by third parties?* Users might request or discover all this information, compile it and add it to the DMP, the privacy policy or to any other document a stakeholder requested. Each change of the data processing entails a repetition of that process and creates new versions of all documents, which introduces even more complexity.

This demo shows our data processing workflow editor. Instead of using dedicated tools to generate DMPs or privacy policies, the proposed tool *SeGoFlow* assists in the creation of data processing workflows. *SeGoFlow* shows that a single semantic description of data processing workflows and result-sets, generated by SPARQL queries over that representation, can be used as base for DMPs.

Since not everyone who models data processing is familiar with Semantic Web technologies, our proposed tool makes use of a graphical workflow language to model the data processing, which also improves the communication between stakeholders [1]. The graphical workflow components, that are described with the OPMW ontology[5], can also be reused, which simplifies the need to request or discover relevant information when modelling data processing of a certain project. The screencast available at https://www.youtube.com/watch?v=6zTRL1WUL5g, demonstrates the generation of a DMP with our tool.

2   Demonstration

This section introduces our proposed tool, *SeGoFlow*, based on a scenario.

Scenario. A researcher performs a study to investigate stress in peoples daily life. Therefore each participant receives multiple wearable devices used to measure values like heart response or skin conductance. The study also involves the processing of participants private data, like their email address. Before the research starts, a DMP needs to be provided to the funding agency. The researcher uses our proposed tool *SeGoFlow* to describe the data processing tasks.

Projects. Our tool allows to create graphical data-driven *workflows*. Multiple workflows can be grouped into a *project* to increase readability of each workflow. The introduced researcher creates one workflow to describe the process of data collection, and another workflow describing the data sharing. Figure 1 shows the data collection workflow of the demonstration.

---

[5] http://www.opmw.org/model/OPMW/.

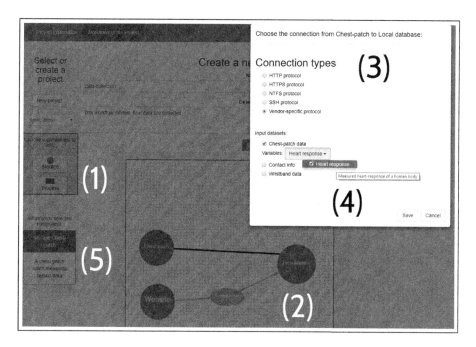

Fig. 1. A screenshot of the user interface. (1) The menu where users can select *data stores* and *processes*. (2) The workflow drawing area in which the workflow is modelled. (3) A connection dialog, asking a user *which* data should be transferred from *chest-patch* to *local database* and *how* it should be transferred. (4) Tooltips when hovering over elements. (5) Detailed information of the currently selected component. (Color figure online)

Workflow Components. The basic components of a workflow are *data stores* and *data processes*. These can be selected from a *repository* and inserted into a *workflow*, part (1) of Fig. 1 shows the components menu. Each component is described semantically to express detailed information of multiple domains in an interoperable way. For example data stores, the semantic model describes their physical location as well as persons and organizations having access. The separation of defining a component and re-using a component, allows users with domain knowledge to create and maintain components, whereas users interested in modelling data processing can focus purely on the workflows. Users with the aim of modelling their data processing are provided with more details about workflow components (part (4) and (5) of Fig. 1).

The introduced researcher finds relevant data stores and processes in the repository and re-uses them. Part (2) of Fig. 1 shows the drawing area of a workflow, containing the three *data stores Chest-patch*, *Local database* and *Website*.

Connections. SeGoFlow offers the functionality to connect selected components of a workflow with each other. One connection symbolizes the flow (transfer) of data. Since the way *how* data are being transferred carries important semantics, these connections are modelled semantically as well. A connection defines which data are being transferred, and also which protocol or communication channel is used. The tool prompts the user to select data and a transfer protocol. These semantically defined data and protocols are available through a repository as well. Part (3) of Fig. 1, shows the dialog where a user has to choose the semantics of a connection. In case of the screenshot, the connection from *Chest-patch* to *Local database* is selected. The connection itself is represented as yellow arrow, containing the name of the transferred dataset.

Data Management Plan Generation. Based on the workflows of a project, a DMP can automatically be generated via a button of the project description view. Figure 2 shows an excerpt of a generated DMP. The question regarding used data stores could be answered based on the used workflow components (see part (1) of Fig. 2). Semantics of data transfers (drawn connections) were used to

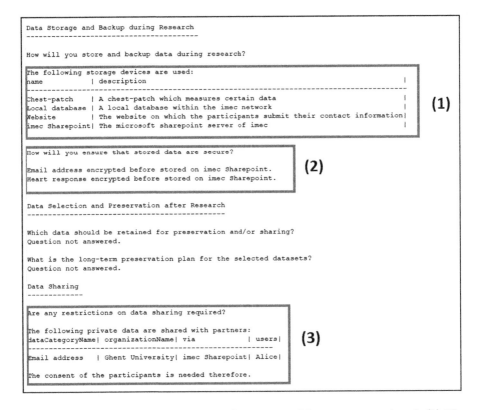

Fig. 2. Excerpt of a data management plan generated by our proposed tool. (1) The answer regarding used data stores is answered based on used workflow components. The semantics of drawn workflow connections contributed to answer questions regarding data sharing (2, 3). The DMP is generated by a text template and SPARQL queries against the workflows created in the demonstration available at https://www.youtube. com/watch?v=6zTRL1WUL5g.

answer the question regarding the secure storage of data (see part (2) of Fig. 2). Finally the semantically encoded legal domain knowledge that *Email address* is considered as personal data, and the technical domain knowledge that the used data store is accessible by a user of another institution, contributes to the answer of data sharing restrictions (see part (3) of Fig. 2).

3   Conclusion and Future Work

With *SeGoFlow*, researchers have a semantically enhanced and a graphical representation of data processing. Such a graphical representation allows, for example, researchers to communicate their research to colleagues or other stakeholders. Researchers create detailed workflows which reflect on their data processing. Workflow components, as well as projects and workflows themselves are described semantically in a provenance-aware way that reduces the overhead and provides valuable information in case of e.g. an audit.

A possible future direction is to further assist users in creating workflows. For instance, to provide directly privacy-related feedback when connecting components, as already proposed for computational workflow tools [2,3].

References

1. Johnston, W.M., Hanna, J.R., Millar, R.J.: Advances in dataflow programming languages. ACM Comput. Surv. (CSUR) **36**(1), 1–34 (2004)
2. Gil, Y., Cheung, W.K., Ratnakar, V., Chan, K.k.: Privacy enforcement in data analysis workflows. In: Proceedings of the 2007 PEAS Workshop, pp. 41–48 (2007)
3. Gil, Y., Fritz, C.: Reasoning about the appropriate use of private data through computational workflows. In: AAAI Spring Symposium: Intelligent Information Privacy Management (2010)

Image User Profiling with Knowledge Graph and Computer Vision

Vincent Lully[1,2(✉)], Philippe Laublet[1], Milan Stankovic[1,2],
and Filip Radulovic[2]

[1] Sorbonne Université, 28 rue Serpente, 75006 Paris, France
{vincent.lully,philippe.laublet}@sorbonne-universite.fr
[2] Sépage, 38 avenue de l'Opéra, 75002 Paris, France
{milstan,filip}@sepage.fr

Abstract. In this paper, we explore the synergy between knowledge graph technologies and computer vision tools for image user profiling. We propose two image user profiling approaches which map an image to knowledge graph entities representing the interests of a user who appreciates the image. The first one maps an image to entities which correspond to the objects appearing in the image. The second one maps to entities which are depicted by visually similar images and which exist in the conceptual scope of the dataset within which further personalisation tasks are conducted. A demo configured with a real and recent commercial travel domain dataset is given at ESWC 2018.

Keywords: Image · User profiling · Knowledge graph · Computer vision
Personalisation · Travel · Recommender system

1 Introduction

Recent research efforts show several interesting convergence points between knowledge graph and computer vision, such as improving object detection with external knowledge graphs [1], scene description with triples [2], knowledge graph completion with visual features [3] and visuo-semantic search [4]. In this paper, we explore their synergy for image user profiling which has not been sufficiently studied so far.

Since several years, knowledge graphs have been leveraged to conduct user profiling through semantic analysis of text and to improve content-based recommendation approaches by providing structured metadata [5–10]. Today, a tremendous amount of multimedia data are available on the web and are being produced continuously. Modern websites should be equipped with systems which can understand users' interests through their interactions with multimedia data and adapt the services accordingly in order to provide a better user experience.

© Springer Nature Switzerland AG 2018
A. Gangemi et al. (Eds.): ESWC 2018 Satellite Events, LNCS 11155, pp. 100–104, 2018.
https://doi.org/10.1007/978-3-319-98192-5_19

Our main contribution is two novel image user profiling approaches:

- The first one maps an image to entities which correspond to the objects appearing in the image.
- The second one maps to entities which are depicted by visually similar images and which exist in the conceptual scope of the dataset within which further personalisation tasks are conducted.

In the rest of the paper, we discuss some related work on image user profiling in Sect. 2, we then present our two image user profiling approaches in Sect. 3, Sect. 4 describes the demonstration given at ESWC 2018 and Sect. 5 concludes the paper.

2   Related Work

We present some existing approaches which create user profiles from images. In [11], the authors try to detect demographic attributes of individual users and group types from the photos posted on photo sharing sites. In [12], the authors derive users' personalities from pictures posted on Instagram. In [13], the authors introduce a picture-based user elicitation and recommendation method for tourism products. The system creates a user profile which consists of 7 traveller types accompanied with a matching degree. A very similar tool is presented in [14] which maps photos to 17 tourist types. In [15], the photos are mapped to several pre-defined categories such as "leisure", "art" and "culture". Different from these existing approaches, the approaches that we propose map images to knowledge graph entities. This choice has been motivated by existing work which has proven the advantages of such semantic user profiling per se and in personalisation systems [5–10].

3   Two Novel Image User Profiling Approaches

In this section, we present two image user profiling approaches which map an input image to knowledge graph entities. A user profile contains top-n entities representing things of interest to a user who appreciates the input image. In this paper, we use DBpedia, knowing that other similar large-scale knowledge graphs like Wikidata can also be used.

The first approach consists of mapping an image to entities which correspond to the objects appearing in the image. There are two main steps: object detection and entity linking. For object detection, we use a computer vision tool named "Inception-V3" [16]. Inception-V3 is a convolutional neural network model trained for the ImageNet Large Visual Recognition Challenge using the data from 2012. The model tries to classify entire images into 1000 classes which are WordNet synsets like "gazelle" and "patio, terrace". At the entity linking step, we map the 1000 synsets to corresponding DBpedia entities. We are completely aware that this is a very basic and obvious approach. We still present it because we did not find it in the state of the art.

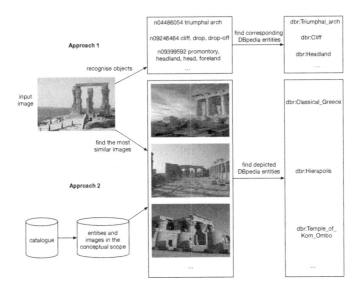

Fig. 1. Example illustrating the two proposed image user profiling approaches

The second approach consists of mapping an image to entities which are depicted by visually similar images and which exist in the conceptual scope of the catalogue within which further personalisation tasks are conducted. The conceptual scope is a new notion that we propose in our work. We assume that the user profiling is not an end in itself but should serve further personalisation tasks. The created user profiles should be useful for these further tasks. Given a catalogue of items, we currently consider that its conceptual scope consists of all knowledge graph entities which directly appear in the catalogue. The entities can be obtained by two means: direct item linking and item description linking as presented in [17]. To compute the visual similarity between images, we rely on the penultimate layer outputted by Inception-V3 which is a 2048-dimensional vector. The similarity between two images is determined by the Euclidean distance between their vectors.

Our second approach requires the following steps:

1. We constitute the conceptual scope of the catalogue.
2. We retrieve the images depicting the entities in the conceptual scope (linked by the property "foaf:depiction").
3. We compute pairwise visual similarity between the input image and the depicting images with the method explained above.
4. We retain the n most similar depicting images and thereafter the entities linked to them.

In Fig. 1, we give an example to illustrate the proposed approaches.

4   Demonstration Given at ESWC 2018

In the demonstration given at ESWC 2018, we showcase the second approach which is more advanced. We configured it with a real and recent commercial catalogue of a popular French travel agency. The catalogue contains 1,357 tours which take place in more than 136 countries and regions. The tours are depicted by 11,614 distinct images. The conceptual scope is obtained by item description linking and contains 13,109 DBpedia entities. We provide a Web interface where users can select an image that he/she is interested in and are then shown the profile (top-3 DBpedia entities) corresponding to the selected image (Fig. 2).

Please click on an image and check the created user profile.

Based on the image that you selected,

we guess you might be interested in:
http://dbpedia.org/resource/Khmer_architecture
http://dbpedia.org/resource/Angkor
http://dbpedia.org/resource/Angkor_Wat

Fig. 2. Screenshots of the demo given at ESWC 2018

5   Conclusion

In this paper, we explored the synergy between knowledge graph technologies and computer vision tools. We proposed two novel image user profiling approaches which map an image to knowledge graph entities representing the interests of a user who appreciates the image. We described the demonstration given at ESWC 2018 which is configured with a real and recent travel domain dataset. As future work, we plan to evaluate our profiling approaches and to apply them in personalisation tasks.

References

1. Fang, Y., Kuan, K., Lin, J., Tan, C., Chandrasekhar, V.: Object detection meets knowledge graphs. In: IJCAI, pp. 1661–1667 (2017)
2. Baier, S., Ma, Y., Tresp, V.: Improving visual relationship detection using semantic modeling of scene descriptions. In: d'Amato, C., et al. (eds.) ISWC 2017. LNCS, vol. 10587, pp. 53–68. Springer, Cham (2017). https://doi.org/10.1007/978-3-319-68288-4_4
3. Thoma, S., Rettinger, A., Both, F.: Towards holistic concept representations: embedding relational knowledge, visual attributes, and distributional word semantics. In: d'Amato, C., et al. (eds.) ISWC 2017. LNCS, vol. 10587, pp. 694–710. Springer, Cham (2017). https://doi.org/10.1007/978-3-319-68288-4_41

4. Ferrada, S., Bustos, B., Hogan, A.: IMGpedia: a linked dataset with content-based analysis of Wikimedia images. In: d'Amato, C., et al. (eds.) ISWC 2017. LNCS, vol. 10588, pp. 84–93. Springer, Cham (2017). https://doi.org/10.1007/978-3-319-68204-4_8

5. Di Noia, T., Mirizzi, R., Ostuni, V.C., Romito, D., Zanker, M.: Linked open data to support content-based recommender systems. In: Proceedings of the 8th International Conference on Semantic Systems, pp. 1–8. ACM, September 2012

6. Lu, C., Stankovic, M., Radulovic, F., Laublet, P.: Crowdsourced affinity: a matter of fact or experience. In: Blomqvist, E., Maynard, D., Gangemi, A., Hoekstra, R., Hitzler, P., Hartig, O. (eds.) ESWC 2017. LNCS, vol. 10249, pp. 554–570. Springer, Cham (2017). https://doi.org/10.1007/978-3-319-58068-5_34

7. Nguyen, P.T., Tomeo, P., Di Noia, T., Di Sciascio, E.: Content-based recommendations via DBpedia and Freebase: a case study in the music domain. In: Arenas, M., et al. (eds.) ISWC 2015. LNCS, vol. 9366, pp. 605–621. Springer, Cham (2015). https://doi.org/10.1007/978-3-319-25007-6_35

8. Piao, G., Breslin, J.G.: Exploring dynamics and semantics of user interests for user modeling on Twitter for link recommendations. In: Proceedings of the 12th International Conference on Semantic Systems, pp. 81–88. ACM, September 2016

9. Ristoski, P., Paulheim, H.: RDF2Vec: RDF graph embeddings for data mining. In: Groth, P., et al. (eds.) ISWC 2016. LNCS, vol. 9981, pp. 498–514. Springer, Cham (2016). https://doi.org/10.1007/978-3-319-46523-4_30

10. Kapanipathi, P., Jain, P., Venkataramani, C., Sheth, A.: User interests identification on Twitter using a hierarchical knowledge base. In: Presutti, V., d'Amato, C., Gandon, F., d'Aquin, M., Staab, S., Tordai, A. (eds.) ESWC 2014. LNCS, vol. 8465, pp. 99–113. Springer, Cham (2014). https://doi.org/10.1007/978-3-319-07443-6_8

11. Chen, Y.Y., Cheng, A.J., Hsu, W.H.: Travel recommendation by mining people attributes and travel group types from community-contributed photos. IEEE Trans. Multimedia 15(6), 1283–1295 (2013)

12. Ferwerda, B., Schedl, M., Tkalcic, M.: Using instagram picture features to predict users' personality. In: Tian, Q., Sebe, N., Qi, G.J., Huet, B., Hong, R., Liu, X. (eds.) MMM 2016. LNCS, vol. 9516, pp. 850–861. Springer, Cham (2016). https://doi.org/10.1007/978-3-319-27671-7_71

13. Neidhardt, J., Seyfang, L., Schuster, R., Werthner, H.: A picture-based approach to recommender systems. Inf. Technol. Tour. 15(1), 49–69 (2015)

14. Berger, H., Denk, M., Dittenbach, M., Pesenhofer, A., Merkl, D.: Photo-based user profiling for tourism recommender systems. In: Psaila, G., Wagner, R. (eds.) EC-Web 2007. LNCS, vol. 4655, pp. 46–55. Springer, Berlin, Heidelberg (2007). https://doi.org/10.1007/978-3-540-74563-1_5

15. Linaza, M.T., Agirregoikoa, A., Garcia, A., Torres, J.I., Aranburu, K.: Image-based travel recommender system for small tourist destinations. In: Law, R., Fuchs, M., Ricci, F. (eds.) Information and Communication Technologies in Tourism 2011, pp. 1–12. Springer, Vienna (2011). https://doi.org/10.1007/978-3-7091-0503-0_1

16. Szegedy, C., Vanhoucke, V., Ioffe, S., Shlens, J., Wojna, Z.: Rethinking the inception architecture for computer vision. In: Proceedings of the IEEE Conference on Computer Vision and Pattern Recognition, pp. 2818–2826 (2016)

17. Di Noia, T., Ostuni, V.C.: Recommender systems and Linked open data. In: Faber, W., Paschke, A. (eds.) Reasoning Web 2015. LNCS, vol. 9203, pp. 88–113. Springer, Cham (2015). https://doi.org/10.1007/978-3-319-21768-0_4

reboting.com: Towards Geo-search and Visualization of Austrian Open Data

Erich Heil[1(✉)] and Sebastian Neumaier[2]

[1] 23°, Vienna, Austria
erich.heil@23degrees.io
[2] Vienna University of Economics and Business, Vienna, Austria
sebastian.neumaier@wu.ac.at
https://www.23degree.org/

Abstract. Data portals mainly publish semi-structured, tabular formats which lack semantic descriptions of geo-entities and therefore, do not allow any exploration and automated visualization of these datasets. Herein, we present a framework to add geo-semantic labels, based on a constructed geo-entity knowledge graph, and a user interface to query and automatically visualize the resources from the Austrian data portals. The web-application is available at https://reboting.com/.

1 Introduction

Governmental Open Data portals such as the Austrian data.gv.at release local, regional and national data to a variety of users. The data is collected as part of census collections, infrastructure assessments or any other, secondary output data; for instance, public transport data of cities, demographic indicators, etc. Making this data accessible, searchable and analyzable to the public is vital to foster an open government [2]. However, geospatial information in Open Data – as it is currently published – mainly still comes in semi-structured and tabular formats, such as CSV or XLS [4] and geo-references in these tabular sources are not encoded structuredly or homogeneously, but using mixes of region names, country codes, or other implicit references. Therefore, these portals do not allow any geo-semantic queries; in fact, the search functionalities are limited to the metadata descriptions only, and hardly provide any visualizations to explore the datasets. Herein, we present a framework to automatically generated visualizations of open datasets based on queries for geo-entities:

1. We integrate Linked Data repositories, geo-reference datasets, and geocode standards in a hierarchical base geo-entities knowledge graph.
2. Using this knowledge graph, we label metadata and data of the Austrian data portals and index all labelled datasets. We provide an API to search over geo-entities, but also full-text search over the content.

This work was supported by the Austrian Research Promotion Agency (FFG) under the projects ADEQUATe (grant no. 849982) and CommuniData (grant no. 855407).

© Springer Nature Switzerland AG 2018
A. Gangemi et al. (Eds.): ESWC 2018 Satellite Events, LNCS 11155, pp. 105–110, 2018.
https://doi.org/10.1007/978-3-319-98192-5_20

3. The user interface at reboting.com offers showcase queries for Austrian geo-entities and displays automatically generated visualizations for any input dataset from the data portals.

2   Approach

In Fig. 1 we display our overall approach: Initially, we crawl CSVs and metadata information (such as title, description, publisher) from the two Austrian data portals data.gv.at and opendataportal.at and label these using our constructed base knowledge graph (cf. Sect. 2.1). The data is stored and indexed in Elastic-Search.[1] The web application at reboting.com (Sect. 2.4) accesses the indexed data via a search API (Sect. 2.3).

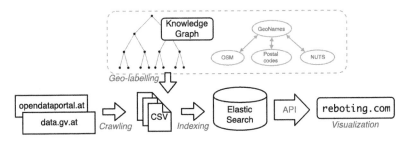

Fig. 1. Process of crawling, labelling, indexing and visualizing datasets from the Austrian Open Data portals.

2.1   Constructing a Base Knowledge Graph of Geo-Entities

Similar to our approach, the 2012 project LinkedGeoData [6] uses Open Street Maps to construct a lightweight ontology and a Link Data resource. In contrast, our geo-entities knowledge graph is based on GeoNames:[2] it contains over 10 million geographical names and provides detailed hierarchical descriptions, e.g., countries, federal states, regions, cities, etc. We enrich the GeoNames graph with three additional sources:

Postal codes: GeoNames also provides a comprehensive collection of postal codes for several countries and the respective name of the places/districts.[3] Additionally, we use codes available in Wikidata to extend and verify the graph.

NUTS is a geocode standard by the European Union (EU). It references the statistical subdivisions of all EU member states in three hierarchical levels.[4] Wikidata includes several links to the GeoNames repository as well as a property

---

[1] https://www.elastic.co/products/elasticsearch.

[2] http://www.geonames.org/.

[3] http://download.geonames.org/export/zip/, last accessed 2018-01-05. Note, that this dataset is not linked to GeoNames entities: We heuristically map the codes to the entities by using the countries and place/district names.

[4] http://ec.europa.eu/eurostat/web/nuts/overview, last accessed 2018-03-05.

for the NUTS classifications of regions, so we can use the Wikidata SPARQL endpoint[5] to add mappings to the corresponding NUTS regions.

OpenStreetMaps (OSM): To cover a more detailed and larger set of labels as it is available in GeoNames, e.g., the set of all street names and local places/POIs of a city, we extract OSM ways and nodes and map these to the GeoNames hierarchy. We use OSM's Nominatim service to get polygons for all district/city-level regions and use these to extract all street names, places, etc. from an OSM country extract (currently Austria).

2.2 Geo-Labelling Algorithm

Our framework crawls the datasets from the two Austrian Open Data portals data.gv.at and opendataportal.at, and annotates (i) the CSVs' columns and (ii) the metadata descriptions using the geo-entities in our base knowledge graph.

(i) *The CSVs'* columns get classified based on regular expressions for NUTS identifier and postal codes. In case a column holds potential postal codes the algorithm tries to map the values to existing postal codes and add the respective semantic labels.

   In case of string columns, we first try to map the column values to GeoNames labels: We collect all possible entity mappings for all column values, and disambiguate values with multiple GeoNames candidates based on the predecessors in the knowledge graph, i.e., we sum up the aggregated counts of these predecessors to resolve a mapping.[6] If no GeoNames mapping was found we try to instantiate the values with the OSM street names and places from our knowledge graph.

(ii) *The Metadata descriptions*, which can be found on the Open Data portals, often give hints about the respective region covering the actual data. Therefore, we try to extract geo-entities from the titles, descriptions and publishers of the dataset. Table 1 lists the total number of indexed CSVs, the number of CSVs with annotated columns (by GeoNames and OSM labels) and the number of datasets where we could annotate the metadata. The source code for the graph construction and the labelling is available on GitHub.[7]

Table 1. Number of CSVs with column and metadata labels.

Portal	Indexed	Columns	GeoNames	OSM	Metadata
data.gv.at	2427	717 *(30%)*	587	185	2391 *(99%)*
opendataportal.at	442	7 *(2%)*	5	3	441 *(99%)*

---

[5] https://query.wikidata.org/ with the following query to get these NUTS-to-GeoNames mappings: `SELECT ?s ?nuts ?geonames WHERE {?s wdt:P605 ?nuts.?s wdt:P1566 ?geonames}`.

[6] This algorithm is based on the assumption that values in the same column have a common context, i.e., common predecessors.

[7] https://github.com/sebneu/geolabelling.

2.3   Search API

An indexed document (i.e., CSV) in Elasticsearch contains all cell values of the table (arranged by columns), the potential geo-labels for the labelled columns, the metadata of the CSV (e.g., the data portal, title, publisher, etc.), and any additional geo-labels extracted from this metadata. The data can be accessed via the ODGraph API (http://data.wu.ac.at/odgraph/):

`/locationsearch?l={GeoNames}&offset={offset}&limit={limit}&q={keyword}`

It takes multiple instances of `GeoNames` identifiers (parameter `l`) and an optional white space separated list of keywords (`q`) as input parameters. The output consists of a list of documents that match the requested entities or keywords.

Alternatively to the document-based Elasticsearch, GeoSPARQL [5] defines a small ontology to represent and query geometries and spatial regions. In future work, we plan to make our base knowledge graph and RDFized linked data points from the CSVs also available via a GeoSPARQL endpoint.

2.4   User Interface and Visualization

Visualizations for Open data are an active area of research. IBM [7] created a free visualization tool for user uploaded open data. Cerami et al. [1] enable everybody to explore cancer data visually. Furthermore, open data portal providers, such as opendataportal.at, provide their own visualization tools.

To enable non-technical users to explore the results of our search API in the context of the nine Austrian federal states, our web application reboting.com parses for categorical and numeric columns and then scans for geo-references and time components that can be visualized on a map or a barchart by the 23degree visualization API.[8] In theory the amount of visualizations that can be generated is huge. For one visualization type it is the amount of string columns multiplied with the amount of numeric columns. To reduce the space of possible visuals we use the string column with the maximum string length as sum of all rows. To further reduce possible visuals we assigned random colors and for maps we use a fixed distribution for the legend depending on the minimum and maximum of the visualized numeric column. With this approach we generated 6117 visuals for 393 datasets. Out of 1321 results for the nine Austrian federal states, 928 results could not be visualized either because of download/parsing errors, or because of the structure of the data. The example visualization in Fig. 2 illustrates the possibility for users to rate shown visualizations. We save the rating information and plan to use it to evaluate and improve our visual generation process. Furthermore, we are evaluating the use of A/B testing [3] to further improve on our knowledge of visualization preferences. Currently, the user cannot choose a specific dataset and the visualization is limited to a random selection. We chose this random approach to get some initial ratings, which will hopefully shed some light on dataset features that are useful for meaningful visualizations.

---

[8] https://23degrees.io.

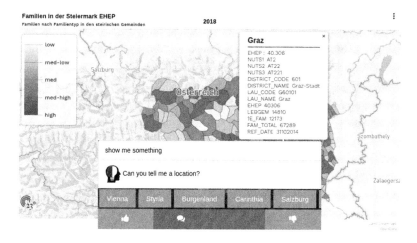

Fig. 2. Example visualization by reboting.com: number of families in Styria, Austria. The color indicates the density; details can be displayed by selecting a subregion. (Color figure online)

3   Conclusions and Outlook

Herein, we have presented reboting.com, an interface that allows geo-queries for Austrian federal states and automatically generates visualization of respective open datasets. The geo-labelling of the dataset is based on a base knowledge graph of geo-entities. In future versions of this framework, we plan to integrate information gathered from the user ratings of the visualizations: In case of inadequate representations we will adapt the visualization (i.e. change the input columns). Also, we plan to scale our systems to datasets/data portals worldwide, so that users can query for any geo-entity/location. Complementary, users might benefit from other dimensions such as temporal and topic filters.

References

1. Cerami, E., Gao, J., Dogrusoz, U., Gross, B.E., Sumer, S.O., Aksoy, B.A., Jacobsen, A., Byrne, C.J., Heuer, M.L., Larsson, E., et al.: The cBio cancer genomics portal: an open platform for exploring multidimensional cancer genomics data. Cancer Discov. **2**, 401–404 (2012)
2. Janssen, M., Charalabidis, Y., Zuiderwijk, A.: Benefits, adoption barriers and myths of open data and open government. Inf. Syst. Manag. **29**(4), 258–268 (2012). https://doi.org/10.1080/10580530.2012.716740
3. Kohavi, R., Longbotham, R.: Online controlled experiments and A/B testing. In: Sammut, C., Webb, G.I. (eds.) Encyclopedia of Machine Learning and Data Mining, pp. 922–929. Springer, Boston (2017). https://doi.org/10.1007/978-1-4899-7687-1
4. Neumaier, S., Umbrich, J., Polleres, A.: Automated quality assessment of metadata across open data portals. J. Data Inf. Qual. **8**(1), 2:1–2:29 (2016). https://doi.org/10.1145/2964909

5. Perry, M., Herring, J.: OGC GeoSPARQL - a geographic query language for RDF data. OGC Implementation Standard, September 2012
6. Stadler, C., Lehmann, J., Höffner, K., Auer, S.: LinkedGeoData: a core for a web of spatial open data. Semant. Web **3**(4), 333–354 (2012)
7. Viegas, F.B., Wattenberg, M., Van Ham, F., Kriss, J., McKeon, M.: ManyEyes: a site for visualization at internet scale. IEEE Trans. Visual. Comput. Graph. **13**(6), 1121–11218 (2007)

Demoing Platypus – A Multilingual Question Answering Platform for Wikidata

Thomas Pellissier Tanon[1,2](✉), Marcos Dias de Assunção[1], Eddy Caron[1], and Fabian M. Suchanek[2]

[1] Université de Lyon, ENS de Lyon, Inria, CNRS,
Univ. Claude-Bernard Lyon 1, LIP, Lyon, France
ttanon@enst.fr
[2] LTCI, Télécom ParisTech, Paris, France

Abstract. In this paper we present Platypus, a natural language question answering system on Wikidata. Our platform can answer complex queries in several languages, using hybrid grammatical and template based techniques. Our demo allows users either to select sample questions, or formulate their own – in any of the 3 languages that we currently support. A user can also try out our Twitter bot, which replies to any tweet that is sent to its account.

1 Introduction

Recent years have seen the rise of systems that can answer natural language questions such as "Who is the president of the United States?". These systems usually rely on *knowledge bases* (KBs) – large, structured repositories of machine-readable facts. In this paper, we propose to demonstrate a question answering system called Platypus. It differs from existing systems in two main aspects. First, it explicitly targets Wikidata, which is one of the largest general purpose knowledge bases. Second, it supports multiple natural languages with minimal adjustments. Our system is available online as an API[1], as a Web interface[2], and as a Twitter bot[3]. A full description of the system is available as a technical report [1].

2 Related Work

Question Answering (QA) has been an active domain of research since the early 1970s. One group of approaches is based on the grammatical structure of the questions, among which one of them [2] uses the formal grammar of the target

---

[1] https://qa.askplatyp.us.
[2] https://askplatyp.us.
[3] https://twitter.com/askplatypus.

© Springer Nature Switzerland AG 2018
A. Gangemi et al. (Eds.): ESWC 2018 Satellite Events, LNCS 11155, pp. 111–116, 2018.
https://doi.org/10.1007/978-3-319-98192-5_21

language. Our work, in contrast, relies solely on semantic parsing models, and does not need expensive adaptations for different languages. Furthermore, the work of [2] targets only domain-specific knowledge, while we target a knowledge base like Wikidata. Another grammar-based approach employs a multilingual semantic parser on top of universal dependencies [3]. Our work differs from this approach, in that (1) we provide a working implementation on Wikidata and (2) our logical representation matches directly the target KB, so that we can work with specific output types such as strings, dates, numbers, and quantities. Our approach differs from [4] in that (1) we provide a method for question answering rather than dispatching to an external service, and (2) we support multiple languages.

Another set of approaches [5–9] relies on machine learning or neural networks in order to build a KB query directly from the question, sometimes using templates. Compared to this previous work, Platypus provides a similar end-to-end learning approach based on templates, but also a grammar-based approach that can answer questions for which there is no template. Furthermore, our work provides easy support for multiple languages, a task that is only starting to be tackled by other works [10,11].

3   Platypus System

Knowledge Base. Platypus works on a knowledge base. We choose Wikidata for two reasons. First, it provides a large set of lexical representations for its properties, in numerous languages [12] (e.g., "was born in", "has the birthplace", and "est né à" for bornIn). Second, Wikidata is one of the largest general purpose knowledge bases on the Semantic Web. We built a specialized service that can perform fast entity-lookups on Wikidata, with support for edit distance and type constraints. In order not to overload the Wikidata SPARQL endpoint, Platypus has its own data storage. To keep our answers accurate, we perform a daily replication of Wikidata to include updates.

Logical Representation. We represent questions not directly in SPARQL, but rather in a custom logical representation. The representation is inspired by dependency-based compositional semantics [13,14], and adapted to work with multiple languages. The advantage of this approach is that it allows the composition of partial representations. For instance, one could give the representation $\{x \mid \langle \texttt{dynamite}, \texttt{inventor}, x\rangle\}$ for "the inventor of dynamite" and $\{y \mid \langle x, \texttt{birthPlace}, y\rangle\}$ for "Where was X born?"; composing the two thus gives the representation $\{y \mid \exists x \, \langle \texttt{dynamite}, \texttt{inventor}, x\rangle \wedge \langle x, \texttt{birthPlace}, y\rangle\}$ for "Where was the inventor of dynamite born?".

Platypus System. Our system takes as input a natural language question, and produces as output a set of answers (RDF terms) from the KB. For this purpose, the question is first transformed into one or several internal logical representations. We provide two different *analyzers* to this end: a primary one (the *grammatical*

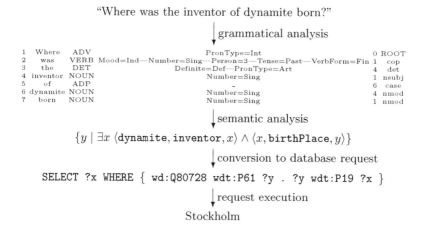

Fig. 1. Pipeline execution using the grammatical analyzer

analyzer) and a secondary one (the *template-based analyzer*). Figure 1 shows the process with the grammatical analyzer.

Grammatical Analyzer. The grammatical analyzer takes as input a natural language question, and translates it into a logical representation. For this purpose, it first parses the question with CoreNLP [15], or Spacy [16], yielding a dependency tree. Then it transforms this tree to the logical representation using manually designed rules. For example, we have the following rule:

$$parse\left(\begin{array}{c} \texttt{Where} \\ | \, \text{nsubj} \\ \texttt{X} \end{array}\right) = \{p \mid \exists x. \, x \in parse_t(X) \wedge \langle x, \texttt{located in}, p\rangle\}$$

This rule allows us to parse the question "Where is Paris?" as follows:

$$parse\left(\begin{array}{c} \texttt{Where} \\ \text{cop}\diagup \quad \diagdown \text{nsubj} \\ \texttt{is} \qquad \texttt{Paris} \end{array}\right) = \left\{p \,\middle|\, \exists x. \begin{array}{c} x \in parse_t(Paris) \wedge \\ \langle x, \texttt{located in}, p\rangle \end{array}\right\}$$

$$= \{p \mid \langle \texttt{Paris}, \texttt{located in}, p\rangle\}$$

Entity lookup is done using a special rule that returns the set of entities matching a given label. When several rules can be applied, the analyzer returns several results. Hence, *parse* does not return a single logical representation but a set of possible representations. We will discuss below how to filter out the wrong representations. Our rules depend as much as possible on the set of POS tags and the set of dependency tags and not on the input language. Both tag sets are language independent. When specific words are needed, e.g. for connection words (such as "in" or "from") and question words (such as "where" or "when"), we use dictionaries. We have developed dictionaries for English and French, which allows Platypus to answer questions in these two languages. Support of Spanish is currently in development and German support is planned. Adding support of a new language only requires to fill the dictionaries and make sure that all grammatical constructions of the language are covered by the existing rules.

Template Analyzer. The second Platypus analyzer is based on templates and implemented using the RasaNLU [17] library. A template is a logical representation with free variables, annotated with natural language questions. For example $\{o \mid \langle$ s , `birth date`, $o\rangle\}$ could be annotated with "When was George⁸ Washington⁸ born?". Our analyzer uses these templates in order to find the logical representation of a given natural language question. For this purpose, the analyzer first finds the template that best matches the question. This is done using a classifier. We encode the question by the average of the word embeddings of its words, and classify them with a linear support vector machine. After this, the analyzer fills the logical representation slots. We use conditional random fields [18] to recognize entity labels in the input sentence, and we match them with the knowledge base entities. We trained this analyzer in English using the WikidataSimpleQuestions dataset [19].

Query Execution. We execute the two analyzers in parallel. The grammatical one is executed for all languages and has the advantage of supporting complex sentences. The template-based one works only in English, but has the advantage of working well with short sentences that are not covered by the implemented grammatical rules.

We rank the logical representations according to their likelihood of being the correct interpretation of the question. For this, we take into account the prominence of the mentioned entities in the KB. Finally, the representations are converted into SPARQL, and executed one after the other on Wikidata, until one of them yields an answer.

4 Demonstration Setting

Our system is available online at https://askplatyp.us (see Fig. 2) and executes the two analyzers. During the demo session, users can either choose from a set of predefined questions, or ask Platypus any question they want. Since Wikidata is quite exhaustive, it is likely that Platypus can answer questions about the city where the user was born, about the author of their favorite books, or the children of a given president. Users can choose to ask in any of the 3 languages that we currently support. The demo interface shows the grammatical analysis of the question, the logical representation, the SPARQL query, as well as the answer to the question – allowing the user to trace the entire process of question analysis in Platypus.

For those conference attendees who cannot make to our demo, we offer a special service: Platypus can also answer questions via Twitter. For this, the user has to send their natural language question to the Twitter handle `@askplatypus`.

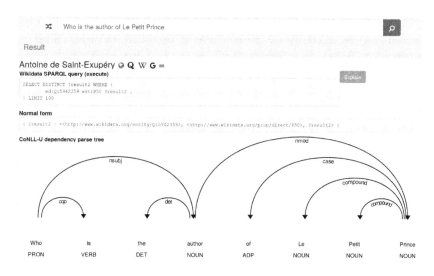

Fig. 2. Platypus Web interface

5   Conclusion

We demonstrate a fully functional multilingual natural language question answering system for Wikidata. Our system can work with both a grammatical analyzer and a template-based analyzer to parse natural language questions. During the demo session, Platypus can be tried out in English, French, and Spanish on our Web page https://askplatyp.us – or via our Twitter bot.

Acknowledgments. We thank the contributors of the first version of the Platypus project: M. Chevalier, R. Charrondière, Q. Cormier, T. Cornebize, Y. Hamoudi, V. Lorentz. Work supported by the LABEX MILYON (ANR-10-LABX-0070).

References

1. Pellissier Tanon, T., Dias De Assuncao, M., Caron, E., Suchanek, F.: Platypus - a multilingual question answering platform for Wikidata. Technical report (2018)
2. Marginean, A.: Question answering over biomedical linked data with grammatical framework. Semant. Web **8**(4), 565–580 (2017)
3. Reddy, S., Täckström, O., Petrov, S., Steedman, M., Lapata, M.: Universal semantic parsing. In: EMNLP (2017)
4. Athreya, R.G., Ngomo, A.C.N., Usbeck, R.: Enhancing community interactions with data-driven chatbots - the DBpedia chatbot. In: WWW Demo (2018)
5. Unger, C., Bühmann, L., Lehmann, J., Ngomo, A.N., Gerber, D., Cimiano, P.: Template-based question answering over RDF data. In: WWW (2012)
6. Sorokin, D., Gurevych, I.: End-to-end representation learning for question answering with weak supervision. In: Dragoni, M., Solanki, M., Blomqvist, E. (eds.) SemWebEval 2017. CCIS, vol. 769, pp. 70–83. Springer, Cham (2017). https://doi.org/10.1007/978-3-319-69146-6_7

7. Yahya, M., Berberich, K., Elbassuoni, S., Ramanath, M., Tresp, V., Weikum, G.: Natural language questions for the web of data. In: EMNLP-CoNLL (2012)
8. Bordes, A., Usunier, N., Chopra, S., Weston, J.: Large-scale simple question answering with memory networks. CoRR (2015)
9. Yin, W., Yu, M., Xiang, B., Zhou, B., Schütze, H.: Simple question answering by attentive convolutional neural network. In: COLING (2016)
10. Hakimov, S., Jebbara, S., Cimiano, P.: AMUSE: multilingual semantic parsing for question answering over linked data. In: d'Amato, C., et al. (eds.) ISWC 2017. LNCS, vol. 10587, pp. 329–346. Springer, Cham (2017). https://doi.org/10.1007/978-3-319-68288-4_20
11. Diefenbach, D., Singh, K., Maret, P.: WDAqua-core0: a question answering component for the research community. In: Dragoni, M., Solanki, M., Blomqvist, E. (eds.) SemWebEval 2017. CCIS, vol. 769, pp. 84–89. Springer, Cham (2017). https://doi.org/10.1007/978-3-319-69146-6_8
12. Kaffee, L., Piscopo, A., Vougiouklis, P., Simperl, E., Carr, L., Pintscher, L.: A glimpse into Babel: an analysis of multilinguality in Wikidata. In: OpenSym (2017)
13. Zelle, J.M., Mooney, R.J.: Learning to parse database queries using inductive logic programming. In: AAAI (1996)
14. Liang, P., Jordan, M.I., Klein, D.: Learning dependency-based compositional semantics. Comput. Linguist. **39**(2), 389–446 (2013)
15. Chen, D., Manning, C.D.: A fast and accurate dependency parser using neural networks. In: EMNLP (2014)
16. Honnibal, M., Johnson, M.: An improved non-monotonic transition system for dependency parsing. In: EMNLP (2015)
17. Bocklisch, T., Faulker, J., Pawlowski, N., Nichol, A.: Rasa: open source language understanding and dialogue management. CoRR (2017)
18. Lafferty, J.D., McCallum, A., Pereira, F.C.N.: Conditional random fields: probabilistic models for segmenting and labeling sequence data. In: ICML (2001)
19. Diefenbach, D., Pellissier Tanon, T., Singh, K.D., Maret, P.: Question answering benchmarks for Wikidata. In: ISWC Poster (2017)

Knowledge Graph Embeddings
with node2vec for Item Recommendation

Enrico Palumbo[1,2,3(✉)], Giuseppe Rizzo[1], Raphaël Troncy[2], Elena Baralis[3],
Michele Osella[1], and Enrico Ferro[1]

[1] ISMB, Turin, Italy
{palumbo,giuseppe.rizzo,osella,ferro}@ismb.it
[2] EURECOM, Biot, France
raphael.troncy@eurecom.fr
[3] Politecnico di Torino, Turin, Italy
elena.baralis@polito.it

Abstract. In the past years, knowledge graphs have proven to be beneficial for recommender systems, efficiently addressing paramount issues
such as new items and data sparsity. Graph embeddings algorithms have
shown to be able to automatically learn high quality feature vectors
from graph structures, enabling vector-based measures of node relatedness. In this paper, we show how node2vec can be used to generate item
recommendations by learning knowledge graph embeddings. We apply
node2vec on a knowledge graph built from the MovieLens 1M dataset
and DBpedia and use the node relatedness to generate item recommendations. The results show that node2vec consistently outperforms a set
of collaborative filtering baselines on an array of relevant metrics.

Keywords: Knowledge graphs embeddings · Recommender systems
node2vec

1 Background

In the past few years, recommender systems leveraging knowledge graphs have
proven to be competitive with state-of-the-art collaborative filtering systems
and to efficiently address issues such as new items and data sparsity [1,7–10,12].
node2vec has shown to be able to effectively learn features from graph structures, outperforming existing systems in node classification and link prediction
tasks [3]. In this paper, we show that node2vec can be effectively used to learn
knowledge graph embeddings to perform item recommendation. node2vec is
applied on a knowledge graph including user feedback on items, modelled by
the special relation 'feedback', and item relations to other entities. Then, recommendations are generated using the relatedness between users and items in the
vector space. The evaluation on the Movielens dataset shows that: (1) node2vec
with default hyper-parameters outperforms collaborative filtering baselines on all
metrics and the MostPop algorithm on most metrics (2) node2vec with optimized
hyper-parameters significantly outperforms all baselines under consideration.

A. Gangemi et al. (Eds.): ESWC 2018 Satellite Events, LNCS 11155, pp. 117–120, 2018.
https://doi.org/10.1007/978-3-319-98192-5_22

2   Approach

Item Recommendation: given a set of items I and a set of users U, the problem of item recommendation is that of ranking a set of N candidate items $I_{candidates} \subset I$ according to what a user may like. More formally, the problem consists in defining a ranking function $\rho(u, i)$ that assigns a score to any user-item pair $(u, i) \in U \times I_{candidates}$ and then sorting the items according to $\rho(u, i)$:

$$L(u) = \{i_1, i_2, ..., i_N\} \tag{1}$$

where $\rho(u, i_j) > \rho(u, i_{j+1})$ for any $j = 1..N - 1$.

   node2vec [3] learns representations of nodes in a graph through the application of the word2vec model on sequences of nodes sampled through random walks (Fig. 1). The innovation brought by node2vec is the definition of a random walk exploration that is flexible and adaptable to the diversity of connectivity patterns that a network may present. Given a knowledge graph K encompassing users U, items I (the object of the recommendations, e.g. a movie) and other entities E (objects connected to items, e.g. the director of a movie), node2vec generates vector representations of the users x_u and of the items x_i (and of other entities x_e). Thus, we propose to use as a ranking function the relatedness between the user and the item vectors: $\rho(u, i) = d(x_u, x_i)$ where d is the cosine similarity in this work.

Knowledge Graph Construction: the dataset used for the evaluation is MovieLens 1M[1] [4]. We used the publicly available mappings from MovieLens 1M items to the corresponding DBpedia entities [8] to create the knowledge graph K using DBpedia data. We split the data into training X_{train}, validation X_{val} and test set X_{test}, containing respectively 70%, 10% and 20% of the ratings for each user. We selected a set of properties based on their frequency of occurrence[2]: ["dbo:director", "dbo:starring", "dbo:distributor", "dbo:writer","dbo:musicComposer", "dbo:producer", "dbo:cinematography", "dbo:editing"]. We add "dct:subject" to this set of properties, as it provides an extremely rich categorization of items. For each property p, we include in K all the triples (i, p, e) where $i \in I$ and $e \in E$, e.g. (dbr:Pulp_Fiction, dbo:director, dbr:Quentin_Tarantino). We finally add the 'feedback' property, modeling all movie ratings that are $r \geq 4$ in X_{train} as triples $(u, feedback, i)$.

Evaluation: we use the evaluation protocol known as AllUnratedItems [11] and we measure standard information retrieval metrics such as P@5, P@10, Mean Average Precision (MAP), R@5, R@10, NDCG (Normalized Discounted Cumulative Gain), MRR (Mean Reciprocal Rank). As baselines, we use collaborative filtering algorithms based on Singular Value Decomposition [6], ItemKNN with baselines [5] and the MostPop item recommendation strategy, which ranks items

---

[1] https://grouplens.org/datasets/movielens/1m/.
[2] We sorted the properties used in DBpedia to describe the Movielens1M items according to their frequency and selected the first K properties so that the frequency of the K + 1 property was less that 50% of the previous one.

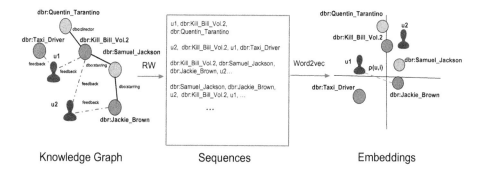

Fig. 1. Node2vec for item recommendation using the knowledge graph. Users are represented in black, items in orange and entities in grey. node2vec learns knowledge graph embeddings by sampling sequences of nodes through random walks and then applying the word2vec model on the sequences. The ranking function for item recommendation is then given by the node relatedness in the vector space.

based on their popularity (i.e. total number of positive ratings). The baselines are implemented using the *surprise* python library[3].

3   Results

The results of the evaluation are reported in Table 1. In "node2vec (default)" the hyper-parameters have been set to their default value as reported in the original paper [3] and in the reference Python implementation available on Github[4] ($p = 1, q = 1, num\_walks = 10, walk\_length = 80, window\_size = 10, iter = 1, dimensions = 128$). We observe that "node2vec (default)" outperforms SVD and ItemKNN on all metrics, but that the MostPop approach performs slightly better on the P@5 and P@10 and on MRR. Note that Most-Pop, although trivial, is known to be quite effective on the Movielens 1M dataset as a consequence of the strong concentration of item feedback on a small number of highly popular items [2]. In "node2vec (opt)" we have optimized the hyper-parameters by a combination of grid-search and manual search over the validation set, exploring the ranges: $p \in \{0.25, 1, 4\}$, $q \in \{0.25, 1, 4\}$, $dimensions \in \{200, 500\}$, $walk\_length \in \{10, 20, 30, 50, 100\}$, $window\_size \in \{10, 20, 30\}$, $num\_walks \in \{10, 50\}$. We found the configuration ($p = 4, q = 1, num\_walks = 50, walk\_length = 100, window\_size = 30, iter = 5, dimensions = 200$) to be optimal on the validation set in the explored range. We observed that the number of walks per node, the walk length, i.e. the maximum length of random walk, and the context size are particularly significant to improve the performance. However, the hyper-parameters optimization is a time consuming endeavor, as it requires running the whole evaluation pipelines with multiple configurations. Thus, in a future work, we will extend the evaluation to other datasets and investigate the relation between hyper-parameters and the graph structure, with the aim of elaborating some indications to guide the hyper-parameter search process.

---

[3] http://surprise.readthedocs.io/en/v1.0.2/matrix_factorization.html.
[4] https://github.com/aditya-grover/node2vec.

Table 1. Results on the MovieLens 1M dataset sorted by NDCG

System	P@5	P@10	MAP	R@5	R@10	NDCG	MRR
node2vec (opt)	**0.224**	**0.196**	**0.153**	**0.092**	**0.155**	**0.482**	**0.441**
node2vec (default)	0.120	0.129	0.117	0.067	0.122	0.438	0.256
MostPop	0.145	0.129	0.092	0.049	0.085	0.406	0.307
SVD	0.068	0.062	0.043	0.020	0.037	0.329	0.164
ItemKNN	0.057	0.054	0.041	0.019	0.032	0.325	0.143
Random	0.007	0.007	0.008	0.002	0.003	0.246	0.030

References

1. Catherine, R., Cohen, W.: Personalized recommendations using knowledge graphs: a probabilistic logic programming approach. In: Proceedings of the 10th ACM Conference on Recommender Systems, pp. 325–332. ACM (2016)
2. Cremonesi, P., Koren, Y., Turrin, R.: Performance of recommender algorithms on top-n recommendation tasks. In: Proceedings of the Fourth ACM conference on Recommender Systems, pp. 39–46. ACM (2010)
3. Grover, A., Leskovec, J.: node2vec: scalable feature learning for networks. In: Proceedings of the 22nd ACM SIGKDD International Conference on Knowledge Discovery and Data Mining, pp. 855–864. ACM (2016)
4. Harper, F.M., Konstan, J.A.: The movielens datasets: history and context. ACM Trans. Interact. Intell. Syst. (TiiS) **5**(4), 19 (2016)
5. Koren, Y.: Factor in the neighbors: scalable and accurate collaborative filtering. ACM Trans. Knowl. Discov. Data (TKDD) **4**(1), 1 (2010)
6. Koren, Y., Bell, R., Volinsky, C.: Matrix factorization techniques for recommender systems. Computer **42**(8), 30–37 (2009)
7. Noia, T.D., Ostuni, V.C., Tomeo, P., Sciascio, E.D.: SPrank: semantic path-based ranking for top-n recommendations using linked open data. ACM Trans. Intell. Syst. Technol. (TIST) **8**(1), 9 (2016)
8. Ostuni, V.C., Di Noia, T., Di Sciascio, E., Mirizzi, R.: Top-n recommendations from implicit feedback leveraging linked open data. In: Proceedings of the 7th ACM Conference on Recommender systems, pp. 85–92. ACM (2013)
9. Palumbo, E., Rizzo, G., Troncy, R.: Entity2Rec: learning user-item relatedness from knowledge graphs for top-n item recommendation. In: Proceedings of the Eleventh ACM Conference on Recommender Systems, pp. 32–36. ACM (2017)
10. Rosati, J., Ristoski, P., Di Noia, T., Leone, R.d., Paulheim, H.: RDF graph embeddings for content-based recommender systems. In: CEUR Workshop Proceedings, vol. 1673, pp. 23–30. RWTH (2016)
11. Steck, H.: Evaluation of recommendations: rating-prediction and ranking. In: Proceedings of the 7th ACM Conference on Recommender systems, pp. 213–220. ACM (2013)
12. Yu, X., et al.: Personalized entity recommendation: a heterogeneous information network approach. In: Proceedings of the 7th ACM International Conference on Web Search and Data Mining, pp. 283–292. ACM (2014)

REDI: A Linked Data-Powered Research Networking Platform

Xavier Sumba[1]([✉]), José Segarra[1], José Ortiz[1], Boris Villazón-Terrazas[2],
Mauricio Espinoza[1], and Víctor Saquicela[1]

[1] Computer Science Department, University of Cuenca, Cuenca, Ecuador
xavier.sumba93@ucuenca.edu.ec
[2] Fujitsu Laboratories of Europe, Madrid, Spain

Abstract. Research networking is a difficult part of academics in spite
of the multiple benefits that the Web has brought within this field in
recent years. Even though scientific and business social networks provide
a medium to discover peers worldwide, their usefulness meets its limits when real-world requirements come in. The broad audience of those
tools and other bibliographic databases lead them to ignore cultural and
geographical aspects such regional indexes, organizational structures,
among others. On this poster, we introduce REDI, a Linked Data -
powered research networking platform which combines both local (insti-
tutional/regional) and external (Web) scholarly sources in a consolidated
knowledge base. Moreover, REDI leverages on its knowledge base to cluster authors within similar research areas easing networking and unveiling
a variety of new information from data for multiple purposes.

Keywords: Data integration · Linked Data · Data mining
Research networking

1 Introduction

The web not only has opened up a new whole world of opportunities to share scientific work but has eradicated the barrier of communication. However, there is
still an open door for the process of research networking. Senior researchers usually create their collaborative networks through the years. Technology and tools
such as ResearchGate have simplified this process but are still limited. Indeed,
young or novice researchers need a mechanism to locate possible collaborators.
For example, some grants are allocated in an inter-institutional approach, so
there is no tool to find potential collaborators in a certain area or institution.
Filling that gap in social research networks will ease the research community the
creation of cross-cultural and interdisciplinary projects.

In addition, the availability of scholarly literature on the web has given
access to researchers a considerable amount of articles or other digital academic
resources. This extremely large amount of scientific publications turns the process of finding an article into a challenging task due to the overwhelming results

© Springer Nature Switzerland AG 2018
A. Gangemi et al. (Eds.): ESWC 2018 Satellite Events, LNCS 11155, pp. 121–125, 2018.
https://doi.org/10.1007/978-3-319-98192-5_23

of well-known search engines or bibliographic repositories. As a consequence of the variety of bibliographic repositories, articles are spread out in different digital repositories, text files, or bibliographic databases, and researchers have to search in a variety of sources.

Further, in some cases, institutions are regulated by a control system. This control system is carried out for external or internal institutions in order to approach a quality assessment of education. For this evaluation, institutions need to generate research-based indicators. Digital repositories provide some indicators, but they target a specific index (e.g. Scopus). On the other hand, bibliographic databases (e.g. Google Scholar) cover a broad range of indexed literature, and as a trade-off of their broad audience, they cannot provide specific indicators for institutions. As a result of the lack of useful features for decision making, institutions need to get indicators manually.

In this poster, we present and describe REDI a research networking platform, outlining its components and main functionalities.

2   What Is REDI?

REDI[1] is an open source platform[2] for scholarly information that is built on top of Apache Marmotta[3]. It allows storing information of authors along with their publications in a *Linked Data* approach. In addition, it supports the discovery of similar areas of knowledge and potential collaboration networks. Finally, it has a web application to navigate information in the repository and generate statistics and reports. The main modules that make REDI are illustrated in Fig. 1. For a detailed description of each component, we refer to [1].

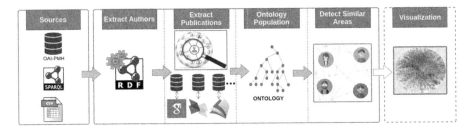

Fig. 1. Main components of the REDI platform.

Authors Sources. As a starting point, there is the need to register a candidate researchers source. These authors will be used for the population of the platform.

---

[1] REDI is a spanish acronym, "Repositorio Ecuatoriano de Investigadores", and stands for the project name where the idea was born (https://redi.cedia.edu.ec/).

[2] https://github.com/ucuenca/redi.

[3] http://marmotta.apache.org/.

Researchers can be imported through a *CSV file, SPARQL Endpoint,* or *DSpace repository.*

Authors Extraction. Given an authors source, this module extracts authors information and transforms to *RDF* if necessary. The information is stored in the repository using FOAF[4] ontology.

Publications Extraction. Each researcher is assigned to his publications. Publications are extracted from digital repositories or bibliographic databases, at the time of writing the ones used are Academics Knowledge, DBLP, DSpace, Google Scholar, Scielo, Springer, and Scopus. Information of each provider is stored in its own graph of the triple-store platform using BIBO[5] ontology.

Ontology Population. Information of each provider and authors is consolidated in a *central graph.* It implies that information is verified; e.g. assigning correctly publications to authors, combine repeated information found in different providers, and disambiguate authors, publications, and co-authors. For a detailed explanation of the author disambiguation process refer to [2].

Similar Areas of Knowledge. Using the information of the central graph, we classify documents based on the UNESCO nomenclature in order to identify knowledge areas. This is done using graph mining, clustering, and DBpedia as a knowledge base, the process is similar to the work of [3]. Once identified those areas, we build potential collaboration networks.

Visualization. Finally, results are shown in a web application that allows exploring information about authors or publications. Most importantly, it suggests potential collaboration networks and similar knowledge areas that authors are working. It shows similar authors working in similar areas even if they have not co-authored before.

3   Platform Overview

REDI gives the facility to store research data of an institution or country. These data are relevant for researchers, regulatory agencies, government agencies, or the general public. The platform has a set of user-friendly interfaces in order to facilitate data accessing and its consumption. These interfaces show information that is collected and summarized, and it is presented to final users in a graphic and intuitive approach through mechanisms such as statistics, author graph-like navigation, authors or publications search, among others. Next, we highlight some features of the platform.

Academic Knowledge Base. REDI collects a large amount of information related to the academic and scientific field. Information that might act as a source of interest for private and public institutions that deal with academic

---

[4] http://xmlns.com/foaf/spec/.
[5] http://bibliontology.com/.

information. The available information is processed, stored and published following the Linked Data principles, thus facilitating the process of data sharing, as well as improving its interpretation as it has a defined ontology and allows linkage through repositories.

Visualization of Authors and Their Associated Elements. The tool has the ability to search for authors and visualize their data. These data are collected from different sources of information, so users can find interesting notions about data that they cannot find when exploring a single source. For instance, resources of scientific works of an author and co-authors can be expanded when exploring a graph, and probably discovering new information given that these associations are not always explicit.

Knowledge Discovery. In the repository of researchers, it is possible to find new information that is not available in other repositories. For example, it is possible to identify the articles of publications that have Latindex index as detailed in [4]. This information is valuable, both for researchers and control agencies because it can help calculate the research impact, for example.

Building Potential Collaboration Networks. Another outstanding functionality of REDI is the identification of possible collaborative networks among researchers. Through this process, researchers can discover people who are working in similar areas of knowledge, or whom have common characteristics for the formulation of joint projects, or simply visualize the knowledge developed in a specific area of knowledge within a region. These networks can also be used by government agencies to visualize the research areas that have greater coverage within the country, and those that have few participants and need to be driven.

4   Conclusions

We introduce REDI a platform for collaboration and networking. Currently, the platform is used in Ecuadorian academic institutions, but we are aiming to expand and adopt through South America. At the time of writing, we are starting three nodes: Colombia, Costa Rica, and Mexico. In addition, we want that each REDI talks to each other through a centralized node and exploit all advantages of Linked Data. For example, every country or institution can host its own data or choose what they share in its networking platform.

Acknowledgments. This work is supported by RED CEDIA in the project "Repositorio Ecuatoriano de Investigadores".

References

1. Sumba, X., Sumba, F., Tello, A., Baculima, F., Espinoza, M., Saquicela, V.: Detecting similar areas of knowledge using semantic and data mining technologies. Electron. Notes Theor. Comput. Sci. **329**, 149–167 (2016)
2. Ortiz, J., Segarra, J., Sumba, X., Cullcay, J., Espinoza, M., Saquicela, V.: Authors semantic disambiguation on heterogeneous bibliographic sources. In: Simposio Latinoamericano de Manejo de Datos e Información (SLMDI)-JAIIO 46 (Córdoba, 2017) (2017)
3. Chicaiza, J., Piedra, N., Lopez-Vargas, J., Tovar-Caro, E.: Domain categorization of open educational resources based on Linked Data. In: Klinov, P., Mouromtsev, D. (eds.) KESW 2014. CCIS, vol. 468, pp. 15–28. Springer, Cham (2014). https://doi.org/10.1007/978-3-319-11716-4_2
4. Cullcay, J., Ortiz, J., Sumba, X., Sumba, F., Saquicela, V.: Identificación automática de artículos indexados en latindex. Maskana **8**, 103–111 (2017)

Combining P-Plan and the REPRODUCE-ME Ontology to Achieve Semantic Enrichment of Scientific Experiments Using Interactive Notebooks

Sheeba Samuel[(⊠)] and Birgitta König-Ries

Heinz-Nixdorf Chair for Distributed Information Systems,
Friedrich-Schiller University, Jena, Germany
{sheeba.samuel,birgitta.koenig-ries}@uni-jena.de

Abstract. End-to-end reproducibility of scientific experiments requires scientists to share their experimental data along with the computational environment. Interactive notebooks have recently gained widespread popularity among scientists because they allow users to document their experiments along with the code, visualize the results inline and selectively execute the code. In a multi-user environment where users can run and modify the shared notebooks, it becomes essential to capture the provenance of notebooks along with the experiments which used them. In this paper, we propose a way to capture provenance of these interactive notebooks and convert them into semantic descriptions so that a user can query the difference between the results, steps, errors and the execution environment of the code. We use the REPRODUCE-ME ontology extended from PROV-O and P-Plan to describe the provenance of notebook execution. We evaluate our prototype in a multi-user environment provided by JupyterHub.

Keywords: Notebooks · Provenance · Reproducibility
Experiments · Ontology

1 Introduction

Scientific experiments are a complex set of processes which involve multiple agents, activities, computational environment, input, and output. Additional challenges emerge with the collaborative and distributed experiment environment in terms of code sharing and execution. The inspiration for our work arises from the Collaborative Research Center (CRC) ReceptorLight[1], where scientists from multiple research institutes collaborate to develop high-performance microscopy techniques to understand the function of membrane receptors. In such a distributed and collaborative environment, it is necessary to understand

---

[1] http://www.receptorlight.uni-jena.de/.

© Springer Nature Switzerland AG 2018
A. Gangemi et al. (Eds.): ESWC 2018 Satellite Events, LNCS 11155, pp. 126–130, 2018.
https://doi.org/10.1007/978-3-319-98192-5_24

the provenance of results generated by the researchers. In our previous work [9], we developed a prototype to capture the non-computational parts of an experiment which includes the descriptions, agents, execution environment, devices, materials and methods used. To capture the provenance of the computational part of an experiment, we use Jupyterhub[2], which is a multi-user version of Jupyter Notebooks. It is an open source initiative which supports centralized deployment, centralized user-authentication and advances collaboration among scientists to document and run the code in any programming languages.

Several tools have been introduced to capture provenance of computational experiments. Scientific Workflow Management Systems capture provenance by running experiments as workflows. But, because of their steep learning curve, scientists still prefer writing scripts [6]. This has motivated approaches that aim to capture provenance from scripts and notebooks [2,5,7]. The YesWorkflow tool [5] is a language-independent tool where provenance data from a script is rendered as a workflow with the help of special annotations added by the user. Another recent approach is to convert notebooks into workflows where notebook developers need to follow a set of guidelines in writing code [2]. Carvalho et al. [1] present a methodology to convert scripts into workflow research objects with the help of tools like YesWorkflow, Research Objects, and PROV. All of these approaches have the limitation that they require changes to scripts by the user. Pimentel et al. [7] collect provenance data from IPython Notebooks by integrating noWorkflow [6] to the notebooks. However, this approach is limited to Python scripts. In our work, we capture and semantically describe the provenance of notebook execution in a multi-user environment using the REPRODUCE-ME ontology [8] by extending PROV-O [4] and P-Plan [3] to give a complete picture of a scientific experiment.

2 Development

We use the REPRODUCE-ME ontology [8] to describe the provenance of a notebook and its execution. In order to do this, we extend P-Plan [3] to represent the steps, plans, input and output variables and their relationship with each other. The prefixes *prov:*, *p-plan:* and *repr:* are used to indicate the namespace of all terms of PROV-O, P-Plan, and REPRODUCE-ME respectively. A *p-plan:Plan* consists of smaller steps *p-plan:Step* which consumes and produces *p-plan:Variable*. A *repr:Experiment* and *repr:Notebook* are the subclasses of *p-plan:Plan* and the *repr:Notebook* is related to *repr:Experiment* using the object property *p-plan:isSubPlanOfPlan*. A cell of the notebook, a *repr:Cell*, is a *p-plan:Step* which generates an output which is described as a *p-plan:Variable*. The source of the cell is described as an input variable. The creation of the notebook is described using *prov:generatedAtTime* and the modification time using *repr:modifiedAtTime*. The order of the execution of cells is described using *p-plan:isPrecededBy*. The *repr:Session*, a subclass of *p-plan:Activity*, describes

---

[2] https://jupyter.org/.

the session of a notebook user who is described using *prov:Agent*. The execution environment of a notebook is described using *repr:Setting* which includes *repr:ProgrammingLanguage*, *repr:Version* and *repr:Kernel*.

JupyterHub is installed and connected to our prototype so that users can create new notebooks, run and share them. The notebooks are stored in a centralized place so that they can be shared and run by scientists that belong to a group. Our prototype fetches the metadata of the notebooks from the Jupyter Notebook and JupyterHub REST APIs which provide details of the notebooks, the kernel, and the programming language used, the sessions and the users. The metadata that is useful for scientists is stored along with the other experimental data. The captured provenance data is then mapped to the ontology using ontology-based data access technique. The prototype provides a dashboard which runs SPARQL queries and visualizes the experimental data including the people who are involved in the experiment, the devices and their settings, publications used in the experiment and the notebook data. Figure 1 shows the project dashboard in our prototype. In this way, the prototype provides a complete picture of an experiment. Listing 1.1 shows an example SPARQL query to find all the notebooks used in an experiment and their metadata.

Fig. 1. The project dashboard in the prototype [9]

```
Select DISTINCT * WHERE {
  ?notebook a :Notebook ; :name ?NotebookName ;
  prov:generatedAtTime ?generatedAtTime ;
  :modifiedAtTime ?modifiedAtTime ;
  p-plan:isSubPlanOfPlan ?experiment .
  ?experiment a :Experiment .
  ?NotebookStep p-plan:isStepOfPlan ?notebook ;
  p-plan:hasOutputVar ?output ; :type ?StepType .
  ?output prov:value ?OutputValue ;
  :type ?OutputType ; :name ?OutputName
}
```

Listing 1.1. SPARQL query for Notebooks used in an experiment

The REPRODUCE-ME ontology, the mappings and the SPARQL queries used for evaluation are publicly available[3].

3   Conclusion and Future Work

The REPRODUCE-ME ontology was initially developed for microscopy-based experiments. Since scientists use scripts to perform data analysis, we decided to expand the ontology by extending W3C vocabularies to describe the widely used notebooks. In this paper, we semantically enrich the scientific experimental data using notebooks in a multi-user environment provided by JupyterHub. The prototype provides a dashboard which visualizes the experimental data along with the notebooks used to generate the final results. This allows the user to visualize the complete path taken for an experiment from its input to its output along with the execution environment. As future work, we aim to evaluate the prototype based on scalability measures.

Acknowledgements. This research is supported by the "Deutsche Forschungsge-meinschaft" (DFG) in Project Z2 of the CRC/TRR 166 "High-end light microscopy elucidates membrane receptor function - ReceptorLight". We thank Christoph Biskup, Kathrin Groeneveld and Tom Kache from University Hospital Jena, Germany, for providing the requirements to develop the proposed approach and evaluating the system.

References

1. Carvalho, L.A.M.C., Belhajjame, K., Medeiros, C.B.: Converting scripts into repro-ducible workflow research objects. In: 2016 IEEE 12th International Conference on e-Science (e-Science), pp. 71–80, October 2016
2. Carvalho, L.A.M.C., Wang, R., Gil, Y., Garijo, D.: NiW: converting notebooks into workflows to capture dataflow and provenance (2017)
3. Garijo, D., Gil, Y.: Augmenting PROV with plans in P-Plan: scientific processes as linked data. In: CEUR Workshop Proceedings (2012)
4. Lebo, T., Sahoo, S., McGuinness, D., Belhajjame, K., et al.: PROV-O: the PROV ontology. W3C Recomm. **30** (2013)
5. McPhillips, T.M., Song, T., Kolisnik, T., Aulenbach, S., Belhajjame, K., et al.: YesWorkflow: a user-oriented, language-independent tool for recovering workflow information from scripts. CoRR abs/1502.02403 (2015)
6. Pimentel, J.F., Murta, L., Braganholo, V., Freire, J.: noWorkflow: a tool for collect-ing, analyzing, and managing provenance from python scripts. Proc. VLDB Endow. **10**(12), 1841–1844 (2017)
7. Pimentel, J.F.N., Braganholo, V., Murta, L., Freire, J.: Collecting and analyz-ing provenance on interactive notebooks: when IPython meets noWorkflow. In: 7th USENIX Workshop on the Theory and Practice of Provenance (TaPP 2015). USENIX Association, Edinburgh (2015)

---

[3] http://fusion.cs.uni-jena.de/fusion/repr/.

8. Samuel, S., König-Ries, B.: REPRODUCE-ME: ontology-based data access for reproducibility of microscopy experiments. In: Blomqvist, E., Hose, K., Paulheim, H., Ławrynowicz, A., Ciravegna, F., Hartig, O. (eds.) ESWC 2017. LNCS, vol. 10577, pp. 17–20. Springer, Cham (2017). https://doi.org/10.1007/978-3-319-70407-4_4
9. Samuel, S., Taubert, F., Walther, D., König-Ries, B., Bücker, H.M.: Towards reproducibility of microscopy experiments. D-Lib Mag. **23**(1/2) (2017)

A Scalable Consent, Transparency and Compliance Architecture

Sabrina Kirrane[1]([envelope]), Javier D. Fernández[1], Wouter Dullaert[2], Uros Milosevic[2], Axel Polleres[1], Piero A. Bonatti[3], Rigo Wenning[4], Olha Drozd[1], and Philip Raschke[5]

[1] Vienna University of Economics and Business, Vienna, Austria
sabrinakirrane@gmail.com
[2] Tenforce, Leuven, Belgium
[3] Universita' di Napoli Federico II, Naples, Italy
[4] W3C, Sophia-Antipolis, France
[5] Technical University Berlin, Berlin, Germany

Abstract. In this demo we present the SPECIAL consent, transparency and compliance system. The objective of the system is to afford data subjects more control over personal data processing and sharing, while at the same time enabling data controllers and processors to comply with consent and transparency obligations mandated by the European General Data Protection Regulation. A short promotional video can be found at https://purl.com/specialprivacy/demos/ESWC2018.

1 Introduction

Data, which is commonly touted as the oil of the 21st century, is not only fueling the success of the tech giants (i.e. Google, Apple, Facebook, Amazon) but also driving innovation in enterprises in general, as evidenced by the rise in data science across a variety of domains. Although personal data is particularly valuable, in Europe the General Data Protection Regulation (GDPR) stipulates obligations with respect to personal data processing and sharing that must be fulfilled by data controllers and processors. Such obligations relate to obtaining consent from data subjects, the provision of transparency with respect to personal data processing and sharing, and ensuring compliance with usage restrictions.

Although a number of tools that focus on GDPR compliance [4–6] have recently been released, such tools are targeted at self assessment, whereby companies are given information on their obligations after completing a standard questionnaire. In contrast the system described herein can be used by companies to automatically check if existing data processing and sharing practices comply with data protection related obligations. In this demo paper, we describe the SPECIAL[1] consent, transparency and compliance system, which can be used not only to record consent but also to provide transparency to data subjects concerning the use of their personal data.

---

[1] https://www.specialprivacy.eu/.

© Springer Nature Switzerland AG 2018
A. Gangemi et al. (Eds.): ESWC 2018 Satellite Events, LNCS 11155, pp. 131–136, 2018.
https://doi.org/10.1007/978-3-319-98192-5_25

The contributions of the paper can be summarized as follows: we (i) demonstrate how usage constraints, data processing and sharing events can be expressed using the Resource Description Framework (RDF); and (ii) propose a transparency and compliance system that can automatically verify that data processing and sharing complies with the relevant usage control policies.

2   Related Work

The traditional way to obtain consent is to have a human readable description of the processing where the data collected is described in some very general terms. *Dynamic consent* is a relatively new framework that refers to the use of modern communication mediums to provide transparency, enable consent management and to elicit greater involvement of data subjects from a consent perspective [3].

When it comes to transparency with respect to data processing, relevant work primarily relates to the re-purposing of existing logging mechanisms as the basis for personal data processing transparency and compliance [2]. Many of the works analyzed by [2] use a secret key signing scheme based on Message Authentication Codes (MACs) together with a hashing algorithm to generate chains of log records that are in turn used to ensure log confidentiality and integrity [1]. MACs are themselves symmetric keys that are generated and verified using collision-resistant secure cryptographic hash functions. However, only a few works [7,8] focused on personal data processing.

As for GDPR compliance, recently the Information Commissioner's Office (ICO) in the UK [4], Microsoft [5], and Nymity [6] have developed compliance tools that enable companies to assess the compliance of their applications and business processes by completing a predefined questionnaire. In contrast to existing approaches, we propose a system that can be used to record both usage policies and data processing and sharing events in a manner that supports automatic compliance checking.

3   RDF Vocabularies for Usage Policies and Events

The vocabularies described in this section are based on the SPECIAL usage policy language[2] and log vocabulary[3], which were derived from in-depth legal analysis of use cases that require the processing and sharing of personal data for improved information and communication technology and financial services. SPECIAL usage policies can be used to denote the following information at different levels of granularity:

- *Data* describes the personal data collected from the data subject.
- *Processing* describes the operations that are performed on the personal data.
- *Purpose* represents the objective of such processing.

---

[2] http://purl.org/specialprivacy/policylanguage.
[3] http://purl.org/specialprivacy/splog.

- *Storage* specifies where data are stored and for how long.
- *Recipients* specifies with whom the data is shared.

In this paper we use the standard namespace prefixes for both rdf and rdfs, and adopt the SPECIAL vocabulary prefixes represented in *Listing* 1.1.

Listing 1.1. SPECIAL Namespace Prefixes

```
PREFIX  spl:  <http://www.specialprivacy.eu/langs/usage-policy#>
PREFIX  splog: <http://www.specialprivacy.eu/langs/splog#>
PREFIX  svd:  <http://www.specialprivacy.eu/vocabs/duration#>
PREFIX  svl:  <http://www.specialprivacy.eu/vocabs/locations#>.
```

Usage Policies. Using the SPECIAL usage policy language it is possible to specify basic usage policies as OWL classes of objects, as denoted in *Listing* 1.2 (represented using the OWL functional syntax for conciseness). Whereby the permission to perform *SomeProcessing* of *SomeDataCategory* for *SomePurpose* has been given to *SomeRecipient* in compliance with *SomeStorage* restrictions.

Listing 1.2. Structure of a Usage Control Policy

```
ObjectIntersectionOf(
    ObjectSomeValuesFrom(spl:hasData SomeDataCategory)
    ObjectSomeValuesFrom(spl:hasProcessing SomeProcessing)
    ObjectSomeValuesFrom(spl:hasPurpose SomePurpose)
    ObjectSomeValuesFrom(spl:hasStorage SomeStorage)
    ObjectSomeValuesFrom(spl:hasRecipient SomeRecipient))
```

Data Processing and Sharing Events. The SPECIAL policy log vocabulary is used to represent data processing and sharing events. The event log extract represented in *Listing* 1.3 (represented using turtle), relates to a new processing event corresponding to a data subject identified as befit:Sue on the 03.01.2018 at 13:20 (i.e., validity time). The event was recorded few seconds later (i.e., transaction time). The actual data captured can be traced via the splog:eventContent property, which is detailed in *Listing* 1.4, and usually stored in a separate knowledge base. While a hash of the content is stored in the event log.

Listing 1.3. A new event for Sue's BeFit device

```
befit:entry3918 a splog:ProcessingEvent;
splog:dataSubject befit:Sue;
dct:description ''Store location in our database in Europe''@en;
splog:transactionTime ''2018-01-10T13:20:50Z''^^xsd:dateTimeStamp;
splog:validityTime ''2018-01-10T13:20:00Z''^^xsd:dateTimeStamp;
splog:eventContent befit:content3918;
splog:inmutableRecord befit:iRec3918.
```

Listing 1.4. The content of a new event for Sue's BeFit device

```
befit:content3918 a splog:LogEntryContent;
    spl:hasData svd:Location;
    spl:hasProcessing befit:SensorGathering;
    spl:hasPurpose befit:HealthTracking;
    spl:hasStorage [spl:haslocation svl:OurServers];
    spl:hasRecipient [a svr:Ours].
```

Compliance Checking. In order to verify that data processing and sharing events comply with the corresponding usage policies specified by data subjects, we use OWL reasoning to decide whether the authorized operations specified by a data subject through their given consent, subsume the specific data processing records in the transparency log.

4   A Scalable Consent, Transparency and Compliance Architecture

The SPECIAL demo system architecture, which is depicted in Fig. 1, enables transparency and compliance checking based on usage policies and events expressed using the aforementioned vocabularies.

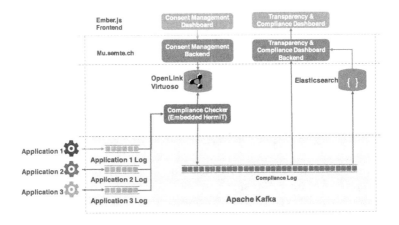

Fig. 1. A scalable consent, transparency and compliance architecture

Kafka and Zookeeper. Data processing and sharing event logs are stored in the Kafka[4] distributed streaming platform, which in turn relies on Zookeeper[5] for configuration, naming, synchronization, and providing group services. Each application log is represented using a distinct Kafka topic, while a separate compliance topic is used to store the enriched log after compliance checks have been completed.

Virtuoso Triple Store Based on our current use case requirements, we assume that consent updates are infrequent and as such usage policies and the respective vocabularies are represented in a Virtuoso triple store.

Compliance Checker. The compliance checker, which includes an embedded HermiT[6] reasoner uses the consent saved in Virtuoso together with the application logs provided by Kafka to check that data processing and sharing

---

[4] https://kafka.apache.org/.

[5] https://zookeeper.apache.org/.

[6] http://www.hermit-reasoner.com/.

complies with the relevant usage control policies. The results of this check are saved onto a new Kafka topic.

Elasticsearch. As logs can be serialized using JSON-LD, it is possible to benefit from the faceting browsing capabilities of Elasticsearch[7] and the out of the box visualization capabilities provided by Kibana.

Consent and Transparency & Compliance Backends. Interaction between the various architectural components is managed by mu.semte.ch[8] an open source micro-services framework for building RDF enabled applications.

Consent and Transparency & Compliance Dashboards. Users interact with the system via the consent management and the transparency and compliance dashboards. The former supports granting and revoking consent for processing/sharing. While, latter provides the data subject with transparency with respect to data processing and sharing events in a digestible manner.

5 Conclusion

The objective of this demo paper is to introduce the SPECIAL consent, transparency and compliance system, which is built around the Kafka distributed streaming platform. Future work includes the benchmarking of the various system components of the SPECIAL system from a performance and a scalability perspective, and the hardening of the system against various security attacks.

Acknowledgments. Supported by the European Union's Horizon 2020 research and innovation programme under grant 731601.

References

1. Bellare, M., Yee, B.: Forward integrity for secure audit logs. Technical report, Computer Science and Engineering Department, University of California at San Diego (1997)
2. Bonatti, P., Kirrane, S., Polleres, A., Wenning, R.: Transparent personal data processing: the road ahead. In: Tonetta, S., Schoitsch, E., Bitsch, F. (eds.) SAFECOMP 2017. LNCS, vol. 10489, pp. 337–349. Springer, Cham (2017). https://doi.org/10.1007/978-3-319-66284-8_28
3. Budin-Ljøsne, I., et al.: Dynamic consent: a potential solution to some of the challenges of modern biomedical research. BMC Med. Ethics **18**(1), 4 (2017)
4. Information Commissioner's Office (ICO) UK. Getting ready for the GDPR (2017). https://ico.org.uk/for-organisations/resources-and-support/data-protection-self-assessment/getting-ready-for-the-gdpr/
5. Microsoft Trust Center. Detailed GDPR Assessment (2017). http://aka.ms/gdprdetailedassessment
6. Nymity. GDPR Compliance Toolkit. https://www.nymity.com/gdpr-toolkit.aspx

---

[7] https://www.elastic.co/products/elasticsearch.

[8] https://mu.semte.ch/.

7. Pulls, T., Peeters, R., Wouters, K.: Distributed privacy-preserving transparency logging. In: Proceedings of the 12th ACM Workshop on Workshop on Privacy in the Electronic Society (2013)
8. Sackmann, S., Strüker, J., Accorsi, R.: Personalization in privacy-aware highly dynamic systems. Commun. ACM **49**(9), 32–38 (2006)

Enabling Conversational Tourism Assistants Through Schema.org Mapping

Oleksandra Panasiuk$^{(\boxtimes)}$, Zaenal Akbar$^{(\boxtimes)}$, Umutcan Şimşek, and Dieter Fensel

Semantic Technology Institute (STI) Innsbruck, Department of Computer Science,
University of Innsbruck, Innsbruck, Austria
{oleksandra.panasiuk,zaenal.akbar,umutcan.simsek,dieter.fensel}@sti2.at

Abstract. An immense effort has been invested so far by the semantic web community to make semantically annotated tourism data available. Naturally, the result of these efforts can only be proven useful if there are applications working on top of the data produced. In this paper we introduce a simple method for developing a conversational agent with state of the art tools by mapping tourism related types and properties to conversational elements in a straightforward and generic way.

Keywords: Intelligent assistant · e-tourism
Conversational mapping · schema.org

1 Introduction

In the Austrian economy, tourism takes an important place, contributing more than 10% to GDP. Every year 41.5 million guests visit Austria giving a total of 141 million overnight stays[1]. This represents a great opportunity to apply Artificial Intelligence (AI) technologies and develop intelligent assistants for tourist needs. AI techniques are used to provide proactive recommendations, automated and optimized travel planning and scheduling, tourist clustering and user preference inferences [2]. Currently one of the most widely used applications is for conversational assistants. The advance of artificial intelligence presents the challenges of providing the content of web pages through semantic annotation to such intelligent personal assistants (IPAs). In this paper we address the challenge of defining a method of developing a conversational agent by using generic mapping from dialogs to schema.org[2] types and properties.

The paper is organized as follows: Sect. 2 describes some related works, Sect. 3 explains our approach for mapping conversations to schema.org. The implementation is explained in Sect. 4 and Sect. 5 concludes our work.

---

[1] https://www.bmnt.gv.at/english/Tourism0/Tourism-Statistics/National-data.html.

[2] http://schema.org/.

© Springer Nature Switzerland AG 2018
A. Gangemi et al. (Eds.): ESWC 2018 Satellite Events, LNCS 11155, pp. 137–141, 2018.
https://doi.org/10.1007/978-3-319-98192-5_26

2   Related Work

Creating natural language interfaces over knowledge bases has drawn a great interest from the semantic web community, mainly in form of question answering systems over linked data sources. The survey in [3] covers many of these applications and the techniques they use for language understanding and query generation. For understanding the entities mentioned in a question, NER and NEL techniques with synonym expansion are used. As for the tourism vertical, most of the effort aligned to our work is in the recommender systems field [2]. These systems use different modalities for interacting with user(s) including text and speech. They mostly benefit from ad-hoc application ontologies for knowledge representation. The dialogue systems in the tourism domain typically connect to a coupled backend system like a Geographic Information System to complete context-aware question answering tasks [4]. To move such dialogue systems beyond question answering, another recent concept has been introduced in [6], that proposes a methodology for benefiting from lightweight web service annotations to extract task related dialogs. Although there have been many advanced efforts, we think that it is important to present a straightforward approach for a simplistic mapping from tourism related schema.org types and properties to natural language expressions by using prominent state of the art tools. Given the popularity of schema.org in industry, we believe this is a good step to enable IT professionals outside of semantic web and NLP community to create applications on semantically annotated data with schema.org.

3   Generic Conversational Mapping

In general, users would interact with a digital personal assistant by asking a series of questions until the users are satisfied with all answers. Most of the existing dialog engines have been powered by NLP combined with AI techniques to perceive the user's intentions. An engine would extract a few essential information items from user's expressions, such as entities, in a way relevant actions can be performed accordingly. To extract those entities correctly, the engine would require a lot of training datasets, which are not always possible to be acquired. Furthermore, different kind of schemas have been proposed in the tourism industry, and having training datasets for every schema is challenging. We solve the challenge by defining a generic mapping for every possible dialog, where schema.org will be used as the main schema.

Table 1 shows an example of the dialog conversation in the tourism domain. A few user intentions can be identified from those questions, including three important information items: (i) concept/class/type, formatted in Italics, as the object of the conversation, (ii) property, formatted in Bold, as a property of the object in the current conversation, (iii) value, formatted in Bold Italics, as the value of the property in the current conversation.

Figure 1 shows our conceptual solution for an intelligent assistant through a generic conversational mapping. It contains two most important aspects: (i) a

Table 1. Mapping user's questions to related types, properties, and values

Dialog conversation	Type	Property	Value
⇒ Find all *sports clubs* in **Seefeld**	SportsClub	not defined	Seefeld
⇐ Please specify what is Seefeld?			
⇒ **Seefeld** is a **town**	SportsClub	address	Seefeld
⇐ There are the following sport clubs:			
⇒ Find *hotels* with **price range** *between 70–150*	Hotel	priceRange	70–150

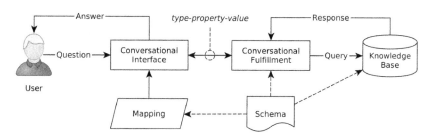

Fig. 1. Conceptual solution for an IPA through a generic conversational mapping

schema is required to feed all components in the solution, including the mapping to be consumed by the conversational interface, (ii) the dialog between conversation interface and fulfillment will be represented in a generic format, namely in a *type-property-value* pattern. The solution employs two types of mapping: (i) Schema Type Mapping, responsible to associate all classes in the schema with possible user's expressions (e.g. "bar" with type "BarOrPub"). (ii) Schema Property Mapping, responsible to associate all properties in the schema with possible user's expressions ("price range" with the property "priceRange").

Representing conversation in a *type-property-value* pattern provides a generic way to build tourism assistants, where: (i) the conversational interface will send a request to the conversational fulfillment only when the pattern has been completed, (ii) the conversational fulfillment would construct a query easily because a request has been structured in a standardized pattern.

4 Implementation

The conceptual solution explained in the previous section is currently implemented with the following technologies: (i) for knowledge base, we utilize a knowledge graph for related touristic information available in the region of Tyrol, Austria [1], which are stored in a GraphDB triplestore[3], (ii) for conversational interface, we utilize the Dialogflow[4], which is supported by Google actions, (iii) for conversational fulfillment, a web service was developed to discover required

---

[3] http://graphdb.ontotext.com/.
[4] https://dialogflow.com.

information from the KB through SPARQL query language, (iv) for schema, we use a subset of schema.org that has been designed especially for tourism [5].

After creating a mapping, we provide a list of user expressions as the training dataset into the conversational interface, where relevant entities will be annotated with either *type*, *property* or *value*. Then, we perform an experiment, where several dialogs are generated. For every received request, the interface would search for the most relevant intent by identifying entities in the request such that actions in the intent can be performed and defined responses can be provided. In some cases, the interface could not find any relevant intent due to its incapability to identify entities in a given request. We define this capability/incapability as the accuracy metric in our experiment. A dialog will be accurate 100% whenever an intent can be identified for every request in the dialog. We generated 51 dialogs that contain a total 200 requests/questions from users (on average 4 requests per dialog). As results, we obtained 67.13% dialog accuracy on average, where more than 90% of the dialogs have 50% or more accuracy, 35% of them were 100% accurate.

5   Conclusion

In this paper, we argue that feeding a dialog engine with a generic conversational mapping would help the engine to recognize users intentions fast and easily. We demonstrated this possibility by defining a generic conversational format as a representation of a triple of type, property, and value from a schema. As use case, we developed an intelligent assistant to explore a knowledge base, which contains tourism related information from the region of Tyrol, Austria.

Acknowledgements. We would like to thank all the members of the Schema-Tourism Working Group (https://schema-tourism.sti2.org) for their valuable feedback and suggestions.

References

1. Akbar, Z., Kärle, E., Panasiuk, O., Şimşek, U., Toma, I., Fensel, D.: Complete semantics to empower touristic service providers. In: Panetto, H., et al. (eds.) Proceedings of the 2017 on the Move Federated Conferences & Workshops (OTM 2017). LNCS, pp. 353–370. Springer, Heidelberg (2017). https://doi.org/10.1007/978-3-319-69459-7_24
2. Borras, J., Moreno, A., Valls, A.: Intelligent tourism recommender systems: a survey. Expert Syst. Appl. **41**(16), 7370–7389 (2014)
3. Diefenbach, D., Lopez, V., Singh, K., Maret, P.: Core techniques of question answering systems over knowledge bases: a survey. Knowl. Inf. Syst. **55**(3), 529–569 (2017)
4. Janarthanam, S., et al.: Integrating location, visibility, and question-answering in a spoken dialogue system for pedestrian city exploration. In: Proceedings of the 13th Annual Meeting of the Special Interest Group on Discourse and Dialogue, pp. 134–136. Association for Computational Linguistics (2012)

5. Panasiuk, O., Kärle, E., Şimşek, U., Fensel, D.: Defining tourism domains for semantic annotation of web content. e-Rev. Tourism Res. **9** (2018). Research notes from the ENTER 2018 Conference on ICT in Tourism. https://ertr.tamu.edu/files/2018/01/ENTER2018_Submission_94-ok.pdf

6. Şimşek, U., Fensel, D.: Now we are talking! Flexible and open goal-oriented dialogue systems for accessing touristic services. e-Rev. Tourism Res. **9** (2018). Research notes from the ENTER 2018 Conference on ICT in Tourism. https://ertr.tamu.edu/files/2018/01/ENTER2018_Submission_91-ok.pdf

A Workflow for Generation of LDP

Noorani Bakerally$^{(\boxtimes)}$, Antoine Zimmermann, and Olivier Boissier

Univ Lyon, IMT Mines Saint-Étienne, CNRS, Laboratoire
Hubert Curien UMR 5516, 42023 Saint-Étienne, France
{noorani.bakerally,antoine.zimmermann,olivier.boissier}@emse.fr

Abstract. Linked Data Platform 1.0 (LDP) is the W3C Recommendation for exposing linked data in a RESTful manner. While several implementations of the LDP standard exist, deploying an LDP is still manual and tighly coupled to the chosen implementation. As a consequence, the same design (in terms of how the data is organised) is difficult to reuse in different LDP deployments. In this paper we propose a workflow for LDP generation to automatize the generation of LDPs from static, dynamic and heterogeneous data sources while keeping the design loosely coupled from the implementation.

Keywords: RDF · Linked data · Linked data platform

1 Introduction

The aim of the Linked Data Platform (LDP) 1.0 W3C Recommendation [7] is to standardize RESTful access to RDF data. Linked data platforms complying with the LDP standard, which we refer to as LDPs, can be useful in different contexts such as open data, where there is need to have a homogeneous view and access to data to facilitate their exploitation.

Currently, a number of LDP implementations exist. They are mostly referenced in the standard conformance report[1]. Yet, deploying an LDP from existing data sources is still complex. Currently, it requires the development of LDP generators to transform data resources from their native structures to LDP resources which can be deployed in LDP stores. Moreover, while doing so, it is possible that design decision related to the final platform are hardcoded in the LDP generator enhancing a tight coupling between the design and implementation complexifying both the maintainability and reusability. In summary, current LDP implementations are in their early stages as there is little to no support for automating the generation and deployment of LDPs from existing data, even if it is already in RDF.

In our previous works, we described an approach [1] for the generation of LDPs and a simple proof of concept [3] of doing so from static and heterogeneous data sources using existing LDP implementations. In this paper, our objective is to present the extension of the former proof of concept as a refined approach that

---

[1] https://www.w3.org/2012/ldp/hg/tests/reports/ldp.html on 11 March 2018.

© Springer Nature Switzerland AG 2018
A. Gangemi et al. (Eds.): ESWC 2018 Satellite Events, LNCS 11155, pp. 142–147, 2018.
https://doi.org/10.1007/978-3-319-98192-5_27

we refer to as the LDP generation workflow. In addition to considering static and heterogeneous data sources, the novelty of this approach is the ability to deploy LDPs on dynamic data sources and to provide fresh data for LDP resources at query time, a feature which is not yet natively supported directly by any existing LDP implementation. To this end, first we provide an overview of our approach (Sect. 2) followed by its implementation (Sect. 3) and demonstration in different scenarios (Sect. 4). Finally, we conclude with an outlook on future works (Sect. 5).

2   Our Approach: The LDP Generation Workflow

Our approach is based on model-driven engineering that involves using models as first-class entities and transforming them into running systems by using generators or by dynamically interpreting the models at run-time [5]. Doing so enables separation of concerns thus guaranteeing higher reusability of systems' models [8].

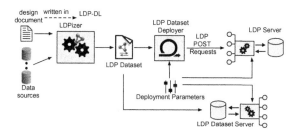

Fig. 1. General overview of the LDP Generation Workflow

Figure 1 shows a general overview of the approach that includes two processes: LDPization and deployment. In the former process, the LDPizer consumes a design document written in our language, LDP-DL, that we use as a domain-specific language, a core component of model-driven engineering, to explicitly describe LDP design models. Concerning LDP-DL, its abstract syntax is described in our technical report [4] while its concrete RDF syntax of LDP-DL is given in its specification [2]. The LDPizer interprets the model and exploits the data sources to generate what we call an LDP dataset, which is a structure to store LDP resources introduced to abstract ways from how current implementations store resources. The deployment process involves configuring the LDP and loading the LDP dataset into it. It can be done in two ways based on the nature of the LDP server. First, if the LDP server accepts POST requests, an LDP Dataset Deployer can generate and send such requests for each resource contained in the LDP dataset. Second, using an LDP server that can directly consume the LDP dataset and expose resources from it. For now, our approach only requires the design document from which the entire LDP can be automatically generated.

3   Implementation

In this section, we describe our implementation which consists of a tool for every component from the LDP generation workflow (Fig. 2).

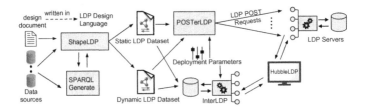

Fig. 2. Implementation of our LDP Generation Workflow

ShapeLDP[2] is an LDPizer that interprets documents written in LDP-DL refered to as *design documents*. To exploit heterogeneous data sources, lifting rules specified for `DataSources` in SPARQL-Generate [6] are used. ShapeLDP can process design documents in *static evaluation* (resp. *dynamic evaluation*) to produce a static (resp. *dynamic*)*LDP dataset*. The difference between these two types of LDP dataset is that the static one contains the materialized RDF graph of the LDP resource while the dynamic one contains the information to generate this RDF graph and can thus be used for dynamic or real-time data sources. The algorithms used in ShapeLDP and the formal models of LDP dataset (static or dynamic) are given in our technical report [4].

InterLDP[3] is an LDP server which can directly consume an LDP dataset (static or dynamic) and expose resources from it. It was validated against the conformance tests of the LDP read interactions.[4] In the static mode, it consumes static LDP dataset and exposes resources from it. In the dynamic mode, it is able to consider dynamic and real-time heterogeneous or RDF data sources and process the request for a particular resource and generate its RDF graph at query time.

POSTerLDP[5] is the implementation of the LDP Dataset Deployer. It consumes a static LDP dataset and deployment parameters: base URL of LDP server and optionally the username and password for basic authentication on the server. It can function in two different modes: *append* and *update*. In the *append mode*, it sends only `POST` request to the server to create resources from the LDP dataset. In the *update mode*, for resources on the LDP having similar URLs with that from the LDP dataset, a `PUT` request with the RDF graph from the LDP dataset is sent for those resources.

HubbleLDP[6] is an LDP browser that can be used to browse resources on an LDP and view their content. Figure 3 shows a screenshot which is actually an instance of it is running at http://bit.ly/2BGYl9X loaded with an LDP[7] about DCAT catalogue[8] and organization of its datasets in different languages.

Fig. 3. Screenshot of HubbleLDP

4   Demonstration

We perform several experiments to show that our approach can significantly automatize the generation of LDPs from static, dynamic and heterogeneous data sources while keeping the design loosely coupled from the implementation. A description of all these experiments can be found on our GitHub page[9]. Below, we describes some of these experiments.

Reusability of Design Documents. We perform two experiments to show that design documents are indeed reusable. In the first experiment[10], we consider 22 DCAT datasets from data portals as input data sources along 5 design documents. Every design document is applied of all data sources showing their

---

[6] https://github.com/noorbakerally/HubbleLDP.

[7] http://opensensingcity.emse.fr/ldpdfend/tourism62/d3/catalog.

[8] https://tourisme62.opendatasoft.com/api/v2/catalog/exports/ttl.

[9] https://github.com/noorbakerally/LDPDatasetExamples.

[10] https://tinyurl.com/y9rhgs6g.

reusability and on every data source, 5 design documents are applied showing the flexibility. In all, 110 LDPs are generated. In the second experiment[11], we consider two generic design documents that can we reused on RDF graph that uses RDFS/OWL vocabularies and apply them on one input data source to generate two LDPs with different designs. These two experiments shows that the design is highly reusable and not tighly coupled to any specific implementation.

Heterogeneous Data Sources[12]. Handling heterogeneity of data portals is demonstrated by doing deploying 2 datasets, in JSON and CSV formats, via an LDP. In the design document, the original data source is specified together with a lifting rule. Using SPARQL-Generate, the RDF data is generated and used by ShapeLDP to generate the LDP dataset which is finally deployed as an LDP using InterLDP.

Dynamic Data Sources[13]. Then, we use a dataset which is being updated on a real-time basis and deploy it via an LDP to show that our approach can cope with hosting constraints. Using dynamic evaluation in ShapeLDP, the dynamic LDP dataset is generated and used by InterLDP to expose the LDP. Generating response for LDP-RSs takes more time because their content are generated at the query time using real-time data from the source.

Compatibility with Existing LDP Implementations[14]. To show that our approach is compatible with existing LDP servers, we use POSTerLDP to deploy 2 LDPs over LDP servers that are instances of Apache Marmotta and Gold, both of them being reference implementation of the LDP standard.

5   Conclusion and Future Work

Linked Data Platforms can potentially ease the work of data consumers, but there is not much support from implementations to automate the generation and deployment of LDPs. Considering this, we proposed an approach, the LDP generation workflow, whose core is a language, LDP-DL, to generate LDPs. We describe the approach, give an implementation of it and demonstrates its ability to generate LDPs from static, dynamic, heterogeneous data sources while keeping the design loosely coupled from the implementation. Several improvements can be envisaged such as considering new design aspects (access rights, pagination etc.), support non-RDF sources and other types of LDP containers which we intend to consider in future versions.

Acknowledgments. This work is supported by grant ANR-14-CE24-0029 from *Agence Nationale de la Recherche* for project OpenSensingCity.

---

[11] https://tinyurl.com/yaoyt6kt.
[12] https://tinyurl.com/yd8auvp2.
[13] https://tinyurl.com/yb6cl3r7.
[14] https://tinyurl.com/yc9yg8nz.

References

1. Bakerally, N.: Towards automatic deployment of linked data platforms. In: ISWC Doctoral Consortium (2017)
2. Bakerally, N.: LDP-DL: RDF syntax and mapping to abstract syntax. Technical report, Mines Saint-Étienne (2018). https://w3id.org/ldpdl
3. Bakerally, N., Zimmermann, A.: A system to automatize the deployment of data in linked data platforms. In: ISWC 2017 Posters & Demo (2017)
4. Bakerally, N., Zimmermann, A., Boissier, O.: LDP-DL: a language to define the design of Linked Data Platforms. Technical report, Mines Saint-Étienne (2018). http://w3id.org/ldpdl/technical_report.pdf
5. France, R.B., Rumpe, B.: Model-driven development of complex software: a research roadmap. In: FOSE (2007)
6. Lefrançois, M., Zimmermann, A., Bakerally, N.: A SPARQL extension for generating RDF from heterogeneous formats. In: ESWC (2017)
7. Speicher, S., Arwe, J., Malhotra, A.: Linked Data Platform 1.0, W3C Recommendation 26 February 2015. Technical report, W3C (2015)
8. Stahl, T., Volter, M., Bettin, J., Haase, A., Helsen, S.: Model-Driven Software Development: Technology, Engineering, Management. Pitman (2006)

Supporting Sustainable Publishing and Consuming of Live Linked Time Series Streams

Julian Andres Rojas Melendez[✉], Gayane Sedrakyan, Pieter Colpaert,
Miel Vander Sande, and Ruben Verborgh

IDLab, Department of Electronics and Information Systems,
Ghent University - IMEC, Ghent, Belgium
julianandres.rojasmelendez@ugent.be

Abstract. The road to publishing public streaming data on the Web is paved with trade-offs that determine its viability. The cost of unrestricted query answering on top of data streams, may not be affordable for all data publishers. Therefore, public streams need to be funded in a sustainable fashion to remain online. In this paper we present an overview of possible query answering features for live time series in the form of multidimensional interfaces. For example, from a live parking availability data stream, pre-calculated time constrained statistical indicators or geographically classified data can be provided to clients on demand. Furthermore, we demonstrate the initial developments of a Linked Time Series server that supports such features through an extensible modular architecture. Benchmarking the costs associated to each of these features allows to weigh the trade-offs inherent to publishing live time series and establishes the foundations to create a decentralized and sustainable ecosystem for live data streams on the Web.

Keywords: Semantic web · Open linked data
Linked Data Fragments · Time series · Data streams

1 Introduction

The development of Internet of Things technologies has fostered the creation of live data streams in multiple domains. Specifically in the public domain, examples of such data streams can be found as sensor observations about air quality, noise level, street occupancy, vacant parking spaces, temperature, river water level, wind speed, state of public lighting systems, traffic lights, among others. Furthermore, in Europe thanks to the European Public Sector Information directive[1], public authorities are required to publish such data in an open fashion on

---

[1] https://ec.europa.eu/digital-single-market/en/european-legislation-reuse-public-sector-information.

© Springer Nature Switzerland AG 2018
A. Gangemi et al. (Eds.): ESWC 2018 Satellite Events, LNCS 11155, pp. 148–152, 2018.
https://doi.org/10.1007/978-3-319-98192-5_28

the Web. This raises new challenges for data publishers as they cannot antici-
pate the amount of users or type of queries required on the Web, and might not
be able to afford expensive infrastructures, required to maintain availability and
scalability.

Studying the trade-offs introduced by Linked Data Fragments [5] to publish
data streams on the Web, helps to understand possible ways to reduce server
costs by transferring query answering related tasks to clients. This requires
clients to implement the logic to answer a given query, increasing their complexity and the time required to process the data on the client side. Anticipating this, data publishers may provide multidimensional interfaces [3] containing
pre-processed data, relevant for answering common queries and offer them as a
service that could benefit clients by reducing query response times and implementation complexity, without limiting query flexibility. The type of interfaces to
offer depend directly on the type of data and the related use-cases. Such an approach may help to create revenue sources for data publishers while contributing
to the sustainability of the Open Data streams on the Web.

In this demo paper we present an overview of possible multidimensional interfaces, containing query answering features, that may be implemented and offered
as a service on different Open Stream data use cases. Furthermore, we introduce
the initial developments of a Live Time Series server that support the creation
of such interfaces through an extensible modular architecture.

2   Related Work

RDF Stream Processing (RSP) [1] defines a framework for continuous query
answering over data streams. RSP engines can take into account one or more
RDF streams to answer queries which results will be computed at several time
instants to consider new available data on the streams. Triple Pattern Fragments
Query Streamer (TPF-QS) [4] was introduced as an alternative to server-side RSP
engines. with the goal of making RDF stream server-side publishing possible at a
low cost, with a client-side RSP engine. In this approach, several time-annotation
techniques were investigated, of which annotation using named graphs caused
the least overhead. The results however showed that this approach has scalability
issues when querying historic data.

The work presented in [2] raises the fundamental question of the sustainability of the Web of data and introduces a marketplace for federated query
answering, giving clients the option to decide from which sources do they want
to retrieve the data needed to answer a certain query and who will process the
data to obtain that answer. The cost of the answer(s) of a given query can be
derived from the cost of hosting the related data. However determining what
is the cost of computing such answer(s) is still an open issue. In this direction,
benchmarking mechanisms could be used to determine it in terms of computational costs. For instance, the solution proposed in the HOBBIT project which
provides a generic platform for benchmarking question/answering processes centered around the challenges of data heterogeneity and scalability could be used
to determine the costs associated to answering a certain query.

3   Multidimensional Interfaces

Multidimensional Interfaces [3] were introduced for generically fragmenting data with a specific order and publishing these fragments in an interface-level index. These interfaces can make multidimensional ordinal data automatically discoverable and consumable by clients using hypermedia controls. The goal of these interfaces is to raise the server expressivity while maintaining low server costs. A vocabulary[2] to formally describe multidimensional interfaces was introduced. It defines the concepts of *Range Fragments* and *Range Gates*. A *Range Fragment* is a Linked Data Fragment that specifies an ordinal interval for a predefined fragmentation strategy. A *Range Gate* is a Linked Data interface which exposes a set of *Range Fragments*. Using these concepts it is possible to define different fragmentation strategies that can be exposed as multidimensional interfaces.

In a general sense, for live time series originated from sensor observations it is possible to define ranges as follows:

Time Ranges. Time constrained intervals can be used to create *Range Fragments* or summaries that compute statistical variables. For example to expose average values of measurements at hour, day, week, month and year level.

Geospatial Ranges. Sensors locations can be used to create Range Fragments that comprises predefined geographical areas. For example, street occupation can be given on a neighborhood, city or country level.

Depending on the type of data and the specific use case other type of fragmentations and even combinations of them can be further defined.

4   Live Time Series Server

The Live Time Series Server is an ongoing implementation that aims on providing a cost efficient interface for Open Stream data publishing. Through an extensible modular architecture we allow data publishers to define multidimensional interfaces to provide query answering functionalities on top of their data. The code is available in a Github repository[3], along with the instructions of how to test it.

As shown in Fig. 1, the server is composed by three main modules:

Data Event Manager. This module receives RDF stream updates and fires an event to notify the availability of new data.

Communications Manager. Handle the communication between the Multidimensional Interfaces and the clients. It can expose the data as Range Fragments, created by each interface through HTTP endpoints or by Websocket channels for publish/subscribe communication.

---

[2] http://semweb.datasciencelab.be/ns/multidimensional-interface/RangeGate.
[3] https://github.com/linkedtimeseries/timeseries-server.

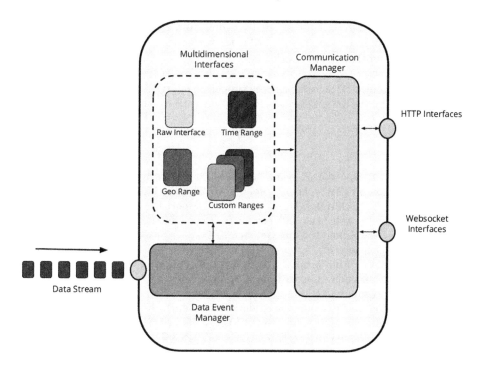

Fig. 1. Modular architecture of the Live Time Series server.

Multidimensional Interfaces. The interfaces expose the data stream according to its predefined logic. Each interface subscribes to a data event with the Data Event Manager and performs a new calculation with each update with the exception of the Raw Interface, which exposes the data as it is received. The data can be exposed as *Range Fragments* through HTTP or pushed to subscribed clients through Websocket channels.

5   Conclusion and Future Work

We introduced Live Time Series server which provides a Linked Data fragments based interface for publishing live time series on the Web. By integrating the concept of multidimensional interfaces data publishers can define modules that perform predefined calculations over the data that suit a given use case. This increases the expressivity of the server while keeping its costs low. It also reduces clients implementation complexity and data processing time to obtain a query answer. Allowing features to be turned off and on on the time series server, helps data owners to define what features they want to support and make the trade-off with their budget. Data reusers may still implement some of these features as a third party, yet then a revenue model should be thought of [2].

In future work we plan to extend this approach by defining a mechanism that allows to calculate computational cost of multidimensional interfaces through benchmarking processes, in order to help determining their economical cost. Integrating mapping capabilities in order to work with non RDF data streams constitutes yet another future work line.

Acknowledgements. This work has been supported by HOBBIT H2020 project (GA no. 688227) and by the Smart Flanders Programme (https://smart.flanders.be).

References

1. Dell'Aglio, D., Della Valle, E., van Harmelen, F.: Stream reasoning: a survey and outlook. **1–2**, 59–83 (2017). https://doi.org/10.3233/DS-170006
2. Grubenmann, T., Dell'Aglio, D., Bernstein, A., Moor, D., Seuken, S.: Decentralizing the semantic web: who will pay to realize it? In: ISWC2017 Workshop on Decentralizing the Semantic Web, October 2017
3. Taelman, R., Colpaert, P., Verborgh, R., Mannens, E.: Multidimensional interfaces for selecting data within ordinal ranges. In: Proceedings of the 7th International Workshop on Consuming Linked Data, October 2016
4. Taelman, R., Verborgh, R., Colpaert, P., Mannens, E.: Continuous client-side query evaluation over dynamic linked data. In: Sack, H., Rizzo, G., Steinmetz, N., Mladenić, D., Auer, S., Lange, C. (eds.) ESWC 2016. LNCS, vol. 9989, pp. 273–289. Springer, Cham (2016). https://doi.org/10.1007/978-3-319-47602-5_44
5. Verborgh, R.: Triple pattern fragments: a low-cost knowledge graph interface for the web. J. Web Semant. **37–38**, 184–206 (2016). https://doi.org/10.1016/j.websem. 2016.03.003

TagTheWeb: Using Wikipedia Categories to Automatically Categorize Resources on the Web

Jerry Fernandes Medeiros[1(✉)], Bernardo Pereira Nunes[2],
Sean Wolfgand Matsui Siqueira[1], and Luiz André Portes Paes Leme[3]

[1] Department of Applied Informatics,
Federal University of the State of Rio de Janeiro (UNIRIO),
Rio de Janeiro, RJ 22290-240, Brazil
{jerry.medeiros,sean}@uniriotec.br
[2] Department of Informatics, Pontifical Catholic University of Rio de Janeiro,
Rio de Janeiro, RJ 22451-900, Brazil
bernardo@ccead.puc-rio.br
[3] Institute of Computing, Fluminense Federal University,
Niterói, RJ 24210-310, Brazil
lapaesleme@ic.uff.br

Abstract. Identifying topics associated with a set of documents is a common task for many applications and can be used to improve various tasks involving documents on the Web, such as search, retrieval, recommendation, and clustering. To address this problem, this paper introduces a tool, called TagTheWeb, as a proposition of a generic classification method, that relies on the knowledge expressed by the taxonomic structure of Wikipedia, based on the generation of a fingerprint through the semantic relation between nodes of the Wikipedia Category Graph. TagTheWeb can be used as a WEB interface or as an API to classify any text based resource.

Keywords: Text categorization · Semantic web · Wikipedia Categories · Category Graph

1 Introduction

Wikipedia is the most substantial encyclopedia freely available on the Web. It has been developed and curated by a large number of users over time and represents the common sense about facts, people and the broadest type of topics currently found on the Web.

One of the outstanding features of Wikipedia is the categorization system used to index its internal content. Very briefly, there are a finite number of top categories that represents the whole Wikipedia content. These top categories, as well as their subcategories, are not fixed and are maintained and curated by Wikipedia users.

© Springer Nature Switzerland AG 2018
A. Gangemi et al. (Eds.): ESWC 2018 Satellite Events, LNCS 11155, pp. 153–157, 2018.
https://doi.org/10.1007/978-3-319-98192-5_29

The primary purpose of this research is to create a general-purpose classification tool based on Wikipedia Categorization scheme that can categorize text-based content on the Web, for instance, scientific articles, web pages or even posts on social media. At the current stage, it is possible to categorize any textual content in different languages via a web interface or API.

2   Related Work

The depth and coverage of Wikipedia has attracted the attention of many researchers who have used it as a knowledge resource for several tasks, including text categorization [2], predicting document topics [8] and computing semantic relatedness [3,6,7].

Halavais and Lackaff [4] quantitatively compared the distribution of 3,000 Wikipedia articles coded into Library of Congress categories with a distribution of published books. They found substantial overlap between Wikipedia categories and topics from other encyclopedias. Kittur [5] demonstrated a simple technique for determining the distribution of topics for articles in Wikipedia, mapping all items to the top categories. The process was based on building the Category Graph of Wikipedia and counting the edges on the shortest paths from the categories of an article to the top categories of Wikipedia. Farina [1] improved this by penalizing edges followed in the wrong direction concerning the hierarchy. Strube and Ponzetto [9] developed a system named WikiRelate!. They used data from Wordnet, Wikipedia, and Google for computing degrees of semantic similarity and reported that Wikipedia outperforms Wordnet. They used different measures for computing semantic relatedness and showed good results with the one based on paths.

3   TagTheWeb - Approach Overview

Our primary goal is to take advantage of the Wikipedia body of knowledge to automatically categorize any text-based content on the Web according to the collective knowledge of Wikipedia contributors. A processing chain to generate a generic categorization was developed based on three steps: (i) Text Annotation; (ii) Categories Extraction; (iii) Fingerprint Generation.

As the basis for our approach, we consider the relationships of Wikipedia Categories as a directed graph. Let $G = (V, E)$ be a graph, where V is the set of nodes representing Wikipedia categories, and E is the set of edges representing the relationships between two categories.

To make it simple to understand, let us illustrate the steps.

3.1   Text Annotation

When dealing with the Web of Documents, we are primarily working with unstructured data, which, in turn, hinders data manipulation and the identification of atomic elements in texts. To alleviate this problem, information extraction (IE) methods, such as Named-Entity Recognition (NER) and name resolution, are employed. These tools automatically extract structured information from unstructured data and link them to external knowledge bases in the Linked Open Data cloud (LOD), which is DBpedia in this case.

For instance, after processing the following Web resource using an IE tool: "I agree with Barack Obama that the whole episode should be investigated.", the entity "Barack Obama" is annotated, classified as "person" and linked to the DBpedia resource <http://dbpedia.org/resource/Barack_Obama>, where structured information about the entity is available.

3.2   Categories Extraction

Given the entities found in the previous step as a starting point, the categories extraction step begins by traversing the entity relationships to find a more general representation of the entity, i.e., their categories. All categories associated with the entities identified in the source of information are extracted.

For instance, for each extracted and enriched entity in a Web resource, we explore the relationships through the predicate [dcterms:subject], which by definition represents the categories of an entity. In that sense, to retrieve the topics, we use SPARQL query language for RDF over the DBpedia SPARQL, where we navigate up in the DBpedia hierarchy to retrieve broader semantic relations between the entities and its topics.

3.3   Fingerprint Generation

The goal of this step is to assign a set of main topics within Wikipedia Categories to a given web resource.

Our approach consists of navigating in the Category Graph from each category extracted in the previous step towards the top of the graph by all the shortest paths between the category and the main topics.

Each time the source category reaches one of the top-level categories, we update the influence of this top category in the composition of the resource classification.

Based on the influence of each main topic category in the resource, we generate a fingerprint, which represents the calculated categorization as a multidimensional vector, making it easy to retrieve and compare documents. For Instance, using a straightforward similarity metric such as cosine.

As a formal definition, let us denote I as the set of categories related to a web resource d, found in the category extraction step. C is the set of all Categories in Wikipedia, and M is the set of categories that represent the main topics. $G = (V, E)$, where $I \subset V; C \subset V; M \subset V$; and $M \subset C$. The parameter t is defined to indicate the broadest t levels to be considered in the set of M. If t is 1, only the main topics previously defined are considered; if t is 2, any category 1 edge away in the graph is also considered as one of the main topics, as represented in Algorithm 1. An example of the tool can be seen in Fig. 1.

Algorithm 1. Fingerprint Generation

1: **procedure** GENERATEFINGERPRINT(G, M, I, t, w)
2:     $E \leftarrow$ a map from a list of categories $m \in M$
3:     **for** $i \in I$ **do**
4:         $S \leftarrow$ the set of shortest paths between i and any category in M
5:         **for** $s \in S$ **do**
6:             $B \leftarrow$ the set of last t vertices in path s
7:             **for** $b \in B$ **do**
8:                 $E[b] \leftarrow E[b] + w$
9:     **return** E

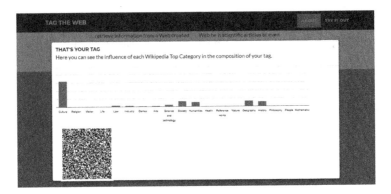

Fig. 1. Categorization for a given page of Obama's Twitter

4   Preliminary Evaluation and Results

The first validation of this work was the analysis of the fingerprint in posts of question and answers communities. Stack Exchange is a network of 133 Q&A (Question and answers) communities on topics in varied fields, each community covering a specific theme, where questions, answers, and users are subject to a reputation award process.

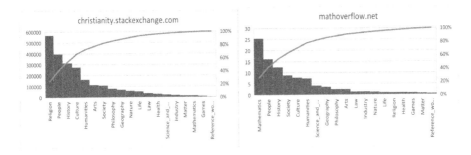

Fig. 2. Distribution of topics along the questions on stack exchange communities

We relied on an anonymized dump of all user-contributed content on the Stack Exchange network, extracted on August 31st. We selected four representative communities on stack exchange to perform this evaluation: (1) Biology; (2) Christianity; (3) Law; and (4) Math. For each row in the Post.xml file of each one of these communities, we executed the three steps of the chain described in Sect. 3. The topic distribution for each community is displayed in Fig. 2.

5   Conclusion and Future Works

This paper introduced TagTheWeb, a tool to automatically categorize resources on the web based on the Wikipedia Category Graph. A preliminary empirical evaluation shows promising results as we can reliably classify question and answers on communities that cover specific themes. As future works, we intend to test TagTheWeb in other scenarios to fine-tune the algorithm. We are also conducting experiments with humans to identify whether they agree or not with the categorization generated by the tool. TagTheWeb is publicly available at tagtheweb.com.br, and the API documentation can be found at https://documenter.getpostman.com/view/1071275/tagtheweb/77bC7Kn.

References

1. Farina, J., Tasso, R., Laniado, D.: Automatically assigning Wikipedia articles to macrocategories (2011)
2. Gabrilovich, E., Markovitch, S.: Overcoming the brittleness bottleneck using Wikipedia: enhancing text categorization with encyclopedic knowledge. In: AAAI, vol. 6, pp. 1301–1306 (2006)
3. Gabrilovich, E., Markovitch, S.: Computing semantic relatedness using Wikipedia-based explicit semantic analysis. In: IJCAI, vol. 7, pp. 1606–1611 (2007)
4. Halavais, A., Lackaff, D.: An analysis of topical coverage of Wikipedia. J. Comput.-Mediat. Commun. **13**(2), 429–440 (2008)
5. Kittur, A., Chi, E.H., Suh, B.: What's in Wikipedia?: mapping topics and conflict using socially annotated category structure. In: Proceedings of the SIGCHI Conference on Human Factors in Computing Systems, pp. 1509–1512. ACM (2009)
6. Milne, D.: Computing semantic relatedness using Wikipedia link structure. In: Proceedings of the New Zealand Computer Science Research Student Conference. Citeseer (2007)
7. Ponzetto, S.P., Strube, M.: Exploiting semantic role labeling, Wordnet and Wikipedia for coreference resolution. In: Proceedings of the Main Conference on Human Language Technology Conference of the North American Chapter of the Association of Computational Linguistics, pp. 192–199. Association for Computational Linguistics (2006)
8. Schönhofen, P.: Identifying document topics using the Wikipedia category network. Web Intell. Agent Syst.: Int. J. **7**(2), 195–207 (2009)
9. Strube, M., Ponzetto, S.P.: Wikirelate! computing semantic relatedness using Wikipedia. In: AAAI, vol. 6, pp. 1419–1424 (2006)

ViziQuer: A Web-Based Tool for Visual Diagrammatic Queries Over RDF Data

Kārlis Čerāns[1,2(✉)], Agris Šostaks[1,2], Uldis Bojārs[1,2],
Jūlija Ovčiņņikova[1,2], Lelde Lāce[1,2], Mikus Grasmanis[1],
Aiga Romāne[1], Artūrs Sproģis[1], and Juris Bārzdiņš[3]

[1] Institute of Mathematics and Computer Science,
University of Latvia, Riga, Latvia
karlis.cerans@lumii.lv
[2] Department of Computing, University of Latvia, Riga, Latvia
[3] Department of Medicine, University of Latvia, Riga, Latvia

Abstract. We demonstrate the open source ViziQuer tool for web-based creation and execution of visual diagrammatic queries over RDF/SPARQL data. The tool supports the data instance level and statistics queries, providing visual counterparts for most of SPARQL 1.1 select query constructs, including aggregation and subqueries. A query environment can be created over a user-supplied SPARQL endpoint with known data schema (a data schema exploration service is available, as well). There are pre-defined demonstration query environments for a mini-university data set, a fragment of synthetic similar to reality hospital data set, and a variant of Linked Movie Database RDF data set.

Keywords: Visual query tool · Ad-hoc queries · Rich queries
RDF data · SPARQL

1 Introduction

The textual SPARQL 1.1 [1] select query language over RDF data allows creating rich data selection queries, possibly involving subqueries, aggregations, unions and rich expression notation. The visual/diagrammatic environments for query creation support, such as Optique VQs [2], Query VOWL [3] and early versions of ViziQuer [4], however, stay significantly behind the expressivity of SPARQL 1.1 select queries by not supporting e.g. the subqueries and aggregation. The possibility of introducing aggregated fields and rich expression notation into a diagrammatic UML-style RDF data query environment has been shown in the earlier work of authors [5, 6], while [7] provides a more refined set of extended UML class diagram constructs for visual SPARQL query definition including: (i) separation of aggregated and grouping fields in query node attribute lists; (ii) visual notation for subqueries, (iii) separate query control nodes for query structuring and (iv) integrated textual SPARQL fragments.

We describe and demonstrate here the web-based open source ViziQuer tool supporting the notation of [7] and providing basic user services both for query environment configuration and visual query creation. The resource point http://viziquer. lumii.lv provides links both to the online tool and the source code repository.

© Springer Nature Switzerland AG 2018
A. Gangemi et al. (Eds.): ESWC 2018 Satellite Events, LNCS 11155, pp. 158–163, 2018.
https://doi.org/10.1007/978-3-319-98192-5_30

We provide preliminary results on query notation and tool usability, as well.

In what follows, Sect. 2 briefly reviews the visual query notation, Sect. 3 describes the query tool usage and implementation and Sect. 4 concludes the paper.

2 Visual Notation Overview

For query notation illustration we use a mini-hospital data schema, extracted from [8] and depicted in UML style notation in Fig. 1. The role names, if not specified, coincide with target class names with lowercase first letter; the attributes and roles are assumed by default to have minimum and maximum cardinalities 1.

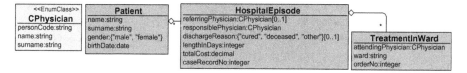

Fig. 1. Mini-hospital data schema

A basic visual query (cf. [4, 7]) is a UML class diagram style graph with the nodes describing data instances, the edges describing their connections and the attributes forming the query selection list from the node instance attributes and their expressions; every node can specify both the instance class and additional conditions on the instance. One of the graph nodes is the main query node (shown as orange round rectangle in the diagram); the structural edges (all edges except the condition ones) within the graph form its spanning tree with the main query node being its root.

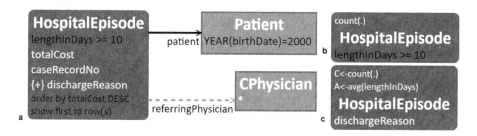

Fig. 2. Class-attribute-link-condition and statistics queries

Figure 2 shows initial query examples following the basic class-attribute-link-condition paradigm (a), similar to [2, 4], and simple statistics queries (b) and (c), as in [7]:

(a) *select top 10 most expensive hospital episodes with discharge reason specified, lasting for at least 10 days, for patients born in 2000; show episode total cost, case record number, discharge reason and all attributes of referring physician, if specified;*

(b) *count the hospital episodes lasting for at least 10 days and*

(c) *compute the hospital episode count and average length in days, grouped by the episode discharge reason.*

The visual notation supports links that are required, optional and negated. The attributes in node fields by default are optional, not to bypass entire solution rows because of missing attribute values, an attribute is marked as required by a {+} decoration in the visual notation is (cf. *dischargeReason* attribute in Fig. 2 (a)).

Figure 3 demonstrates more advanced query examples using subqueries (edges with black bullets at the end) (a), control nodes ([] stands for an outer query scope for collecting, filtering, projecting, further aggregating of subquery result lists) and non-model links (denoted by ++ in (b)), as well as schema-level variables (c):

(a) *count the patients with at least 3 hospital episodes having at least 5 wards each;*

(b) *count all wards with more than 1000 treatment in ward cases, and*

(c) *select all data classes together with their instance count.*

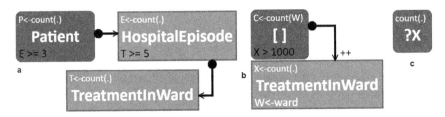

Fig. 3. Advanced query constructs

For more details and further notation examples one may consult [7], as well as the demonstration examples provided within the query environment.

3 Query Tool Usage and Implementation

The user's work with the ViziQuer tool is arranged in projects. Users can create projects that consist of query diagrams each capable of hosting multiple queries. Each project needs a supplied data schema and a SPARQL endpoint (pre-configured Vizi-Quer instances with built in schema and endpoint information are possible, as well). There are prototype services for ViziQuer schema extraction from an OWL ontology and from SPARQL endpoint data.

A ViziQuer project needs also a SPARQL engine type to enable query translation optimizations for vendor-specific SPARQL endpoints. The practical tool usage up to now has been oriented towards OpenLink Virtuoso SPARQL endpoints, although a "General SPARQL" option is available, as well.

Each query diagram allows for new query creation, starting from a query symbol selection from the symbol palette (cf. Fig. 4), followed by class name condition, plain and aggregate attribute setting using the property dialogues (there are basic suggestion services for class and attribute names). Adding of another class into the query can be performed by introducing the class via symbol palette, or by using the offered "Add Link" service (cf. Fig. 4) offering the link names and their target classes making sense in the context of the selected host class. The defined queries in the diagrams (either the connected components or parts thereof) can be either translated into the textual SPARQL form, or directly executed over the specified SPARQL endpoint.

There are available demonstration query environments for a mini-university data set, a fragment of synthetic hospital data set resembling the data of Children's hospital in Riga, Latvia [8] and a variant of Linked Movie Database RDF data set [9].

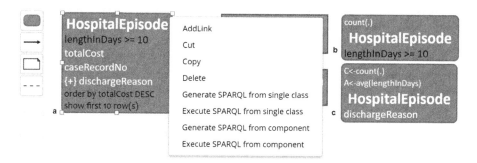

Fig. 4. Basic working environment

The tool is created using *ajoo* – a generic platform for web-based diagrammatic tool building [10]. The ViziQuer tool is defined within the platform by creating a JSON-style configuration for the node, edge and compartment types in the diagrams, and writing JavaScript functions for the tool specific functionality, including query translation into SPARQL. Ajoo and ViziQuer use Meteor framework [11] and MongoDB for diagram storage and exchange, and for user management and collaboration features.

The ajoo framework and ViziQuer query tool are open source and have been made available on GitHub, so enabling local installations of the ViziQuer query engine.

The tool architecture allows for de-coupling of the ajoo platform and custom diagram handling code from the Meteor server, should there a need arise for integrating it into some other diagram serving infrastructure.

4 Conclusions

The presented ViziQuer tool demonstrates the feasibility of visual querying of the RDF data just from a web browser window. The supported query notation allows visual creation of most of the SPARQL select query language constructs, including aggregates, subqueries and query structuring [7]. The initial experiments with potential tool end users without a formal IT background have indicated that this user group could well read and understand e.g. the queries involving subquery construct formerly considered to be out of scope for visual query formulation systems (cf. e.g. [2]).

A preliminary query composition experiment with undergraduate 4th year IT students at University of Latvia has indicated a potential usability of the visual notation and tool for generally IT literate persons. The 14 student participants (with some background in SQL and no specific training in RDF/SPARQL) were given brief introductions about the hospital data model, RDF, SPARQL and ViziQuer (each about 10 min) and then were split into two groups of 7 and given 10 query writing tasks. One group was asked to create queries in ViziQuer and the other – using textual SPARQL notation. After the training period students had 60 min to work on the assigned tasks. The numbers of successfully completed tasks by the students in the visual notation group were 10, 5, 5, 4, 4, 3, 2 (in average 4.7), while in the SPARQL group there were 5, 5, 3, 3, 2, 2, 1 completed tasks (in average 3.0). The ViziQuer group outperformed the SPARQL group on all query subsets of data instance queries, simple aggregate queries and queries with subquery structure.

It can be expected that the tool interface re-work that is to be provided as a future work (the property sheets with very basic name suggestion services currently available) would make the notation and tool a potential alternative or complement to other SPARQL query creation approaches both for semantic technology experts and lay users. This future work involves also more definite usability tests that are to be run.

Acknowledgements. This work has been partially supported by research organization base financing at Institute of Mathematics and Computer Science, University of Latvia and the University of Latvia project AAP2016/B032 "Innovative information technologies".

References

1. SPARQL 1.1 Query Language. W3C Recommendation 21 March 2013. http://www.w3.org/TR/2013/REC-sparql11-query-20130321/
2. Soylu, A., Giese, M., Jimenez-Ruiz, E., Vega-Gorgojo, G., Horrocks, I.: Experiencing OptiqueVQS: a multi-paradigm and ontology-based visual query system for end users. Univ. Access Inf. Soc. **15**(1), 129–152 (2016)
3. Haag, F., Lohmann, S., Siek, S., Ertl, T.: QueryVOWL: visual composition of SPARQL queries. In: Gandon, F., Guéret, C., Villata, S., Breslin, J., Faron-Zucker, C., Zimmermann, A. (eds.) ESWC 2015. LNCS, vol. 9341, pp. 62–66. Springer, Cham (2015). https://doi.org/10.1007/978-3-319-25639-9_12
4. Zviedris, M., Barzdins, G.: ViziQuer: a tool to explore and query SPARQL endpoints. In: Antoniou, G., et al. (eds.) ESWC 2011. LNCS, vol. 6644, pp. 441–445. Springer, Heidelberg (2011). https://doi.org/10.1007/978-3-642-21064-8_31
5. Cerans, K., Ovcinnikova, J., Zviedris, M.: SPARQL aggregate queries made easy with diagrammatic query language ViziQuer. In: Proceedings of the ISWC 2015 Posters & Demonstrations Track, CEUR, vol. 1486 (2015). http://ceur-ws.org/Vol-1486/paper_68.pdf
6. Čerāns, K., Ovčiņņikova, J.: ViziQuer: notation and tool for data analysis SPARQL queries. In: Proceedings of VOILA 2016, Kobe, Japan, CEUR Workshop Proceedings, CEUR-WS. org, vol. 1704, pp. 151–159 (2016). http://ceur-ws.org/Vol-1704/paper15.pdf
7. Cerans, K., et al.: Extended UML class diagram constructs for visual SPARQL queries in ViziQuer/web. In: Voila!2017, CEUR Workshop Proceedings, vol. 1947, pp. 87–98 (2017)

8. Barzdins, J., Grasmanis, M., Rencis, E., Sostaks, A., Barzdins, J.: Ad-Hoc querying of semistar data ontologies using controlled natural language. In: Frontiers of AI and Applications, Databases and Information Systems IX, vol. 291, pp. 3–16. IOS Press (2016). http://ebooks.iospress.com/volumearticle/45695

9. Linked Movie Database. http://www.cs.toronto.edu/~oktie/linkedmdb/

10. Sprogis, A.: ajoo: WEB based framework for domain specific modeling tools. In: Frontiers of AI and Applications, Databases and Information Systems IX, vol. 291, pp. 115–126. IOS Press (2016). http://ebooks.iospress.com/volumearticle/45704

11. Strack, I.: Getting Started with Meteor JavaScript Framework. Packt Publishing Ltd, Birmingham (2012)

EventKG+TL: Creating Cross-Lingual Timelines from an Event-Centric Knowledge Graph

Simon Gottschalk[✉] and Elena Demidova

L3S Research Center, Leibniz Universität Hannover, Hannover, Germany
{gottschalk,demidova}@L3S.de

Abstract. The provision of multilingual event-centric temporal knowledge graphs such as EventKG enables structured access to representations of a large number of historical and contemporary events in a variety of language contexts. Timelines provide an intuitive way to facilitate an overview of events related to a *query entity* - i.e. an entity or an event of user interest - over a certain period of time. In this paper, we present EventKG+TL - a novel system that generates cross-lingual event timelines using EventKG and facilitates an overview of the language-specific event relevance and popularity along with the cross-lingual differences.

Demo URL: http://eventkg.l3s.uni-hannover.de/eventkg_tl.

1 Introduction

The amount of event-centric information regarding contemporary and historical events of global importance, such as Brexit and the migration crisis in Europe, constantly grows on the Web, in Web archives, in the news as well as within emerging event-centric collections [2] and knowledge graphs generated from these sources (e.g. [4,7]). An important research area in this context is cross-cultural and cross-lingual event analytics (e.g. see [5,6] for case studies, and [3] for a cross-lingual user interface). These studies aim to analyze language-specific and community-specific representations and perceptions of historical and contemporary events including their popularity and relations in a language context as well as to better understand the cross-lingual differences.

EventKG [4] - a recently proposed multilingual event-centric temporal knowledge graph incorporating over 690 thousand events in five languages - is an important knowledge source that can facilitate a variety of studies and applications related to cross-cultural and cross-lingual event analytics. However, given a *query entity*, i.e. an entity or an event of user interest, EventKG can contain hundreds of related events along with their descriptions in several language contexts, which makes the provision of a comprehensive cross-lingual overview and a selection of relevant events for further detailed analysis challenging.

© Springer Nature Switzerland AG 2018
A. Gangemi et al. (Eds.): ESWC 2018 Satellite Events, LNCS 11155, pp. 164–169, 2018.
https://doi.org/10.1007/978-3-319-98192-5_31

Timelines are an intuitive way to provide an overview of events related to a *query entity* over a certain period of time. Timeline generation is an active research area [1], where the focus is to generate a timeline (i.e. a chronologically ordered selection) of events related to the *query entity* from a knowledge graph. However, existing timelines do not explicitly support a cross-lingual comparison of language-specific event representations, including their popularity and relation to the *query entity* in different language contexts.

EventKG+TL presented in this paper is a timeline generator that creates cross-lingual timelines for a *query entity*, while relying on EventKG to provide language-specific information with respect to the event popularity and the relation strength between the events and the *query entity*. To this extent, EventKG+TL conducts a language-specific event ranking and complements this ranking with a cross-lingual visual representation. The timelines generated by EventKG+TL facilitate efficient identification of relevant events based on their language-specific popularity, relation strength and the cross-lingual differences.

2   Scenarios and Timelines

A *multilingual event-centric temporal knowledge graph* $kg = (L, E, R)$ is a labeled directed multigraph, where L is a set of language contexts, E is a set of nodes (i.e. events or entities), and R is a multiset of directed edges (i.e. relations).

Given a *query entity* $q \in E$, the timelines generated by EventKG+TL can assist users in answering questions such as:

Q_1: *What are the most popular events related to q?*
Q_2: *Which events are the most closely related to q?*
Q_3: *Which of the most popular events are the most closely related to q?*
Q_4: *How does the popularity of the identified events and the strength of their relations to the query entity q differ across the language contexts?*

The provision of EventKG+TL facilitates users to answer these questions with respect to a particular language context $l \in L$ and enables a visual cross-lingual comparison. To answer these questions, the user of EventKG+TL can issue a *timeline query* that includes the following parameters:

- a *query entity* $q \in E$;
- a set of the language contexts of user interest $L' \subseteq L$;
- the maximum number k of the events to be selected per language context;
- the ranking criterion rc_i to identify the top-k most relevant events among all events $E' \subset E$ related to q in kg according to the questions $Q_1 - Q_3$.

The ranking criteria include:

rc_1: *popularity(e, l)* is the popularity of an event $e \in E'$ in $l \in L'$;
rc_2: *relation strength(q, e, l)* is the relation strength between the *query entity* q and an event $e \in E'$ in a language context $l \in L'$; and

rc_3: $combined(q, e, l)$ is a combination of the event popularity of $e \in E'$ and the relation strength between e and the *query entity* q in $l \in L'$.

The timelines generated by EventKG+TL complement the language-specific event ranking with a cross-lingual visual representation to address the question Q_4. To this extent, EventKG+TL utilizes labeled pie charts located on a timeline, where each pie chart represents an individual event. The size of the pie chart corresponds to an overall (i.e. language independent) relevance of the event according to the ranking criterion rc_i. Each slice of the pie chart represents a language context. The area of each slice is proportional to the contribution of the corresponding language context to the ranking criterion rc_i.

Figure 1 exemplifies a Brexit timeline. We can observe that the most important event according to rc_3 is the "*United Kingdom European Union membership referendum, 2016*" that is nearly equally important in all considered language contexts. Some of the events are more important in the specific language contexts, e.g. "*European Migrant Crisis*" in the German and "*Dutch Ukraine-European Union Association Agreement referendum 2016*" in the Russian context.

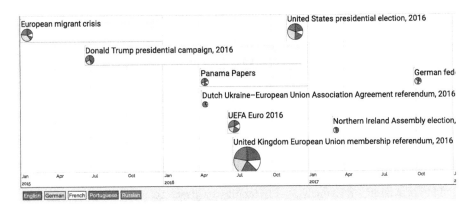

Fig. 1. An excerpt of an EventKG+TL timeline representing events related to the *query entity* "Brexit" in the time interval 01/2015–01/2018, overall including the top-8 events from each of the five language contexts in EventKG ranked according to rc_3 - i.e. a combination of the popularity and the relation strength of the events towards Brexit. Each event is represented by a labeled pie chart. The size of the pie chart corresponds to the language independent event relevance according to rc_3. The colored slices determine the ratio of the relevance in a language context (see the legend for the color encoding). The duration of events that lasted for more than a day is marked by a yellow interval. Upon click on a timeline entry, detailed information, including scores and link counts, is shown. (Color figure online)

3   Timeline Generation

The Knowledge Graph. To answer a *timeline query*, EventKG+TL utilizes EventKG [4]. EventKG is a multilingual RDF knowledge graph incorporating over 690 thousand events and over 2.3 million temporal relations in V1.1 extracted from several large-scale entity-centric knowledge graphs (i.e. Wikidata, DBpedia in five language editions and YAGO), Wikipedia Current Event Portal (WCEP) and Wikipedia event lists. One of the key features of EventKG is the provision of event-centric information for historical and contemporary events, including their interlinking in the language-specific contexts to facilitate an assessment of relation strength and event popularity. The information on language-specific interlinking provided by EventKG is based on the corresponding Wikipedia language editions.

Event and Relation Retrieval. To retrieve relevant information from EventKG, EventKG+TL adopts SPARQL queries. First, EventKG+TL retrieves the *query entity* q, including its existence time, if available. Second, EventKG+TL retrieves a set of events $E' \subset E$ that are connected to q via an EventKG relation as the subject or the object, along with the time information associated with these events. Third, the interlinking information related to the events in E' is retrieved from EventKG's link relations and their `eventKG-s:links` and `eventKG-s:mentions` property values.

Event Ranking and Timeline Creation. The top-k events related to q are selected according to the ranking criterion. For each event $e \in E'$ and language $l \in L'$, the language-specific relevance score is computed using the interlinking information provided by EventKG. The following link counts are used:

- $count_{links}(e, l)$: Event link count, i.e. the number of links pointing to the event e in a language context l (via `eventKG-s:links`).
- $count_{pair}(q, e, l)$: Pair count, i.e. the number of links from q to e plus the number of links from e to q in l, denoted by `eventKG-s:links` values.
- $count_{mentions}(q, e, l)$: Mention count, i.e. the number of sentences in a language context l that jointly link to q and e, denoted by `eventKG-s:mentions`.

Each count is normalized to $[0, 1]$ by dividing its value by the highest value of this count related to the events in E' in the respective language. That way, the bias resulting from the differences in the language-specific coverage is reduced. To avoid the domination of the disproportionately often linked events (e.g. the World War II), a smoothing parameter α, experimentally set to 0.25, is adopted. The scores are computed as follows:

$$\text{popularity}(e, l) = \left(\frac{count_{links}(e, l)}{max\{count_{links}(e', l) | e' \in E'\}} \right)^{\alpha} \tag{1}$$

$$\text{relation strength}(q, e, l) = \frac{1}{2} \cdot \left(\frac{count_{pair}(q, e, l)}{max\{count_{pair}(q, e', l) | e' \in E'\}} \right)^{\alpha}$$
$$+ \frac{1}{2} \cdot \left(\frac{count_{mentions}(q, e, l)}{max\{count_{mentions}(q, e', l) | e' \in E'\}} \right)^{\alpha} \quad (2)$$

The *combined* score (rc_3) is computed as a linear combination of the two ranking criteria. We experimentally set its weight to $w = 1/3$.

$$\text{combined}(q, e, l) = w \cdot \text{popularity}(e, l)$$
$$+ (1 - w) \cdot \text{relation strength}(q, e, l) \quad (3)$$

The resulting timeline consists of a chronologically ordered list of the top-k highest ranked events per language with respect to the ranking criterion.

System Implementation. The EventKG+TL system is accessible as an HTML5 website. It is implemented using the Java Spark web framework[1]. The timeline is visualized through the browser-based Javascript library vis.js[2], the pie charts are created using the Google Charts Javascript library[3] and pop-ups showing detailed event information are based on Twitter Bootstrap[4].

4   Demonstration

In our demonstration we will primarily show how EventKG+TL works and how users can use it to create cross-lingual timelines. To highlight the advantages of our approach, we will ask our audience to create timelines for the entities and events of their choice using EventKG+TL based on the language-specific information contained in EventKG. Through the visual cross-lingual comparison provided by EventKG+TL, the audience can get an impression of the language-specific event representations, as well as their relation to the *query entity* and popularity in different language contexts.

Acknowledgements. This work was partially funded by the ERC ("ALEXANDRIA", 339233) and BMBF ("Data4UrbanMobility", 02K15A040).

References

1. Althoff, T., Dong, X.L., Murphy, K., Alai, S., Dang, V., Zhang, W.: TimeMachine: timeline generation for knowledge-base entities. In: Proceedings of SIGKDD 2015 (2015)
2. Gossen, G., Demidova, E., Risse, T.: iCrawl: improving the freshness of web collections by integrating social web and focused web crawling. In: JCDL 2015 (2015)

---

[1] http://sparkjava.com/.
[2] http://visjs.org/timeline_examples.html.
[3] https://developers.google.com/chart/interactive/docs/gallery/piechart.
[4] https://getbootstrap.com/.

3. Gottschalk, S., Demidova, E.: MultiWiki: interlingual text passage alignment in Wikipedia. TWEB **11**(1), 6:1–6:30 (2017)
4. Gottschalk, S., Demidova, E.: EventKG: a multilingual event-centric temporal knowledge graph. In: Proceedings of the ESWC 2018 (2018)
5. Gottschalk, S., Demidova, E., Bernacchi, V., Rogers, R.: Ongoing events in Wikipedia: a cross-lingual case study. In: Proceedings of WebSci 2017, pp. 387–388 (2017)
6. Rogers, R.: Digital Methods. MIT Press, Cambridge (2013)
7. Rospocher, M., et al.: Building event-centric knowledge graphs from news. Web Semant. **37**, 132–151 (2016)

ABSTAT 1.0: Compute, Manage and Share Semantic Profiles of RDF Knowledge Graphs

Renzo Arturo Alva Principe, Blerina Spahiu$^{(\boxtimes)}$, Matteo Palmonari,
Anisa Rula, Flavio De Paoli, and Andrea Maurino

University of Milano-Bicocca, Milano, Italy
{renzo.alvaprincipe,blerina.spahiu,matteo.palmonari,anisa.rula,
flavio.depaoli,andrea.maurino}@unimib.it

Abstract. As Linked Data available on the Web continue to grow, understanding their structure and content remains a challenging task making such the bottleneck for their reuse. ABSTAT is an online profiling tool which helps data consumers in better understanding the data by extracting ontology-driven patterns and statistics about the data. This demo paper presents the capabilities of the new added feature of ABSTAT.

1 Introduction

Knowledge Graphs (KGs) in the Linked Open Data cloud[1] define possible classes and relations in a schema or ontology, and mainly describe instances and inter-link entities through relations. KGs cover different domains and are widespread, for example, in the EuBusinessGraph project[2], several parties contribute their data into the KG of the company. Despite the gross amount of data available on the Web, the selection of the data suitable for a given task is not straightforward as many data discovery steps have to be performed in order to understand data set's content and their characteristics. Thus, in order to use a data set, one needs to know which classes and properties are most commonly used, which predicates are generally associated with an instance of a given class, the potential domain and range of a given predicate, the cardinality of a predicate, etc. ABSTAT is an ontology-driven linked data summarization model which helps users in an effortless understanding of the data [5]. Given a RDF data set and, optionally, an ontology (used in the data set), ABSTAT computes a semantic profile which consists of a summary and statistics. ABSTAT's summary is a collection of patterns known as Abstract Knowledge Patterns (AKPs) of the form <subjectType, pred, objectType>, which represent the occurrence of triples <sub, pred, obj> in the data, such that subjectType is a minimal type of the subject and objectType is a minimal type of the object. With the

---

[1] http://lod-cloud.net/.
[2] http://eubusinessgraph.eu/.

© Springer Nature Switzerland AG 2018
A. Gangemi et al. (Eds.): ESWC 2018 Satellite Events, LNCS 11155, pp. 170–175, 2018.
https://doi.org/10.1007/978-3-319-98192-5_32

term type we refer to either an ontology class (e.g., foaf:Person) or a datatype (e.g., xsd:DateTime). By considering only minimal types of resources, computed with the help of the data ontology, we exclude several redundant AKPs from the summary making them compact and complete. Summaries are published and made accessible via web interfaces, in such a way that the information that they contain can be consumed by users and machines (via APIs). The user interface is available and can be used to explore summarized datasets[3]. Several approaches to profile RDF data have been proposed, we refer to our research papers [1,5] for a detailed discussion of state-of-the-art. While many of these approaches publish and make accessible the computed profiles, only a few are open source and, to the best of our knowledge, none of them provide support for the summarization process to the user. Based on requirements collected in the two industry-driven innovation projects EW-Shopp[4] and EuBusinessGraph we have built ABSTAT 1.0, a tool to compute, manage and make accessible to humans and machines semantic profiles of RDF graphs. Compared to the ABSTAT research prototype [2], ABSTAT 1.0 not only provides more features, which are used in different applications scenarios [1,3,5] but it has also developed into a tool that lays on a more scalable modular and effective architecture, and is endowed with a user interface to help the management of the profiling process. ABSTAT 1.0 is released as open source[5] under the GNU Affero General Public License v3.0[6].

In this paper, we make the following contributions: (i) Minimalization over properties; (ii) AKPs inference and instance count; (iii) Cardinality extraction; (iv) Configuration and launch of the summarization via GUI; (v) Indexing of summaries via GUI; (vi) Browsing and full-text search; (vii) Access to summaries via APIs (viii) Autocomplete service over arbitrary strings.

2   Exploring and Understanding a Data Set with ABSTAT

ABSTAT controller[7] is designed to be modular and decoupled as in Fig. 1. The modules of ABSTAT 1.0 are the following:

– **ABSTAT Viewer** provides a graphic user interface to serve different types of tasks such as summary exploration, execution of the summarization process using a wizard and summaries indexing. Summary exploration can be performed using constrained queries (a desired subject and/or predicate and/or object) and full-text search. The summarization wizard provides a GUI to let users select datasets/ontologies from a populated list or using an upload module, configure and execute the summarization process. After the semantic profile is computed, the user can load/index it on a persistent storage/search engine in order to support its access through APIs or GUI.

---

[3] http://abstat.disco.unimib.it.

[4] http://www.ew-shopp.eu.

[5] https://bitbucket.org/disco_unimib/abstat.

[6] https://www.gnu.org/licenses/.

[7] http://backend.abstat.disco.unimib.it.

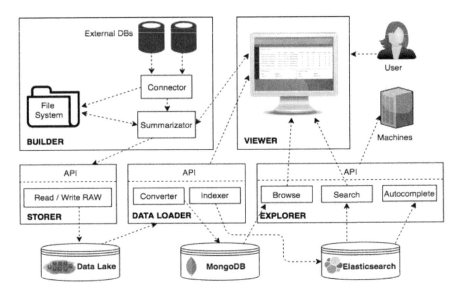

Fig. 1. ABSTAT architecture

- **ABSTAT Builder** is the module that executes the summarization algorithms and produces the profiles. The Summarizator component requires as input a dataset (in N3 format) and an ontology (in OWL format) along with the configuration chosen by the user. If the data are in an external DB, the Connector component allows extracting a dump and storing it in the correct file to serve as input to the Summarizator.
- **ABSTAT Storer** component feeds a data lake storage with the raw data produced by the Builder. It also receives download requests from users who want to get raw summaries.
- **ABSTAT Loader** contains the Converter component, which converts the data formats in the Data Lake in a format suitable for the Explorer module. The Indexer component indexes summaries in a search engine. Note that the Loader component receives the control input from the Viewer.
- **ABSTAT Explorer** is organized as a set of APIs to satisfy profile exploration requests from Viewer or users who want to use them directly.

3   Demonstration

ABSTAT is a framework that computes and provides access to semantic profiles that consist in an RDF summary and statistics. The summary of a data set describes its content by listing every schema-level pattern that occur in the data. In addition, semantic profiles provide several statistics about the occurrence of patterns, types and properties and cardinality statistics. During the summarization process if the user specifies the main pay-level domain of the data set (e.g., dbpedia.org for DBpedia), ABSTAT can distinguish between resources (patterns, types and properties) that are internal (resources having the specified pay-level domain) and external (resources having a pay-level domain different from the one specified by the user). This distinction has the only purpose of letting users filter out patterns that include some external resource (e.g., hide all patterns that contain the type foaf:Person when looking at patterns extracted from DBpedia).

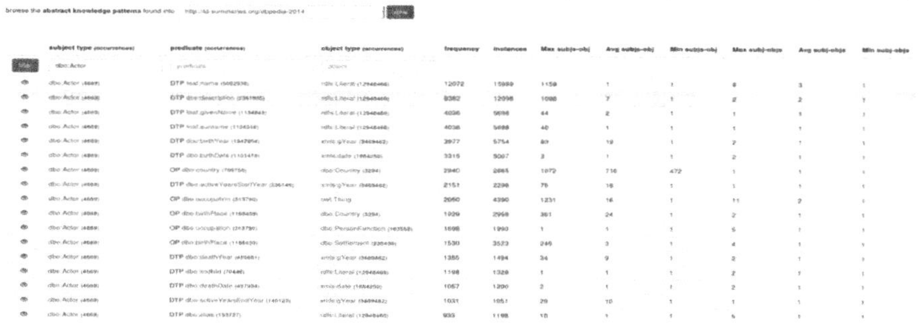

Fig. 2. ABSTAT browse GUI

Figure 2 shows the home page of ABSTAT. The menu on the left side can be used to explore semantic profiles. The **Overview** page gives an overview of the uploaded data sets, ontologies and computed profiles. **Summarize** page gives a configuration interface for custom summarizations including data sets and ontologies uploading. **Consolidate** allows to persist and index the computed profiles into the search engine. **Browse** is the GUI for constraint-based pattern exploration. **Search** is the GUI for full-text searching. Patterns, predicates and types that match the keyword will be returned. Search can be processed over the whole set of indexed profiles or on those originated from a specif data sets. Statistics, data set names and pattern symbols will be shown in the results of the query. **Manage** allows to remove data sets, ontologies and profiles. **APIs** lists the available APIs for machine-friendly profile exploration.

Patterns of the semantic profile are sorted by frequency in descendant order. The user can also put constraints on subjects and/or predicates and/or objects. In every text box a simple suggestion menu will recommend types/predicates that occur in the patterns. Then patterns are filtered in order to match the user constraints. Figure 3 shows the patterns that match the predicate dbo:knownFor and the object type dbo:Film. For each pattern several statistics are returned. Considering the one in the black box, the frequency of the pattern shows how many times does this pattern occur in the data set. The number of instances shows how many instances have this pattern including those for which the types Person and Film and the predicate knownFor can be inferred. Max (Min, Avg) subjs-obj cardinality is the maximal (minimal, average) number of distinct entities of type Person linked to a single entity of type Film through the predicate `knownFor`. Max (Min, Avg) subj-objs is the maximal (minimal, average) number of distinct entities of type `Film` linked to a single entity of type `Person` through the predicate `knownFor`. Frequency is given also for types and predicates.

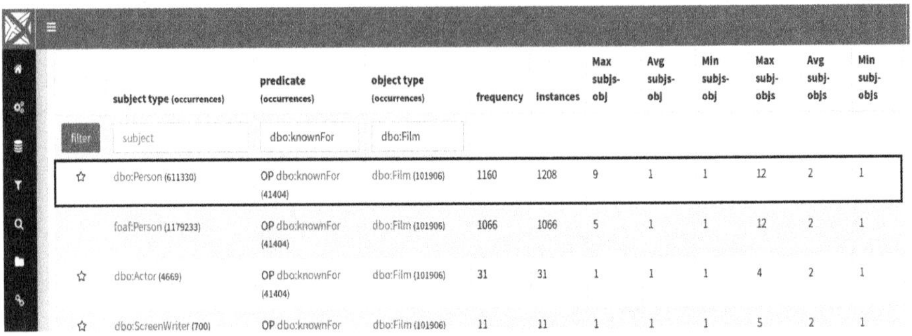

Fig. 3. Semantic profile of DBpedia 2014 data set

Previous experiments suggest that ABSTAT summaries help users in understanding a data set, e.g., by facilitating query formulation, and provide support to the assessment of data quality by finding outliers in the vocabulary usage [5]. In addition, we have recently found that rich profiles as the ones computed in ABSTAT 1.0 support automatic feature selection for semantic recommender systems, outperforming other purely statistical measures like Information Gain [1,3]. Finally, ABSTAT 1.0 supports vocabulary suggestions, similarly to [4]. In the future, ABSTAT will provide more significant statistics such statistics about class hierarchy depth, classes and properties per entity, etc.

Acknowledgements. This research has been supported in part by EU H2020 projects EW-Shopp - Grant n. 732590, and EuBusinessGraph - Grant n. 732003.

References

1. Di Noia, T., Magarelli, C., Maurino, A., Palmonari, M., Rula, A.: Using ontology-based data summarization to develop semantics-aware recommender systems. In: Gangemi, A., et al. (eds.) ESWC 2018. LNCS, vol. 10843, pp. 128–144. Springer, Cham (2018). https://doi.org/10.1007/978-3-319-93417-4_9
2. Palmonari, M., Rula, A., Porrini, R., Maurino, A., Spahiu, B., Ferme, V.: ABSTAT: linked data summaries with ABstraction and STATistics. In: Gandon, F., Guéret, C., Villata, S., Breslin, J., Faron-Zucker, C., Zimmermann, A. (eds.) ESWC 2015. LNCS, vol. 9341, pp. 128–132. Springer, Cham (2015). https://doi.org/10.1007/978-3-319-25639-9_25
3. Ragone, A.: Schema-summarization in linked-data-based feature selection for recommender systems. In: Proceedings of the Symposium on Applied Computing, SAC 2017, Marrakech, Morocco, 3–7 April 2017, pp. 330–335 (2017)

4. Schaible, J., Gottron, T., Scherp, A.: *TermPicker*: enabling the reuse of vocabulary terms by exploiting data from the linked open data cloud. In: Sack, H., Blomqvist, E., d'Aquin, M., Ghidini, C., Ponzetto, S.P., Lange, C. (eds.) ESWC 2016. LNCS, vol. 9678, pp. 101–117. Springer, Cham (2016). https://doi.org/10.1007/978-3-319-34129-3_7

5. Spahiu, B., Porrini, R., Palmonari, M., Rula, A., Maurino, A.: ABSTAT: ontology-driven linked data summaries with pattern minimalization. In: Sack, H., Rizzo, G., Steinmetz, N., Mladenić, D., Auer, S., Lange, C. (eds.) ESWC 2016. LNCS, vol. 9989, pp. 381–395. Springer, Cham (2016). https://doi.org/10.1007/978-3-319-47602-5_51

Entity Linking in 40 Languages
Using MAG

Diego Moussallem[1]([✉]), Ricardo Usbeck[2]🆔, Michael Röder[2],
and Axel-Cyrille Ngonga Ngomo[2]

[1] AKSW Research Group, University of Leipzig, Leipzig, Germany
moussallem@informatik.uni-leipzig.de
[2] Data Science Department, Paderborn University, Paderborn, Germany
{ricardo.usbeck,michael.roeder,axel.ngonga}@upb.de

Abstract. A plethora of Entity Linking (EL) approaches has recently been developed. While many claim to be multilingual, the MAG (Multilingual AGDISTIS) approach has been shown recently to outperform the state of the art in multilingual EL on 7 languages. With this demo, we extend MAG to support EL in 40 different languages, including especially low-resources languages such as Ukrainian, Greek, Hungarian, Croatian, Portuguese, Japanese and Korean. Our demo relies on online web services which allow for an easy access to our entity linking approaches and can disambiguate against DBpedia and Wikidata. During the demo, we will show how to use MAG by means of POST requests as well as using its user-friendly web interface. All data used in the demo is available at https://hobbitdata.informatik.uni-leipzig.de/agdistis/

1 Introduction

A recent survey by IBM[1] suggests that more than 2.5 quintillion bytes of data are produced on the Web every day. Entity Linking (EL), also known as Named Entity Disambiguation (NED), is one of the most important Natural Language Processing (NLP) techniques for extracting knowledge automatically from this huge amount of data. The goal of an EL approach is as follows: Given a piece of text, a reference knowledge base K and a set of entity mentions in that text, map each entity mention to the corresponding resource in K [4]. A large number of challenges has to be addressed while performing a disambiguation. For instance, a given resource can be referred to using different labels due to phenomena such as synonymy, acronyms or typos. For example, `New York City`, `NY` and `Big Apple` are all labels for the same entity. Also, multiple entities can share the same name due to homonymy and ambiguity. For example, both the state and the city of Rio de Janeiro are called `Rio de Janeiro`.

Despite the complexity of the task, EL approaches have recently achieved increasingly better results by relying on trained machine learning models [6]. A portion of these approaches claim to be multilingual and most of them rely

---

[1] https://tinyurl.com/ibm2017stats.

© Springer Nature Switzerland AG 2018
A. Gangemi et al. (Eds.): ESWC 2018 Satellite Events, LNCS 11155, pp. 176–181, 2018.
https://doi.org/10.1007/978-3-319-98192-5_33

on models which are trained on English corpora with cross-lingual dictionaries. However, MAG (Multilingual AGDISTIS) [4] showed that the underlying models being trained on English corpora make them prone to failure when migrated to a different language. Additionally, these approaches hardly make their models or data available on more than three languages [6]. The new version of MAG (which is the quintessence of this demo) provides support for 40 different languages using sophisticated indices[2]. For the sake of server space, we deployed MAG-based web services for 9 languages and offer the other 31 languages for download. Additionally, we provide an English index using Wikidata to show the knowledge-base agnosticism of MAG. During the demo, we will show how to use the web services as well as MAG's user interface.

2   MAG Entity Linking System

MAG's EL process comprises two phases, namely an offline and an online phase. The sub-indices (which are generated during the offline phase) consist of surface forms, person names, rare references, acronyms and context information. During the online phase, the EL is carried out in two steps: (1) candidate generation and (2) disambiguation. The goal of the candidate generation step is to retrieve a tractable number of candidates for each mention. These candidates are later inserted into the disambiguation graph, which is used to determine the mapping between entities and mentions. MAG implements two graph-based algorithms to disambiguate entities, i.e., PageRank and HITS. Independently of the chosen graph algorithm, the highest candidate score among the set of candidates is chosen as correct disambiguation for a given mention [4].

3   Demonstration

Our demonstration will show the capabilities of MAG for different languages. We provide a graphical, web-based user interface (GUI). In addition, users can choose to use the REST interface or a Java snippet. For research purposes, MAG can be downloaded and deployed via Maven or Docker. Figure 1 illustrates an example of MAG working on Spanish. The online demo can be accessed via http://agdistis.aksw.org/mag-demo and its code can be downloaded from https://github.com/dice-group/AGDISTIS_DEMO/tree/v2.

We have set up a web service interface for each language version. Each of these interfaces understands two mandatory parameters: (1) `text` and (2) `type`.

1. `text` accepts an UTF-8 and URL encoded string with entities annotated with XML-tag `<entity>`. It is also capable of recognizing NIF [3] or txt files.
2. `type` accepts two different values. First, '`agdistis`' to disambiguate the mentions using the graph-based algorithms, but also '`candidates`' which list all possible entities for a given mention through the depth-candidate selection of MAG.

---

[2] The quality of indices is directly related to how much information is provided by Wikipedia and DBpedia.

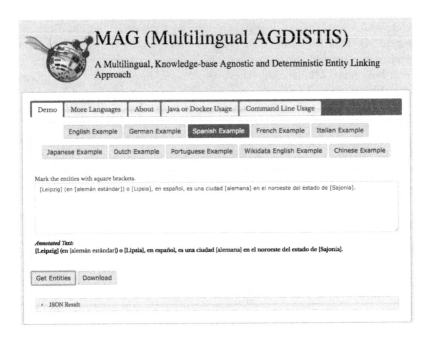

Fig. 1. A screenshot of MAG's web-based demo working on Spanish.

Other Parameters. The user can also define more parameters to fine-tune the disambiguation. These parameters have to be set up within the properties file[3] or via environment variables while deploying it locally. Below, we describe all the parameters.

- **Popularity** - The user can set it as `popularity=false` or `popularity=true`. It allows MAG to use either the Page Rank or the frequency of a candidate to sort while candidate retrieval.
- **Graph-based algorithm** - The user can choose which graph-based algorithm to use for disambiguating among the candidates per mentions. The current implementation offers HITS and PageRank as algorithms, `algorithm=hits` or `algorithm =pagerank`.
- **Search by Context** - This boolean parameter provides a search of candidates using a context index [4].
- **Acronyms** - This parameter enables a search by acronyms. In this case, MAG uses an additional index to filter the acronyms by expanding their labels and assigns them a high probability. For example, PSG equals Paris Saint-Germain. The parameter is `acronym=false` or `acronym=true`.
- **Common Entities** - This boolean option supports finding common entities, in case, users desire to find more than ORGANIZATIONs, PLACEs and PERSONs as entity type.

---

[3] https://tinyurl.com/agdistis-properties.

- **Ngram Distance** - This integer parameter chooses the ngram distance between words, e.g., bigram, trigram and so on.
- **Depth** - This parameter numerically defines how deep the exploration of a semantic disambiguation graph must go.
- **Heuristic Expansion** - This boolean parameter defines whether a simple co-occurrence resolution is done or not. For instance, if Barack and Barack Obama are in the same text then Barack is expanded to Barack Obama.

Knowledge-base Agnosticism. Fig. 2 shows a screen capture of our demo for disambiguating mentions using Wikidata. We also provide a web service to allow further investigation. In addition, MAG is used in a domain specific problem using a music Knowledge Base (KB) [5].

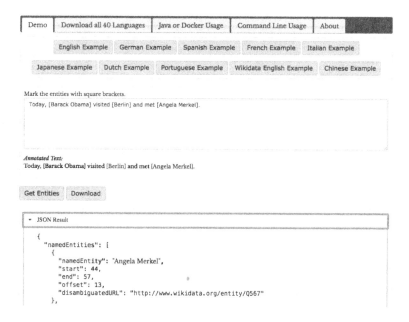

Fig. 2. MAG working on Wikidata as Knowledge base.

4   Evaluation of the User Interface

We performed a system usability study (SUS)[4,5] to validate the design of our user interface. 15 users - with a good or no knowledge of Semantic Web, EL or knowledge extraction - selected randomly from all departments at Leipzig University answered our survey. We achieved a SUS-Score of 86.3. This score assigns the mark S to the current interface of MAG and places it into the *category*

---

[4] http://www.measuringu.com/sus.php.
[5] https://goo.gl/forms/01kpxBf24pjbsWUV2.

of the 10% interfaces, meaning that users of the interface are likely to recommend it to a friend. Figure 3 shows the average voting per question and its standard deviation.

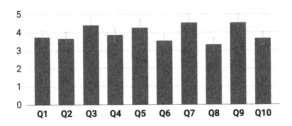

Fig. 3. Standard Usability Score results. The vertical bars show the standard deviation

5   Summary

In this demo, we will present MAG, a KB-agnostic and deterministic approach for multilingual EL on 40 different languages contained in DBpedia. Currently, MAG is used in diverse projects[6] and has been used largely by the Semantic Web community. We also provide a demo/web-service using Wikidata for supporting an investigation of the graphs structures behind DBpedia and Wikidata pertaining to Information Extraction tasks [1,2]. The indexes we provided will be used in future work to investigate the EL problem in low-resource languages. Our next step will hence be to evaluate EL on all 40 languages presented in this demo.

Acknowledgements. This work has been supported by the BMVI projects LIMBO (project no. 19F2029C) and OPAL (project no. 19F20284) as well as by the German Federal Ministry of Education and Research (BMBF) within 'KMU-innovativ: Forschung für die zivile Sicherheit' in particular 'Forschung für die zivile Sicherheit' and the project SOLIDE (no. 13N14456). This work has also been supported by the Brazilian National Council for Scientific and Technological Development (CNPq) (no. 206971/2014-1). The authors gratefully acknowledge financial support from the German Federal Ministry of Education and Research within Eurostars, a joint programme of EUREKA and the European Community under the project E! 9367 DIESEL and E! 9725 QAMEL.

---

[6] For example, http://diesel-project.eu/, https://qamel.eu/ or https://www.limbo-project.org/.

References

1. Färber, M., Ell, B., Menne, C., Rettinger, A.: A comparative survey of dbpedia, freebase, opencyc, wikidata, and yago. Semant. Web J. **1**, 1–5 (2015)
2. Geiß, J., Spitz, A., Gertz, M.: NECKAr: a named entity classifier for wikidata. In: Rehm, G., Declerck, T. (eds.) GSCL 2017. LNCS (LNAI), vol. 10713, pp. 115–129. Springer, Cham (2018). https://doi.org/10.1007/978-3-319-73706-5_10
3. Hellmann, S., Lehmann, J., Auer, S., Brümmer, M.: Integrating NLP using linked data. In: Alani, H., Kagal, L., Fokoue, A., Groth, P., Biemann, C., Parreira, J.X., Aroyo, L., Noy, N., Welty, C., Janowicz, K. (eds.) ISWC 2013. LNCS, vol. 8219, pp. 98–113. Springer, Heidelberg (2013). https://doi.org/10.1007/978-3-642-41338-4_7
4. Moussallem, D., Usbeck, R., Röeder, M., Ngomo, A.-C. N.: MAG: a multilingual, knowledge-base agnostic and deterministic entity linking approach. In: Proceedings of the Knowledge Capture Conference, p. 9. ACM (2017)
5. Oramas, S., Ferraro, A., Correya, A., Serra, X.: Mel: a music entity linking system. In: 18th International Society for Music Information Retrieval Conference (ISMIR17) (2017)
6. Röder, M., Usbeck, R., Ngonga Ngomo, A.-C.: GERBIL–benchmarking named entity recognition and linking consistently. Semant. Web, 1–21 (2017, Preprint)

Ulysses: An Intelligent Client
for Replicated Triple Pattern Fragments

Thomas Minier[1($\boxtimes$)], Hala Skaf-Molli[1], Pascal Molli[1], and Maria-Ester Vidal[2]

[1] LS2N, University of Nantes, Nantes, France
{Thomas.Minier,Hala.Skaf-Molli,Pascal.Molli}@univ-nantes.fr
[2] TIB Leibniz Information Centre For Science and Technology,
University Library & Fraunhofer IAIS, Sankt Augustin, Germany
Maria.Vidal@tib.eu

Abstract. Ulysses is an intelligent TPF client that takes advantage of replicated datasets to distribute the load of SPARQL query processing and provides fault-tolerance. By reducing the load on a TPF server, Ulysses improves the Linked Data availability and distributes the financial costs of queries execution among data providers. This demonstration presents the Ulysses web client and shows how users can run SPARQL queries in their browsers against TPF servers hosting replicated data. It also provides various visualizations that show in real-time how Ulysses performs the actual load distribution and adapts to network conditions during SPARQL query processing.

Keywords: Semantic Web · Triple pattern fragments
Intelligent client · Load balancing · Fault tolerance · Data replication

1 Introduction

We proposed Ulysses [1], a replication-aware intelligent TPF client that distributes the load of SPARQL query processing across heterogeneous replicated TPF servers. Ulysses relies on a light-weighted cost-model for computing servers processing capabilities and a client-side load balancer to distribute SPARQL query processing and provides fault tolerance during query processing.

Consider the SPARQL query Q_1 in Fig. 1, and the two servers S_1 and S_2 publishing a replica of the DBpedia 2015 dataset, hosted by DBpedia[1] and LANL Linked Data Archive[2], respectively. Executing Q_1 with the regular TPF client [4] on S_1 alone generates **442 HTTP calls**, takes **7 s** in average, and returns 222 results. Executing the same query as a federated SPARQL query on both S_1 and S_2 generates **478 HTTP calls** on S_1 and **470 HTTP calls** on S_2, returns 222 results, and takes **25 s** in average. This is because *existing TPF clients do not support replication nor client-side load balancing* [1].

---

[1] http://fragments.dbpedia.org/.
[2] http://fragments.mementodepot.org/.

© Springer Nature Switzerland AG 2018
A. Gangemi et al. (Eds.): ESWC 2018 Satellite Events, LNCS 11155, pp. 182–186, 2018.
https://doi.org/10.1007/978-3-319-98192-5_34

As Ulysses is aware that datasets hosted at S_1 and S_2 are replicated, it only generates **442 HTTP calls** that are distributed between servers according to their processing capabilities and network latencies. If the servers are not loaded, the performances of Ulysses are similar to those of the regular TPF client ($7\,s$) without replication. However, if the servers are loaded, Ulysses improves significantly the performances thanks to load-balancing.

```
PREFIX dbo: <http://dbpedia.org/ontology/>
PREFIX rdfs: <http://www.w3.org/2000/01/rdf-schema#>
SELECT DISTINCT ?software ?company WHERE {
  ?software dbo:developer ?company. # tp1
  ?company dbo:locationCountry ?country . # tp2
  ?country rdfs:label "France"@en . # tp3
}
```

Fig. 1. SPARQL query Q_1 that finds all softwares developed by French compagnies

Using replicated servers, Ulysses prevents a single point of failure server-side, improves the overall availability of data, and distributes the financial costs of queries execution among data providers.

This demonstration presents the Ulysses web client. It details which informations are collected by Ulysses about servers in real-time, how the cost model is recomputed, and how the load of SPARQL query processing is balanced among replicated servers through different real-time visualizations. Finally, Ulysses reactions in presence of servers failure are illustrated.

2   Overview of Ulysses Client

The Ulysses web client is available online at http://ulysses-demo.herokuapp.com. In order to distribute the load of SPARQL query processing across heterogeneous TPF servers hosting replicated data, it relies on three key ideas detailed in [1]. In next sections, we provides a brief overview of key ideas and how they are integrated in the Ulysses web client[3].

2.1   Replication-Aware Source Selection

Ulysses uses a *replication-aware source selection* algorithm to identify which TPF servers can be used to distribute evaluation of triple patterns during SPARQL query processing, based on the replication model introduced in [2,3].

This replication model allows to describe replicated datasets using *replicated fragment* and a *fragment mapping*. A fragment is defined as 2-tuple: the authoritative source of the fragment, and a triple pattern met by the fragment's triple. A fragment mapping is a function that maps each fragment to a set of TPF

---

[3] The open-source Ulysses client is available at https://github.com/Callidon/ulysses-tpf, under MIT license.

servers. Using these information, ULYSSES is able to compute relevant sources for all triple pattern in a SPARQL query.

Consider again the two servers S_1, S_2 and the SPARQL query Q_1 in Fig. 1. Only one fragment $f_1 = \langle$http://fragments.dbpedia.org/2015-10/en, ?s ?p ?o$\rangle$ is defined to indicate a total replication. A fragment mapping $\mathcal{F}$ maps f_1 to the set $\{S_1, S_2\}$. Thus, all RDF triples met by every triple pattern of Q_1 are replicated by both DBpedia and LANL servers.

For simplicity, in this demonstration we only consider the scenario with total replication. Consequently, the evaluation a triple pattern of the query Q_1 will be distributed between servers DBpedia and LANL.

2.2   A Cost-Model for Estimating Servers Processing Capabilities

ULYSSES uses response times of HTTP requests performed against TPF servers during query processing as probes to accurately estimate the *processing capabilities* of a server. The response time of each request is used to compute the throughput of a server, *i.e.*, the number of results server per unit of time by a server. As SPARQL query processing with the TPF approach requires to send many requests to a server in order to evaluate triple patterns, ULYSSES can keep the servers throughputs updated in real-time without additional probing. This can also easily detect load spikes or server failures.

Servers' throughputs are used to compute a *cost-model* that define a *capability factor* of each TPF server. This capability factor determines the load distribution among servers: a server with a high capability factor has more chance to be selected to evaluate a triple pattern as detailed in Sect. 2.3.

.ıl Real-time statistics

Estimated load

Server	Access time	Page size	Throughput	Server capability factor	Estimated load
http://fragments.dbpedia.org/2015-10/en	139ms	100 triples	0.714 triple/ms	1	25%
http://fragments.mementodepot.org/dbpedia_201510	264ms	500 triples	2.392 triple/ms	3	75%

Fig. 2. ULYSSES cost-model, updated in real-time

Figure 2 shows a real-time estimation of servers loads during execution of query Q_1 of Fig. 1 against S_1 and S_2. S_1 is slightly faster to access than S_2, but as the latter serves five times more results per access (**Page size** column), S_2 has a better throughput than S_1. As, S_2 has a better capability factor than S_1, it will receive approximately 75% of the query load, while S_1 will approximately receive the remaining 25% (**Estimated load** column).

2.3   Adaptive Client-Side Load Balancing with Fault Tolerance

ULYSSES uses an *adaptive load-balancer* to perform load balancing among replicated servers. Each evaluation of a triple pattern scheduled by the client is sent to a server selected using a weighted random algorithm, inspired by the Smart clients approach [5]. The probability of selecting a server is proportional to its processing capabilities, according to Ulysses cost-model.

This probability distribution ensures that each TPF server will only process an amount of requests proportional to its processing capabilities, without concentrating all the load of query processing on the most performant servers. Ulysses load-balancer also provides *fault-tolerance*, by re-scheduling failed HTTP requests using available replicated servers.

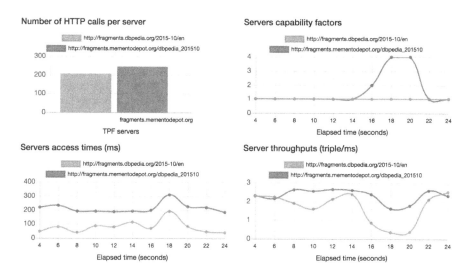

Fig. 3. Metrics recorded by Ulysses and used to perform load-balancing during SPARQL query processing

Figure 3 shows the metrics displayed in real-time by the Ulysses web client during SPARQL query processing of Q_1, distributed among S_1 and S_2. We see that the server throughputs and capability factors of both servers remain close at the start of query processing (**Server access times** and **Servers capability factors**). However, after 18 seconds, S_1 access times increase, so S_2 became more efficient than S_1, causing its capability factor to rise. Thus, the load distribution is affected in real-time, and, at the end of query processing, we see that S_2 has received more HTTP requests (**Number of HTTP requests per server**).

3   Demonstration Scenario

In the context of ESWC 2018, we would like to run a live experiment that anyone can join. We will tweet a link that participants can click to access Ulysses online demonstration, using their laptops or smartphones. Then, they will be able to submit SPARQL queries against a set of TPF servers hosting replicated data.

We will provide a selection of replicated TPF servers, hosting replicas of DBpedia and WatDiv datasets, with some SPARQL queries as a quick-start. Participants will also be able to use their own set of TPF servers and SPARQL queries.

In this scenario, participants will be able to see how ULYSSES keeps its cost-model updated in real-time and how it benefits of this to distribute the load of query processing, using visualizations presented in Figs. 2 and 3. Additionally, we will also provide replicated TPF servers that can be shutdown in order to simulate failures. Participants will be able to see how ULYSSES is able to continue query processing after a server failure, by re-distributing the load using available servers.

4   Conclusion

In this demonstration, we presented the ULYSSES web client that enables Web Browsers to perform client-side load balancing and provides fault tolerance when evaluating SPARQL queries against TPF servers hosting replicated data. Real-time visualizations allow to observe how ULYSSES distributes the load of SPARQL query processing across replicated TPF servers according to their processing capabilities, and adapts to failures or variations in network conditions.

Acknowledgments. This work is partially supported through the FaBuLA project, part of the AtlanSTIC 2020 program.

References

1. Minier, T., Skaf-Molli, H., Molli, P., Vidal, M.-E.: Intelligent clients for replicated triple pattern fragments. In: Gangemi, A., et al. (eds.) ESWC 2018. LNCS, vol. 10843, pp. 400–414. Springer, Cham (2018). https://doi.org/10.1007/978-3-319-93417-4_26
2. Montoya, G., Skaf-Molli, H., Molli, P., Vidal, M.-E.: Federated SPARQL Queries processing with replicated fragments. ISWC 2015. LNCS, vol. 9366, pp. 36–51. Springer, Cham (2015). https://doi.org/10.1007/978-3-319-25007-6_3
3. Montoya, G., Skaf-Molli, H., Molli, P., Vidal, M.E.: Decomposing federated queries in presence of replicated fragments. Web Semant. Sci. Serv. Agents World Wide Web **42**, 1–18 (2017)
4. Verborgh, R., et al.: Triple pattern fragments: a low-cost knowledge graph interface for the web. Web Semant. Sci. Serv. Agents World Wide Web **37**, 184–206 (2016)
5. Yoshikawa, C., Chun, B., Eastham, P., Vahdat, A., Anderson, T., Culler, D.: Using smart clients to build scalable services. In: Proceedings of the 1997 USENIX Technical Conference, CA, p. 105 (1997)

Bridging Web APIs and Linked Data with SPARQL Micro-Services

Franck Michel$^{(\boxtimes)}$, Catherine Faron-Zucker, and Fabien Gandon

Université Côte d'Azur, Inria, CNRS, I3S (UMR 7271), Nice, France
`franck.michel@cnrs.fr`, `faron@i3s.unice.fr`, `fabien.gandon@inria.fr`

Abstract. Web APIs are a prominent source of machine-readable information that remains insufficiently connected to the Web of Data. To enable automatic combination of Linked Data (LD) interfaces and Web APIs, we present the SPARQL Micro-Service architecture. A SPARQL micro-service is a lightweight SPARQL endpoint that provides access to a small, resource-centric, virtual graph, while dynamically assigning stable, dereferenceable URIs to Web API resources that do not have URIs in the first place. We believe that the emergence of an ecosystem of SPARQL micro-services could enable LD-based applications to glean pieces of data from a wealth of distributed, scalable and reliable services from independent providers. We describe an experimentation where we dynamically augment biodiversity-related LD resources with data from Flickr, MusicBrainz and the Macauley scientific media library.

Keywords: Web API · SPARQL · Micro-service · Linked Data
JSON-LD

1 Introduction

Web APIs are commonly used to enable HTTP-based, machine-processable access to all sorts of data. Similarly, Linked Data (LD) seek the publication of machine-readable data on the Web while connecting related resources across datasets. Several approaches have been proposed to bridge these two worlds, based on bespoke wrappers, SPARQL extensions or RESTful APIs. Until now however, several challenges hinder the definition of standard approaches to enable automatic reconciliation of LD and Web APIs. Firstly, Web APIs usually rely on proprietary vocabularies documented in Web pages meant for developers but hardly machine-readable. Secondly, on-the-fly SPARQL querying of non-RDF data sources proves to be difficult, as attested by the many works on SPARQL-based access to legacy databases.

The *SPARQL Micro-Service* architecture aims to address this issue. The term *micro-service* refers to an increasingly popular architectural style where an application consists of a collection of lightweight, loosely-coupled, fine-grained services that are deployed independently [2]. They improve applications modularity thereby speeding up the development, testing and deployment process.

© Springer Nature Switzerland AG 2018
A. Gangemi et al. (Eds.): ESWC 2018 Satellite Events, LNCS 11155, pp. 187–191, 2018.
https://doi.org/10.1007/978-3-319-98192-5_35

Leveraging these principles may help in the design of modular LD-based applications structured as a collection of services such as RDF stores, SPARQL endpoints, SPARQL micro-services or other services based on LD REST APIs for instance. A SPARQL micro-service is a lightweight method to query a Web API using SPARQL. It provides access to a small RDF graph describing the targeted resources from the data available at the API, while dynamically assigning dereferenceable URIs to Web API resources that do not have URIs beforehand.

2 SPARQL Micro-services Principles

A SPARQL micro-service S_μ is a wrapper of a Web API service S_w. It complies with the SPARQL Query Language and protocol, and accepts a set Arg_w of arguments that are specific to S_w. These arguments are passed to S_μ as parameters on the HTTP query string, *e.g.* "http://hostname/sparql?param=value". S_μ evaluates a SPARQL query Q against an RDF graph that it builds at runtime as follows: it invokes the Web API service S_w with the arguments in Arg_w, translates the response into RDF triples (in an implementation-dependent manner), evaluates Q against these triples and returns the result to the client.

The semantics of a SPARQL micro-service differs from that of a standard SPARQL endpoint insofar as the SPARQL protocol treats a service URL as a black box, *i.e.* it does not interpret URL parameters. By contrast, a SPARQL micro-service is a configurable SPARQL endpoint whose arguments delineate the virtual graph being queried. Thence, each pair (S_μ, Arg_w) is a standard SPARQL endpoint. Arguably, other options may be adopted to pass the arguments to S_μ, that we discuss in details in [1].

Furthermore, bridging Web APIs and LD requires to create stable, dereferenceable URIs for Web API resources that are generally identified by mere proprietary identifiers. This is implemented quite easily with SPARQL micro-services: once a stable URI scheme is decided, a Web server is set up to handle look-ups for URIs matching that scheme: for each look-up, it invokes a suitable SPARQL micro-service along with an appropriate CONSTRUCT or DESCRIBE query form. Hence, by smartly designing services, we can come up with a consistent ecosystem where some micro-services respond to SPARQL queries while translating Web API identifiers into URIs that, in turn, are made dereferenceable by other micro-services.

3 Implementation and Experimentation

To evaluate this architecture, we have developed a prototype implementation[1] depicted in Fig. 1, that handles JSON-based Web APIs. It maps a Web API response to RDF triples in two steps. First, the response is translated to JSON-LD by applying a JSON-LD profile. The resulting graph G is stored in an in-memory triple store. Then, for mapping cases that JSON-LD cannot describe

---

[1] https://github.com/frmichel/sparql-micro-service.

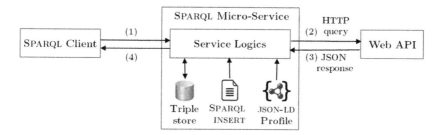

Fig. 1. Example SPARQL micro-service implementation for JSON-based Web APIs.

(involving *e.g.* string manipulations), a SPARQL INSERT query augments G with triples based on well-adopted or domain vocabularies. Lastly, S_μ evaluates the client's SPARQL query against G and returns the response following a regular content negotiation.

Listing 1.1 exemplifies the use of SPARQL micro-services in a biodiversity-related use case. The query retrieves the URI of a resource representing the common dolphin (species *Delphinus delphis*) from a taxonomic register. Then, it invokes SPARQL micro-services to retrieve additional data from three Web APIs: photos from the Flickr photography social network[2], audio recordings from the Macaulay Library[3] and music tunes from MusicBrainz[4]. Figure 2 portrays a snippet of the response to this query in the Turtle syntax, along with photos, audio recordings pictures and a MusicBrainz Web page.

Fig. 2. Snippet of the response to query Q (Listing 1.1) along with snapshots of the images, audio recordings and Web page whose URLs are part of the response.

---

[2] https://www.flickr.org/.
[3] https://www.macaulaylibrary.org/.
[4] https://musicbrainz.org/.

```
prefix rdfs:   <http://www.w3.org/2000/01/rdf-schema#>
prefix owl:    <http://www.w3.org/2002/07/owl#>
prefix foaf:   <http://xmlns.com/foaf/0.1/>
prefix schema: <http://schema.org/>

CONSTRUCT {
  ?species
    schema:subjectOf ?photo; foaf:depiction ?img;      # from Flickr
    schema:contentUrl ?audioUrl;  # from the Macaulay Library
    schema:subjectOf ?page.       # from MusicBrainz
} WHERE {
  SERVICE <https://taxref.mnhn.fr/sparql>
    { ?species a owl:Class; rdfs:label "Delphinus delphis". }
  SERVICE <https://example.org/sparql-ms/flickr/getPhotosByGroupByTag
            ?group_id=806927@N20&tags=taxonomy:binomial=Delphinus+delphis>
    { ?photo foaf:depiction ?img. }
  SERVICE <https://example.org/sparql-ms/
            macaulaylibrary/getAudioByTaxon?name=Delphinus+delphis>
    { [] schema:contentUrl ?audioUrl. }
  SERVICE <https://example.org/sparql-ms/
            musicbrainz/getSongByName?name=Delphinus+delphis>
    { [] schema:sameAs ?page. } }
```

Listing 1.1. Querying SPARQL micro-services to enrich a LD resource with data from Flickr, the Macaulay Library and MusicBrainz.

4   Future Works

For an ecosystem of SPARQL micro-services to emerge from independent service providers, two crucial issues shall be tackled. Firstly, to enable services discovery, SPARQL micro-services should provide self-describing metadata such as the query string parameters or the types of triples generated. In this respect, the smartAPI metadata specification may be leveraged [4]. Secondly, it should be possible to retrieve fragments by smaller pieces using a paging mechanism. To tackle those issues, *Triple Patterns Fragments* (TPF) expose a self-describing, uniform interface consisting of metadata and hypermedia controls [3]. A perspective would be to extend this approach to the case of SPARQL micro-services, stemming some sort of *Graph Pattern Fragment* interface, *i.e.* a generalized TPF interface able to process regular graph patterns instead of only triple patterns, but still complying with the TPF metadata and hypermedia controls specification. Let us finally mention that we have focused specifically on consuming Web APIs data with SPARQL, although the principles presented in this work could apply to other types of APIs. Furthermore, many APIs empower users not only to read but more importantly to interact with data. Hence, an interesting perspective would be to think of SPARQL micro-services as a way to support distributed SPARQL Update over Web APIs, thus eventually contributing to build an actual read-write Web of Data.

References

1. Michel, F., Faron-Zucker, C., Gandon, F.: SPARQL micro-services: lightweight integration of web APIs and linked data. In: Proceedings of LDOW 2018 (2018)
2. Newman, S.: Building Microservices. O'Reilly Media, Sebastopol (2015)
3. Verborgh, R., et al.: Triple pattern fragments: a low-cost knowledge graph interface for the web. J. Web Semant. **37–38**, 184–206 (2016)
4. Zaveri, A., et al.: smartAPI: towards a more intelligent network of web APIs. In: Blomqvist, E., Maynard, D., Gangemi, A., Hoekstra, R., Hitzler, P., Hartig, O. (eds.) ESWC 2017. LNCS, vol. 10250, pp. 154–169. Springer, Cham (2017). https://doi.org/10.1007/978-3-319-58451-5_11

Grasping Metaphors: Lexical Semantics in Metaphor Analysis

Enrico Mensa, Aureliano Porporato, and Daniele P. Radicioni[✉]

Dipartimento di Informatica, Università degli Studi di Torino, Turin, Italy
{mensa,radicion}@di.unito.it, aureliano.porporato@edu.unito.it

Abstract. Metaphors represent to date an extraordinary challenge for computational linguistics. Dealing with metaphors has relevant consequences on our ability to build agents and systems that understand Natural Language and text documents: annotating metaphoric constructions by linking the metaphor elements to existing resources is a crucial step to make text documents more easily accessible by machines. Our approach tackles metaphors by considering concepts and their abstractness. We report the encouraging results obtained in a preliminary experimentation; we elaborate on present limitations, and individuate the needed improvements, which will be the base for future work.

Keywords: Metaphors · Figurative language · Lexical semantics
Natural language semantics · Lexical resources

1 Introduction

Metaphors can be seen as mechanisms for delivering semantic content in a concise way. More concise than with literal, plain language. Metaphors are highly pervasive in both language and thought [5], to such an extent that more than 30% sentences in the British National Corpus contain a metaphor [9]. It is thus easy to foresee that the capacity of recognizing and elaborating metaphorical uses will become more and more essential for building computational systems to deal with Natural Language, such as, e.g., conversational agents underlying chat bots, automatic summarization systems, and in general for extracting information from text documents and in making text documents machine readable. A metaphor is a mechanism to quickly deliver some information: some abstract concept (*explanandum*) is explained by referring to something else (*explanans*), which is more directly understood. Typically, the latter element comes from a more direct physical experience of the real world. The *abstractness* of involved concepts seems to play a major role in metaphors creation and understanding. This work investigates the interplay between metaphor detection and the lexical semantics underlying the terms involved in the metaphorical construction. Our approach consists of two main steps: *(i)* we extend the conceptual representation contained in COVER—a recently proposed lexical resource [6]— by automatically annotating information on concepts' abstractness, and *(ii)* we propose an

© Springer Nature Switzerland AG 2018
A. Gangemi et al. (Eds.): ESWC 2018 Satellite Events, LNCS 11155, pp. 192–195, 2018.
https://doi.org/10.1007/978-3-319-98192-5_36

algorithm to detect metaphors and investigate whether some kinds of metaphors can be understood based on abstractness. In particular, we are presently concerned with illustrating how metaphors are identified and mapped onto concept identifiers, which is a relevant step towards the semantic annotation of text documents and the encoding of meaningful pieces of information in machine readable format, such as RDF triples, linked to encyclopedic resources such as DBpedia.

2   Metaphors Detection

The COVER lexical resource was originally conceived as part of a larger project aimed at combining ontological inference and common-sense reasoning [7]. COVER has been built by merging BabelNet [8] and ConceptNet [1], and is composed by a list of vectors, each reporting information about a single concept. The representation of concepts rather than just terms requires the adoption of a set of concept identifiers (so to define a uniform naming space), and COVER relies on the sense inventory provided by BabelNet. BabelNet is a *semantic network* where each node (called synset, that is 'set of synonyms') represents a unique meaning, identified through a BabelNet synset ID (e.g., BN:00008010N). Furthermore, most BabelNet synset IDs are directly linked to the corresponding DBpedia URIs via the EXTERNAL LINKS relation in BabelNet: this connects COVER with the Semantic Web. The conceptual information borrowed from BabelNet has been coupled to common-sense knowledge, that has been extracted from ConceptNet. The ConceptNet relationships have been set as the skeleton of the vectors in COVER, that is the set dimensions upon which a vector describes the represented concept. More precisely, each vector dimension contains a set of values that are concepts themselves, identified through their own BabelNet synset IDs.

We extended the conceptual representation in COVER by enriching each concept herein with information on its *abstractness*[1] [2]; due to the lack of space, we defer to a future work the description of how this annotation was automatically performed. We focus instead on showing how abstractness information is used by the algorithm for the metaphors detection.

2.1   Metaphor Detection Algorithm

Provided that different categorizations of metaphors can be drawn, we refer to the threefold (not exhaustive) categorization of metaphors proposed in [3]. In this view, *Type I* metaphors are in the form "*smb/sth* is *sth*" (e.g., "He is a monster"), in which something or somebody is said to be of a kind that is not correct in a literal sense; *Type II* metaphors are in the form "*smb/sth verb sth*" (e.g., "I shot down all his arguments"), where an action is performed by or on something that cannot properly perform an action of that sort; *Type III* metaphors are in the form "*adj noun*" (e.g., "A brilliant idea"), where an adjective is associated to a

---

[1] The enriched resource can be downloaded at http://ls.di.unito.it.

concept that cannot have the quality expressed in a literal sense. We focus on metaphors of Types I and II, and presently disregard those of any different type.

Given a sentence $\mathcal{S}$ along with its parse tree $\triangle(\mathcal{S})$, we individuate the dependency patterns corresponding to Type I and II metaphors, which we denote as $\overline{\wedge}(\mathcal{S}) \subset \triangle(\mathcal{S})$. We note that Type I metaphors have a direct counterpart in terms of RDF triples (e.g., "The baby is a new arrival" is represented as ISA(BABY,NEW ARRIVAL)). Conversely, in the case of Type II some further effort is needed in order *(i)* to map the verb onto some predicate; and *(ii)* to split verbal subcategorization frames with more than two dependents into an appropriate set of triples, according to the semantics of each verb (e.g., "Laughter filled the room in few moments." is represented as FILL(LAUGHTER, ROOM) and FILL(LAUGHTER, [IN] MOMENTS)). However, in all cases the nouns involved in such triples can be mapped onto DBpedia nodes by means of their identifiers.

Some preprocessing steps are performed, basically involving syntactic parsing and word sense disambiguation. Namely, given in input the sentence $\mathcal{S} = \{t_1, t_2, \ldots, t_n\}$ composed of n input terms, we parse it and obtain the parse tree $\triangle(\mathcal{S})$; we then perform the word sense disambiguation of the terms in $\mathcal{S}$,[2] thus obtaining the set of concepts $\mathcal{C}(\mathcal{S}) = \bigcup_{i=1}^{n} \mathrm{WSD}(t_i)$.

The metaphor detection algorithm consists of the following steps:

1. Given the dependency patterns $\overline{\wedge}(\mathcal{S}) \subset \triangle(\mathcal{S})$ on the parse tree, we retain the corresponding concepts (thus dropping patterns whose elements were not disambiguated), $\mathcal{C}' = \bigcup_{\mathcal{C}} \overline{\wedge}(\mathcal{S})$;
   among concepts $c' \in \mathcal{C}'$, we select *target* (that is, *subj* in both Type I and II metaphors) and *source* (*dir-obj* in Type I metaphors, and *verb* in Type II metaphors) of the metaphorical expression;
2. We label as metaphorical a sentence if the target concept is more abstract than the source concept.

3   Pilot Experimentation

The aim of this experimentation is to test in how far combining syntactic, conceptual and abstractness information can be helpful in unveiling the presence of metaphors. We experimented on the Master Metaphors List (MML), a set of metaphors compiled by Lakoff and others in the '80s [4]. This corpus contains 1728 sentences, each sentence with at least one metaphor. From this set we extracted 75 sentences: we selected 40 sentences containing a metaphor of Type I, and 35 with a metaphor of Type II. We then collected 75 additional non metaphoric sentences (so to be able to compute the *precision* metrics, too); syntactic constructions similar to those characterizing sentences with Type I and Type II metaphors were preserved. The final data set is available at the URL ls.di.unito.it.

The system obtained a Recall of 0.70 and 0.74 on Type I and Type II, respectively, and a Precision of 0.56 (Type I) and 0.77 (Type II). The higher accuracy

---

[2] We presently used Babelfy, http://babelfy.org for the WSD and the Stanford CoreNLP, https://goo.gl/yxcRPF as our parser.

on Type II metaphors corroborates our hypothesis, thereby showing that for such (simpler) cases the comparison between target and source abstractness works fine. An explanation for the lower figures on Type I may stem from the fact that some Type I metaphors require *projecting* some features from the source onto the target (e.g., *lawyers are sharks*). In such cases, we conjecture that just considering the abstractness of the involved terms does not suffice, since the metaphor is best recognized by projecting the features of ferocity and dangerousness —which is proper to sharks— onto lawyers, as well. Remarkably, these are typically common-sense traits.

4 Conclusions

The experimental results seem to support the proposed approach, that puts together deep parsing, word sense disambiguation, common-sense knowledge and abstractness information. However, it also emerged that such approach needs further, substantial, efforts in order to deal with the widely varied linguistic constructions actually underlying metaphoric language. Grasping the semantics hidden in metaphors may be seen as the task of making explicit how abstract concepts, actions and properties can be explained through less abstract entities, or by resorting to common-sense traits that are transferred from the source to the target. The issue of explanation comes, in other words, together with the detection itself. Improving the whole system and providing it with explanatory skills will be the focus of our future work.

References

1. Havasi, C., Speer, R., Alonso, J.: ConceptNet: a lexical resource for common sense knowledge. Sel. Pap. RANLP **309**, 269–280 (2007)
2. Iliev, R., Axelrod, R.: The paradox of abstraction: precision versus concreteness. J. Psycholinguist. Res. **46**(3), 715–729 (2017)
3. Krishnakumaran, S., Zhu, X.: Hunting elusive metaphors using lexical resources. In: Proceedings of the Workshop on Computational Approaches to Figurative Language, pp. 13–20 (2007)
4. Lakoff, G., Æspenson, J., Schwartz, A.: The master metaphor list. University of California at Berkeley, Technical report, October 1991
5. Lakoff, G., Johnson, M.: Metaphors We Live By. The University of Chicago Press, Chicago (2003)
6. Lieto, A., Mensa, E., Radicioni, D.P.: A resource-driven approach for anchoring linguistic resources to conceptual spaces. In: Adorni, G., Cagnoni, S., Gori, M., Maratea, M. (eds.) AI*IA 2016. LNCS (LNAI), vol. 10037, pp. 435–449. Springer, Cham (2016). https://doi.org/10.1007/978-3-319-49130-1_32
7. Lieto, A., Radicioni, D.P., Rho, V.: Dual PECCS: a cognitive system for conceptual representation and categorization. JETAI **29**(2), 433–452 (2017)
8. Navigli, R., Ponzetto, S.P.: BabelNet: building a very large multilingual semantic network. In: Proceedings of the 48th ACL, pp. 216–225. ACL (2010)
9. Shutova, E.: Design and evaluation of metaphor processing systems. Comput. Linguist. **41**(4), 579–623 (2015)

The Unified Code for Units of Measure in RDF: `cdt:ucum` and other UCUM Datatypes

Maxime Lefrançois[(✉)] and Antoine Zimmermann

Univ Lyon, MINES Saint-Étienne, CNRS,
Laboratoire Hubert Curien UMR 5516, 42023 Saint-Étienne, France
{maxime.lefrancois,antoine.zimmermann}@emse.fr

Abstract. Being able to describe quantity values and their units is a requirement that is common to many applications in several industrial sectors such as manufacturing, transport and logistics, personal and public health, smart cities, energy, environment, buildings, agriculture. Different ontologies have been developed to describe units, their relations, and quantities with their values. In this paper we propose an alternative approach that leverages the Unified Code of Units of Measure, a code system intended to include *all* units of measures being contemporarily used in international sciences, engineering, and business. Our approach consists of a main UCUM datatype identified by IRI http://w3id.org/lindt/custom_datatypes#ucum, abbreviated as cdt:ucum. This datatype can be used for lightweight encoding and querying of quantity values, in a wide range of applications where representing and reasoning with quantity kinds and values is more important than reasoning with units. We compare our approach with existing approaches, and demonstrate it with our implementation on top of Apache Jena and an online testing tool.

1 Introduction

Applications in many industry sectors rely on quantity values with units of measures, for sensor observations, actuation, design calculations/simulations, quantitative general knowledge, etc. A typical way to convey the value of a quantity in RDF consists in using a structure with one triple providing a numerical value as a literal in standard datatypes (xsd:float, xsd:double, xsd:decimal), and a triple with an IRI identifying the unit. A dedicated ontology can define the properties that connect the quantity value to the numerical value and the unit. An alternative approach relies on custom datatypes [5].

In this paper, we introduce an RDF datatype, cdt:ucum, that transposes to RDF the full expressive power of the Unified Code for Units of Measure (UCUM [8]), enabling lightweight descriptions and querying of physical quantities using a single datatype. We currently provide 32 more specific datatypes such as cdt:speed and cdt:length to further specify the quantity kind of quantity values, but more datatypes may be introduced in the future.

© Springer Nature Switzerland AG 2018
A. Gangemi et al. (Eds.): ESWC 2018 Satellite Events, LNCS 11155, pp. 196–201, 2018.
https://doi.org/10.1007/978-3-319-98192-5_37

We first show in Sect. 2 how quantity values are typically described in RDF with existing ontologies or custom datatypes. Then, in Sect. 3, we introduce the cdt:ucum datatype, highlighting the conciseness of the representation with many examples. Finally, in Sect. 4, we describe our implementation as an extension of Apache Jena with support for cdt:ucum in SPARQL queries, with an online testing tool.

2   Related Work

We identify two approaches to represent physical quantities in RDF: using ontologies, or using custom datatypes.

Using ontologies of units of measurements. The classical approach consists in using an ontology to describe units, their relations, and measurements. A recent survey [4] compares and evaluates eight well known ontologies for units of measurements, among which MUO [6], QUDV [1], OM [7], QUDT [3]. This survey also report on the Wikidata corpus[1] that currently contains over 4.4 k measurement units and 4.1 k non-prefixed units. Using such ontologies, quantity values are usually represented as OWL individuals linked to some numeric value and to some individual representing a unit of measure. For example, Listing 1.1 represents the quantity value 29 °C using QUDT 1.1.

Listing 1.1. Description of a quantity value using QUDT 1.1

```
@prefix qudt−1−1: <http://qudt.org/1.1/schema/qudt#> .
@prefix qudt−unit−1−1: <http://qudt.org/1.1/vocab/unit#> .
[ ]  a  qudt−1−1:QuantityValue ;
     qudt−1−1:unit  qudt−unit−1−1:DegreeCelsius ;
     qudt−1−1:numericValue  "29"^^xsd:double  .
```

Not all possible units of measurement are (or will be) defined in these ontologies, for example QUDT 1.1 defines a unit for kilowatt hour, but not megawatt hour. Application developers in the energy domain can force themselves to use units they are not used to, or they can define missing units using the definition mechanism provided by QUDT. This extension mechanism uses concepts such as base units, conversion offsets and multipliers, numerator and denominator. For example, Listing 1.2 illustrates how the unit megawatt hour may be defined. Even then, two energy operators may define the same unit using different URIs, leading to potential interoperability issues.

Listing 1.2. Description of a new unit using QUDT 1.1

```
ex:Megawatthour  a  qudt−1−1:EnergyAndWorkUnit ;
     rdfs:label  "Megawatthour" ;
     qudt−1−1:symbol  "MW-hr" ;
     qudt−1−1:conversionOffset  "0.0"^^xsd:double ;
     qudt−1−1:conversionMultiplier  "3.6E9"^^xsd:double ;
```

---

[1] https://www.wikidata.org/.

Datasets using quantity values defined with such ontologies require 4 triples every time a quantity needs to be linked to a quantity value, and complex mechanisms are needed to canonicalize quantity values so as to query them uniformly. We are not aware of any existing support of QUDT or OM custom units in any RDF or SPARQL engine.

Using datatypes. DBpedia has many datatypes[2], which are hard-coded in OntologyDatatypes.scala and listed in the DBpedia Mappings Wiki for reference. Dbpedia defines datatypes for physical dimensions (http://dbpedia.org/datatype/Area) along with datatypes for specific units of measures (http://dbpedia.org/datatype/cubicInch). Yet, these datatypes do not dereference, so one cannot understand if Inch here is in the international customary units, U.S. survey lengths, British Imperial lengths, for example. Again, not all possible units of measurement are (or will be) defined in the Dbpedia ontology, and complex mechanisms are needed to canonicalize quantity values so as to query them uniformly.

We previously proposed an approach for RDF and SPARQL engines to support arbitrarily complex custom datatypes on-the-fly by dereferencing their URIs and retrieving specifications in JavaScript [5]. In this paper we are exclusively interested in datatypes for quantity values, and do not consider on-the-fly support capabilities.

3   Specification of **cdt:ucum** and other UCUM Datatypes

The Unified Code for Units of Measure (UCUM) [8] is a code system intended to include *all* units of measures being contemporarily used in international science, engineering, and business.

We define a RDF datatype UCUM identified by IRI http://w3id.org/lindt/custom_datatypes#ucum, abbreviated as cdt:ucum. Its lexical space is the concatenation of an xsd:decimal, optionally followed by e or E and the lexical form of an xsd:integer, at least one space, and a unit chosen in the case sensitive version of the UCUM code system. The value space corresponds to the set of measures, or quantity values as defined by the International Systems of Quantities. The lexical-to-value mapping maps lexical forms with a UCUM unit to their corresponding measures according to the International Systems of Quantities.

We also define a set of additional datatypes such as cdt:length and cdt:speed that further specify the quantity kind of quantity values. Their lexical spaces, value spaces, and lexical-to-value mappings are subsets of those of cdt:ucum. More such datatypes may be defined in the future. Table 1 lists examples of valid cdt:ucum literals, and their equivalent using more specific datatypes.

---

[2] http://mappings.dbpedia.org/index.php/DBpedia_Datatypes.

Table 1. Some valid UCUM literals.

"1 mA"^^cdt:ucum	1 milli ampère. Same value as "1e-3 C/s"^^cdt:ucum and "1 mA"^^cdt:electricCurrent
"1 MW.h"^^cdt:ucum	1 mega watt hour.
"1 [nmi_i]"^^cdt:ucum	1 nautical mile, international customary unit. Same value as "1852.0 m"^^cdt:length, or "0.9993618864985154 [nmi_br]"^^cdt:length (nautical mile, British imperial unit)
"1 cd/cm2/[pi]"^^cdt:ucum	1 candela per square centimeter and divided by Pi: Valid UCUM unit definition equivalent to the Lambert brightness unit. Same value as "1 Lmb"^^cdt:ucum
"1.8 [ppm]"^^cdt:ucum	1.8 parts per million. Literals may be formed with stranger units such as "1.8 M[ppm]"^^cdt:ucum (mega parts per million, which is equal to 1). Same value as "1.8 [ppm]"^^cdt:dimensionless

4 Implementation of UCUM Datatypes on Apache Jena

The UCUM specification has implementations in different languages. We used the latest version of systems-ucum-java8[3], an implementation leveraging the recent Java units of measurement API 2.0 (JSR 385), to add support of the 33 datatypes specified above on top of Apache Jena. Our extension, named jena-ucum, is open-source and available online[4]. It overloads native SPARQL operators (=, ¡, etc.) to compare UCUM literals, and arithmetic functions (+, −, *, /) to manipulate quantity value literals: 1. Add two commensurable quantity value literals; 2. Subtract a quantity value literals to a commensurable one; 3. Multiply two quantity value literals, or a quantity value literal and a scalar (xsd:int, xsd:decimal, xsd:float, xsd:double); 4. Divide a quantity value literal by a quantity value literal, a quantity value literal by a scalar, or a scalar by a quantity value literal. We additionally define a custom SPARQL function with IRI: http://w3id.org/lindt/custom_datatypes#sameDimension which takes two parameters and returns true if they are commensurable quantity values.

5 Demonstration

We demonstrate the UCUM datatypes using a playground illustrated on Fig. 1 and accessible online.[5] The user can enter a SPARQL Construct or Select query and the default graph of the RDF Dataset on which it is evaluated. The result is computed in real-time and returned to the user using the WebSocket protocol.

Queries are predefined to progressively introduce the use of SPARQL comparison operators, arithmetic functions, solution sequence modifiers (ORDER BY).

---

[3] Implementation of UCUM we used: https://github.com/unitsofmeasurement/uom-systems/tree/master/ucum-java8.

[4] Our implementation on Jena: https://github.com/OpenSensingCity/jena-ucum.

[5] UCUM Datatype playground https://w3id.org/lindt/playground.html.

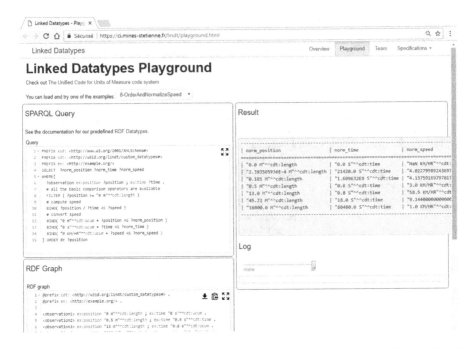

Fig. 1. Screenshot of the UCUM datatypes playground https://w3id.org/lindt/playground.html.

Other predefined queries are predefined to illustrate each of the 33 currently defined UCUM datatypes. We will also showcase how the UCUM datatypes may be used in combination with other vocabularies such as SOSA/SSN [2].

6   Conclusion

Using the UCUM datatypes, one only requires 1 triple to link a quantity to a fully qualified value, and one does not require custom mechanisms to canonicalize literals based on external descriptions of units of measurements. Using UCUM Datatypes, datasets are therefore drastically lightened, and queries are also simpler. The UCUM datatype can inherently represent an infinite set of custom units, and is therefore suitable for an open set of application domains.

A similar datatype could be defined to support amounts of money, potentially with any type of currencies and a timestamp for this currency.

Acknowledgments. This work has been partly funded by the ANR 14-CE24-0029 OpenSensingCity project.

References

1. Quantities, Units, Dimensions, Values (QUDV). SysML 1.2 Revision Task Force Working draft, Object Management Group, October 30 2009
2. Haller, A., Janowicz, K., Cox, S.J.D., Le Phuoc, D., Taylor, K., Lefrançois, M.: Semantic Sensor Network Ontology. W3C Recommendation, W3C, 19 October 2017
3. Hodgson, R., Keller, P.J., Hodges, J., Spivak, J.: QUDT - Quantities, Units. Dimensions and Data Types Ontologies. Technical report, NASA (2014)
4. Keil, J.M., Schindler, S. Comparison and evaluation of ontologies for units of measurement. Semant. Web J. (2018, to appear). http://www.semantic-web-journal.net/content/comparison-and-evaluation-ontologies-units-measurement-1
5. Lefrançois, M., Zimmermann, A.: Supporting arbitrary custom datatypes in RDF and SPARQL. In: Sack, H., Blomqvist, E., d'Aquin, M., Ghidini, C., Ponzetto, S.P., Lange, C. (eds.) ESWC 2016. LNCS, vol. 9678, pp. 371–386. Springer, Cham (2016). https://doi.org/10.1007/978-3-319-34129-3_23
6. Polo, L., Berrueta, D.: MUO - Measurement Units Ontology, Working Draft - DD April 2008. Working draft, Fundación CTIC (2008)
7. Rijgersberg, H., van Assem, M., Top, J.L.: Ontology of units of measure and related concepts. Semant. Web J. **4**(1), 3–13 (2013)
8. Shadow, G., McDonald, C.J.: The Unified Code for Units of Measure. Technical report, Regenstrief Institute Inc., 22 October 2013

Deep Linking Desktop Resources

Markus Schröder[1,2(✉)], Christian Jilek[1,2], and Andreas Dengel[1,2]

[1] Smart Data & Knowledge Services Department,
DFKI GmbH, Kaiserslautern, Germany
{markus.schroeder,christian.jilek,andreas.dengel}@dfki.de
[2] Computer Science Department, TU Kaiserslautern, Kaiserslautern, Germany

Abstract. Deep Linking is the process of referring to a specific piece of web content. Although users can browse their files in desktop environments, they are unable to directly traverse deeper into their content using deep links. In order to solve this issue, we demonstrate "DeepLinker", a tool which generates and interprets deep links to desktop resources, thus enabling the reference to a certain location within a file using a simple hyperlink. By default, the service responds with an HTML representation of the resource along with further links to follow. Additionally, we allow the use of RDF to interlink our deep links with other resources.

Keywords: Deep link · Desktop · URI · Fragment identifier · RDF

1 Introduction

Internet resources are commonly identified using URIs[1] which contain the information to look them up. In this context, "deep linking"[2] is the practice of generating a hyperlink to link to a specific piece of web content. For example, https://en.wikipedia.org/wiki/Deep_linking#Example refers to the Example section of Wikipedia's Deep Linking page. Similarly, desktop resources, like files (in various formats[3]) and folders, are typically addressed with their absolute paths or file URI schemata[4]. Although users can browse a file in this way, they are unable to directly descend deeper into its content. As a result, users cannot refer to a certain location deep inside their desktop resources, for example, referring to a shape in a slide of a presentation. This is due to a missing definition and standardisation, and as a consequence, absent implementations of common desktop applications such as editors or readers.

Allowing deep linking of desktop resources enables several possibilities. Instead of manually traverse complex structures, a link automatically lead to a desired fragment. In addition, such links serve as unique identifiers which can

---

[1] https://tools.ietf.org/html/rfc3986.

[2] https://www.w3.org/2001/tag/doc/deeplinking.html (Sect. 2).

[3] In addition to files, other resources may reside on the desktop as services like, for example, mails (IMAP), databases (SQL) or on other external endpoints.

[4] https://tools.ietf.org/html/rfc8089.

© Springer Nature Switzerland AG 2018
A. Gangemi et al. (Eds.): ESWC 2018 Satellite Events, LNCS 11155, pp. 202–207, 2018.
https://doi.org/10.1007/978-3-319-98192-5_38

be used to annotate resources (e.g. by using RDF). Services (or agents) can use deep links to precisely refer to a resource's part (e.g. in search results). The same way, in collaborative scenarios users are able to share links to shared resource fragments instead of explaining how to reach them.

Thus, in this paper we demonstrate "DeepLinker" which allows browsing desktop resources to an arbitrary depth using deep links. The core idea is to generate, interpret and maintain the URIs referring to a certain location within desktop resources as well as showing an HTML representation of the browsed fragment in order to provide a visualization. For better demonstration an online prototype is available[5].

2   Related Work

To satisfy the need for identifying subordinate resources in the web, the URI standard defines fragment identifiers[6]. However, usual desktop applications are not aware of the fragment identifier concept. One would have to reimplement or extend all of them (e.g. with plug-ins) to enable a similar behaviour. That is why we decided to write our own application. To simulate a Desktop application rendering resources we convert and present them using HTML.

Other approaches like the LEMO annotation framework [1] use fragment identification for MPEG resources[7] as well as other fragment identifiers. A 2007 survey [2] showed that fragmentation links for complex documents (e.g. spreadsheets, charts, presentations and word processing documents) do not exist. In fact, current media fragments[8] solely focus on image, audio and video.

3   DeepLinker

Our tool generates and interprets deep links to desktop resources, thus making it possible to refer to a certain location within a file using a simple hyperlink. An HTML page presents the referred part to the users.

For a first impression, Fig. 1 exemplifies four deep links together with the web sites they refer to. In general, the pages show the accessed link and a simple form to add and list RDF triples below. The images depict the following cases each having a different highlighting: (a) a part of an image, (b) a shape in a presentation slide (text in red), (c) a line in a text file, and (d) an element in a web page.

Figure 2 shows the environment in which DeepLinker is used together with additional example links. Usually, our tool runs locally on the users' PCs. A DeepLinker resource is requested by using its hyperlink (deep link) in a web browser. Our tool responds with an HTML representation of the resource along

---

[5] www.dfki.uni-kl.de/~mschroeder/demo/deeplinker.

[6] https://tools.ietf.org/html/rfc3986#section-3.5.

[7] https://www.iso.org/standard/42075.html.

[8] https://www.w3.org/TR/media-frags/.

(a) `/filesystem/a.png/content/to@image`
`/rect@600,109,188,36`

(b) `/filesystem/b.pptx/content/to@powerpoint`
`/index@3/cssSelector@svg%2B%253E%2Bg%2B%253E`
`%2Bg%253Anth-child%252843%2529`

(c) `/filesystem/c.txt/content/to@string`
`/line@2`

(d) `/remote/download@http%253A%252F%252F`
`w3c.org,*%252F*/content/to@html/cssSelector@`
`%2523w3c_nav%2520%253E%2520form%253...`

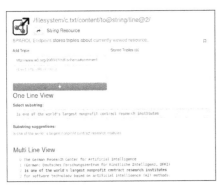

Fig. 1. (a) Focusses the word "Artificial" in DFKI's logo which is annotated with an `rdfs:comment` "Artificial", (b) highlights the shape "Fehler vermeiden" in the 4th slide of the Powerpoint presentation `b.pptx`, (c) selects the 3rd line of a text file, (d) refers to the "Participate" element in the downloaded w3c.org page. (Color figure online)

Fig. 2. DeepLinker browses usual desktop resources by using various path segments. Usually, our app returns an HTML representation of the fragment with further links to follow. Hyperlinks: (1) returns file information of `note.txt` (not its content), (2) presents the name of the file, (3) highlights its 6th line. (4) draws a rectangle on image `a.png`. (5) shows the 4th slide of `b.pptx`.

with links pointing deeper into the file. As a result, instead of just stopping at the resource's content (surface link), users can traverse further into the resources enabling a more fine-grained selection of a desired fragment. Users generate deep links by browsing desktop resources (like usual websites) and copy links from their browser's address bar.

Our approach allows for a hierarchical drill-down using the absolute URI's path segments. The deep links are processed by the server at runtime in the following way: Each path segment is implemented as a parametrized method returning a DeepLinker resource. Thus, they can be chained in order to traverse arbitrarily deep. The segments are serialised in the URI in the following way: /<method>@<param1>,...,<paramN>/. DeepLinker parses on every request segment-by-segment the whole deep link. Parameters are URL encoded in order to avoid clashes with the predefined @ and , symbols. Whenever a requested resource does not exist or a method is not implemented, an exception is thrown. Because our links are composed of resource names, indices or selectors they are not robust against modified data sources (e.g. when a resource is moved). For demonstration purpose we implemented nine path segment methods along with 14 resource types.

Path Segment Methods. The child[9] and index methods are convenient ways to select a sub-resource by name or sequence number. line and substring select corresponding parts of a string. rect is meant to highlight a part of an image, while cssSelector is used to refer to an element in an XML-like structure. download retrieves an external file using its URL. In order to acquire a value for a given key the property method can be used. In contrast to the previous read-only methods, the to method allows for transforming resources from one format to another (if this functionality is available for the respective DeepLinker resource type).

Resource Types. Currently 14 resource types are supported. Collection and Map store resources the same way known from programming languages. File holds a local file's meta data but not its content. The latter is represented by String (plain text), JSON, Image, PDF, Powerpoint(Slide) and RDF depending on its associated format. The raw content can also be represented using the Binary resource type. A special Rect type models the actual highlighted area. Xmlish is a more general resource type covering XML and XML-based structures like HTML or SVG. The Remote resource serves as an entry point to upload and download files.

Annotations via RDF. Like stated before in more detail, DeepLinker generates and interprets deep links to desktop resources. Having these links now enables us to make statements about them using RDF. This approach is comparable with the Annotea project [3] which stores meta data about websites. Similarly, Deeplinker additionally allows to store and retrieve RDF using an external SPARQL endpoint. For demonstration purposes, DeepLinker is equipped with a Fuseki endpoint running localhost at /fuseki/annotation. In the resource's

---

[9] If no method is given, child is assumed to be the default.

HTML representation, our prototype provides a form to add RDF statements and inspect stored ones. With this capability it is possible to annotate any desktop resource (and especially their fragments) with further meta data. The resources' literals are searchable in order to find associated DeepLinker links. In order to simulate bookmarking, users may conveniently add a triple of the form `<DeepLinkerLink> rdf:type` https://www.w3.org/2002/01/bookmark# Bookmark with a single click. Bookmarks are queried and listed using a separate resource page.

Content Negotiation. By default, DeepLinker returns an HTML page rendering the resource and providing further links. Users may thus browse their desktop resources in a familiar way. However, DeepLinker supports content negotiation based on the provided accept header in the request (if the requested resource type implements it). For example, given the accept header `application/json` returns the resource serialized as JSON. In case of `text/turtle`, the resource is converted to RDF and serialized in Turtle format (currently only implemented for file resources). Following the third Linked Data principle, additional statements about the resource queried using the SPARQL endpoint are added, too.

4   Conclusion and Outlook

In this paper, we demonstrated DeepLinker, a tool that allows for browsing usual desktop resources arbitrarily deep, enabling users to refer to any desired fragment. This is accomplished by generating and interpreting deep links. Currently, our prototype implements nine path segment methods together with 14 resource types, especially making it possible to use RDF to annotate the now existing links with further meta data. Our prototype can be tested online (see footnote 5).

In the future, we think of supporting data scientists in business and data understanding phases of data mining processes. Using our tool they would then be able to browse and annotate their database content and CSV files in order to store newly acquired knowledge. In this regard, we also think of collaborative scenarios in which users create and share deep links among each other. For example, a user's generated deep link refers to a text section of a shared PDF document which can easily be opened by another user's local DeepLinker.

Acknowledgements. Parts of this work have been funded by the German Federal Ministry of Food and Agriculture in the project SDSD (2815708615) and by the DFG in the project Managed Forgetting (DE 420/19-1).

References

1. Haslhofer, B., Jochum, W., King, R., Sadilek, C., Schellner, K.: The LEMO annotation framework: weaving multimedia annotations with the web. Int. J. Digit. Libr. **10**(1), 15–32 (2009)
2. Jochum, W.: Requirements of fragment identification. In: Proceedings of I-Media 2007 and I-Semantics 2007, pp. 172–179 (2007)
3. Koivunen, M.R.: Annotea and semantic web supported collaboration. In: Workshop on End Users Aspects of the Semantic Web, pp. 5–16 (2005)

VocRec: An Automated Vocabulary Recommender Tool

Wagner G. do Amaral[1], Bernardo Pereira Nunes[1,2],
Sean W. M. Siqueira[1(✉)], and Luiz André P. Paes Leme[3]

[1] Department of Applied Informatics,
Federal University of the State of Rio de Janeiro (UNIRIO),
Rio de Janeiro, RJ, Brazil
{wagner.amaral,bernardo.nunes,sean}@uniriotec.br
[2] Department of Informatics,
Pontifical Catholic University of Rio de Janeiro (PUC-Rio),
Rio de Janeiro, RJ, Brazil
bnunes@inf.puc-rio.br
[3] Institute of Computing,
Fluminense Federal University (UFF), Niterói, RJ, Brazil
lapaesleme@ic.uff.br

Abstract. A common problem faced by data publishers is how to semantically represent data and how to find vocabularies that best represent their data to publish in the Web. To address these problems, this paper introduces a tool, called VocRec, which can be used for recommending vocabularies for relational data that will be published as Linked Data on the Web. Preliminary evaluation using educational databases shows promising results in terms of precision and its ability on assisting data publishers in the task of dataset publication.

Keywords: Vocabulary recommendation · Linked data

1 Introduction

With the increasing adoption of Linked Data (LD) standards for publishing and connecting structured data on the Web, a global data space has been created covering a large variety of domains (e.g. Government, Life Sciences, Linguistics, etc.) as shown in the LOD cloud [1]. Additionally, LD has also led to the creation of a number of cross-domain and domain-specific applications [2, 3], allowing the interlinking of heterogeneous applications at the data level.

Despite the many benefits of using LD, a number of challenges arises when one wants to publish data following the LD standards. A common problem faced by data publishers is how to semantically represent data – one of the first steps when publishing linked data [4]. For this task, a data publisher needs to either create his own vocabulary or to reuse one or more of the existing vocabularies published on the Web. The latter takes data publishers to a prior problem, that is, how to find vocabularies that best represent their relational data? This is the problem addressed in this paper.

A. Gangemi et al. (Eds.): ESWC 2018 Satellite Events, LNCS 11155, pp. 208–212, 2018.
https://doi.org/10.1007/978-3-319-98192-5_39

Vocabularies are responsible for adding semantics to data, defining and characterizing concepts, relationships and constraints [5]. The use of well-known and largely adopted vocabularies is key to enable data integration and interoperability [6]. Following the recommendation provided by [7], a new vocabulary should only be defined if there is no other mix of existing vocabularies that can represent your data. However, there exists a thousand of vocabularies [8] representing multiple areas of concern and very often a single vocabulary is not sufficient to entirely represent a dataset. For instance, suppose that a data publisher wants to publish a relational database with hundreds of entities following the LD standards. The mapping between the entities and the most adequate vocabularies would be time-consuming and very hard even for specialists.

This paper introduces a tool named VocRec, an automated vocabulary recommender tool, to assist data publishers in selecting vocabularies to represent their relational data. The tool follows a 5-step process chain starting from the extraction of syntactical information from relational databases until the actually vocabulary recommendation after passing through clustering and a semantic processing. A preliminary evaluation shows promising results on the recommendation of vocabularies.

2 VocRec – Automated Vocabulary Recommender Tool

This section introduces the VocRec tool through a running example. We use a database schema from a well-known learning management system called Moodle [9] to exemplify the whole recommendation process. Its database schema contains a total of 2,840 attributes scattered into 314 tables. The choice of this schema is motivated by its complexity and the diverse knowledge it represents.

Figure 1 illustrates the tool and overviews the process chain responsible for recommending vocabularies to data publishers. The process is split into five main steps, namely: (i) Data Extraction; (ii) Data Preprocessing; (iii) Contextual Clustering; (iv) Semantic Expansion; and (v) Vocabulary Recommendation. In what follows we describe the vocabulary recommendation process chain and instantiate each step based in Moodle's relational database used as input to the process:

(i) **Data Extraction**. This step is responsible for the extraction of schema information [10] from relational database (e.g. tables, attributes and relationships).

   Given the Moodle schema, this step outputs the names of tables (e.g., *mdl_user, mdl_course_categories*) and attributes (e.g., *fullname* and *course_description*). After extracting schema information, a preprocessing step is required to clean up messy data.

(ii) **Data Preprocessing.** This step is responsible for cleaning and preparing the data for the next steps. For this, Apache OpenNLP toolkit[1] is used to detect the language, tokenize, and stemming.

---

[1] https://opennlp.apache.org/.

Continuing with the running example, after data preprocessing, the entities *mdl_user, mdl_course_categories* are represented by [*user*] and [*course, category*]. Note that "*mdl_*" is a prefix and is removed during the preprocessing, and *categories* is now in its singular form after stemming.

(iii) **Contextual Clustering.** This step is responsible for grouping related entities for further recommendation of vocabularies. There are at least two possible ways to group related entities: (a) using the existing relationships (e.g. *foreign keys)* between entities in a database; and/or (b) using (semantic) similarity between terms. VocRec implements the latter approach. For this, we use semantic similarity and relatedness measures from the lexical database WordNet through the API WS4 J[2], and based on the similarity of the terms the clusters are formed using the K-Means algorithm.

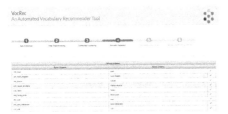

Fig. 1. The automated processing chain of VocRec to recommending vocabularies.

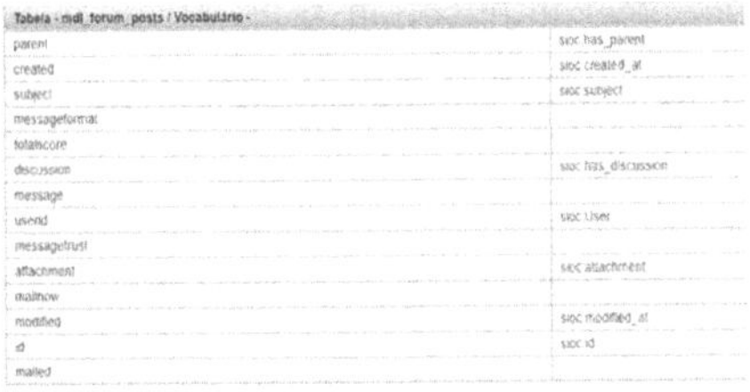

Fig. 2. Vocabulary recommendation for the table *mdl_forum_posts*. The recommended vocabulary is SIOC (Semantically-Interlinked Online Communities).

For instance, assume that the previous steps extracted information about the entities: *mdl_user, mdl_course_modules* and *mdl_course_category.* So, after preprocessing, the following vectors are generated: [*user*], [*course, module*] and [*course, category*]. Clearly, two clusters should be generated based on the semantic similarity between the vectors: Cluster 1: {[*user*]}, and Cluster 2: {[*course, module*], [*course, category*]}.

iv **Semantic Expansion.** This step is responsible for automatically extracting semantic relationships from the clusters generated in the previous step. Here, we use the MIT Java Wordnet Interface to synsets and sense index from Wordnet based on the terms representing the clusters. A cluster is represented by the most occurring terms, so, for instance, the term representing Cluster 2 is *course.* Based on the synsets and the sense of the term *course,* we expand the cluster representative terms by using their synonyms and hypernyms. For example, the term *user* found in Cluster 1 has as its hypernym the term "Person", which can

---

[2] https://github.com/Sciss/ws4j.

be used to find related vocabularies in the next and final step. So, the output of this step is a set of related terms that represent a group of entities extracted from a relational database schema.

v **Vocabulary Recommendation.** This step is responsible for recommending vocabularies. Based on the set of terms generated in the previous step, the terms are used to query a vocabulary repository. Two queries are issued, one containing the hypernym term as a class, and another with all expanded terms. The vocabulary repository used is LOV. Three different strategies are available to the vocabulary recommendations: (i) Popular Vocabularies; (ii) Minimize the number of vocabularies; and (iii) Maximize the number of vocabularies. The first strategy takes into account the usage of the vocabularies in order to recommend the most popular ones (thus, the most probable to be used) whereas the second and the third strategies use the minimum/maximum number of vocabularies to represent the data. Figure 2 shows the recommended vocabulary for the entity *mdl_forum_posts* using the *popular* strategy.

3   Preliminary Evaluation and Results

The preliminary evaluation of the quality of the results obtained were conducted based on precision and used databases from the Education field. Table 1 summarizes the results. Although, on average, the best strategy is based in the popular vocabularies, the other two strategies may show to data publishers other vocabularies that may also represent the data.

Table 1. Table results the vocabulary recommendation to two groups of databases.

DB schema	Popular Vocabularies			Minimize vocabularies			Maximize vocabularies		
	Moodle	Sakai	Atutor	Moodle	Sakai	Atutor	Moodle	Sakai	Atutor
Precision	0.58	0.7	0.72	0.34	0.46	0.66	0.27	0.4	0.78

4   Conclusion and Future Works

This paper introduced VocRec a tool used for recommending vocabularies for relational data that will be published as LD in the Web. Preliminary evaluation shows promising results and its ability on assisting data publishers in the task of dataset publication. The recommendation of vocabularies for Atutor reached 78% of precision using the maximize strategy whereas the precision for Moodle and Saki reached 58% and 70%, respectively, using the popular strategy. As future works, we intend to test VocRec in other scenarios other than Educational, perform in-depth evaluation and include an additional step to perform property alignment. We also intend to evaluate the usability of the tool. VocRec is publicly available at: https://tinyurl.com/y8m5pvtv.

References

1. Cyganiak, R., Jentzsch, A.: The Linking Open Data cloud diagram. http://lod-cloud.net/. Accessed 15 July 2017
2. Heath, T., Bizer, C.: Linked data: evolving the web into a global data space. Synth. Lect. Semant. Web Theory Technol. **1**, 1–136 (2011)
3. Mouromtsev, D., D'Aquin, M.: Open data for Education Linked, Shared, and Reusable Data for Teaching and Learning. Springer, Switzerland (2016). https://doi.org/10.1007/978-3-319-30493-9
4. Best Practices for Publishing Linked Data. https://www.w3.org/TR/ld-bp/. Accessed 15 July 2017
5. W3C. https://www.w3.org/standards/semanticweb/ontology. Accessed 15 July 2017
6. Data on the Web Best Practices. https://www.w3.org/TR/dwbp/. accessed 15 July 2017
7. Bizer, C., Cyganiak, R., Heath, T.: How to Publish Linked Data on the Web. http://wifo5-03.informatik.uni-mannheim.de/bizer/pub/LinkedDataTutorial/#whichvocabs. Accessed 15 July 2017
8. Vandenbussche, P.-Y., Atemezing, G.A., Poveda-Villalón, M., Vatant, B.: Linked Open Vocabularies (LOV): a gateway to reusable semantic vocabularies on the Web. Semant. Web **8**, 437–452 (2017)
9. Moodle - Modular object-oriented dynamic learning environment https://moodle.org/. Accessed 15 July 2017
10. Rahm, E., Bernstein, P.A.: A survey of approaches to automatic schema matching. VLDB J. **10**, 334–350 (2001)

Declarative Rules for Linked Data Generation at Your Fingertips!

Pieter Heyvaert[✉], Ben De Meester, Anastasia Dimou, and Ruben Verborgh

Department of Electronics and Information Systems,
Ghent University – imec – IDLab, Ghent, Belgium
{pheyvaer.heyvaert,ben.demeester,anastasia.dimou,
ruben.verborgh}@ugent.be

Abstract. Linked Data is often generated based on a set of declarative rules using languages such as R2RML and RML. These languages are built with machine-processability in mind. It is thus not always straight-forward for users to define or understand rules written in these languages, preventing them from applying the desired annotations to the data sources. In the past, graphical tools were proposed. However, next to users who prefer a graphical approach, there are users who desire to understand and define rules via a text-based approach. For the latter, we introduce an enhancement to their workflow. Instead of requiring users to manually write machine-processable rules, we propose writing human-friendly rules, and generate machine-processable rules based on those human-friendly rules. At the basis is YARRRML: a human-readable text-based representation for declarative generation rules. We propose a novel browser-based integrated development environment (IDE) called *Matey*, showcasing the enhanced workflow. In this work, we describe our demo. Users can experience first hand how to generate triples from data in different formats by using YARRRML's representation of the rules. The actual machine-processable rules remain completely hidden when editing. Matey shows that writing human-friendly rules enhances the workflow for a broader range of users. As a result, more desired annotations will be added to the data sources which leads to more desired Linked Data.

1 Introduction

Linked Data is often generated based on data derived from certain data sources. Initially, custom tools and scripts were used that incorporate directly in their implementation how Linked Data is generated. Updating the semantic annotations resulted in dedicated software development cycles to adjust the implementations. This was circumvented through the use of rules that are defined according to a specific language syntax, such as R2RML [2] or RML [3].

The described research activities were funded by Ghent University, imec, Flanders Innovation & Entrepreneurship (AIO), the Research Foundation – Flanders (FWO), and the European Union.

A. Gangemi et al. (Eds.): ESWC 2018 Satellite Events, LNCS 11155, pp. 213–217, 2018.
https://doi.org/10.1007/978-3-319-98192-5_40

These languages define *declaratively* how Linked Data is generated from corresponding data sources using annotations provided through vocabulary terms. Rules are detached from the implementation that executes them, thus, the implementation does not need to be updated when the rules are updated. As such Linked Data generation languages are built foremost with machine-processability in mind, it is not always straightforward for users to define or understand rules written in these languages. This prevents the users from specifying the desired annotations for the data sources. In the past, graphical editors were proposed, e.g., the RMLEditor [4] and Map-On [7], to enhance the workflow of defining rules. However, next to users who prefer a graphical approach, there are users who desire a text-based approach. For the latter, we introduce an enhancement to their workflow. At the basis of this enhancement is YARRRML[1], a human-readable text-based representation for declarative generation rules.

To investigate a human-readable text-based representation in the workflow, we propose a novel browser-based integrated development environment (IDE) called *Matey*[2]. Even though other IDEs and text editors can be used to work with YARRRML, Matey showcases the enhanced workflow of the rules generation process, such as the samples of the data sources, the generation of the machine-processable generation rules, and the corresponding Linked Data. Through the use of YARRRML, the underlying languages' complexity and verbosity are hidden.

In this work, we describe our demo, during which participants can have a hands-on experience with Matey to define machine-processable rules from data in different formats by using YARRRML's representation of the rules. With Matey we show that a broader range of users can enhance their workflow for defining rules via writing human-friendly rules. As a result, more desired annotations will be added to the data sources which leads to more desired Linked Data. In Sect. 2, we briefly summarize YARRRML, and in Sect. 3, we discuss and demonstrate Matey. Matey is available at https://w3id.org/yarrrml/matey/ and a screencast is available at https://w3id.org/yarrrml/matey/screencast.

2   Human-Readable Text-Based Representation

YARRRML is a human readable text-based representation for declarative Linked Data generation rules. It is expressed in YAML [1], a widely used data serialization language designed to be human-friendly. It is already specified how YARRRML can be used to represent R2RML and RML rules. Through the example in Listing 1, we summarize YARRRML's basic concepts[3].

All rules that state how subjects, predicates, and objects are generated are found under the `mappings` key, which is attached to the root of the YARRRML document (Listing 1, line 4). Per set of rules that state how an entity is generated together with its corresponding attributes, a user-chosen key is added to the

---

[1] https://w3id.org/yarrrml/.
[2] From *mate* + $-y$ (pronounced *M-eighty*), i.e., a fellow pirate.
[3] The specification is available at https://w3id.org/yarrrml/spec/.

```
1   prefixes:
2     ex: "http://example.com/"
3
4   mappings:
5     person:
6       sources:
7         - ['data.json~jsonpath', '$.persons[*]']
8       s: ex:$(firstname)
9       po:
10        - [a, foaf:Person]
11        - [foaf:givenName, $(firstname)]
```

Listing 1. example YARRRML rules that annotate the data in Listing 2

```
1   {
2       "persons": [
3           {"firstname": "John",  "lastname": "Doe"     },
4           {"firstname": "Jane",  "lastname": "Smith"   },
5           {"firstname": "Sarah", "lastname": "Bladinck"}
6       ]
7   }
```

Listing 2. example JSON file (data.json) detailing people's first and last name

mappings key. In Listing 1, you can find such a set of rules for the generation of Linked Data from the JSON file in Listing 2. The file contains metadata information about people, including their first and last name. The user-chosen key person has as value all the rules related to the entity that represents a person. That key can be reused in other rules when there is a relationship between the different entities. The key sources has as value all the data sources that are used to generate the person entities, which includes the name of the file and an optional iterator. The latter determines the records that represent the different entities.

The key s has as value the rules that state how subject-IRIs are generated for the different entities (Listing 1, line 8). In this example, each IRI is constructed by appending the first name of every person to http://example.com/. The key po has as value the rules that state how combinations of predicates and objects are generated (Listing 1, line 9). For example, the rule at Listing 1, line 10 states that the class of every person is foaf:Person. The rule at line 11 states that for every person the value in the JSON attribute firstname is related to a person via the predicate foaf:givenName[4].

3   Matey

YARRRML's Matey is a browser-based IDE[5] for viewing and defining Linked Data generation rules in a YARRRML representation, while the corresponding

---

[4] The prefix foaf is short for http://xmlns.com/foaf/0.1/, as YARRRML by default includes the predefined prefixes of RDFa (see https://www.w3.org/2011/rdfa-context/rdfa-1.1).

[5] https://w3id.org/yarrrml/matey/.

RML rules can be exported. Additionally, the rules can be executed in Matey on a sample of the data, which allows users to inspect the generated Linked Data. Through the use of a YARRRML representation the underlying language's complexity and verbosity are hidden. Although other IDEs and text editors can be used to work with YARRRML, Matey pays special attention to the specific aspects of the rules generation process, such as the samples of the data sources, the generation of the machine-processable generation rules, and the corresponding Linked Data.

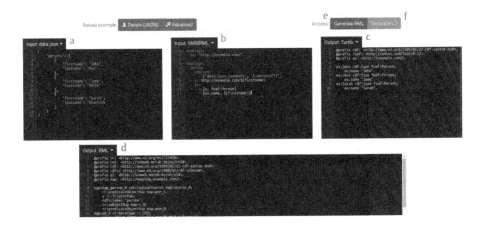

Fig. 1. GUI of Matey

The Graphical User Interface (GUI) of Matey is visible at Fig. 1. It fulfills the seven requirements for GUIs for the creation of Linked Data generation rules we introduced in previous work [5]: is independent of the underlying language (R1) and rule execution (R2); supports multiple data sources (R3), heterogeneous data formats (R4), and multiple ontologies (R5); and enables multiple alternative modeling approaches (R6) and non-linear workflows (R7).

The GUI consists of two rows: the top row contains three panels (the editing area), and the bottom row contains a single panel (the results). Matey's top row follows the RMLEditor's layout [4]. The **top left panel** is an editing area showing a sample of the data sources from which Linked Data is generated (see Fig. 1, a). Multiple data sources can be added through the use of a drop down menu (R3) with data in different formats, such as CSV, JSON, and XML (R4).

The **top middle panel** is an editing area showing the YARRRML representation of the rules (see Fig. 1, b). The representation is independent of RML, the underlying mapping language (R1). It automatically generates the RML rules based on the YARRRML representation, and no restrictions are enforced by the GUI on which and how many ontologies are used (R5).

In the **top right panel**, the resulting Linked Data is shown (see Fig. 1, c).

In the **bottom panel**, the RML rules corresponding with the YARRRML representation are shown (see Fig. 1, d). They can be exported and reused by existing tools supporting such rules (R2). Thanks to the layout of these panels, users can follow different rules creation approaches, such as the data-driven and schema-driven approach [6] (R6). Furthermore, users can inspect the panels, and optionally update their content, independently at any time (R7).

During an example workflow, users add their data in the top left panel and define the rules in the middle panel. Next, either they generate the corresponding RML rules by clicking "Generate RML" (see Fig. 1, e) or they generate Linked Data by clicking "Generate LD" (see Fig. 1, f). During the former, the rules appear in the bottom panel. During the latter, the generated Linked Data appears in the top right panel. In case the Linked Data is not as desired, users update the rules in the middle panel. Once users are satisfied with the rules, they export them as YARRRML and RML rules via their respective panels.

During the demo participants will be able to have a hands-on experience with Matey. They will be able to define their own rules on their own data. Matey is publicly available at https://w3id.org/yarrrml/matey/ and a screencast is available at https://w3id.org/yarrrml/matey/screencast. The demo showcases – next to manually defining machine-processable rules and using a graphical tool – a textual human-friendly alternative to understanding and defining rules. The complexity of the machine-processable rules are hidden and remain interoperable with existing tools that use Linked Data generation rules.

References

1. Ben-Kiki, O., Evans, C., Ingerson, B.: YAML Ain't Markup Language (YAML) Version 1.2. Technical report (2009)
2. Das, S., Sundara, S., Cyganiak, R.: R2RML: RDB to RDF mapping language. In: Working Group Recommendation, World Wide Web Consortium (W3C), September 2012
3. Dimou, A., Vander Sande, M., Colpaert, P., Verborgh, R., Mannens, E., Van de Walle, R.: RML: a generic language for integrated RDF mappings of heterogeneous data. In: Proceedings of the 7th Workshop on Linked Data on the Web, vol. 1184 of CEUR Workshop Proceedings (2014)
4. Heyvaert, P., Dimou, A., De Meester, B., Seymoens, T., Herregodts, A.-L., Verborgh, R., Schuurman, D., Mannens, E.: Specification and implementation of mapping rule visualization and editing: MapVOWL and the RMLEditor. In: Science, Services and Agents on the World Wide Web, Web Semantics (2018)
5. Heyvaert, P., Dimou, A., Verborgh, R., Mannens, E., Van de Walle, R.: Towards a uniform user interface for editing mapping definitions. In: Proceedings of the 4th International Workshop on Intelligent Exploration of Semantic Data (IESD 2015). CEUR-WS.org (2015)
6. Heyvaert, P., Dimou, A., Verborgh, R., Mannens, E., Van de Walle, R.: Towards approaches for generating RDF mapping definitions. In: Proceedings of the ISWC 2015 Posters & Demonstrations Track. CEUR Workshop Proceedings (2015)
7. Sicilia, Á., Nemirovski, G., Nolle, A.: Map-On: a web-based editor for visual ontology mapping. Semant. Web 8(6), 969–980 (2017)

Modeling and Reasoning
over Data Licenses

Oleksandra Panasiuk[1(✉)], Simon Steyskal[2,3(✉)], Giray Havur[2,3(✉)],
Anna Fensel[1(✉)], and Sabrina Kirrane[2(✉)]

[1] STI Innsbruck, Department of Computer Science,
University of Innsbruck, Innsbruck, Austria
{oleksandra.panasiuk,anna.fensel}@sti2.at
[2] Vienna University of Economics and Business, Vienna, Austria
{simon.steyskal,giray.havur,sabrina.kirrane}@wu.ac.at
[3] Siemens AG Österreich, Vienna, Austria

Abstract. In this paper, we propose an extension of the Open Digital
Right Language for modeling well-known licenses and propose an approach to automatically check license compatibility.

1 Introduction

Copyright is a legal right, under Intellectual Property law, that enables creators
of artistic works to specify how their work is used and distributed. When it
comes to information available on the Internet there is often a misconception
that public information can be freely copied and downloaded, however creative
works available online are also protected via copyright, irrespective of whether a
license is present or not. In order to support the automatic checking of licenses,
it is necessary to model licenses in a manner such that it is possible to automatically verify if it is permissible to combine and reuse different datasets or software
libraries. When it comes to machine readable licenses, there have been a number of Rights Expression Languages standardisation initiatives (e.g. the Open
Digital Rights Language(ODRL)[1] and the Creative Commons Rights Expression Language (ccREL)[2]). In addition, there have been a number of works that
demonstrate how RDF can be used to represent and reason over licenses [2,4,7].
In this paper, we describe work conducted by the Data Licenses Clearance Center
(DALICC) project[3], which focuses on extending existing vocabularies to enable
modeling and reasoning over well-known license texts. Herein we make the following contributions: (i) we extend ODRL so that it can be used to model several
standard license families (CC, BSD, MIT, BSD, GPL); and we propose a system
to automatically check license compatibility.

---

[1] https://www.w3.org/TR/odrl-model/.
[2] https://www.w3.org/Submission/ccREL/.
[3] https://www.dalicc.net/.

© Springer Nature Switzerland AG 2018
A. Gangemi et al. (Eds.): ESWC 2018 Satellite Events, LNCS 11155, pp. 218–222, 2018.
https://doi.org/10.1007/978-3-319-98192-5_41

2   Related Work

Rights Expression Languages (RELs) are used to explicate machine-readable rights for purposes of Digital Asset Management. Among the most prominent REL vocabularies are ccREL (which is a W3C member submission) and ODRL (a W3C recommendation from February 2018), and a derivative RightsML[4]. Besides standardization other work includes: an OWL ontology that can be used to describe the copyright domain [2], a framework for adding licensing terms to web data [7] and a license composition tool for derivative works [4].

3   License Modeling

An example output from our modeling process, which is comprised of three parts: (i) analysis of license text; (ii) defining vocabularies to express licenses; and (iii) deriving modeling and mapping mechanisms, can be seen in *Listing* 1.1.

Analysis of the License Text Representation. For our analysis we selected 14 commonly used licenses, namely: CC BY, CC BY-SA, CC BY-NC, CC BY-ND, CC BY-NC-ND, CC BY-NC-SA, APACHE, BSD-2, BSD-3, GNU GPL-2, GNU GPL-3, APGL, LGPL and MIT, which can be applied to the different assets, such as creative works, software and datasets. From the text representation we identified important concepts, requirements, and conflicts between licenses.

Defining Vocabularies. Based on research conducted on the genealogy of RELs [5] we chose ODRL as it is particularly suitable for modeling licenses in the form of *policies*. The *policy* expresses *permissions*, *prohibitions* and *duties* related to the usage of *assets* (e.g. actions `odrl:reproduce`, `odrl:distribute` can be applied to the target "Image"). To represent the main asset targets we used the Dublin Core vocabulary[5], which covers such concepts as: software, dataset, sound, text and image. Furthermore, the ODRL vocabulary includes terms that are depreciated by terms from ccREL (e.g. `odrl:commercialize` by `cc:CommercialUse`) or are supplemented by terms from ccREL (e.g. `cc:Notice` to capture copyright information). However, given that together the ODRL and ccREL vocabularies are not able to represent all of the necessary license concepts, we constructed a DALICC vocabulary[6] in order to fill this gap (e.g. `dalicc:perpetual` as a validity period of the license, `dalicc:worldwide` as a juris- dictional property, `dalicc:modificationNotice` as an action to state changes, see in *Listing* 1.1).

Modeling and Mapping Mechanisms. When it comes to modeling licenses, we use provenance to model information about assets (e.g. `odrl:target`

---

[4] https://iptc.org/standards/rightsml/.
[5] http://dublincore.org/documents/dcmi-type-vocabulary/.
[6] https://dalicc.poolparty.biz/DALICCVocabulary.

dct:Software) and additional information about the license (e.g.cc:jurisdiction dalicc:worldwide) and ODRL rules to represent common licensing conditions divided into three categories: permissions, duties and prohibitions. An RDF representation of the APACHE 2.0 license[7] is shown *Listing* 1.1. The license permits redistribution, reproduction, modification, public presentation of the asset, commercial use, charging a distribution fee, creation of a new derivative, distribution and changing the license for a derivative work, but prohibits the charge of a licensing fee. The license requires the user to post a notice of the type of license, to give attribution to the creator and to state changes.

Listing 1.1. Excerpt RDF serialisation of the APACHE 2.0 license

```
[...]
:APACHE_v2 a odrl:Set ;
   odrl:permission [
      a odrl:Permission ;
   odrl:target dct:Software ;
   odrl:action odrl:distribute, odrl:reproduce, odrl:modify, odrl:present,
         cc:CommercialUse, dalicc:chargeDistributionFee, odrl:derive,
         cc:DerivativeWorks, odrl:grantUse ;
   odrl:duty [
            a odrl:Duty ;
            odrl:action cc:Notice, cc:Attribution, dalicc:modificationNotice ]] ;
   odrl:prohibition [
      a odrl:Prohibition ;
      odrl:target <http://purl.org/dc/dcmitype/Software> ;
      odrl:action dalicc:chargeLicenseFee] ;
   dalicc:validityType dalicc:perpetual ;
   cc:jurisdiction dalicc:worldwide ;
   dct:title "Apache License , Version 2.0"@en ;
[...]
```

4   Verifying License Compatibility

The license compatibility check is performed by a reasoning engine, which uses Answer Set Programming (ASP) [1], a declarative knowledge representation and reasoning formalism that is supported by a wide range of efficient solvers. An ASP program consists of rules: $Head \leftarrow A_1, ..., A_m, not\ A_{m+1}, ..., not\ A_n$ where $m, n \geq 0$, $Head$ and each A_i are atoms. A rule is called a *fact* if $m = n = 0$. Sets of rules are evaluated in ASP under the stable-model semantics which allows several models, i.e. "answer sets" [1]. We use the CLINGO [3] ASP solver for our experiments, as it is one of the most efficient implementations available.

Licences should be understood as a set of rules derived from the RDF graphs of the licenses. Herein, a rule that permits or prohibits the execution of an action on certain assets does not only affect other rules that govern the execution of the same action on the same asset(s) but also those permitting or prohibiting related actions on the same asset(s). DALICC utilises a dependency graph for representing the semantic relationship between defined actions (cf., Listing 1.2). The function of this graph is to encode expert knowledge on the implicit and explicit dependencies between actions. Following the work of

---

[7] http://www.apache.org/licenses/LICENSE-2.0.

Steyskal and Polleres [6], the corresponding dependency graph represents hierarchical relationships (e.g., present *includes* display), implications derived from a specific action (e.g., share *implies* distribute), equalities (e.g., copy *equals* reproduce), and contradictions between specific actions (e.g., non-derivative *contradicts* derivative).

Listing 1.2. ASP encoding of an excerpt of DALICC's dependency graph

```
[...]
action(odrl_display;odrl_present;odrl_reproduce;odrl_derive).
includedIn(odrl_display,odrl_present).
[...]
```

In order to verify license compatibility, the RDF representation of the licenses are first translated into an ASP program as follows: (i) `rule`(l, c, i, α, t), a rule in a licence l of category c (i.e. permission, prohibition or duty) is granted to an assignee i for executing an action α on the asset t; (ii) `action`(α), α is an action; (iii) `sameAs`(α_1, α_2), α_1 and α_2 are the same action; (iv) `includedIn`(α_1, α_2), action α_1 is included in action α_2; (v) `implies`(α_1, α_2), action α_1 implies action α_2.

Our ASP program returns an answer set that consists of the predicate `conflict`$(rule_1(l_1, c_1, i_1, \alpha_1, t_1), rule_2(l_2, c_2, i_2, \alpha_2, t_2))$ which means $rule_1$ is in conflict with $rule_2$ (i.e., l_1 does not comply with l_2). In ODRL, if an action α_1 is included in or equal to another action α_2 (α_1 `odrl:includedIn|owl:sameAs` α_2), all the rules defined for α_2 must also hold for α_1 and vice versa. Moreover, if an action α_1 implies another action α_2 (α_1 `odrl:implies` α_2), a prohibition of α_2 conflicts a permission of α_1 (but not necessarily vice versa).

An extended version of this program is – given multiple licenses as input – capable of finding all non conflicting sets of permissions, prohibitions, and duties of those licenses. These reasoning functionalities are accessed via an UI in a web service.

5 Conclusion

In this paper, we discussed how well-know licenses can be modeled using ODRL. We analyzed 14 licenses in total and extended existing vocabularies so that we can both model and check the compatibility of licenses automatically.

Acknowledgments. Funded by the Austrian Federal Ministry of Transport, Innovation and Technology (BMVIT) DALICC project https://www.dalicc.net.

References

1. Brewka, G., Eiter, T., Truszczyński, M.: Answer set programming at a glance. Commun. ACM **54**(12), 92–103 (2011)
2. García, R., Gil, R.: Copyright licenses reasoning using an OWL-DL ontology. Law Ontol. Semant. Web Channelling Legal Inf. Flood **188**, 145–162 (2009)
3. Gebser, M., Kaminski, R., Kaufmann, B., Schaub, T.: Clingo = asp+ control: extended report (2014)

4. Governatori, G., Lam, H.-P., Rotolo, A., Villata, S., Atemezing, G.A., Gandon, F.L.: Live: a tool for checking licenses compatibility between vocabularies and data. In International Semantic Web Conference (2014)
5. Pellegrini, T., et al.: A genealogy and classification of rights expression languages - preliminary results. In: Data Protection/LegalTech - Proceedings of the 21st International Legal Informatics Symposium IRIS 2018, pp. 243–250 (2018)
6. Steyskal, S., Polleres, A.: Towards formal semantics for ODRL policies. In: Bassiliades, N., Gottlob, G., Sadri, F., Paschke, A., Roman, D. (eds.) RuleML 2015. LNCS, vol. 9202, pp. 360–375. Springer, Cham (2015). https://doi.org/10.1007/978-3-319-21542-6_23
7. Villata, S., Gandon, S.: Licenses compatibility and composition in the web of data. In: Third International Workshop on Consuming Linked Data (2012)

PhD Symposium Track

Recommending Spatial Classes for Entity Interlinking in the Web of Data

Vasilis Kopsachilis$^{(\boxtimes)}$ (iD)

University of Aegean, Mytilene, Greece
vkopsachilis@geo.aegean.gr

Abstract. Recent advances in the web informatics domain bring closer the realization of Web of Data, a global interconnected data space where richer entity descriptions are easily retrievable and reusable. A key Web of Data component is the establishment of links between related entities. Link Discovery tools can be utilized for the (semi) automatic identification and linkage of related entities between a pair of entity sets. However, they require the manual examination and selection of Web of Data datasets (or sub parts of them) that will be used for link establishment. This research focuses on proposing automated methods, which search in Web of Data datasets and recommend pairs of classes that may contain related entities and thus can be used as input in Link Discovery tools. We approach the problem from a geographical perspective by exploiting the spatial information of classes i.e. the location of their instances. We intuitively believe that classes that present similar spatial distribution is likely to contain related entities. To achieve scalability at web scale, we study and implement spatial summarization methods that capture the spatial distribution of each class. To identify relevant classes, we investigate and propose techniques that act on the summaries to compute their similarity. We (a) evaluate two aspects of our methodology, namely the ability of identifying relevant classes effectively and performing at web scale efficiently and (b) compare our approach with other state of the art dataset recommendation for interlinking approaches.

Keywords: Web of Data · Spatial data · Dataset recommendation
Entity interlinking

1 Introduction

Over the last years many data providers have been publishing their data on the web according to the Linked Data principles [1] weaving the Web of Data, a global entity-centric data space where entities across the web are more discoverable and easier reusable [2]. A fundamental prerequisite for the realization of the Web of Data is the establishment of links between, dispersed across different datasets, entities for which a kind of relation is hold (e.g. they refer to the same real world object). Towards the goal of link establishment, Linked Data best practices suggest data providers to apply to their data Link Discovery methodologies, implemented by tools such as SILK [3] or LIMES [4]. Link Discovery refers to the process of identifying and interlinking related entities between two (or more) given datasets (or more abstractly entity sets) [5].

© Springer Nature Switzerland AG 2018
A. Gangemi et al. (Eds.): ESWC 2018 Satellite Events, LNCS 11155, pp. 225–239, 2018.
https://doi.org/10.1007/978-3-319-98192-5_42

A preprocessing step in the Link Discovery workflow requires data providers to provide as input a pair of entity sets that will be used for link establishment. Therefore, data providers should have prior knowledge of the available in the Web of Data datasets and their sub parts that may contain related entities. This PhD focuses on this preprocessing step of Link Discovery workflow, i.e. the identification of Web of Data datasets and sub parts of them that may contain related entities for interlinking. The identified entity sets can be then used as input in Link Discovery tools.

Several works give insights about the Web of Data size and connectivity status. The last version of LOD cloud diagram [6], created in 2017, was including 1.163 datasets. LODStats [7], in order to generate Web of Data statistics, parsed about 3.000 datasets containing in total approximately 50 million entities. A deeper Web of Data analysis [8] reveals that 44% of datasets do not contains links to other datasets. Furthermore, only a small number of datasets is highly linked while the majority is only sparsely linked [9]. Data providers tend to link their datasets with well-known datasets (such as DBpedia or GeoNames) and ignore less well known datasets which may also contain related entities for interlinking [10]. As [11] points linkage with popular datasets is favored because of two main reasons: (i) the difficulty in finding related datasets; and (ii) the strenuous task of discovering instance mappings between different datasets. Data providers can look up for relevant datasets by examining the LOD cloud diagram, which provides an overview of the datasets domain and connectivity, or by querying dataset catalogs, such as datahub.io,[1] which preserve user submitted datasets metadata. However, since Web of Data is continuously expanding (LOD cloud reports a 294% increase in the number of the LOD cloud diagram datasets during the period 2011–2017 [9]) the task of manual examining and selecting datasets that can be used for entity linking will become even more challenging. In this work, we argue that data providers will benefit from automating the process of examining datasets and their contents for interlinking.

Recently, methodologies that automatically recommend datasets for entity interlinking have been proposed. They adopt techniques which mainly exploit dataset's instance/schema keywords [10], graph structure [12] or existing links [11] in order to determine the relevancy of datasets for interlinking. Even though a significant number of Web of Data entities are geo-located, to the best of our knowledge, no approach so far makes use of the spatial information available in datasets to recommend relevant datasets for interlinking. According to [8], W3C BasicGeo vocabulary,[2] one of the most well-known spatial vocabularies, is used for assigning coordinates to entities in more than 25% of datasets. In this work, we introduce the exploitation of the spatial information available in datasets for recommending relevant classes for entity interlinking and we examine how geographic approaches can contribute to the problem. We are based on the hypothesis that entity sets (classes) which contain entities that present similar spatial distribution is likely to contain related entities. We argue that comparing the spatial distribution of classes can be identify relevant classes effectively and additionally can reveal relations that cannot be captured by other approaches.

---

[1] http://datahub.io/.

[2] https://www.w3.org/2003/01/geo/.

For example, it can reveal the topological relation of two, at first sight irrelevant, "Airports" and "Weather Stations" classes. Since many weather stations are located inside airport premises, a data provider might find useful to connect weather stations and their associating airports by a "LocatedIn" relation. Other cases where a geographical approach might be proved useful includes the comparison of datasets that use different languages, schemas or labels to describe related entities.

The goal of our research is to facilitate data providers in the process of discovering Web of Data spatial datasets and classes which may contain related entities with their spatial data. Data providers can then enrich their data by establishing entity links with the identified datasets. Driven by that motivation, we study and propose spatial dataset and class recommendation for entity interlinking methods. Proposed methods will be integrated in a tool that, given as input a spatial entity set, will automatically return a list of Web of Data datasets and their classes that may contain related entities. To fulfill this goal, we firstly parse available in the Web of Data datasets and extract their spatial classes i.e. classes that contain geo-located entities, represented as points. Since the goal of our methodology is to operate at web scale, rather than capturing the actual locations (points) of entities, we propose summarization techniques that capture the spatial distribution of each class. Finally, we apply methods that compare the spatial distributions of the classes in order to identify relevant spatial classes for entity interlinking. In this paper, we also describe our initial experiments that show that our approach can be effective in recommending relevant spatial classes for entity interlinking.

2   State of the Art

Our research addresses the dataset recommendation for entity interlinking problem, which aims at the discovery of Web of Data datasets (or subparts of them) that may contain related entities so as to be used by link discovery methodologies. Typically, the input in dataset recommendation methodologies is a source dataset that is compared against a set of target datasets. The outcome is a (usually ranked) list of relevant (with the source dataset) datasets from the set of target datasets. We identify three main approaches in the existing literature, based on the source of evidence that is used for determining dataset relevancy: (a) keyword based (b) graph based and (c) linkage based approaches. Keyword based approaches measure the string similarity of instance/ schema information between datasets. [13] identifies an initial set of candidate datasets by issuing, relevant to the input dataset, keyword queries to a semantic web index (Sigma). Then, they rank the initial set of candidate datasets by applying ontology matching techniques that assess the semantic similarity between classes (e.g. string similarity of labels, semantic relations defined in WordNet etc.). Similarly to our approach, they recommend relevant classes for entity interlinking. [14] adopts dataset profiling techniques for characterizing datasets through a set of class labels and they use these profiles to identify schema overlap between datasets. Initially, they identify a cluster of datasets that share schema classes with a given dataset by the help of a semantico-frequential similarity measure. Then, for each dataset in the identified cluster they compute a dataset relevancy ranking score based on tf*idf cosine similarity. As an additional contribution, their method also returns the mappings between the schema classes across datasets. A dataset recommendation tool, called DRX, which is also based on dataset profiles, was proposed in [15]. Other keyword based methodologies were proposed in [16, 17]. Graph based approaches compare the similarity of datasets ontology graphs to determine whether two datasets contain related entities. For example, [12] combine Frequent Subgraph Mining techniques to find similarities among datasets. Their approach built on the assumption that "similar datasets should have a similar structure and include semantically similar resources and relationships". They extract frequent subgraphs from RDF datasets and then evaluate the cost of transforming one graph to another. The lower the cost the higher the probability that the two datasets are relevant. Linkage based approaches recommend relevant datasets by using as source of evidence existing links between datasets. [11] develops a Bayesian classifier for ranking datasets according to the probability to define links between URIs of two datasets. The technique uses as evidence of relevance metadata about existing links between all catalogued datasets. [18] uses ranking techniques from social networks for link prediction; the estimation of the likelihood of the existence of an edge between two nodes is based on the already existing links and on the attributes of the nodes. A similar methodology, based on link prediction techniques, was proposed in [19]. We should note that often methodologies use a combination of the above described approaches. For example in [13], additionally to string similarity metrics, they also exploit existing sameAs relations between datasets to determine their relevancy. As pointed earlier, our work is the first that deals with the dataset recommendation for interlinking problem by using as evidence of relevance datasets spatial information.

Another research domain that is closely related to our work is that of dataset summarization. Since capturing analytical information for all Web of Data entities is impractical, Dataset Recommenders usually calculate dataset relevancy based on summarized descriptions of datasets. Dataset profiling is the task of generating a summarized description of a dataset using a set of dataset characteristics [20]. They sketch a taxonomy that discriminates dataset profiles approaches depending on the dataset characteristic they describe. They point that approaches that describe dataset's Domain/Topic [15, 21, 22], Contextual Connectivity [23, 24] or Index/Representative elements [14, 25, 26] can be used for the dataset recommendation for entity interlinking problem. Nevertheless, most works on dataset profiling focus on the profile generation task and do not provide methods for comparing the similarity between dataset profiles. In the geospatial domain, [27] present and compare summarization techniques, distinguished as geometric, space partitioning and hybrid approaches for describing the geographical footprints of point datasets. These summaries are used for answering range and kNN queries. [28] proposes 27 spatial statistics metrics to describe the spatial distribution of feature types and evaluate their discriminative power for the identification of similar feature types. These statistics calculate spatial point patterns (e.g. local intensity, Ripley's K), spatial autocorrelation (e.g. Moran's I) and spatial interactions with other geographic feature types (e.g. count of distinct nearest feature types). However, as they state, these statistics are mostly descriptive and cannot be used in isolation for effective feature type similarity.

A third related research domain is that of point set similarity which refers to the calculation of a similarity score between two sets of points. In [29] some well know point set distance measures such as Mean, Max, Average, Link and Hausdorff distance are compared regarding their effectiveness for link discovery. These measures calculate the distance between two point sets (in their work a point set represent the vector geometry of an entity) based on the actual point locations and not on summarized descriptions of point sets. [30] applies modified Hausdorff distance measures on Minimum Bound Rectangle (MBR)-based point set summarizations to efficiently cal- culate similarity on large collections of point sets. Other approaches apply point set similarity techniques to identify similar social network users based on the locations of their activities. [31] proposes and evaluate two distance measures for finding the k-most similar users of a given one: the mutually nearest distance and a QuadTree-based. [32] introduces the Spatio-Textual Point-Set Similarity Join (STPSJoin) query: Given sets of Spatio-Textual objects, each one belonging to a specific type, this query seeks pairs of types that have similar Spatio-Textual objects. Their similarity algorithm uses a similar to Jaccard coefficient metric to measure the overlap of grid based indexed point sets. In this PhD, we examine the applicability of point set similarity methods to the dataset recommendation for entity interlinking problem.

3 Problem Statements and Contributions

The problem of dataset recommendation for entity interlinking can be formulated as follows: Given a source dataset (S) and a set of target datasets (T), identify those $Ti \in T$ which may contain related entities for interlinking with S. We intent to contribute to that problem by exploiting the spatial information available in datasets. We extract the spatial classes from each dataset i.e. classes that contain instances for which their geographic location is available, and we compare them to identify the relevant ones for interlinking. We note that we focus on classes which contain instances whose locations are represented as points, excluding thus more complex geometry representations such as lines and polygons. Then, we reformulate the problem: Given a source spatial class (S) and a set of target spatial classes (T), identify those $Ti \in T$ which may contain related entities for interlinking with S.

Since this work is the first that exploit the geospatial characteristics of datasets in order to recommend the relevant classes for interlinking, the central research query of this PhD is "How the spatial information of classes can be used for the effective identification of classes that may contain related entities for interlinking". We capture and compare the spatial distribution of classes i.e. the set of the entities' locations which are contained in a class. Our main hypothesis is that "Classes that present similar spatial distribution contain related entities for interlinking". In order to answer our main research question and validate our hypothesis we have to answer the following two questions:

Q1: How to effectively and efficiently summarize the spatial distribution of a spatial class. The goal of our work is to recommend relevant spatial classes for entity interlinking at web scale. A naïve approach would be to capture and operate on the actual entity locations. However, at this scale this seems inefficient and impractical. We, therefore, need to operate on more abstract spatial classes characteristics, like descriptions of the spatial distribution of their entities. We study and evaluate spatial summarization techniques, such as MBRs, spatial indexes and histograms, for their applicability in the dataset recommendation for entity interlinking problem. Proposed spatial summaries should be: (a) effective; the description of a class spatial distribution is accurate and (b) efficient; summary creation, storage and maintenance costs are low.

Q2: How to compare spatial summaries to effectively determine class relevancy for interlinking. We need metrics that will be applied on the spatial summaries to identify classes that contain related entities. To answer this question we study and evaluate set similarity, distance and probability theory metrics. The proposed metrics should effectively (a) identify the relevant pairs of classes and (b) rule out the irrelevant classes.

In this research, we argue that our geographical approach may reveal relations between classes that other dataset recommendation for entity interlinking approaches could not identify. For instance, it may identify classes that contain non sameAs but topologically related entities (e.g. Libraries and Universities) or classes that contain sameAs entities described in different languages. Therefore, an additional research question that we target is "Whether a geographical approach can contribute to the dataset recommendation for entity interlinking problem by capturing kinds of relations between datasets that other approaches could not identify". An affirmative answer would be an indication that geographic approaches can be used in combination with other approaches for increasing dataset recommendation for entity interlinking methodologies effectiveness.

The main contributions of this PhD to the research community are:

- We introduce the exploitation of spatial information for recommending Web of Data datasets and classes for entity interlinking and we examine how a geographic approach contributes to the problem
- We propose spatial summarizations techniques and metrics for identifying datasets and classes that may contain related entities
- We provide an easy to use online tool to data providers for the automated and quick discovery of spatial datasets and classes that may contain related entities, facilitating them in the Link Discovery process.

4   Research Methodology and Approach

Our overall methodology is mainly divided in five parts: (a) spatial class collection (b) spatial summaries creation and (c) metrics development (d) matching algorithm and (e) online tool implementation, which are described below.

4.1   Spatial Class Collection

In the first part we identify and collect available Web of Data spatial classes. Collected spatial classes form our basis (database) for the rest parts of our research. Spatial classes are identified and collected automatically according to the following steps:

1. List Web of Data datasets that are provided via a SPARQL Endpoint or as an RDF dump. We acquire this information by automatically parsing CKAN based data catalogs, such as datahub.io. After the execution of this step, we have collected some basic metadata about Web of Data datasets like their name and online resource (e.g. SPARQL Endpoint URL).

2. Identify spatial datasets. Spatial datasets contain spatial entities i.e. entities for which their geographic location, in the form of coordinates, is available. The geographic location of entities is typically described with the use of spatial ontologies. Some well-known spatial ontologies, listed in LOV[3] and LOV4IoT,[4] are W3C Basic Geo, NeoGeo,[5] GeoSPARQL,[6] OrdnanceSurvey,[7] GeoNames[8] and GeoRSS.[9] To identify spatial datasets we issue queries directly to datasets' online resources to check whether they use one of the well-known spatial ontologies. For example, the SPARQL query "ASK {?s <http://www.georss.org/georss/point> ?o}" asks an endpoint whether it uses the point predicate of the GeoRSS ontology. We ask datasets in similar fashion for the remaining spatial ontologies listed above. In this step, we preserve in our database only the detected spatial datasets along with the spatial ontologies that they use. We remind that, as we stated in Sect. 3, we collect only datasets that contain point spatial entities and use the WGS84 coordinate reference system.

3. Identify datasets spatial classes. A dataset may contain one or more classes. Each class contains entities (defined at instance level by the predicate rdf:type) that may be or not spatial. A spatial class is a class that contains spatial entities. Since non spatial classes are irrelevant for our methodology, we maintain only the spatial classes from each dataset. We issue queries directly to datasets online resources to get the list of classes that contain spatial entities using the ontologies that were identified in step 2. For example, the query "SELECT DISTINCT ?class WHERE {?s <http://www.georss.org/georss/point> ?o. ?s <rdf:type> ?class}" returns the list of the dataset's classes that contain entities that use the GeoRSS ontology. To rule out classes that contain very few spatial entities we maintain only those classes that contain 5 or more spatial entities.

---

[3] http://lov.okfn.org.

[4] http://lov4iot.appspot.com/?p=ontologies.

[5] http://geovocab.org/.

[6] http://www.geosparql.org/.

[7] http://data.ordnancesurvey.co.uk/ontology.

[8] http://www.geonames.org/ontology/.

[9] http://www.georss.org/rdf_rss1.html.

The output of the spatial class collection is a list of all the identified Web of Data spatial classes. Each spatial class is described by its URI, the dataset it belongs and the spatial ontology it uses.[10]

4.2 Spatial Summaries Creation

In the second part of our research, we create summaries for the collected spatial classes. We study state of the art spatial summarization techniques and evaluate them for their applicability to the dataset recommendation for entity interlinking problem. Geometric approaches, such as Minimum Bounding Rectangle (MBR), summarize point sets by generating one or multiple geometric shapes that enclose all dataset's points [27]. These techniques are relatively cheap to compute and require low storage, however they do not provide rich dataset descriptions. Space Partitioning approaches, such as spatial indexing, segments the data space into cells. A dataset is summarized by the list of the index cells IDs that are occupied by dataset's points [27]. Compared to the Geometric approaches, they are usually more expensive and require more storage space but they provide richer dataset descriptions. As stated in Sect. 3, Q1 is one of our main research questions. In this PhD, we will develop and compare different spatial summarization techniques.

Currently, we are working on an approach that use both MBR and spatial indexes. For each spatial class we compute and maintain its MBR. Also, we summarize the spatial distribution of the classes trying two spatial indexes: (a) a Regular Grid, which partition the global space in equally sized cells (10×10 km) and (b) a QuadTree, which splits space into 4 sub cells recursively according to a criterion (in our case the split criterion is a fixed number of Web of Data spatial entities that occupy a cell, such that high density areas, e.g. city centers, correspond to small sized cells and low density areas, e.g. oceans, correspond to large sized cells). For each indexing method, we use the same index to summarize all spatial classes. For each spatial class, we generate a list of the index cells IDs that intersect with the locations (points) of its entities (we retrieve the entity locations of a class by issuing a SPARQL query to its corresponding endpoint). For example, using the regular grid index (Fig. 1a), the summaries of the triangle and square classes are {2, 8, 9, 11, 14, 15, 16, 20} and {6, 7, 9, 13, 15, 17, 20, 22} respectively. Using the QuadTree index (Fig. 1b), the summaries of the triangle and square classes are {1, 6, 11, 14, 16, 17} and {1, 5, 6, 9, 13, 16, 17, 18} respectively.

The result of this methodology part is that each spatial class is described by its summaries which in our case are its MBR, its Regular Grid-based and its QuadTree-based summary.

---

[10] The SPARQL queries that were used for the spatial classes collection and the list of the collected spatial datasets and classes are available in: https://github.com/vkopsachilis/WoDSpatialClass Recommender.

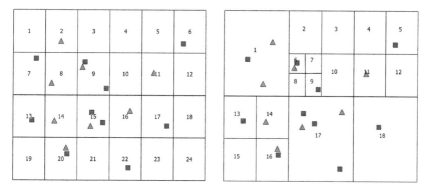

Fig. 1. (a) Regular Grid summarization (b) QuadTree summarization

4.3 Metrics Development

This part refer to the development of metrics that will be applied on the class spatial summaries to compute their similarity. If two classes present similar spatial summaries (which as stated earlier represent classes spatial distributions), then it is likely that they contain related entities for interlinking. Proposed metrics should have the discriminative power to accurately and precisely identify relevant classes. We study and evaluate state of the art metrics from different domains (e.g. set similarity, probability theory) for their suitability to the dataset recommendation problem. For our first experiments (Sect. 5) we adapted and evaluated four metrics. We use the following notation: e represents the total number of the index cells (e.g. QuadTree) contained in a given geographic area; a and b the number of the class A and B summary cells respectively contained in a given geographic area; and c the number of the cells that the two classes have in common. In the example of Fig. 1b, these number would be e = 18, a = 6 (triangles), b = 8 (squares) and c = 4.

- *Jaccard Similarity:* calculates the number of the common cells divided by the size of the union cells of two classes. *JS* returns values between 0 and 1. Values approaching 1 means high similarity while values approaching 0 means low similarity.

$$JS = \frac{c}{a+b-c}$$

- *Overlap Coefficient:* calculates the number of the common cells divided by the cells number of the smallest class summary. *OC* returns values between 0 and 1. Values approaching 1 means high similarity and values approaching 0 means low similarity.

$$OC = \frac{c}{\min(a, b)}$$

- *HyperGeometric Distribution Cumulative Probability:* estimates the probability of existing c or more common cell when class A occupies a cells and class B occupies b cells in a given area covered by e cells. *HG* returns values between 0 and 1.

Low probability values imply that is unlikely for two (random) classes to have c or more common cells, therefore they must be related.

$$P(X \geq c) = \sum_{c}^{min(a,b)} P(X = c) \text{ where } P(X = c) = \frac{\binom{a}{c}\binom{e-a}{b-c}}{\binom{e}{b}}$$

- *Independent Events Probability Ratio:* calculates the ratio of the common cells to the number of the expected common cells (c_{exp}). IR values have no upper limit. High IR values imply that two classes are likely to contain related entities. Expected common cells is the number of the common cells that two classes would have if they were not related (independent). We calculate c_{exp} by adapting the independent event probability formula: the probability for two not related (A and B) classes to have common cells in a given area (c_{exp}/e) is the product of the probabilities of class A (a/e) and class B (b/e) (i.e. the number of cells that a class occupies in a given area).

$$IR = \frac{c}{C_{exp}} \text{ where } C_{exp} = \frac{ab}{e}$$

4.4   Matching Algorithm

The goal of the matching algorithm is to identify spatial classes that may contain related entities and thus are relevant for interlinking. Below, we sketch the execution order of the algorithm:

Input: A source spatial class and a set of target spatial classes (formed by the set of already collected classes in the spatial class collection part). The source class can be selected from the list of the already collected classes or might be a new one. In the latter case, we create the summaries for the new class according to the methodology described in the spatial class summarization part.

1. Filter out as irrelevant, target classes with non-overlapping MBR with the source class in order to identify an initial set of candidate classes.
2. Compare the spatial index summary (e.g. QuadTree-based) of the source class with the respective summary (i.e. QuadTree-based) of each candidate class in the overlapping MBR area by calculating the values of the metrics described in Sect. 4.3.
3. Determine whether the source class is relevant for interlinking with a candidate class by checking if the calculated metrics values for this pair of classes satisfy some criteria e.g. exceed a metric threshold.

Output: A list of the relevant classes for interlinking with the source class. Part of future work is to provide a ranked list of relevant classes.

4.5   Online Tool

The last part of our work refer to the development of an online tool that will be the entry point to the matching algorithm, allowing data providers to easily discovery relevant spatial classes for entity interlinking.

5   Preliminary Results

At this point of our research we have identified and created summaries for about 20700 spatial classes from 57 different datasets provided via SPARQL endpoints. The three datasets that contain the most spatial classes (collected as described in Sect. 4.1) are DBpedia, an online repository of links between Knowledge Bases called LinkLion,[11] and a service that delivers RDF based descriptions of Web addressable resources called URIBurner[12] (15488, 898 and 544 spatial classes respectively).

We conducted a first experiment to assess the effectiveness of the developed spatial summaries and metrics for discovering classes that contain related entities on a randomly selected set of 100 spatial classes. We examined them manually to identify pairs of classes that contain related entities. We found that 20 pairs of classes contain related entities while the rest pairs (4930) are irrelevant for interlinking. We, then applied our matching algorithm using as input each time a different source class and comparing it with the rest sample classes, thus resulting in 100 runs and 4950 pair comparisons in total. For each pair of classes comparison, we calculated all possible metric/summary values (e.g. Jaccard Similarity for Regular Grid summaries, Jaccard Similarity for QuadTree summaries, Overlap Coefficient for Regular Grid summaries and so on) and we manually defined some metrics thresholds to determine whether a pair of class should be returned as relevant for interlinking or not. To assess the effectiveness of the various metric/summary and thresholds combinations we calculated their Recall and Precision for all runs. Recall calculates the number of the correctly identified relevant pairs of classes divided by the number of the total relevant pairs of classes in our sample (that is 20), while precision calculates the number of the correctly identified pairs of classes divided by the number of total identified pairs of classes.[13]

The results of the first experiment showed that the 10×10 km Regular Grid is ineffective (averaging 0.03 precision and 0.71 recall for all the regular gird/metric combinations that we tested) for identifying relevant datasets for interlinking. Of course, using a Regular Grid with smaller sized cells would increase its precision but this would explode storage requirements and computational costs. On the other hand, QuadTree summaries proved effective for identifying relevant classes, since they averaged 0.56 precision and 0.74 recall for all QuadTree/metric combinations that we tested. Concerning the metrics, the HyperGeometric Distribution Cumulative Probability (HG) and Independent Events Probability Ratio (IR) achieved better F-scores

---

[11] http://www.linklion.org/.

[12] http://uriburner.com/.

[13] Sample classes, ground truth pairs of relevant classes and analytical results for the experiments are available in https://github.com/vkopsachilis/WoDSpatialClassRecommender/tree/master/Experiments.

than the Jaccard Similarity (JS) and Overlap Coefficient (OC) metrics for the various thresholds that we tested. The best score for each metric when applied on QuadTree summaries is: HG scored 0.80 recall and 0.51 precision when the threshold set to HG < 0.00001 and IR scored 0.95 recall and 0.54 precision when the threshold set to IR > 5. JS scored 0.20 recall and 1 precision when the threshold set to JS > 0.2 and OC scored 0.80 recall and 0.23 precision when the threshold set to OC > 0.1. The above results indicate that applying HG and IR metrics on QuadTree summaries is the most effective combination that we tested so far for recommending relevant classes for entity interlinking.

We conducted a second experiment using a different sample to confirm the methodology effectiveness. To form our sample we selected 25 classes and we took care to include pairs of relevant classes that belong to different datasets and pairs of relevant classes with different class labels (e.g. "Cathedrals" and "PlaceOfWorship"). In this sample 28 pairs of classes were identified as relevant and the rest 272 pairs as irrelevant. Similar to the first experiment, we applied our matching algorithm using as input a different source class each time and we compare it with the rest sample classes, thus resulting in 25 runs and 300 pairs comparison in total. For each pair of class comparison, we calculated metric values only for QuadTree summaries (since regular grid was proved ineffective) and we used the metrics thresholds from the first experiment. Similarly to the first experiment, we were based on the recall and precision metrics to evaluate the methodology effectiveness. The results of the second experiment confirmed the finding that HG and IR metrics perform better than the JS and OC metrics. HG scored 0.79 recall and 0.58 precision when the threshold set to HG < 0.00001 and IR scored 0.64 recall and 0.95 precision when the threshold set to IR > 5. JS scored 0.07 recall and 1 precision when the threshold set to JS > 0.2 and OC scored 0.71 recall and 0.65 precision when the threshold set to OC > 0.1. The results of our initial experiments indicate that the exploitation of the dataset's spatial information can contribute to the dataset recommendation for entity interlinking problem. Part of this research we will dedicated in the research and development of more effective and efficient summaries and metrics.

6   Evaluation Plan

In the future, we plan to perform more experiments that would enables us to draw safer conclusion regarding the effectiveness of our approach for recommending relevant class for interlinking. For instance, in subsequent experiments we will formulate more unbiased sample class sets by including classes from more datasets and taking into account factors like class size and geographical extent diversity. A method that will return a ranked list of relevant datasets will be integrated and evaluated using appropriate metrics such as Precision@N. Moreover, Data Mining techniques can be used for determining metrics thresholds. As our research evolves, we will be based on a bigger training set of classes that will help in the methodology optimization. Finally, we will compare our approach with other state of the art works, particularly for answering the question of how a spatial approach differentiates, regarding the kind of relations that can identify, from other dataset recommendation for entity interlinking approaches.

7 Conclusion

Our research focuses on recommending Web of Data spatial datasets and classes that can be used for entity interlinking. To achieve this, we propose a methodology that exploits the spatial information available in datasets. We are based on the assumption that classes that present similar spatial distribution is likely to contain related entities. We identify Web of Data spatial classes, we capture their spatial distributions and we compare them to identify the relevant classes for interlinking. Our initial experiments indicate that our spatial approach can contribute to the problem. We continue our research for the development of more effective and efficient summaries and metrics and for drawing conclusions about what kind of insights to the dataset recommendation problem can a spatial approach provide.

Acknowledgements. This research is being completed under the supervision of Ass. Prof. Michail Vaitis and is being supported by the funding program "YPATIA" of University of Aegean.

References

1. Berners-Lee, T.: Linked Data. https://www.w3.org/DesignIssues/LinkedData.html. Accessed 05 Mar 2018
2. Heath, T., Bizer, C.: Linked data: evolving the web into a global data space. In: Synthesis Lectures on the Semantic Web: Theory and Technology. Morgan & Claypool Publishers (2011)
3. Volz, J., Bizer, C., Gaedke, M., Kobilarov, G.: Discovering and maintaining links on the web of data. In: Bernstein, A., et al. (eds.) ISWC 2009. LNCS, vol. 5823, pp. 650–665. Springer, Heidelberg (2009). https://doi.org/10.1007/978-3-642-04930-9_41
4. Ngomo, A.C.N., Auer, S.: LIMES - a time-efficient approach for large-scale link discovery on the web of data. In: Proceedings of the Twenty-Second International Joint Conference on Artificial Intelligence, pp. 2312–2317. AAAI Press (2011)
5. Nentwig, M., Hartung, M., Ngomo, A.C.N., Rahm, E.: A survey of current link discovery frameworks. Semant. Web **8**(3), 419–436 (2017)
6. The Linking Open Data cloud diagram. http://lod-cloud.net/. Accessed 05 Mar 2018
7. LODStats. http://stats.lod2.eu/. Accessed 05 Mar 2018
8. State of the LOD Cloud 2014. http://lod-cloud.net/state/state_2014/. Accessed 05 Mar 2018
9. Schmachtenberg, M., Bizer, C., Paulheim, H.: Adoption of the linked data best practices in different topical domains. In: Mika, P., et al. (eds.) ISWC 2014. LNCS, vol. 8796, pp. 245–260. Springer, Cham (2014). https://doi.org/10.1007/978-3-319-11964-9_16
10. Nikolov, A., D'Aquin, M.: Identifying relevant sources for data linking using a semantic web index. In: Workshop: Linked Data on the Web, WWW 2011 (2011)
11. Leme, L.A.P.P., Lopes, G.R., Nunes, B.P., Casanova, M.A., Dietze, S.: Identifying candidate datasets for data interlinking. In: Daniel, F., Dolog, P., Li, Q. (eds.) ICWE 2013. LNCS, vol. 7977, pp. 354–366. Springer, Heidelberg (2013). https://doi.org/10.1007/978-3-642-39200-9_29
12. Emaldi, M., Corcho, O., López-de-Ipiña, D.: Detection of related semantic datasets based on frequent subgraph mining. In: IESD@ISWC (2015)

13. Nikolov, A., d'Aquin, M., Motta, E.: What should I link to? Identifying relevant sources and classes for data linking. In: Pan, J.Z., et al. (eds.) JIST 2011. LNCS, vol. 7185, pp. 284–299. Springer, Heidelberg (2012). https://doi.org/10.1007/978-3-642-29923-0_19

14. Ben Ellefi, M., Bellahsene, Z., Dietze, S., Todorov, K.: Dataset recommendation for data linking: an intensional approach. In: Sack, H., Blomqvist, E., d'Aquin, M., Ghidini, C., Ponzetto, S.P., Lange, C. (eds.) ESWC 2016. LNCS, vol. 9678, pp. 36–51. Springer, Cham (2016). https://doi.org/10.1007/978-3-319-34129-3_3

15. Arturo, A., Caraballo, M., Nunes, B.P., Casanova, M.A.: DRX: a LOD dataset interlinking recommendation tool (2015)

16. Mehdi, M., Iqbal, A., Hogan, A., Hasnain, A., Khan, Y., Decker, S., Sahay, R.: Discovering domain-specific public SPARQL endpoints: a life-sciences use-case. In: Proceedings of the 18th International Database Engineering and Applications Symposium, pp. 39–45. ACM, New York (2014)

17. Martins, Y.C., da Mota, F.F., Cavalcanti, M.C.: DSCrank: a method for selection and ranking of datasets. In: Garoufallou, E., Subirats Coll, I., Stellato, A., Greenberg, J. (eds.) MTSR 2016. CCIS, vol. 672, pp. 333–344. Springer, Cham (2016). https://doi.org/10.1007/978-3-319-49157-8_29

18. Lopes, G.R., Leme, L.A.P.P., Nunes, B.P., Casanova, M.A., Dietze, S.: Recommending tripleset interlinking through a social network approach. In: Lin, X., Manolopoulos, Y., Srivastava, D., Huang, G. (eds.) WISE 2013. LNCS, vol. 8180, pp. 149–161. Springer, Heidelberg (2013). https://doi.org/10.1007/978-3-642-41230-1_13

19. Liu, H., Wang, T., Tang, J., Ning, H., Wei D.: Link prediction of datasets sameAS interlinking network on web of data. In: 3rd International Conference on Information Management (2017)

20. Ben Ellefi, M., Bellahsene, Z., Breslin, J.G., Demidova, E., Dietze, S., Szymaski, J., Todorov, K.: RDF dataset profiling - a survey of features, methods, vocabularies and applications. Semant. Web J. (2017)

21. Lalithsena, S., Hitzler, P., Sheth, A., Jain, P.: Automatic domain identification for linked open data. In: 2013 IEEE/WIC/ACM International Joint Conferences on Web Intelligence (WI) and Intelligent Agent Technologies (IAT) (2013)

22. Fetahu, B., Dietze, S., Nunes, B.P., Taibi, D., Casanova, M.A.: Generating structured profiles of linked data graphs. In: Proceedings of the 12th International Semantic Web Conference (ISWC). Springer (2013)

23. Mountantonakis, M., et al.: Extending VoID for expressing connectivity metrics of a semantic warehouse. In: 1st International Workshop on Dataset Profiling and Federated Search for Linked Data (2014)

24. Wagner, A., Haase, P., Rettinger, A., Lamm, H.: Entity-based data source contextualization for searching the web of data. In: Presutti, V., Blomqvist, E., Troncy, R., Sack, H., Papadakis, I., Tordai, A. (eds.) ESWC 2014. LNCS, vol. 8798, pp. 25–41. Springer, Cham (2014). https://doi.org/10.1007/978-3-319-11955-7_3

25. Böhm, C., Lorey, J., Naumann, F.: Creating VoID descriptions for web-scale data. J. Web Semant. 9(3), 339–345 (2011)

26. Hasnain, A., Zainab, S., Hasnain, A., Hogan, A.: SPORTAL: profiling the content of public SPARQL endpoints. Int. J. Semant. Web Inf. Syst. 12(3), 134–163 (2016)

27. Kufer, S., Henrich, A.: Hybrid quantized resource descriptions for geospatial source selection. In: International Conference on Information and Knowledge Management, pp. 17–24 (2014)

28. Zhu, R., Hu, Y., Janowicz, K., McKenzie, G.: Spatial signatures for geographic feature types: examining gazetteer ontologies using spatial statistics. Trans. GIS 20(3), 333–355 (2016)

29. Sherif, M.A., Ngomo, A.N.: A systematic survey of point set distance measures for link discovery. Semant. Web **1**(2013), 1–5 (2014)
30. Adelfio, M.D., Nutanong, S., Samet, H.: Similarity search on a large collection of point sets. In: Proceedings of the 19th ACM SIGSPATIAL International Conference on Advances in Geographic Information Systems - GIS 2011, pp. 132–141 (2011)
31. Kanza, Y., Kravi, E., Safra, E., Sagiv, Y.: Location-based distance measures for geosocial similarity. ACM Trans. Web **11**(3). (2014)
32. Efstathiades, C., Belesiotis, A., Skoutas, D., Pfoser, D.: Similarity search on spatio-textual point sets. In: 19th International Conference on Extending Database Technology (2016)

Ontology ABox Comparison

Jan Martin Keil[(✉)] [iD]

Heinz Nixdorf Chair for Distributed Information Systems,
Institute for Computer Science, Friedrich Schiller University Jena, Jena, Germany
jan-martin.keil@uni-jena.de

Abstract. Correctness and completeness of facts are relevant criteria
for the evaluation and selection of ontologies. They can be determined
through the comparison with a gold standard. But a gold standard is usually not available. Hence, we propose to determine these criteria through
the comparison of ontology ABoxes. However, the comparison of ontology ABoxes is only rarely addressed in the literature. We aim to identify
appropriate methods and criteria for the semi-automatic comparison of
the ABox of ontologies. They will be integrated into an ontology comparison framework. This framework will provide novel opportunities to
assess and improve the correctness and completeness of ontologies.

Keywords: Ontology ABox · Ontology comparison
Ontology evaluation · Ontology quality · Ontology selection

1 Introduction

Ontologies can provide domain knowledge in various applications. The accuracy
of the provided knowledge is important for their faultless operation. Ideally, an
ontology has been carefully evaluated before its employment. The correctness
and completeness of facts are relevant criteria for the evaluation and selection
[1,2]. For example, before using an ontology of measurement units in a data
transformation application, the correctness of conversion factors and the wide
coverage of units should have been evaluated by the ontology developer or the
user. The further rise of knowledge available in ontologies [3] increasingly compli-
cates the determination of correctness and completeness. The manual review of
large ontologies is possible only at great expense. Hence, automation is required.

Earlier research provided methods to verify the inferential consistency [4]
or the compliance with given constraints [1]. However, an inferential consistent
and constraint compliant ontology is not necessarily in line with the real world.
Therefore, an additional method is required to complement existing methods for
the evaluation of ABox rich ontologies. To verify correctness and completeness,
modeled facts must be compared to actual facts. As it is impossible to directly
compare the facts with the real world, a trusted data source representing the
real world is required. An ontology could be automatically compared with this

---

The original version of this chapter was revised: this chapter was previously published
non-open access. The correction to this chapter is available at
https://doi.org/10.1007/978-3-319-98192-5_62

A. Gangemi et al. (Eds.): ESWC 2018 Satellite Events, LNCS 11155, pp. 240–250, 2018.
https://doi.org/10.1007/978-3-319-98192-5_43

data source to determine the correctness and completeness of facts. However, the aim of building an ontology is to create such a trusted data source. Therefore, it seems unlikely to having another trusted data source available.

Alternatively, multiple ontologies of the same domain could be compared to each other. Even if they have only a partial overlap, a comparison can provide valuable information about the correctness and completeness. As the number of available ontologies is continuously increasing, the existence of several ontologies of the same domain is becoming more likely. For example, several ontologies provide knowledge about measurement units [5]. To select the most appropriate ontology for the application at hand, all of them have to be analyzed anyway. Thus, the additional effort during the ontology selection is low. However, methods for comparing the facts in ontologies have not previously been investigated.

To fill this gap, we aim to identify appropriate methods and criteria for the semi-automatic comparison of the ABox of ontologies. Moreover, we will provide a framework implementing these methods. In the remainder of this article we will summarize the state of the art in Sect. 2, formulate the problem in Sect. 3, present our approach in Sect. 4, present preliminary results in Sect. 5, and describe the evaluation plan in Sect. 6.

2   State of the Art

The term *comparison* is ambiguously used in the context of ontologies and semantic web technologies. We will use the term to describe (a) the comparison of entire ontologies regarding certain aspects to evaluate or select ontologies. This is in contrast to other notions of the term to describe (b) the comparison of different versions of one ontology to highlight changes [6], (c) the comparison of single entities or sets of entities to calculate recommendations of entities [7–9], or (d) the calculation of the similarity of single or a few entities from different ontologies to match or merge these ontologies [10–12].

Visser et al. [13] compared four law ontologies regarding the dimensions *epistemological adequacy*, *operationality*, and *reusability*. The criteria for adequacy included the *epistemological completeness*. However, they concluded that the assessment of the completeness is difficult due to the lack of a gold standard.

Botke et al. [14] compared two ontologies regarding their expressive power. To achieve this, they tested if the ontologies can be expressed using the other ontology. An ontology is more powerful if it can express the other ontology, but not vice versa.

Xue et al. [10] proposed an algorithm to calculate the similarity of trees, which could be used to compare ontologies. They focused on the application of their algorithm for ontology integration. Beside that, they claimed that it can be used to evaluate ontologies: An ontology is considered more trustworthy, if it is more similar to other domain ontologies.

Blázquez et al. [15] presented an approach to compare three hydrographical ontologies. The criteria mainly focus on the ontology development process and used data sources that could justify trust into an ontology.

Kretz et al. [16] described a system to select, compare and align ontologies. The comparison is based on observational, structural, functional, processing time, usability, and domain relevance criteria. They named some example criteria without further explanation. Most of these criteria have been described in [17]. Further, the system generates additional candidate ontologies by combining two candidate ontologies. The selection of combination pairs is based on the similarity of the ontologies which is calculated using the confidence of matches between contained entities.

Steinberg et al. [18] compared the schemata of seven unit ontologies based on a set of 16 use cases. A metric was developed to measure the suitability of an ontology with respect to those use cases.

Katsumi et al. [19] designed a procedure to compare candidate ontologies for reuse. The comparison is based on competency questions that specify the intended models of an ontology. They state, that it is easier to address errors of omitted models than superfluous models. Therefore, an ontology is preferred for reuse if it omits the fewest intended models and has no superfluous models.

Färber et al. [20] provided an extensive comparison of DBpedia, Freebase, OpenCyc, Wikidata, and YAGO. They applied 34 metrics covering eleven data quality dimensions like accuracy, consistency, completeness, and accessibility. This included metrics for *semantic validity of triples*, *population completeness*, and *column completeness*. *Semantic validity of triples* is the proportion of correct triples compared to a gold standard. Due to the lack of a comprehensive gold standard the evaluation of the semantic validity of triples remains "very challenging" and it is hard to reveal meaningful differences. Therefore they proposed to use test cases [1] to check the semantic validity of triples, although this would not detect all wrong values. *Population completeness* is the coverage of a basic population, which is defined by a gold standard. *Column completeness* is the proportion of the individuals of a class that have a property that is dedicated to this class. Due to properties that do not apply for each individual of the class (e.g., :hasChild), they only used a subset of the properties.

The metric for *column completeness* in [20] is similar to the methods presented in [21–23]. Galárraga et al. [21] proposed to use mined rules to assess the completeness of entities. Ahmeti et al. [22] presented a tool to asses the completeness of entities in Wikidata, based on a comparison with similar entities. Similarly, Hitz-Gamper [23] proposed to compare entities of the same class for the detection of missing facts in Wikidata. More general, Razniewski et al. [2] discussed the challenges regarding the completeness of knowledge bases. They proposed to use *mark and recapture* techniques from the field of ecology to estimate the size of a population.

The ABox comparison of ontologies is also related to the field of *data integration*. Naumann et al. [24] described data integration as a process of the three main steps (1) schema matching, (2) duplicate detection, and (3) data fusion. Their work is focused on the integration of databases. Therefore *schema matching* is the process of detecting corresponding tables and attributes. *Duplicate detection* refers to the detection of rows from multiple sources describing the same real-world entity. *Data fusion* is the step of integrating corresponding rows and resolving contradictions. Methods from this field could be adapted for the usage in the ABox comparison of ontologies.

3   Problem Statement and Contributions

The purpose of our work is to explore appropriate methods and criteria for the semi-automatic comparison of the ABox of ontologies to aid ontology evaluation and selection. The lack of a gold standard to evaluate ontologies has already been identified as a problem in early work on ontology comparison [13]. Still 20 years later this remains an open issue [20]. We aim to contribute on this issue by employing the comparison of the ABox of ontologies.

The ABox of an ontology consists of membership, property, and equality assertions about individuals. The TBox describes available vocabulary by defining relations and constraints of classes and properties. ABox rich ontologies contain many ABox axioms compared to the number of TBox axioms. As the vocabulary used in the ABox is defined in the TBox, the comparison of ABoxes must take place in context of the according TBoxes: The comparison of ABoxes requires a matching of the according TBoxes to identify corresponding assertion axioms. Constraints defined in the TBoxes might imply particular comparison rules. Further, the TBoxes can be used to restrict the ABox comparison on a reasonable set of assertions. It is unlikely to find corresponding property assertions without a corresponding property. Neither can it be expected to find corresponding individuals without a corresponding class.

We assume that the ontologies to compare are given by the user. If the ontologies have been independently developed, it is unlikely that the same accidental error occurred multiple times at the same fact. Therefore we expect that the replacement of a gold standard by competing ontologies will uncover a relevant number of issues. Even if not all wrong facts will be discovered, this will enable ontology authors to correct their ontologies. The results of our preliminary work in the domain of measurement units show promise [5]. Further, the number of errors can be used to assess the quality of an ontology. Ontology users can involve this assessment in their choice of an ontology.

Equally, it is unlikely that independent ontologies contain the same subset of individuals and facts of an unknown population. Therefore we expect that the replacement of a gold standard by competing ontologies will uncover a relevant number of missing individuals and facts. In extreme case, two ontologies do not share any corresponding individuals and facts and therefore, all of them will be treated as missing in the other ontology. Even if not all missing entities and facts will be discovered, this will enable ontology authors to further enrich their ontologies. Further, the number of missing entities and facts can be used to assess the completeness of an ontology. Ontology users can involve this assessment in their choice of an ontology.

Hence we believe that the semi-automatic comparison of ontology ABoxes helps improve these ontologies or to select a suitable ontology:

Hypothesis 1. *Given two different ontologies that are overlapping, ABox rich, and **flawed**: The encountered number of **errors** in these ontologies after limited time using semi-automatic comparison of the ABoxes is greater than the encountered number of **errors** in these ontologies and after the same time using manual review.*

Hypothesis 2. *Given two different ontologies that are overlapping, ABox rich, and **incomplete**: The encountered number of **missing facts** in these ontologies after limited time using semi-automatic comparison of the ABoxes is greater than the encountered number of **missing facts** in these ontologies and after the same time using manual review.*

Hypothesis 3. *Given two different ontologies that are overlapping, ABox rich, and **incomplete**: The encountered number of **missing individuals** in these ontologies after limited time using semi-automatic comparison of the ABoxes is greater than the encountered number of **missing individuals** in these ontologies and after the same time using manual review.*

The comparison of the ABox requires to identify the corresponding facts of the ontologies. However, different ontologies of the same domain might use different approaches to model certain aspects of the domain. For example, there might be (a) properties corresponding to a chain of properties, (b) anonymous individuals corresponding to named individuals, (c) data properties corresponding to annotation properties, or (d) classes corresponding to individuals. This leads to the question:

Research Question 1. *How can different modeling approaches used in the ontologies be (semi-)automatically handled during the comparison of the ABox of ontologies?*

OWL 2 [25] allows the logical description of properties, such as the definition as functional or inverse functional properties. These might imply particular rules on the comparison of the ABox of ontologies. This motivates the question:

Research Question 2. *How can OWL 2 Object Property Axioms, Data Property Axioms, and Key Axioms be (semi-)automatically utilized in the comparison of the ABox of ontologies?*

The comparison of the facts about entities requires to match the corresponding entities. However, the matching relies on analogous facts about the entities. This might reflect the classic 'chicken and egg' problem. Hence, one question is:

Research Question 3. *Are general ontology matching methods sufficient for the comparison of ontology ABoxes to match incorrect entities or are specialized entity resolution methods required?*

The involvement of reasoning in the comparison process might, on the one hand, provide the implicit facts in ontologies for comparison too. On the other hand, high computational effort or inconsistencies could intercept the comparison process. However, the extend of reasoner usage is adjustable. Reasoning could be used for (a) at least each single ontology, to produce the implicit facts, (b) each single ontology and the according mappings to other ontologies, to also produce a schema translation, (c) each pair of ontologies and the according mappings, to also produce implicit facts implied by axioms from both ontologies, or (d) all ontologies and mappings at once, to also produce implicit facts implied by axioms from at least three ontologies. Therefore, a question is:

Research Question 4. *To which extent should reasoning be incorporated into the comparison of the ABox of ontologies?*

The comparison of the ABox of ontologies is supposed to complement other comparison methods. A general interpretation requires the result integration of all methods. Therefore the results of the ontology ABox comparison have to be embedded into an general ontology quality model. Thus, one question is:

Research Question 5. *How can the comparison of the ABox of ontologies be embedded into a general ontology quality model?*

4   Research Methodology and Approach

We propose a framework for the ABox comparison of ontologies. This framework will be implemented to verify our hypotheses. The implementation requires to answer the research questions. Our framework consist of five components, as shown in Fig. 1.

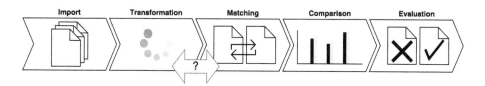

Fig. 1. Schematic of the ABox comparison framework. The order of the transformation component and the matching component is open regarding to Research Question 4.

The *import component* imports ontologies from the web or a local file. Further data sources like SPARQL endpoints, CSV files, or databases are also conceivable, but must be converted into RDF graphs during the import. One data source might have several versions, which in turn might consist of several files. The versions used in the further process can be selected.

The *transformation component* allows to generate additional axioms, to enable the user to employ domain knowledge that is not formalized in the ontology to deduce additional facts. The user could, e.g., provide SPARQL construct queries to generate axioms. This provides high flexibility, which is important for the applicability in a wide range of domains. Further, reasoning could be employed to deduce facts that are not explicitly formalized in the ontology. However, it is open for evaluation if reasoning should better be involved after the matching of the ontologies. Therefore, the final cooperation and order of these components depends on the answer to Research Question 4.

The *matching component* matches the entities of all data sources. We will employ well known matching libraries using the Alignment API [26]. However, the suitability of general ontology matching methods is open for evaluation regarding to Research Question 3. It might be necessary to implement other, fault-tolerant entity resolution methods. This would employ adapted duplicate detection methods known from the field of data integration. Regardless of the method used, the automated matching could be complemented by user defined mappings and mapping exclusions. The matching of properties is a special issue at this component. The knowledge of the relation of the properties is essential for the further process. However, this might be hampered by different modeling approaches whose mapping goes beyond simple relations. Therefore, a special approach for the property mapping is required, as outlined in Research Question 1.

The *comparison component* provides comparative statistics of the ontologies. It automatically selects relevant classes and properties to compare. This might benefit from an analysis of property definitions, as outlined in Research Question 2. Additionally, classes and properties can be manually (de-)selected. It will compare the number of property assignments and individuals. *Mark and recapture* techniques could be used to estimate the total completeness of each ontology [2]. Finally, it will generate a report containing the comparison results. Regarding to Research Question 5, it remains open how to transfer the statistical values into quality metrics. This is required to embed the comparison into a quality model.

The *evaluation component* highlights deviations between property values of mapped individuals. It will use the classes and properties selected in the comparison component. Methods from the field of data integration could be adapted for this, depending on the aims of the user. If users wants to debug the ontologies, they must explicitly flag conflicting facts as wrong or correct. These flags can be reused for new versions. Therefore, facts do not need to be assessed twice. If users need a quality overview, a completely automated strategy, like a majority voting or a preferred ontology [24], might be sufficient. Wrong facts that have been generated in the transformation component are not a failure of the ontology, but they might hint to wrong source facts. Therefore, the provenance of these facts needs to be provided for assessment. Finally, the component will generate a report with missing, deviating, and wrong property values and missing or duplicated individuals. Regarding to Research Question 5, the evaluation results must be aggregated into meaningful metrics, too.

5   Preliminary Results

We performed a semi-automatized comparison of nine ontologies and knowledge bases in the domain of measurement units [5]. We used a collection of scripts to automatize a majority of the work. While we did not utilize the presented framework, our experiences from that work influenced our framework design. The comparison uncovered a surprisingly low overlap of the ontologies. Further more, we discovered several issues in all analyzed ontologies. The issues have been reported to the ontology authors. For some ontologies, this triggered new releases. The results of this work support the importance of ontology ABox comparison.

Challenges and Lessons learned. Due to the ongoing development of some of the analyzed ontologies, it was necessary on several occasions to reevaluate all ontologies considering a newly published version of one ontology. Even if a majority of the work was automatized, we had to reevaluate possible issues, because our scripts did not take earlier decisions into account. Hence the implementation of our framework should record decisions about potential issues to avoid repeated manual effort.

To improve the comparison of conversion values, we calculated their transitive closure inside each ontology. The localization of the actual causes of errors required to keep the provenance of the calculated values. Hence the implementation of the presented comparison framework should, on the one hand, allow to calculate further facts that have not been formalized in the ontologies, but, on the other hand, also record the provenance of these generated facts.

6   Evaluation Plan

In a first step, we plan to perform a further iteration of the comparison and evaluation of ontologies for measurement units. This is to prove the suitability of the framework in an already investigated context. Several ontologies in this domain are under active development. Therefore, this also provides an opportunity to evaluate the consideration of different versions in the framework. Subsequently, we will perform further ontology comparisons in other domains to prove the general applicability of the framework. Candidate domains are, e.g., species, chemical substances, publications, famous persons, locations, or diseases.

In addition, we intend to test our hypotheses by a series of experiments. Several test persons will inspect two ontologies without using our methods and two other ontologies using our methods. All ontologies will be based on the same set of artificial facts, but with different schemata, omissions and errors. To test the hypotheses we will measure the number of (1) errors, (2) missing facts, (3) missing individuals that a test person detects in a specific time. It is important that it is easy for the test person to validate the facts, but also that it is difficult to automatize the validation. However, the detailed design of this experiments remains open for future work.

7 Conclusions

The presented framework will provide novel opportunities to strengthen the trustworthiness of ontologies. Ontology developers will be able to keep track on the correctness and completeness of facts in their work. The framework will allow them to regularly compare their ontology with their competitors' ontologies and further data sources. Users of ontologies will be empowered to easily compare available ontologies. They will not longer have to blindly trust the represented facts or to perform a tedious manual review of each axiom. The framework will highlight questionable facts. That way, users will be able to take a more educated decision on the selection of ontologies for their projects.

Acknowledgments. This work was funded by DFG in the scope of the LakeBase project within the Scientific Library Services and Information Systems (LIS) program. Many thanks to my supervisor Birgitta König-Ries for her valuable feedback. I also thank the reviewer Agnieszka Ławrynowicz and one anonymous reviewer for their helpful comments.

References

1. Kontokostas, D., Westphal, P., Auer, S., et al.: Test-driven evaluation of linked data quality. In: Chung, C., Broder, A.Z., Shim, K., Suel, T. (eds.) 23rd International World Wide Web Conference, WWW 2014, pp. 747–758. ACM (2014). https://doi.org/10.1145/2566486.2568002

2. Razniewski, S., Suchanek, F.M., Nutt, W.: But what do we actually know? In: Pujara, J., Rocktäschel, T., Chen, D., Singh, S. (eds.) Proceedings of the 5th Workshop on Automated Knowledge Base Construction, AKBC@NAACL-HLT 2016, pp. 40–44. The Association for Computer Linguistics (2016)

3. Abele, A., McCrae, J.P., Buitelaar, P., et al.: The Linking Open Data Cloud Diagram (2017)

4. Sirin, E., Parsia, B., Grau, B.C., et al.: Pellet: A practical OWL-DL reasoner. J. Web Sem. **5**(2), 51–53 (2007). https://doi.org/10.1016/j.websem.2007.03.004

5. Keil, J.M., Schindler, S.: Comparison and evaluation of ontologies for units of measurement. In: Semantic Web (2018, in press)

6. Noy, N.F., Musen, M.A.: Using prompt ontology-comparison tools in the EON ontology alignment contest. In: Sure, Y., Corcho, Ó., Euzenat, J., Hughes, T. (eds.) Evaluation of Ontology-based Tools EON 2004 at ISWC 2004, vol. 128. CEUR Workshop Proceedings. CEUR-WS.org (2004)

7. Weinstein, P.C., Birmingham, W.P.: Comparing concepts in differentiated ontologies. In: Proceedings of the Twelfth Workshop on Knowledge Acquisition, Modeling and Management (KAW 1999) (1999)

8. Giménez-Lugo, G.A., Amandi, A., Simão Sichman, J., Godoy, D.: Enriching information agents' knowledge by ontology comparison: a case study. In: Garijo, F.J., Riquelme, J.C., Toro, M. (eds.) IBERAMIA 2002. LNCS (LNAI), vol. 2527, pp. 546–555. Springer, Heidelberg (2002). https://doi.org/10.1007/3-540-36131-6_56

9. Bieliková, M., Andrejko, A.: Comparing instances of ontological concepts for personalized recommendation in large information spaces. Comput. Inf. **28**(4), 429–452 (2009)

10. Xue, Y., Wang, C., Ghenniwa, H.H., Shen, W.: A tree similarity measuring method and its application to ontology comparison. J. UCS **15**(9), 1766–1781 (2009). https://doi.org/10.3217/jucs-015-09-1766

11. Maedche, A., Staab, S.: Comparing Ontologies — Similarity Measures and a Comparison Study. Internal Report. 408. Institute AIFB, University of Karlsruhe, 76128 Karlsruhe, Germany, March 2001

12. Wang, J.Z., Ali, F.: An efficient ontology comparison tool for semantic web applications. In: Skowron, A., Agrawal, R., Luck, M., et al. (eds.) IEEE/WIC/ACM International Conference on Web Intelligence (WI 2005) IEEE Computer Society 2005, pp. 372–378. https://doi.org/10.1109/WI.2005.28

13. Visser, P.R.S., Bench-Capon, T.J.M.: A comparison of four ontologies for the design of legal knowledge systems. Artif. Intell. Law **6**(1), 27–57 (1998). https://doi.org/10.1023/A:1008251913710

14. Botke, M., Hoede, C.: A comparison of two ontologies of regions. Memorandum 1511. Department of Applied Mathematics, University of Twente (2000)

15. Vilches-Blázquez, L.M., Ramos, J.A., López-Pellicer, F.J., Corcho, O., Nogueras-Iso, J.: An approach to comparing different ontologies in the context of hydrographical information. In: Popovich, V.V., Claramunt, C., Schrenk, M., Korolenko, K.V. (eds.) Information Fusion and Geographic Information Systems. Lecture Notes in Geoinformation and Cartography, pp. 193–207. Springer, Heidelberg (2009). https://doi.org/10.1007/978-3-642-00304-2_13

16. Kretz, D.R., Phillips, W.D., Peoples, B.E., Toennies, J.W.: Method and system for ontology candidate selection, comparison, and alignment. US Patent 8,655,882. 18 February 2014 (2014)

17. Gangemi, A., Catenacci, C., Ciaramita, M., Lehmann, J.: Ontology evaluation and validation. An integrated formal model for the quality diagnostic task. Technical report Laboratory for Applied Ontology, Institute of Cognitive Sciences and Technologies, Italian National Research Council, 6 September 2005 (2005)

18. Steinberg, M.D., Schindler, S., Keil, J.M.: Use cases and suitability metrics for unit ontologies. In: Dragoni, M., Poveda-Villalón, M., Jimenez-Ruiz, E. (eds.) OWLED/ORE -2016. LNCS, vol. 10161, pp. 40–54. Springer, Cham (2017). https://doi.org/10.1007/978-3-319-54627-8_4

19. Katsumi, M., Grüninger, M.: Choosing ontologies for reuse. In: Applied Ontology, November 2016, pp. 1–27 (2016). https://doi.org/10.3233/AO-160171

20. Färber, M., Bartscherer, F., Menne, C., Rettinger, A.: Linked data quality of DBpedia, Freebase, OpenCyc, Wikidata, and YAGO. Semantic Web **9**(1), 77–129 (2018). https://doi.org/10.3233/SW-170275

21. Galárraga, L., Razniewski, S., Amarilli, A., Suchanek, F.M.: Predicting completeness in knowledge bases. In: Rijke, M. de Shokouhi, M., Tomkins, A., Zhang, M. (eds.) Proceedings of the Tenth ACM International Conference on Web Search and Data Mining (WSDM 2017), pp. 375–383. ACM (2017). https://doi.org/10.1145/3018661.3018739

22. Ahmeti, A., Razniewski, S., Polleres, A.: Assessing the completeness of entities in knowledge bases. In: Blomqvist, E., Hose, K., Paulheim, H., Ławrynowicz, A., Ciravegna, F., Hartig, O. (eds.) ESWC 2017. LNCS, vol. 10577, pp. 7–11. Springer, Cham (2017). https://doi.org/10.1007/978-3-319-70407-4_2

23. Hitz-Gamper, B.: What do others say about similar things - predicate comparing for a linked data quality boost. In: Aroyo, L., Gandon, F. (eds.) Proceedings of the Doctoral Consortium at the 16th International Semantic Web Conference (ISWC 2017), vol. 1962. CEUR Workshop Proceedings (2017). CEUR-WS.org

24. Naumann, F., Bilke, A., Bleiholder, J., Weis, M.: Data fusion in three steps: resolving schema, tuple, and value inconsistencies. IEEE Data Eng. Bull. **29**(2), 21–31 (2006)
25. Motik, B., Patel-Schneider, P.F., Parsia, B., eds.: OWL 2 Web Ontology Language Structural Specification and Functional-Style Syntax, 2nd edn. 11 December 2012. http://www.w3.org/TR/2012/REC-owl2-syntax-20121211/
26. David, J., Euzenat, J., Scharffe, F., dos Santos, C.T.: The Alignment API 4.0. Semantic Web **2**(1), 3–10 (2011). https://doi.org/10.3233/SW-2011-0028

Modeling and Querying Versioned Source Code in RDF

Jacob Bellamy-McIntyre[✉]

University of Auckland, Auckland, New Zealand
jbel071@aucklanduni.ac.nz

Abstract. Source code management is an active and fundamental area of research where one of the key challenges is allowing developers to maintain an understanding of software projects when it is being actively developed in a distributed setting. Despite a number of well established practices and tools to help keep track of modifications to a project, there is a lack of a standard representation and query mechanism to integrate different repositories and serve fine-grained retrieval tasks. In this paper we propose modeling source code in resource description framework (RDF) triples as it is the main standard for sharing semantic information over the web. To support temporal queries over different source code versions we present a temporal extension of SPARQL that uses an in memory index of changes generated from a standard transaction log. We have built a prototype system to demonstrate that the approach is feasible, and present some preliminary results on query execution.

Keywords: Temporal databases · RDF · SPARQL · Static analysis

1 Introduction and Motivation

One of the key challenges in software engineering is supporting developers so they can understand and maintain software projects under active development. This problem is known as program comprehension and is especially challenging for developers new to a project. When reading source code it is natural for questions such as "which lines affect the value of this variable?", or "does this method call modify any data structure in addition to returning a value?". While different developer tools exist that aid in answering these kinds of questions, more expressive information needs cannot be resolved in a standardised way. This issue is aggravated when dealing with distributed source code that exists with multiple versions as they may apply to different systems and use different formats.

The Resource Description Framework (RDF) could be a suitable foundation for building a standardised source code model that allows for queries over these different formats using the SPARQL query language. As an increasing number of projects are hosted on public software repositories it makes sense to share information about those projects across the semantic web following linked data principles, and doing so gives access to a wide range of existing semantic web tools.

© Springer Nature Switzerland AG 2018
A. Gangemi et al. (Eds.): ESWC 2018 Satellite Events, LNCS 11155, pp. 251–261, 2018.
https://doi.org/10.1007/978-3-319-98192-5_44

In this work we specifically wish to give support for temporal source code queries, where one can run their queries over the history of a project from its version control repository, and determine when different changes occurred to different source code artifacts. Being able to see the history of changes made to say, a class, can aid in program comprehension as it allows one to see the iterative process that went into building that class. Alternatively, one can use these queries to search for the introduction of bug patterns to a project in an automated fashion.

Our contributions are as follows: we propose a general RDF schema for source code based on abstract semantic graphs, we have developed a triplestore that maintains an index of all changes made to the store, we present the query language LSPARQL that allows for temporal queries using that index and which can be applied to typical triplestore transaction logs, and we have developed a prototype of our system focusing on Java source code to show that our approach can be practical. Our paper is structured as follows: Sect. 2 covers the state of the art on querying source code and temporal RDF, Sect. 3 discusses more in depth the problem we are trying to address, Sect. 4 describes our approach in terms of our implementation, Sect. 5 gives some preliminary results in terms of query execution speed on our prototype, Sect. 6 details how we wish to further evaluate our approach in the future, and lastly Sect. 7 summaries and concludes the work of this paper.

2   State of the Art

2.1   Querying Source Code

There have been numerous systems that have been developed to allow one to perform queries over source code artifacts. Early examples include OMEGA [1] and CIA [2] which used the relational model to represent the relationships between different source code artifacts, and allowed queries via SQL. Over the years several alternatives have been developed, such as the system ASTLog [3] which used an abstract syntax tree representation of source code with queries based around tree traversals, and CodeQuest [4] which was based on Datalog. Rather than use an underlying database to store a source code model, the JQuery eclipse plugin [5] instead answers queries directly against the eclipse API. More recently, the Wiggle system [6] implemented source code queries with Neo4J which uses the property graph model and the Cypher query language.

There have also been some implementations of modeling source code in RDF, for instance CodeOntology [7] and Evolizer [8]. In the case of CodeOntology there is no support for modeling multiple versions or supporting temporal queries over them. For Evolizer, while the authors do briefly describe how multiple versions of a project may be stored, there is no discussion on how one may form temporal queries or how they maintain the identity of individual artifacts across changes. The work of Ghezzi et al. [9] and Iqbal and Decker [10] allow higher level queries on software evolution by modeling the meta data of open source projects. EvoOnt [11] modeled entire source code repositories in RDF for the purpose of performing repository mining tasks such as detecting the introduction of code smells, but their model remains relatively coarse-grained and does not support queries on the statement level.

2.2   Temporal RDF

There has been some work on modeling time in RDF to be queried by SPARQL. The work of Guiterrez et al. [12] introduced Temporal RDF where every RDF triple additionally receives a temporal label describing the point in time or interval in which it is valid. They described how temporal labeling could be represented in standard RDF by performing reification on every triple.

While one could represent temporal triples in this way using any standard RDF triple store unfortunately it requires six additional triples for each triple that requires a temporal label describing an interval.

Besides being less space efficient than they could be, it also makes SPARQL queries cumbersome to write as they also need to refer to those six additional temporal triples per underlying triple in each query. The problem is compounded when we want the matched triples to be valid over some common overlapping interval. This is because it would require comparing the valid intervals of each matched triple with all the other matched intervals. The cumbersomeness of the queries can be somewhat overcome by using a more concise language that translates temporal queries into regular SPARQL, as in [13], though efficiently answering these queries likely requires a specialised temporal index like tGrin [14].

There are a few alternatives to reification that have been explored, such as singleton properties where a unique predicate is used to denote a specific context to a relationship [15], and the work of Welty and Fikes [16] which instead represented fluents by giving a unique identifier to individuals depending on context. A separate approach again is to extend the basic RDF triple to also include an annotation which can describe its valid interval, such as is done with stRDF [17], aRDF [18] and AnQL [19]. The fundamental issue of this kind of solution is that these extended RDF triples are no longer standard RDF and so are not supported by standard tools, and are much less suited for sharing across the semantic web. Tappolet et al. [20] suggested using a separate named graph containing all the triples that hold for a specific interval and to use an index which specifies which named graphs apply for any particular time instant. This approach however is less applicable when few triples are valid for the same intervals.

Temporal queries also arise in the context of data archiving and versioning. The X-RDF-3x system [21] maintains an in memory index for triples that also includes when each triple was added or deleted, which they use for single version 'time travel' queries. R&WBase [22] similarly supports single version queries, but also takes into account standard version control operations like branching and merging to determine whether a triple holds for a particular version. The BEAR test suite [23] evaluates different archiving strategies over different stores using temporal queries written in AnQL.

3   Problem Statement and Contributions

The goal of our research was to create a system that can parse source code from a repository into RDF which would allow us to use source code queries with SPARQL. The challenge was designing our system in such a way that we could run queries to find changes made to specific source code artifacts in the repository, and to allow queries over any historic state without needing to materialize past versions. This presents three key problems:

1. Source code projects can span hundreds of thousands of lines. If we directly represent the abstract syntax tree of each class in RDF, this can easily become tens of millions of artifacts.
2. We require a means of supporting efficient temporal queries. Temporal reification would require a large number of additional triples. Extending triple patterns into quadruples with timestamps means that our triples would not be consumable by standard RDF triplestores.
3. When presented with two separate versions of the same source code, we require a way to associate artifacts in one version to the other. If we do not, then practically we cannot track changes to artifacts.

The major contributions of the PhD are a new schema for modeling source code in RDF and an extension to the SPARQL query language that allows for temporal queries over a triplestores transaction log. We have additionally created a proof of concept prototype system for Java source code.

4   Research Methodology and Approach

4.1   Overview

Our system has three major components. The first major component is our parser, which takes abstract syntax trees generated by a public library and uses those to construct an abstract semantic graph represented in RDF triples. The second is the underlying triplestore which we have developed ourselves called PDStore which uses a hash based indexing scheme. A key feature of PDStore is that by default it indexes all changes that are made in the transaction log so that queries can be run against any historic state. The query language LSPARQL is the last major component, and it allows one to specify temporal queries which are run against the changes described in the transaction log.

We parse all the classes of that project into abstract syntax trees, which our parser then uses to generate an abstract semantic graph represented as a set of RDF triples. Once all the classes have been parsed, we commit all the RDF triples in a single transaction which adds them to the log and assigns each the timestamp of the commit. We then sequentially repeat this process for each subsequent version we wish to run queries over. When generating a new abstract semantic graph after the first, we have to compare with the previous version to identify triples that need to be removed as they no longer exist in the current version.

Artifacts which are unchanged naturally gain no new triples. Once all versions have been parsed they can be queried using LSPARQL. While currently our implementation focuses on Java, this process can be straight forwardly repeated for other declarative programming languages.

4.2   Abstract Semantic Graph Representation

An abstract syntax tree is a common representation of source code that is based on the parse tree used by compilers that prunes away much of the low level parsing such as punctuation. An abstract semantic graph (ASG) is a further abstraction that treats the program as one expression, and each vertice is a subexpression. Abstract semantic graphs differ from abstract syntax trees in that there can be additional edges to different vertices (for instance denoting invocation) and may contain back edges such as with recursion. Furthermore, duplicate subexpressions that occur in different portions of the program can reuse the same vertices. In our prototype system we currently parse all Java artifacts down to the statement level. Figure 1 shows an example of an ASG we create, with simplified identifiers.

We assume the abstract syntax tree for the source code is available as they are a standard feature of source code parsing libraries. Given an abstract syntax tree, generating an abstract semantic graph is not particularly difficult. It just requires performing name resolution to associate the usage of some identifier with its definition. Common subexpressions could be identified by using a hashing scheme like what is done with merkle trees. What is much more difficult is determining the changes made to specific artifacts across subsequent graphs.

Analogous to the notion of a superkey in the relational model, different artifacts can have different properties which we can use to define a unique identity for that artifact, and if two artifacts across two different versions have these same

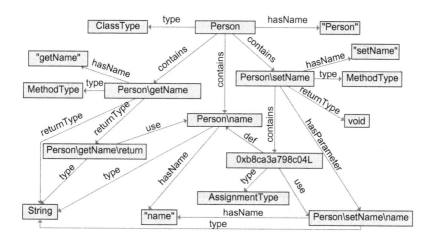

Fig. 1. ASG of a simple class

properties then they are the same artifact. The most obvious of these are identifiers, such as class names, method names, and variable names. If two classes in separate versions have the same fully qualified name including the package, we can be fairly certain that they are the same artifact regardless of whichever changes have been made. Likewise we can do the same with methods if we include the method signature and containing class, and for variable declarations if we include the scope of the variable. These same names can straightforwardly be used in defining the IRIs used in RDF to identify them. For example, the bar() method in the foo class could be recorded as "projectURI:foo/bar()". The deficiency of doing this is that if an artifact is renamed it assumes a new identity. If the rename is of the class, then this will also change the identity of all containing methods and variables.

For artifacts that cannot be uniquely identified by a name we see two viable options. The first is to use a combination of type and position. For example "the first while loop in the bar() method in the Foo class". The second would be to define its identity by all of its properties and sub properties, such as "the while loop with this condition and these statements". The former approach is a straight forward way of tracking the identity of artifacts without identifiers for which we can still create meaningful IRIs, but its identity can be usurped by the insertion of another artifact of the same type before it and its identity will not persist through a rename of a parent artifact or if the artifact is moved. The latter approach essentially would give us hash based identifiers that are immutable and so the only change of them that we can query is which artifacts contain them. They are perfectly suited for representing common subexpressions though, and can be recycled for representing reused code fragments across a project. While there is some flexibility as to which identity scheme to use, the decision we made with respect to this implementation which we used for our evaluation was to use type and positional identification for block constructs like for loops and while loops as well as variable assignments, and use hash based identifiers for other statements and expressions. In our prototype, we have used string based IRIs for representing the mutable artifacts, and hash-based integer identifiers for the immutable expressions.

4.3   PDStore

PDStore is an RDF triplestore that uses a hash based index for all triples added and deleted from the store. The standard (s, p, o) triple is instead represented with a quintuple (t, c, s, p, o) where t is a timestamp and c is a change type that is either an add change $+$ or a removal change $-$. The modification of a triple is represented by the deletion of the original triple, and the addition of a new triple. This representation corresponds to the minimum amount of information one would expect from a standard triplestore's transaction log. Internally String literal values such as URI identifiers are represented with 128 bit integers, with the strings mapped to them using a dictionary.

Indexing is performed using a pair of hash based indexes called the InstanceInstance index, and the RoleInstance index. The InstanceInstance index is a

Table 1. Index query efficiency

Change patterns	Iterator retrieval	Get next
All queries with variable timestamp	$O(1)$	$O(1)$
$(t, +, s, p, o)$, $(t, +, s, ?p, o)$, $(t, +, ?s, p, o)$, $(t, +, s, p, ?o)$	$O(\log n)$	$O(1)$
$(t, +, ?s, ?p, ?o)$, $(t, +, s, ?p, ?o)$, $(t, +, ?s, ?p, o)$	$O(n)$	$O(n)$
$(t, e, s, ?p, o)$, $(t, e, ?s, p, o)$, $(t, e, s, p, ?o)$	$O(\log n)$	$O(n)$
(t, e, s, p, o), $(t, e, ?s, ?p, ?o)$, $(t, e, ?s, ?p, o)$, $(t, e, s, ?p, ?o)$	$O(n)$	$O(n)$

hashmap that takes as a key both a subject and object pair, and has as its value a list of all triples added and deleted that used both that subject and object in temporal order. As such, it is used directly to answer $(?t, ?c, s, ?p, o)$ queries. The RoleInstance index takes the predicate as a key, and has a second hashmap as its value. The second hashmap takes either a subject or object as a key, and once again returns a list of all corresponding triples that were added or deleted in temporal order. As such, it answers directly both $(?t, ?c, ?s, p, o)$ queries and $(?t, ?c, s, p, ?o)$ queries[1]. Table 1 describes the runtime complexity of the different query patterns over our log. Of note are queries where the change type is denoted by e which is used for queries on a single snapshot. For all patterns the runtime complexity for $+$, $-$, and $+-$ (wildcard) change types is unchanged, so we only list those for $+$. As in our prototype system there is a small finite number of roles, we assume the time it takes to iterate over all roles to take $O(1)$ time.

The $O(n)$ complexity can arise for those patterns having to visit multiple buckets in the hashmap. It might be that the earliest change in a bucket occurs after the specified timestamp and so would need to be skipped. In the worst case, the number of buckets which would have to be checked and then skipped is proportional to n. For a case like $(t, e, s, ?p, o)$ only a single bucket needs to be visited, but it is possible that a triple might be added and removed repeatedly but only a single one of those changes is related to the specified timestamp. Practically however, the expected complexity $O(\log n)$ in normal use cases.

4.4   LSPARQL

As mentioned in the previous subsection, PDStore uses a quintuple representation of triples of the form (t, c, s, p, o), where t is a timestamp, and c is a change type. For LSPARQL queries, the valid change types are $+$, to denote an added triple, $-$ to denote a deleted triple, e which means 'exists' and which is used for queries on a specific snapshot. Regular SPARQL queries which do not specify a timestamp and change type run the query on the most recent state, and are equivalent to a query that uses the most recent timestamp with a change type of e and thus give the same results as it would on a conventional triplestore

---

[1] When a predicate/object pair is added to the roleInstance index the predicate provides a slightly different key than if the object was given as a subject.

that just had the latest snapshot. Currently LSPARQL is limited to conjunctive queries with FILTER.

The temporal variable $?t$ is assigned a single timestamp denoting a point in time in the case of patterns with change types $+$, $-$, and $+-$, and a pair of timestamps denoting a valid interval in the case of e patterns. Computing the valid interval for a given change takes $O(1)$ time, as we store a reference from an added change to one that removes it, and vice versa. Performing a temporal join with two single timepoints requires them to be the same time point. When performing a temporal join on two intervals however, we get the intersection of those intervals. For instance, given the triple $(Bob, likes, Alice)$ valid in the interval $(1, 4)$, and $(Alice, likes, Bob)$ valid in the interval $(2, 5)$, the query $(?t, e, ?x, likes, ?y)$, $(?t, e, ?y, likes, ?x)$ then the corresponding mapping μ would give $\mu(?t) = (2, 4)$. Sometimes a temporal join must be performed between a single time point and an interval, as would be the case in a query like $(?t, +, ?x, likes, ?y)$, $(?t, e, ?y, likes, ?x)$. In which case the mapping μ for this query would give $\mu(?x) = Alice$, $\mu(?y) = Bob$, and $\mu(?t) = 2$.

We support the standard SPARQL filters, and additionally have incorporated filters for the different temporal relations described in Alan's Interval Algebra, such as meets, overlaps, and during.

Table 2. Query evaluation

Query #	Time (seconds)	Query description
1	0.16	All recursive methods in the latest version
2	0.9	All classes in the current version which previously removed a method
3	0.11	All classes which implemented an interface that had some methods that were later removed
4	3.97	All methods whose return type changed at some point
5	0.02	All variables that had at some point been both incremented and decremented
6	0.09	SwitchTypes that later added a new SwitchCase
7	2.02	All pairs of assignments that modified the same variable at different points in time
8	0.007	All classes that existed when the 'HashQuery' class was added

5   Current Results

To demonstrate that our approach is viable, we have opted to parse the Chronicle Map project, a Java based key-value store publicly available on Github[2]. The latest version of the project consists of 381 Java files over 57603 lines of code.

___
[2] https://github.com/OpenHFT/Chronicle-Map.

While the project itself is only modestly large, the abstract semantic graph model we are using is fairly fine grained, and we are also wishing to account for every historical version which was developed over 2330 commits. In total our in memory indexes account for around nine million separate triples.

We present our proof of concept by showing that our query system can answer some ad hoc temporal queries in a reasonable amount of time. The machine running our implementation has an intel I7-2600 cpu and 12 gigabytes of RAM. For each temporal query we test the time taken to execute the query, and then iterate over all of the results. The recorded time for each query is the average over ten separate runs. The total in memory usage was 3.7 gigabytes. The results we can see in Table 2 demonstrates our proof of concept, as all queries were answered within a few seconds.

6 Evaluation Plan

Our current evaluation is very limited as it is simply a proof of concept. A proper evaluation would consist of evaluating several different metrics. Firstly, a performance evaluation should compare our query evaluation with other implementations. For other source code query systems we should compare the speed of query execution using a single version, using a much larger set of queries, and with projects of varying size. To evaluate our temporal queries, we can potentially compare it to different repository mining tools to see if we can generate a comparable amount of information about the repository in a faster amount of time, or we could compare against temporal databases using more general temporal datasets.

Secondly, we need to consider expressibility. We need to consider other temporal SPARQL implementations, and determine whether LSPARQL can formulate equivalent queries by way of a formal comparison of our semantics. For our source code model, we should try to establish which patterns of changes we can easily capture and those we cannot.

The last main metric we would want to evaluate our system is usability. We would like to do a study where we provide some software developers a sample project repository, and we ask them to perform some tasks such as bug and feature location, as well as determine when and by whom those features or bugs were implemented. We would then introduce them to our query language, teach them how to write our queries, and ask them to perform the same tasks using our query language. We would record the time to do these tasks with both approaches, and give a questionaire asking whether they found using our queries easier or harder, and whether they could practically see themselves ever wanting to use it.

7 Conclusion

In this paper we have presented our proposal for using RDF for modeling versioned source code. In Sect. 4.1 we described how we can accomplish this using an abstract semantic graph representation. Incorporating temporal information into RDF triplestores is an open research problem, and in Sect. 4.3 we described a simple hash based temporal index based on entries in a standard transaction log. Then, in Sect. 4.4 we proposed the language LSPARQL, a natural temporal extension of SPARQL that can use such a temporal index to answer temporal queries over transaction time. In Sect. 5 we described a prototype system we have developed that parses Java source code into RDF and which we query with LSPARQL, and have provided some preliminary results. In Sect. 6 we describe how in the near future we wish to improve the evaluation.

References

1. Linton, M.A.: Implementing relational views of programs. In: ACM SIGSOFT Software Engineering Notes, vol. 9, pp. 132–140. ACM (1984)
2. Chen, Y.F., Nishimoto, M.Y., Ramamoorthy, C.: The C information abstraction system. IEEE Trans. Software Eng. **3**, 325–334 (1990)
3. Crew, R.F., et al.: ASTLOG: a language for examining abstract syntax trees. DSL **97**, 18–18 (1997)
4. Hajiyev, E., Verbaere, M., de Moor, O.: *codeQuest*: scalable source code queries with datalog. In: Thomas, D. (ed.) ECOOP 2006. LNCS, vol. 4067, pp. 2–27. Springer, Heidelberg (2006). https://doi.org/10.1007/11785477_2
5. Janzen, D., De Volder, K.: Navigating and querying code without getting lost. In: Proceedings of the 2nd International Conference on Aspect-Oriented Software Development, pp. 178–187. ACM (2003)
6. Urma, R.G., Mycroft, A.: Source-code queries with graph databases-with application to programming language usage and evolution. Sci. Comput. Program. **97**, 127–134 (2015)
7. Atzeni, M., Atzori, M.: CodeOntology: RDF-ization of source code. In: d'Amato, C., et al. (eds.) ISWC 2017. LNCS, vol. 10588, pp. 20–28. Springer, Cham (2017). https://doi.org/10.1007/978-3-319-68204-4_2
8. Würsch, M., Ghezzi, G., Reif, G., Gall, H.C.: Supporting developers with natural language queries. In: 2010 ACM/IEEE 32nd International Conference on Software Engineering, vol. 1, pp. 165–174. IEEE (2010)
9. Ghezzi, G., Würsch, M., Giger, E., Gall, H.C.: An architectural blueprint for a pluggable version control system for software (evolution) analysis. In: Proceedings of the Second International Workshop on Developing Tools as Plug-Ins, pp. 13–18. IEEE Press (2012)
10. Iqbal, A., Decker, S.: Integrating open source software repositories on the web through linked data. In: 2015 IEEE International Conference on Information Reuse and Integration (IRI), pp. 114–121. IEEE (2015)
11. Tappolet, J., Kiefer, C., Bernstein, A.: Semantic web enabled software analysis. Web Semant. Sci. Serv. Agents World Wide Web **8**(2–3), 225–240 (2010)
12. Gutierrez, C., Hurtado, C.A., Vaisman, A.: Introducing time into RDF. IEEE Trans. Knowl. Data Eng. **19**(2) (2007)
13. Perry, M., Jain, P., Sheth, A.P.: SPARQL-ST: extending sparql to support spatiotemporal queries. In: Ashish, N., Sheth, A. (eds.) Geospatial Semantics and the Semantic Web. Semantic Web and Beyond (Computing for Human Experience), vol. 12, pp. 61–86. Springer, Boston (2011). https://doi.org/10.1007/978-1-4419-9446-2_3

14. Pugliese, A., Udrea, O., Subrahmanian, V.: Scaling RDf with time. In: Proceedings of the 17th International Conference on World Wide Web, pp. 605–614. ACM (2008)
15. Nguyen, V., Bodenreider, O., Sheth, A.: Don't like RDF reification? Making statements about statements using singleton property. In: Proceedings of the 23rd International Conference on World Wide Web, pp. 759–770. ACM (2014)
16. Welty, C., Fikes, R., Makarios, S.: A reusable ontology for fluents in OWL. FOIS **150**, 226–236 (2006)
17. Koubarakis, M., Kyzirakos, K.: Modeling and querying metadata in the semantic sensor web: the model stRDF and the query language stSPARQL. In: Aroyo, L., et al. (eds.) ESWC 2010. LNCS, vol. 6088, pp. 425–439. Springer, Heidelberg (2010). https://doi.org/10.1007/978-3-642-13486-9_29
18. Udrea, O., Recupero, D.R., Subrahmanian, V.: Annotated RDF. ACM Trans. Comput. Logic (TOCL) **11**(2), 10 (2010)
19. Lopes, N., Polleres, A., Straccia, U., Zimmermann, A.: AnQL: SPARQLing up annotated RDFS. In: Patel-Schneider, P.F., et al. (eds.) ISWC 2010. LNCS, vol. 6496, pp. 518–533. Springer, Heidelberg (2010). https://doi.org/10.1007/978-3-642-17746-0_33
20. Tappolet, J., Bernstein, A.: Applied temporal RDF: efficient temporal querying of RDF data with SPARQL. In: Aroyo, L., et al. (eds.) ESWC 2009. LNCS, vol. 5554, pp. 308–322. Springer, Heidelberg (2009). https://doi.org/10.1007/978-3-642-02121-3_25
21. Neumann, T., Weikum, G.: x-RDF-3X: fast querying, high update rates, and consistency for RDF databases. Proc. VLDB Endowment **3**(1–2), 256–263 (2010)
22. Vander Sande, M., Colpaert, P., Verborgh, R., Coppens, S., Mannens, E., Van de Walle, R.: R&Wbase: git for triples. In: LDOW (2013)
23. Fernández, J.D., Umbrich, J., Polleres, A., Knuth, M.: Evaluating query and storage strategies for RDF archives. In: Proceedings of the 12th International Conference on Semantic Systems, pp. 41–48. ACM (2016)

Linkflows: Enabling a Web of Linked Semantic Publishing Workflows

Cristina-Iulia Bucur$^{(\boxtimes)}$

Department of Computer Science, Vrije Universiteit Amsterdam,
Amsterdam, The Netherlands
c.i.bucur@vu.nl

Abstract. In recent decades, the prevalence of the Internet and Semantic Web technologies has shifted the traditional scientific journal publishing framework towards the digital environment. In support of this, ontologies on digital publishing and new forms of granular provenance modeling have been built to support digital publishing. These fine-grained technologies facilitate the decomposition of traditional science articles in constituent machine-readable parts that are linked not only with one another, but also to other related fine-grained parts of knowledge on the Web following the Linked Data principles. However, these resulting digital artifacts of fine-grained knowledge are static objects that do not take dynamic processes, or *scientific workflows*, into account. Additionally, *scientific workflows* are important because they directly produce and consume digital artifacts. In this project, we enable the decentralized execution of scientific workflows of digital artifacts across platforms such that individual steps of single workflows can be distributed. By considering these *scientific workflows*, we can further find new dimensions with respect to the quality and impact of digital artifacts. In our preliminary results we have developed a model that is able to support Linked Data Notifications to demonstrate the feasibility of our approach.

Keywords: Digital publishing workflows · Scientific workflows
Semantic publishing · Semantic web

1 Introduction

Publishing is an important practice, not only in the world of science, but also in everyday life. In the recent years, with the pervasiveness of technology and the Internet, we changed not only the way we do science, but also how we perform and disseminate science. As such, scientific publishing became a more versatile and multifaceted process, but the initial paradigm of publishing has stayed the same despite moving towards a digital environment with new methods of electronic publication including scientific workflows, research protocols and standard operating procedures [25]. Especially in the sciences, moving towards

© Springer Nature Switzerland AG 2018
A. Gangemi et al. (Eds.): ESWC 2018 Satellite Events, LNCS 11155, pp. 262–271, 2018.
https://doi.org/10.1007/978-3-319-98192-5_45

a more digital environment and generating digital content seems to be more the rule and challenges the classic ways of publishing.

In this rather new digital publishing context, Linked Data is a framework that supports scientific publications by enabling the exchange, reuse and linking of data on the Web [11]. While the Linked Data set of best practices to connect and publish structured data on the Web is not enough to enable the entire scientific publication process, it is an important layer that facilitates it. The Linked Data principles encourage using dereferenceable HTTP URIs for things like datasets, services, tools, etc. and including links to other URIs. Linked Data also supports provenance (meta-)information about the resources that are linked, thus giving a way to locate various versions of data and access information like ownership and copyright. In turn this would sustain reproducibility.

Reproducibility plays a crucial role in scientific research because it allows others to test, check and verify the validity of one's claims and methods [19] and it permits further collaboration and reuse of scientific discoveries. Unfortunately, according to a recent study published in Nature [23], over 70% of the 1500 interrogated scientists admitted to have failed to reproduce the work of other researchers at some point in time. The FAIR principles for scientific information [22] can be key factors in guiding towards reproducible research. According to these, data should be (i) findable both for humans and machines; (ii) accessible on the long term; (iii) interoperable by the use of shared vocabularies, for example; and (iv) reusable for both humans and machines. And, following these guidelines should, in turn, support reproducibility.

As Mons [10] notices, an important problem with traditional articles and another hurdle in the way of reproducibility is the process of "Knowledge Burying". That is all information is written and published in one bulk of text - the article - that contains the scientific hypotheses, arguments, methods and results. So, in order to extract knowledge from an article and have information in a structured form, additional methods like text mining need to be applied, thus resulting in a loss of knowledge.

In this project we want to investigate new approaches in the digital environment of scientific publishing by combining Linked Data principles to address problems like "Knowledge Burying" of traditional articles. Furthermore, we want to provide a framework that supports scientific workflows for digital artifacts. As such, we aim to link and connect the static products of dynamic processes - digital artifacts - to the processes that produce and consume them. The main innovative aspect of this research is the fact that scientific workflows are executed decentrally and linked across platforms, such that individual steps of a single workflow can be distributed. Moreover, these scientific workflows will be used to create new quality dimensions of digital artifacts that take into consideration the dynamic processes that produce and consume them. Thus, by using new and existing Semantic Web technologies we will support the reproducibility of scientific research, the exchange, reuse and linking of all digital artifacts involved in scientific workflows.

2   State of the Art

In the last 25 years, scientific publishing has evolved from the form of a traditional, paper-printed article, to electronic publishing of scholarly journals. Accessing research publications without the restriction of subscriptions is the idea behind Open Access journals. These journals have been growing in number faster than traditional subscription journals [1]. Consequently, debates were raised whether the Open Access system is damaging the peer-review system and puts the quality of scientific journal publishing at risk [24]. In [13] the authors mention that semantic publishing is inevitable and that it will happen in incremental steps as it is already possible to publish data as RDF statements in the Linked Open Data Cloud [21]. Semantic Web technologies have launched a revolution in the field of scientific publishing and the idea is to create and facilitate an open access ecosystem where both content and metadata of scientific articles is accessible, together with formalized internal structures of the documents and components, enriched and with semantic connections to other related or similar documents.

In the view of the prevalence of the Semantic Web, considerable research has been done in enriching the meaning of a traditional article in the digital publishing environment, facilitating its automatic discovery, having access in a semantic way to and within the article and also being able to link to other related articles or other related parts of articles. Especially notable in this sense are the SPAR ontologies [27], the ontologies central to the task of semantic publishing. All these techniques, methods and approaches can facilitate the scientific publishing domain and our research.

As datasets, documents and, in general, knowledge is spread in the web of the Internet, where everything can be shared and reused and linked, decentralization is a key concept. Decentralization implies that there is no control of a central authority anymore, e.g. a publishing house, over the open content that exists on the Web. There is a lot of research in this area of computer science, but we will focus especially on technologies related to the field of digital scientific publishing. In the past, techniques to ensure the functioning of a secure and decentralized global file system over the Internet to entice collaborations have been described in [12]. Then, the BitTorrent communication peer-to-peer file sharing protocol over the Internet to distribute and access data in the digital publishing environment was studied in [20], while peer-to peer networks for RDF data were developed in [17] and a decentralized architecture to support nanopublications, scientific RDF snippets, was built in [30].

In terms of assessing the quality of scientific publications, the most widely used indicator is the Journal Impact Factor (JIF) [15], but this metric has been the subject of multiple debates in the past as it was shown that it can be favourably manipulated [28]. For example, the JIF can be biased towards journals that publish high number of non-research items (e.g. research notes, comments) and have higher publishing numbers [14]. So, new ways of rating the quality of scientific publications is needed. Semantic Web technologies with ontologies like the Dataset Quality Information (daQ) [18] can support better and unbiased measures of quality, while new dimensions of quality that consider these technologies need to be taken into account.

In order to support provenance and reproducibility in scientific publications, we consider the notion of scientific workflows. While *scientific computational workflows* are mechanisms to specify and automate repetitive tasks for computational science or in silico science [16], we take into account not only these fully automated and computational workflows, but a more general concept of scientific workflows. Mainly, a *scientific workflow* as a set of inter-connected steps that produce and consume objects or digital artifacts that together combine for a certain result goal. This provides concrete specifications of workflows involved in scientific publishing that can be digitally stored themselves and allow for their automated execution. Additionally, we allow for abstract definitions or templates of scientific workflows or scientific workflow steps that can be executed by users.

3   Problem Statement and Contributions

This research PhD project will be guided by a main research question:

How can scientific workflows that produce and consume digital artifacts be assessed, linked and decentrally executed across platforms, such that individual steps of a single workflow can be distributed?

Digital artifacts can be considered all objects or resources that belong to a scientific publication, such as text, datasets, code, multimedia objects, spreadsheets, reviews, figures, methods, protocols, and results. The *scientific workflows* refer to processes, actions or operations that produce or consume these *digital artifacts* like authoring, revising, editing, reviewing, commenting and annotating. A single scientific workflow can be composed of multiple steps and we argue that these various steps can be spread on various platforms like repositories, code bases and collaboration platforms. The innovative aspect of the project is that one platform would not be in full control of the complete workflow, but would provide the means to link to a workflow step as it is produced. Thus, a complete scientific workflow of a digital artifact would then be composed of these workflow steps that are distributed on different platforms. As such, the static digital objects will be linked to the dynamic processes that contain them. Another innovative aspect lies in the fact that new quality and impact measures of digital artifacts can be derived by considering the workflows that consume and produce them.

Different aspects of the main research question are captured by four sub-research questions:

1. *How can we model the decentralized execution of workflows by using Linked Data principles and tools?*
   First, we would like to be able to model scientific workflows. For this, we will provide and build the necessary framework based on PROV-Pings [3] and Linked Data Notifications (LDN) [4], to enable notifications across platforms and tracking of provenance of various scientific workflows. We will use Linked Data principles like dereferenceable URIs using open standards like RDF to

publish and link workflows. When workflows are modelled using the Linked Data principles and tools, we call them linkflows, the Linked Data version of workflows. To evaluate the model we will use a case study of at least 20 scientific articles together with their scientific workflows including reviewing and authoring. The innovative aspect is that workflow steps that are produced on various platforms are linked and then they are reused and consumed on other platforms.

2. *How can we execute workflows that produce and consume digital artifacts?*
This research question allows the creation and execution of the workflow steps modelled previously. Through a software prototype, users will be able to create workflows for a selected corpora of digital artifacts, for example to generate a review. This software prototype will connect and enable linked workflows to flow across platforms and as such involve resources without involving the platform that contains a certain workflow step. This means, for example that the review that was created can be accessed by various interested parties, like online journal editors, who can consume it further by including the review in their own submission system. The innovative aspect that this sub-research question addresses is the same as in the first sub-research question, producing and linking workflows across platforms and consuming them on other platforms. The difference here is that the scientific workflows will be created in an automated manner with a focus on workflow decentralization and the small granularity of digital artifacts.

3. *How can we automatically analyze digital artifacts and assess their quality and impact based on the linked workflows that produce and consume them?*
In this research question we want to analyze the workflows in which digital artifacts were produced and consumed. The goal is to evaluate the quality and impact that these digital artifacts have based on the workflows they are part of. For this, we will build a prototype of a user interface that makes visible the connection between the digital artifact and the workflow that generated it. Next, we will develop metrics to measure the quality of a digital artifact based on the linked workflows that produced it. Moreover, analyzing the workflows that consume the digital artifact, we would be able to measure the impact of the artifact. The innovative aspects here are two-fold: first, tracking and visualizing the workflow steps and the digital artifacts that contain them and second, enabling new ways of measuring quality and impact of digital artifacts that do not rely only on the analysis of their provenance, but how they participate in the flow of dynamic processes, thus in linked workflows across platforms.

4. *Can we use digital artifacts and the linked workflows that contain them to support inquires from users?*
This last sub-research question will bridge and blend all previous aspects together. An inquiry consists of searches of digital artifacts. The search results will contain not only the static object, the digital artifact, that is relevant for the inquiry, but also the workflow(s) that produce and consume that digital artifact, together with metrics like quality and impact. Moreover, users would be able to generate workflows for digital artifacts at the same time.

So, a comment or a review could be added for a digital artifact, opening the execution of workflow steps for users. The innovative aspect would be two-fold: first, the inquiry responses will contain not only the corresponding digital artifact(s) of interest, but also the linked workflows that contain them and second, users would be able to produce, consume and execute workflows for digital artifacts on the fly.

4   Research Methodology and Approach

In order to answer the research questions from Sect. 3, we will move away from the idea of a traditional scientific article. We will consider digital artifacts as "universal entities" or objects that can be in the form of text, figures, datasets, code, presentation slides, multimedia objects, etc. as represented in Fig. 1. Each of these digital artifacts can be represented in the form of a node in a network. As such, a classical scientific PDF article is comprised of various digital artifacts like text, figures, datasets, code, etc. that are inter-connected. These digital artifacts are considered first class citizens and all bear the same importance. Connections between the nodes of this network of digital artifacts are links, as in Web links.

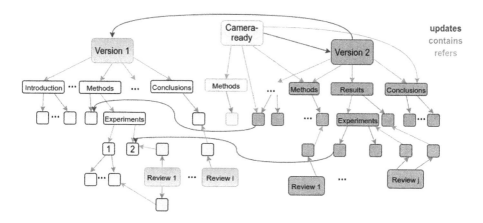

Fig. 1. Traditional scientific article represented as interconnected digital artifacts.

The digital artifacts that connect together to form a scientific contribution are involved in specific scientific workflows for their production and even when they are consumed by various systems, platforms and users. A scientific workflow involving a digital artifact is the collection of processes and actions that the digital artifacts undergo in science, like reviewing, commenting, annotating, etc. The linked workflows of a digital artifact are called linkflows. As such, either small steps of these workflows or entire workflows on a digital artifact are open and distributed in the sense that they can be produced on one platform and consumed on another, thus allowing the smooth flow of a workflow across platforms. This means, for example, that a review of a digital artifact can be produced on platform A, but platforms B and C can get notified of this review and consume or use it on these platforms. In the same way, a scientific workflow can contain multiple steps and these steps can be executed on different platforms, but linked together to form a coherent flow.

Considering this networked structure, when modifications are made in the network of a scientific contribution, notifications can be sent around about the changes as these propagate through the network. Here PROV-Pings [3] and Linked Data Notifications [4] technologies will help in sending notifications to the interested parties. But, every node in the network, thus each digital artifact, can be considered a fixed and immutable entity making provenance and versioning possible. Using Trusty URIs [29] and the use of hashes can help in establishing and tracking the changes that a digital artifact goes through.

In this project we will collaborate closely with two organizations:

Use case 1: The Netherlands Institute of Sound and Vision[1] - the biggest audio-visual cultural archive in the Netherlands having almost 70% of the Dutch audio-visual heritage under its tutelage. For this project, we will work closely with two open access media historical e-journals: VIEW Journal of European Television History and Culture and Tijdschrift voor Mediageschiedenis.

Use case 2: IOS Press[2] - an independent publishing house that has about 100 journals (mainly focused on medicine, but also from scientific and technical domains) and around 130 books published annually. For this project we will consider two of the open access journals that are printed by IOS Press: one in the computer science domain, the Data Science Journal, and a journal from the medical domain, the Journal of Alzheimer's Disease Reports (JAD Reports).

Throughout this project, we will implement, test and evaluate the linked workflows (linkflows) on the journals or datasets described in the use cases above. The diversity of the domains, ranging from audio-visual and multimedia to computer science and medicine will ensure a complex coverage of our project.

5   Preliminary Results

For answering the first sub-research question, we model the workflow steps of a journal submission using the Linked Data Notifications (LDNs) protocol [4]. To support this, we use the LDN protocol, but we might also consider OWL-S ontology [5] in the future to describe in more detail the semantic web services that are used.

First, we chose a PDF article from the Data Science journal from IOS Press [26]. This article has two versions, three reviews for each version and a final, camera-ready, version. Next, in order to analyze the publishing workflow of this

---

[1] https://beeldengeluid.nl/en.
[2] https://www.iospress.nl/.

article at a more granular level, we decomposed it into more fine-grained inter-connected parts or digital artifacts and represented them as nodes in a network. For this we mainly used the SPAR ontology suite [8] to decompose the bulk of PDF text into separate paragraphs with semantic meaning, used PROV-O [7] to model the provenance of these digital artifacts, the FAIR* reviews ontology [2] for modeling the reviews and the Web Annotation Data Model [9] for modeling information or connections between certain nodes in this network. The online repository of the model can be found online [6]. In total we had 284 nodes and 685 links. In the future we will use the LDNs protocol to model all the workflow steps in which the digital artifacts that comprise this article are involved.

6   Evaluation Plan

Throughout the various stages of our research methodology we will perform various evaluations to assess the validity of our results. For this we will mostly consider the use cases provided by the Netherlands Sound and Vision and IOS Press.

For the first sub-research question, where we want to model the decentralized execution of workflows, for a more complex evaluation we will use two different use cases: (i) we will manually model around 20 published scientific articles together with their scientific workflows; (ii) we will use the automated extraction of information from a bioinformatics repository already curated by experts, e.g. DisGeNET, "one of the largest and comprehensive repositories of human gene-disease associations currently available". For the evaluation we will conduct a qualitative analysis on the corpus of selected scientific papers and on the bioinformatics repository. We will consider reviews content, comments and annotations and how these relate to the structured parts of the article or of the bioinformatics repository.

For the second sub-research of how we can execute workflows that produce and consume digital artifacts, we will use the manually created model from the first step. The prototype that we will build will provide the software means to create a fully decentralized reviewing workflow. For evaluation purposes, we will conduct a controlled user experiment where we will ask participants to evaluate both the user interfaces, as well as the new way the reviews are conducted and how these reviewing workflows are generated by comparing it with how this process was carried on previously.

The third sub-research question addresses new ways of evaluating the quality and impact of a digital artifact based on the analysis of the workflows that produced and consumed the respective artifact. Here, we will develop new metrics for quality assessment of digital artifacts based on the scientific workflows that produce them, like reviewing. We will also develop a metrics for the impact that a digital artifact has based on the workflows that consume it. To evaluate these two metrics, we will first use nichesourcing (crowdsourcing with experts). At the same time, we will use existing data to import workflows and use it as a ground truth for generating the workflows.

For the fourth sub-research question, where we want to be able to provide answers to inquiries made by users, we will develop a prototype that can return digital artifacts in response to user queries, together with the linked workflows that contain them. Furthermore, users would be able to create on the fly workflows for digital artifacts. For evaluation, we will use crowdsourcing to evaluate the software prototype in terms of the relevancy and the results that are returned as answers to user inquiries and also for rating the creation and execution of workflows on digital artifacts.

7   Conclusions

This project address issues like provenance and reproducibility in scientific publications and the support for a descentralized system of publishing in which scientific workflows can be modeled using Semantic Web technologies. We also define alternative ways of assessing the quality of scientific publications based on the more granular representation of digital artifacts involved in scientific workflows. This fine-grained representation of digital artifacts in the form of a continuously-expanding network of digital artifacts supports in turn the more granular execution of scientific workflows and workflow steps, allowing for greater transparency and descentralization of scientific workflows like the peer review process. This new way of publishing digital artifacts by considering the *scientific wokflows* that produce and consume them will improve the dissemination, transparency and reproducibility of science in the future.

Acknowledgements. We would like to thank Tobias Kuhn, Davide Ceolin, Lora Aroyo, Johan Oomen, Erwin Verbruggen, Maarten Frohlich and Stephanie Delbecque for helping in writing this research proposal, for their valuable and constant feedback and ideas.

References

1. Budapest Open Access Initiative. http://www.budapestopenaccessinitiative.org/
2. FAIR* Reviews ontology. http://fairreviews.linkeddata.es/def/core/index.html
3. PROV-Pings. http://git2prov.org:8902/prov-pings/
4. Linked Data Notifications. https://www.w3.org/TR/ldn/
5. OWL Web Ontology Language for Services (OWL-S). https://www.w3.org/Submission/2004/07/
6. Linkflows model. https://github.com/LaraHack/linkflows_model
7. PROV-O: The PROV Ontology. https://www.w3.org/TR/prov-o/
8. SPAR ontologies. http://www.sparontologies.net/ontologies
9. Web Annotaion Data Model. https://www.w3.org/TR/annotation-model/
10. Mons, B.: Which gene did you mean? BMC Bioinform. **6**, 142 (2005). https://doi.org/10.1186/1471-2105-6-142
11. Bizer, C., Heath, T., Berners-Lee, T.: Linked Data - the story so far. Int. J. Semant. Web Inf. **5**(3), 1–22 (2009). https://doi.org/10.4018/jswis.2009081901

12. Mazieres, D., Frans Kaashoek, M.: Escaping the evils of centralized control with self-certifying pathnames. In: Proceedings of the 8th ACM SIGOPS European Workshop on Support for Composing Distributed Applications, pp. 118–125 (1998)

13. Shotton, D.: Semantic publishing: the coming revolution in scientific journal publishing. Learn. Publ. **22**(2), 85–94 (2009). https://doi.org/10.1087/2009202

14. Dissecting our impact factor. In: Nature Materials (2011). https://www.nature.com/articles/nmat3114

15. Garfield, E.: The history and meaning of the journal impact factor. JAMA **295**(1), 90–93 (2006). https://doi.org/10.1001/jama.295.1.90

16. Taylor, I.J., Deelman, E., Gannon, D.B., Shields, M.: Workflows for e-Science: Scientific Workflows for Grids. Springer, London (2014). ISBN: 1849966192

17. Filali, I., Bongiovanni, F., Huet, F., Baude, F.: A survey of structured P2P systems for RDF data storage and retrieval. In: Hameurlain, A., Küng, J., Wagner, R. (eds.) Transactions on Large-Scale Data- and Knowledge-Centered Systems III. LNCS, vol. 6790, pp. 20–55. Springer, Heidelberg (2011). https://doi.org/10.1007/978-3-642-23074-5_2

18. Debattista, J., Lange, C., Auer, S.: daQ, an ontology for dataset quality information. In: Proceedings of the Workshop on Linked Data on the Web 1184 (2014)

19. Mesirov, J.P.: Accessible reproducible research. Int. J. Semant. Web Inf. **327**(5964), 415–416 (2010). https://doi.org/10.1126/science.1179653

20. Cohen, J.P., Lo, H.Z.: Academic torrents: a community-maintained distributed repository. In: Proceedings of the 2014 Annual Conference on Extreme Science and Engineering Discovery Environment (2014). https://doi.org/10.1145/2616498.2616528

21. Janowicz, K., Hitzler, P.: Open and transparent: the review process of the Semantic Web journal. Learn. Publ. **25**, 48–55 (2012). https://doi.org/10.1087/20120107

22. Wilkinson, M., et al.: The FAIR Guiding Principles for scientific data management and stewardship. Scie. Data **3** (2016). https://doi.org/10.1038/sdata.2016.18

23. Baker, M.: 1,500 scientists lift the lid on reproducibility. Nature **533**(7604) (2016). https://doi.org/10.1038/533452a

24. Murray-Rust, P.: Open data in science. Ser. Rev. **34**(1), 52–64 (2008). https://doi.org/10.1016/j.serrev.2008.01.001

25. Bechhofer, S., et al.: Why linked data is not enough for scientists. Future Gener. Comput. Syst. **29**(2), 599–611 (2013). https://doi.org/10.1016/j.future.2011.08.004

26. Peroni, S.: Automating semantic publishing. Data Sci. J. (2017). https://doi.org/10.3233/DS-170012

27. Peroni, S.: The semantic publishing and referencing ontologies. In: Semantic Web Technologies and Legal Scholarly Publishing, pp. 121–193 (2014). https://doi.org/10.1007/978-3-319-04777-5_5

28. Kiesslich, T., Weineck, S.B., Koelblinger, D.: Reasons for journal impact factor changes: influence of changing source items. PLOS One (2016). https://doi.org/10.1371/journal.pone.0154199

29. Kuhn, T., Dumontier, M.: Trusty URIs: verifiable, immutable, and permanent digital artifacts for linked data. In: Proceedings of the 11th Extended Semantic Web Conference (2014). https://doi.org/10.1007/978-3-319-07443-6_27

30. Kuhn, T., et al.: Decentralized provenance-aware publishing with nanopublications. In: PeerJ Comput. Sci. (2016). https://doi.org/10.7717/peerj-cs.78

Adaptive Anomaly Detection and Root Cause Analysis by Fusing Semantics and Machine Learning

Bram Steenwinckel$^{(\boxtimes)}$ (iD)

Ghent University - imec, IDLab, Ghent, Belgium
`Bram.Steenwinckel@ugent.be`

Abstract. Anomaly detection (AD) systems are either manually built by experts setting thresholds on data or constructed automatically by learning from the available data through machine learning (ML). The first requires profound prior knowledge and are non-adaptive to changing environments but can perform root cause analysis (RCA) to give an understanding of the detected anomaly. The second has a huge need for data, is unable to perform RCA and is often only trained once and deployed in various contexts, leading to a lot of false positives. Fusing the prior knowledge with ML techniques could resolve the generation of these alarms and should define the causes. The primary challenges to create such a detection system are: (1) Augmenting the current ML techniques with prior knowledge to enhance the detection rate. (2) Incorporate knowledge to interpret the cause of a detected anomaly automatically. (3) Reduce of human-involvement by automating the design of detection patterns.

Keywords: Anomaly detection · Root cause analysis
Machine learning · Expert knowledge · Semantic web
Knowledge graphs

1 Introduction

In recent years, there is an increasing interest in Internet-connected devices and sensors, called the Internet of Things (IoT). These IoT devices continuously generate data that describe their state and their context or environment. Sensor monitoring systems have found their way into almost all industries and a variety of research fields and applications such as transportation [5] and healthcare [19]. Such systems can yield valuable insights into a company's physical assets and the interaction between these assets. However, awareness is growing across industries that strategically placed sensors have small added value without data analysis. Companies that invest in and successfully derive value from their data hold a distinct advantage over their competitors [29]. Both Anomaly detection (AD) and root cause analysis (RCA) are methods to investigate irregularities in the

© Springer Nature Switzerland AG 2018
A. Gangemi et al. (Eds.): ESWC 2018 Satellite Events, LNCS 11155, pp. 272–282, 2018.
https://doi.org/10.1007/978-3-319-98192-5_46

data. They are becoming more accessible as more relevant data is generated and tools for data analysis becoming widely available.

AD is the identification process of events or observations, which do not correspond to an expected pattern or other items inside a dataset [19]. RCA helps to guide the problem solver understand the real causes of detected anomalies [17]. The detection process visualised in Fig. 1 represents the usual workflow. First, historical data from different sources are used in a préprocessing step to make sure that all the available records are uniform. Based on this cleaned data, algorithms will learn the regular patterns and will detect the most relevant characteristics. This pattern can now be used to identify different anomalies in newly, unseen data. When the learned patterns diverge from this new data, an action mechanism will be able to alert this anomalous behaviour, or the cause of this unusual event can be investigated to resolve it. More concrete, suppose for example a fully automated ventilation system available in modern houses today. Historical sensor data will be used to determine the average levels of CO_2. New sensor data will be used to determine which room is currently underventilated and the system acts by adapting the fan speed to resolve the high level of CO_2. Modern techniques monitor the household's behaviour to react to the possible causes of the detected anomalies. In our example, self-learning techniques optimise the performance of the fan to get the house fully ventilated when people arrive after work.

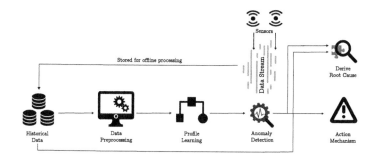

Fig. 1. Overview of the workflow of current anomaly detection systems

However, the AD and RCA tools of today have difficulties to adapt to changing behaviours. If in our ventilation example, a person works at home, the ventilation system will detect abnormal behaviour and will be unable to react to this new situation or is even unable to derive the cause if it is not explicitly programmed or taught. Human-involved tuning is, therefore, frequently needed to adapt these systems to multiple environments. Sensors can produce new information at a fast pace, while enhanced analysis is needed to investigate whether current observations are anomalous, resulting in many false alerts and undetected events [6].

There is a need for adaptive, but still, accurate AD and RCA system that can take directly into account the prior knowledge to optimise the detection of anomalies and identify their causes. In our example, work schedules and agendas could be used as prior knowledge to optimise the ventilation process.

In summary, the challenges this research will tackle are: (1) Reducing the number of falsely generated anomalies by incorporating available prior knowledge (2) Automatic determination of the most plausible cause of the detected anomalies, to give additional interpretability to human operators. (3) Adaptively change the detection behaviour to a various number of contexts to reduce the human-involvement during the design of such detection techniques.

2   State of the Art

Different research domains make use of the available prior knowledge to improve AD and RCA. This section gives an overview of (1) learning models which uses the available knowledge as input. (2) techniques which work directly with the available information. (3) rule-based detection mechanisms.

2.1   Knowledge Incorporation in Data-Driven AD and RCA

Approaches for detecting anomalies in a dataset which do not require any pre-defined rules, models, or prior knowledge limit the efforts needed for systems designed by experts [8]. Most of these approaches are based on machine learning (ML) techniques and can process vast amounts of data. ML models can be supervised or unsupervised, based on the availability of labelled data. Labelling a significant amount of data for a domain-specific problem requires much human involvement. Therefore, most AD problems belong to the category of unsupervised learning due to unpredictable aspects of the data. In critical domains, where faults have a significant impact, the primary goal of AD is not the speed of the detection, but the accuracy or the reduction of the false negative and positive rates [23].

The goal of AD detection technique is, therefore, to model the normal behaviour. Statistical tests can be devised to determine if this behavioural model explains the data samples, uncovering both temporal and spatial anomalies when it does not succeed [20,28]. The detected anomalies are mostly hard to interpret [22]. RCA techniques are therefore based on detection models using tree structures and logics [2,30]

Knowledge nowadays is usually represented as a mesh of information, linked up in such a way that it should be interpretable by machines. Such a mesh of information is more generally known as the semantic web [3]. Many of the semantic concepts inside various domains are described in so-called ontologies, providing structured relations and the ability to reason on these concepts. Data annotated by these ontologies is stored using node-edge triples in a knowledge graph, relating prior information over multiple domains [14]. ML methods, in general, are currently not able to take advantage of these graphical knowledge representations. Therefore, techniques to transform graphs into a vectorial representation are becoming more popular, resulting in embedding techniques [11].

Knowledge graph embeddings usually map entities and relations to a vector space and predict unknown triples by scoring the candidate triples [21]. Embeddings are mostly designed to perform a single statistical relational learning task, like predicting missing edges or predicting properties of nodes [12]. Recently designed embedding techniques transform the graph triples (subject, object and relation pairs) directly into vectors which can be reused for various tasks [15]. These more general embeddings are particularly attractive for cross-domain knowledge graphs, which can be used in a variety of scenarios and applications. Constructing embeddings for dynamic knowledge graphs is, however, still problematic. High variable behaviour, such as in sensor data streams, usually involve recalculations due to the changed graphical representation.

Embedding techniques used in combination with the traditional ML techniques usually have a low level of interpretability because decisions are based on the vectors themselves, not on the interpretable initial graphical data. Techniques to resolve this loss in interpretability are usually expensive and do not scale for large graphs [25]. Song et al. [18] gave a broad overview of how to use the existing general-purpose knowledge to enhance the ML processes, by enriching the features or reducing the labelling work using prior knowledge. No efforts within this research domain are taken to use such an approach for developing AD systems to our knowledge, probably due to the unsupervised nature of the original detection problems.

2.2 Knowledge-Based Machine Learning

While embeddings translate the information into a manageable form for which we already have many methods available, techniques exist to learn directly over the knowledge graphs without any loss of information due to embedding transformations. One such technique is the Relational Graph Convolutional Network (RGCN), a method similar to neural networks but operating on graphs, developed specifically to deal with the highly multi-relational data characteristic of realistic knowledge graphs [10]. Another research area focuses on the development of predicate descriptions, using the available data and the existing prior knowledge. This Inductive Logic Programming (ILP) techniques are based on sound principles from both Logic and Statistic. Other combinations of ML techniques and prior knowledge models exist [1,5], but none of them is currently adapted to work with sensor streams or highly variable data because the evaluation of the prediction also requires the additional prior knowledge.

2.3 Defining Prior Knowledge into Rule-Based Systems

Rule-based detection systems utilising expert information have the advantage of being explainable and can determine the cause of the problem. They are however language dependent, do not scale with the increasing amount of data, and the development is time-consuming because much human involvement is needed [1,17]. Detection systems use techniques which track unwanted patterns in a data stream to provide more scalable solutions to the highly variable data of today.

Complex Event Processing (CEP) can be used to identify these abnormal events using pattern matching techniques such as rule-based, model-based or parametric statistical approaches [19]. These approaches, however, lack of expressiveness and flexibility to cope with complex events in different situations or different contexts. Therefore, semantic complex event processing (SCEP) proposes the semantic enrichment of the event streams, in which derived events are added in addition to the already observed pattern [19]. SCEP has been used in diverse applications comprising a variety of complex events including security and threat detection events [7,13], sensor networks [4,26] and eHealth or ambient assisted living [16,27]. SCEP systems make self-constrained decisions using a rule base, making them ideal candidates to perform RCA in data streams. Despite the benefits of SCEP, most patterns are static, and the anomalies must be defined upfront to work correctly. It requires some human involvement to adapt and update these patterns inside the multiple processing units [19].

3   Problem Statement

By analysing the state of the art methods, the following open problems can be identified:

P1 Current AD techniques only use the data itself to determine the occurrence of the unwanted behaviour.

P2 The frequently used accuracy metric misleads the functioning of the models due to the high impact of the falsely generated alarms.

P3 AD and RCA techniques are optimised for offline purposes, making them inappropriate to work with variable data, such as streaming environments.

P4 AD en RCA models are usually trained once and are therefore hard to adapt to new contexts, sensors or environments.

P5 The design of RCA models for a specific domain requires much human involvement.

P6 Most AD methods do not make interpretable decisions, reducing the ability to perform RCA.

From this, the following hypotheses can be deducted:

H1 Incorporating prior knowledge in learning and reasoning algorithms will outperform the detection rate of original AD ML techniques by at least 1% in real-life cases.

H2 The F1-score, which relates the number of false negatives and false positives, will be increased at least by 3% by incorporating the prior knowledge.

H3 Techniques which are adaptable to changing environments will reduce the human involvement by more than 50%.

H4 Designed techniques must be applicable in streaming contexts, without causing any data-driven congestions.

The following research question will be resolved to deliver the hypotheses proves:

Q1 Can prior knowledge, in the form of knowledge graphs or linked datasets, be incorporated as simple input features in the currently existing AD ML models to improve the detection of both false positives and false negatives?

Q2 Can current AD outcomes be transformed to enable RCA-based reasoning for finding the cause with the highest probability of an anomalous observation or be representative for the decision they make?

Q3 Is it possible to reduce the human involvement by deriving explainable rules from existing AD models inside a data stream and detect newly derived types of events without retraining or increasing the computational costs?

4   Research Methodology and Approach

A system which fuses both ML and semantics will be designed to improve the detection of anomalies together with the ability to determine their causes inside a stream of data accurately. An overview of such a system is given in Fig. 2. Prior knowledge will be used to derive rule patterns directly from the data stream and improve both the AD and RCA to address the research questions defined in Sect. 3. How this prior knowledge is incorporated in each of these three parts is discussed in the following sections.

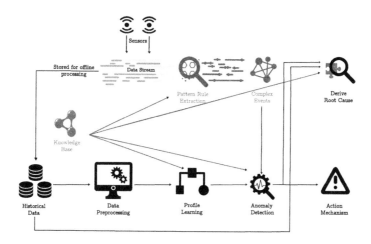

Fig. 2. Overview of the enhanced AD and RCA system

4.1   Improved Feature Selection for Enhanced AD

Embeddings can be used to incorporate prior knowledge into ML models as discussed in Sect. 2.1. These embeddings can be used as features for anomaly-based ML systems but will operate in a pipeline of discrete steps. More concretely, the detection models will no further improve once the feature vectors are extracted because the error signal from the performed detection task can no longer be used to fine-tune the extraction step further. Instead of using the embedded representation of the knowledge graph directly, a new technique will transform the knowledge graph directly into a matrix formation. Rows will represent subject-object pairs, while the columns represent the relation types. Analysing this matrix can require some computational effort because the computations scale linearly with the number of cells or thus the number of links within the knowledge graph. There is a high probability that important information is scattered all over the matrix. The proposed technique will extract information from this matrix by adaptively selecting a sequence of regions of interest. These regions of interest represent the cells within the matrix with the most valuable information concerning the anomalous links. A (bandit) reinforcement learning (RL) agent is, therefore, an excellent candidate to control the choice of the region of interest, as it can work with partially available information. The agent will select actions related to the number of regions and the location in the matrix. The feedback on the correctly detected anomalies will improve the region selection process of the RL agent. Figure 3 gives an overview of this process. The detection rate can be improved because the extracted information only focusses on the informative links within the available prior knowledge.

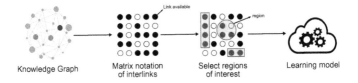

Fig. 3. Overview of the matrix knowledge learning process.

4.2   Interpretable Knowledge for RCA

ML-based detections reveal the relations between the selected features and the provided outcome. Most of these feature vectors have, however, a low level of interpretability, reducing the capability of determining the underlying cause of the detected anomaly. The generated vectors, both from Sect. 4.1 and the previously mentioned embedding techniques, are called black-box features due to the reduced interpretation of the generated values. Research is needed to reproduce valuable information, which was available in the original knowledge graph, from these embedded vectors. One method based on Generative Adversarial Networks (GAN) can be used to transform the vectors back into an interpretable graph, giving back the power to determine the cause of an anomaly. In such a GAN network, the generator network constructs a graphical representation from a generated vector and inputs these graph structures to the discriminative network. The discriminative system is supposed to detect whether the structure generated by the generative network resembles a part of the original knowledge graph. Both networks update their performance until a low number of faults are generated, and the discriminative system has difficulties in finding differences between fake subgraphs from the original subgraphs. An overview of such a GAN process is given in Fig. 4. Further analysis to determine the cause of the detected anomalies is possible with these embedding interpretations.

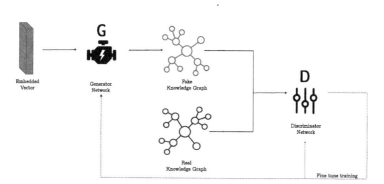

Fig. 4. Overview of knowledge graph embedding using a Generative Adversarial Network.

4.3   Adaptive Detection and Analysis for Streaming Data

Techniques to incorporate prior knowledge directly into data streams resulted in the design of SCEP systems. Problems arise when many different anomalous events need to be tracked. Rules are human maintained and can contradict. The correct functioning of the system can, therefore, not be guaranteed. Rules should be able to directly derivable from the ML-learning techniques used for the detection of anomalies in Sect. 4.1. White-box models can be translated easily into rules and benefit from the ease of interpretability. In contrast, black-box models do not have this interpretability, but methods exist to convert these models to a set of rules [24]. To cope with the adaptive character of adding and removing these generated model-based rules, a RL agent will decide which rules to activate. The pattern rule extractor in Fig. 2 will still test a subset of rules (actions) using this approach, while adaptations and further improvements are ensured. Feedback based on the number of rules or the complexity of the rule tests guarantees the efficiency of the RL agent. An overview of the learning agent is given in Fig. 5. The designed technique will be able to operate in a changing environment where high variable data, such as in data streams, need to be analysed. Automatic derivation of simple rules reduces the human involvement and can be explainable, making RCA possible after the detections took place.

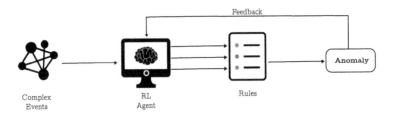

Fig. 5. RL agent for rule selection.

5   Evaluation Plan

Each phase of Sect. 4 can be evaluated separately. The proposed technique of Sect. 4.1 will be compared with existing embedding techniques, to show the advantages. A comparison using the prior knowledge directly and the technique proposed in Sect. 4.2 will reveal the benefits of fusing semantics with ML for RCA. At last, evaluation of models using the original rule sets and the technique proposed in Sect. 4.3 will be made to determine their adaptiveness and scalability. All this will be done using standardised benchmark RDF datasets used for classification purposes in [15], but adapted here to detect the minority classes as anomalies. The functioning of the full system will be tested using two different proof of concepts:

- **Pervasive Healthcare:** In the eHealth domain, the available data from intelligent devices and sensors correlate to prior knowledge. Profile information of the patients can improve the detection of anomalies. The imec SWEET study[1] is such a case were stress analyses with sensor data can be improved by incorporating additional context. Data will be used during this research containing both raw sensor data available from wearables and context parameters based on the person's habits.
- **Transport and maintenance:** In the transport and ventilation sector, many devices are equipped with different types of sensors, investigating the onboard electronics and engines [9]. Televic[2] is such a partner in the railway domain, utilising a high number of sensors on trains which produce floats of data for further analysis. Renson[3] controls the airflow of many households, based on sensor observations per room. Several contextual parameters, such as the weather, influence the measures. To reduce these unwanted alerts, this prior knowledge must be fused with the available sensor data.

---

[1] https://www.imec-int.com/en/articles/imec-s-sweet-study-collects-world-s-largest-dataset-on-stress-detection.
[2] https://www.televic-rail.com.
[3] https://www.renson.eu.

6   Conclusions

In this proposed research, techniques will be developed for improved AD and RCA in a sensor stream environment. While current techniques only focus on the data themselves, the proposed methods will incorporate prior knowledge to reduce the number of false positive and negatives. Analysing the cause of an anomaly will be possible with the design of an interpretable embedding technique. At last, adaptiveness with less human involvement can be achieved in data streams by automatic derivation of learning rules from already existing models. The full system will be evaluated with two use cases for two different domains. I would like to thank my promotors prof. dr. ir. Filip De Turck and dr. Femke Ongeae for their support and valuable input in the realisation of this work. I would also like to thank Televic, Renson and imec for participating in this research.

References

1. Abele, L., et al.: Combining knowledge modeling and machine learning for alarm root cause analysis. IFAC Proc. **46**(9), 1843–1848 (2010)
2. Smith, B.A., et al.: Fault diagnosis using first order logic tools. In: Proceedings of the 32nd Midwest Symposium on Circuits and Systems, vol. 1, pp. 299–302, August 1989
3. Berners-Lee, T., Hendler, J., Lassila, O.: The semantic web. Sci. Am. **284**(5), 34–43 (2001)
4. Calvier, FÉ., Kammoun, A., Zimmermann, A., Singh, K., Fayolle, J.: Ontology driven complex event pattern definition (Short Paper). In: Debruyne, C., et al. (eds.) On the Move to Meaningful Internet Systems: OTM 2016 Conferences. OTM 2016. Lecture Notes in Computer Science, vol. 10033. Springer, Cham (2016). https://doi.org/10.1007/978-3-319-48472-3_31
5. Camossi, E., et al.: Semantic-based Anomalous Pattern Discovery in Moving Object Trajectories, pp. 1–20. CoRR abs/1305.1 (2013)
6. Ehsani-Besheli, F., Zarandi, H.R.: Context-aware anomaly detection in embedded systems. In: Zamojski, W., Mazurkiewicz, J., Sugier, J., Walkowiak, T., Kacprzyk, J. (eds.) DepCoS-RELCOMEX 2017. AISC, vol. 582, pp. 151–165. Springer, Cham (2018). https://doi.org/10.1007/978-3-319-59415-6_15
7. Hammar, K.: Modular semantic CEP for threat detection. In: Operations Research and Data Mining ORADM 2012 workshop proceedings (2012). ISBN: 978–607-414-284-6
8. Huang, H., et al.: Streaming anomaly detection using randomized matrix sketching. Proc. VLDB Endow. **9**(3), 192–203 (2015)
9. Kdouh, H., et al.: Wireless sensor network on board vessels. In: 2012 19th International Conference on Telecommunications, ICT 2012, pp. 1–6. IEEE, April 2012
10. Schlichtkrull, M.S., et al.: Modeling relational data with graph convolutional networks. CoRR abs/1703.06103 (2017)
11. Nguyen, D.Q.: An overview of embedding models of entities and relationships for knowledge base completion. arXiv preprint arXiv 1703.08098 (2017)
12. Nickel, M., et al.: A review of relational machine learning for knowledge graph. Proc. IEEE **104**(28), 1–23 (2015)

13. Patri, O., et al.: Sensors to events: semantic modeling and recognition of events from data streams. Int. J. Semant. Comput. **10**, 461–501 (2016)
14. Paulheim, H., et al.: Exploiting linked open data as background knowledge in data mining. In: International Workshop on Linked Data, pp. 1–10 (2013)
15. Ristoski, P., et al.: RDF2Vec: RDF Graph Embeddings and Their Applications. IOS Press (2016)
16. Sandha, S.S., et al.: Complex Event Processing of Health Data in Real-time to Predict Heart Failure Risk and Stress (2017)
17. Solé, M., et al.: Survey on models and techniques for root-cause analysis. In: Clinical Orthopaedics and Related Research (CoRR), pp. 1–18 (2017)
18. Song, Y., et al.: Machine Learning with World Knowledge: The Position and Survey, pp. 1–20. arXiv preprint arXiv 1705.02908 (2017)
19. Souiden, I., Brahmi, Z., Toumi, H.: A survey on outlier detection in the context of stream mining: review of existing approaches and recommadations. In: Madureira, A.M., Abraham, A., Gamboa, D., Novais, P. (eds.) ISDA 2016. AISC, vol. 557, pp. 372–383. Springer, Cham (2017). https://doi.org/10.1007/978-3-319-53480-0_37
20. Ahmad, S., et al.: Unsupervised real-time anomaly detection for streaming data. Neurocomputing **262**, 134–147 (2017)
21. Ebisu, T., et al.: Toruse: Knowledge graph embedding on a lie group. CoRR abs/1711.05435 (2017)
22. Ademujimi, T.T., Brundage, M.P., Prabhu, V.V.: A review of current machine learning techniques used in manufacturing diagnosis. In: Lödding, H., Riedel, R., Thoben, K.-D., von Cieminski, G., Kiritsis, D. (eds.) APMS 2017. IAICT, vol. 513, pp. 407–415. Springer, Cham (2017). https://doi.org/10.1007/978-3-319-66923-6_48
23. Ukil, A., et al.: IoT healthcare analytics: the importance of anomaly detection. In: Conference on Advanced Information Networking and Applications, pp. 994–997 (2016)
24. Uzun, Y., et al.: Rule extraction from training artificial neural network. Multi. Eng. Sci. Technol. **3**(8), 2458–9403 (2016)
25. Wang, Q., et al.: Knowledge base completion via coupled path ranking. In: ACL, pp. 1308–1318 (2014)
26. Xiao, F., et al.: New parallel processing strategies in complex event processing systems with data streams. Distrib. Sens. Netw. **13**(8), 1–15 (2017)
27. Xu, Y., et al.: Semantic-based complex event processing in the AAL domain. In: 9th International Semantic Web Conference (ISWC2010) (2010)
28. He, Y., et al.: Mechanism-indepedent outlier detection method for online experimentation. In: IEEE International Conference on Data Science, pp. 640–647 (2017)
29. YE: Big data: Changing the way businesses compete and operate (2014)
30. Zheng, A.X., et al.: Failure diagnosis using decision trees. In: Proceedings of the First International Conference on Autonomic Computing (2004)

Question Answering over Knowledge Bases

Lucia Siciliani[✉]

Department of Computer Science, University of Bari Aldo Moro, Bari, Italy
lucia.siciliani@uniba.it

Abstract. The fast growth of the Semantic Web has unleashed its potentialities, leading to the development of many tools and services that can exploit the huge amount of information it contains. As more semantic information is available online, mainly in the form of ontology based Knowledge Bases the process of searching and querying this content has become more and more challenging. Question Answering, which defines the task of retrieving an answer to a question formulated using natural language, can make the Semantic Web easily accessible by anyone, even by those users that do not know how to use a specific data query language or are unaware of the structure of the KB they want to query. Moreover, in the same way the Semantic Web can benefit in its spread from Question Answering, also Question Answering systems can improve their outcome since Knowledge Bases can be exploited to retrieve a concise answer for complex questions. Although several approaches have been proposed by the research community in the field, the experimental results show that the performance are still far from optimal. Following the future directions presented in the latest works about this field, we outline an approach for Question Answering over structured data applicable to Knowledge Bases whose aim is to overcome the main issues that affect the research in this area.

Keywords: Question Answering · Semantic Web
Natural language processing · Machine learning · Knowledge Bases

1 Introduction

Question Answering (QA) has the purpose of retrieving an answer to a question written in natural language by a user. To a certain extent QA systems can be considered as a particular kind of Information Retrieval (IR) systems, since in both the cases the goal is to find an answer to a specific information need expressed in textual form. The main difference between them regards the kind of output: in an IR system the output is usually represented by a subset of the overall corpus of documents, ordered according to a criterion of relevance, meanwhile in QA systems the output can take the form of a concise fact, in the case of factoid QA, or other kind of formats such as lists, short passages, and so on.

© Springer Nature Switzerland AG 2018
A. Gangemi et al. (Eds.): ESWC 2018 Satellite Events, LNCS 11155, pp. 283–293, 2018.
https://doi.org/10.1007/978-3-319-98192-5_47

Among several different classifications for Question Answering, one of the most discriminating concerns the type of data sources. According to such taxonomy, the data stored into the resource exploited by the QA system can be either unstructured or structured. Unstructured data, as the name suggest, takes the form of free text without any kind of arrangement. The source text can be pre-processed using a wide range of techniques of various complexity, in order to facilitate the retrieval of the query keywords in the following steps. On the other hand, structured data is already organized in data structures which allow the system to leverage them almost directly. Obviously, many combination are possible and one opportunity is also represnted by web services, from which both structured and unstructured data can be obtained and exploited by a question answering system by applying different kind of techniques.

QA over structured data is rooted in the late sixties and early seventies, when the first Natural Language Interfaces were developed as a way to access data contained into databases [1]. Later on, the attention focused over the extraction of relevant information from free text. In the last two decades, the birth of the Semantic Web (SW) [2] has opened up new paths for QA.

SW was born as an extension of the so called Web 2.0 with the aim of enriching the huge amount of data already available online with a meaning. Thanks to SW an increasing amount of information is accessible on the Web in the form of Knowledge Bases, such as DBpedia [3], YAGO [4] and Wikidata [5], which collect huge amounts of information using the ontology model. Nowadays all these projects are still ongoing, with a steady effort to further extend and improve the quality of data that they include. A crucial aspect to consider in order to exploit such amount of information is how to actually access it and this is where QA systems prove to be useful.

Moreover QA systems over structured data can benefit in several ways by the use of KBs: first of all, they can allow the system to enhance the answer with contextual informations (e.g.: images, infoboxes), secondly, it is possible to aswer more complex questions by combining information coming from different KBs.

The format chosen to model data in the SW is the Resource Description Framework (RDF) and the query language associated to it is the SPARQL Protocol and RDF Query Language. Although those models have been properly designed to guarantee the automated processing of Web resources and the interoperability among applications that use this kind of information, they still represent an obstacle for many users who are not accustomed to such formalisms. Thus, QA systems can be used to overcome such limits and disclose to a greater variety of users the information encoded into KBs.

2   State of the Art

The problem of QA over KBs has been addressed in a wide variety of ways. Until the last decade there was still no official benchmark for evaluating those systems, hence a comparison was almost infeasible. However, the growing interest towards the potentialities of the SW has raised the need to guide the efforts made in this research field and try to find a solution for this problem. At the moment there are three major benchmarks for QA system over KBs, namely: QALD [6–11], WebQuestions [12] and SimpleQuestions [13]. Further details about those datasets will be provided in Sect. 6.

QA systems share the common feature to be very complex since transforming a question in natural language to its equivalent in SPARQL is not a straightforward task.

Such conversion must start from the analysis of the user question via different techniques, whose aim is to catch the overall meaning of the question and collect information which facilitate the following phases. The methods than can be adopted include Part-Of-Speech tagging, parsing, the identification of the kind of question or of the expected answer type. Next, the phrases contained in the questions must be mapped with the entities or relations belonging to RDF datasets. Selecting the right resource is crucial since even a slight error could greatly affect the meaning of the final query that could return a wrong answer.

Each of these phases can obviously be further decomposed in smaller subtasks and all of them can be performed using a plethora of methods. For this reason is really hard to categorize the approaches proposed in the literature, even though there are some surveys that accomplished this difficult goal.

In [14], the authors give an overview of the topic describing the actual state of the research, categorizing the main approaches proposed in the literature, giving information about the available tools which can be used to design a novel system and providing a description of the evaluation metrics along with the available benchmarks.

In [15], the authors tackle the problem from an interesting perspective, focusing the attention over the main challenges related to this field and describing each one of the selected publications according to them.

One of the latest survey [16], provides an accurate analysis of the state of the art, listing almost all the systems proposed for every benchmark. After having traced the overall structure of a QA system, each component is further analyzed to describe the different approaches that have been employed and which systems have used them.

Since in this context an exhaustive description of all the work proposed until now is infeasible due to space constraints, we will focus the attention on the systems that achieved the most significant results in QALD (starting from its fourth edition), SimpleQuestions and WebQuestions.

Xser [17] is the system that obtained the best performance in both QALD-4 and QALD-5. To retrieve the answer for a given question it utilizes two different stages: the first one which is KB-independent and the second one which is KB-dependent. In the first phase, the user query is subdivided into phrases and to each of them a semantic label (i.e. entity, relation, category, variable) is assigned. Those labels are then used to construct a Directed Acyclic Graph (DAG) which encodes the query intention. The main advantage of performing those steps independently from the KB is that the method can be more easily adapted to any new KB. The KB-dependent phase has the aim of instantiating the query intention with regard to the chosen KB. For each semantic label, different tools are used to create a list of possible candidates in the KB and to disambiguate among them. Once this step is completed, the query can finally be translated into its structured equivalent form. The main disadvantage of this approach is that the semantic parser used to produce the DAG must be trained with a corpus of questions that must be manually annotated with the corresponding labels.

CANaLI [18] achieved an outstanding result during the sixth edition of QALD, proposing an approach based on controlled natural languages. A controlled natural language can be seen as a restricted version of a certain natural language, obtained by considering only a subset of its vocabulary and its grammar rules. The analysis of the question is then performed by exploiting a finite state automata. CANaLI progressively considers each phrase in the question and, if it belongs to those accepted by the system, it shifts the state of the automata accordingly to the chunk in input. Once all the question is analyzed, the history of all the states that have been reached by the automata along with the transition rules that have been applied are used to construct the SPARQL query. Since this process is deterministic, the query generation step can be performed without mistakes. However this approach reveals some drawbacks: first of all, if a certain phrase is not recognized by the automata then the final state is never reached and the computation can not go on; secondly the question must be formulated using the grammar rules which are accepted by the system. This is why the authors performed a rephrasing of the questions that belonged to the QALD, adapting the vocabulary and the syntactic structure when possible.

In QALD-7 [11] the task of English QA over Wikipedia was introduced for the first time along with the one of multilingual QA over DBpedia which appeared in every edition of the challenge.

The best performances in the task using DBpedia as RDF dataset were obtained by ganswer2 [19]. The authors propose a solution where the answer to the user question is obtained without generating the SPARQL query. The natural language query is interpreted as a semantic query graph and then the system tries to match such structure in the overall RDF graph of the KB. In this way it is also possible to postpone the disambiguation of possible candidates for the matching, thus decreasing the response time.

Regarding the task focused on Wikidata instead, WDAqua [20] managed to obtain a better result compared with the other participants. The system is language and KB independent, meaning that it can answer to a question formulated in different languages and can exploit different KBs. In order to achieve this result, the authors start from the assumption that what really encloses the meaning of a question is the semantic of the words that compose it rather than its syntactic features. Following this assumption, all the candidate entities, properties and classes which can be extracted by analyzing the source question are extracted, while stopwords are removed. Next, following different patterns, a set SPARQL queries is constructed and each query is then ranked according its capability of covering the meaning of the original question. Finally, using a model based on logistic regression, the system estimates the confidence in the retrieved answers. If such value is greater than a certain threshold, the answer is given, otherwise it is rejected.

Regarding SimpleQuestions and WebQuestions, the system that performed the best on these datasets are [21] and [22], respectively.

SimpleQuestions contains a big amount of questions, so most of the systems that have been evaluated on this dataset use an approach based on neural networks. [21] makes no exception, making use of a two step approach. Since all the questions only involve a single binary relation, the first step consists in identifying the phrases which can correspond to the subject and the predicate of the question. Next, entity linking and relation detection are performed to actually map those phrases to entities and relations in the KB. Those steps are not sequential, but they are handled together using a Recurrent Neural Network.

[22] use a Memory Network to answer questions over WebQuestions. First all the possible n-grams of words in the question within the dataset are matched against the entities in the KB. This list of matching items is used to construct a set of hypothetical questions that are compared to the upcoming question using a similarity measure, which is then exploited to find out the correct answer.

3 Problem Statement and Contributions

As previously stated in Sect. 1, the growth of the Semantic Web has raised the problem of how effectively exploit this huge amount of information.

One of the main problems which prevents the spread of this technology among common users is represented by the difficulty of extracting the information contained in a KB. In fact in order to do this, it is necessary to know the vocabulary adopted in the KB and use a specific Data Query Language (i.e. SPARQL) that can be challenging to use, especially when trying to satisfy complex information needs.

QA systems aim to free users from these constraints allowing them to query a KB using natural language. In most cases, the question is formulated using a terminology which is greatly different from the vocabulary of the knowledge base since the user is completely unaware of it. For example, given the question *"Who is the writer of Neuromancer?"* and DBpedia as the only KB to be queried, it is not possible to find an answer if only the label of each resource is considered as valid. Infact, the entity *Neuromancer* has no property labeled *writer* and the right term that should be used in accordance to the structure of DBpedia is *author*. This issue is known in literature with as lexical gap. Finding an effective way to bridge this gap is the primary problem that we want to deal with.

The problem represented by the lexical gap is intertwined to another important issue: ambiguity. Ambiguity can be considered as an intrinsic feature of natural language, where the meaning of a word is deeply influenced by the context in which it occurs. Considered by itself, ambiguity is not a negative characteristic: it adds syntactic sugar to a language and is the fundamental element to all the figures of speech which enrich our cultural heritage. However, going back to the context of QA over KBs, ambiguity is something that we want to avoid, since it can lead to an incorrect answer. In the question *"What is the genre of Chicago?"* the entity *Chicago* could refer to the city, the band or the musical, however the word *genre* can give a good hint about which option is the correct one. A QA system has to cope with polysemous words performing a disambiguation step, which obviously must be executed after entity linking and relation prediction that allow to collect a set of candidate resources related to the phrases within the question.

Even if the lexical gap and the ambiguity issues appear to be more focused on the semantics of the user question, its syntactic structure must not be underrated. This is particularly true when handling articulated questions. SPARQL is a powerful query language, which allows to express even complex constructs using a wide range of query forms (e.g.: SELECT, ASK), patterns (e.g.: ORDER BY, DISTINCT) and modifiers (e.g.: GROUP BY, HAVING, FILTER, OPTIONAL). The main problem is that with natural language these constructs can be formulated using a considerable number of expressions that share the same meaning but can have very little in common from a lexical point of view. The goal then is to identify those expressions in the question and properly translate them using SPARQL.

Therefore, the aforementioned issues can be summarized through the following questions:

RQ1 What methods can help bridging the gap between the vocabulary of the user and the one used within a KB? Which one is most suitable method for entities and which one for relations?

RQ2 How to disambiguate among different resources that can be connected to the same phrase in the question?

RQ3 How to understand the overall meaning of the user query and translate it into a proper SPARQL query?

4   Research Methodology and Approach

With our work we want to further extend the results already put forward in literature, trying to face the challenges that are still open in this field.

We can split the architecture of the QA system to be proposed in two distinct pipelines: one for data preprocessing and the other one for the answer retrieval.

The information contained in the KB is essential in the last step of those QA systems that first perform the translation of the user question in a SPARQL query which is then ready to be submitted to the underlying data resource.

Nevertheless this data play a key role in the answer retrieval pipeline, especially when trying to perform entity linking and relation prediction. For this reason it is really important to perform a data preprocessing step.

First of all, the RDF triples of the KB must be collected and indexed in proper data structures. In this way they can be retrieved more quickly when needed, leading to an improvement of the performance of the system.

Secondly, we want to add more information to those structure, by performing a proper augmentation of the KB. In order to do this we could exploit the mappings between questions and query that can be found in the datasets available in literature and even employ some external corpora of text. From this point of view our research could benefit from a focused analysis of the state of the art systems in the fields of entity linking and relation prediction.

The second pipeline is related to answer retrieval, i.e. performing the steps needed to actually find an answer for the question issued by a user.

Given a natural language question we must perform a syntactic and semantic analysis which consists of Part of Speech tagging, semantic parsing and Named Entity Recognition among the others. In literature there are several tools that can be used to perform this analysis, one of them being Stanford Core NLP [23].

Next, we have to map the phrases contained in the question to resources within the knowledge base and disambiguate between them if more than one option is available. This step will be deeply influenced by the preprocessing one, however we plan to make use of word embeddings and other distributional semantic models.

Lastly, the question must be converted into a SPARQL query. We intend to explore the benefits that would come from the introduction of an hybrid approach.

In literature this step has been performed in several ways, but the interesting fact is that, to the best of our knowledge, every system adopts the same mechanism for any kind of query.

We want to combine different approaches in order to mitigate the shortcomings that would descend from the use of a unique method. Usually simpler questions share a similar structure and the differences among them concern only the subject and the relation being involved. An approach based on pre-defined templates to be instantiated in real time has proven to be effective, but it is not as adequate when handling complex queries. For articulated questions, we could exploit as much as possible the output of the semantic analysis using a set of compositional rules.

The combination of these two techniques will allow our system to answer a broader variety of questions, accordingly to their complexity.

5   Preliminary Results

We have already developed a QA system over KBs enhancing the work presented in CANaLI [18].

As described in Sect. 2, an approach using controlled natural language suffers of some drawbacks connected to the constraints imposed on the vocabulary and the applicable grammar rules.

In particular, the vocabulary accepted by the finite state automata used in CANaLI is created by collecting the labels of the resources in the KB and hence only those labels can be employed in the question. For this reason we have decided to extend this vocabulary using Word2Vec (W2V) [24]. In the offline phase, we applied W2V to Wikipedia abstracts to create a word embedding for each term. Then, in the online phase, when a phrase is not recognised by the automata, it is projected in the same distributional space created from the Wikipedia abstract to retrieve all the semantically similar words. The top ten ranked words are selected as suitable candidates and the system substitutes the original word with candidate until the right one is found.

Another issue that we tried to solve is connected to the transition mechanism of the automata, which stops the computation for misinterpreted tokens. To avoid this problem we strengthened the automata with a backtracking algorithm which allows to cancel the last state shift and choose another interpretation the previous phrase.

Although these changes led to an improvement of the system, they could not completely overcome the limits imposed by the adoption of a controlled natural language. When trying to test the result of our version of the system over the QALD-6 dataset, we could avoid the rephrasing of several questions, but still an evaluation on the questions as they are provided by the proposer of the challenge is infeasible and did not produce promising results. Indeed, as shown in [18], this kind of systems prove to be really effective in real use cases when combined with a query autocompletion module, able to guide the user in formulating a query compliant with the controlled natural language, otherwise it requires a manual rephrasing of the question.

Since we want to evaluate our system on benchmarks like QALD, Simple-Question and so on, we want to avoid the rephrasing step which could be infeasible for large datasets and could not guarantee a fair comparison with other QA systems. For these reasons, we decided to investigate other approaches.

6   Evaluation Plan

As introduced in Sect. 2 the three main benchmarks for QA over KBs are QALD, SimpleQuestions and WebQuestions. QALD is actually a series of evaluation campaigns for Question Answering over Linked Data which first started in 2011. Every year a new edition of the challenge has been proposed with more enlarged datasets and new tasks. The main RDF dataset used in the QALD challenges is DBpedia even if in the current edition there is a specific task focused on Wikidata. The question comprised in QALD are manually created by the organizers for each edition and they include questions of varying difficulty that can range from simple ones, involving only one binary relation, to complex, which require to handle specific modifiers.

On the other hand, SimpleQuestions and WebQuestions make use of Freebase [25] which has currently been discontinued and is part of Wikidata. These two dataset contain more questions than those in QALD since they are created through a crowd-sourcing method. SimpleQuestions owes its name to the structure of its questions that usually follow a similar pattern and does not involve any kind of reification, unlike what happens for WebQuestions.

Considering the features of these three datasets, the idea is to make an initial evaluation starting from SimpleQuestion: in this way we might exploit the rich dataset of questions and focus the attention on the resolution of the lexical gap and the ambiguities. In a second phase, we can shift our attention over articulated queries involving more than a single relation, testing our system over QALD and WebQuestions.

For the comparison with other systems we will use the standard measures adopted in this field, i.e.: error count, precision, recall and f-measure.

7   Conclusions

In this work we provide an overview of QA over KBs, ranging from a description of the most relevant systems that have been proposed until now, to an analysis of the main issues related to this topic.

Being in an early stage, our work is still focused on the analysis of the approaches proposed by the state of the art system.

Based on our current knowledge, we outline an architecture whose aim is to resolve three principal problems: bridging the lexical gap, resolving the ambiguities and handling complex queries. We expect to achieve good performance by making use of external corpora to facilitate the phrase mapping step and adapting the methods used to retrieve an answer accordingly to the question complexity.

The future step of our research program is to convert this architecture into an actual prototype with the aim of addressing the aforementioned issues in an incremental fashion.

References

1. Androutsopoulos, I., Ritchie, G.D., Thanisch, P.: Natural language interfaces to databases-an introduction. Nat. Lang. Eng. **1**(1), 29–81 (1995)
2. Berners-Lee, T., Hendler, J., Lassila, O.: The semantic web. Sci. Am. **284**(5), 34–43 (2001)
3. Auer, S., Bizer, C., Kobilarov, G., Lehmann, J., Cyganiak, R., Ives, Z.: DBpedia: a nucleus for a web of open data. In: Aberer, K., et al. (eds.) ASWC/ISWC -2007. LNCS, vol. 4825, pp. 722–735. Springer, Heidelberg (2007). https://doi.org/10.1007/978-3-540-76298-0_52
4. Suchanek, F.M., Kasneci, G., Weikum, G.: Yago: a core of semantic knowledge. In: Proceedings of the 16th International Conference on World Wide Web, pp. 697–706. ACM (2007)
5. Vrandečić, D., Krötzsch, M.: Wikidata: a free collaborative knowledgebase. Commun. ACM **57**(10), 78–85 (2014)
6. Lopez, V., Unger, C., Cimiano, P., Motta, E.: Evaluating question answering over linked data. Web Seman. Sci. Serv. Agents World Wide Web **21**, 3–13 (2013)
7. Cimiano, P., Lopez, V., Unger, C., Cabrio, E., Ngonga Ngomo, A.-C., Walter, S.: Multilingual question answering over linked data (QALD-3): lab overview. In: Forner, P., Müller, H., Paredes, R., Rosso, P., Stein, B. (eds.) CLEF 2013. LNCS, vol. 8138, pp. 321–332. Springer, Heidelberg (2013). https://doi.org/10.1007/978-3-642-40802-1_30

8. Unger, C., Forascu, C., Lopez, V., Ngomo, A.C.N., Cabrio, E., Cimiano, P., Walter, S.: Question answering over linked data (QALD-4). In: Working Notes for CLEF 2014 Conference (2014)
9. Unger, C., Forascu, C., Lopez, V., Ngomo, A.C.N., Cabrio, E., Cimiano, P., Walter, S.: Question answering over linked data (QALD-5). In: Cappellato, L., Ferro, N., Jones, G.J.F., SanJuan, E. (eds.) CLEF (Working Notes), vol. 1391, CEUR Workshop Proceedings, CEUR-WS.org (2015)
10. Unger, C., Ngomo, A.-C.N., Cabrio, E.: 6th open challenge on question answering over linked data (QALD-6). In: Sack, H., Dietze, S., Tordai, A., Lange, C. (eds.) SemWebEval 2016. CCIS, vol. 641, pp. 171–177. Springer, Cham (2016). https://doi.org/10.1007/978-3-319-46565-4_13
11. Usbeck, R., Ngomo, A.-C.N., Haarmann, B., Krithara, A., Röder, M., Napolitano, G.: 7th open challenge on question answering over linked data (QALD-7). In: Dragoni, M., Solanki, M., Blomqvist, E. (eds.) SemWebEval 2017. CCIS, vol. 769, pp. 59–69. Springer, Cham (2017). https://doi.org/10.1007/978-3-319-69146-6_6
12. Berant, J., Chou, A., Frostig, R., Liang, P.: Semantic parsing on freebase from question-answer pairs. In: Proceedings of the 2013 Conference on Empirical Methods in Natural Language Processing, pp. 1533–1544 (2013)
13. Bordes, A., Usunier, N., Chopra, S., Weston, J.: Large-scale simple question answering with memory networks. arXiv preprint arXiv:1506.02075 (2015)
14. Unger, C., Freitas, A., Cimiano, P.: An introduction to question answering over linked data. In: Koubarakis, M., et al. (eds.) Reasoning Web 2014. LNCS, vol. 8714, pp. 100–140. Springer, Cham (2014). https://doi.org/10.1007/978-3-319-10587-1_2
15. Höffner, K., Walter, S., Marx, E., Usbeck, R., Lehmann, J., Ngonga Ngomo, A.C.: Survey on challenges of question answering in the semantic web. Semantic Web 8(6), 895–920 (2017)
16. Diefenbach, D., Lopez, V., Singh, K., Maret, P.: Core techniques of question answering systems over knowledge bases: a survey. Knowl. Inf. Syst. 1–41 (2017)
17. Xu, K., Feng, Y., Zhao, D.: Xser@ qald-4: answering natural language questions via phrasal semantic parsing. In: Working Notes for CLEF 2014 Conference, pp. 15–18 (2014)
18. Mazzeo, G.M., Zaniolo, C.: Answering controlled natural language questions on RDF knowledge bases. In: EDBT, pp. 608–611 (2016)
19. Zou, L., Huang, R., Wang, H., Yu, J.X., He, W., Zhao, D.: Natural language question answering over RDF: a graph data driven approach. In: Proceedings of the 2014 ACM SIGMOD International Conference on Management of Data, pp. 313–324. ACM (2014)
20. Diefenbach, D., Singh, K., Maret, P.: WDAqua-core0: a question answering component for the research community. In: Dragoni, M., Solanki, M., Blomqvist, E. (eds.) SemWebEval 2017. CCIS, vol. 769, pp. 84–89. Springer, Cham (2017). https://doi.org/10.1007/978-3-319-69146-6_8
21. Lukovnikov, D., Fischer, A., Lehmann, J., Auer, S.: Neural network-based question answering over knowledge graphs on word and character level. In: Proceedings of the 26th International Conference on World Wide Web, International World Wide Web Conferences Steering Committee, pp. 1211–1220 (2017)
22. Jain, S.: Question answering over knowledge base using factual memory networks. In: Proceedings of the NAACL Student Research Workshop, pp. 109–115 (2016)
23. Manning, C., Surdeanu, M., Bauer, J., Finkel, J., Bethard, S., McClosky, D.: The stanford CoreNLP natural language processing toolkit. In: Proceedings of 52nd Annual Meeting of the Association for Computational Linguistics: System Demonstrations, pp. 55–60 (2014)

24. Mikolov, T., Chen, K., Corrado, G., Dean, J.: Efficient estimation of word representations in vector space. arXiv preprint arXiv:1301.3781 (2013)
25. Bollacker, K., Evans, C., Paritosh, P., Sturge, T., Taylor, J.: Freebase: a collaboratively created graph database for structuring human knowledge. In: Proceedings of the 2008 ACM SIGMOD International Conference on Management of Data, pp. 1247–1250. ACM (2008)

Semantic Query Federation for Scalable Security Log Analysis

Kabul Kurniawan[✉]

Multimedia and Information System Group, University of Vienna,
Wahringerstrasse 29, 1190 Vienna, Austria
kabulk87@univie.ac.at

Abstract. The digitalization of business processes increasingly exposes organizations to sophisticated cyber-security threats. To contain attacks and minimize their impact, it is essential to detect them early. To this end, it is necessary to analyze a wide range of log files that potentially provide clues about malicious activity. However, these logs are typically voluminous, heterogeneous, difficult to interpret, and stored in disparate locations, which makes it difficult to analyze them. Current approaches to analyze security logs mainly focus on regular expressions and statistical indicators and do not directly provide actionable insight to security analysts. To address these limitations, we propose a distributed approach that enables semantic querying of dispersed log sources in large-scale infrastructures. To automatically integrate and reason about security log information, we will leverage linked data technologies and state-of-the-art federated query processing systems. In this proposal, we discuss the research problem, methodology, approach and evaluation plan for scalable federated semantic security log analysis.

Keywords: Security log analysis · Semantic query federation
Linked data · Semantic reasoning

1 Introduction

Today, most organizations depend strongly upon information technology (IT) systems. While these IT systems provide a lot of benefits, they also have their drawbacks in the form of increasing non-trivial cyber-security threats. These threats manifest as specialized, sophisticated and non-trivial cyber attacks across network and region, which multiply the complexity and difficulty of the effort to keep the system safe. Organizations are now threatened by serious losses from these threats, such as business process disruptions, sensitive data thefts, and reputational damages [1].

IT Systems produce security logs that contain important information within the systems. Security log data can be utilized for supporting security analysis in order to address these threats. By extracting and mining those data, users can reveal events occurred on a certain system [2]. Log data are typically written in various data structures and formats (e.g. plain-text, XML, CSV etc.),

© Springer Nature Switzerland AG 2018
A. Gangemi et al. (Eds.): ESWC 2018 Satellite Events, LNCS 11155, pp. 294–303, 2018.
https://doi.org/10.1007/978-3-319-98192-5_48

coming from heterogeneous data sources (e.g. operating system logs, application logs, database logs, router logs, switch logs, firewall logs, etc.) and result in an enormous size (e.g. gigabyte, terabyte) of log data, which makes it difficult for users to comprehend. In addition, Cyber-attacks launched by adversaries, typically leave digital traces spread across machines in an organization's IT system, makes comprehensive manual security log analysis infeasible [3].

Current approaches in security log analysis mainly focus on system anomaly detection through log parsing and log mining [4]. These approaches typically encounters challenges with incomplete information of logs, which limits the extent of analysis [5]. These challenges emerge due to the difficulty of getting the relevant information from incomplete log sources, as an event occurred in a machine is typically distributed into different log sources in a networked IT systems. Another challenge is on the semantic information from security logs, which is not yet addressed in the current approaches. Without a correct understanding of information contained in logs, it is difficult to infer the causally related events from security logs.

To address these challenges, we propose an innovative approach leveraging linked data technology. Linked data is part of the semantic web technology stack [6], which provides a method of publishing structured data so that it can be interlinked and become more useful through semantic queries [7]. On the security domain, linked data can be applied to provide a conceptual model that can semantically lift heterogeneous security log data, integrate them, and support reasoning to infer implicit causally-related events.

The remainder of this paper is structured as follows: In Sect. 2 we will describe the state of the art and related work. The problem statement and contributions follow in Sect. 3. The methodology and approach to this problem are described in Sect. 4. The preliminary results are shown in Sect. 5 and the evaluation plan that is outlined in Sect. 6. Section 7 concludes the paper.

2   State of the Art

As we plan to leverage linked data technology in our research, in this section we provide the state-of-the-art from two different research domains, cyber-security and semantic web. For the cyber-security domain, we present the state-of-the-art on security log analysis research while on the semantic web research, we provide the state-of-the-art of semantic query federation.

Research on security log analysis has been conducted by several researchers for many years. Some of them have been launched as commercial products (e.g. ArcSight, SplungES, QRadar, LogRhythm, McAfee ESM, etc.). They are mostly implemented based on the Security Information and Event Management (SIEM) approach. SIEM is a combination approach of security information management (SIM) and security event management (SEM) [8]. The goal of this approach is to aggregate relevant information from the extracted log data from multiple different sources in order to provide system administrators access to logging information in a convenient way. SIEM employs statistical correlation engines to generate relationships between event log entries. The main difference between SIEM and our proposed approach is that we provide semantic information and background knowledge of extracted log data and events so that it has capability to infer implicit semantic relationships between those events in which this capability is not provided yet by SIEM systems.

Intrusion detection systems (IDS) are a mechanism to monitor networks or systems for malicious activities. There are two main detection approaches [9] (1) signature-based-detection (2) anomaly-based detection. The signature-based detection is used to detect known attacks by comparing event against a database of signature of malicious activities while the anomaly-based detection is used to detect not only an unknown pattern but also previously unseen pattern using statistical techniques. Machine learning techniques have recently been successfully applied to this context [10]. In our proposed approach, we also aim to identify malicious activities with the main focus on the context-rich high-level understanding of complete attacks.

Another conceptual approach to network security assessment has also been recently proposed in [11]. It performs network information acquisition by collecting attributes of network including topology, service, vulnerabilities and configuration. The results of the network information acquisition are used as a basic security ontology to generate attack graphs iteratively and to infer potential attack using a reasoning engine. Compare to our proposed approach, we plan to use empirical research rather than just a conceptual research. We will use security log data as the main data sources and build background knowledge to infer causally-related events.

On the semantic web domain, we particularly focus on the state-of-the-art of semantic query federation approach. Semantic query federation is an approach to query linked data from multiple distributed datasets [19]. There are several existing approaches in terms of semantic query federation. Link Traversal [12] is a semantic query federation approach to discover potentially relevant data during the query execution. It provides high fresh data since the data is directly accessed from a data source. The query execution is initially from one single triple pattern as starting point. FedX [13] is an optimization SPARQL query processing on multiple distributed RDF datasets which are known and accessible via SPARQL Endpoint. SPLENDID [14] provides transparent query federation over distributed SPARQL endpoints. In order to achieve a good query execution performance, data source selection and query optimization are based on basic statistical information which is obtained from VOID descriptions. ANAPSID [15] employs VoiD (Vocabulary of Interlinked Datasets) as data catalogue that is loaded when the system is started and submit ASK SPARQL query to each dataset verification. ANAPSID provides hash join and bind join to merge result locally. Triple pattern fragment (TPF) [16] is a linked data interface which use triple pattern, metadata and controller to query linked dataset. TPF performs with an average speed in running time and top rank in precision-recall (compared with another federated system). TPF offers low-cost and scalable query processing of multiple distributed interlinked datasets.

3   Problem Statement and Contribution

The effort to keep systems safe from cyber-security threats requires comprehensive security analyses to precisely understand malicious events that occurred within them. Logs produced by the systems can be used to support security analyses as they record important system's information. System's logs are composed of log entries in which contain information related to events occurred in a systems or networks [2]. For instance, log messages describe user's activities when they attempt to gain access of a certain system via a networks (e.g. SSH access, FTP access, web portal access etc.). This activity will then be stored as a set of information including date, time-stamp, username, type of access, message etc.

As depicted in Fig. 1, there is a wide variety of structural schemas among log messages. For instance, the 'date' written in the SSH log message is different from the one which is written in the Firewall log (and two others). As illustrated by this example, different systems typically generate different structure of log messages. We can also find other differences between log messages such as the structure order and the attributes' name.

```
SSH Invalid user login attempt:

Jul  7 10:51:24 chaves sshd[19537]: Invalid user admin from spongebob.lab.ossec.net
Jul  7 10:53:24 chaves sshd[12914]: Failed password for invalid user test-inv from spongebob.lab.ossec.net
Jul  7 10:53:24 kiko sshd[3251]: User dcid not allowed because listed in DenyUsers
```

```
Firewall Accept (Windows):

2006-09-19 03:04:29 OPEN TCP 192.168.72.12 10.20.72.204 3599 445 - - - - - - - - - -
2006-09-19 03:04:29 OPEN TCP 192.168.72.12 10.20.72.204 3600 139 - - - - - - - - - -
```

```
Apache access log (success - code 200):

192.168.2.20 - - [28/Jul/2006:10:27:10 -0300] "GET /cgi-bin/try/ HTTP/1.0" 200 3395
127.0.0.1 - - [28/Jul/2006:10:22:04 -0300] "GET / HTTP/1.0" 200 2216
```

```
useradd&passwd fail (Linux):

May 28 16:04:10 server2 useradd[30245]: failed adding user 'avahi', data deleted
May 28 16:04:10 server2 passwd[30246]: password for 'avahi' changed by 'root'
May 28 16:04:12 server2 passwd[30263]: password for 'hal' changed by 'root'
May 28 16:07:10 server2 useradd[30523]: failed adding user 'mysql', data deleted
May 28 16:11:48 server2 passwd[32532]: password for 'gdm' changed by 'root'
May 28 16:16:07 server2 useradd[633]: failed adding user 'privoxy', data deleted
```

Fig. 1. Security log messages generated from heterogeneous applications and systems

Figure 2 provides an example case about data theft. There is a user who gets access to a certain system on a local computer using either legitimate or illegitimate credentials. This event will be recorded in a pertinent log (e.g. Win Even Log). After the user gets access to a certain server e.g. (file server, web server, database server etc.), the user may download a credential file or dump a database from the database server. These events will then be recorded to a relevant log (e.g. Webserver log, Share-point logs, Sys-logs on endpoint hosts, the file system operation auditing for downloaded files or database backup, DB audit logs, Firewall logs etc.). Subsequently, the user may attach any removable storage (e.g. USB flash-drive) to copy or move the downloaded files to her or his own storage. These events (attach and copy activity) will then be recorded in a system log (e.g. Win Event log). To this end, this example shows that a single case may generate several different logs and it may separately distributed to different systems and locations, depending on the activity of the user.

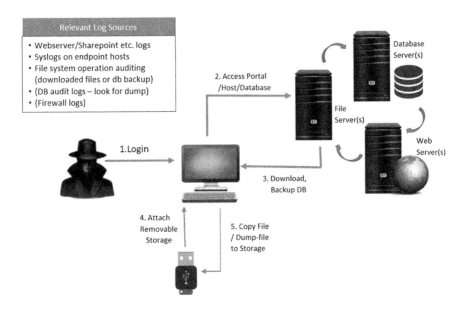

Fig. 2. An example of data theft case

Security logs are important sources for security analysts who tackle such security issue. However, log data typically have characteristics which can be problems in security log analysis. These characteristics include but are not limited to (1) heterogeneity (e.g. different terms of terminology, structure, format etc.) (2) separated (coming from different log sources e.g.operating system, application, databases, routers, switches, firewall etc.) (3) enormous sizes (systems may generated vast amount of log data: gigabyte, terabyte etc.) [2].

Thus, in order to address these challenges, we propose an innovative approach of security log analysis by leveraging the potential and the capability of linked data technology. We define a number of research questions based on the consideration of several hypotheses.

RQ1: *How to semantically integrate heterogeneous security log information?*

Although traditional security log analysis approaches and other academic research [17] have tackled the problem of "normalizing" log messages into a common format as mentioned in Sect. 2, they do not address the semantic aspect of log processing. They lack constructing formal conceptualization of security log data. Conceptualization of a domain knowledge can be used to support unambiguous and useful interlinking between log data so that it can be understood by a machine. A uniform conceptual model can semantically lift heterogeneous security log data from diverse sources. Therefore, our first research question based on the hypothesis:

Hypothesis 1: *Security log data can be structured and enhanced by semantics, to support unambiguous and useful interlinking between logs in a knowledge graph. A uniform conceptual model can semantically lift heterogeneous security log data from diverse sources.*

Distributed enormous sizes of security log data separated from different applications, system and host remains a problem. Traditional security log analyses typically tackle this problem through centralized data integration (e.g. log server, SIEM system, etc.). Centralized data analyses such as ETL (extract-transform-load) [18] style is a typical method for traditional data analytics, in which it doesn't solve the problems of highly verbose, redundant and incoherent and poorly structured information. As systems typically generate high-frequency, fine-grained and vast amounts of log data, analyzing data by means of a centralized method is not ideal for real-time processes or on-demand access, where fast response is required.

RQ2: *How to support analysis of scalable and separated security log information?*

Consider another example case about network interruption. When an interruption happens in a working network of a large system, it then will trigger to put different log messages to various related system logs with the same meaning. Hence, without a automated scalable integration, security analyst may loss of keeping track of log data, particularly when the interruption happens suddenly or in an emergency situation.

We expect that semantic query federation, through decentralized semantic data integration, can retrieve meaningful results from large-scale, dispersed security logs. We expect that it can overcome scalability issues [18] and flexibly combine different datasets to improve attack detection and causal analysis. Thus, we consider that RQ2 is fit with the Hypothesis 2.

Hypothesis 2: *Multiple distributed security log datasets can be retrieved* in a scalable manner *by means of semantic query federation.*

The growing amounts of log data available for security analyses inhibits a timely detection and response to attacks. Current security analysis processes typically rely on human intelligence rather than systems to perform better task inference. Although human experts typically are better to perform inference tasks, they are easily over-burdened by the vast amounts of data. Therefore, security analysts often find it difficult to identify the potential impact of a security incident. Current security log analyses systems provide insufficient inference capabilities as they typically do not provide semantic reasoning.

RQ3: *How to represent and infer causally-related events from security log information?*

Semantic reasoning, in the security domain, can be applied to enable identification of potential attacks by exploiting property chains, transitive and reflexive properties of interlinked security log data. Moreover, semantic reasoning can also be processed in a streaming way by means of an RDF stream reasoner [20] which will allow us to perform continuous queries over incoming log event streams. Stream reasoning will hence allow us to detect potential attacks and suspicious behavior in real-time. Therefore, RQ3 is fit with Hypothesis 3.

Hypothesis 3: *Semantic reasoning can be used to infer causally-related events from security log data. Furthermore, by means of an RDF stream reasoning will allow us to identify potential attacks and suspicious behavior in real-time.*

Our research will propose an innovative security log analysis approach which will contribute results at the intersection between semantic web and cybersecurity research. By providing theory, models and techniques to this approach we expect that the research will have a high-impact on cybersecurity research domain. We expect to obtain these following contributions: (1) conceptualization of security domain (e.g. system, log and event vocabulary, (2) semantic modeling approach of infrastructure and attack patterns (e.g. background knowledge), (3) a framework for data acquisition, integration and semantic reasoning of large-scale and disparate security log information. Our proposed approach will allow experts without particular skills in semantic web and query language to easily analyze large-scale disparate log information and to improve the identification of potential attacks and suspicious behavior in real-time. Therefore, it can improve situational security awareness.

4   Research Methodology and Approach

Based on the research questions we have defined, we decide to apply iterative research methodology Action Research (AR) described by Checkland and Holwell [19]. This method allows us to start research with a literature review, analyze examples of real-world security issues and evaluate existing technologies (e.g. approaches, frameworks, tools, etc.) which are used to tackle these issues in order to analyze their advantages and drawbacks. By this evaluation, we can consider whether we can adapt them in our research or not. We define our research method as three aspects: conceptual model, prototyping and evaluation. Both conceptual model and prototyping are discussed in this section, while evaluation aspect is discussed in Sect. 6.

For the conceptual model, we will conceptualize the architecture of our semantic log processing framework that includes test specification and metrics that can be used to validate our developed framework. We will develop ontologies that represent concepts of system infrastructure, log events, attack patterns and background knowledge. We will also reuse existing upper ontologies to facilitate semantic interoperability and cross-domain knowledge sharing.

As a prototype of our proposed framework, we will instantiate our developed ontologies (e.g. system, log events, patterns) and include several steps such as log extraction, event extraction and integration, and semantic log analysis. Log extraction process will cover log sources acquisition, extraction and conversion from raw data to a certain RDF serialization (e.g. XML/RDF, JSON-LD). By leveraging background knowledge, We will extract explicit events to discover new patterns as they appear in log messages and learn a new type of previously unseen log entries. Event integration process will cover the integration of related events from multiple different sources so that we will have a complete event pattern. Regarding the semantic log analysis, we will implement semantic query federation over distributed event datasets and stream reasoning to infer and discover potential attacks and suspicious behavior in real-time.

Furthermore, this research is related to a research project called SEPSES (Semantic Processing of Security Event Streams) which also serves as a source for ideas of how to approach problems arising on semantic processing of security log data. This project also serves as result comparison to evaluate the proposed approach.

5   Preliminary Result

As explained in Sect. 2, we have surveyed the state-of-the-art research from two different domains: security domain and semantic web domain. On the security domain, we found several existing approaches, both semantic and non - semantic, to analyze the security logs. We have investigated the gaps in security log analyses and formulated a number of research questions. On the semantic web domain, we also conducted surveys of the current semantic query federation approaches.

As a first step, we have already started evaluating several log parsing tools and libraries (e.g. Plaso, Splunk, Logstash) to acquire and parse different log sources from different machines (e.g. Syslog, Authlog, Apachelog etc.). From there, we got several terms (e.g. host, message, timestamps, etc.) and focused to find the most important terms which can generalize the informations of log sources. Then, by those terms we started to define our log vocabularies.

We realize that there are a lot of different type of log sources which might come from different platforms and machines. Therefore, we defined our log vocabulary modularly. It means that we have one log vocabulary as a core and on top of that we have another specific log vocabulary which fit with a certain type of log. We also reused several existing vocabularies that are relevant to our vocabulary concept by attaching them in the log extraction process and we got results as RDF-based log entries on JSON-LD format [21]. We also have already submitted our first paper on log extraction to the upcoming 2018 SEMANTICS Conference.

6   Evaluation Plan

We will continuously evaluate the results of each part of our developed framework. The evaluation will be conducted to measure and to check whether the results have met our research goals. We will assess the ability of our developed framework to evaluate performance characteristics such as throughput and latency. The research will be started with a simple scenario (e.g. login scenario) and implement elaborate data generator that simulate real-world event data (e.g. Syslog, Apachelog, Sys-Log etc.). We will setup a system with various log sources in a virtual environment. Regarding to the semantic stream processing, we will conduct the evaluation using live data that generated by several tester's actions. We will also conduct evaluation towards the addition of new scenarios in order to measure the scalability performance. Based on the evaluation results, we will able to draw conclusions about accuracy, latency and completeness of detection and the overall scalability of our research approach.

7   Conclusion

In this proposal, we provide a research roadmap for security log analysis based on federated linked data querying technology. We outline the problem of technical, syntactical and semantical heterogeneity, physical and logical separation of log data, and the enormous size of security log data that hinders efficient and effective analysis of security log information. Based on our analysis of the state-of-the-art, we formulate three specific research questions, for which we provide our initial hypotheses in this proposal. We describe our research methodology and approach that will guide our research. To conclude, we aim to contribute both to the cyber-security and semantic web domains by developing a novel method that improves the current state of the art in security log analyses.

Acknowledgement. This work was supported by the Ministry of Education and Culture, Indonesia. Furthermore, support for project SEPSES by the Austrian Science Fund (FWF) and netidee SCIENCE: P 30437-N31 is gratefully acknowledged. I want to thank my supervisors, Prof. A Min Tjoa, Prof. Gerald Quichmayr, Dr. Elmar Kiesling and my colleague Fajar Ekaputra, Peb Aryan and Niina Novak for their helpful discussion, comments and feedback.

References

1. FT Services: Cybercrime survey report insight and perspective (2017)
2. Calvanese, D., Montali, M., Syamsiyah, A., Van Der Aalst, W.M.P.: Ontology-driven extraction of event logs from relational databases **256**, 140–153 (2016)
3. Kent, K., Souppaya, M.: Guide to computer security log management. National Institute of Standards and Technology, pp. 1–72 (2006)
4. He, P., Zhu, J., He, S., Li, J., Lyu, M.R.: An evaluation study on log parsing and its use in log mining. In: Proceedings - 46th Annual IEEE/IFIP International Conference on Dependable Systems and Networks, DSN 2016, pp. 654–661 (2016)

5. Xu, W.: Advances and challenges in log analysis. Commun. ACM **55**(2), 55–61 (2012)
6. Berners-Lee, T., Hendler, J., Lassila, O.: The semantic web. Sci. Am. **284**, 34–43 (2001)
7. Bizer, C., Heath, T., Berners-Lee, T.: Linked data-the story so far. Int. J. Semant. Web Inf. Syst. **5**(3), 1–22 (2009)
8. Miller, D.R., Harris, S., Harper, A., VanDyke, S., Blask, C.: Security Information and Event Management. McGraw-Hill Osborne Media (2010)
9. Axelsson, S.: Intrusion detection systems: a survey and taxonomy. Department of Computer Engineering (2009)
10. Gander, M., Felderer, M., Katt, B., Tolbaru, A., Breu, R., Moschitti, A.: Anomaly detection in the cloud: detecting security incidents via machine learning. In: Moschitti, A., Plank, B. (eds.) EternalS 2012. CCIS, vol. 379, pp. 103–116. Springer, Heidelberg (2013). https://doi.org/10.1007/978-3-642-45260-4_8
11. Wu, S., Zhang, Y., Cao, W.: Network security assessment using a semantic reasoning and graph based approach. Comput. Electr. Eng. **64**, 96–109 (2017)
12. Hartig, O.: Zero-knowledge query planning for an iterator implementation of link traversal based query execution. In: Antoniou, G., et al. (eds.) ESWC 2011. LNCS, vol. 6643, pp. 154–169. Springer, Heidelberg (2011). https://doi.org/10.1007/978-3-642-21034-1_11
13. Schwarte, A., Haase, P., Hose, K., Schenkel, R., Schmidt, M.: FedX: optimization techniques for federated query processing on linked data. In: Aroyo, L., et al. (eds.) ISWC 2011, Part I. LNCS, vol. 7031, pp. 601–616. Springer, Heidelberg (2011). https://doi.org/10.1007/978-3-642-25073-6_38
14. Gorlitz, O., Staab, S.: SPLENDID: SPARQL endpoint federation exploiting VOID descriptions. In: Proceedings of the 2nd International Workshop on Consuming Linked Data, Bonn, Germany (2011)
15. Acosta, M., Vidal, M.-E., Lampo, T., Castillo, J., Ruckhaus, E.: ANAPSID: an adaptive query processing engine for SPARQL endpoints. In: Aroyo, L., et al. (eds.) ISWC 2011. LNCS, vol. 7031, pp. 18–34. Springer, Heidelberg (2011). https://doi.org/10.1007/978-3-642-25073-6_2
16. Verborgh, R., et al.: Triple pattern fragments: a low-cost knowledge graph interface for the web. J. Web Semant. **37–38**, 184–206 (2016)
17. Azodi, A., Jaeger, D., Cheng, F., Meinel, C.: Pushing the limits in event normalisation to improve attack detection in IDS/SIEM systems. In: Proceedings of the 2013 International Conference on Advanced Cloud and Big Data, pp. 69–76. IEEE (2013)
18. Kimball, R., Caserta, J: The Data Warehouse ETL Toolkit. Wiley Publishing, Inc., Indianapolis (2004)
19. Della Valle, E., Ceri, S., van Harmelen, F., Fensel, D.: It's a streaming world! Reasoning upon rapidly changing information. IEEE Intell. Syst. **24**(6), 83–89 (2009)
20. Checkland, P., Holwell, S.: Action research: its nature and validity. Syst. Pract. Action Res. **11**(1), 9–21 (1989)
21. Sporny, M., et al.: A JSON-based serialization for linked data (2014)

Assessing the Quality
of owl:sameAs Links

Pierre-Henri Paris[(✉)]

Conservatoire National des Arts et Métiers, CEDRIC,
292 rue saint martin, Paris, France
pierre-henri.paris@upmc.fr

Abstract. *owl:sameAs* is one of the most important properties of the
Linked Open Data domain. The property is used to indicate that two
things are the same and when these two things come from two different
datasets. But unfortunately, there is a gap between the purpose of this
property, the way it was conceived and designed, and the way it is used
in the wild. This deficiency is mainly due to the misuse of *owl:sameAs*
because its strict semantics is not always taken into account or well
understood and there may be no clear alternative. As a result, inaccurate data can be either crawled or inferred from incorrect (or at least
questionable) links. Depending on the need for high quality data, the
impact on the end users of the data can be considerable. This is why we
propose to study how erroneous links can influence data, how to repair
such cases, or even better, how to prevent the production of these links.
We want to assess wrong links impact (e.g. at which points they decrease
overall quality) and how they can be addressed.

Keywords: Linked Open Data · Identity · sameAs · OWL

1   Introduction

Linked Open Data[1] (LOD) is an initiative proposed by Tim Berners-Lee to
publish data on the Web. Such datasets use standards from the Semantic Web
(SW) like the Resource Description Framework[2] (RDF) to represent data. RDF
is an oriented and labeled multi-graph model. LOD datasets are graphs and thus
can be linked together through the addition of statements having one node in
one dataset and another node in a different dataset. This is the linking part of
Linked Open Data.

There are more and more LOD datasets published and linked together. Linking datasets is a powerful way to enable retrieving knowledge from other datasets.
This enables the ability of crawl various datasets to discover new facts. Thanks
to ontologies using OWL [16], it is even possible to use reasoners based on, e.g.,
Description Logics (DL), to infer new things from data.

---

[1] http://5stardata.info/en/.
[2] https://www.w3.org/TR/2004/REC-rdf-primer-20040210/.

ⓒ Springer Nature Switzerland AG 2018
A. Gangemi et al. (Eds.): ESWC 2018 Satellite Events, LNCS 11155, pp. 304–313, 2018.
https://doi.org/10.1007/978-3-319-98192-5_49

There are many ways to link two datasets. Many properties can be used to do so, since virtually any object property[3] can be used. One of the most employed is the famous *owl:sameAs* property from the OWL ontology. To create a link with *owl:sameAs* between two instances is stating that these two instances are the same. It is an identity link. For example, let us say that we have two instances *ds1:Paris* and *ds2:CityOfParis* of Paris, the French capital. Each one of these instances is in one dataset (*ds1* and *ds2* here). It is possible to link *ds1* and *ds2* by simply adding this fact: *owl:sameAs(ds1:Paris, ds2:CityOfParis)*.

Because *owl:sameAs* has a very strict semantics, creating such links among instances has consequences. *owl:sameAs* semantics is based upon Leibniz's principle of indiscernibility. Therefore if two things are identical they must share the same values for the same properties. If in *ds1* the population of Paris is not filled out but is given in *ds2*, then the population can be used in *ds1*. More formally, the indiscernibility of identicals is: $owl:sameAs(a, b) \rightarrow (p(a, o) \rightarrow p(b, o))$. This is how one can discover new knowledge through the use of *owl:sameAs* links, by either retrieving or inferring new data. An erroneous link can lead to inaccurate inferred data and consequently it is very important to have high quality *owl:sameAs* links in order to maintain the overall quality of the datasets. As stated in Ding et al. [6] and Halpin et al. [12], there are many misuses of *owl:sameAs* in current LOD, which undermines the quality of the data it provides.

2   State of the Art

There are many facets to the interlinking problem. We want to underline four of them in this section.

2.1   Instance Matching

The term instance matching refers to the problem of finding equivalent resources. As stated in Hogan et al. [15], the search for identity links among instances of the *LOD* has several names in literature such as *data linking* [10], *data reconciliation* [25], *record linkage* [21], *duplicate identification* [7], *object consolidation* [14], *instance matching* [3], *link discovery*, or *Co-reference resolution*. Those approaches are historically the first ones to emerge. The goal is to produce links between a source dataset and a target dataset. For each potential link a similarity score is produced and if the score is above some threshold, the link is validated. Ferraram et al. [8] published a complete survey and more recently Achichi et al. [1] and Nentwig et al. [20] propose complementary surveys.

2.2   Knowledge Enrichment

Because several approaches used to match instances benefit from semantics features like inverse functional properties or cardinality restrictions, knowledge

---

[3] https://www.w3.org/TR/owl-guide/.

enrichment approaches are tangential to our domain of concern. For example, if one can find that a property is inverse functional, then any subjects related to the same object by this property have to be the same. More formally: $InverseFunctional(P) \land P(a,c) \land P(b,c) \rightarrow owl{:}sameAs(a,b)$. Thus, the addition of new knowledge to the $TBox$[4] of an ontology might, hypothetically, lead to finding novel $owl{:}sameAs$ links. Völker and Niepert [27] propose the induction of a schema (i.e. an ontology) for a given KB by using statistics. Association rules are mined and then translated into OWL2 axioms, but some interesting features cannot be mined, e.g. inverse properties, cardinal restrictions or property disjointness. Töpper et al. [26] also use statistical methods but from the Inductive Logical Programming (ILP) field, where only property domain, property range and class disjointness are computed. With AMIE [9], the authors use an assumption called the partial completeness assumption (PCL) and calculate scored rules under this assumption. PCL assumes that if a subject-predicate pair is present in the KB, then all possible objects for that pair are in the dataset. This method does not take into account any existing ontological knowledge nor use reasoning capabilities of Description Logics (DL). The approach of d'Amato et al. [4] is able to use ontological knowledge to produce rules.

2.3   Identity Crisis

Since several works, like Halpin et al. [12] or Ding et al. [6], raised the misuse of identity links, proposals have been made to circumvent this problem. Halpin et al. [12] propose to use weaker versions of $owl{:}sameAs$ (e.g. from $SKOS$ vocabulary) but with a loss of inference capabilities. There are also proposals for new properties to represent identity relations by McCusker and McGuinness [19] and Halpin et al. [12], where $owl{:}sameAs$ is a sub property of a more specific and more relaxed list of (semi-)identity properties. [12] by using a new ontology where $owl{:}sameAs$ is a sub property of more specific and more relaxed link of (semi-)identity links. In this hierarchy each property has a combination of reflexivity, symmetry and/or transitivity. McCusker and McGuinness [19] propose a local and domain-specific approach where one can specialize $owl{:}sameAs$ property in a particular domain (e.g. using a $biomedidentity{:}sameAsBioSource$ property in the biology domain) but link usability thus becomes only local. At the intersection of link invalidation and contextual identity links, De Melo [5] propose to use a property to assert proven identity links on the basis that $owl{:}sameAs$ might contain erroneous links. That is if an $owl{:}sameAs$ link between a and b is proven to be right then one can have a $lvont{:}strictlySameAs$ link between a and b. In Halpin et al. [13], authors propose to manage the context of identity links through the addition of a formal context. Several ideas are proposed, but none of them has been widely adopted. Beek et al. [2] propose to manage the context as a set of properties. Therefore two things are equal if they share the same property-value pairs where properties are defined by the context. Idrissou et al. [17] extends the proposition of Beek et al. [2] by adding operators other than the

---

[4] https://www.lesliesikos.com/tbox/.

intersection between the sets of properties representing different contexts. Raad et al. [24], also based on Beek et al. [2] work, propose an algorithm to compute those contexts, i.e. contexts based on sets of properties where identity holds.

2.4 Identity Link Assessment

Identity link assessment approaches consist of checking if a link is true or false. It does not create any link but does evaluate existing ones. Guéret et al. [11] propose to use classical network measures to assess existing links. De Melo [5] propose an approach using the unique name assumption within datasets (i.e. an instance has one name in a dataset) to spot sets of instances linked by *owl:sameAs* where at least one link is presumed to be wrong. Next, a linear programming algorithm is used to compute the wrong link. In Papaleo et al. [22], the authors propose a logical approach to detect such wrong statements. The algorithm tries to detect logical conflicts by using semantics features like functional properties in small sub-graph containing the two involved instances to assess. Thus, this approach strongly relies on semantics. Paulheim [23] propose to use data mining methods. First, links are represented in an embedded space. Second, an outlier detection algorithm is used to detect links that may be erroneous.

3 Problem Statement and Contributions

As we have seen in Sect. 1, a wrong *owl:sameAs* link can lead to inferring wrong data and therefore reduce the overall quality of datasets. As stated by Halpin et al. [12] there is an identity crisis in the sense that the *owl:sameAs* strict semantics is not always respected when used. To state that two things are the same is a very strong statement in LOD domain, with huge consequences. It is common to find instances that are nearly the same but not quite. For example, the city of Paris is **geographically the same** as the administrative department of Paris (it is an administrative subdivision). But in a **legal** context they are **two completely different things**. Another example is a glass of water belonging to a set of glasses. All glasses look the same and in most contexts they certainly are interchangeable but two glasses of this set are two physically different objects. What is identical or not is a philosophical question.

So there is confusion regarding how the *owl:sameAs* property has been defined and how it has been used. *owl:sameAs* has been created to be used only when things are really the same, **in all contexts**. But in the wild it is used in a more relaxed context, leading users to infer inaccurate facts.

There is a need to know how incorrect *owl:sameAs* links decrease the overall quality, and how frequent such incorrect links are. Also it is important to investigate the use of semantic features among LOD datasets. Because *owl:sameAs* links computation also relies on semantics features (e.g. functional properties, maximum cardinality, etc.).

Our goal is to identify quality defects related to data interlinking, then to assess them and finally, propose a way to correct them. Some questions that this work proposes to address include: How to evaluate a *owl:sameAs* link? What is the impact of erroneous links of this type on datasets? How to measure this impact and how to reduce the negative effect on dataset quality?

4 Research Methodology and Approach

For now, the approach we consider is the following, depending on preliminary results:

1. The first step consists in identifying quality defects due to data interlinking. As pointed out by several authors, *owl:sameAs* links are far from sure things. They can be incorrect and therefore produce incoherence in datasets. Thus, we propose to investigate several domains and try to find the nature of the underlying quality defects such as incompleteness (missing links) or incoherence. We will have to define efficient algorithms for data exploration and defect detection.

   But before before diving deeper into quality defects, we plan to reproduce independently some results from previous work (like in Halpin et al. [12]) and to gather useful and precise statistics about *owl:sameAs* links and semantics in general. By semantics we mean OWL properties or classes, because *owl:sameAs* links rely a lot on them. Moreover we need to establish how much this identity crisis is a problem.

2. For each type of defect, we need to associate a set of assessment methods and algorithms. The proposal of Papaleo et al. [22] relies mainly on semantic features like functional or inverse functional properties. Problems arise when semantic features are not sufficiently present in the vocabulary or the data. For example, according to the last version of DBpedia (October-2016), the ontology contains only 30 functional properties (1%) and zero inverse functional property (out of more than 2860 properties). 1.6M out of 4.6M instances (34%) use at least one of the functional properties. Conversely, other approaches rely on statistical, graph or mining techniques. A hybrid approach using semantics, statistics on data and vocabulary, network or graphs measures (etc.) could be used successfully.

3. The next logical step is to be able to correct detected quality defects. Such defects decrease data quality and hence, finding how to correct them can improve data quality. There are, at this time, not so many propositions to deal with existing defects, where the balance tends to lean towards the creation of links in the literature.

4. We want to implement the proposed solutions through a Web application and/or a Web service to support Data Interlinking evaluation and improvement. This is an important point because if the tooling is not good enough, we cannot expect people to adopt our work.

5. Finally, with the high volume of data composing the LOD cloud[5], it is not only a matter of Open Data but also a Big Data issue. Hence, the developed solutions should scale well.

---

[5] http://lod-cloud.net/.

5   Preliminary or Intermediate Results

Until now, we have focused primarily on related work. Nevertheless, we have written two articles to study some ideas related to our problem.

One of the interesting aspects of linking datasets is that one can complete data in a dataset thanks to another one. Therefore, studying completeness might be interesting because to understand the impact of interlinking between two datasets one has to know more about completeness of datasets. Once two instances are connected thanks to an *owl:sameAs* link, one can retrieve properties from the first instance towards the second one (and conversely). As a consequence, completeness might be subject to variation and to be able to assess this variation before and after interlinking is important information. We want to be able to check how the *owl:sameAs* property, used to connect a local dataset to external datasets, can help improve the completeness of this given local dataset. Furthermore, even if it might not be obvious at the first look, completeness is also a very important part to interlink two datasets, i.e. to produce links. In fact, the more complete the datasets, the easier it is to find proof that two instances are the same. For example, with only the last name we can not tell if two persons are the same or not. But in addition with their first names and birth dates, we have more hints to decide whether they are the same or not. Hence, a method for assessing completeness can be very interesting given the two previous points. We published a study [18] to assess the completeness evolution of DBpedia. In this work we proposed to assess completeness by using a mining-based approach. Using a given set of instances ($\mathcal{I}$) of the same class, the first step consists in computing a set of properties that are frequently found among instances of $\mathcal{I}$. For each instance, the corresponding transaction is all its properties. Here we use frequent-itemset algorithm to do so. Once those set of properties (or transactions) found, we can compute the completeness $\mathcal{CP}$ of the set of instances $\mathcal{I}$:

$$\mathcal{CP}(\mathcal{I}) = \frac{1}{|\mathcal{T}|} \sum_{k=1}^{|\mathcal{T}|} \sum_{j=1}^{|\mathcal{MFP}|} \frac{\delta(\mathcal{P}(t_k), \hat{P}_j)}{|\mathcal{MFP}|} \tag{1}$$

such that $\mathcal{T}$ is the set of transactions associated with $\mathcal{I}$ (see second column of Table 2). $\mathcal{MFP}$ is the set of maximal frequent patterns computed in the first step, $\mathcal{P}(t_k)$ is the power set of the transaction t_k and δ is equal to one if the frequent pattern $\hat{P}_j$ is in $\mathcal{P}(t_k)$, zero otherwise.

Example 1. The completeness of the subset of instances in Table 1 regarding their transactions in Table 2 and $\mathcal{MFP} = \{\{director, musicComposer\}, \{director, editing\}\}$, would be:

$$\mathcal{CP}(\mathcal{I}') = (2 * (1/2) + (2/2))/3 = 0.67$$

This value corresponds to the completeness average value for the whole dataset regarding the inferred patterns in $\mathcal{MFP}$.

Table 1. A sample of DBpedia triples

Subject	Predicate	Object
The_Godfather	director	Francis_Ford_Coppola
The_Godfather	musicComposer	Nino_Rota
Goodfellas	director	Martin_Scorsese
Goodfellas	editing	Thelma_Schoonmaker
True_Lies	director	James_Cameron
True_Lies	editing	Conrad_Buff_IV
True_Lies	musicComposer	Brad_Fiedel

Table 2. Transactions corresponding to triples from Table 1

Resource	Transaction
The_Godfather	{director, musicComposer}
Goodfellas	{director, editing}
True_Lies	{director, editing, musicComposer}

We apply this approach on several versions of DBpedia, thus allowing us to study evolution when new data is added or changed. This permits us to have an efficient way to characterize an important aspect of data quality, i.e. completeness.

We are also investigating the way *owl:sameAs* links are created. We are currently writing a proposition that takes into account the structure of data (both TBox and ABox[6]) in a dataset. We believe that not all evidence (in one direction or another) have the same strength. To compare two instances from two distinct datasets we want to collect evidences. Evidence is either a proof of identity or a proof of difference between those two instances. If the two instances share a property and an object, it is therefore a proof they may be the same. Rather, if they share a property but the objects are different, this evidence will tend to prove that the instances are different. The strength of this proof depends on the weight of the property among instances of the same class, and it also depends on the discriminating power of the object(s). The higher the weight and discriminating power are, the stronger the evidence. This approach can help us determine whether an existing relationship has a justification.

6   Evaluation Plan

The rudimentary version of our evaluation plan is as follows:

1. In order to validate our work, we will first select several interlinked datasets from the LOD. Datasets will have to cover different domains, with different sizes and vocabularies to ensure a large number of situations to be tested.

---

[6] https://www.lesliesikos.com/abox/.

For the moment, DBpedia and Wikidata are good candidates to be used as a playground since both datasets are cross-domain, well known and well interconnected. Datasets in a specific domain should also be part of our assessment. Therefore, we also plan to use life sciences datasets, as there has been an explosion in the number of interlinked datasets in this area. Datasets from other domains can be used later if necessary.

2. For each dataset, we will have to evaluate several dimensions of data quality (still to be chosen).
3. The third step is to apply our approach. We will assess the interlinked datasets and modify them based on the experience gained in previous steps (e.g., to help determine which links can be safely deleted, which are useful in one context but not in another, etc.). This step will depend in large part on our future findings, so it may be subject to change.
4. Finally, we will again compute the same data quality dimensions. At this stage, we will have assessed several dimensions of data quality before and after the application of our approach, and so we can compare the situation before and after, hoping that there will be an improvement.

7   Conclusions

Being able to identify inaccurate links is a first step towards improving the overall quality of the data, since the data producer could be notified at the time of publication. Moreover, since the correction of links is not sufficiently addressed in the literature, if we achieve this objective, improving existing data sets would be a significant breakthrough in the identity crisis of the LOD.

Acknowledgements. We would like to thank the anonymous reviewers for their helpful comments. We also sincerely thank Aidan Hogan for his expert advice.

References

1. Achichi, M., Bellahsene, Z., Todorov, K.: A survey on web data linking. Revue des Sciences et Technologies de l'Information-Série ISI: Ingénierie des Systèmes d'Information (2016)
2. Beek, W., Schlobach, S., van Harmelen, F.: A contextualised semantics for owl:sameAs. In: Sack, H., Blomqvist, E., d'Aquin, M., Ghidini, C., Ponzetto, S.P., Lange, C. (eds.) ESWC 2016. LNCS, vol. 9678, pp. 405–419. Springer, Cham (2016). https://doi.org/10.1007/978-3-319-34129-3_25
3. Castano, S., Ferrara, A., Montanelli, S., Lorusso, D.: Instance matching for ontology population. In: Italian Symposium on Advanced Database Systems, pp. 121–132 (2008)
4. d'Amato, C., Staab, S., Tettamanzi, A.G., Minh, T.D., Gandon, F.: Ontology enrichment by discovering multi-relational association rules from ontological knowledge bases. In: Proceedings of the 31st Annual ACM Symposium on Applied Computing, pp. 333–338. ACM (2016)

5. De Melo, G.: Not quite the same: Identity constraints for the web of linked data. In: AAAI National Conference of the American Association for Artificial Intelligence (2013)
6. Ding, L., Shinavier, J., Finin, T., McGuinness, D.L.: owl: sameAs and linked data: an empirical study (2010)
7. Elmagarmid, A.K., Ipeirotis, P.G., Verykios, V.S.: Duplicate record detection: a survey. IEEE Trans. Knowl. Data Eng. **19**(1), 1–16 (2007)
8. Ferraram, A., Nikolov, A., Scharffe, F.: Data linking for the semantic web. Semant. Web Ontol. Knowl. Base Enabled Tools Serv. Appl. **169**, 326 (2013)
9. Galárraga, L., Teflioudi, C., Hose, K., Suchanek, F.M.: Fast rule mining in ontological knowledge bases with amie + +. VLDB J. **24**(6), 707–730 (2015)
10. Giannopoulou, I., Saïs, F., Thomopoulos, R.: Linked data annotation and fusion driven by data quality evaluation. In: EGC French Speaking Conference on the Extraction and Management of Knowledge, pp. 257–262 (2015)
11. Guéret, C., Groth, P., Stadler, C., Lehmann, J.: Assessing linked data mappings using network measures. In: Simperl, E., Cimiano, P., Polleres, A., Corcho, O., Presutti, V. (eds.) ESWC 2012. LNCS, vol. 7295, pp. 87–102. Springer, Heidelberg (2012). https://doi.org/10.1007/978-3-642-30284-8_13
12. Halpin, H., Hayes, P.J., McCusker, J.P., McGuinness, D.L., Thompson, H.S.: When owl:sameAs Isn't the same: an analysis of identity in linked data. In: Patel-Schneider, P.F., et al. (eds.) ISWC 2010. LNCS, vol. 6496, pp. 305–320. Springer, Heidelberg (2010). https://doi.org/10.1007/978-3-642-17746-0_20
13. Halpin, H., Hayes, P.J., Thompson, H.S.: When owl:sameAs isn't the same redux: towards a theory of identity, context, and inference on the semantic web. In: Christiansen, H., Stojanovic, I., Papadopoulos, G.A. (eds.) CONTEXT 2015. LNCS (LNAI), vol. 9405, pp. 47–60. Springer, Cham (2015). https://doi.org/10.1007/978-3-319-25591-0_4
14. Hogan, A., Decker, S., Harth, A.: Performing object consolidation on the semantic web data graph (2007)
15. Hogan, A., Polleres, A., Umbrich, J., Zimmermann, A.: Some entities are more equal than others: statistical methods to consolidate linked data. In: 4th International Workshop on New Forms of Reasoning for the Semantic Web: Scalable and Dynamic (NeFoRS2010) (2010)
16. Horrocks, I., Kutz, O., Sattler, U.: The even more irresistible SROIQ. KR **6**, 57–67 (2006)
17. Idrissou, A.K., Hoekstra, R., van Harmelen, F., Khalili, A., van den Besselaar, P.: Is my: sameAs the same as your: sameAs? Lenticular lenses for context-specific identity. In: Proceedings of the Knowledge Capture Conference, p. 23. ACM (2017)
18. Issa, S., Paris, P.-H., Hamdi, F.: Assessing the completeness evolution of DBpedia: a case study. In: de Cesare, S., Frank, U. (eds.) ER 2017. LNCS, vol. 10651, pp. 238–247. Springer, Cham (2017). https://doi.org/10.1007/978-3-319-70625-2_22
19. McCusker, J.P., McGuinness, D.L.: Towards identity in linked data. In: OWLED Proceedings of OWL Experiences and Directions Seventh Annual Workshop (2010)
20. Nentwig, M., Hartung, M., Ngonga Ngomo, A.C., Rahm, E.: A survey of current link discovery frameworks. Semant. Web **8**(3), 419–436 (2017)
21. Newcombe, H., Kennedy, J., Axford, S., James, A.: Automatic linkage of vital records (1967)
22. Papaleo, L., Pernelle, N., Saïs, F., Dumont, C.: Logical detection of invalid SameAs statements in RDF data. In: Janowicz, K., Schlobach, S., Lambrix, P., Hyvönen, E. (eds.) EKAW 2014. LNCS (LNAI), vol. 8876, pp. 373–384. Springer, Cham (2014). https://doi.org/10.1007/978-3-319-13704-9_29

23. Paulheim, H.: Identifying wrong links between datasets by multi-dimensional out-lier detection. In: WoDOOM Third International Workshop on Debugging Ontologies and Ontology Mappings-WoDOOM14, pp. 27–38 (2014)
24. Raad, J., Pernelle, N., Saïs, F.: Detection of contextual identity links in a knowledge base. In: Proceedings of the Knowledge Capture Conference, p. 8. ACM (2017)
25. Saïs, F., Pernelle, N., Rousset, M.C.: Combining a logical and a numerical method for data reconciliation. J. Data Semant. **12**(12), 66–94 (2009)
26. Töpper, G., Knuth, M., Sack, H.: DBpedia ontology enrichment for inconsistency detection. In: Proceedings of the 8th International Conference on Semantic Systems, pp. 33–40. ACM (2012)
27. Völker, J., Niepert, M.: Statistical schema induction. In: Antoniou, G., et al. (eds.) ESWC 2011. LNCS, vol. 6643, pp. 124–138. Springer, Heidelberg (2011). https://doi.org/10.1007/978-3-642-21034-1_9

SHARK: A Test-Driven Framework for Design and Evolution of Ontologies

Gustavo Correa Publio[✉]

Institut für Informatik, AKSW Group, Universität Leipzig, Leipzig, Germany
gustavo.publio@informatik.uni-leipzig.de

Abstract. In the Semantic Web, the sharing and reuse of knowledge are made possible by ontologies which establish common vocabularies and semantic interpretations of terms. Over the last years, the LOD cloud has been growing substantially in size of each ontology and the total number of objects. In order to ensure a certain level of data quality, several methods have been proposed so far, with different characteristics and approaches, demanding the composition of different tools to ensure a full validation and continuous integration with hosting solutions. In this paper, we present SHARK, a single framework capable to test an ontology using formally pre-defined guidelines or custom SHACL tests, and can also be used for continuous testing during the ontology development process.

Keywords: Ontology evolution · Test driven
Ontology development · SHACL

1 Introduction

The Linked Open Data Cloud [2] is growing exponentially in the last few years. Besides the increase in the number of available datasets, each of them also evolves and grows in size and amount of data in an accelerated speed, often in a crowd-sourced and collaborative environment – which makes virtually impossible to find an error-free dataset. In order to achieve a sustainable growth, such amount of data demands methods for effective control of data quality and conformance.

Over the last years, many approaches aiming the description and validation of ontologies have been proposed, including methodologies, frameworks, tools, and languages. Among the last group, we can cite the Shape Expression (ShEx) [3], a language that attempted to develop the same function for RDF graphs that languages like XML Schema do for XML; and the Shapes Constraint Language (SHACL) [9], created in 2014 by the W3C Working Group on RDF Data Shapes [1].

In "*Validating RDF Data book*" [7], authors demonstrate several SHACL applications, including "Ontology Validation with SHACL" - a starting point to this work.

Aiming to a new approach for data validation that benefits from SHACL advantages, we present SHARK (SHACL Reasoning over Knowledge-graphs),

© Springer Nature Switzerland AG 2018
A. Gangemi et al. (Eds.): ESWC 2018 Satellite Events, LNCS 11155, pp. 314–324, 2018.
https://doi.org/10.1007/978-3-319-98192-5_50

a SHACL-based ontology validation framework. This framework aims to (1) provide a continuous-integration test solution for ontology evaluation; (2) support ontology review and design through a simple web interface, by allowing pre-selected tests based on several ontology development guidelines to be run against user-submitted ontologies; and (3) allow advanced users to run their own custom SHACL tests against any ontology, through the web interface or web service API.

The remainder of this paper is organised as follows. Section 2 reviews the related literature. The research problems and expected contributions are presented in Sect. 3. Section 4 outlines the research methodology and approach. Section 5 discuss the preliminary tests, while Sect. 6 discuss the evaluation plan. The paper is finally concluded in Sect. 7.

2   State of the Art

Several languages, methodologies, frameworks, and tools have been proposed in the last twenty years to evaluate ontologies. Tomaszuk [17] makes a comparison of different languages for RDF Validation including SHACL [9], as well as ReSh [16], DSP [4], SPIN [8], OWL [6] and RDFs [5]. In the evaluation, SHACL stands out as the fastest and most complete processing language.

In [14] and as of 2012, the author made an extensive literature review that found relevant dependencies between ontology development methodologies,[1] ontology evaluation frameworks[2] and evaluation tools.[3] The author also showed that although ontology development methodologies had served as key reference for ontology evaluation (mainly by spreading the use of *Competency Questions* - CQ), they were not a requirement for the implementation of evaluation frameworks and tools.

In general lines, CQs consist in questions that a specific ontology must be able to answer. In [15] authors claims that it is difficult to either specify the requirements for an ontology, or to test their satisfaction. Thus, they propose a novel approach to address this problem by leveraging the ideas of competency questions and test-before software development. A key benefit of this approach is to easily guide ontology authoring, especially for authors that are not proficient in logic.

In [14] is also proposed OOPS! (OntOlogy Pitfall Scanner!), a diagnosis tool to both detect potential errors (*pitfalls*) in ontologies and recommend some tips to repair them. The detection methods are mainly based on structural pattern matching and linguistic analysis. OOPS counts with a catalog of errors obtained by manual review where each error is classified as critical, important or minor according its importance level. Although OOPS provides a wider range of known ontology issues, it has some drawbacks: (a) its catalog of *pitfalls* is not exhaustive, (b) it only deals with the conceptual schema level of OWL DL ontologies

---

[1] The seminal work of Gruninger and Fox, Methontology, On-To-Knowledge, DILIGENT and Neon.

[2] OntoClean, OntoQA, Unit Tests, OQuaRE, Neon Guidelines, etc.

[3] ODEClean, ODEval, AEON, Eyeball, Moki, OQuare, OntoCheck, XD-Analyzer.

(TBox) and (c) it only checks explicit knowledge, i.e. it does not perform inference. In addition, since those *pitfalls* were not been formalized, the tool cannot be integrated smoothly into a *continuous ontology quality assurance process*.

Unit Tests, one of the ontology evaluation frameworks enumerated above, is a well-known technique in test-driven software development and has also been applied to the ontology evaluation field. In a framework initially proposed in [19] and enhanced in [18], the working ontology is validated against a positive and a negative test ontology. Each unit test controls that each axiom in the positive test ontology be inferred by the working ontology and that each axiom in the negative test ontology be not inferred by the working ontology. Thus, if a unit test fails, an error might exist in the working ontology. Notice that the proposed framework formalizes competency questions but does not formalize all ontology requirements.

In [10], a test-driven approach to evaluate Linked Data quality is described. This approach encodes data quality constraints in generic SPARQL query templates which in turn are instantiated automatically into specific quality test queries for a particular ontology or dataset. The data quality constraints are compiled as a reusable set of Data Quality Test Patterns (DQTP) ready to be integrated as automated test-methods.

3   Problem Statement and Contributions

The following examples illustrates some of the problems that might raise during the ontology development process. As stated in [15], authoring ontologies is a non-trivial task as ontology authors are usually domain experts but not necessarily proficient in logic. This may cause misleading in following the best practices in ontology authoring, as for instance missing useful metadata. In fact, [11] shows that a significant part of datasets available in the LOD cloud lack or has incorrect/incomplete basic metadata information. Besides the metadata at the dataset level, according to [13] the lack of label or comment in the schema level (classes and/or properties) also deviates best practices.

In [12], authors define two distinct modes of ontology evolution: *traced* and *untraced* evolution. In the first mode we treat the evolution as a series of documented changes in the ontology. Those can be structural changes in the schema level (TBox) or in the individuals of the ontology (ABox). On the other hand, due to the extremely distributed nature of ontologies, we must also account for the fact that we will not always have the trace of changes that led from one version to another, leading to the untraced mode. In any case, it is expected that the data keeps consistent in the new version of the ontology in order to keep the compatibility between those versions, but such consistency is difficult to be assured.

Finally, impacts of ontology evolution may be of interest to data authors, consumers, reviewers, system developers, and so on, but they might be difficult to trace, especially in crowd-sourced ontology edition. An approach to preview or detect such impacts in any ontology must be public available to general purpose, so users can try to mitigate such impacts prior to publish a new version of the ontology.

3.1 Research Questions

To solve the identified problems in the ontology design and evolution process, the following research questions are intended to be addressed with the proposed approach:

1. Regardless of prior technical knowledge in logic, authoring or programming languages, how can any user evaluate whether his or her ontology addresses the best practices of ontology design w.r.t. the data structure, metadata, and so on?
2. How can non-conformance data inserted between two distinct versions of ontology (whether in traced or untraced evolution) be detected at ABox or TBox level?
3. In order to assure data quality, how can ontology evolution be evaluated prior to final publication?
4. In a community-based crowd-sourced environment, how is it possible to mitigate data quality issues?

3.2 Contributions

In order to solve the mentioned research questions, this paper presents the SHARK framework with the following respective contributions:

1. a novel web-based application that (a) allows users to select relevant tests among predefined guidelines based on best practices of ontology design, and (b) allows users to run custom SHACL tests against any given ontology;
2. for any given ontology and test set, a report at instance level for every violation found;
3. a web API enabled through a web service endpoint that allows users to run tests against any ontology at any phase of development;
4. a continuous-integration test solution for ontologies hosted in version-control environments (e.g. GitHub).

4 Research Methodology and Approach

To achieve the intended contribution goals, the SHARK framework consists in an environment as pictured in Fig. 1. The only external dependency, that was not developed in the context of this work, is the RDFUnit tool[4], which provides the SHACL implementation, running the SHACL tests in the provided ontology and giving the results.

---

[4] http://rdfunit.aksw.org/.

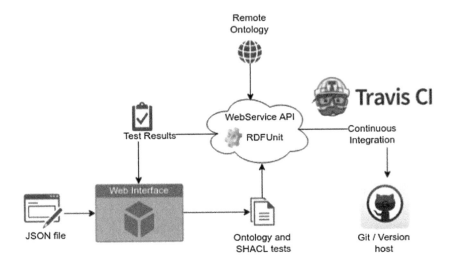

Fig. 1. The SHARK framework architecture

4.1 Technologies

The front-end Web application under development uses HTML5 and Javascript ES6, and also the Bootstrap framework.[5] The Web Service and its API is being written in Java, with support of Springboot framework.[6] It runs in the backend the RDFUnit tool. Finally, the developed continuous integration system integration was preliminary tested with Travis-CI[7] (as shown in Fig. 3) and GitHub[8] for hosting and version control.

4.2 Web Application Home

The web application consists of a three-step-process. As seen in Fig. 2[a], the initial screen of the web-based application offers to the user to select between uploading an ontology from his local computer or specifying the remote URL of the ontology to be tested.

In the second step (Fig. 2[b]), users can either select which pre-defined guidelines they want to test against the provided ontology or define custom SHACL tests in the second tab (Fig. 2[c]). There are 20 distinct pre-defined guidelines that can be tested in the provided ontology. To make it easier to update such guidelines, they are described in a separated JSON file that contains the SHACL tests and generates the HTML form. When selecting each of them, the user is indirectly generating (internally by the tool) a SHACL test which can be either a SHACL Core-based test or a SHACL SPARQL-based one. Such tests were

---

[5] https://getbootstrap.com/.
[6] https://spring.io/.
[7] https://travis-ci.org.
[8] https://github.com/.

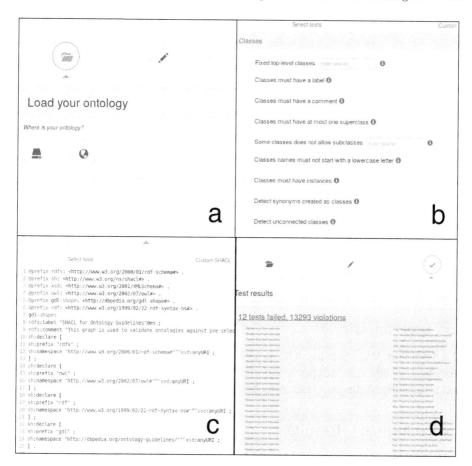

Fig. 2. The SHARK web tool interface, with (a) ontology selection screen, (b) guidelines selection, (c) custom SHACL editor and (d) test results report.

designed based on the best practices reviewed in the literature, such as OOPS! framework [14], or those included in *Validating RDF Data book* [7].

To the users, there are two different types of tests: those that they can only select and activate, and those that demands an extra, custom text input. The latter are the "*Fixed top-level classes*" test, where users can specify whether the first layer of the class hierarchy of the ontology is fixed and cannot be changed by simply listing those fixed classes, and the "*Some classes does not allow subclasses*" test, which in the same way, requires as text input a list of classes that does not allow subclasses.

Finally, in the third step (Fig. 2[d]), the report with the test results is presented, showing all the elements that violates any of the selected guidelines/SHACL tests.

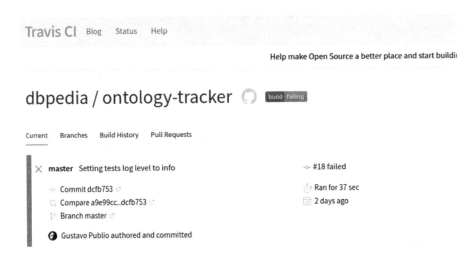

Fig. 3. The SHARK continuous integration, showing a build that failed due to a test violation.

4.3 RESTful API

The RESTful Web Service API is described in the SwaggerHub service.[9] It provide methods that supports different input formats of the ontology file, as well as all output formats that Apache Jena[10] supports.

5 Preliminary Results

5.1 Guidelines Evaluation

In order to evaluate the usefulness of the pre-selected guideline tests, we run most of them (18 out of 20 - except the two that requires custom user input) against the ontologies available in the LOV Cloud.[11] As provided by LOV vocabulary list API,[12] we found 633 ontologies in the cloud. From those, 237 ontologies were not tested due to different reasons: broken (Error 404) or non-public (Error 401) URI, connection timeout, empty ontologies (model with 0 elements), etc. Thus, 396 ontologies were effectively tested.

Given that the tested ontologies are public available in the LOV list, and that this test set consists in ontologies of different domains and authors, the idea is that each of the designed tests should neither fail or pass in 100% of the ontologies, otherwise that test would not be useful for generic guidelines purposes. Table 1 shows the test results. The most frequent violation is classes/properties

---

[9] https://app.swaggerhub.com/apis/gcpdev/SHARK/0.1.

[10] http://jena.apache.org/documentation/io/rdf-output.html#normal-printing.

[11] https://lov.okfn.org.

[12] http://lov.okfn.org/dataset/lov/api/v2/vocabulary/list.

Table 1. Compilation of test results over 396 different ontologies streamed from the LOV Cloud. The second column shows the absolute number of ontologies where the test failed; the third one shows the average frequency of element violations, and the last column shows the percentage of ontologies that failed the test with at least one violation

Test	#Occurr.	Av. Freq. (%)	Ontologies occurr. (%)
Classes must have a label	363	12.04	92.37
Classes must have a comment	363	12.04	92.37
Classes must have at most one superclass	170	3.27	43.26
Classes names must not start with a lowercase letter	4	3.87	1.02
Classes must have instances	282	9.46	71.76
Detect synonyms created as classes	12	0.75	3.05
Detect unconnected classes	129	1.14	32.82
Detect cycles in the class hierarchy	14	0.91	3.56
Properties must have a label	359	15.26	91.35
Properties must have a comment	359	15.26	91.35
Properties must have at most one domain	68	0.93	17.30
Properties must have at least one class as domain	359	20.77	91.35
Properties must have at most one range	62	0.65	15.78
Properties must have at least one class as range	359	20.77	91.35
Properties must have at most one superproperty	60	2.83	15.27
Properties names must not start with a capital letter	19	4.23	4.83
Detect relationships inverse to themselves	15	0.50	3.82
Detect wrongly defined relationship 'is'	23	0.36	5.85

must have a label/comment, which shows that unfortunately the metadata of ontology elements still lack in most of the available datasets. On the other hand, tests like *"Detect relationships inverse to themselves"*, *"Detect cycles in the class hierarchy"* or *"Detect synonyms created as classes"* have only a few occurrences, but they point out critical structural problems in each ontology they occur.

6   Evaluation Plan

6.1   User Interface Evaluation

In order to obtain a deeper, critical evaluation of the SHARK web based tool, we plan to make an evaluation of its web user interface with a group of users through surveys, rating the usability and relevance/usefulness of those predefined guidelines.

6.2   Improve Guidelines

The literature review and guidelines maintenance will be periodically revisited, in order to improve the actual tests according to users feedback and add new predefined guidelines.

6.3   Better Evolution/Alignment Evaluation

The evolution process of ontologies are very related to the alignment process, as both of them deals with the differences and compatibility between two different ontology versions. Both process demand a better evaluation, with study cases and practical examples of the impact of the SHACL tests over each of them.

7   Conclusion

In this paper, we presented SHARK, a test-driven framework for design and evolution of ontologies. The framework consists in a Web-based interface where users can either choose between 20 different pre-defined guidelines to test their ontology, or run their own custom SHACL tests. The pre-defined tests were run successfully against 396 different ontologies, demonstrating their usefulness against real data. The framework has also an web service API, and a continuous integration system setup for automatic evaluation of ontology evolution.

Finally, all the SHARK framework code is open-source and available in the GitHub.[13]

Acknowledgements. This paper's research activities were funded by grants from the Smart Data Web BMWi project (GA-01MD15010B) and CNPq foundation (scholarship 201808/2015-3). The author also acknowledges the support of Adam Sanchez, Sebastian Hellmann, Magnus Knuth, and Rafael Peñaloza in the development of this paper.

---

[13] https://github.com/gcpdev/shark.

References

1. Rdf data shapes working group. https://www.w3.org/2014/data-shapes/wiki/Main_Page. Accessed 29 Jan 2018
2. Abele, A., McCrae, J.P., Buitelaar, P., Jentzsch, A., Cyganiak, R.: Linking open data cloud diagram (2017). http://lod-cloud.net/
3. Boneva, I., Gayo, J.E.L., Hym, S., Prud'hommeau, E.G., Solbrig, H., Staworko, S.: Validating RDF with shape expressions. arXiv preprint arXiv:1404.1270 (2014)
4. Bosch, T., Eckert, K.: Towards description set profiles for RDF using SPARQL as intermediate language. In: International Conference on Dublin Core and Metadata Applications, pp. 129–137 (2014)
5. Brickley, D., Guha, R.V.: Resource description framework (RDF) schema specification 1.0: W3c candidate recommendation 27 March 2000 (2000)
6. Dean, M., et al.: OWL web ontology language reference. W3C Recommendation February 10 (2004)
7. Gayo, J.E.L., Prud'Hommeaux, E., Boneva, I., Kontokostas, D.: Validating RDF Data, vol. 7. Morgan & Claypool Publishers, San Rafael (2017)
8. Knublauch, H., Hendler, J.A., Idehen, K.: Spin-overview and motivation. W3C Member Submission 22 (2011)
9. Knublauch, H., Kontokostas, D.: Shapes constraint language (SHACL). https://www.w3.org/TR/shacl/. Accessed 29 Jan 2018
10. Kontokostas, D., et al.: Test-driven evaluation of linked data quality. In: 23rd International World Wide Web Conference, WWW 2014, Seoul, Republic of Korea, 7–11 April 2014, pp. 747–758 (2014). http://doi.acm.org/10.1145/2566486.2568002
11. Neto, C.B., Kontokostas, D., Kirschenbaum, A., Publio, G.C., Esteves, D., Hellmann, S.: IDOL: comprehensive & complete LOD insights. In: Proceedings of the 13th International Conference on Semantic Systems, Semantics 2017, pp. 49–56. ACM, New York (2017). http://doi.acm.org/10.1145/3132218.3132238
12. Noy, N.F., Klein, M.: Ontology evolution: not the same as schema evolution. Knowl. Inf. Syst. **6**(4), 428–440 (2004)
13. Poveda, M., Suárez-Figueroa, M.C., Gómez-Pérez, A.: Common pitfalls in ontology development. In: Meseguer, P., Mandow, L., Gasca, R.M. (eds.) CAEPIA 2009. LNCS (LNAI), vol. 5988, pp. 91–100. Springer, Heidelberg (2010). https://doi.org/10.1007/978-3-642-14264-2_10
14. Poveda-Villalón, M.: Ontology evaluation: a pitfall-based approach to ontology diagnosis. Ph.D. thesis, Departamento de Inteligencia Artificial, Universidad Politécnica de Madrid, February 2016
15. Ren, Y., Parvizi, A., Mellish, C., Pan, J.Z., van Deemter, K., Stevens, R.: Towards competency question-driven ontology authoring. In: Presutti, V., d'Amato, C., Gandon, F., d'Aquin, M., Staab, S., Tordai, A. (eds.) ESWC 2014. LNCS, vol. 8465, pp. 752–767. Springer, Cham (2014). https://doi.org/10.1007/978-3-319-07443-6_50
16. Ryman, A.G., Le Hors, A., Speicher, S.: OSLC resource shape: a language for defining constraints on linked data. LDOW 996 (2013)
17. Tomaszuk, D.: RDF validation: a brief survey. In: Kozielski, S., Mrozek, D., Kasprowski, P., Małysiak-Mrozek, B., Kostrzewa, D. (eds.) BDAS 2017. CCIS, vol. 716, pp. 344–355. Springer, Cham (2017). https://doi.org/10.1007/978-3-319-58274-0_28

18. Vrandecic, D.: Ontology evaluation. Ph.D. thesis, Departamento de Inteligencia Artificial, Fakultät für Wirtschaftswissenschaften des Karlsruher Instituts für Technologie (KIT), June 2010
19. Vrandečić, D., Gangemi, A.: Unit tests for ontologies. In: Meersman, R., Tari, Z., Herrero, P. (eds.) OTM 2006. LNCS, vol. 4278, pp. 1012–1020. Springer, Heidelberg (2006). https://doi.org/10.1007/11915072_2

3rd Workshop on Geospatial Linked Data

Using Linked Open Geo Boundaries for Adaptive Delineation of Functional Urban Areas

Ali Khalili[1]([✉]), Peter van den Besselaar[2], and Klaas Andries de Graaf[1]

[1] Department of Computer Science, Vrije Universiteit Amsterdam,
Amsterdam, Netherlands
{a.khalili,ka.de.graaf}@vu.nl
[2] Department of Organization Sciences, Vrije Universiteit Amsterdam,
Amsterdam, Netherlands
p.a.a.vanden.besselaar@vu.nl

Abstract. The concentration of people, companies, research organizations and other activities in urban areas is a key process in the development of economies and societies. In order to investigate how these urban systems function, the OECD (Organization for Economic Co-operation and Development) in collaboration with EC (European Commission) and Eurostat have introduced the concept of Functional Urban Areas (FUAs). FUAs consider a preliminary set of socio-economic and environmental factors and provide a basis for an agreed definition for measuring development of metropolitan areas. However, because FUAs are predefined they do not meet the need for designing policies and research questions involving different types of urban areas that are defined by weighting some factors more than others or by using additional factors. Therefore, providing an adaptive approach for dynamic and multi-faceted delineation of FUAs, rather than merely relying on a rigid schema with a fixed list of FUAs per country, allows to more flexibly reflect the socio-economic geography of where people live and work. This adaptive definition of FUAs demands integration of data from multiple up-to-date linked data sources. In this paper, we describe an approach and implementation for a Linked Open Geo-Data space, which combines openly available spatial and non-spatial resources on the Web to classify urban areas with the aim to more flexibly monitor and research urban development.

1 Introduction

The concentration of people, companies, research organizations and other activities in urban areas is a key process in the development of economies and societies. How urban systems function is crucial to future economic prosperity and better quality of life for more than three billion people [1]. In order to investigate how these urban systems function, the OECD (Organization for Economic Co-operation and Development) in collaboration with EC (European Commission) and Eurostat have developed a new approach to classifying urban areas with the aim to better monitor urban development within and across countries.

© Springer Nature Switzerland AG 2018
A. Gangemi et al. (Eds.): ESWC 2018 Satellite Events, LNCS 11155, pp. 327–341, 2018.
https://doi.org/10.1007/978-3-319-98192-5_51

The new notion of urban areas called *Functional Urban Areas* (FUAs) considers several factors beyond the formal city boundaries such as population, area, GDP, environment (CO_2 emissions and air pollution), labour market (employment and unemployment growth), innovation (patent intensity), urban form and territorial organization to develop a harmonized definition of urban areas in 28 OECD countries. Even though this new way to measure metropolitan areas provides a basis for an agreed definition of functional urban areas, to support the design of better policies for different types of urban areas, one needs to weight some factors more than others or use additional factors, which are not predefined in the current OECD methodology. Governments and policy makers need a way to dynamically redefine different types of urban areas [2]. Therefore, providing an adaptive approach for dynamic and multi-faceted delineation of FUAs, rather than merely relying on a rigid schema with a fixed list of FUAs per country, allows to more flexibly reflect the socio-economic geography of where people live and work. This adaptive definition of FUAs demands integration of data from multiple up-to-date linked data sources. Spatial data often has a temporal component; things move, and boundaries change over time.

Tackling the challenges of data integration on a dynamic environment such as WWW has been the mission of Linked (Open) Data technologies since the introduction of Semantic Web in 2001. Providing a *Linked Open Data* space, which brings together structured and interlinked geospatial data on the Web, facilitates delineating of FUAs. Currently, access to the micro data used by OECD for calculating different indicators of FUAs is limited, and negotiation with OECD is required to retrieve detailed data for regeneration of OECD FUAs.[1] On the other hand, openly available geospatial datasets on the Web such as *OpenStreetMap*[2] are already interlinked with existing structured data published on the Linked Open Data (LOD) cloud and provide the opportunity to reproduce a more flexible and dynamic list of FUAs. For example, the public sector in Europe creates lots of statistical data on different levels of administrative boundaries such as *NUTS* (Nomenclature of Units for Territorial Statistics), *LAU* (Local Administrative Unit), *HASC* (Hierarchical Administrative Subdivision Codes) and *ISO 3166* country codes which could be utilized to dynamically identify FUAs adapted to the context of the corresponding policy studies.

In this paper we propose a Linked Data approach and implementation which combines openly available spatial and non-spatial resources on the Web to more flexibly classify urban areas. To achieve this goal, we followed methodology described in the LOD Lifecycle [4], consisting of several steps (cf. Fig. 1) for geospatial data collection, extraction, storage, linkage and exploitation which are discussed in the following sections of this paper. This paper makes the following contributions:

– Report an approach and implementation for dynamically defining FUAs based on linked open data.

---

[1] http://www.oecd.org/cfe/regional-policy/functionalurbanareasbycountry.htm provides the shapefiles for FUAs together with some descriptions in PDF format.

[2] http://www.openstreetmap.org.

– Use linked open data to reconstruct the closed OECD FUA dataset.
– Report a use case on the implemented approach.

Fig. 1. An overview of the steps for adaptive delineation of FUAs.

2   Step 1 - Data Discovery and Collection

As first step (step '*search/browse/exploration*' in LOD Lifecycle [4]), we performed an extensive offline/online search to find existing relevant geospatial datasets, which provide data for world-wide administrative boundaries. We were particularly looking for datasets that contain shapefiles for those boundaries. For the offline search, we used our network to find research groups working on spatial data infrastructures and through them either get access to available geospatial datasets or find other related institutes that publish geospatial data related to urban areas. For the online search, we used both general-purpose search engines (e.g. Google) as well as search engines indexing only structured content (DataHub[3], LOTUS[4] and EU Open Data Portal[5]). Progressive moves toward Open Data are creating frameworks through which geographic data assets that have often previously not been in the public domain, or been in the public domain under more restrictive licenses, can be released for free to re-use in either commercial or non-commercial applications [11]. As result of our search for open geo data, we discovered the following resources on the Web providing geospatial data for administrative boundaries:

OpenStreetMap (OSM) Data. OSM is a collaborative project to build a free editable map of the world. OSM offers up to 10 administrative boundary levels

---

[3] http://datahub.io.
[4] http://lotus.lodlaundromat.org.
[5] https://open-data.europa.eu/en/data/.

as subdivisions of areas/territories/jurisdictions recognized by governments or other organizations for administrative purposes.[6] And for these administrative units, all kind of socio-economic, demographic, and other data are available. These administrative boundaries range from large groups of nation states right down to small administrative districts and suburbs. There are different methods to access the properties (including the shape coordinates) of administrative boundaries in OSM. Nominatim Web API[7] allows querying OSM for a name or address(forward search) or look up data by its geographic coordinate(reverse search). The Overpass API[8] allows fetching selected parts of the OSM map data by search criteria such as location, type of objects, tag properties, proximity, or combinations of them. In addition to the API access, users can directly download the latest data dump of the OSM through Planet.osm mirrors[9] in two main available formats namely PBF and compressed OSM XML.

Database of Global Administrative Areas (GADM). GADM[10] provides a curated database of the administrative areas in the world. GADM provides some properties of these administrative areas such as name, variant names and "spatial features" about the location of the areas. Administrative areas in this database include up to 6 levels of details starting from level 0 which refers to countries. Level 1 to 5 cover lower level subdivisions such as provinces, departments, counties, etc. depending on the size and availability of data for the underlying country. The GADM data are publicly available for download by country or the whole world in different formats such as shapefile, ESRI geodatabase, RData, and Google Earth kmz format.

Flickr Shapefiles Dataset. Flickr Shapefiles Public Dataset[11] provides data from 190M geo-tagged photos on Flickr. The shapefiles are generated by plotting all the geotagged photos associated with a particular place and by generating a mostly accurate contour of that place. Flickr offers 6 levels of boundaries identified by so called Where On Earth (WOE) IDs. The levels range from country (level 1), region (level 2) county (level 3), locality (level 4) to neighborhood (level 5). The dataset is publicly available for download in GeoJSON format.

Published Shapefiles for Individual Countries. In addition to crowd-sourced and curated datasets on global administrative boundaries, local administrative offices or geo-related research centres in specific countries provide shapefiles and other properties related to the administrative units in that country. For example, *Centraal Bureau voor de Statistiek* (CBS) or *Bundesamt für Kartographie und Geodäsie* (BKG) provide shapefiles of administrative boundaries for the Netherlands and Germany respectively.

---

[6] for some specific countries level 11 is also defined. Check http://wiki.openstreetmap. org/wiki/Template:Admin_level_11.

[7] http://nominatim.openstreetmap.org/.

[8] http://overpass-api.de/api/.

[9] http://wiki.openstreetmap.org/wiki/Planet.osm.

[10] http://www.gadm.org.

[11] http://www.flickr.com/services/shapefiles/2.0/.

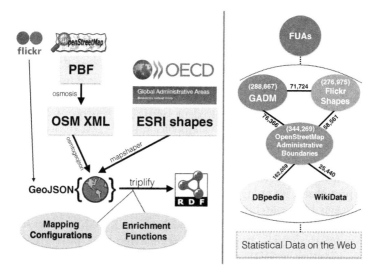

Fig. 2. (left) Steps to convert geospatial data to RDF. (right) General and domain-specific interlinked datasets for delineating FUAs.

Published Geospatial RDF Datasets. There are already several efforts to implement a spatial dimension on the Web of Data (a.k.a. Semantic Web). Geo-Know [3][12] and LinkedGeoData projects [12][13] collect and publish the information extracted from the INSPIRE [8] and OpenStreetMap data sources as an RDF knowledge base interlinked with other knowledge bases in the Link Open Data initiative. To the best of our knowledge, LinkedGeoData dataset[14] does not provide "relations" elements for OSM administrative units which are required to create precise polygon or multi-polygon shapes for them. GeoVocab.org is another related effort which provides an RDF spatial representation of the administrative boundaries represented in the GADM database called *GADM-RDF*[15]. We also found several geo datasets on particular countries, for instance Spanish open geo datasets [13] or Ecuadorian geospatial Linked Data [10], etc.

3   Step 2 - Data Extraction and Conversion

The existing diverse landscape of standards for spatial data on the Web makes the task of data extraction and conversion very cumbersome and time-consuming. The left side of Fig. 2 depicts our implemented approach to deal with spatial data extraction, processing and conversion. This corresponds to step '*extraction*' in the LOD Lifecycle [4]. We used *GeoJSON* as our terminal data format for the conversion to RDF. The Flickr Shapefiles Dataset was

---

[12] http://geoknow.eu.
[13] http://linkedgeodata.org/.
[14] http://downloads.linkedgeodata.org/releases/2015-11-02/.
[15] http://gadm.geovocab.org/.

already available in GeoJSON format. Additional processing and conversion to GeoJSON format was needed for some of the other collected data. We downloaded the OSM dataset in PBF (Protocolbuffer Binary Format) which provides a more compressed format comparing to the XML format. We then used the Osmosis[16] tool to process the data and to only extract the data about administrative boundaries in OSM format. The OSMtoGeoJSON[17] tool was then applied on the extracted subset which resulted in GeoJSON version of data. We used MapShaper[18] to convert the OECD shapefiles and GADM dataset from ESRI format to GeoJSON format.

We utilized a set of *Mapping Configurations* and *Enrichment Functions* to convert spatial data encoded in GeoJSON to RDF format. The Mapping configurations provided a mapping between the given properties of data in original dataset and their best matching RDF properties expressed in the Linked Open Data cloud. Linked Open Vocabularies[19] were used to produce suggestions from existing vocabularies on the Web. In case no existing RDF properties are available, a new proprietary RDF property is created and defined as part of our proposed vocabulary.

Enrichment functions were defined to clean up, standardize, and enrich the property values. For example, we added the ISO 3166 code of the countries by processing the given country names and converted the given Wikipedia URLs to their corresponding DBpedia URIs. We also set the right data types for the converted literal values. The convertor scripts are available as separate repositories on Github[20]. In addition to the spatial data, we extracted tabular data about the OECD list of municipalities and FUAs[21], as well as metadata on different OSM levels provided as HTML tables on Wikipedia[22], and converted this data to RDF. The final RDF dataset consisted of 344,269 administrative boundaries from OSM, 288,668 from GADM and, 276,975 from Flickr.

4   Step 3 - Data Storage and Querying

We used Openlink Virtuoso triple store for storing the generated RDF data. The main reason for using Virtuoso was its extensive support for geometry data types and spatial indexing[23]. At the time of conversion to RDF, we adapted all the GeoJSON shapes coordinates to WKT (Well-Known Text) `Polygon` and `MultiPolygon` representations. Virtuoso's stored procedures such as

---

[16] http://wiki.openstreetmap.org/wiki/Osmosis.
[17] https://github.com/tyrasd/osmtogeojson.
[18] https://github.com/mbloch/mapshaper.
[19] http://lov.okfn.org/.
[20] https://github.com/ali1k/osm-rdf
       https://github.com/ali1k/gadm-rdf
       https://github.com/ali1k/flickrshapes-rdf.
[21] http://www.oecd.org/gov/regional-policy/List-municipalities.xls.
[22] http://wiki.openstreetmap.org/wiki/Template:Admin_level_10.
[23] http://docs.openlinksw.com/virtuoso/sqlrefgeospatial.html.

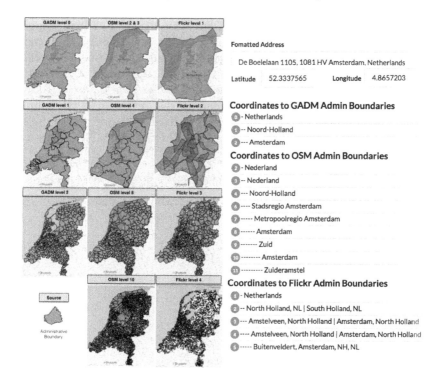

Fig. 3. Example mapping of an address to the extracted administrative boundaries.

st_intersects, st_contains and st_within were then used to test whether two geometries overlap in different ways. For example to find all the administrative boundaries which contain a certain point. This step corresponds to step 'Storage/Querying' in the LOD Lifecycle [4].

5   Step 4 - Data Linking

In order to exploit the power of Linked Data, we established links between the converted RDF datasets and other open datasets available on Linked Open Data cloud. This corresponds to step 'Interlinking/Fusing' in the LOD Lifecycle [4]. The right side of Fig. 2 shows the connectivity of the main datasets. The OSM dataset already contains links to general knowledge bases, e.g., DBpedia and WikiData, which serve as hubs to interlink with other open statistical datasets.

In order to compute direct links between OSM, GADM and Flickr, we followed a hybrid approach combining string similarity with the geometric overlapping of administrative boundaries. We first created a mapping between different levels of boundaries provided in OSM, GADM and Flickr by comparing the granularity of divisions in different countries. We took into account the provided OSM metadata per country for each administrative boundary level. Figure 3 shows a sample of extracted administrative boundaries for the Netherlands which reflects the possible mappings at different levels for a specific address (top-right of Fig. 3). Secondly, we checked the overlaps of areas at the similar level, and for the matching areas we applied string matching to make sure that they refer to the same administrative boundary. Code 1.1 brings an example of CONSTRUCT queries used to create linksets between the OSM and GADM datasets. To showcase the output of our query, for Amsterdam in the Netherlands, the approach will result in the following linked entities: oecd:NL002, gadm:158-9-266, hasc:NL-NH-AD, osm:relation_47811, flickr:727232, dbpedia: Amsterdam, wikidata:Q9899 and geonames:2759794.

Code 1.1. An example of making links between OSM and GADM datasets.

```
1  PREFIX GADMV: <http://geo.risis.eu/vocabulary/gadm/>
2  PREFIX OSMV: <http://geo.risis.eu/vocabulary/osm/>
3
4  CONSTRUCT {?s1 owl:sameAs ?s2 .} WHERE {
5    graph <http://geo.risis.eu/osm> {
6      ?s1 a OSMV:AdministrativeArea ;
7         OSMV:level "2"^^xsd:integer ;
8         dcterms:title ?title1 ;
9         geo:geometry ?polygon1 . }
10   graph <http://geo.risis.eu/gadm> {
11     ?s2 a GADMV:AdministrativeArea ;
12        GADMV:level "0"^^xsd:integer ;
13        dcterms:title ?title2 ;
14        geo:geometry ?polygon2 . }
15   FILTER (regex(?title1,?title2, "i") && bif:st_intersects (?
          polygon1,?polygon2)) }
```

6   Step 5 - Data to Service

In addition to a SPARQL endpoint[24] provided for Semantic Web users, we also exposed a set of predefined SPARQL query templates as RESTful Web services to facilitate use of the interlinked data by developers who are unfamiliar with the SPARQL query language. The Web services also allow for better management of data access (in case authentication and authorization are needed) whilst monitoring the data usage to optimize the queries and to provide load balancing on the services infrastructure (due to reasons of data size and performance of the respective geospatial queries, scalability of Linked Geo Data platforms is a critical issue [6]). We used Swagger[25] to document the APIs of the exposed Linked Geo Data services[26]. The APIs are generally categorized as following:

- Find administrative boundaries containing a given point (e.g. Point ToOSMAdmin).

---

[24] http://sparql.sms.risis.eu/.
[25] http://swagger.io.
[26] http://api.sms.risis.eu/#/Geo-Services.

- Find details of a given administrative boundary (e.g. `OSMAdmin`).
- Find (multi-)polygon shapes of a given administrative boundary (e.g. `OSMAdminToPolygon`).
- Find FUAs related to a given administrative boundary (e.g. `BoundaryToOECDFUA`) or a given point (e.g. `PointToOECDFUA`). In case of adaptive FUAs, for a given indicator, the service will return its corresponding FUA.

Invoking the services will result in executing the SPARQL query templates filled in with the given input.

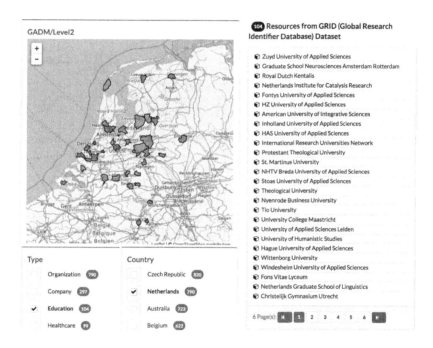

Fig. 4. Exploring http://grid.ac dataset using the extracted geo boundaries.

7   Step 6 - Service to Application

An important benefit of exposing data as service is the ability to combine one or more services with other existing services and applications to build novel and innovative applications. With regards to our domains of interest, we created several applications to better demonstrate the value of the provided services[27]. Utilizing GoogleMap and Mapbox APIs to explore a dataset based on the extracted boundaries was one example of these applications. For instance, Fig. 4 shows our geo-boundaries faceted browser [5] which allows users to browse a map with areas delineated based on different attributes of a dataset.

---

[27] http://sms.risis.eu/demos.

Fig. 5. The screenshot of the Google spreadsheet add-ons for geocoding addresses using SMS Web services (available at http://sms.risis.eu/demos).

Another practical application we built for batch processing of addresses was a Google spreadsheet add-on, depicted in Fig. 5, which chains Google Geocoding API with our `PointToAdmin` and `AdminToFUA` services (see Sect. 6). Given addresses in a spreadsheet are enriched with different levels of administrative boundaries and FUAs. The users are then able to export the extracted boundaries and process them in geodata analysis tools such as CartoDB[28].

In order to evaluate our spreadsheet add-ons, we performed a controlled usability case study with 20 participants of the RISIS geo summer school[29]. Participants included researchers in the science & technology domain from different European research institutes with no knowledge of Semantic Web and Linked Data who wanted to enrich their datasets using our proposed Linked Data services. In the first part of the evaluation, we explained the idea of Linked Open Data in general and then specific Linked Geo Data services provided by our SMS platform were presented. We then asked them to install our spreadsheet add-ons and follow the steps to geocode their datasets using different sources and levels of administrative boundaries and then connect them to FUAs. In the second part, we asked them to fill in the questions recommended by *System Usability Scale* (SUS) [7] system to grade the usability of the app. SUS is a standardized, simple, ten-item Likert scale-based questionnaire[30] giving a global view of subjective assessments of usability. It yields a single number in the

---

[28] https://carto.com/.
[29] http://risis.eu/event/geography-training/.
[30] www.usabilitynet.org/trump/documents/Suschapt.doc.

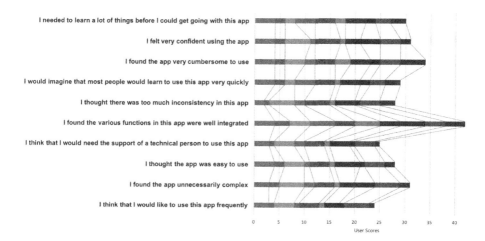

Fig. 6. Result of the SUS questionnaire evaluating our spreadsheet add-ons.

range of 0 to 100 which represents a composite measure of the overall usability of the system. The results of our questionnaire filled by 10 of the participants showed a mean usability score of **71.5** for our add-ons which indicates a good level of usability. Figure 6 shows the scores per user for the SUS questions. In addition to quantitative results, we also collected a number of user suggestions to further improve the application. For instance, to Important feedback from participants include; facilitate initial setup, add more metadata for GADM and Flickr boundaries, and clarify possible level of detail of an address field.

8   In-Use Case Study: Adaptive Delineation of FUAs

We applied the provided services and applications of linked geo-boundaries to several use cases within the context of the RISIS project. RISIS EU project[31] aims to build a distributed infrastructure on data relevant for research and innovation dynamics and policies [9]. One of the objectives in the project is to integrate different science and technology (S&T) datasets centered on the geographical dimension and thereby propose a S&T map of Europe. To achieve this goal, geographical harmonization of different datasets in the S&T domain seems necessary. Therefore, Functional Urban Areas (FUAs) are employed as unit of harmonization. To create an S&T map of Europe we reconstructed and dynamically delineated FUAs from open datasets, starting with the following actions (linked to the steps in our approach described in previous sections):

– Find S&T related indicators which refer to different levels of administrative boundaries; and are suitable for the underlying study.
– Identify a weighted subset of open geo boundaries called adaptive FUAs to serve as unit of geo harmonization (Using steps 1–3 in Sects. 2, 3 and 4).

---

[31] http://risis.eu.

- Geocode addresses in the targeted datasets to enrich the datasets with geo coordinates (Using steps 4 & 5 in Sects. 5 and 6).
- Identify the corresponding adaptive FUAs in different sources/levels surrounding the extracted coordinates (Using steps 6 in Sect. 7).
- Compare datasets based on the identified FUAs (Using step 6 in Sect. 7).

We conducted a concrete case study in this direction which is both exploratory, to gain insight into how a researcher in the science & technology domain (a co-author of this paper) can create an S&T map, and descriptive in nature, to illustrate what results (delineation in an S&T map based on different attributes) are achieved and how these results can be interpreted. We investigated the effect of socio-economic and structural properties of the urban areas on innovative activities, as stimulated by recent RTD[32] policies in the Netherlands. This policy is oriented at the 'top sectors' of the economy, which were selected in a consultation of policy makers, representatives of the research system and entrepreneurs in the country. After selecting these 'top sectors', a large part of public research funding was devoted to this new policy. Consortia can apply for funding, and they should exist of companies and research organizations (such as universities) with a company as main applicant. Because of this context, the funded projects can be considered as a useful representation of *RTD collaboration* for innovation.

In this use case we were interested in the geographical properties of these collaboration networks. In order to investigate this we needed data about the projects, and statistical data about the characteristics of the geographical units. These data are openly available on The Dutch data portal[33]. In this case, we employed the following open datasets:

- *RVO dataset*[34] provides a list of R&D projects that have received subsidies and financial support from the Netherlands Enterprise Agency[35]. Projects information includes companies and research institutes which are collaborating on the project together with the geographical coordinates of the projects.
- *CBS dataset*[36] published by the statistics office of the Netherlands[37] provides different types of statistical information on dimensions such as labour, income, economy, society and regional aspects of regions in the Netherlands.

As we did not know ex ante what the level of geographical organization of the consortia was, we needed to define these in different granularities. This enabled us to find out at what geo-level the consortia were organized. We could then identify the characteristics of these geographical 'containers' of the projects. To realize that, we first calculated different sets of Urban Areas based on different statistics

---

[32] Research and Technology Development.
[33] https://data.overheid.nl.
[34] http://www.rvo.nl/open-data-van-rvonl.
[35] Rijksdienst voor Ondernemend Nederland: RVO.nl.
[36] https://www.cbs.nl/en-gb/our-services/open-data.
[37] Het Centraal Bureau voor de Statistiek: CBS.nl.

Fig. 7. An example of the adaptive delineation of FUAs for the Netherlands based on the open statistical data (populations, business establishments, hybrid and OECD).

Fig. 8. Amount of RVO project subsidies mapped to the dynamically delinated FUAs defined based on the CBS open statistical data and OpenStreetMap boundaries.

provided by the CBS dataset and different levels of open administrative boundaries. Figure 7 shows the delineation of these Urban Areas through population, business establishment, and combinations of these two indicators in the municipality level. Boundaries typically differ when defined by different characteristics. When compared to the OECD FUAs[38] (right map in Fig. 7), the adaptive Urban Areas take into account additional regions (administrative boundaries) and enable the user to put different weights for the delineated boundaries which could be used for focused analysis of specific factors.

Our open data linking (step 4 in Sect. 5) allowed us to then map geographical coordinates of RVO projects to these FUAs (as a baseline for analysis of different S&T indicators) using SPARQL queries, to analyse the correlation of projects to the designated socio-economic factors. Figure 8 shows the result of the mapping where frequency of the projects on different factors are highlighted: the darker the color, the higher the number of awarded projects. As can be seen when comparing Figs. 6 and 7, by far not all (Functional) Urban Areas have projects. But more importantly, the different ways the Urban Areas are defined leads

---

[38] We used the shapefile from the Eurostat used in the large study named urban audit: http://ec.europa.eu/eurostat/web/cities/data/database.

to different outcomes. Using the OECD FUAs (right map), or the population density based FUA (left map) would miss some of the relevant areas[39].

As an additional use case, we also worked on exploiting background knowledge provided by DBpedia, WikiData and other open datasets to find the relation between the structural properties of the universities (e.g. number of students and size, or position on rankings) and properties of their container FUAs (e.g. various demographic and socio-economic characteristics). For example, have the locations of the higher ranked universities systematically different characteristics than lower ranked universities? Describing this use case is beyond the scope of this paper.

9 Conclusion and Future Work

With more than half the world's population now living in urban areas, defining a metropolitan area is critical to reflect the reality of where people live and work as well as the connections between surrounding cities, educational institutes, and businesses. The issue of comparability of metropolitan areas needs an in-depth, dynamic and multi-faceted analysis of administrative boundaries bringing together data about all the influencing factors. The OECD has already defined functional urban areas to address factors beyond the predefined city boundaries, and to better reflect the economic geography of where people live and work.

In this work we report an approach, implementation, and case study on the use of Semantic Web and Linked Data technologies to establish an open data space to more flexibly delineate FUAs by intergrating spatial and non-spatial data from the openly available data sources on the Web. We describe how our approach allows dynamic recreation of FUAs using linked open data and we illustrate our implementation in case studies involving researchers in the science & technology domain. In addition to better geographical coverage, our integration of Flickr, OpenStreetMap, and GADM open boundaries enables researchers and government policy makers to have different views on urban areas[40]. GADM as a curated dataset focuses mainly on formal administrative boundaries while OpenStreetMap and Flickr boundaries as social crowdsourced datsets provide more details and flexibility in defining boundaries.

As future work, we envisage to (1) analyze the quality of data by applying the services to several real-world scenarios defined in the RISIS[41] project; (2) create more connections to the relevant datasets on Linked Open Data cloud; (3) design intuitive user interfaces for end-users to explore FUAs while combining several indicators.

---

[39] in this case South-West Friesland is missing in population based indiators because it is less populated but still hosts a large set of businesses.

[40] We write about *urban* areas because we reconstructed FUAs, however, our approach and implementation supports delineation of any functional area.

[41] http://risis.eu.

Acknowledgement. We would like to thank our colleagues from the Knowledge Representation & Reasoning research group at Vrije Universiteit Amsterdam for their helpful comments during the development of our approach for delineation of functional urban areas. This work was supported by a grant from the European Union's 7th Framework Programme provided for the project RISIS (GA no. 313082).

References

1. Redefining "Urban": A New Way to Measure Metropolitan Areas. OECD (2012)
2. Definition of Functional Urban Areas (FUA) for the OECD metropolitan database. OECD (2013)
3. Athanasiou, S., Hladky, D., Giannopoulos, G., García-Rojas, A., Lehmann, J.: GeoKnow: making the web an exploratory place for geospatial knowledge. ERCIM News **96**, 2014 (2014)
4. Auer, S., Lehmann, J., Ngonga Ngomo, A.-C., Zaveri, A.: Introduction to linked data and its lifecycle on the web. In: Rudolph, S., Gottlob, G., Horrocks, I., van Harmelen, F. (eds.) Reasoning Web 2013. LNCS, vol. 8067, pp. 1–90. Springer, Heidelberg (2013). https://doi.org/10.1007/978-3-642-39784-4_1
5. Khalili, A., Loizou, A., van Harmelen, F.: Adaptive linked data-driven web components: building flexible and reusable semantic web interfaces. In: Sack, H., Blomqvist, E., d'Aquin, M., Ghidini, C., Ponzetto, S.P., Lange, C. (eds.) ESWC 2016. LNCS, vol. 9678, pp. 677–692. Springer, Cham (2016). https://doi.org/10.1007/978-3-319-34129-3_41
6. Kritikos, K., Rousakis, Y., Kotzinos, D.: Linked open GeoData management in the cloud. In: Proceedings of the 2nd International Workshop on Open Data, WOD 2013, pp. 3:1–3:6, New York, NY, USA, 2013. ACM (2013)
7. Lewis, J.R., Sauro, J.: The factor structure of the system usability scale. In: Kurosu, M. (ed.) HCD 2009. LNCS, vol. 5619, pp. 94–103. Springer, Heidelberg (2009). https://doi.org/10.1007/978-3-642-02806-9_12
8. Patroumpas, K., Georgomanolis, N., Stratiotis, T., Alexakis, M., Athanasiou, S.: Exposing INSPIRE on the semantic web. Web Semant. Sci. Serv. Agents World Wide Web **35**(Part 1), 53–62 (2015). Geospatial Semantics
9. van den Besselaar, P., Khalili, A., Koudous Idrissou, A., Schlobach, S., van Harmelen, F.: SMS: a linked open data infrastructure for science and innovation studies. In: Peripheries, Frontiers and Beyond; proceedings of the 21st STI Conference, pp. 106–114. University Valencia (2016). https://www.dropbox.com/s/u5rk2bzxaupssdn/20160914%20SMS%20STI.pdf?dl=0
10. Saquicela, V., Espinoza, M., Piedra, N., Terrazas, B.V.: Ecuadorian geospatial linked data (2014)
11. Singleton, A.D., Spielman, S.E., Brunsdon, C.: Establishing a framework for open geographic information science. Int. J. Geogr. Inf. Sci. **30**(8), 1507–1521 (2016)
12. Stadler, C., Lehmann, J., Höffner, K., Auer, S.: LinkedGeoData: a core for a web of spatial open data. Semant. Web J. **3**(4), 333–354 (2012)
13. Vilches-Blázquez, L.M., Villazón-Terrazas, B., Saquicela, V., de León, A., Corcho, O., Gómez-Pérez, A.: Geolinked data and inspire through an application case. In: 18th SIGSPATIAL International Conference on Advances in Geographic Information Systems, pp. 446–449. ACM (2010)

4th Workshop on Sentic Computing, Sentiment Analysis, Opinion Mining, and Emotion Detection

A Study of the Similarities of Entity Embeddings Learned from Different Aspects of a Knowledge Base for Item Recommendations

Guangyuan Piao$^{(\boxtimes)}$ and John G. Breslin

Insight Centre for Data Analytics, Data Science Institute,
National University of Ireland, Galway, Ireland
guangyuan.piao@insight-centre.org, john.breslin@nuigalway.ie

Abstract. The recent development of deep learning approaches provides a convenient way to learn entity embeddings from different aspects such as texts and a homogeneous or heterogeneous graph encoded in a knowledge base such as DBpedia. However, it is unclear to what extent domain-specific entity embeddings learned from different aspects of a knowledge base reflect their similarities, and the potential of leveraging those similarities for item recommendations in a specific domain has not been explored. In this work, we investigate domain-specific entity embeddings learned from different aspects of DBpedia with state-of-the-art embedding approaches, and the recommendation performance based on the similarities of these embeddings. The experimental results on two real-word datasets show that recommender systems based on the similarities of entity embeddings learned from a homogeneous graph via the dbo:wikiPageWikiLink property provides the best performance compared to the ones learned from other aspects.

Keywords: Deep learning · Semantic similarity · Knowledge base
Entity embeddings · Recommender systems · Knowledge graph

1 Introduction

Knowledge bases (KBs) such as DBpedia [12] and Wikidata [29] have received great attention in the past few years due to the embedded knowledge which is useful for a wide range of tasks including recommender systems [3]. For example, Linked Open Data-enabled recommender systems (LODRS) aim to utilize the background knowledge about items (entities) from linked datasets such as DBpedia for improving the quality of recommendations [6,7]. However, most previous studies on LODRS view a KB as a heterogeneous knowledge graph (KG) based on the domain-specific entities and properties defined in an ontology (e.g., DBpedia ontology). Take DBpedia as an example, the heterogeneous KG can be

© Springer Nature Switzerland AG 2018
A. Gangemi et al. (Eds.): ESWC 2018 Satellite Events, LNCS 11155, pp. 345–359, 2018.
https://doi.org/10.1007/978-3-319-98192-5_52

seen as one aspect of a knowledge base, and a KB can contain several aspects of knowledge with respect to entities (see Fig. 1) such as:

- *Textual knowledge*: This type of knowledge denotes textual knowledge about entities, e.g., the abstracts of movies via dbo[1]:`abstracts` property.
- *Knowledge from a homogeneous graph*: This type of knowledge denotes the inherited knowledge from Wikipedia[2] based on the dbo:`wikiPageWikiLink` property, which provides a set of connected entities via the same property.
- *Knowledge from a heterogeneous graph*: This type of knowledge is powered by the heterogeneous graph, which consists of domain-specific entities and other nodes connected to those entities via different properties defined in the ontology of a KB, and has been widely used for extracting background knowledge about items (entities) for LODRS.
- *Visual knowledge*: This denotes visual information about entities, e.g., the thumbnails of movies via dbo:`thumbnail` property.

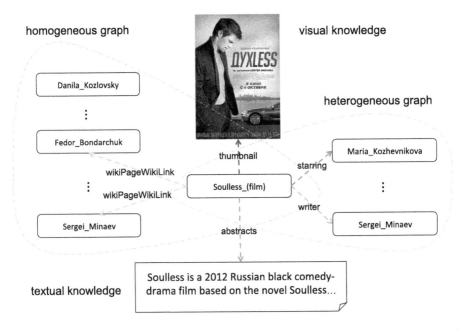

Fig. 1. Knowledge about the movie entity `Soulless_(film)` from different aspects of DBpedia.

Recently, a great number of studies have been proposed to learn entity embeddings in a KG for the KG completion task [4] or for other classification or recommendation tasks using those low-dimensional representations of entities as

---

[1] The prefix dbo denotes http://dbpedia.org/ontology/.

[2] https://www.wikipedia.org.

features [26,27] based on deep learning approaches. While related work reveals several insights regarding the entity embeddings learned from the heterogeneous graph of a KB, there exists little research on understanding the similarities between those entity embeddings learned from other aspects of KBs. There has been considerable semantic similarity/distance measures which were designed for measuring the similarity/distance between entities in the same domain in linked datasets such as DBpedia for various purposes such as item recommendations in a cold start. This preliminary work can be seen as being in the same direction as these studies but with the focus on investigating the similarities between entity embeddings learned from embedding approaches using deep learning or factorization models with domain knowledge.

In this preliminary work, we aim to investigate the semantic similarities of entity embeddings learned from different aspects of a KB, and evaluate them in the context of item recommendations in the music and book domains. Specifically, we focus on the textual knowledge, knowledge from a homogeneous or heterogeneous graph based on dedicated embedding approaches including deep learning techniques. Deep learning approaches have been proved to be effective on learning the latent representations of various forms of data such as images, texts, as well as nodes in networks. Therefore, we use `Doc2Vec` [10] and `Node2Vec` [8] to learn the entity embeddings based on the textual knowledge and the knowledge from a homogeneous graph, and use an embedding model for knowledge graph completion to learn the entity embeddings based on the heterogeneous graph of a KB. We use DBpedia as our knowledge base in this work. In particular, we are interested in investigating the following research questions with results in Sect. 5:

- *How do those entity embeddings learned from different aspects of a KB reflect the similarities between items (entities) in a specific domain in the context of item recommendations in a cold start?*
- *Do those entity embeddings learned from different aspects complement each other?*

To the best of our knowledge, this is the first work on investigating the semantic similarities between entity embeddings learned from different aspects of a KB, and exploring their usages in the context of recommender systems. A shorter version of this paper was published in the CEUR proceedings of the 1st Workshop on Deep Learning for Knowledge Graphs and Semantic Technologies [23].

2   Related Work

Here we review some related work on linked data similarity/distance measures for measuring the similarity/distance between two entities in a specific domain for recommendation purposes, and the approaches exploring entity embeddings for item recommendations.

2.1   Linked Data Similarity/Distance Measures

LDSD [19, 20] is one of the first approaches for measuring the linked data semantic distance between entities in a linked dataset such as DBpedia. Leal et al. [11] proposed a similarity measure which is based on a notion of *proximity*. This method measures how connected two entities are (e.g., based on the number of paths between two entities), rather than how distant they are. Piao et al. [21] revised LDSD in order to satisfy some fundamental axioms as a distance-based similarity measure, and further improved it based on different normalization strategies [22]. More recently, Alfarhood et al. [1] considered additional resources beyond the ones one or two hops away in LDSD, and the same authors also proposed applying link differentiation strategies for measuring the linked data semantic distance between two entities in DBpedia [2]. In contrast to aforementioned approaches, Meymandpour et al. [14] proposed a information content-based semantic similarity measure for measuring the similarity between two entities in linked open data cloud, which can consider multiple linked datasets for measuring the similarity. In this work, we are interested in the similarities of entity embeddings learned from different aspects of a knowledge base, and compare those similarities with one of the semantic similarity/distance measures [22].

2.2   Exploring Entity Embeddings for Item Recommendations

Recently, entity embeddings learned from a knowledge graph using deep learning approaches have been used for item recommendations. In [27], the authors proposed RDF2Vec, which runs random walks on a heterogeneous RDF[3] graph in DBpedia, and then applies Word2Vec [15, 16] techniques by treating the sequences of triples as sentences. The learned entity embeddings based on the whole KG were then used to find the k-nearest neighbors of items. Afterwards, those neighbors were used as side information for factorization machines [25] for providing item recommendations. In contrast to [27] which uses the whole KG for learning entity embeddings, we learn domain-specific entity embeddings from different aspects of a KB. The entity embeddings learned from the whole KG might reflect relatedness of entities instead of their similarities as they are learned by incorporating all properties and nodes from other domains. However, related entities are not always similar, e.g., a musical artist and his/her spouse are related but not similar.

Zhang et al. [30] proposed collaborative knowledge base embedding, which jointly learn the latent representations in collaborative filtering for item recommendations as well as the ones for a knowledge base. However, those entity embeddings were used as features and the similarities between them were not investigated. Palumbo et al. [18] used domain-specific triples from DBpedia for learning entity embeddings with Node2Vec for item recommendations. In order to use Node2Vec for the heterogeneous graph based on domain-specific properties, the authors applied Node2Vec to each heterogeneous graph which consists

---

[3] https://www.w3.org/RDF/.

of all triples based on a single property. Afterwards, those property-specific similarity scores were used as features for a learning-to-rank framework with the training dataset. In contrast, we are interested in the entity embeddings learned from the heterogeneous graph and the similarities between those embeddings.

3   Learning Entity Embeddings from Different Aspects of DBpedia

In this section, we discuss three state-of-the-art embedding/vectorization approaches that we adopted for learning entity embeddings based on different aspects of knowledge from DBpedia.

3.1   Entity Embeddings with Textual Knowledge

Doc2Vec [10], which is inspired by Word2Vec [15,16], was devised for learning embeddings for larger blocks of text such as documents or sentences. This model uses document vectors and contextual word vectors to predict the next word, which is a multi-class classification task. Figure 2 shows the Doc2Vec model, where each document/paragraph is mapped to a latent vector which is a column in a document/paragraph matrix D, and each word has its embedding which is a column in a word embedding matrix W. As we can see from the figure, the document vector and word vectors are concatenated to predict the next word in a context. The document and word vectors can be learned by optimizing the classification error in a given set of documents. For example, with a window size 8, the model predicts the 8th word based on the document and 7 contextual word vectors. We used the gensim [24] implementation of Doc2Vec for our experiment.

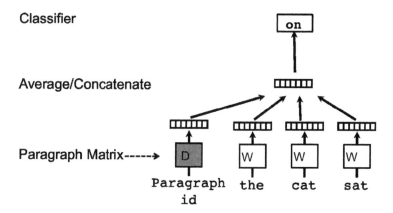

Fig. 2. Doc2Vec model for learning document/paragraph vector [10].

In our experiment, each abstract of an entity in a specific domain is a document, which is provided by the `dbo:abstracts` property, and the set of all abstracts is used for learning entity embeddings in a specified domain with the `Doc2Vec` model. The window size is set to 8 in the same way as [10].

3.2 Entity Embeddings with a Homogeneous Graph

`Node2Vec` [8], which is also inspired by `Word2Vec` [15], aims to learn latent representations of nodes for a homogeneous network. It extends the Skip-gram architecture (see Fig. 3) to networks, and optimizes the (log) probability of observing a network neighborhood for each node. To apply the Skip-gram model for networks, `Node2Vec` first executes random walks based on a defined searching strategy, and the sequence of nodes obtained via the search is used for the Skip-gram model. We used the author's implementation[4] for our experiment.

In our study, we treat the graph which consists of all items in a specific domain and other connected nodes to those items via the `dbo:wikiPageWikiLink` property as the homogeneous graph from DBpedia, and apply `Node2Vec` to learn the entity embeddings based on this homogeneous graph.

Parameters. We choose smaller values for some parameters compared to the settings in the original paper as there is a great number of `dbo:wikiPageWikiLink` relationships, which takes a long time for training the model due to its expensiveness. Our settings for the main hyperparameters of `Node2Vec` are as follows:

- `walk_length=10`: The length of walk for each node.
- `num_walks=10`: The number of walks per node.
- `p=q=1`: p and q denote the return and in-out hyperparameters for random walks, respectively.
- `window_size=5`: The context size for optimization.

3.3 Entity Embeddings with a Heterogeneous Graph

`TransE` [4] is a translation-based model for knowledge graph completion by learning the embeddings of entities and their relationships. In short, `TransE` learns those embeddings in order to satisfy $E(s) + E(p) \approx E(o)$ for a valid triple (s, p, o) in a knowledge base, where $E(x)$ denotes x's embedding. Although `TransE` has been used for learning entity embeddings for KG completion by considering all triples in a KG, for item recommendations in a specific domain, most previous studies extract the domain-specific DBpedia graph which consists of all entities in that domain and incoming or outgoing nodes via domain-specific properties [19, 22]. Therefore, to learn domain-specific entity embeddings, we extract all triples for the entities/items in that domain with relevant properties. In consistence with a previous work [22], we used the top-15 properties for each domain in order to obtain all triples for the subjects in that domain. Table 1 shows those properties we used to extract domain knowledge about items for our experiment in Sect. 4.

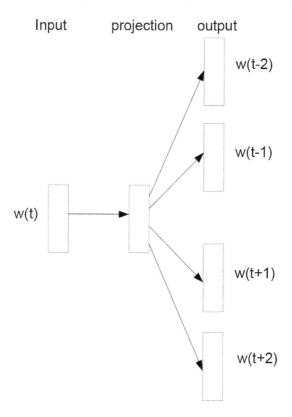

Fig. 3. The Skip-gram model architecture from [16], which aims to learn word vector representations that are good at predicting the nearby words.

The dimensionality of entity embeddings is set to 100 for all three approaches, and the trained embeddings are available at https://github.com/parklize/DL4KGS. For our experiment, we used the HDT [5] dump for the DBpedia 2016-04 version, which is available at http://www.rdfhdt.org/datasets/.

4   Experiment Setup

We evaluate the similarities of entity embeddings learned from different aspects of DBpedia in the context of cold-start scenarios in recommender systems where the top-N items are recommended based on the cosine similarities between entity embeddings, which are learned from different aspects of DBpedia.

---

[4] http://snap.stanford.edu/node2vec.

Table 1. The top-15 domain-specific properties used for extracting valid triples from DBpedia and for training `TransE`.

Music	Book
– dct:subject	– dct:subject
– dbo:genre	– dbo:author
– dbo:associatedBand	– dbo:publisher
– dbo:associatedMusicalArtist	– dbo:literaryGenre
– dbo:instrument	– dbo:mediaType
– dbo:recordLabel	– dbo:subsequentWork
– dbo:occupation	– dbo:previousWork
– dbo:hometown	– dbo:country
– dbo:bandMember	– dbo:series
– dbo:formerBandMember	– dbo:nonFictionSubject
– dbo:currentMember	– dbo:coverArtist
– dbo:influencedBy	– dbo:illustrator
– dbo:pastMember	– dbo:genre
– dbo:associatedAct	– dbo:translator
– dbo:influenced	– dbo:recordLabel

4.1 Datasets

We use two real-world datasets in the music and book domains for our experiment. The first dataset is a last.fm dataset from [17], which consists of 232 musical artists, and the top-10 similar artists for each of the 232 artists obtained from last.fm. Those top-10 similar artists provided in last.fm for each artist are used as the ground truth. The second dataset is a dbbook dataset[5] in the book domain, which consists of 6,181 users and 6,733 items which have been rated by at least one user. We randomly selected 300 users who have liked at least 10 books for our experiment. For each user, we randomly chose one item and recommended items similar to the chosen one based on their similarities. Therefore, the other books liked by each user except the chosen one are used for our ground truth here. For both datasets, all items in each dataset are considered as candidate items for recommendations.

To learn domain-specific entity embeddings, we extracted background knowledge from DBpedia for all entities/items in two domains: the music and book domains. The subjects in the music domain are the entities that have their `rdf:type`(s) as `dbo:MusicalArtist` and `dbo:Band`, and the subjects in the book domain are the ones that have their `rdf:type`(s) as `dbo:Book`. After obtaining all subjects, we further obtain their abstracts, connected nodes (entities and categories) via the `dbo:wikiPageWikiLink` property, and the connected nodes

---

[5] http://challenges.2014.eswc-conferences.org/index.php/RecSys#DBbook_dataset.

via those properties defined in Table 1. Table 2 shows the details of the domain knowledge with respect to the music and book domains.

Table 2. The statistics of background knowledge about items from different aspects of DBpedia.

	Music	Book
# subjects	171,812	76,639
# abstracts	131,622	70,654
# wikiPageWikiLinks	5,480,222	2,340,146
# triples	1,481,335	316,969

4.2   Evaluation Metrics

The recommendation performance is evaluated by the evaluate metrics below:

– **P@N**: Precision at rank N (P@N) is the proportion of the top-N recommendations that are relevant to the user, which is measured as follows:

$$P@N = \frac{|\{relevant\ items@N\}|}{N}$$

– **R@N**: Recall at rank N (R@N) represents the mean probability that relevant items are successfully retrieved within the top-N recommendations.

$$R@N = \frac{|\{relevant\ items@N\}|}{|\{relevant\ items\}|}$$

– **nDCG@N**: nDCG (Normalized Discounted Cumulative Gain) takes into account rank positions of the relevant items. nDCG@N can be computed as follows:

$$nDCG@N = \frac{1}{IDCG@N} \sum_{k=1}^{N} \frac{2^{\hat{r}_{uk}} - 1}{\log_2(k+1)}$$

where $\hat{r}_{uk}$ is the relevance score of the item at position k with respect to a user u in the top-N recommendations, and the normalization factor IDCG@N denotes the score obtained by an ideal top-N ranking.

We used the paired t-test in order to test the statistical significance where the significance level is set to 0.05.

4.3   Compared Methods

We compare the similarity measures below to evaluate the similarities of item embeddings based on different aspects of DBpedia:

- Resim [22]: This is a semantic distance/similarity measure for LOD dataset such as DBpedia, which measures the similarity based on the direct and indirect properties between two entities. We use the implementation from our previous work[6] for our experiment.
- $Cos(V_{tk:Doc2Vec})$: This method uses the cosine similarity measure for the entity embeddings learned from textual knowledge of entities from DBpedia using Doc2Vec.
- $Cos(V_{hmk:Node2Vec})$: This method uses the cosine similarity measure for the entity embeddings learned from homogeneous graph knowledge of entities from DBpedia using Node2Vec.
- $Cos(V_{htk:TransE})$: This method uses the cosine similarity measure for the entity embeddings learned from heterogeneous graph knowledge of entities from DBpedia using TransE.
- $Cos([V_x, V_y])$: This method uses the cosine similarity measure for the concatenated entity embeddings learned from several aspects of entities from DBpedia. For example, $Cos([V_{htk:TransE}, V_{tk:Doc2Vec}])$ denotes the method using the cosine similarity measure for the concatenated entity embeddings based on TransE and Doc2Vec, and Cos([all]) denotes the concatenated ones based on all embedding approaches.

5   Results

Figures 4 and 5 show the nDCG@N results and the precision-recall curve of item recommendations based on the similarities of different entity embeddings in the music and book domains. Overall, we observe that the recommendations based on the entity embeddings with Node2Vec provide the best performance followed by the ones with TransE and Doc2Vec.

In both datasets, the results using the embeddings learned from Node2Vec significantly outperform the ones learned from TransE and Doc2Vec, which show that the great amount of information provided by dbo:wikiPageWikiLink reflects the similarities between entities better than other aspects of DBpedia. We also observe that combining the embeddings based on TransE and Doc2Vec improves the recommendation performance significantly compared to using the embeddings learned from TransE or Doc2Vec. However, combining all embeddings learned from the three different aspects do not provide further improvement on the recommendation performance. Also, the concatenated embeddings with Node2Vec and other embeddings do not provide better performance compared to using the ones learned from Node2Vec alone, and the results are omitted from Figs. 4 and 5 for clarity.

---

[6] https://github.com/parklize/resim.

In the last.fm dataset, we observe some significant improvement of Node2Vec and Cos([all]) over Resim. For example, the recommendation performance is improved by 25.4% and 11.1% with Node2Vec and Cos([all]) compared to using Resim. In contrast, there is no statistical difference between the recommendation performance using those embeddings and using Resim in the dbbook dataset. This might be due to the relatively small size of subjects in the book domain and their related aspects for training those embeddings.

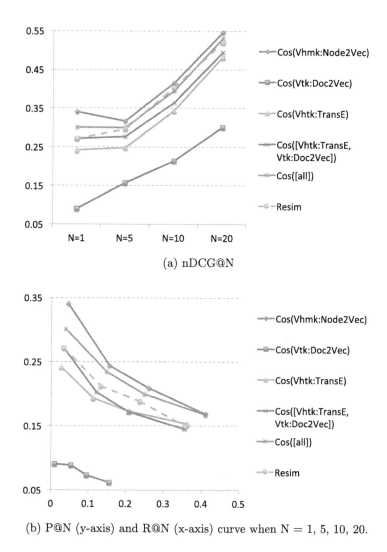

(a) nDCG@N

(b) P@N (y-axis) and R@N (x-axis) curve when N = 1, 5, 10, 20.

Fig. 4. The performance of item recommendations on the last.fm dataset with all methods compared.

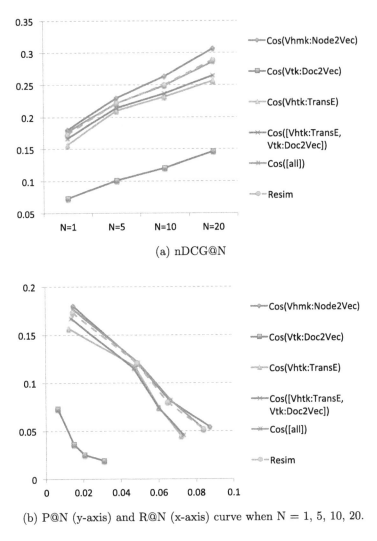

(a) nDCG@N

(b) P@N (y-axis) and R@N (x-axis) curve when N = 1, 5, 10, 20.

Fig. 5. The performance of item recommendations on the dbbook dataset with all methods compared.

6   Conclusions and Future Work

In this paper, we investigated the embeddings learned from three different aspects of DBpedia using state-of-the-art deep learning and embedding-based approaches, and the recommendation performance based on the similarities captured by those embeddings in two real-world datasets. The preliminary results indicate that the entity embeddings learned from the homogeneous graph powered by the `dbo:wikiPageWikiLink` property provide the best performance in the context of item recommendations compared to the ones learned from other aspects of DBpedia. We further explored potential synergies that exist by combining those embeddings learned from different aspects. The concatenated embeddings with the ones learned from textual knowledge (using `Doc2Vec`) and the heterogeneous graph (using `TransE`) significantly improves the performance. This preliminary study can be seen as a first step towards investigating the similarity between entity embeddings learned from different aspects of a knowledge base for item recommendations, and also poses many research questions for future work.

First, although we used state-of-the-art approaches for learning entity embeddings from different aspects, there are many other state-of-the-art alternatives for learning entity embeddings such as `Tweet2Vec` [28] for learning entity embeddings based on their abstracts, and `ETransR` [13] for learning the embeddings based on the heterogeneous graph. A further investigation of using other deep learning and embedding-based approaches for learning entity embeddings for different aspects of a knowledge base is required.

Secondly, how to choose domain-specific triples out of all triples in the knowledge base is a remaining question. Using triples extracted with domain-specific properties might lead to a smaller number of triples for those embedding-based approaches to learn good entity embeddings. In contrast, using the whole heterogeneous graph might lead to general entity embeddings which tend to capture their relatedness instead of the similarities. Further research is needed to confirm the hypothesis, and a recent approach such as [9] for extracting domain-specific subgraphs can be further explored for extracting domain-specific triples for training the entity embeddings in that domain.

Finally, the results of this study showed that concatenating all embeddings does not further improve the performance, and those results suggest more research is needed for combining those entity embeddings which are learned from different aspects of a knowledge base.

Acknowledgments. This publication has emanated from research conducted with the financial support of Science Foundation Ireland (SFI) under Grant Number SFI/12/RC/2289 (Insight Centre for Data Analytics).

References

1. Alfarhood, S., Labille, K., Gauch, S.: PLDSD: propagated linked data semantic distance. In: 2017 IEEE 26th International Conference on Enabling Technologies: Infrastructure for Collaborative Enterprises (WETICE), pp. 278–283 (2017)
2. Alfarhood, S., Gauch, S., Labille, K.: Employing link differentiation in linked data semantic distance. In: Różewski, P., Lange, C. (eds.) KESW 2017. CCIS, vol. 786, pp. 175–191. Springer, Cham (2017). https://doi.org/10.1007/978-3-319-69548-8_13
3. Blomqvist, E.: The use of Semantic Web technologies for decision support - a survey. Semant. Web 5(3), 177–201 (2014). https://doi.org/10.3233/SW-2012-0084
4. Bordes, A., Usunier, N., Garcia-Duran, A., Weston, J., Yakhnenko, O.: Translating embeddings for modeling multi-relational data, pp. 2787–2795 (2013)

5. Fernández, J.D., Martínez-Prieto, M.A., Gutiérrez, C., Polleres, A., Arias, M.: Binary RDF representation for publication and exchange (HDT). Web Semant. Sci. Serv. Agents World Wide Web **19**, 22–41 (2013). http://www.sciencedirect.com/science/article/pii/S1570826813000036

6. Figueroa, C., Vagliano, I., Rodríguez Rocha, O., Morisio, M.: A systematic literature review of Linked Data-based recommender systems. Concurrency Comput. **27**(17), 4659–4684 (2015)

7. de Gemmis, M., Lops, P., Musto, C., Narducci, F., Semeraro, G.: Semantics-aware content-based recommender systems. In: Ricci, F., Rokach, L., Shapira, B. (eds.) Recommender Systems Handbook, pp. 119–159. Springer, Boston (2015). https://doi.org/10.1007/978-1-4899-7637-6_4

8. Grover, A., Leskovec, J.: node2vec: Scalable Feature Learning for Networks. CoRR abs/1607.0 (2016). http://arxiv.org/abs/1607.00653

9. Lalithsena, S., Kapanipathi, P., Sheth, A.: Harnessing relationships for domain-specific subgraph extraction: a recommendation use case. In: IEEE International Conference on Big Data, Washington D.C. (2016)

10. Le, Q.V., Mikolov, T.: Distributed Representations of Sentences and Documents. CoRR abs/1405.4 (2014). http://arxiv.org/abs/1405.4053

11. Leal, J.P., Rodrigues, V., Queirós, R.: Computing semantic relatedness using DBpedia (2012)

12. Lehmann, J., et al.: DBpedia-a large-scale, multilingual knowledge base extracted from wikipedia. Semant. Web J. **6**(2), 167–195 (2013)

13. Lin, H., Liu, Y., Wang, W., Yue, Y., Lin, Z.: Learning entity and relation embeddings for knowledge resolution. Procedia Comput. Sci. **108**, 345–354 (2017)

14. Meymandpour, R., Davis, J.G.: A semantic similarity measure for linked data: an information content-based approach. Knowl. Based Syst. **109**, 276–293 (2016)

15. Mikolov, T., Chen, K., Corrado, G., Dean, J.: Efficient Estimation of Word Representations in Vector Space. CoRR abs/1301.3 (2013). http://arxiv.org/abs/1301.3781

16. Mikolov, T., Sutskever, I., Chen, K., Corrado, G.S., Dean, J.: Distributed representations of words and phrases and their compositionality. In: Advances in Neural Information Processing Systems, pp. 3111–3119 (2013)

17. Oramas, S., Sordo, M., Espinosa-Anke, L., Serra, X.: A semantic-based approach for artist similarity. In: ISMIR, pp. 100–106 (2015)

18. Palumbo, E., Rizzo, G., Troncy, R.: Entity2Rec: learning user-item relatedness from knowledge graphs for top-N item recommendation. In: Proceedings of the Eleventh ACM Conference on Recommender Systems, RecSys 2017, pp. 32–36. ACM, New York (2017). https://doi.org/10.1145/3109859.3109889

19. Passant, A.: dbrec — music recommendations using DBpedia. In: Patel-Schneider, P.F., et al. (eds.) ISWC 2010. LNCS, vol. 6497, pp. 209–224. Springer, Heidelberg (2010). https://doi.org/10.1007/978-3-642-17749-1_14

20. Passant, A.: Measuring semantic distance on linking data and using it for resources recommendations. In: Proceedings of the AAAI Spring Symposium: Linked Data Meets Artificial Intelligence. vol. 77, pp. 93–98 (2010). files/129/display.html

21. Piao, G., Ara, S., Breslin, J.G.: Computing the semantic similarity of resources in dbpedia for recommendation purposes. In: Qi, G., Kozaki, K., Pan, J.Z., Yu, S. (eds.) JIST 2015. LNCS, vol. 9544, pp. 185–200. Springer, Cham (2016). https://doi.org/10.1007/978-3-319-31676-5_13

22. Piao, G., Breslin, J.G.: Measuring semantic distance for linked open data-enabled recommender systems. In: Proceedings of the 31st Annual ACM Symposium on Applied Computing, 04–08 April 2016, pp. 315–320. ACM, Pisa (2016)

23. Piao, G., Breslin, J.G.: A study of the similarities of entity embeddings learned from different aspects of a knowledge base for item recommendations. In: 1st Workshop on Deep Learning for Knowledge Graphs and Semantic Technologies at the 15th Extended Semantic Web Conference (2018). CEUR-WS.org

24. Radim Rehurek, P.S.: Software framework for topic modelling with large corpora. In: Proceedings of the LREC 2010 Workshop on New Challenges for NLP Frameworks, pp. 45–50. ELRA, Valletta, May 2010

25. Rendle, S.: Factorization machines with libFM. ACM Trans. Intell. Syst. Technol. **3**(3), 57:1–57:22 (2012)

26. Ristoski, P., Paulheim, H.: RDF2Vec: RDF graph embeddings for data mining. In: Groth, P., et al. (eds.) ISWC 2016. LNCS, vol. 9981, pp. 498–514. Springer, Cham (2016). https://doi.org/10.1007/978-3-319-46523-4_30

27. Ristoski, P., Rosati, J., Di Noia, T., De Leone, R., Paulheim, H.: RDF2Vec: RDF graph embeddings and their applications. Semant. Web J. (2018). http://www.semantic-web-journal.net/system/files/swj1495.pdf

28. Vosoughi, S., Vijayaraghavan, P., Roy, D.: Tweet2Vec: learning tweet embeddings using character-level CNN-LSTM encoder-decoder. In: Proceedings of the 39th International ACM SIGIR Conference on Research and Development in Information Retrieval, SIGIR 2016, pp. 1041–1044. ACM, New York (2016). https://doi.org/10.1145/2911451.2914762

29. Vrandečić, D., Krötzsch, M.: Wikidata: a free collaborative knowledgebase. Commun. ACM **57**(10), 78–85 (2014)

30. Zhang, F., Yuan, N.J., Lian, D., Xie, X., Ma, W.Y.: Collaborative knowledge base embedding for recommender systems. In: Proceedings of the 22nd ACM SIGKDD International Conference on Knowledge Discovery and Data Mining, KDD 2016, pp. 353–362. ACM, New York (2016)

2nd Workshop on Querying the Web of Data

MAS: A Corpus of Tweets
for Marketing in Spanish

María Navas-Loro[1]([✉])[ID], Víctor Rodríguez-Doncel[1][ID],
Idafen Santana-Pérez[1][ID], Alba Fernández-Izquierdo[1][ID], and Alberto Sánchez[2]

[1] Ontology Engineering Group, Universidad Politécnica de Madrid, Madrid, Spain
{mnavas,vrodriguez,isantana,albafernandez}@fi.upm.es
[2] Havas Media, Madrid, Spain
alberto.sanchezsf@dbi.io

Abstract. This paper presents a corpus of tweets in Spanish language which were manually tagged for marketing purposes. The used tags describe three aspects of the text of each Twitter post. First, the emotions a brand caused to the author from among a taxonomy of emotions designed by marketing experts. Also, whether it mentioned any element of the *marketing mix* (including various relevant marketing concepts such as *price* or *promotion*). Finally, the position of the author of the tweet with respect to the acquisition process (or *purchase funnel*). Each Twitter post is related to only one brand, which is also indicated in the corpus. The corpus presented in this article is published in a machine-readable format as a collection of RDF documents with links to additional external information. The paper also includes details on the used vocabulary and the tagging criteria, as well as a description of the annotation process followed to tag the tweets.

Keywords: Corpus · Marketing · Marketing mix
Sentiment analysis · NLP · Purchase funnel · Emotion analysis

1 Introduction

Twitter is a source of valuable feedback for companies to probe the public perception of their brands. Whereas sentiment analysis has been extensively applied to social media messages (see [17] among many), other dimensions of brand perception are still of interest and have received less attention [13], specially those related to marketing. In particular, marketing specialists are highly interested in: (a) knowing the position of a tweet author in the purchase funnel (this is, where in the different stages of the customer journey is the author in); (b) knowing to which element or elements of the marketing mix[1] the text refers to and (c) knowing the author's affective situation with respect to a brand in the tweet.

This paper presents the MAS Corpus, a Spanish corpus of tweets of interest for marketing specialists, labeling messages in the three dimensions aforementioned. The corpus is freely available at http://mascorpus.linkeddata.es/ and has

---

[1] http://economictimes.indiatimes.com/definition/marketing-mix.

© Springer Nature Switzerland AG 2018
A. Gangemi et al. (Eds.): ESWC 2018 Satellite Events, LNCS 11155, pp. 363–375, 2018.
https://doi.org/10.1007/978-3-319-98192-5_53

been developed in the context of the Spanish research project LPS BIGGER[2], which analyzed different dimensions of tweets in order to extract relevant information on marketing purposes. A first version of the corpus containing only the sentiment analysis annotations was released as the Corpus for Sentiment Analysis towards Brands (SAB) and was described in [16]. Following this work, we have expanded the corpus tagging the messages in the two remaining dimensions described before: the purchase funnel and the marketing mix. Tweets that were almost identical to others have been removed. Categories of each of the three aspects tagged in the corpus (Sentiment Analysis, Marketing Mix and Purchase Funnel) can be found in Fig. 1.

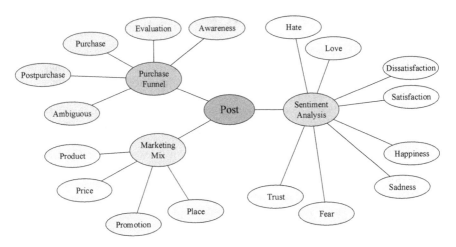

Fig. 1. The three different aspects in an opinion of interest for marketing: Purchase Funnel (*when* is the opinion emitted with regard to the purchase journey), Marketing Mix (*what* is evaluated in the opinion) and Sentiment Analysis (*emotions* expressed with regard to the brand).

2   Related Work

2.1   Sentiment Analysis

Even when Sentiment Analysis is a major field in Natural Language Processing, most of works in Spanish tend to focus on polarity [6,11], being the efforts towards emotions really scarce [23]. Sources of corpora also differ to our aims, since they tend to use specific websites [15,18] and different social networks [6,11,23], and limit to domains such as tourism [15] and medical opinions [18]. Twitter publicly available corpus scarcity is mainly due to two related facts; first, its policy on text dissemination (just the ID of the tweets can be provided, no text nor username). Second, that Twitter deletes periodically deletes tweets

---

[2] http://www.cienlpsbigger.es.

from their servers; these two facts lead that, even when having the IDs, texts in corpora become impossible to retrieve and therefore the corpus is not available as resource for test anymore. An extended review of works in Spanish Sentiment Analysis with regard to our needs can be found in [16].

2.2 Purchase Funnel

Although different purchase funnel interpretations have been suggested in literature [4, 7], we have based our approach on the one defined in the LPS BIGGER project and already used in [26]. This purchase funnel consists of four different stages (*Awareness, Evaluation, Purchase* and *Postpurchase*), that reflect how the client gets to know the product, investigates or compares it to other options, acquires it and actually uses and reviews it, respectively.

To the best of our knowledge, there are not public Spanish corpora available containing purchase funnel annotations, since the only work in Spanish on this topic the authors are aware of did not release the dataset used [26]. Nevertheless, the concept of Purchase Intention has been widely covered in literature, especially for marketing purposes in English language. Differently to Sentiment Analysis, Purchase Intention tries to detect or distinguish whether the client intends to buy a product, rather than whether he likes it or not [27]. Starting with the WISH corpus [9], covering wishes in several domains and sources (including product reviews), most works aim to discriminate between different kinds of intentions of users: in [22], the analysis focuses in suggestions and wishes for products and services both in a private dataset and in a part of the previously mentioned WISH corpus; also an analysis performed on tweets about different intentions can be found in [14].

Finally, the most similar categories to the ones in our purchase funnel interpretation are the ones in [5], where the authors differentiate between several kinds of intention, being some of them (such as *wish, compare* or *complain*) easy mappable to our purchase funnel stages. Also the corpus used in [10], that classifies into pre-purchase and post-purchase reviews, shares our "timeline" interpretation of the purchase funnel. Out of the marketing domain, corpora labeled with purchase funnel tags for an specific domain have also been published, e.g., for the London musicals and recreational events [8].

2.3 Marketing Mix

Although the original concept of marketing mix [3] contained twelve elements for manufacturers, the most extended categorization for marketing is the one proposed by [12], consisting of four aspects (*price, product, promotion, place*) often known as "the four Ps" (or 4Ps) and revisited several times in literature [25]. Nevertheless, while marketing mix is a well-known and extended concept in the marketing field, in NLP the task of identifying these facets is often simply referred as detecting or recognizing "aspects", excepting some cases in literature [2]. This task has been often tackled in English [19,21], while in Spanish corpora we can find a few datasets containing information about aspects, such as those in [6,20].

3   Tagging Criteria

The corpus consists of more than 3k tweets of brands (see Fig. 1) from different sectors, namely *Food, Automotive, Banking, Beverages, Sports, Retail* and *Telecom*. When several brands appear in one tweet, just one of them is considered in the tagging process (the marked one); at the same time, the same tweet can appear several times in the corpus considering different brands. Every tweet is tagged in the dimensions exposed in Fig. 1; more than one tag is possible in sentiment and marketing mix dimensions (except simultaneously tagging the pairs of directly opposed emotions), while the purchase funnel, as representing a path on the purchase journey, only presents a tag per tweet. We describe below each dimension, along with a brief report on the criteria used for tagging each category (the complete criteria document, along with statistics on the corpus, can be downloaded with it) (Table 1).

Table 1. Sectors and Brands in the corpus.

Sector	Brand
BEBIDAS (BEVERAGES)	Cruzcampo, Heineken, Estrella Galicia, Mahou
AUTOMOCIÓN (AUTOMOTIVE)	Citroën, Fiat, Hyundai, Kia, Peugeot, Toyota
BANCA (BANKING)	Bankia, Bankinter, BBVA, Sabadell, ING, La Caixa/Caixabank, Santander
ALIMENTACIÓN (FOOD)	Auchan, Bimbo, Hacendado, Milka, Pascual, Puleva
RETAIL	Alcampo, Carrefour, Decathlon, Ikea, Leroy Merlin, Mediamarkt, Mercadona
TELCO (TELECOM)	Amena, Lowi, Movistar, Orange, Vodafone, Yoigo
DEPORTES (SPORTS)	Adidas, Nike, Reebok

3.1   Sentiment Analysis

A tweet can be tagged with one or several emotions, as long as it does not contain directly opposite emotions, or with a *NC2* label meaning there are no emotions on it. Each basic emotion embraces also secondary emotions in it (described in Table 2, and also used by Aguado [1]), and a combination of them can express more complex feelings often seen in customers, such as shown in the following examples:

– When a customer is unable to find a desired product, the post is tagged as *sadness* (for the unavailability) and *satisfaction* (because it reveals previous satisfaction with the brand that deserves the effort of keep looking exactly for it instead of switching to one from another brand).

- When a post shows that a purchase is recurrent, it is tagged as *trust*, referring to the loyalty of the client.
- Emoticons of love are tagged as *love* and musical ones as *happiness* (unless irony happens). *Love* typically implies *happiness*.
- *Happiness* can only be tagged for an already acquired product or service, not for future purchases. The wish for a brand (*"I would like to have X"*) is tagged as *trust* and *satisfaction*, and possibly *love* (depending on the degree of the desire).
- A deep *dissatisfaction* is *hate*, a deep *satisfaction* is *love*.
- *Fear* is understood as the opposite of *trust*.
- The document *"I am satisfied with X but..."* is tagged as *satisfaction*, *trust* plus whichever negative sentiment follows.
- When the emotion is not obvious, the message must be marked as *NC2* (sometimes the meaning is not evident from the message alone). Messages that are evident advertising by the brand community managers, automatic messages or messages related to brand-events are also tagged as *NC2*.
- The emotion must be sparked by the brand/product, and it is not necessarily the same as the message. If the author of a message says that he is sad and he is going to have a *Mahou* (Spanish beer brand), the tag should not be *sadness*, but a positive emotion.
- A deep *dissatisfaction* is *hate*, a deep *satisfaction* is *love*. *Fear* is understood as the opposite of *trust*.

3.2   Purchase Funnel

Each tweet can belong to a stage in the purchase funnel, be ambiguous or be related to a brand without the author being involved in the purchase (such as is the case of posts of the brand itself). Different phases and concrete examples are tagged in the corpus as follows:

Awareness. The first contact of the client with the brand (either showing a willingness to buy or not), usually expressed in first person and mentioning advertising, videos, publicity campaigns, etc. Some examples of awareness would be:

(1) *I just loved last Movistar ad.*
(2) *I like the videos in Nike's YouTube channel.*

Evaluation. The post implies some research on the brand (such as questions or seek of confirmation) or comparison to others (by showing preferences among them, for instance), and some interest in acquiring a product or service. Examples of evaluation would be the following:

(3) *I prefer Citroen to more expensive brands, such as Mercedes or BMW.*
(4) *Looking for a second-hand Kia Sorento in NY, please send me a DM.*

Table 2. Main emotions and their secondary emotions.

Emotion	Related emotions
Trust	Optimism, Hope, Security
Satisfaction	Fulfillment, Contentment
Happiness	Joy, Gladness, Enjoyment, Delight, Amusement, Joviality, Enthusiasm, Jubilation, Pride, Triumph
Love	Passion, Excitement, Euphoria, Ecstasy
Fear	Nervousness, Alarm, Anxiety, Tenseness, Apprehension, Worry, Shock, Fright, Terror, Panic, Hysteria, Mortification
Dissatisfaction	Dislike, Rejection, Revulsion, Disgust, Irritation, Aggravation, Exasperation, Frustration, Annoyance
Sadness	Depression, Defeat, Hopelessness, Unhappiness, Anguish, Sorrow, Agony, Melancholy, Dejection, Loneliness, Humiliation, Shame, Guilt, Regret, Remorse, Disappointment, Alienation, Isolation, Insecurity
Hate	Rage, Fury, Wrath, Envy, Hostility, Ferocity, Bitterness, Resentment, Spite, Contempt, Vengefulness, Jealously

Purchase. There is a direct reference to the moment of a purchase or to a clear intention of purchase (usually in first person). Some examples:

(5) *I've finally decided to switch to Movistar.*
(6) *Buying my brand new blue Citroen right now!*

Postpurchase. Texts referring to a past purchase or to a current experience, implying to own a product. This class presents a special complexity, since interpretation on the same linguistic patterns change depending on the kind of product, as already exposed in [26] and exemplified in the sentences below:

(7) *I like Heineken, the taste is so good.*
    I would love a Heineken!
(8) *I like BMWs, they are so classy!*
    I would love a BMW!

In (7), the client has likely tasted that beer brand before; people does not tend to like or want beverages they have no experience with (at least without mentioning, such as in *"I want to taste the new Heineken."*). But the same fact is not derived from more expensive items, even when expressed the same way, such as happens in (8): someone can like a car (such as its appearance or its engine) without having used it or intending to. This is why our criteria states that these kind of expressions must be tagged as *Postpurchase* for some brands (depending on the sector) and others must be tagged as *Ambiguous*, since there can be several possible and equally likely interpretations. This is kind of expressions has been tagged therefore:

- As *ambiguous* for more expensive products of which people tend to give opinion without acquiring them. In our case, this applies just to the *AUTOMOTIVE* sector.
- As *postpurchase* for products that are easier to acquire, and are likely to have been tried before talking about them. This include the sectors *BEVERAGES, BANKING, FOOD, RETAIL, TELECOM* and *SPORTS*.

Ambiguous. This category includes critical posts, suggestions and recommendations, along with posts where it is not clear in which stage the customer is (such as the case mentioned above).

(9) *Do not buy Milka!*
(10) *Loving the new Kia!*

NC2. Includes impersonal messages without opinions (such as corporative news or responses of the brand to clients), questions implying no personal evaluation or intention (for instance, involving a third person), texts with buy or rental offers with no mention to real use experience, etc.

(11) *2008 Hyundai for sale.*
(12) *My aunt didn't like the Kia.*

3.3 Marketing Mix

We have added a *NC2* class to the four original McCarthy's Ps to indicate none of the four aspects is treated in the tweet. It must be noted that, differently than the purchase funnel, several marketing mix tags can appear in the same tweet (except of the *NC2*). Brief explanation of each of the categories tagged for marketing mix, along with examples and part of the criteria, are exposed below:

Product. This category encompasses texts related to the features of the product (such as its quality, performance or taste), along with references to design (such as size, colors or packing) or guaranty, such as in the following examples:

(13) *I find the new iPhone too big for my pocket.*
(14) *I love the new mix Milka Oreo!*

Note that when someone loves/likes something (such as food), we assume it refers to some feature of a product (such as its taste), so we tag it as *Product*.

Promotion. Texts referring to all the promotions and programs of the brand channeled to increase sales and ensure visibility to their products or the brand, such as advertisements, sponsorships (such as prices, sport teams or events), special offers, work offers, promotional articles, etc.

(15) *Freaking out with the new 2x1 @Ikea!*
(16) *La Liga BBVA is the best league in the world.*

Price. Includes economical aspects of a product, such as references to its value or promotions involving discounts or price drops (that must also be tagged as *Promotion*). Examples of texts that should be tagged as *Price* would be the following:

(17) *I'm afraid that I can't afford the new Toyota.*
(18) *Yesterday I saw the same Adidas for just 40e!*

Place. Aspects related to commercialization, such physical places of distribution of the products (for instance, if a product is difficult to find) and customer service (in every stage of the purchase: information, at the point of sale, postpurchase, technical support, etc.).

(19) *I love the new Milka McFlurry at McDonalds*
(20) *Already three malls and unable to find the new Nike Pegasus!*

NC2. Impersonal messages of the brand, news or texts that include none of the aspects mentioned before.

(21) *Nike is paying no tax!*
(22) *I can't decide between Puleva and Pascual.*

4   The MAS Corpus

4.1   Building the Corpus

A different approach was used for Marketing Mix and the Purchase Funnel tagging with respect to the Sentiment Analysis tagging procedure (where three taggers acted independently with just a common criteria document) exposed in [16]. This meets the need of streamlining the whole tagging process, that happens to be both difficult and time-consuming for taggers. This new procedure is briefly exposed below:

1. A first version of the criteria document was written, based on the study of literature and previous experience within the LPS BIGGER project.
2. Then Tagger 1 tagged a representative part of the corpus (about 800 tweets), highlighting main doubts and dubious tweets with regard to the criteria, that are revised; new tagging examples are added, and some nuances and special cases are rewritten.
3. Taggers 2 and 3 revise the tags by Tagger 1, paying special attention to tweets marked as dubious: if an agreement is reached, the tagging is updated consequently; otherwise, the tweet is tagged as *Ambiguous* or *NC2*.
4. Then each tagger takes a part of the corpus to tag it following the new criteria and highlighting doubts again; these tweets will be revised with remaining taggers, reaching an agreement on the final unique tags in the corpus.

4.2 Publishing the Corpus as Linked Data

We maintain the RDF representation used in the previous version of the corpus, using again our own vocabulary[3] to express the purchase funnel and the marketing mix. We also reuse Marl [28] and Onyx [24] for emotions and polarity, and SIOC[4] and GoodRelations[5] for post and brand representation. Also links to the entries of brands and companies in external databases such as Thomson Reuters' PermID[6] and DBpedia[7] extend the information in the tweets. Figure 2 shows an example of a tweet tagged in the dimensions extracted from the corpus, while Fig. 3 shows information on the company. An overview of this example is depicted in Fig. 4.

4.3 Corpus Description

Final corpus contains 3,763 tweets. Statistics on linguistic information in the corpus can be found in Table 3, along with specific data relevant for Social Media, such as the amount of hashtags, user mentions and URLs. The distribution of categories varies depending on the sector. Mentions of *Place* are for instance more common in *Sports* than in other categories, such as *Beverages* or *Telecom*, as shown in Table 4. Also when opinions are expressed differs: tweets in the *Food*

Table 3. Total and average (per tweet) statistics on the corpus. Stanford CoreNLP was used for POS information, while patterns were used for detecting hashtags ('#'), mentions ('@') and URLs ('www.*'/'http*').

	TOTAL	AVG
Tweets	3,763	—
Sentences	5,189	1.38
Tokens	59,555	15.83
Hashtags	1,819	0.48
Mentions	2,306	0.61
URLs	2,111	0.56
Verbs	6,971	1.85
Nouns	8,353	2.22
NPs	6,952	1.85
Adjectives	2,761	0.73
Adverbs	1,584	0.42
Neg. adverbs	560	0.15

---

[3] http://sabcorpus.linkeddata.es/vocab.
[4] https://www.w3.org/Submission/sioc-spec/.
[5] http://purl.org/goodrelations/.
[6] https://permid.org/.
[7] http://dbpedia.org/.

Table 4. Statistics on the corpus for the Marketing Mix dimension. Each column represents the percentages of *NC2* (none of the others) and each of the four Ps described in Sect. 3, namely *Product* (PROD), *Price* (PRI), *Promotion* (PROM) and *Place* (PLA)

	NC2	PROD	PRI	PROM	PLA
FOOD	48.80	30.84	2.10	15.27	7.49
AUTOMOTIVE	77.56	4.67	2.00	16.00	1.56
BANKING	53.33	8.50	7.83	21.17	13.17
BEVERAGES	19.85	70.37	2.22	8.59	8.59
SPORTS	54.98	6.43	17.76	0.92	30.32
RETAIL	72.17	12.56	2.09	8.62	7.51
TELECOM	91.63	1.26	1.67	4.60	0.00

Table 5. Statistics on the corpus for the Purchase Funnel categories. Each column represents the percentages of each of the tags described in Sect. 3, namely *NC2* (none of the others) *Evaluation* (EVA), *Awareness* (AWA), *Purchase* (PUR), *Postpurchase* (POS) and *Ambiguous* (AMB).

	NC2	AWA	EVA	PUR	POS	AMB
FOOD	43.41	3.59	3.29	4.19	40.72	5.09
AUTOMOTIVE	85.56	2.67	4.00	0.22	4.44	3.33
BANKING	58.50	5.83	2.00	0.00	7.83	25.67
BEVERAGES	33.63	0.44	13.33	8.44	11.26	32.74
SPORTS	63.09	2.91	4.29	1.84	7.50	19.75
RETAIL	89.29	2.71	4.80	0.62	1.97	1.60
TELECOM	94.14	0.42	0.42	0.00	4.60	0.00

Table 6. Statistics on the emotions in the corpus. Column *ANY* shows the percentage of posts with any emotion (this is, non neutral posts); remaining columns show the percentage of each category among these non neutral posts: *Hate* (HAT), *Sadness* (SAD), *Fear* (FEA), *Dissatisfaction* (DIS), *Satisfaction* (SAT), *Trust* (TRU), *Happiness* (HAP) and *Love* (LOV).

	ANY	HAT	SAD	FEA	DIS	SAT	TRU	HAP	LOV
FOOD	54.79	1.50	1.20	0.00	8.08	45.21	44.01	14.67	12.87
AUTOMOTIVE	9.11	0.00	0.22	1.11	2.44	6.89	3.33	1.11	0.89
BANKING	24.67	5.33	1.00	15.00	23.83	1.33	0.50	0.00	0.00
BEVERAGES	63.11	2.07	1.19	0.74	19.11	44.00	32.74	7.26	7.70
SPORTS	34.15	2.45	2.60	0.31	13.32	18.84	11.94	4.90	11.33
RETAIL	33.00	3.20	1.11	1.48	11.95	14.53	14.41	3.69	3.45
TELECOM	40.17	12.97	0.84	0.00	30.13	8.79	6.28	3.35	1.26

```
mas:827146264517165056 a sioc:Post ;
  sioc:id "827146264517165056" ;
  sioc:content "Las camisetas nike 2002~2004 y las adidas 2006~2008
  son el amor de mi vida"@es ;

  marl:describesObject mas:Nike ;
  sabd:isInPurchaseFunnel sabv:postPurchase;
  sabd:hasMarketingMix sabv:product;
  onyx:hasEmotion sabv:love, sabv:satisfaction, sabv:happiness ;
  marl:hasPolarity marl:positive ;
  marl:forDomain "SPORT" .
```

Fig. 2. Sample tagged post *"Nike's 2002–2004 T-shirts and Adidas' 2006–2008 are the love of my life"*, with information such as the tweet ID (*sioc:id*), the text (*sioc:content*, if available), emotion and polarity expressed towards the brand (*marl* and *onyx*), and Purchase Funnel and Marketing Mix tags (*sabd*).

```
mas:Nike a gr:Brand ;
  rdfs:seeAlso <http://dbpedia.org/resource/Nike> ;
  sabd:1-5000062703 a gr:Business ;
  rdfs:label "Nike Inc", "Nike" ;
  owl:sameAs permid:1-4295904620 .
```

Fig. 3. Extra information on a brand (Nike) and its company (Nike Inc).

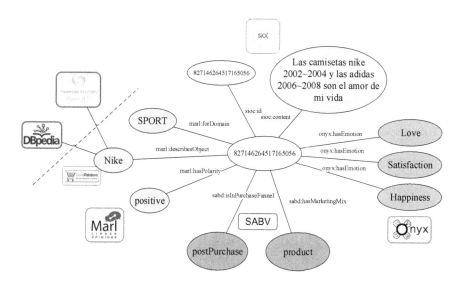

Fig. 4. Example of a tweet using our vocabulary and reusing ontologies (*marl, onyx, good relations* and *sioc*) and linking to external resources (*DBpedia* and *PermID*) as exposed in Sect. 4.2.

sector tend to refer to the *Postpurchase* phase, while others tend to be more ambiguous or refer to previous phases, as shown in Table 5. Regarding emotions, some of them just appear in certain domains, such as *Fear* for *Banking*, as shown in Table 6.

5   Conclusions

Whereas the SAB corpus provided a collection of tweets tagged with labels useful for making Sentiment Analysis towards brands, this new corpus is of interest for the marketing analysis in a broader way. Using categories specially designed for marketing, such as the four Ps, the MAS Corpus allows marketing professionals to have additional information of habits and behaviors, strong and weak points of the whole purchase experience, and also full insights on concrete aspects of each client reviews.

Acknowledgments. This work has been partially supported by LPS-BIGGER (IDI-20141259), esTextAnalytics project (RTC-2016-4952-7), a Predoctoral grant by the Consejo de Educación, Juventud y Deporte de la Comunidad de Madrid partially founded by the European Social Fund, two Predoctoral grants from the I+D+i program of the Universidad Politécnica de Madrid and a Juan de la Cierva contract. We would also want to thank Pablo Calleja for his help in corpora statistics extraction.

References

1. Aguado, G., et al.: Análisis de sentimientos de un corpus de redes sociales. In: Actas del 31er Congreso Asociación Española de Lingüística Aplicada. Comunicación, Cognición y Cibernética, pp. 522–534 (2013). http://oa.upm.es/20092/
2. Bel, N., Diz-pico, J., Pocostales, J.: Classifying short texts for a Social Media monitoring system. Clasificación de textos cortos para un sistema monitor de los Social Media. Procesamiento del Lenguaje Nat. **59**, 57–64 (2017)
3. Borden, N.H.: The concept of the marketing mix. J. Advertising Res. **4**(2), 2–7 (1964)
4. Bruyn, A.D., Lilien, G.L.: A multi-stage model of word-of-mouth influence through viral marketing. Int. J. Res. Mark. **25**(3), 151–163 (2008)
5. Cohan-Sujay, C., Madhulika, Y.: Intention analysis for sales, marketing and customer service. In: Proceedings of COLING 2012, Demonstration Papers, pp. 33–40, December 2012
6. Cumbreras, M.Á.G., Cámara, E.M., et al.: TASS 2015 - The evolution of the Spanish opinion mining systems. Procesamiento de Lenguaje Nat. **56**, 33–40 (2016)
7. Elzinga, D., Mulder, S., Vetvik, O.J., et al.: The consumer decision journey. McKinsey Q. **3**, 96–107 (2009)
8. García-Silva, A., Rodríguez-Doncel, V., Corcho, Ó.: Semantic characterization of tweets using topic models: a use case in the entertainment domain. Int. J. Semantic Web Inf. Syst. **9**(3), 1–13 (2013)
9. Goldberg, A.B., Fillmore, N., Andrzejewski, D., Xu, Z., Gibson, B., Zhu, X.: May all your wishes come true : a study of wishes and how to recognize them. In: Proceedings of Human Language Technologies: NAACL 2009 (June), pp. 263–271 (2009)

10. Hasan, M., Kotov, A., Mohan, A., Lu, S., Stieg, P.M.: Feedback or research: separating pre-purchase from post-purchase consumer reviews. In: Ferro, N., et al. (eds.) ECIR 2016. LNCS, vol. 9626, pp. 682–688. Springer, Cham (2016). https://doi.org/10.1007/978-3-319-30671-1_53

11. Martínez-Cámara, E., Martín-Valdivia, M.T., et al.: Polarity classification for Spanish Tweets using the COST corpus. J. Inf. Sci. **41**(3), 263–272 (2015)

12. McCarthy, E.: Basic Marketing, A Managerial Approach, 6th edn. Richard D. Irwin, Inc., Homewood (1978)

13. Moghaddam, S.: Beyond sentiment analysis: mining defects and improvements from customer feedback. In: Hanbury, A., Kazai, G., Rauber, A., Fuhr, N. (eds.) ECIR 2015. LNCS, vol. 9022, pp. 400–410. Springer, Cham (2015). https://doi.org/10.1007/978-3-319-16354-3_44

14. Mohamed, H., Mohamed, S.G., Lamjed, B.S.: Customer intentions analysis of twitter based on semantic patterns, pp. 2–6 (2015)

15. Molina-González, M.D., Martínez-Cámara, E., et al.: Cross-domain sentiment analysis using Spanish opinionated words. In: Proceedings of NLDB, pp. 214–219 (2014)

16. Navas-Loro, M., Rodríguez-Doncel, V., Santana-Perez, I., Sánchez, A.: Spanish corpus for sentiment analysis towards brands. In: Proceedings of the 19th International Conference on Speech and Computer (SPECOM), pp. 680–689 (2017)

17. Pak, A., Paroubek, P.: Twitter as a corpus for sentiment analysis and opinion mining. In: LREc, vol. 10 (2010)

18. Plaza-Del-Arco, F.M., Martín-Valdivia, M.T., et al.: COPOS: corpus of patient opinions in Spanish. Application of sentiment analysis techniques. Procesamiento de Lenguaje Nat. **57**, 83–90 (2016)

19. Pontiki, M., Galanis, D., Pavlopoulos, J., Papageorgiou, H., Androutsopoulos, I., Manandhar, S.: Semeval-2014 task 4: aspect based sentiment analysis, pp. 27–35, January 2014

20. Pontiki, M., et al.: Semeval-2016 task 5: aspect based sentiment analysis. In: Proceedings of SemEval-2016, pp. 19–30. ACL, San Diego, June 2016

21. Pontiki, M., et al.: SemEval-2016 task 5: aspect based sentiment analysis. In: ProWorkshop SemEval-2016, pp. 19–30. ACL (2016)

22. Ramanand, J., Bhavsar, K., Pedanekar, N.: Wishful thinking: finding suggestions and 'buy' wishes from product reviews. In: Proceedings of the NAACL HLT 2010 Workshop (CAAGET 2010) (June), pp. 54–61 (2010)

23. Rangel, F., Rosso, P., Reyes, A.: Emotions and irony per gender in facebook. In: Proceedings of Workshop ES3LOD, LREC-2014, pp. 1–6 (2014)

24. Sánchez Rada, J.F., Torres, M., et al.: A linked data approach to sentiment and emotion analysis of twitter in the financial domain. In: FEOSW (2014)

25. Van Waterschoot, W., Van den Bulte, C.: The 4P classification of the marketing mix revisited. J. Mark. **56**, 83–93 (1992)

26. Vázquez, S., Muñoz-García, O., Campanella, I., Poch, M., Fisas, B., Bel, N., Andreu, G.: A classification of user-generated content into consumer decision journey stages. Neural Networks 58(Suppl. C), 68–81 (2014). Special Issue on "Affective Neural Networks and Cognitive Learning Systems for Big Data Analysis"

27. Vineet, G., Devesh, V., Harsh, J., Deepam, K., Shweta, K.: Identifying purchase intent from social posts. In: ICWSM 2014, pp. 180–186 (2014)

28. Westerski, A., Iglesias, C.A., Rico, F.T.: Linked opinions: describing sentiments on the structured web of data. In: Proceedings of the 4th International Workshop Social Data on the Web, vol. 830 (2011)

4th Workshop on Social Media World Sensors

Benchmarking Commercial RDF Stores with Publications Office Dataset

Ghislain Auguste Atemezing[(✉)] and Florence Amardeilh

Mondeca, 35 Boulevard de Strasbourg, 75010 Paris, France
ghislain.atemezing@mondeca.com

Abstract. This paper presents a benchmark of RDF stores with real-world datasets and queries from the EU Publications Office (PO). The study compares the performance of four commercial triple stores: Stardog 4.3 EE, GraphDB 8.0.3 EE, Oracle 12.2c and Virtuoso 7.2.4.2 with respect to the following requirements: bulk loading, scalability, stability and query execution. The datasets and the selected queries (44) are used in the Linked Data publication workflow at PO. The first results of this study provides some insights into the quantitative performance assessment of RDF stores used in production environment in general, especially when dealing with large amount of triples. Virtuoso is faster in querying and loading scenarios while GraphDB shows better results regarding stability.

Keywords: Benchmarking · Triple stores · RDF · Semantic web
Knowledge management · SPARQL · Stardog · GraphDB
Enterprise RDF store

1 Introduction

The adoption of semantic technologies for data integration has evolved in the recent years, thus the use of triple stores as back-end for data publishers has become popular. Triple stores stability and robustness are then critical in production environment where many thousands of users need to have access to fresh data, such as the case of the Publications Office (PO)[1]. In this article, we propose a quantitative analysis of four popular commercial triple stores (POSB); Stardog, GraphDB, Oracle 12c and Virtuoso. The initial list of triple stores also included Blazegraph and Neo4j. The latter were not included in this final article for two reasons: (i) It was not possible to load the dataset with Neo4j and (ii) Although we succeeded in loading the dataset with Blazegraph, we were not satisfied with the high number of time-outs (15) for the first set of queries, and the vendor was taking too long to answer technical inquiries. The benchmark is based on queries that are actually issued by PO employees to manage and create applications using their own dataset related to legal publications in all the languages of the European Union. This benchmark is motivated by PO requirements

---

[1] https://publications.europa.eu.

© Springer Nature Switzerland AG 2018
A. Gangemi et al. (Eds.): ESWC 2018 Satellite Events, LNCS 11155, pp. 379–394, 2018.
https://doi.org/10.1007/978-3-319-98192-5_54

to evaluate and document the advances on triple stores performance compared to their current solution adopted some years ago. The results show that a real-world SPARQL benchmark gives some indicators for comparing enterprise-based triple stores and provide insightful output for their quantitative-based analysis. The comparison of our results with other benchmark studies confirms that the performance of triple stores is not always homogeneous and depends on many parameters such as the types of queries, the characteristic of the datasets and more importantly the underlying hardware set up. Triple stores are used to store knowledge bases in RDF for data management and data web applications. The W3C SPARQL recommendation [10] is the vendor-independent query language to build more effective queries. It is clearly important for data integration applications to assess the performance of triple store implementations. Publications Office produces and publishes legal information and official journal of the European Union, in more than 20 languages in RDF. Currently, Virtuoso is part of their publishing architecture. After some years, PO wants to reevaluate the current state of the art of triple stores with respect to their use case. This paper contributes to give an overview of the status of Virtuoso compared to other commercial triple stores regarding bulk loading, benchmarking and stability. The results presented here are subsets of criteria needed by a data producer to assess the strengths and weaknesses of RDF triple stores. To mitigate the Virtuoso-Bias, we asked to other vendors if they could provide us with reformulated queries. Unfortunately, only Oracle gave us some recommendations that we implemented and reported as "oracle 12c optimized". This paper[2] presents the results of the evaluation of four popular commercial RDF stores conducted in 2017: Virtuoso, Stardog, Oracle 12c and GraphDB using the datasets from the PO and 44 queries used daily in production. The fraction of the commercial RDF stores covered in this paper is a subset of an initial list of seven triple stores including Marklogic, Blazegraph and Neo4J. PO suggested the list of the RDF stores for the benchmark. The results for Marklogic 8 are not presented because we did not have all the results at the time of writing the paper. It does not intend to be yet another benchmark, but rather a quantitative assessment by a data publisher for evaluating existing commercial triple stores. The paper describes a general purpose benchmarking with real datasets and queries by looking at bulk loading time, stability test and multi-client benchmark for 20 queries from the "instantaneous queries". The first results show that Virtuoso and Stardog are faster in bulk loading, while Virtuoso outperforms respectively to GraphDB, Stardog and Oracle in query-based performance. GraphDB shows to be the winner in the stability test performed in this benchmark.

The rest of the paper is structured as follows: Sect. 2 presents an overview of the ontology and the datasets. Section 3 describes the selected queries and analyses the features form and Basic Graph Pattern (BGP)[3] involve in their

---

[2] We would like to highlight that the conclusions reached are exclusively those of the authors, not necessarily those of the Publications Office.

[3] https://www.w3.org/TR/rdf-sparql-query/#BasicGraphPatterns.

construction. Section 4 describes the set up of the benchmark, followed by Sect. 5 and discussions. Section 7 presents some related works and Sect. 8 concludes the paper and highlights future work.

2   PO Semantic Datasets

This section presents an overview of the ontology used to model the datasets at PO, with an analysis of the nquads dataset used for the benchmarking.

2.1   Ontology

The Common Metadata Model (CDM) is the ontology used by the Publications Office to generate data in RDF. CDM[4] is an ontology based on the Functional Requirements for Bibliographic Records (FRBR) model described in RDF(S)/OWL to represent the relationships between the resource types managed by the PO and their views according to the FRBR model in terms of Work, Expression, Manifestation and Item.

2.2   Datasets

Two original datasets are used for the loading experiment, a normalized dataset with 2,195 nquads files representing a dump of the production environment [11], and a non-normalized dataset from 64 nquads files. PO uses "normalization" to replace all subjects by URIs to avoid the use of owl:sameAs pragma in Virtuoso. We loaded 727,442,978 triples from the normalized dataset, while 728,163,464 triples from the non-normalized dataset. For querying, we also add the CDM ontology and the Named Authority Lists (NAL). The Name Authority List (NAL) are SKOS [7] concepts representing categories such as events, countries, organizations, treaties, etc. In the production dataset (PROD data), 187 CDM classes are instantiated, which represents 60.71% of the ontology. Additionally, 198 distinct object properties are present in the dataset.

Furthermore, the dataset contains around 4,958,220 blank nodes. This number is quite high as it implies the presence of 7 blank nodes on every 1,000 triples.

2.3   Generated Datasets

We generated extra datasets based on original data to perform scalability test during the loading process. We implemented a script to generate the new datasets without modifying the structure of the initial data. Our algorithm postfixes all the resources of the type <http://publications.europa.eu/resource/cellar> by new ones of the form <http://publications.europa.eu/resource/cellar/$i/gen/g> where $i was incremented according to the desired size. We generated datasets for 2 billion (2Bio) and 5 billion (5Bio) triples respectively.

---

[4] http://publications.europa.eu/mdr/cdm/.

3   Query Description and Analysis

The queries used in this benchmark were received from the employees of PO working directly in the publication workflow of RDF data. Additionally the current endpoint used to publish the dataset at PO is Virtuoso, which means the queries are optimized for Virtuoso. We identified two categories of queries based on the goal achieved and the expected response time:

- Instantaneous queries[5]: These queries are generally used to dynamically generate dynamic visualizations on the website. Thus, they should be faster. In this group, we got 20 queries, divided into SELECT(16), DESCRIBE(3) and CONSTRUCT(1). Figure 1 depicts the Basic Graph Pattern (BGP) count per query.
- Analytical queries: These queries are used for validation and mapping purposes, where the most important feature is the quality of the results, not only the time to answer the query. In a total of 24 validation and mappings queries, 100% are SELECT queries. Table 1 depicts the number of BGP detected in each query of this category.

Table 2 shows the use of the 4 SPARQL query forms, i.e., SELECT, DESCRIBE, ASK, and CONSTRUCT in the whole set of queries used in POSB.

Query	1	2	3	4	5	6	7	8	9	10	11	12	13	14	15	16	17	18	19	20
BGP	2	2	2	5	7	6	7	7	7	7	11	17	12	3	1	4	17	3	11	3

Fig. 1. BGP repartition of SPARQL queries in Category 1.

For each of the query in the two categories, we analyze the features in the SPARQL query syntax. Tables 3 and 4 depicts the forms used in the queries where column GRBY is GROUP BY, GRPC is GROUP CONCAT and ORBY is ORDER BY. Queries in category 2 contain less combination of SPARQL features, with only two queries Q13 and Q14 with 8 different number of features.

We define the notion of "Feature Mix per Query (FMpQ)" which is the number of distinct form of a query. The maximum number is set to be 14. As described in [13], the most important constructs are the following: UNION, DISTINCT, ORDERBY, REGEX, LIMIT, OFFSET, OPTIONAL, FILTER and GROUPBY.

Based on the above definition, we obtained 7 queries (IQ5, IQ6, IQ7, IQ8, IQ9, IQ10 and IQ19) with more than 7 number of features. They might be "slow" according to the threshold in the average response time set for each category as presented in Sect. 5.2. Query IQ10 contains the highest number of features, without UNION, VALUES and ORDER BY.

---

[5] https://github.com/gatemezing/posb/tree/master/bench/queries/category1.

Table 1. BGP repartition of SPARQL queries in Category 2.

Query	#BGP	Query	#BGP
AQ1	1	AQ13	6
AQ2	1	AQ14	7
AQ3	2	AQ15	7
AQ4	5	AQ16	1
AQ5	5	AQ17	1
AQ6	4	AQ18	7
AQ7	5	AQ19	1
AQ8	4	AQ20	1
AQ9	1	AQ21	6
AQ10	15	AQ22	1
AQ11	16	AQ23	1
AQ12	2	AQ24	1

Table 2. SPARQL query forms detected for the PO SPARQL benchmark (POSB).

Query form	Total	Percentage (%)
SELECT	40	90.9%
DESCRIBE	3	6.81%
CONSTRUCT	1	2.27%
ASK	-	-

Table 3. Queries form detected in instantaneous queries. The last column shows the total number of distinct element forms for each query.

ID	DISTINCT	FILTER	OPTIONAL	UNION	LANG	REGEX	STR	LIMIT	OFFSET	GRBY	VALUES	GRPC	ORBY	FMpQ
IQ1	-	-	X	-	-	-	-	-	-	-	X	-	-	2
IQ2	-	-	X	-	-	-	-	-	-	-	X	-	-	2
IQ3	-	-	X	-	-	-	-	-	-	-	X	-	-	2
IQ4	-	X	-	X	X	-	-	-	-	-	X	-	-	4
IQ5	X	X	X	-	-	-	-	X	X	X	-	X	X	8
IQ6	X	-	X	-	-	-	-	X	X	X	-	X	X	7
IQ7	X	-	X	-	-	-	-	X	X	X	-	X	X	7
IQ8	X	X	X	-	-	-	-	X	X	X	-	X	X	8
IQ9	X	-	X	-	-	-	-	X	X	X	-	X	X	7
IQ10	X	X	X	-	X	X	X	X	X	X	-	X	-	10
IQ11	X	-	-	-	-	-	-	-	-	-	-	-	X	2
IQ12	X	X	X	-	-	X	-	-	-	-	-	X	X	6
IQ13	X	X	X	-	-	X	-	-	-	-	-	-	X	5
IQ14	X	X	X	-	-	X	-	-	-	-	-	-	-	4
IQ15	X	-	X	-	-	-	-	-	-	-	-	-	-	2
IQ16	-	X	X	-	-	-	X	-	-	-	X	-	X	5
IQ17	X	X	X	-	-	X	-	-	-	-	-	X	X	6
Q18	-	X	X	-	-	X	-	-	-	-	-	-	X	4
IQ19	X	X	X	X	-	X	-	-	X	-	-	-	X	7
IQ20	-	X	X	-	-	X	-	-	-	-	-	-	-	3

4 Experimental Setup

This section presents the setup we used for benching four triple stores commonly used in production environment. We first describe the triple stores and their configuration, followed by our experimental strategy and finally the results. The experiments were conducted on a server with the following characteristics: (i) Model: DELL PowerEdge R730; processor: Intel(R) Xeon(R) CPU E5-2620 v3 @ 2.40 GHz, 6C/12T; (ii) RAM: 128 GB DDR4 ECC; (iii) Disk capacity: 4 TB

Table 4. Queries form detected in analytical queries with the FMpQ for each query.

ID	DIS-TINCT	FIL-TER	OPT-IONAL	UNION	LANG	REGEX	STR	LIMIT	OFF-SET	GRBY	VAL-UES	GRPC	ORBY	FMpQ
AQ1	X	X	-	-	-	X	X	-	-	-	-	-	-	4
AQ2	X	X	-	-	-	X	X	-	-	-	-	-	-	4
AQ3	X	X	X	-	-	X	X	-	-	X	-	-	-	6
AQ4	-	X	X	-	-	-	-	-	-	-	-	-	-	2
AQ5	-	X	X	-	-	-	-	-	-	-	-	-	-	2
AQ6	-	X	X	-	-	-	-	-	-	-	-	-	-	2
AQ7	-	X	X	-	-	X	X	-	-	-	-	-	-	4
AQ8	X	X	-	-	-	X	X	-	-	-	-	-	-	4
AQ9	X	X	-	-	-	X	X	-	-	-	-	-	-	4
AQ10	X	X	X	-	X	-	X	-	-	-	-	X	-	6
AQ11	X	X	X	-	X	-	X	-	-	-	-	-	-	5
AQ12	X	X	X	-	-	-	-	-	-	-	-	X	X	5
AQ13	X	-	X	X	-	-	-	X	X	X	-	X	X	8
AQ14	X	-	X	X	-	-	-	X	X	X	-	X	X	8
AQ15	X	X	X	-	-	X	X	-	-	-	-	-	X	6
AQ16	X	X	-	-	-	X	-	-	-	-	-	-	X	4
AQ17	X	X	-	-	-	X	-	-	-	-	-	-	X	4
AQ18	X	X	X	-	-	X	X	-	-	-	-	-	X	6
AQ19	X	X	-	-	-	X	-	-	-	-	-	-	X	4
AQ20	X	X	-	-	-	X	-	-	-	-	-	-	X	4
AQ21	-	X	X	-	-	X	X	-	-	-	-	-	-	4
AQ22	X	X	-	-	-	X	-	-	-	-	-	-	X	4
AQ23	X	X	-	-	-	X	-	-	-	-	-	-	X	4
AQ24	X	X	-	-	-	-	-	-	-	-	-	-	-	3

SATA; RAID: Dell PERC H730p, (Raid 0/1) and (iv) Operating System: CentOS 7, 64 bits and Java 1.8.0 running. The system settings follow the best practices recommended by the vendors and double checked by the experts team. The material is available online at https://github.com/gatemezing/posb/.

4.1 Triples Store Setup

We carried out our experiments using Virtuoso [5], Stardog [15], Oracle [9] and GraphDB [2]. The configuration and the version of each triple store were the following:

– Virtuoso: Open-Source Edition version 7.2.4: We set the following memory-related parameters: NumberOfBuffers = 5450000, MaxDirtyBuffers = 4000000.
– Stardog: Stardog Enterprise Edition version 4.2.3. We set the Java heap size to 16 GB and MaxDirectMemorySize to 8 GB. We deactivate the strict parsing option and use the default SL reasoning inference during the loading process of dataset.
– GraphDB: GraphDB Enterprise Edition version 8.0.3. We use a configuration file with entity index size set to 500000000 with entity predicate list enabled, disabling the content index. We use two different rulesets: one empty and the other set to "rdfs-optimized".
– Oracle: Oracle 12.2 database. We set the following parameters in the pfile.ora file: pga_max_size set to 2 G, pga_aggregate_limit set to 64 G and pga_aggregate_target set to 32 G. The configurations are available online for further exploitation.[6]

---

[6] https://github.com/gatemezing/posb/tree/master/config.

4.2 Query Validation

For avoiding parsing errors with other triple stores, the first step before launching the bench tool is the validation the queries with the Jena ARQ tool[7]. The command to parse is: *qparse –query query.rq*. This step aims at providing with standardized SPARQL queries to be used across different RDF stores.

4.3 Benchmark Execution

The benchmark starts once the datasets are loaded into the RDF stores. Each run of loading the dataset is performed in a unique process running on the server. The benchmark comprises the following steps:

1. **Configuration step**: We set in the corresponding configuration file the timeout value for the queries. This forces the store to abort or kill the process running the query.
2. **Warm-up step**: In order to measure the performance of a triple store under operational conditions, a warm-up phase is used. In the warm-up phase, query mixes are posed to the triple store. We used a warm-up set to 20, meaning that we run 20 times the set of queries in a given category before starting the run phase.
3. **Hot-run step**: During this phase, the benchmark query mixes were sent to the tested store. We keep track of each run and output the results in a CSV file containing the statistics. We perform 5 runs in this stage, adding also the timeout value similar to the corresponding configuration file setup of the RDF store. We also set the max delay between query is set to 1000 s.

5 Results

In the section we present the results of the loading process for the datasets, according to the settings described in Sect. 4.

5.1 Bulk Loading

We found the best configuration for the bulk loading with two specificities in Stardog and GraphDB. In the latter, we load in a repository with inference set to RDFS optimized ruleset while in the former, we remove the strict parser option. Figure 2 shows the overall time taken by each RDF store, with the fastest being the one with less time. In GraphDB, the `rdfs-optimized`[8] ruleset is an optimized version of RDFS with the support of subClassOf and related type inference subPropertyOf, symmetric, inverse and transitive properties.

Figure 2 depicts the performance time in hours taken by the four RDF stores. Regardless of data volume, the fastest RDF store to load the datasets is

---

[7] https://jena.apache.org/.

[8] http://graphdb.ontotext.com/documentation/enterprise/reasoning.html.

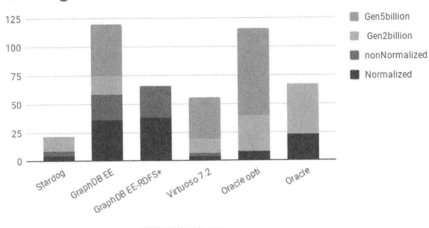

Fig. 2. Performance time during bulk loading of PO datasets and generated ones up to 5Billion triples

Virtuoso, followed closely by Stardog. Oracle optimized is slower compared to GraphDB for loading 2Bio and 5Bio datasets. Stardog failed to load 5Bio dataset. The loading process with GraphDB of 2Bio and 5Bio uses a different loader (8.0.6-SNAPSHOT), optimized by the support team for this specific task. Regarding the bulk loading of PROD dataset, Virtuoso and Stardog are very closed and are faster than the two other stores, achieving all the loads in less than 5 h. This result is useful in case of a database corruption with a need to reload the dataset from scratch within a reasonable exploitation time frame.

5.2   Benchmarking

We use the Sparql Query Benchmarker tool[9], an open-source tool based on Jena, with 20 runs per categories to warm up the server in a mix queries order, with an actual benchmark with 5 runs. The timeout settings are 60 s for instantaneous queries and 600 s for analytical queries. Furthermore we use three datasets, each of them loaded in a dedicated named graph: (i) the normalized dataset, (ii) the NAL dataset and (iii) the CDM ontology. We use the methodology presented in [12] to perform the benchmark and gather the results output in CSV files for further analysis.

Benchmarking Instantaneous Queries. We proceed to compare the results of querying the RDF stores using the benchmarker tool. We gathered the output of each run in CSV files.

---

[9] https://github.com/rvesse/sparql-query-bm.

Table 5. Runtime, standard deviation and QMpH when benchmarking instantaneous queries for PROD dataset

RDF store	Average runtime (s)	Standard deviation	QMpH
Virtuoso 7.x	1.10	0.01	3, 246.82
GraphDB EE	240.29	0.01	14.98
GraphDB RDFS+	240.30	0.02	14.98
Stardog 4.x	253.00	5.99	14.23
Oracle 12c	269.73	2.15	13.34
Oracle 12c optimized	112.75	.59	31.92

Single Thread. Virtuoso is faster compared to GraphDB and Stardog. The last two RDF stores have similar number of QMpH values as shown in Table 5. There were no time outs when querying Virtuoso. However, two queries timed out with Oracle (IQ3 and IQ9), three queries timed out (IQ3, IQ10 and IQ19) with Stardog, while four queries timed out with GraphDB (the same as Stardog plus IQ4). The optimized queries for Oracle permits to double the speed of the queries. Table 6 presents the average runtime execution for queries in category 1.

All the queries in Virtuoso finished in less than 1 s. IQ3 timed out for GraphDB and Stardog, while it finishes in 0.02 s with Virtuoso. GraphDB shows also slower query time except when the queries timed out. Query IQ4 timed out with GraphDB, but faster with Virtuoso. Stardog presents 3 timed out and slower than GraphDB and Virtuoso. There were 6 queries in category 1 that finished in more than 1 s (IQ8, IQ12, IQ14, IQ15, IQ16, IQ18). IQ19 timed out for GraphDB and Stardog, while it finishes in 0.11 s with Virtuoso. Oracle takes particularly long time in average execution for queries IQ5-IQ9; IQ11 and IQ13 compared to the rest of the RDF stores.

Multi-threading. Table 7 presents the results of QMpH values in case of multithread benchmark for instantaneous queries. Virtuoso performs again by far better, follows by GraphDB and Oracle. In general Virtuoso performs 10x slower than in the single thread, compared to GraphDB and Oracle which is only 7x slower. The results also shed lights on the likely constant behavior of GraphDB and Oracle when it comes to concurrent access, one of a key criteria for SPARQL endpoints usage.

Bench for Analytical Queries. We set 600 s for timeout because the queries in this category are more analytical-based queries. Virtuoso is faster than all the other triple stores (cf. Table 8). Stardog reveals 4 timed out queries (AQ15, AQ16, AQ19 and AQ22), 1 timed out query (AQ10) for Oracle. No timed out in GraphDB even when reasoning in RDFS+ activated in the repository. This shows that inferences can be activated in this category of queries in GraphDB without altering the performance of the queries.

Table 6. Average response time in second per queries and RDF stores in the case of instantaneous queries

Query	Virtuoso	Stardog	GraphDB	GraphDBRDFS+	Oracle
IQ1	**.02**	.03	**.02**	.04	.10
IQ2	.02	**.01**	.03	.04	.07
IQ3	**.02**	60	60	60	60
IQ4	**.009**	.35	60	60	.04
IQ5	.09	.82	**.01**	**.01**	31.35
IQ6	.28	.10	**.01**	**.01**	39.35
IQ7	.06	**.01**	**.01**	**.01**	34.82
IQ8	.10	1.35	**.01**	**.01**	31.88
IQ9	.05	.20	**.01**	**.01**	60
IQ10	**.12**	60	60	60	3.64
IQ11	**.004**	.01	.02	.006	.11
IQ12	.06	49.17	.05	**.04**	2.93
IQ13	.03	**.01**	**.01**	**.01**	.14
IQ14	**.01**	5.52	**.01**	**.01**	19.53
IQ15	**.006**	5.28	.009	.009	.08
IQ16	.01	1.50	.01	**.008**	.02
IQ17	.03	.06	**.01**	**.01**	.25
IQ18	**.06**	1.64	.07	.07	.09
IQ19	.11	60	60	60	**.04**
IQ20	**.006**	.02	.009	.008	.15

Table 7. QMpH values in multi-threading bench for instantaneous queries

RDF store	5clients	20clients	50clients	70clients	100clients
Virtuoso 7.2.4.2	367.22	358.27	371.76	354.60	341.02
GraphDB EE	2.13	2.12	2.13	2.12	2.13
GraphDB EE RDFS+	2.13	2.13	2.13	2.36	2.13
Stardog 4.3	1.973	1.94	1.97	1.96	1.95
Oracle 12c	2.10	1.99	2.01	2.01	2.02

Virtuoso is faster than all the rest of the triple stores as shown in Table 9 with the values of QMpH. The slowest query AQ10 involves DISTINCT, FILTER and OPTIONAL. However, this same query is 4x slower on GraphDB, 20x slower on Stardog and timed out in Oracle. Also, the well performing query AQ20 involves the DISTINCT feature.

Table 8. Average response time in second per queries and RDF stores in analytical queries

Query	Virtuoso	Stardog	GraphDB	GraphDBRDFS+	Oracle 12c
AQ1	10.72	**.16**	5.96	7.31	4.24
AQ2	9.87	**9.66**	9.94	12.30	29.13
AQ3	33.52	**15.84**	26.38	31.74	590.37
AQ4	1.65	15.42	.01	**.009**	.09
AQ5	**.677**	12.16	20.89	15.09	39.78
AQ6	.66	22.29	**.15**	.16	.27
AQ7	**.01**	26.27	**.01**	**.01**	.52
AQ8	**.04**	27.11	.48	.51	14.22
AQ9	**.02**	.11	1.7	1.96	.46
AQ10	**16.97**	314.39	60.05	65.56	600
AQ11	**.602**	57.51	2.92	2.43	2.42
AQ12	**7.15**	14.52	60.02	65.64	82.95
AQ13	.06	26.28	**.01**	**.01**	85.19
AQ14	.06	.10	**.01**	**.01**	206.308
AQ15	.72	600	.06	**.05**	3.74
AQ16	.01	600	.01	**.009**	.09
AQ17	.01	14.87	.01	**.008**	.06
AQ18	.06	292.24	.01	**.009**	2.93
AQ19	.01	600	.008	**.007**	.62
AQ20	.01	16.34	.008	**.007**	.60
AQ21	.02	23.00	.02	**.01**	.98
AQ22	.01	600	.01	**.008**	.70
AQ23	.01	15.70	.01	**.007**	.68
AQ24	.03	45.73	**.01**	.012	1.33

Table 9. Runtime, standard deviation and QMpH when benchmarking analytical queries

RDF store	Avg. runtime (s)	Std. deviation	QMpH
Virtuoso 7.2.4.2	44.86	0.14	80.23
GraphDB EE RDFS+	134.95	3.98	36.67
GraphDB EE	180.50	1.02	19.94
Stardog 4.3	4000.26	1226.11	0.89
Oracle 12c	1490.53	67.88	2.41

GraphDB is the second fastest triple store for this set of queries. The slowest query AQ10 involves DISTINCT, FILTER and OPTIONAL features. Also, the fastest query AQ20 involves DISTINCT.

Four analytical queries timed out with Stardog (AQ15, AQ16, AQ19 and AQ22) whereas no query timed out with GraphDB and Virtuoso. All the queries that timed out in Stardog involved FILTER. Additionally, AQ15 also involves OPTIONAL. This indicates that using complex FILTER in conjunction with additional OPTIONAL might affects the overall runtime of the query.

5.3   Stability Test

We perform a stress test on the triple stores to have a quantitative indication related to stability. For this purpose, the queries of category 1 are run continuously under a progressively increasing load to see how the system reacts to high load. The test starts by specifying the number of parallel clients in the script. Each client completes the run of the mix queries in parallel. The number of parallel clients is then multiplied by the ramp up factor which defaults to 2 and the process is repeated. This repeats until either the maximum runtime or the maximum number of threads are reached. We set the maximum runtime to 180 min (3 h) and set the maximum parallel threads to 128.

Table 10. Results of the stress test on triple stores using instantaneous queries.

RDF store	#mix runs	#op. run	Max.//.threads	# Errors
Stardog	92	1,840	128	576
Virtuoso	255	5,100	256	4,732
GraphDB	255	5,100	256	139
Oracle	63	1,260	128	1,009

The results in Table 10 show that Stardog and Oracle finished with the limit of the parallel threads. On the other hand, Virtuoso and GraphDB have completed the test after 180 min, reaching 256 parallel threads. In this scenario, GraphDB shows fewer errors compared to Virtuoso. Based on the total execution errors encountered for this stress experiment, we can conclude that GraphDB is likely to be more stable respectively in this order to Stardog, Oracle and Virtuoso.

6   Discussion

The results indicate that no single RDF store is the absolute winner across different queries. For instantaneous queries, Stardog and GraphDB timed out for queries with REGEX, DISTINCT, FILTER, OPTIONAL and GROUP BY, whereas Oracle was able to finish without time out. However, Oracle timed out in IQ9 containing OPTIONAL and DISTINCT (Table 11). GraphDB performs better in analytical queries, while having timed out in instantaneous queries. Stardog and Oracle are the only RDF stores not able to have "zero time-outs" according to our settings, and sometimes extremely slow for some queries involving complex FILTER and OPTIONAL.

Regarding the bulk loading, Virtuoso and Stardog are faster than the other systems. This has an advantage in case of crashes with a need to reload the whole dataset from scratch within a normal working day time frame. Also, we are aware that the figures obtained in this benchmark might have different values if SSD disks were used instead in our server. However, we argue that this benchmark gives an overview of the current state of the triple stores based on the PO datasets.

In Table 12, we present the time for querying those queries with a combination of at least three of the SPARQL forms REGEX, DIST, FLT, OPT and GRBY. Stardog timed out in AQ15, and took almost 5 min for AQ18.

Table 11. Comparison results time execution (in second) of the seven instantaneous queries with at least seven SPARQL features and BGP.

Query	Virtuoso	GraphDB	Stardog	Oracle	#FMpQ	#BGP
IQ5	.09	.01	.82	31.35	8	7
IQ6	.28	.01	.10	39.35	7	6
IQ7	.06	.01	.01	34.82	7	7
IQ8	.10	.01	1.35	31.88	8	7
IQ9	.05	.01	.20	>60 s	7	7
IQ10	.12	>60 s	>60 s	3.64	10	7
IQ19	.11	>60 s	>60 s	.04	7	11

Table 12. Comparison results of analytical queries with a combination of at least three of the SPARQL forms REGEX, DIST, FLT, OPT and GRBY.

Query	Virtuoso	GraphDB	Stardog	Oracle	#FMpQ	BGP
AQ13	0.06	0.01	26.28	85.19	8	6
AQ14	0.06	0.01	0.10	206.308	8	7
AQ15	0.72	0.06	>600	3.74	6	7
AQ18	0.06	0.01	292.24	2.93	6	7

In summary, this benchmark shows the following insights:

- Overall Virtuoso is the fastest system followed by Stardog in the bulk loading scenario.
- No single system is unique winner across all queries. For instantaneous queries, Virtuoso is faster in 9 queries, followed by GraphDB in 8 queries. Stardog is faster in 3 queries. Oracle is faster in 1 query for which Stardog and GraphDB timed out.
- In analytical queries, Virtuoso is the fastest system in not more than 25% of the queries, while GraphDBRDFS+ is the fastest in almost 42% of the queries.

7   Related Work

In the literature, several general purpose RDF benchmarks were developed on both artificial data and real datasets. The Lehigh University Benchmark (LUBM) [6] uses small number of classes, with plain SPARQL queries. The dataset generated are for the university domain. In LUBM, each query is executed 10 times and the average response time of the query is reported. In the publication domain, the SP2Bench [14] benchmark uses a synthetic test data and artificial queries. However it uses a very limited number of triples (25M) compared to the dataset used in this work.

The Berlin SPARQL Benchmark (BSBM) [3] applies a use case on e-commerce in various triple stores. It tests the SPARQL features on the triple stores, with the particularity of simulating operations performed by a human user. However, BSBM data and queries are artificial, with very limited classes and properties.

The DBpedia SPARQL Benchmark (DBPSB) [8] is another more recent benchmark for RDF stores. Its RDF data is DBPedia with up to 239M triples, starting with 14M to compare the scalability. It uses 25 heterogeneous queries. The procedure for benchmark includes the query log mining, clustering and SPARQL feature analysis for the popular triple stores Virtuoso, Sesame, Jena-TDB and BigOWLIM. POSB shares in common with DBPSB the relative high number of classes, real-world dataset and queries. However, POSB differs in having more heterogeneity in the dataset, the selected queries are SPARQL queries used in production using very large mixture of SPARQL features. Also the benchmark does not assess the comparison in multi-client scenario. The overall results with Virtuoso the fastest store with DBpedia dataset converge with our findings, albeit the diverse set of queries. Our work differs from the above in that the goal is to evaluate four commercial triple stores with dataset in production at PO, with given set of real-world queries not generated from logs. The Waterloo SPARQL Diversity Test Suite (WatDiv) [1] addresses the stress testing of five RDF stores for diverse queries and varied workloads. WatDiv introduces two classes of query features (structural and data-driven) to evaluate previous four benchmarks: LUBM, BSBM, SP2Bench and DBPSB. The systems evaluated two prototype stores (RDF-3X and gStore) and three industrial systems

(Virtuoso 6.1.8, Virtuoso 7.1.0 and 4Store). Their results and findings highlight good results of Virtuoso compared to other RDF system, although remarking that one system may win in one query and timeout in another. This latter remark also applies to our findings for Stardog, GraphDB and Oracle. Recently, Iguana framework [4] provides with a configurable and integrated environment for executing SPARQL benchmark. It also allows a uniform comparison of results across different benchmarks. However, we use for this benchmark a different tool and plan to use Iguana to better mitigate the virtuoso-bias in the input queries and have comparable results with previous benchmarks only with commercial triple stores.

8   Conclusions and Future Work

We have presented in this paper a comparison of four RDF stores Virtuoso, GraphDB Stardog and Oracle, with real datasets and SPARQL queries from Publications Office. The results highlighted that according to our settings, Virtuoso performs better in loading and benching queries in both categories, with a total of 44 queries tested. GraphDB handles more queries mix per hour than Stardog, but shows more timed out queries (instantaneous queries). Inversely, Stardog loads datasets faster than GraphDB, but was unable to succeed "zero time-outs" during the benchmark, showing some weakness in handling queries with complex FILTER and OPTIONAL. This study helps assessing RDF triple stores with datasets with similar characteristics than the one discussed here. However, any comparison depends on the type of queries, the server settings to decide on which RDF store to use in production.

It should be noted that this work has helped to improve the bulk loading mechanism of GraphDB and Oracle and the query engine of Stardog that will be available in their respective future major releases. We plan to add to this benchmark other RDF stores such as Marklogic 8 and Neptune[10], as well as to include SPARQL update queries and qualitative features. We are convinced that such studies shed lights to publishers willing to create enterprise knowledge graph to easily assess which RDF store can fit their needs. Also, we plan to find the impacts of using different storage in the back-end such as binary RDF (e.g., HDT) and client side approach with Linked Data fragments.

Acknowledgments. We would like to thank all the interviewees at the Publications Office for their valuable input. We also thank Oracle, Ontotext and Stardog Union for all their support.

---

[10] http://blog.mondeca.com/2018/02/09/requetes-sparql-avec-neptune/.

References

1. Aluç, G., Hartig, O., Özsu, M.T., Daudjee, K.: Diversified stress testing of RDF data management systems. In: Mika, P., et al. (eds.) ISWC 2014. LNCS, vol. 8796, pp. 197–212. Springer, Cham (2014). https://doi.org/10.1007/978-3-319-11964-9_13
2. Bishop, B., Kiryakov, A., Ognyanoff, D., Peikov, I., Tashev, Z., Velkov, R.: OWLIM: a family of scalable semantic repositories. Semant. Web **2**(1), 33–42 (2011)
3. Bizer, C., Schultz, A.: Benchmarking the performance of storage systems that expose SPARQL endpoints. In: World Wide Web Internet and Web Information Systems (2008)
4. Conrads, F., Lehmann, J., Saleem, M., Morsey, M., Ngonga Ngomo, A.-C.: IGUANA: a generic framework for benchmarking the read-write performance of triple stores. In: d'Amato, C., et al. (eds.) ISWC 2017. LNCS, vol. 10588, pp. 48–65. Springer, Cham (2017). https://doi.org/10.1007/978-3-319-68204-4_5
5. Erling, O., Mikhailov, I.: RDF support in the virtuoso DBMS. In: Pellegrini, T., Auer, S., Tochtermann, K., Schaffert, S. (eds.) Networked Knowledge - Networked Media. SCI, vol. 221, pp. 7–24. Springer, Heidelberg (2009). https://doi.org/10.1007/978-3-642-02184-8_2
6. Guo, Y., Pan, Z., Heflin, J.: LUBM: a benchmark for owl knowledge base systems. Web Semant. Sci. Serv. Agents World Wide Web **3**(2), 158–182 (2005)
7. Isaac, A., Summers, E.: SKOS simple knowledge organization system. In: Primer, World Wide Web Consortium (W3C) (2009)
8. Morsey, M., Lehmann, J., Auer, S., Ngonga Ngomo, A.-C.: DBpedia SPARQL benchmark – performance assessment with real queries on real data. In: Aroy, L., et al. (eds.) ISWC 2011. LNCS, vol. 7031, pp. 454–469. Springer, Heidelberg (2011). https://doi.org/10.1007/978-3-642-25073-6_29
9. Oracle. Oracle 12 manual (2017). http://docs.oracle.com/database/122/index.htm
10. Prud'hommeaux, E., Seaborne, A.: SPARQL query language for rdf. w3c recommendation (2008)
11. Office Publications, Mondeca: Dump of RDF dataset used for RDF benchmark (2017). https://doi.org/10.5281/zenodo.1036739
12. Revelytix: Triple store evaluation - performance testing methodology. Technical report, Revelytix Inc. (2010)
13. Saleem, M., Mehmood, Q., Ngonga Ngomo, A.-C.: FEASIBLE: a feature-based SPARQL benchmark generation framework. In: Arenas, M., et al. (eds.) ISWC 2015. LNCS, vol. 9366, pp. 52–69. Springer, Cham (2015). https://doi.org/10.1007/978-3-319-25007-6_4
14. Schmidt, M., Hornung, T., Lausen, G., Pinkel, C.: SP² Bench: a SPARQL performance benchmark. In: IEEE 25th International Conference on Data Engineering, ICDE 2009, pp. 222–233. IEEE (2009)
15. Stardog. Stardog 4.2.x: The manual (2017). https://docs.stardog.com/

1st Workshop on Semantic Web of Things for Industry 4.0

Such a Wonderful Place: Extracting Sense of Place from Twitter

Giovanni Siragusa[1] and Valentina Leone[1,2(✉)]

[1] Department of Computer Science, Univesity of Turin, Turin, Italy
{siragusa,leone}@di.unito.it
[2] CIRSFID, University of Bologna, Bologna, Italy

Abstract. The concept of *Place* has a structured meaning that involves three different aspects: *location, locale* and *sense of place*. The definition of *sense of place* for a specific location requires the analysis of a large amount of data, and social networks are good sources for their extraction since users act as social sensors on them. In this paper, we want to detect the *sense of place* defined by Twitter's users for the city of New York using Latent Dirichlet Allocation (LDA). Our assumption is that LDA could be used to summarise the several *sense of place* shared by users.

Keywords: Geography · Place · Tweets · LDA · NLP

1 Introduction

Place is an underestimated concept frequently used in every-day life in sentences as *"This is my favourite place"*, *"I finally found my place in the world"*, *"Lay a place at the table for Mr. Twist"*. In the commonsense language, we use the word *place* to refer to a city (e.g., New York), a public space (e.g., Central Park), a shop or even to the seat we usually take at the table. From these examples it is easy to understand that the concept of *place* has a high width degree which ranges from a punctual space to a wide area.

Place is also one of the main concepts in Geography, but it assumes in this field a more structured representation. In particular, according to Cresswell [6,7] the concept of place embodies three different aspects:

- *location*: the physical absolute point in the space, identified by a set of coordinates;
- *locale*: the visible features and settings of a place, such as streets, shops, parks and so on;
- *sense of place*: the set of emotions and feelings that a place inspires in people. These sentiments can be subjective or shared: they are subjective when they are based on someone's personal biography, and shared when a group of people feels the same sentiment towards a place.

© Springer Nature Switzerland AG 2018
A. Gangemi et al. (Eds.): ESWC 2018 Satellite Events, LNCS 11155, pp. 397–405, 2018.
https://doi.org/10.1007/978-3-319-98192-5_55

Starting from the intuition of Cresswell, it is clear that a complete definition of a place can't ignore a systematic analysis of the three aspects listed above. First of all, they involve the identification of a place to focus on and the subsequent collection of a set of observations about the chosen place as for example feelings and emotions. Finally the data must be processed in order to find the *sense of place* (SOP).

To accomplish such a task automatically, it is necessary to analyse a large amount of data which must encompass enough information to define a place in terms of its three composing aspects. Social networks are good sources for the extraction of data suitable to carry on this analysis. Millions of users post their activities, their emotions, their interests and their opinions every day. This is the reason why the scientific community has become increasingly interested on these data, considering people in social network acting as social sensors in different fields such as politics, economics and sociology. Moreover, the possibility to associate a geographical reference to a post (the so called geo-tags) or to infer the location starting from significant hash-tags allowed scientists to develop map-based data analysis which can also be used to identify disaster-affected areas or regions with high crime rates, as respectively in the works of Cerutti et al. [5] and Ristea et al. [12].

In our aim to detect the SOP, we used Twitter as our source of information. Since Twitter allows to extract tweets posted within a specific geographical region, it was easy for us to fix both *location* and *locale*, leaving free the SOP that we extracted from the tweets. We collected all tweets containing the word *nyc* (New York city) and located over the area of New York[1]. Then, following the idea proposed in [14], we applied Latent Dirichlet Allocation (LDA) over the collected data. The assumption is that topics generated by LDA can summarise the several SOP shared by social sensors, since topics capture words that frequently co-occur each other. The topics are used both to select tweets expressing the SOP and to visualise them on a map.

The remain of this paper is structured as follows: Sect. 2 describes some works which use georeferenced data extracted from the social networks and some applications of LDA on them; Sect. 3 describes the experiment we made and the results we obtained in order to detect the SOP for the city of New York applying LDA; finally, in Sect. 4 the article concludes.

2   Related Works

The specification of a geographical reference in a shared post is nowadays an habit for the users of the most famous social networks as *Twitter*[2], *Facebook*[3] and *Instagram*[4]. In addition to these well-known platforms, other new

---

[1] We used both the word and the geo-tag because not all tweets contain the latter information.

[2] www.twitter.com.

[3] www.facebook.com.

[4] www.instagram.com.

location-based services emerged in the last years. Among them, we mention *Trendsmap*[5] which shows on a map the latest trends emerging from Twitter, *Ushahidi*[6] which collects and visualises information about crisis witnesses providing the users the possibility to respond and *FixMyStreet*[7] which allows the UK citizens to signal streets problems (pot holes, unsafe walls, not working lampposts) to the local authorities. *FirstLife*[8] [2] is a more interactivity-oriented service which focuses its attention on the user intended as citizen, giving him the possibility to interact with a map on which he can share events, news and even aggregate people. Moreover, the data are associated with a temporal dimension which allows users to filter and order the information according to time.

As previously mentioned, the mass dissemination of social networks and the possibility to acquire the data posted by users trough the RESTful API provided by the social-networks themselves encouraged the scientific community to analyse these data in different fields of interest.

In their work, Sakaki et al. [13] used the intuition of considering the users as social sensors in order to implement event detection. Through a semantic analysis of a collection of tweets and the application of location estimation methods, they were able to approximate the earthquakes' centre and the typhoons' trajectories. Cataldi et al. [4] extracted in real time the most emerging topics expressed by the community based on the interests of a specific user in a particular temporal frame. Allisio et al. [1] exploited the temporal and spacial information associated with the tweets in order to produce a daily estimation of the degree of happiness of the main Italian cities. An interactive map shows the data obtained combining Sentiment Analysis and visualisation techniques. Referring to the definition of places given by Cresswell, this work can be considered as an experiment designed to the extraction of the sense of place associated to a location.

Besides the Sentiment Analysis techniques, also Latent Dirichlet Allocation (LDA) [3] was successfully applied on data extracted from social networks. LDA is a probabilistic generative model that treats a document as a finite mixture of topics, where a topic is a distribution over the vocabulary. In details, each topic captures words co-occurrences inside documents, allowing to explore the document collection. In the work of Pennacchiotti and Gurutmundi [11], the authors used LDA to discover users' interests. In their model, users are represented as a mixture of topics. Thus, it can be used to suggest friends or people to follow just comparing the topics. Zhang et al. [15] proposed a model called *SSN-LDA* (Simple Social Network LDA) which is able to find communities. In this case, the latent variables (topics) are the communities. Eisenstein et al. [9] argue that words co-occurrences are corrupted by geographical information. According to the authors, people living in a certain geographical region use a different vocabulary from the people that live in a different one. Thus, they treat the geographical area as a latent variable. Lau et al. [10] proposed a method to

---

[5] www.trendsmap.it.

[6] www.ushahidi.com.

[7] www.fixmystreet.com.

[8] www.firstlife.org.

track emerging events in microblogs based on LDA. Finally, Di Caro et al. [8] proposed a framework called TMine which defines a navigable tag-flag: a kind of topic with the associated words.

3   Experiments

As previously described in the Introduction, we would like to extract the SOP defined by Cresswell [6,7] from social networks. To accomplish this research question, we applied Latent Dirchlet Allocation (LDA) [3] to find common topics expressed in users' posts. Our idea is that topics can capture the SOP expressed by people regarding a place or a city. For instance, we may capture that there is an ongoing concert in a park. To validate our assumption, we fixed location and locale to New York, searching all tweets containing the word *nyc* (New York City) with the constraint that they are geo-located over the area of New York. The only free parameter is the SOP which is extracted from the tweets.

3.1   Dataset Creation

We downloaded a set of 449054 tweets using Twitter APIs. This set includes all the tweets in which the *"nyc"* chars sequence appears somewhere in the tweet (it could be into the text or into the hash-tags).

Then, analysing the tweets, we noticed that some of them reported news or irrelevant information for our task. Since SOP regards the sentiments expressed toward the city (e.g., a street, a park or a monument), we decided to filter those ones that express a neutral sentiment. To perform sentiment classification, we used Python's TextBlob library which comprises a pre-trained classifier. After the classification, we found 395467 tweets expressing a non-neutral sentiment. However, many of them were duplicated tweets due to re-tweets. For instance, we found the tweet *"So this happened, gotta love NYC"* 1620 times. We decided to filter those tweets to create a dataset containing unique ones. Such dataset is composed by 120538 tweets.

Finally, we used a regular expression to remove from the set of tweets those in which the *"nyc"* chars sequence was part of another word and was not used as the acronym of "New York City". We applied this regular expression both on the text and the hash-tags of the tweets. Thus, we obtained the final dataset of 21808 tweets from which we extracted the topics using LDA. Table 1 contains some statistics about the collected dataset: the average length of tweets (expressed in

Table 1. Some statistics about the dataset

Tweets number of the dataset	21,808
Words average number in the tweets text	17
Average number of hash-tags per tweet	0.7
Number of words in the vocabulary	22,879

terms of number of words, including hash-tags); the average number of hash-tags per tweet; and the vocabulary dimension of the collected dataset, that is the number of different words which appear in the tweets.

We then extracted the frequent words contained in those tweets to see if there exist words that express a sentiment towards New York City and to analyze the content of the dataset. We started removing stopwords, user names and links. Then, we lowercased the text of those tweets and we stemmed the words. To extract and plot the frequent words we used the WordCloud tool[9]. The produced wordcloud is depicted in Fig. 1. From the image, we can find words that express a sentiment towards *New York City*, such as: *"love"*, *"happen"* and *"deadly"*. Furthermore, the wordcloud shows words related to *weather, school* and a *march* against weapon, meaning that in the days we collected the tweets, those three topics were the most discussed ones.

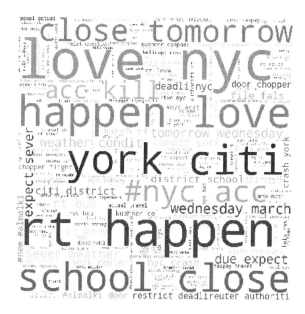

Fig. 1. The figure represents the frequent words (unigrams and bigrams) present in the tweet dataset.

3.2 Topic Extraction

We used Latent Dirchlet Allocation (LDA) model to extract the underline tweets present in the dataset. LDA requires in input the number of topics and extract, for each topic, a probability distribution over the vocabulary. Then, the top-k words of each distribution are selected to represent the topic.

In details, our pipeline to extract the topics is the following one: first, each tweet text has been lowercased and tokenized, preserving users name,

---

[9] http://amueller.github.io/word_cloud/index.html.

hash-tags and urls. Then, we filtered out stopwords, usernames and urls. Finally, we stemmed the words. We also filtered those words that have a globally frequency less than 5. The constructed Bag-Of-Words are given in input to the LDA model.

We used Gensim implementation of LDA, tuning its hyperparameters. We randomly searched the number of topics in output (trying 5, 10, 20 and 50 topics), the number of passes through the corpus (trying 1, 10, 50, 100), and the number of steps of the Expectation-Maximization Algorithm (trying 100, 500 and 1000). We found good results setting the number of topics to 20, the number of passes to 50 and the number of steps to 1000.

3.3 Topic Selection and Analysis

Once we extracted the topics, we had to select those ones that express the *sense of place*. We gave to two annotators the extracted topics with some tweets associated to them (to understand the topics), asking to judge if a topic expresses the SOP. We then considered only those topics that for both annotators express the SOP. Table 2 shows some selected topics and an associated tweet.

Table 2. The table reports six topics with the first 5 words. We also included a tweet associated to the topic that expresses the sense of place.

Topic	Tweet
time, trip, black, gt, brooklyn	i finally had the chance to stop by meow palour, a #catcafe in #nyc it's a great place for...
miss, start, move, train, hour	@nyctsubway a 45 min ride is now taking an hour and a half on the 5 train, which is stopping in every possible...
amaz, perform, amp, music, support	having an amazing time being back in nyc, focusing on some new music...
york, citi, #nyc, ny, #newyork	public transportation should be open to everyone. #nyc, one of the greatest cities in the world, can do better than that!...
love, #nyc, amp, home, win	fallin in love with nyc... probably never going home
#nyc, day, happi, morn, world	5 reasons to stay at the conrad New York

We decided to perform some analysis on the tweets associated to the selected topics to deeply understand how the SOP is spatially and temporally distributed over the city. We started plotting the tweets that have a geographical information on a map labelling them with their associated topic. From Fig. 2, we can notice that the dominant topic is the blue one, which expresses the love of the people towards the city (see the pop-up in the image).

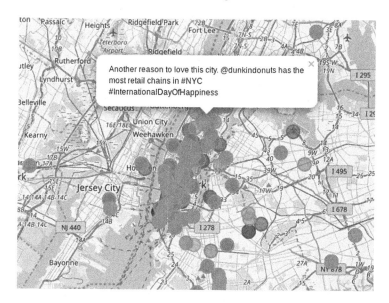

Fig. 2. The figure shows the tweets over New York. The colours represent the topics. From the map, we can see that the dominant topic is the blue one. (Color figure online)

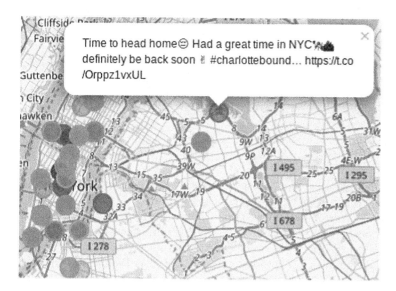

Fig. 3. The figure shows the tweets posted on Monday 19/03/2018.

We conducted a second analysis dividing the tweets by posted date and by posted hour to see if a SOP could emerge in a particular day of the week (e.g., Monday) or time (e.g., from 4 pm to 8 pm). From the split of tweets by day, we noticed that on Monday tourists tweetted that they'll miss New York (see Fig. 3) and that the schools will be closed due to snow (see Fig. 4) on Wednesday.

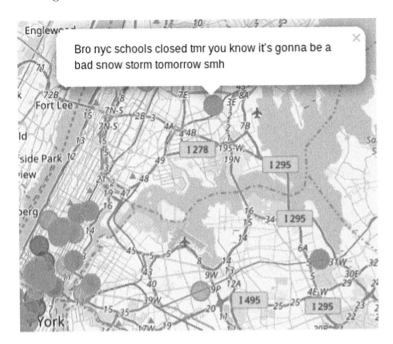

Fig. 4. The figure shows the tweets posted on Friday 16/03/2018.

For the daytime analysis, unfortunately we did not find a set of tweets that expresses the same content. We thought that this is due to the nature of Twitter, whereby people tend to express their opinions, thoughts and news during all the day.

4 Conclusions

In this paper, we created a dataset of tweets regarding New York City in order to extract the sense of place defined by Cresswell [6,7]. In detail, we fixed *location* and *locale* to New York and we tried to extract the *sense of place* (SOP) from the users posts. The detection of the SOP is performed by using Latent Dirchlet Allocation (LDA) [3] in order to extract topics that summarise the several sentiments that people expressed towards the city. Finally, we showed that is possible to capture the SOP from tweets and that it could depend by the day of the week.

As future works, we are planning to improve the pre-processing phase, since some unfiltered tweets do not express the SOP. Furthermore, we are interest to apply other LDA models to unveil information present inside tweets.

References

1. Allisio, L., Mussa, V., Bosco, C., Patti, V., Ruffo, G.F.: Felicittà: visualizing and estimating happiness in Italian cities from geotagged tweets. In: CEUR Workshop Proceedings, vol. 1096, pp. 95–106. CEUR Workshop Proceedings (2013)
2. Antonini, A., et al.: First life, from the global village to local communities. In: 1st IASC Thematic Conference on Urban Commons (2015)
3. Blei, D.M., Ng, A.Y., Jordan, M.I.: Latent Dirichlet Allocation. J. Mach. Learn. Res. **3**, 993–1022 (2003)
4. Cataldi, M., Caro, L.D., Schifanella, C.: Personalized emerging topic detection based on a term aging model. ACM Trans. Intell. Syst. Technol. (TIST) **5**(1), 7 (2013)
5. Cerutti, V., Fuchs, G., Andrienko, G., Andrienko, N., Ostermann, F.: Identification of disaster-affected areas using exploratory visual analysis of georeferenced tweets: application to a flood event, p. 5. Association of Geographic Information Laboratories in Europe, Helsinki, Finland (2016)
6. Cresswell, T.: Place. In: International Encyclopedia of Human Geography, vol. 8, pp. 169–177. Elsevier (2009)
7. Cresswell, T.: Place-part i. In: The Wiley-Blackwell Companion to Human Geography, pp. 235–244 (2011)
8. Di Caro, L., Candan, K.S., Sapino, M.L.: Navigating within news collections using tag-flakes. J. Visual Lang. Comput. **22**(2), 120–139 (2011)
9. Eisenstein, J., O'Connor, B., Smith, N.A., Xing, E.P.: A latent variable model for geographic lexical variation. In: Proceedings of the 2010 Conference on Empirical Methods in Natural Language Processing, pp. 1277–1287. Association for Computational Linguistics (2010)
10. Lau, J.H., Collier, N., Baldwin, T.: On-line trend analysis with topic models: #twitter trends detection topic model online. In: COLING, pp. 1519–1534 (2012)
11. Pennacchiotti, M., Gurumurthy, S.: Investigating topic models for social media user recommendation. In: Proceedings of the 20th International Conference Companion on World Wide Web, pp. 101–102. ACM (2011)
12. Ristea, A., Kurland, J., Resch, B., Leitner, M., Langford, C.: Estimating the spatial distribution of crime events around a football stadium from georeferenced tweets. ISPRS Int. J. Geo-Inf. **7**(2), 43 (2018)
13. Sakaki, T., Okazaki, M., Matsuo, Y.: Earthquake shakes twitter users: real-time event detection by social sensors. In: Proceedings of the 19th International Conference on World Wide Web, pp. 851–860. ACM (2010)
14. Siragusa, G.: Place as topics: analysis of spatial and temporal evolution of topics from social networks data. In: SIDEWAYS@ LREC, pp. 32–35 (2016)
15. Zhang, H., Qiu, B., Giles, C.L., Foley, H.C., Yen, J.: An LDA-based community structure discovery approach for large-scale social networks. In: ISI, p. 200 (2007)

3rd Workshop on Semantic Web for Cultural Heritage

IoT Semantic Interoperability
with Device Description Shapes

Aparna Saisree Thuluva[1,2(✉)], Darko Anicic[1(✉)], and Sebastian Rudolph[2(✉)]

[1] Siemens AG - Corporate Technology, Munich, Germany
{aparna.thuluva,darko.anicic}@siemens.com
[2] TU Dresden, Dresden, Germany
sebastian.rudolph@tu-dresden.de

Abstract. The Internet of Things (IoT) promises easy integration of connected physical devices at a large scale. Use of semantic technologies are widely acknowledged for this purpose as they enable devices to understand meaning of data being exchanged. W3C Web of Things (WoT) Working Group is standardizing Thing Description (TD) which is a machine-readable interface of a thing. Further on, iot.schema.org specifies semantics for capabilities of physical devices. Using these models it is possible to describe devices. However, they do not constrain semantics of IoT devices. For example, iot.schema.org provides one capability for a class of devices. Same-class devices, produced by different manufacturers, differ in certain feature or data they offer. In order to represent device variants we propose to extend iot.schema.org Capabilities with RDF Shapes. In our approach, TDs for device variants are automatically generated. It also enhances device discovery, semantic interoperability, validation of TDs and accelerates IoT application development.

1 Introduction

The Internet of Things (IoT) promises techniques which will enable integration of connected physical devices with less effort, and as a consequence this will enable new added-value services at a large scale [1,2]. The integration of two or more physical devices should not only happen at the level of data exchange but the devices should also understand the meaning of exchanged data. That is, instead of mere interoperability IoT devices are required to achieve semantic interoperability [3,4]. Only then, it would be possible for machines to discover devices relevant for an added-value service, and further to understand their capabilities, to integrate and process their data, and to ultimately create a new value.

The promise of IoT has not been delivered yet. The current focus in the IoT is merely to connect heterogeneous devices to a common IoT platform.[1,2] Once connected, devices are capable to exchange data. But semantics of data and capabilities of devices, which generate this data, are not described in a

---

[1] www.evrythng.com.
[2] www.xively.com.

© Springer Nature Switzerland AG 2018
A. Gangemi et al. (Eds.): ESWC 2018 Satellite Events, LNCS 11155, pp. 409–422, 2018.
https://doi.org/10.1007/978-3-319-98192-5_56

machine-interpretable form. What is generated by each IoT platform is essentially a data silo that yet needs to be integrated. This situation hinders the potential of IoT to enable added-value services at large scale.

In order to improve this, W3C Web of Things (WoT) Working Group[3] is developing a new standard which addresses the challenge of heterogeneous IoT platforms, communication protocols, and data formats. Among others, WoT Group proposes the so-called protocol binding to bring disparate IoT platforms and devices to the Web as a common application layer. Once connected to the Web, devices can be accessed and programmed with a standardized Application Programming Interface (API). However the most important aspect of the upcoming standard is provision of Thing Description[4] (TD). TD is a machine-readable description of an IoT thing (e.g., a physical device or virtual thing residing in a cloud). It abstracts an IoT thing in terms of its interactions and data it consumes or produces. Interactions, data and the thing itself may be marked-up with semantic terms from an ontology or a schema [5,6]. iot.schema.org is a community effort[5] which is developing exactly one such IoT schema to be used with TD. iot.schema.org abstracts the functionality of IoT devices via so-called Capabilities. Capability is a semantic model to formally describe traits of a class of physical devices (e.g., thermostat provides temperature data and it can be set to a target temperature). iot.schema.org exposes capabilities of an IoT device in order to simplify the development of an application. The schema is developed as an IoT extension to the widely-used schema.org.

WoT TD and Capabilities from iot.schema.org offer a solid basis to achieve IoT semantic interoperability. Semantics specified by an iot.schema.org Capability can be used to mark-up a TD. The TD is then used to generate a code-skeleton of the thing. This can be done, for example, with the WoT reference implementation. Once the code-skeleton has been implemented for device, it can be exposed as an IoT thing, i.e., accessible over a Web API and discoverable thanks to its TD. Such an IoT thing can also be easily integrated with other things since its capability, interactions, and data are all semantically described and machine interpretable. With WoT TD and iot.schema.org Capabilities in place we are capable of creating semantically described IoT things and realize them in an efficient manner. This is unfortunately not so easy in practice as an iot.schema.org Capability is always overspecified. It provides one Capability per class of devices. However in real-world there exists multiple device variants from different manufacturers in a class of devices.

1.1 Motivating Example

Consider a widely used industrial device such as a pump, whose functionality should be semantically described and exposed over an IoT API. For this purpose

---

[3] https://www.w3.org/WoT/WG/.

[4] https://www.w3.org/TR/2017/WD-wot-thing-description-20170914/#type-system-object.

[5] https://github.com/iot-schema-collab/iotschema.

one can use pump Capability[6] specified in iot.schema.org. It includes semantic description of pump interactions and their data such as *TurnOn, TurnOff, PumpStatus, PumpRunMode* (such as fixed speed mode, variable speed mode etc.), *FlowRate, Pressure, Temperature* and *PumpSpeed*. The Pump Capability can be used to semantically describe a pump and expose it as an IoT Thing. However not all pumps in the world implement all the interactions described in pump Capability. In the real world, pumps from different manufactures differ in certain feature or data they offer. Consider the following use case where there are two pump manufacturers. Manufacturer 1 produces pumps which can be operated in fixed speed operating mode. In this mode, the speed of a pump cannot be changed by a user. On the other hand manufacturer 2, produces pumps which can run in variable speed operating mode. In this mode, a user can set the speed of a pump by changing the pressure and flow rate of the pump. In such a case, the pump Capability of iot.schema.org should be tailored to fit the requirements of pumps from each manufacturer. This means, we should be able to shape iot.schema.org Capabilities to represent several device variants in a class of devices.

1.2   Contributions

In this work, we address the problem of creating tailored Thing Description templates for specific device variants from overspecified iot.schema.org Capabilities. The goal of this work is to extend semantics of iot.schema.org Capabilities in such a way that it enables specification of variants of Capabilities, and automate the generation of TD for so-extended device Capabilities. In particular, we propose to use RDF Shape languages [7–9] to specify constraints on Capabilities. Shape constraints help to adapt an iot.schema.org Capability to represent several device variants. We model the constraints in both Shape Constraint Languages (W3C SHACL) and Shape Expressions (ShEx). However, in this paper we will present the shapes created for pump use case in ShEx only. Shapes created in SHACL can be found online. After modeling the constraints as RDF shapes, TD templates can be generated from a Capability and its shapes. This is a very important extension to iot.schema.org and WoT TD as it is ensures rich semantic descriptions for IoT device variants, while keeping the overall process easy, e.g., with respect to automatically-generated TD, TD validation, and automatically-generated user interfaces for IoT things.

The main contributions of this paper are the following: (1) we describe a procedure to specify shape constraints on iot.schema.org Capabilities using ShEx [7–9] in Sect. 3; (2) in Sect. 4 we provide a mapping from SHACL to JSON Schema and, from ShEx to JSON Schema as TD uses JSON Schema [10] to model constraints on data consumed or produced by interactions; (3) we provide implementation of the tool to generate semantically enriched TD templates from an iot.schema.org Capability shapes in Sect. 5. In Sect. 6 we will discuss about

---

[6] https://github.com/aparnasai/iotschema/tree/iotschema-TDGenerator/Pump.
jsonld.

pros and cons of our approach and also present our lessons learned by using SHACL and ShEx for creating device variants. We conclude in Sect. 7 and present ideas for future work.

2   Background and Related Work

W3C Web of Things Working Group is developing a standard to create interoperability between physical things on the Web. For this, WoT Group is developing a protocol binding to enable interoperability between various protocols such as OCF, OPC-UA [11], BacNet [12] and so on. Apart from the protocol binding, WoT Group also proposes Thing Description, which is a platform independent description of a physical device. Thing Description describes a device in terms of its interactions such as *Properties*, *Events* and *Actions*. A Thing Description is serialized in JSON-LD [13] format. Further on, Thing Description uses JSON Schema [10] to model syntactical constraints on data. JSON Schema provides simple data types such as *integer*, *number*, *string*, *boolean* and complex data types such as *object*, *array* and *enumeration*.

In order to provide semantic discovery and interoperability between devices, Thing Description is supposed to be extended with external ontologies and schemas [5,6]. Many ontologies are developed for IoT. Domain-independent ontologies such as W3C Semantic Sensor Networks (SSN) [14], M3 [15] to model sensors, their observations and their domain. QUDT [16] to model physical quantities and Units of measurement. WGS84 [17] describes concepts to define spatial features of IoT things. IoT Ontology [18] which models IoT entity features required for their automated deployment. There also exists several domain ontologies such as SAREF[7] for Smart appliances, Brick [19] for Building Management Systems (BMS) domain. There exists eCl@ssOWL ontology [20] for industry domain and so on. A TD can be semantically enriched by marking up with the terms defined in these ontologies. More recently, community work on iot.schema.org (currently referred to as iotschema.org[8]) has started which provides lightweight RDFS semantics to expose capabilities of a device in order to simply IoT application development. iot.schema.org Capability model is aligned with WoT TD model [5]. In order to model domain features of a physical device, iot.schema.org normalizes semantics from existing standards such as OneM2M[9], OpenT2T[10], OCF[11], IPSO Objects[12]. Moreover, the semantics of Capability model can be further extended with existing IoT semantics. For example, Capability model can be extended with Feature of Interest model defined in W3C SSN/SOSA ontology.

---

[7] https://w3id.org/saref.

[8] http://iotschema.org/.

[9] http://www.onem2m.org/.

[10] https://github.com/openT2T/translators.

[11] https://oneiota.org/.

[12] https://github.com/IPSO-Alliance/pub/tree/master/reg.

RDF Shape Languages are used to define constraints on RDF graphs. These constraints can be used for purposes such as generating and validating RDF data, or generating user interfaces [9]. They bring closed-world assumption to RDF data and captures data in a predictable way [21]. This allows to safely process data being exchanged between programs, humans or IoT things. There are two RDF Data shape languages: SHACL and ShEx. Both SHACL and ShEx can be used to express constraints on RDF graphs. We model the constraints on iot.schema.org Capabilities in both languages and the implementation can be found in the following GitHub repository.[13]

3   RDF Constraints Modeling on iot.schema.org Capabilities

In this section, we will consider the pump use case presented in Sect. 1 and present the following: (1) an iot.schema.org Capability for a pump, (2) a procedure to model ShEx constraints on an iot.schema.org Capability to specify device variants of different manufacturers (e.g., pump specification for manufacturer 1 and manufacturer 2 in our use case). Shape constraints modeled in SHACL can be found in git repository mentioned above.

3.1   iot.schema.org Capability

An iot.schema.org Capability models a semantic description of a physical device in terms of its interaction patterns and their input and output data. Here we present an iot.schema.org Capability defined for a pump. This Capability is created referring to eCl@ss description of a centrifugal pump.[14] Due to space constraints, we present a part of the Capability in Listing 1.1. The complete specification of the pump Capability, its interaction patterns and data can be found in the GitHub repository mentioned above. Among others, the pump Capability provides the following interaction patterns (1) *TurnOn*, an action to turn on a pump; (2) *TurnOff*, an action to turn off a pump; (3) *PumpStatus*, a property to check the current status of a pump; (4) *PumpRunMode*, an action to set the operating mode of a pump to *FixedSpeed* or *VariableSpeed*. These interaction patterns are further described in terms of its input and/or output data as shown in Listing 1.2.

Data Description. The Data of an interaction pattern is well-defined in terms of the value type, allowed values for the data, units of measurement, minimum and maximum range of the data. Listing 1.2 shows the definition of data for each interaction pattern of the pump Capability. Let us consider *FlowRate* interaction pattern. It has input and output data called *FlowRateData* which is well-defined

---

[13] https://github.com/aparnasai/iotschema/tree/iotschema-TDGenerator.
[14] http://www.eclasscontent.com/index.php?id=36410108&version=10_1& language=en&action=det.

```
1   {      "@context" :  [{
2        "schema": "http://schema.org/",
3        "iot": "http://iotschema.org/"   }],
4        "@id" :  "iot:Pump",
5        "rdfs:subClassOf": { "@id": "iot:Capability" },
6        "rdfs:label": "Pump_Capability",
7        "iot:domain": {"@id": "iot:Industry"},
8        "iot:providesInteractionPattern": [{
9            "@id": "iot:TurnOn",
10           "@id": "iot:TurnOff",
11           "@id": "iot:PumpStatus",
12           "@id": "iot:PumpRunMode",
13           "@id": "iot:PumpSpeed",
14           "@id": "iot:Pressure",
15           "@id": "iot:FlowRate",
16           "@id": "iot:Temperature" }] }
```

Listing 1.1. Specification of iot.schema.org Pump Capability

```
1   {
2   "@context" :  [{
3   "schema": "http://schema.org/",
4   "iot": "http://iotschema.org/"  }],
5   "@graph": [{
6   "@id": "iot:FlowRate",
7   "iot:acceptsInputData": {
8   "@id": "iot:FlowRateData",
9   "rdfs:label": "FlowRate Data",
10  "rdfs:subClassOf": { "@id": "schema:PropertyValue" },
11  "schema:propertyType": { "@id": "schema:Float" },
12  "schema:unitCode": { "@id": "iot:FlowRateUnit" },
13  "schema:minValue": "schema:Float",
14  "schema:maxValue": "schema:Float"            },
15  "iot:providesOutputData": { "@id": "iot:FlowRateData" },
16  "rdfs:label": "FlowRate",
17  "rdfs:subClassOf": { "@id": "iot:Property" } },
18  {
19  "@id": "iot:TurnOn",
20  "rdfs:label": "Turn On",
21  "iot:acceptsInputData": { "@id": "schema:True" },
22  "rdfs:subClassOf": { "@id": "iot:Property" } }] }
```

Listing 1.2. Specification of Pump interaction patterns and data

in the capability. *FlowRateData* provides a value of type *float*. Minimum and maximum range for *FlowRate* of a pump can be specified in *float*. And also the unit of measurement for *FlowRate* such as *GallonsPerMinute*, *CubicMeterPerSecond*, *CubicYardPerMinute* etc.[15] can be specified for a pump using pump Capability model. Similarly, *PumpRunModeData* defines a set of pre-defined operating modes of a pump such as *FixedSpeedMode*, *VariableSpeedMode*. Data description for all interaction patterns of the pump Capability can be found in the GitHub repository.

In this manner an iot.schema.org Capability provides a well-defined semantic description for a class of physical devices. In the next section, we will describe a procedure to model constraints on an iot.schema.org Capability to model device variants.

3.2 Modeling of ShEx Constraints

Shape constraints on an iot.schema.org Capability are specified at two levels: (1) at the level of a Capability in order to constrain the interaction patterns supported a device variant, (2) at the level of data of an interaction pattern to specify constraints on complex data of an interaction pattern. Listing 1.3 shows a part of ShEx constraints modeled on the pump Capability. ShEx has several serialization formats such as ShExC, which is compact representation of ShEx Shapes. ShExJ is a JSON syntax, which serves as abstract syntax.[16] And ShExR is a RDF syntax generated from ShExJ. In Listing 1.3 shapes are defined in ShExC format. This shape represents the specification of pump features for manufacturer 2 in our use case. That is the pumps which can be operated in variable speed mode.

Constraints on Interaction Patterns. The pump Capability shown in Listing 1.1 defines that a physical device of type pump should implement all eight interactions as specified in the Capability. However, in the real world all the pumps may not provide all these eight interactions. Therefore, using shape constraints we can specify several variants of pumps by modeling constraints on interaction patterns. Listing 1.3 shows ShEx constraints modeled for this pump variant specified by manufacturer 2. Lines 4–11 in the listing present the constraints on interaction patterns. These lines show that a physical device, which implements this shape should implement only a subset of interaction patterns of a pump Capability such as *TurnOn*, *TurnOff*, *PumpStatus*, *PumpRunMode*, *FlowRate* and *Pressure*. Therefore, it represents a variation of pump. In the similar manner, another shape with a different set of interaction patterns can be defined on the pump Capability representing one more variation. Further on, data of the interaction patterns can also be constrained to represent a device variant.

---

[15] https://github.com/iot-schema-collab/iotschema/blob/master/unit.jsonld.
[16] https://shexspec.github.io/spec/#dfn-shexj.

```
1    prefix  schema:  <http://schema.org/>
2    prefix  sh:  <http://www.w3.org/ns/shacl#>
3    base  <http://iotschema.org/>
4    <Pump>
5      {:providesInteractionPattern  [  :TurnOn  ]  }
6      AND  {:providesInteractionPattern  [  :TurnOff  ]  }
7      AND  {:providesInteractionPattern  [  :PumpStatus  ]  }
8      AND  {:providesInteractionPattern  [  :PumpRunMode  ]  }
9      AND  {:providesInteractionPattern  [  :PumpSpeed  ]  }
10     AND  {:providesInteractionPattern  [  :FlowRate  ]  }
11     AND  {:providesInteractionPattern  [  :Pressure  ]  }
12     AND  {  :domain  [:Industry]  }
13   <PumpRunMode>
14   {  :acceptsInputData  [:VariableSpeedMode]   ;
15     :providesOutputData  [:VariableSpeedMode]  }
16   <FlowRate>
17   {  :acceptsInputData  [:FlowRateData]  ;
18     :providesOutputData  [:FlowRateData]  }
19   <FlowRateData>
20   {  schema:propertyType  xsd:float
21       MinInclusive  7.5  MaxInclusive  295.0;
22       schema:unitCode  :CubicMeterPerHour  }
```

Listing 1.3. Shape Expressions on iot.schema.org Pump Capability, Interaction patterns and Data

Constraints on Interaction Pattern's Data. Lines 14–15 and 19–22 in Listing 1.3 shows ShEx constraints on pump interaction patterns data. Constraints for *PumpRunModeData* are modeled in lines 14–15. It specifies that a pump from manufacturer 2 can be operated only in *VariableSpeedMode*. Further on, constraints on *FlowRateData* are also defined to represent pump specification from manufacturer 2. Lines 19–22 present this constraints. It specifies that a pump should be operated within the flow rate range 7.5 and 295.0. It further specifies that flow rate of the pump is measured in *CubicMeterPerHour* unit.

4   Mappings Between SHACL, ShEx and JSON Schema

Having a device variant model in place, our goal is to automate the generation of semantically enriched TD template for a device variant. In a TD constraints on interaction patterns data are modeled using JSON Schema [10]. Therefore in order to generate JSON Schema constraints from SHACL or ShEx constraints, we created a mapping from Shape constraint languages (SHACL and ShEx) to JSON Schema.

ShEx defines RDF shapes as Node constraints, Triple constraints and Shape expressions. On the other hand, SHACL defines two types of shapes such as node shapes and property shapes. Here, we will present different elements of ShEx, SHACL and a possible conversion to JSON Schema. The table in Fig. 1

Concept	SHACL	ShEx	JSON Schema
1. xsFacet: stringFacet	{ sh:datatype xsd:string sh:minLength X ; sh:maxLength Y ; sh:pattern '/regex/'; sh:flags xsd:string ? } **String Length:** { sh:datatype xsd:string sh:length X }	{ :valueType xsd:string MinLength X MaxLength Y pattern '/regex/'; sx:flags xsd:string ? } **String Length:** { :valueType xsd:string Length X }	"valueType": {"type": "string" "minLength": X, "maxLength": Y, "pattern": '/regex/' } **String Length:** "valueType": {"type": "string" "minLength": X, "maxLength": X }
2. xsFacet: Numeric Facet	**Data type:** { :valueType xsd:decimal } OR { :valueType xsd:float } OR { :valueType xsd:double } **MinInclusive & MaxInclusive:** { : valueType xsd:integer sh:minInclusive X sh:maxInclusive Y } **MinExclusive & MaxExclusive:** { : valueType xsd:double sh:minExclusive X sh:maxExclusive Y }	**Data type:** { :valueType xsd:decimal } OR { :valueType xsd:float } OR { :valueType xsd:double } **MinInclusive &** **MaxInclusive:** { : valueType xsd:integer MinInclusive X MaxInclusive Y TotalDigits N FractionDigits M } **MinInclusive &** **MaxExclusive:** { : valueType xsd:double MinExclusive X MaxExclusive Y }	**Data type:** "valueType": { "type": "number"} **MinInclusive & MaxInclusive:** "valueType": { "type": "integer", "minimum": X, "maximum": Y } **MinExclusive & MaxExclusive:** "valueType": { "type": "number", "exclusiveMinimum": M, "exclusiveMaximum": N }
3. Boolean	{:booleanLiteral "true"} {:booleanLiteral "false"}	{:booleanLiteral "true"} {:booleanLiteral "false"}	"booleanLiteral" : {"type" : "boolean"}
4. Value Set Enumeration	sh:path :value ; sh:in (:X :Y)	{:value [:X :Y]}	"value": { "type": "string", "enum" : ["X", "Y"] }
5. Cardinality Zero or More	{ sh:path :zeroUnbounded ; sh:datatype xsd:string }	{:zeroUnbounded xsd:string * }	"zeroUnbounded" : { "type" : "array", "items": { "type": "string" }, "minitems":0}
One or More	{ sh:path :oneUnbounded ; sh:datatype xsd:string ; sh:minCount 1 }	{:oneUnbounded xsd:string + }	"oneUnbounded" : { "type" : "array", "items": { "type": "string" }, "minitems" : 1}
Zero or one	{ sh:path : ZeroOrOne ; sh:datatype xsd:string ; sh:maxCount 1}	{:zeroOrOne xsd:string ? }	{ "type": "array", "items": { "type": "string" }, "minitems" : 0, "maxitems" : 1}
Exactly m repetitions	{ sh:path :mRepetitions ; sh:datatype xsd:string ; sh:minCount m ; sh:maxCount m }	{:mRepetitions xsd:string {m} }	"mRepetitions" : { "type" : "array", "items": { "type": "string" }, "minitems" : m, "maxitems" : m }
Between m and n repetitions	{ sh:path : mTonRepetitions ; sh:datatype xsd:string ; sh:minCount m ; sh:maxCount n }	{:mTonRepetitions xsd:string {m, n}}	"mTonRepetitions" : { "type" : "array", "items": { "type": "string" }, "minitems" : m, "maxitems" : n }
m or more repetitions	{ sh:path : mOrMoreRepetitions; sh:datatype xsd:string ; sh:minCount m }	{:mOrMoreRepetitions xsd:string {m, } }	"mOrMoreRepetitions" : { "type" : "array", "items": { "type": "string" }, "minitems" : m}
Exactly one	{ sh:path : mOrMoreRepetitions; sh:datatype xsd:string ; sh:minCount 1 ; sh:maxCount 1 }	**default cardinality** {:exactlyOne xsd:string }	"exactlyOne" : { "type" : "array", "items": { "type": "string" }, "minitems" : 1, "maxitems" : 1 }

6. Logical Constraints	**ShapeOr**
	sh:or (
	[sh:property [sh:path :X ;
	sh:datatype xsd:string]]
	[sh:property [sh:path :Y ;
	sh:datatype xsd:string]]).
	
	ShapeAnd:
	(a) When objects are shapes
	sh:and (
	[sh:property [sh:path
	:UserShape ;]]
	[sh:property [sh:path
	:IssueShape ;]]) .
	
	(b) When objects are not shapes
	< ShapeAnd> {
	{ :X xsd:string } AND
	{ :Y xsd:string }}
	
	ShapeNot
	: S a sh:NodeShape ;
	sh:not [
	sh:property [
	sh:path :p ;
	sh:class :S ;] ;].
		ShapeOr
		<OrShape> {
		{ :X xsd:string } OR
		{ :Y xsd:string }}
		
		ShapeAnd:
		(a) When objects are shapes
		<ShapeAnd> {
		{ :X @<UserShape> } AND
		{ :Y @<IssueShape> }}
		
		(b) When objects are not shapes
		< ShapeAnd> {
		{ :X xsd:string } AND
		{ :Y xsd:string }}
		
		ShapeNot
		:S {:p NOT @:S}
			anyOf
			{ "anyOf": [
			"properties": {
			"X": { "type": "string" },
			"Y": { "type": "integer" } }]}
			
			allOf
			{ "allOf": [
			"properties": {
			"X": { "$ref": "#/definitions/user" },
			"Y": { "$ref": "#/definitions/issue" } }
			]}
			
			object
			"shapeAnd": {
			"type": "object" {
			"properties": {
			"X": { "type": "string" },
			"Y": { "type": "string" } }
			"required" : ["X", "Y"] }}
			
			Not
			"S": {"not": { "p": "S" }}

7. OneOf	:User a sh:NodeShape ; sh:xone ([sh:property [sh:path :X; sh:datatype xsd:string;]] [sh:property [sh:path :Y ; sh:datatype xsd:string;]]).	<OneOfShape> { :X xsd:string | :Y xsd:string }	{ "oneOf": ["properties": { "X": { "type": "string" }, "Y": { "type": "integer" } }]}

8. EachOf	**(a) when objects are shapes**
	:User a sh:NodeShape ;
	sh:and (
	[sh:property :UserShape;]]
	[sh:property :IssueShape];]).
	(b) When objects are not shapes
	:User a sh:NodeShape ;
	sh:property [sh:path : X;
	sh:datatype xsd:string ;
	sh:minCount 1 ;]
	sh:property [sh:path :Y;
	sh:datatype xsd:string ;
	sh:minCount 1 ;].
		(a) when objects are shapes
		<EachOfShape>
		{ :X @<UserShape> }
		:Y @<IssueShape> }
		
		(b) When objects are not shapes
		<EachOfShape> {
		:X xsd:string ;
		:Y xsd:string }
			(a) when objects are shapes
			{ "allOf": [
			"properties": {
			"X": { "$ref": "#/definitions/user" },
			"Y": { "$ref": "#/definitions/issue" }
			}]}
			(b) When objects are not shapes
			"eachOfShape": {
			"type": "object"
			"properties": {
			"X": { "type": "string" },
			"Y": { "type": "integer" } }
			"required" : ["X", "Y"]
			}}

Fig. 1. Mapping between SHACL, ShEx and JSON Schema

shows this mapping. In the table all the examples use default prefix ":" for URIs. This default prefix can be replaced by other prefixes depending on the use case. ShEx and SHACL uses XML schema datatypes. In this examples we use *xsd* prefix for XML datatypes. Firstly, the table presents elements such as *xsFacet* (*StringFacet, NumericFacet*) and *ValueSet* and their conversion to JSON Schema. Inside each facet we also present the constraints that are applicable to it. For example, constraints such as *MinInclusive, MaxInclusive, MinExclusive, MaxExclusive, TotalDigits, FractionDigits* are presented in *NumericFacet* as they are applicable only to numeric RDF literals. In some cases, there is no JSON Schema equivalent for ShEx and SHACL. *TotalDigits, FractionDigits* in *NumericFacet* and *flags* in *StringFacet* are such examples. The ShEx and SHACL logical operator *And* can be converted to a JSON Schema *allOf* if the shape is combining more than one shapes as shown in row 6(a) of Fig. 1. Alternatively, *AND* can be converted to a JSON Schema *object*, if it combines more than one Triple constraints as shown in row 6(b) of Fig. 1. This mapping from SHACL to JSON Schema and ShEx to JSON Schema are implemented in the TD template generator.

5   Thing Description Template Generation

We developed two implementations of TD template generator in JavaScript. One implementation takes ShEx shapes on an iot.schema.org Capability as input and generates a semantically enriched TD template from it. The second implementation takes SHACL shapes on an iot.schema.org Capability as input and generates a semantically enriched TD template. The code for TD template generator is available online.[17]

The mappings from an iot.schema.org Capability shape to TD model are done at two levels. (1) mapping from iot.schema.org Capability model to WoT TD model [5]. This is a direct mapping as iot.schema.org Capability model is aligned with WoT TD model. This mapping generates semantically enriched interaction templates of a TD, (2) mapping from ShEx to JSON Schema and mapping from SHACL to JSON Schema. This mappings generates input and output data of an interaction pattern.

For ShEx implementation, the tool is built on top of shex.js, which is a JavaScript implementation of ShEx.[18] A Capability shape in ShEx compact format (ShExC) format is given as input to shex.js which verifies the shape and converts it into ShEx JSON format (ShExJ).[19] ShExJ file is given as input to the TD template generator tool. The tool recursively converts shape constraints on a Capability to TD format and gives as output a TD template with semantic markups from iot.schema.org Capability model. In case of SHACL implementation also the TD generator tool recursively converts SHACL shapes to semantically enriched TD template.

---

[17] https://github.com/aparnasai/iotschema/tree/iotschema-TDGenerator.

[18] https://github.com/shexSpec/shex.js.

[19] https://shexspec.github.io/spec/#shape-expressions-shexj.

```
1    {  "name":"Pump",
2       "@type":["Thing","Pump"],
3       "base":  "",
4       "interaction":[{
5        "name":"FlowRate",
6        "outputData":{
7         "type":"object",
8         "properties":{
9          "FlowRateData":{
10          "type":"number", "minimum":7.5, "maximum":295.0  },
11         "unit":"CubicMeterPerHour"  }},
12        "@type":["Property","FlowRate"],
13        "writable":false,
14        "link":[{"href":"  ","mediaType":"  "}]  }],
15       "Domain":["Industry"],
16       "@context":[
17        "https://w3c.github.io/wot/w3c-wot-td-context.jsonld",
18        "https://github.com/iot-schema-collab/iotschema/
19         iotschema-context.jsonld"]  }
```

Listing 1.4. Semantically enriched Pump Thing Description Template

We implemented and tested mappings from all types of ShEx and SHACL shapes to JSON Schema (as presented in the mapping table in previous section). The result is that the tool generates valid TD templates with semantic mark-ups. The resulting semantically enriched TD templates can be found in the GitHub repository. The TD template generated for our pump use case is shown in Listing 1.4.

A generated TD template should be instantiated with the attributes of a physical device. For example, *base* field should be filled by the *uri* where the thing can be accessed. *link* section of the interaction patterns should be filled with the *href* of the interaction, that is the link where an interaction can be accessed and the *mediaType* which indicates the format of data consumed or produced by an interaction. After filling this information, the template becomes a TD which can be validated using thingweb-playground tool.[20] Such a semantically marked-up TDs enhance discovery of devices and semantic interoperability between devices.

6   Discussion

The proposed approach presents a solution to a real-life engineering problem by automatically generating semantically-enriched device descriptions for specific IoT device variants. This approach is tested in W3C WoT Plugfest during the WoT meeting in March, 2018.[21] The results were very encouraging, Thing

---

[20] https://github.com/thingweb/thingweb-playground.

[21] https://github.com/w3c/wot/blob/master/plugfest/2018-prague/result-siemens. md.

Descriptions from various manufacturers were easily discoverable based on terms from iot.schema.org. The discovery process is important as it precedes the development of a new application. An efficient discovery significantly reduces the time required for application development. The work in this paper further simplifies the application development by automating the generation of semantically-enriched TDs. Moreover, it enables specification of variants of TDs to capture differences in physical devices of the same class. Shape Constraints are created based on well-defined semantic terms from iot.schema.org, rather than on strings (as it is the case in JSON).

iot.schema.org tend to overspecify capabilities of physical devices, as capabilities need to capture all possible features of one class of devices. On the other hand, it is desirable to be able to constrain such specification for devices that do not support all features. Before RDF Shape languages it was a challenge to constrain RDF graphs under the Open World Assumption of OWL. On the other hand, in IoT it is critical to restrict the interface of a device to exact requirements of the device (e.g., input/output data provided in certain range). Only then, interoperability with that device is possible. This is the reason why we propose RDF Shape languages to be used for constraining overspecified iot.schema.org Capabilities. Therefore, RDF Shape languages bring a closed-world assumption flavor to the interpretation of semantics of iot.schema.org Capabilities, which is important for building clients that interact with IoT devices.

The process of semantic mark-up of TDs is error-prone. By automating this process, we avoid these errors. Our approach is domain-independent. Device variants to iot.schema.org Capabilities from any domain can be created using our approach. The shape constraints act as constructors for TDs. We believe that this work is a good contribution to both iot.schema.org and W3C WoT communities, as it provides an engineering solution for a real-world problem, and it helps for the adoption of the technologies developed by these communities.

On the other hand, the limitation of this approach is that in some cases, there is no mapping from SHACL and ShEx to JSON Schema, which may lead to loss of information in generated TDs.

Our lessons learned from using RDF shape languages SHACL and ShEx are the following. We first implemented the approach in ShEx as it has very compact syntax and it is easy to parse. However ShEx validates a data graph in Turtle format only. On the other hand, a TD is serialized in JSON-LD format, therefore a semantically enriched TD cannot be validated against ShEx shapes on an iot.schema.org Capability. Moreover, default values for a property cannot be expressed in ShEx. Therefore, we extended our implementation to support SHACL. We modeled shapes on an iot.schema.org Capability in SHACL and implemented TD template generation using SHACL shapes. The advantages of using SHACL are: SHACL can validate a data graph serialized in Turtle or JSON-LD. Default values for a property can be expressed in SHACL. However, SHACL syntax is not very compact. On the whole, the implementation of both SHACL and ShEx should be improved for better usability.

7 Conclusions and Future Work

In summary we addressed the problem of modeling device variants in a class of physical devices and generating semantically enriched TDs for the device variants. For this purpose, we employed SHACL and ShEx RDF shape languages to model device variants. In order to generate TDs from SHACL and ShEx shapes we created a mapping from SHACL and ShEx to JSON Schema. We developed an algorithm to automatically generate semantically enriched TD templates from device variants. We discussed the pros and cons of our approach and also presented our lessons learned on using SHACL and ShEx for modeling constraints on RDF graphs. The future directions of the work are the following: (1) offer TD template generator as an online tool to simplify the usage of the tool and to evaluate the approach by getting user's feedback; (2) in the current work, we developed a top-down approach to generate semantically-enriched TDs from iot.schema.org Capabilities. In the future we will work on bottom-up approach to generate TDs marked-up with iot.schema.org semantics, from existing device descriptions from oneM2M, OCF, IPSO and so on.

References

1. Atzori, L., Iera, A., Morabito, G.: The Internet of Things: a survey. Comput. Netw. **54**(15), 2787–2805 (2010)
2. Aggarwal, C.C., Ashish, N., Sheth, A.: The Internet of Things: a survey from the data-centric perspective. In: Aggarwal, C. (ed.) Managing and Mining Sensor Data, pp. 383–428. Springer, Boston (2013). https://doi.org/10.1007/978-1-4614-6309-2_12
3. Miorandi, D., Sicari, S., De Pellegrini, F., Chlamtac, I.: Internet of Things: vision, applications and research challenges. Ad Hoc Netw. **10**(7), 1497–1516 (2012)
4. Barnaghi, P., Wang, W., Henson, C., Taylor, K.: Semantics for the Internet of Things: early progress and back to the future. Int. J. Semant. Web Inf. Syst. (IJSWIS) **8**(1), 1–21 (2012)
5. Serena, F., Poveda-Villalón, M., García-Castro, R.: Semantic discovery in the web of things. In: Garrigós, I., Wimmer, M. (eds.) ICWE 2017. LNCS, vol. 10544, pp. 19–31. Springer, Cham (2018). https://doi.org/10.1007/978-3-319-74433-9_2
6. Charpenay, V., Käbisch, S., Kosch, H.: Introducing thing descriptions and interactions: an ontology for the web of things. In: SR+ SWIT@ ISWC, pp. 55–66 (2016)
7. Knublauch, H., Ryman, A.: Shapes constraint language (SHACL). W3C Candidate Recommendation 11, p. 8 (2017)
8. Prud'hommeaux, E., Labra Gayo, J.E., Solbrig, H.: Shape expressions: an RDF validation and transformation language. In: Proceedings of the 10th International Conference on Semantic Systems, pp. 32–40. ACM (2014)
9. Gayo, J.E.L., Prud'Hommeaux, E., Boneva, I., Kontokostas, D.: Validating RDF data. Synth. Lect. Semant. Web Theory Technol. **7**(1), 1–328 (2017)
10. Wright, A.e.: JSON Schema: a media type for describing JSON documents (2016)
11. Mahnke, W., Leitner, S.H.: Introduction. In: OPC Unified Architecture, pp. 1–17. Springer, Heidelberg (2009). https://doi.org/10.1007/978-3-540-68899-0_1

12. Merz, H., Hansemann, T., Hübner, C.: Building Automation: Communication Systems with EIB/KNX, LON and BACnet. Springer, Heidelberg (2009). https://doi.org/10.1007/978-3-319-73223-7
13. World Wide Web Consortium, et al.: JSON-LD 1.0: a JSON-based serialization for linked data (2014)
14. Compton, M., et al.: The SSN ontology of the W3C semantic sensor network incubator group. Web Semant. Sci. Serv. Agents World Wide Web **17**, 25–32 (2012)
15. Gyrard, A., Bonnet, C., Boudaoud, K.: Enrich machine-to-machine data with semantic web technologies for cross-domain applications. In: 2014 IEEE World Forum on Internet of Things (WF-IoT), pp. 559–564. IEEE (2014)
16. Hodgson, R., Keller, P.J., Hodges, J., Spivak, J.: QUDT-quantities, units, dimensions and data types ontologies. USA, March 2014. http://qudt.org
17. Brickley, D.: Basic geo (WGS84 lat/long) vocabulary. Documento informal escrito en colaboración (2006)
18. Kotis, K., Katasonov, A.: An ontology for the automated deployment of applications in heterogeneous IoT environments. Semant. Web J. (SWJ) (2012)
19. Balaji, B., et al.: Brick: towards a unified metadata schema for buildings. In: Proceedings of the 3rd ACM International Conference on Systems for Energy-Efficient Built Environments, pp. 41–50. ACM (2016)
20. Hepp, M.: eClassOWL: a fully-fledged products and services ontology in OWL. In: Poster Proceedings of ISWC, Galway (2005)
21. Patel-Schneider, P.F.: Using description logics for RDF constraint checking and closed-world recognition. In: AAAI, pp. 247–253 (2015)

Exploring Linked Data for the Automatic Enrichment of Historical Archives

Gary Munnelly$^{(\boxtimes)}$, Harshvardhan J. Pandit, and Séamus Lawless

Adapt Centre, Trinity College Dublin, Dublin, Ireland
{gary.munnelly,harshvardhan.pandit,seamus.lawless}@adaptcentre.ie

Abstract. With the increasing scale of online cultural heritage collections, the efforts of manually adding annotations to their contents become a challenging and costly endeavour. Entity Linking is a process used to automatically apply such annotations to a text based collection, where the quality and coverage of the linking process is highly dependent on the knowledge base that informs it. In this paper, we present our ongoing efforts to annotate a corpus of 17th century Irish witness statements using Entity Linking methods that utilise Semantic Web techniques. We discuss problems faced in this process and attempts to remedy them.

Keywords: Entity linking · Ontology creation · Automatic enrichment

1 Introduction

The promise of Semantic Web [1] is an attractive one for any individual who is involved in cultural heritage research. It is a promise of powerful search, seamless integration and informed, reasoned decision making between the many siloed instances of data which prevail across domains. Unfortunately, before a collection can take advantage of the benefits gained by being a part of the Semantic Web, it must be annotated with a suitable vocabulary. This annotation process can be an expensive and challenging task for a number of reasons, not least of which is the time and labour cost of employing people to read and manually annotate the contents of the collection. Given the exponential effort of a manual annotation process, it is not surprising that there has been some interest in the effectiveness of applying automatic annotation tools to cultural heritage collections [2–4].

Of the variety of tools and methods that exist for extracting information from a collection, this paper focuses on those concerned with the problem of Entity Linking (EL) [5]. While EL has seen much research in recent years, the lack of suitable semantic web resources to inform the EL process is often a notable weakness which undermines efforts to apply EL methods to cultural heritage resources. To some extent we may accept this as an inevitable limitation due to the immense variety of cultural heritage collections that exist. It is improbable that we will ever have a single centralised source of information which covers all aspects of cultural heritage. However, as the scale of digitised cultural heritage collections grow (Europeana[1] alone currently curates more than 50 million

---

[1] https://www.europeana.eu/portal/en.

© Springer Nature Switzerland AG 2018
A. Gangemi et al. (Eds.): ESWC 2018 Satellite Events, LNCS 11155, pp. 423–433, 2018.
https://doi.org/10.1007/978-3-319-98192-5_57

different items and DPLA[2] hosts almost 21 million resources), it becomes increasingly worthwhile to consider how we might deal with these limitations for collections both great and small.

In this paper we present a discussion on the role of semantic web resources in the task of automatically enriching digitised cultural heritage collections using EL methods. Our discussion is motivated by ongoing efforts to annotate a collection of 17th century Irish witness statements so that they may be integrated as semantic web resources and avail of benefits such enrichment provides. We present some of the challenges faced and lessons learned in the course of this endeavour. We also describe a process by which we are attempting to construct a knowledge base for Entity Linking using record resolution methods. The contribution of this paper is to demonstrate and emphasise the importance of structure in Semantic Web resources. With due consideration it is possible to create new ontologies which may help to facilitate the EL process.

2   Related Work

2.1   Entity Linking

Entity Linking (EL) refers to a specific challenge in computer science whereby a series of unknown textual mentions of entities (commonly termed "surface forms") are provided as input to a disambiguation service. The service is tasked with mapping each of the surface forms to an unambiguous referent entity. To provide a concrete example, given the input sentence, "*I Henry Jones Doctor in Divinity in obedience to his majesties Commission...*" and a request to identify the entity "Henry Jones", an EL service might return a reference to the URI http://dbpedia.org/page/Henry_Jones_(bishop), identifying the subject of the reference as the 17th century Anglican Bishop, as opposed to the fictional character played by Séan Connery in the 1989 film "Indiana Jones and the Last Crusade".

In order to perform this mapping process, an EL system fundamentally requires two components:

1. a knowledge base that stores information about all the entities of which the system is aware, and
2. a referent selection method, which uses evidence extracted from the knowledge base and present in any prevailing information surrounding the surface form to arrive at a set of likely referents for each ambiguous mention.

Given an ambiguous set of mentions, the EL system retrieves from the knowledge base, a set of candidate referents to which an entity mention many be referring. This is usually based on some fuzzy retrieval method. A variety of heuristics are applied and the system eliminates candidate referents which are unlikely to be the subjects of the mentions. Eventually it arrives at a set of mappings from textual mentions to knowledge base URIs which unambiguously identifies the referents.

---

[2] https://dp.la/.

Numerous different methods and approaches to EL may be freely found in the literature [6–8]. Almost universally, these methods use some form of graph based measure as one of the heuristics in the referent selection process. After the candidates have been retrieved from the knowledge base, a graph derived from the relationships between the entities may be constructed. The nature of these relationships varies, but usually it is based on links between corresponding Wikipedia pages. If a strong network exists between a number of candidate referents, then there is a good chance that they are the correct disambiguation choice for the given set of mentions.

It is also common to augment the graph weights using contextual cues derived from the words surrounding an entity mention [8,9]. We note this because systems which consider this feature are based on the assumption that some contextual description of each entity exists in the knowledge base.

The structure and content of the knowledge base is crucial, not only for informing the disambiguation service that an entity exists, but also for providing information which helps the the disambiguation algorithm to distinguish good referents from poor referents. Many modern systems make use of DBpedia[3] [10] and YAGO[4] [11] for this task. These are a good choice for most problems due to the prevalence of links between entities and the long form descriptions of entities obtained from their corresponding Wikipedia articles. However, for cultural heritage collections it is often the case that the range of information contained in these Semantic Web resources are not complete enough to capture the variety of entities we see in cultural heritage collections.

EL systems have the potential to be extremely helpful when enriching cultural heritage collections with semantic data. These fully automated systems are capable of deducing suitable annotations for raw, flat, textual documents based on information that is fed to them via a knowledge base. It is easy to see how a suitably informed EL system might dramatically ease the process of semantically linking new cultural heritage artifacts as they are digitised.

Further discussion could be had surrounding the precise point in the digitisation process at which EL is applied. Are we linking metadata which has already been normalised by an expert, or is the system capable of dealing with the noisy, original, primary source content from which the digital artifact is derived? In the case of the latter, how does the system manage archaic references, evolving entities and other such anomalies present in the source collection?

2.2   Automatic Enrichment in Cultural Heritage

There have been a number of efforts to investigate the effectiveness of EL methods in the automatic enrichment of cultural heritage collections.

A Europeana led task force produced a series of reports in 2015 which document their experience with evaluating different cultural heritage enrichment

---

[3] http://wiki.dbpedia.org/.

[4] https://www.mpi-inf.mpg.de/departments/databases-and-information-systems/ research/yago-naga/yago/#c10444.

services and sourcing different descriptive vocabularies as targets for the annotation process. Their focus was on annotating metadata for digitised artifacts. The content of this metadata ranged from specific fields comprised of a single entity e.g. `dc:creator`, `dc:publisher` to more general, free-form data such as `dc:description`.

As part of the investigation, a comparative evaluation of seven cultural heritage EL services was conducted [12]. Each service used a different vocabulary for enrichment, however the investigators were able to normalise the annotations by exploiting the fact that many of them made reference to corresponding DBpedia and Geonames entities. Using an evaluation dataset that was developed based on a combination of automatic enrichment tools and manual human investigation the report showed that the accuracy of the targeted EL tools was extremely high for the chosen collections.

However, as a variety of previous studies have shown, while the accuracy of EL methods may be high, quite often only a very small percentage of entities contained in cultural heritage datasets may actually be linked with a referent. A recent study we performed on the 1641 depositions (see Sect. 3) showed that a human annotator could only identify referents for 33% of the people and locations in the depositions [13]. We would compare this to efforts by other scholars such as Agirre [14], who attempted to link Europeana artifacts to Wikipedia articles and discovered that only 22% of entities that he identified could be annotated in this manner. This is an important limitation of which we must be aware.

One aspect of the problem is simply that cultural heritage collections are so incredibly diverse, complicated and unique that finding a suitable Semantic Web resource with adequate coverage for all purposes is nigh impossible. This presents the question, how should we annotate a cultural heritage collection when an appropriate Semantic Web resource cannot be found? Moreover (and of particular importance to our own research) how should these new Semantic Web resources be structured in order to aid the automatic enrichment process?

Of particular note for this discussion is the work of Brando et al. [15] on the REDEN project which investigated methods of using multiple knowledge bases for disambiguation. This is an interesting approach which may help to fill the gaps in popular knowledge bases using the information contained in more tailored ones. In their experiments DBpedia was used in conjunction with the Bibliothèque Nationale de France (BnF) ontology on a collection of French literary works.

REDEN's candidate selection phase is based on a literal string comparison between the surface form and entities in the knowledge base. All candidates from all source ontologies are retrieved and a resolution step based on `owl:sameAs` and `skos:exactMatch` properties resolves duplicate mentions into a single reference. Once the candidates have been appropriately pruned, a degree centrality measure is used to select the referents.

REDEN demonstrated that developing EL methods which can avail of multiple knowledge bases may help with poor coverage, but this requires that it be possible to establish reliable, accurate mappings between ontologies. Indeed, this property also facilitated the evaluation conducted by the Europeana task force. This is an important consideration when developing new vocabularies for cultural heritage collections.

3   The 1641 Depositions

Our own research has focused on attempts to automatically annotate a collection of 17th century manuscripts using EL methods. This has been extremely challenging for a variety of reasons. However, we believe our experiences are a reasonably typical example of problems faced in this field.

The 1641 depositions are a collection of letters and witness statements taken from the people of Ireland during the 1641 Irish rebellion. The physical manuscripts are comprised of approximately 19,000 pages bound in 31 volumes. Ireland in 1641 was a tumultuous place, and while the accuracy of some of the witness statements may be questionable, the depositions provide an unparalleled window into this dark chapter in Irish history.

The depositions have been digitised, transcribed and annotated by a team of historical scholars who extracted references to people and locations, tagged depositions based on the nature of their contents, and preserved as much information about the physical manuscripts as possible including margin notes, original spelling etc. The resulting documents are stored in a combination of TEI annotated files and an SQL database. This data rich digital resource presents many interesting and exciting opportunities for computer scientists to begin experimenting with methods of analysing and extracting new information from this historical collection.

Working with the digital versions of the depositions comes with a number of challenges, not least of which is the inconsistent nature of the spelling and grammar used throughout. English was still a developing language in 1641, which means that a vast array of variant spellings for names and common words exist across the documents. The below extract from *The Deposition of Phillip Sergeant*[5] provides an example of these anomalies:

> *"And by those faire promises the said ffitzpatrick getting possession both of their persons & goodes, they there behoulding daily cruelties & murthers vpon other English and belike suspecting the like to be exercised against themselues, ~~desired~~ fled away secretly ~~o n to~~ to Mountrath"*

From the historians' work, we find that the depositions contain references to more than 60,000 people and 7,000 locations. The people in question range from individuals of great historical importance such as Sir Oliver Cromwell, Sir Phelim O'Neill, and King Charles I, to individual servants and common folk who were affected by the rebellion. Locations similarly range from cities such as Dublin which still flourish today, to small plots of land which have been lost either as their names changed or borders shifted.

---

[5] http://1641.tcd.ie/deposition.php?depID=815351r406.

We know that several of the entities extracted from the depositions are duplicates. However, the huge range in spelling variations and naming conventions makes it extremely difficult to determine which mentions of entities in the depositions might be references to the same person or place. Compounding this problem is the fact that the severity of textual noise means that standard NLP tools can struggle with simpler tasks such as sentence chunking or Named Entity Recognition. Performing reliable analysis based on the language of the depositions is, to say the least, difficult.

We are not the first to attempt to decipher the contents of the depositions using computational methods. The CULTURA project [16] developed and applied a range of tools to provide a personalised experience for individuals who are interested in exploring the collection. This project was extremely successful and produced a number of valuable utilities for working with collections of this nature. However, the depositions' content remains in its original SQL database, disconnected from the Semantic Web.

An earlier study conducted on a manually annotated subset of the depositions attempted to assess the feasibility of automatically enriching the collection using standard Entity Linking tools [13]. From this study it was shown that only 33% of entities in the annotated subset had a corresponding referent in DBpedia. It was also observed that, of the eight Entity Linkers evaluated, no single tool could satisfactorily annotate the test corpus. Individually some did show promise on specific aspects of the linking problem, but these were undermined by weaknesses elsewhere. For example, AGDISTIS [7] often correctly abstained from annotating where no referent existed in DBpedia. Yet when considering the accuracy of the systems on entities that should have been annotated, the highest performing system achieved an F1 score of only 0.33, indicating that EL systems are greatly challenged by the depositions.

To some extent, the problems faced by the EL systems can be ascribed to the knowledge base. First, it is clear that the coverage of DBpedia is not sufficient due to the vast proportion of entities in the gold standard which were given a NIL label. It is also worth investigating whether a more tailored knowledge base might improve the F1 score of annotation systems on entities which should have been annotated.

4   Identifying Candidate Knowledge Bases

When investigating Entity Linking for the depositions, we focus on people and places due to their perieved importance in the documents. For historians there are still a number of unanswered research questions about the motivations and influences behind the rebellion. A linked data solution may assist them when investigating these questions. However, modelling the depositions is extremely challenging for a number of reasons.

First, there is no true, definitive list of people and places on which to base the ontology. Ideally any ontology that we create would be populated with a set of distinct entities that can be found in the depositions. While there are resources which can help us to determine this set of entities (as discussed below), there is still noise present in these sources. Sometimes people are referred to by lineage rather than their actual name, e.g. "the heirs of Mr. Gale", or even by title e.g. "Bishop of Meath". Given these ambiguities, there is much risk of accidentally omitting or conflating entities when the ontology is being constructed.

Second, the inconsistent language of the depositions means that multiple variant spellings for people and places can be found throughout the collection. If a suitable ontology can be constructed to represent each entity, discovering all the possible variant names by which it may be referenced would be a monumental task. Sometimes these variations are minor spelling differences e.g. "Florence FitzPatrick" being referred to as "Fflorenc Ffitz Patrick", but some are more severe, such as the "Barony of Fassadinin" being referred to as the "Barrony of ffassa and Dyninge". Detecting such differences is difficult through an automated process and requires an expert to assess its correctness.

Third, if we are to construct this ontology with an eye to automatic enrichment, then the inclusion of links between entities and how to establish them is an important consideration. We could use familial connections, but we are not aware of any reliable sources which document these in a readily adoptable manner. On what basis then are we to establish relationships between our entities? Currently, there is no reliable way to specify that a relation is likely without stating it as a fact in an ontology.

We must also exercise some degree of caution in our attempts to annotate the depositions. If the intention is to assist scholars with their research, then the information conveyed by the proposed solution must be accurate. This can be a subtle problem. For example, if we consider the entity "the Pope", should this be used to describe the role of the head of the Catholic Church, or should it describe an individual who held that role? If we assume the latter, then we must be sure to refer to the correct pope for the source document, which involves additional knowledge that may not be readily available in the knowledge base. Pope Urban VIII held the position until 1644 when he passed away and was replaced by Pope Innocent X. Modelling evolving entities such as these is a common problem in the cultural heritage domain.

In spite of these challenges, resources do exist which can help us to generate lists of distinct entities. Three primary sources at our disposal are:

- The Down Survey: A complete national survey of land in Ireland after the rebellion. The survey was conducted in order to establish which lands should be forfeited as penalty for crimes during the rebellion.
- The Statute Staple: A record of transactions between individuals. The staple documents goods bought and sold, and provides information about debts owed between various parties before the rebellion
- The Books of Survey and Distribution: A list of properties held by various land owners. These documents were used to determine taxes based on land ownership.

These documents have been the subject of historical research for a number of years and were some of the major contributing sources for the Petty Maps project[6]. Notably, The Down Survey and The Books of Survey and Distribution provide lists of important land owners resident in Ireland during the 1641 rebellion, possibly providing a definitive list of both people and locations. Statute Staple may be used to reveal relationships between these entities. We believe that it is possible to structure this information such that an EL system may use it for automatic enrichment of Irish cultural heritage resources.

We also note that two secondary sources which may be helpful are the Oxford Dictionary of National Biography (ODNB)[7] and the Dictionary of Irish Biography (DIB)[8]. These resources are comprised of a number of biographies about significant figures in the history of the British Isles. These resources have the advantage that they are better structured than the primary sources identified above, but they are not as complete with respect to the entities that interest us. We have conducted a separate investigation into the construction of knowledge bases using these resources [17] as they present a different set of challenges to the three primary sources.

5   Resolving Entities Across Sources

Given the three primary sources described in Sect. 4, we have begun the process of constructing an ontology to model the entities present in the depositions. In order to facilitate EL methods, we are attempting to capture features that are commonly used by EL algorithms.

In the simplest terms, our objective is to construct a list of unique entities which are present in each of the records. Such a list would form the basis of a knowledge base by providing a set of entities which we expect to find in the depositions. Through further examination of the available sources e.g. Statute Staple, we may extract additional information about entities, such as relationships, providing more evidence which an EL system might use when investigating the content of a collection.

Effectively, this is a record resolution problem. We have a set of disparate records and our objective is to determine which records refer to the same individuals. The initial phase of this resolution was performed manually by a team of historians working with The Down Survey. The historians extracted two lists of unique landowners for the periods surrounding 1641 and 1670. They also extracted a list of townlands and parishes which were annotated with corresponding longitude and latitude coordinates. This provides a reliable foundation on which we can build our knowledge base, but the list is known to be incomplete. In particular, because the focus of the list of people is on landowners, many of the more common individuals in the depositions (servants, etc.) are not present.

---

[6] http://downsurvey.tcd.ie/index.html.

[7] http://www.oxforddnb.com.

[8] http://dib.cambridge.org/.

Given the historians' lists of landowners, we have attempted to identify instances of these entities in Statute Staple and The Books of Survey and Distribution. There is often little evidence available for this process beyond the name of an individual. We have found that the Fellegi-Sunter method of comparing records [18] is an effective means of filtering candidate resolutions to a manageable pool. However, ultimately, a manual check by a trained historian is required to select which record resolutions are valid.

Gradually this process yields a list of unique entities, a variety of surface forms by which they may be referenced and relationships which exist between the entities in question. Note that we are not necessarily concerned with the nature of a relationship from the perspective of EL. Most Entity Linking algorithms which use relationships between entities are only concerned with the binary presence or absence of a connection. For the purposes of transparency, we state that the relationships in our knowledge base are derived from financial records documenting debts between parties, but this information is not captured by the knowledge base we have created.

We have made use of the DBpedia and FOAF vocabularies to model the properties of individuals extracted thus far. The information available to us is reasonably simple and these vocabularies are adequate for capturing properties such as names of an individual. The DBpedia ontology's `dbo:related` property is used to capture relationships between entities.

The nature of the depositions themselves yields information about the lifespan of entities in our knowledge base. While we do not know the precise dates of birth and death for the entities extracted from the records, we do know that they were alive in 1641. This is analogous to the concept of "floruit", which is essentially a fuzzy time period during which an individual is known to have existed. The vocabularies chosen so far are not adequate for capturing this uncertainty. However, we have found that CIDOC-CRM's timespans allow us to express uncertainty around an individual's lifespan. Although not a typically feature of EL systems, capturing temporal information such as this makes it possible to quickly filter a knowledge base to a range of feasible referents for a given surface form given the period of the text from which it was extracted. Hence it is of benefit to capture some aspect of the temporal properties of entities in the depositions, however crude the representation may be.

This process of constructing a knowledge base is admittedly slow. What we have found is that the features we must extract in order to inform an EL system are reasonably simple – surface forms and relationships. Context vectors for an entity are also a common feature for many EL systems, but given the linguistic anomalies of the depositions this is unlikely to be a helpful property to capture. It is frustrating to observe in the case of the depositions that the knowledge we require exists in digital format. It is simply distributed across a number of disparate repositories. Constructing semantic resources which structure this data requires us to tackle record linkage problems before we can focus on the task of automatic enrichment. We are confident, however, that the resulting resource will be useful for EL, not only on the depositions, but on other cultural heritage archives for the British Isles.

6   Discussion

Performing automatic enrichment of cultural heritage collections is challenging for a variety of reasons. As evidenced by our own experience, and the documented experience of other researchers, finding knowledge bases with adequate coverage for a given cultural heritage resource is extremely difficult. While developing an entirely new ontology that does not reuse existing knowledge is a solution, if not done properly it can lead to inaccurate or incompatible knowledge representations that negate one of the greatest benefits of linked data i.e. connectivity among disparate collections. It is of far greater benefit to the community if these new vocabularies can be integrated with existing semantic web resources in a seamless fashion.

Due to the issue with well-known knowledge bases not covering a large percentage of the entities in specialised cultural heritage collections, it is likely that curators of such resources will need to develop their own ontologies in order to accurately represent the semantics of their data. While it is good to expand the web of knowledge with this new information, we suggest that due care be given to the structure of these resources and to how this structure may lend itself to informing automatic enrichment processes going forward. Methods such as REDEN may exploit `owl:sameAs` or similar relationships between a new ontology and more established ones in order to knit together various knowledge bases for the EL process. If automatic enrichment services can make use of the information in new linked data resources, then future annotation processes may be expedited as new collections are digitised and made available.

At present, the ontology we are constructing is disconnected from the greater semantic web. Our focus has been on the resolution of entities across the resources available to us. However, once this process is completed and important next step will be to associate entities in our knowledge base with their corresponding entities in more established knowledge bases such as Geonames or DBpedia.

Acknowledgements. The ADAPT Centre for Digital Content Technology is funded under the SFI Research Centres Programme (Grant 13/RC/2106) and is co-funded under the European Regional Development Fund.

References

1. Berners-Lee, T., Hendler, J., Lassila, O.: The semantic web. Sci. Am. **284**(5), 34–43 (2001)
2. Van Hooland, S., De Wilde, M., Verborgh, R., Steiner, T., Van de Walle, R.: Exploring entity recognition and disambiguation for cultural heritage collections. Digital Sch. Humanit. **30**(2), 262–279 (2015)
3. Wilde, M.: Improving retrieval of historical content with entity linking. In: Morzy, T., Valduriez, P., Bellatreche, L. (eds.) ADBIS 2015. CCIS, vol. 539, pp. 498–504. Springer, Cham (2015). https://doi.org/10.1007/978-3-319-23201-0_50

4. Stiller, J., Petras, V., Gäde, M., Isaac, A.: Automatic enrichments with controlled vocabularies in europeana: challenges and consequences. In: Ioannides, M., Magnenat-Thalmann, N., Fink, E., Žarnić, R., Yen, A.-Y., Quak, E. (eds.) EuroMed 2014. LNCS, vol. 8740, pp. 238–247. Springer, Cham (2014). https://doi.org/10.1007/978-3-319-13695-0_23

5. Shen, W., Wang, J., Han, J.: Entity linking with a knowledge base: issues, techniques, and solutions. IEEE Trans. Knowl. Data Eng. **27**(2), 443–460 (2015)

6. Ganea, O.E., Ganea, M., Lucchi, A., Eickhoff, C., Hofmann, T.: Probabilistic bag-of-hyperlinks model for entity linking. In: Proceedings of the 25th International Conference on World Wide Web, International World Wide Web Conferences Steering Committee, pp. 927–938 (2016)

7. Usbeck, R., et al.: AGDISTIS - graph-based disambiguation of named entities using linked data. In: Mika, P., et al. (eds.) ISWC 2014. LNCS, vol. 8796, pp. 457–471. Springer, Cham (2014). https://doi.org/10.1007/978-3-319-11964-9_29

8. Yosef, M.A., Hoffart, J., Bordino, I., Spaniol, M., Weikum, G.: AIDA: an online tool for accurate disambiguation of named entities in text and tables. Proc. VLDB Endowment **4**(12), 1450–1453 (2011)

9. Zwicklbauer, S., Seifert, C., Granitzer, M.: Robust and collective entity disambiguation through semantic embeddings. In: Proceedings of the 39th International ACM SIGIR Conference on Research and Development in Information Retrieval, SIGIR 2016, pp. 425–434. ACM, New York (2016)

10. Lehmann, J., Isele, R., Jakob, M., Jentzsch, A., Kontokostas, D., Mendes, P.N., Hellmann, S., Morsey, M., Van Kleef, P., Auer, S., et al.: DBpedia-a large-scale, multilingual knowledge base extracted from wikipedia. Semant. Web **6**(2), 167–195 (2015)

11. Suchanek, F.M., Kasneci, G., Weikum, G.: YAGO: a core of semantic knowledge. In: Proceedings of the 16th International Conference on World Wide Web, WWW 2007, pp. 697–706. ACM, New York (2007)

12. Manguinhas, H., et al.: Exploring comparative evaluation of semantic enrichment tools for cultural heritage metadata. In: Fuhr, N., Kovács, L., Risse, T., Nejdl, W. (eds.) TPDL 2016. LNCS, vol. 9819, pp. 266–278. Springer, Cham (2016). https://doi.org/10.1007/978-3-319-43997-6_21

13. Munnelly, G., Lawless, S.: Investigating entity linking in early English legal documents. In: ACM/IEEE Joint Conference on Digital Libraries (JCDL) (2018)

14. Agirre, E., Barrena, A., Lacalle, O.L.D., Soroa, A., Fern, S., Stevenson, M.: Matching cultural heritage items to wikipedia. In: LREC, pp. 1729–1735 (2012)

15. Brando, C., Frontini, F., Ganascia, J.G.: REDEN: named entity linking in digital literary editions using linked data sets. Complex Syst. Inform. Model. Q. **7**, 60–80 (2016)

16. Steiner, C.M., Agosti, M., Sweetnam, M.S., Hillemann, E.C., Orio, N., Ponchia, C., Hampson, C., Munnelly, G., Nussbaumer, A., Albert, D., et al.: Evaluating a digital humanities research environment: the CULTURA approach. Int. J. Digit. Libr. **15**(1), 53–70 (2014)

17. Munnelly, G., Lawless, S.: Constructing a knowledge base for entity linking on Irish cultural heritage collections. In: Proceedings of the 14th International Conference on Semantic Systems (in press)

18. DuVall, S.L., Kerber, R.A., Thomas, A.: Extending the fellegi-sunter probabilistic record linkage method for approximate field comparators. J. Biomed. Inform. **43**(1), 24–30 (2010)

4th Workshop on Managing the Evolution and Preservation of the Data Web

nlGis: A Use Case in Linked Historic Geodata

Wouter Beek[1](✉) and Richard Zijdeman[2,3](✉)

[1] Department of Computer Science, VU University Amsterdam,
Amsterdam, The Netherlands
w.g.j.beek@vu.nl

[2] International Institute for Social History (IISH), Amsterdam, The Netherlands
richard.zijdeman@iisg.nl

[3] Faculty of Social Sciences, University of Stirling, Stirling, UK

Abstract. While existing Linked Datasets provide detailed representations of Cultural Heritage objects, the locations where the objects originate from is often not accurately represented. Countries, municipalities, and excavation sites are commonly represented by geospatial points, and the fact that countries and municipalities change their geometry over time is not reflected in the data.

We present *nlGis*, a collection of existing geo-historic datasets that are now published as Linked Open Data. The datasets in *nlGis* contain detailed geographic information about historic regions, with an emphasis on the Netherlands. We describe the creation of this Linked Geodataset and how it can be used to enrich Cultural Heritage data. We also distill several 'lessons learned' that can guide future attempts at publishing detailed Linked Geodata in the Cultural Heritage domain.

Keywords: Geodata · Linked Data · Cultural Heritage
GeoSPARQL · GIS

1 Introduction

Linked Open Data (LOD) is a flexible data representation paradigm that combines the expressive graph-based RDF data model with a distributed publication approach. Because it is grounded in Knowledge Representation, Linked Data allows heterogeneous data sources to be described with semantic detail. Furthermore, instead of making wholesale copies of the data, detailed fragments of data can be retrieved from the source location where the data is curated and maintained.

Because of these properties, LOD is well-suited for the publication of datasets in the Cultural Heritage [4] and Humanities [6] domain. Indeed, an increasing number of Cultural Heritage datasets is being disseminated as Linked Open Data, and initiatives exist to increase the publication of Linked Open Datasets in the humanities even further [3].

© Springer Nature Switzerland AG 2018
A. Gangemi et al. (Eds.): ESWC 2018 Satellite Events, LNCS 11155, pp. 437–447, 2018.
https://doi.org/10.1007/978-3-319-98192-5_58

While existing Linked Datasets provide detailed representations of Cultural Heritage objects, the *locations* where these objects originate from, are often not accurately represented. Even when places are assigned unique identifiers, e.g., from GeoNames, they often do not provide detailed geographic information. At the same time, the geographic extent is one of the most important – if not *the* most important – aspect of a location. Finally, often the same identifier is used to denote the same location through time, even though the geographic extent of that location may have changed.

When we look at the state of the LOD Cloud, it is not so strange that geographic information in Linked Cultural Heritage Datasets is often of limited quality or detail. There are very few LOD resources readily available that provide such detailed historic geometries. In fact, even datasets that focus specifically on representing (historic) geographic locations, represent such locations with very little detail, almost exclusively resorting to singular points and/or very rough bounding boxes. Finally, not all datasets use standardized vocabularies in order to represent geographic information. This severely reduces interoperability, since it no longer allows geometric information to be meaningfully queried across datasets. At the same time, geographic knowledge forms an important component of the context of Cultural Heritage object, and the need for Geographic Information Systems (GIS) support in the humanities has been recognized [7].

This paper presents *nlGis*, a collection of existing geo-historic datasets that are now published as Linked Open Data. The datasets in *nlGis* contain detailed geographic information about historic regions, with an emphasis on the Netherlands. The datasets in *nlGis* allow, for instance, a historic event to be located in a municipality at the time at which the event occurred, even though the municipality may no longer exist, or may have changed its geographic extent over time. Since almost every cultural object is related to a geographic location, either for its creation, performance, or conception, the potential applicability for these Linked Geodatasets within the Cultural Heritage domain is enormous.

While, the datasets in *nlGis* only provide a first step towards the full coverage of geographic information in Linked Data, we believe that the here described approach can be used to inform the publication process for other (historic) geographic datasets in the LOD Cloud. We specifically identify the weaknesses of existing Linked Geographic Datasets, their lack of detail, lack of temporality, and the fact that they are often not standards-compliant. The three source datasets that serve as input for the *nlGis* dataset are very different from one another: syntactically, semantically, and topically. We have formulated recurring issues and observations as lessons learned for others to use.

The rest of this paper is structured as follows: the next section presents related work on historic Linked Geodata, as well as related work on Linked Geodata standardization. Section 3 describes our approach of creating, storing, and querying the *nlGis* datasets. To conclude, we formulate lessons learned in Sect. 4.

2   Related Work

Geographical depictions of past events and contexts are important for historical scholars. Knowles et al. [5] distinguish between three mainstream applications of GIS in the first decade of the 21st century: the study of the history of land use, the visualization of changing landscapes and urbanization, the construction of infrastructures that provide historical GIS data for others to visualize. Today, a fourth application called 'deep maps' can be added to this list. Deep maps are maps that connect multiple layers of information (e.g. photographs or people's experiences related to a specific location).

Instances of these four applications of GIS are not always disseminated in an optimal way. Products of historical GIS have been provided as images, as content inside viewer software (e.g. on a CD-ROM accompanying a book), or as downloads (ShapeFiles and tables) to be processed by special-purpose software such as QGIS[1]. The first two, images and interactive viewers, do not allow researchers to process or evaluate the data, whereas ShapeFiles and tables can only be easily linked if common vocabularies are applied. Moreover, web infrastructures are sometimes unable to disseminate data in the long run, as the historical GIS of Belgium[2]) sadly exemplifies.

While many Linked Datasets exist that include geographic information, such information is generally not very detailed. For example, the geographic region of France in today's DBpedia is the point at 2.35 longitude and 48.86 latitude. The historic dimensions of geographies of countries and places are even less well recorded. Even though geographic datasets have occupied a prominent position in different renditions of the LOD Cloud picture[3], even the most popular and comprehensive Linked Geodatasets, e.g., GeoNames, only contain simple point geometries. Even Linked Historic Datasets that focus on geographic information specifically are not very detailed and/or do not follow open standards, which makes them difficult to reuse.

2.1   Linked Geo-Historic Datasets

Portable Antiquities Scheme. The British Museum and National Museum Wales host the Portable Antiquities Scheme website, providing support for the registration of archaeological objects found (by the public) in England and Wales. It provides a database of more than one million objects and uses the Heritage Data vocabulary[4] to describe objects and periods. To communicate the positions of findings, it relies on the Ordnance Survey Linked Data, consisting of a Gazatteer, postcode centroids and administrative boundaries. Unfortunately, there is no temporal variation in the spatial descriptions. So while it is possible to query for a finding from a particular region and period, the geographical result would

---

[1] https://qgis.org.
[2] http://hisgis.be.
[3] http://lod-cloud.net/.
[4] http://heritagedata.org.

always be depicted using contemporary information. Moreover, entities such as rivers, roads and districts are not described by detailed shapes such as lines or polygons, but by points.

Nomisma. Nomisma[5] aims to provide a vocabulary of numismatic concepts. While not specifically engaged with describing locations, concepts such as `nmo:hasFindspot` are used to describe finding places of coins and hoards. Such spots are – especially in the case of archaeological excavations – unlikely to be mere points, yet they are represented as such in the data. The Nomisma documentation does highlight the possibility of describing such points as having an approximate value, exemplifying the use of "a single point in lieu of the boundaries of a region".

Periodo. Periodo[6] is an ontology published by the Institute of Museum and Library services, and focuses on transposing qualitative descriptions of time into Linked Data. It specifically raises awareness for time-specific descriptions of entities, in our case: changing boundaries. Unfortunately the ontology is geographically limited to `periodo:spatialCoverageDescription` in order to capture qualitative descriptions of geographical spaces and `dct:spatial` to link periods to locations in gazettteers.

Pleiades. Pleiades is an RDF dataset that describes ancient geographic places [8]. This is one of the few Linked Historic Datasets that contains polygon geometries of the locations it describes. Unfortunately, it does not use a standardized vocabulary. As a result, this dataset cannot be queried with GeoSPARQL, and standards-conforming Linked Data tools cannot recognized that it contains geodata. Finally, the polygons described by the Pleiades RDF are rough bounding boxes that consist of four coordinates.

2.2   Linked Geodata Standards

WGS84 Geo Positioning. The WGS84 Geo Positioning vocabulary was created in 2003 by the W3C Semantic Web Interest Group[7]. While this vocabulary only allows the description of 2D and 3D points in the WGS84 coordinate reference system, it is used by a large number of Linked Open Datasets today.

GeoSPARQL. GeoSPARQL [2] is an extension to the standard Semantic Web query language SPARQL, and has been standardized by the Open Geospatial Consortium (OGC)[8]. It contains a vocabulary for expressing topological relationships and functions (e.g., `geo:sfWithin`, `geof:sfEquals`), and the ability to represent various geometries (e.g., polygons, lines) in either the Well-Known

---

[5] http://nomisma.org.

[6] http://perio.do/technical-overview/#spatial-extent.

[7] https://www.w3.org/2003/01/geo/.

[8] http://www.opengeospatial.org/standards/geosparql.

Text (WKT) or the Geographic Markup Language (GML) format. By default, GeoSPARQL geometries use the WGS84 coordinate reference system, but allows other coordinate reference systems to be described on a per-geometry basis.

3   Approach

This section presents the approach taken in creating *nlGis*, describing the transformation from source datasets to RDF (Sect. 3.1), the representation of geographic properties (Sect. 3.2), and how the data is published online for other to reuse (Sect. 3.3).

3.1   Transformation to RDF

The source datasets that are used in *nlGis* are published as ESRI ShapeFiles, CSV tables, and GeoJSON. Since Open Source resources for parsing the proprietary ESRI ShapeFile format are limited, we first convert this format into the XML-based Geographic Markup Language (GML) using GDAL[9]. This means that we have a variety of input data formats that all have to be converted into RDF.

While many tools exist that aim to support the conversion from source data into RDF, such conversion tools come with non-trivial limitations that make them impractical to use. In the construction of *nlGis*, we have come across the following teo main limitations. Firstly, existing conversion tools are memory-based. This means that they load the entire source dataset into memory before performing the specified transformation. Since memory is the most costly hardware resource (at least ten times more expensive than disk), this induces an unnecessarily high cost for the transformation process. Moreover, the vast majority of data transformation tasks do not require the entire dataset. Instead, they can be formed at the level of individual statements (e.g., when converting a GeoJSON arrary of floating point values into a Well-Known Text literal), or at the level of individual records (e.g., when asserting a relationship between two geometries of the same object). Secondly, existing transformation tools do not support a wide enough variety of input formats. For the creation of *nlGis*, we already use XML, JSON, and CSV input formats. In the case of GeoJSON and GML, there are non-trivial extensions to the base languages – JSON and XML, respectively – that would ideally also be covered by transformation tools.

A full analysis of existing tools for data transformation, including a comparison of their respective benefits and shortcomings, is outside the scope of this paper. We therefore resort to custom scripts in order to create *nlGis*. While a process that is as open-ended as data transformation may in the end require a full programming language, we believe that the main contribution of transformation tools lies in the ability to describe a transformation process in a way that can be shared with others who are using the same tools. The benefit is not

---

[9] http://gdal.org.

necessarily ease of use or automation, but improved documentation and communication with others. RML[10] provides such a declarative representation format for expressing transformations, but RML tools do not yet meet the above stated requirements.

In addition to the datasets we transform, the Historic Dutch municipalities dataset[11] was already published as Linked Data. This has a tremendous benefit, since this dataset can be downloaded using the Follow Your Nose principle. According to this principle, it is possible to start at some online location within the dataset, and traverse the entire online graph in order to obtain all information.

3.2 Geographic Representation

In the conversion to RDF, we specifically want to focus on how geographic data is best represented. The two most popular vocabularies for representing geographic Linked Data are the WGS84 Geo Positioning vocabulary and GeoSPARQL (Sect. 2.2. We perform measurements on a very large (>650 K documents, >38B triples), but also somewhat outdated (late 2015), LOD Cloud scrape performed by the LOD Laundromat[12]. Unfortunately, there is not a more recent scrape of comparable size to perform a more up-to-date analysis on.

Within this scrape, the WGS84 Geo Positioning vocabulary is used in many more documents (11,235) than GeoSPARQL (47). Table 1 gives an overview of the use of the various properties. While individual longitude (`wgs85:long`) and individual latitude (`wgs84:lat`) are both asserted approximately 43M times in 11 K documents, there are 33,422 more assertions of the former. Since there are very few cases where asserting a longitude without a latitude makes sense, this may indicate a geo-specific data quality issue. While property `wgs84:lat_long` has modeling benefits over the use of individual longitude and latitude properties, it is almost never used (283 statements; 173 documents). The altitude property (`wgs84:alt`) is used relatively frequently (2.3 M triples; 9.8 K documents), especially given the fact that Linked Geodata is not often visualized on a map that is able to display altitude.

Even though GeoSPARQL is used in only 47 documents, these documents contain relatively many GeoSPARQL assertions. In fact, overall there are more GeoSPARQL (188 M) than WGS84 Geo Positioning (42 M) geometries, even though they appear in a relatively tiny amount of documents. Most GeoSPARQL geometries are points (165,875,711 statements, or 88%), 6% are polygons, and the remaining 6% are linestrings. All geometries are serialized in Well-Known Text (WKT), and none are serialized in GML. Notice that it is possible for `geo:asGML` to never be used, but still appear in one document: it appears in the GeoSPARQL vocabulary itself.

---

[10] http://rml.io.

[11] http://gemeentegeschiedenis.nl.

[12] http://lodlaundromat.org.

Table 1. Overview of the use of standardized vocabularies, based on the LOD Laundromat scrape. Usage is quantified in terms of (i) the number of documents and (ii) the number of triples, in which the respective properties appear.

Property	№ statements	№ documents
`wgs84:alt`	2,349,607	9,843
`wgs84:lat`	42,883,363	11,134
`wgs84:lat_long`	283	173
`wgs84:location`	14,688,561	117
`wgs84:long`	42,916,785	11,134
`geo:asGML`	0	1
`geo:asWKT`	188,427,329	50
`geo:hasGeometry`	28,366,268	7

Table 2. Statistical overview of the *nlGis* datasets.

Dataset	№ statements	Main concepts	№ geometries
CShapes	6,120	Countries, cities	510
Mint Authorities	6,987	Authorities, houses	950
Gemeentegeschiedenis	46,929	Municipalities, provinces	3,219
Total	60,036	Features, geometries	4,679

3.3   Data Publication

An overview of the *nlGis* datasets is given in Table 2. CShapes [9] encodes detailed historical maps of state boundaries and capital cities from the second World War onward. Countries are coded according to the Correlates of War and the Gleditsch & Ward state lists. The RDF version of CShapes contains information about 207 countries and 201 capital cities. The historic Dutch municipalities dataset[13] contains 1,679 historic municipalities, including the relationships between them, e.g., two or municipalities are often merged into one. The Mint Authorities of the Low Countries[14] contains the polygons of the major coin issuing authorities that existed in the Low Countries in the Middle Ages. Each authority is paired with begin and end dates. Starting from the twelfth century onward, most authorities are included, except for small authorities such as towns.

The *nlGis* datasets are stored on the Druid Linked Data platform[15], where the data can be browsed and queried online. Druid is developed within the CLARIAH project[16], and is hosted by the Royal Dutch Academy of Arts

---

[13] http://gemeentegeschiedenis.nl.
[14] https://datasets.socialhistory.org/dataverse/lowcountries_GIS.
[15] https://druid.datalegend.net/nlgis.
[16] https://clariah.nl.

and Sciences (KNAW). Datasets are stored using Header Dictionary Triples (HDT)[17], which allows them to be stored on disk rather that in memory (which incurs a relatively low hardware cost).

The writing of complex queries is an iterative process, in which inspection of the results for the previous query inform the (re)writing of the next query. For querying Linked Geodata, it is important to use a GeoSPARQL-compliant editor like GeoYASGUI [1] (Fig. 1).

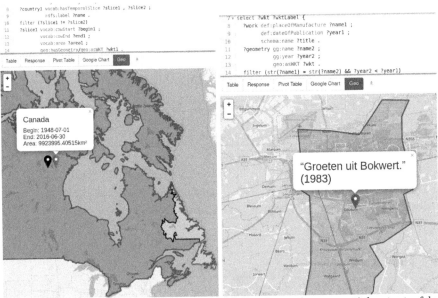

(a) Retrieves the change in Canada's geospatial extent: Newfoundland and Labrador were added to Canada in 1948.

(b) Retrieves the geospatial extent of locations in the Netherlands where cultural heritage objects are published.

Fig. 1. The results of two GeoSPARQL queries over *nlGis* data. Results are displayed in the GeoYASGUI result set viewer.

Figure 1a gives an example of how the data in *nlGis* can be used in practice. This example shows how the geospatial extent of Canada changes over time. Figure 1b shows how *nlGis* can be used to enrich Cultural Heritage data. This query is written over the knowledge graph of the International Institute for Social History (IISH), which records information about hundreds of thousands of cultural history objects. The geospatial extents from *nlGis* are queried through SPARQL federation, which allows data that is published in a distributed way to be integrated on a per query basis. In fact, this query specifically retrieves the geo-temporal extent that coincides with the date of publication of the particular cultural heritage object.

---

[17] http://www.rdfhdt.org/.

4   Lessons Learned and Conclusion

We conclude by identifying the main lessons we have learned during the creation, publication, and use of *nlGis*. The following lessons learned can be used in order to ease future publications of Linked Geodata in the Cultural Heritage domain:

Combine Components that Belong Together. Source data often stores components of values that conceptually belong together in separate properties. For example, CShapes stores the begin and end dates of geo-temporal extensions in one, two, or three properties (depending on their availability: the year, month, and day property). Another example is the separate storage of longitude and latitude properties that together represent a point geometry.

It is better, e.g., more fault tolerant, to represent values that conceptually belong together with one property. *nlGis* stores the begin and end dates of geo-temporal extents in one property, whose value is of type `xsd:gYear`, `xsd:gYearMonth`, or `xsd:date`, depending on how many date components are specified. No functionality is lost, since SPARQL contains functions that return the constituent components of dates (`year()`, `month()`, and `day()`). The longitude and latitude of a point geometry can are also stored together in *nlGis*, using one WKT literal. In some cases, combining longitude and latitude solves an important data quality issue: if a location has more than one point geometry, it is no longer clear which `wgs84:long` and `wgs84:lat` values belong together.

Do not use Ambiguous Default Values. Default values are very popular in non-RDF sources. Default values are most commonly represented by values that are (assumed to be) nonsensical within a certain context. For example, in CShapes the year -1 denotes the fact that a year is not known. This convention makes some sense in the context of CShapes, which only contains geographic locations after 1945. However, in Linked Data we cannot rely on such dataset-specific disambiguation assumptions. For example, the LOD Cloud may well contain geometries whose begin date is the year -1. This is why we try to detect and remove ambiguous default values within the transformation process. If a property has a default value in the source data, we simply do not generate a triple for that particular property in the RDF data.

No Perfect Tool for Data Transformation. It is not easy to find a data transformation tool that 'does the job' (see Sect. 3.1.

No Perfect Triple Store for GeoSPARQL. We tried out three production-grade triple stores that claim to support GeoSPARQL, but did not find one that is able to do so correctly and with good performance. Table 3 enumerates our findings in terms of (i) standards-compliance, (ii) correctness, and (iii) performance. As with data transformation tools, a detailed comparison of GeoSPARQL support in different triple stores is outside the scope of this paper. Even through GeoSPARQL support is not yet perfect, it certainly is usable, and the here mentioned three triple stores are specifically working on improving the support over time.

Table 3. Experience-based comparison of GeoSPARQL support in three production-grade triple stores.

Triple store	Standards-compliance	Correctness	Performance
Virtuoso	Uses custom relations and functions	Uses bounding boxes rather than the geometries themselves	Can be used interactively and/or to power an application
GraphDB	Compliant	Once a result is obtained it seems to be correct	Cannot be used interactively; many queries receive a timeout
Stardog	Only few functions are implemented; some are not part of GeoSPARQL	Could not test	Geographic queries with polygons do not terminate

Direct Geospatial Feedback. Use a SPARQL editor that is able to detect and display geospatial data for direct feedback.

Interoperable Representation. In order to make geospatial data interoperable with others, and directly useful in standards-compliant tools, it is best to use widely supported and standardized representations. There is no reason to the use the WGS84 Geo Positioning vocabulary anymore: WGS84 point geometries can also be expressed in the standardized GeoSPARQL vocabulary. In GeoSPARQL, use WKT in order to serialize geometries, since GML is (almost) never used (see Sect. 3.2).

References

1. Beek, W., Folmer, E., Rietvel, L., Walker, J.: GeoYASGUI: the GeoSPARQL query editor and result set visualizer. Int. Arch. Photogrammetry Remote Sens. Spat. Inf. Sci. **42**, 39–42 (2017)
2. Open Geospatial Consortium et al.: OGC GeoSPARQL-a geographic query language for RDF data (2012)
3. Hoekstra, R., Meroño-Peñuela, A., Rijpma, A., Zijdeman, R., Ashkpour, A., Dentler, K., Zandhuis, I., Rietveld, L.: The datalegend ecosystem for historical statistics. Science, Services and Agents on the World Wide Web, Web Semantics (2018)
4. Hyvönen, E.: Publishing and using cultural heritage linked data on the semantic web. Synth. Lect. Semant. Web Theory Technol. **2**(1), 1–159 (2012)
5. Knowles, A.K., Hillier, A.: Placing history: How maps, spatial data and GIS are changing historical scholarship. ESRI (2015)
6. Meroño-Peñuela, A., Ashkpour, A., Van Erp, M., Mandemakers, K., Breure, L., Scharnhorst, A., Schlobach, S., Van Harmelen, F.: Semantic technologies for historical research: a survey. Semant. Web **6**(6), 539–564 (2015)

7. Owens, J.B., et al.: Visualizing historical narratives: geographically-integrated history and dynamics GIS (2009)
8. Simon, R., Isaksen, L., Barker, E.T.E., de Soto Cañamares, P.: The Pleiades gazetteer and the Pelagios project. Placing Names: Enriching and Integrating Gazetteers (2015)
9. Weidmann, N.B., Kuse, D., Gleditsch, K.S.: The geography of the international system: the cshapes dataset. Int. Interact. **36**(1), 86–106 (2010)

2nd Semantic Web Solutions for Large-Scale Biomedical Data Analytics

Distributed RDF Archives Querying with Spark

Afef Bahri[1], Meriem Laajimi[2], and Nadia Yacoubi Ayadi[3(✉)]

[1] MIRACL Laboratory, University of Sfax, Sfax, Tunisia
afef.bahri@gmail.com
[2] High Institute of Management Tunis, Tunis, Tunisia
laajimimeriem@yahoo.fr
[3] RIADI Research Laboratory, ENSI, University of Manouba,
2010 Manouba, Tunisia
nadia.yacoubi.ayadi@gmail.com

Abstract. The prevalence of open data and the expansion of published information on the web have engendered a large scale of available RDF data. When dealing with the evolution of the published datasets, users may need to access to not only the actual version of a dataset but equally the previous ones and would like to track the evolution of data over time. To this direction, single-machine RDF archiving systems and Benchmarks have been proposed but do not scale well to query large RDF archives. Distributed data management systems present a promising direction for providing scalability and parallel processing of large volume of RDF data. In this paper, we study and compare commonly used RDF archiving techniques and querying strategies with the distributed computing platform Spark. We propose a formal mapping of versioning queries defined with SPARQL into SQL SPARK. We make a series of experimentation of these queries to study the effects of RDF archives partitioning and distribution.

Keywords: RDF archives · Distributed systems · Versioning queries
SPARQL · SPARK · SPARK SQL

1 Introduction

The Linked Data paradigm promotes the use of the RDF model to publish structured data on the Web. As a result, several datasets have emerged incorporating a huge number of RDF triples. The Linked Open Data cloud [3], as published in 22 August 2017 illustrates the important number of published datasets and their possible interconnections (1,184 datasets having 15,993 links). LODstats, a project constantly monitoring statistics reports 2,973 RDF datasets that incorporate approximately 149 billion triples. As a consequence, an emerging interest on what we call archiving of RDF datasets [5,9,15] has emerged raising several challenges that need to be addressed. Moreover, the emergent need for efficient

© Springer Nature Switzerland AG 2018
A. Gangemi et al. (Eds.): ESWC 2018 Satellite Events, LNCS 11155, pp. 451–465, 2018.
https://doi.org/10.1007/978-3-319-98192-5_59

web data archiving leads to recently developed Benchmarking RDF archiving systems such as BEAR (BEnchmark of RDF ARchives) [5] and EvoGen [9]. More recently, the EU H20205 HOBBIT[1] project is focusing the problem of Benchmarking Big Linked Data. A new Benchmark SPBv was developed with some preliminary experimental results [12].

Obviously, the fast increasing size of RDF datasets raises the need to treat the problem of RDF archiving as a Big data problem. Many efforts have been done to processes RDF data with distributed framework (MapReduce, Hadoop and Spark) [1]. Nevertheless, no works have been realized for managing RDF archives on top of cluster computing engine. The problem is more challenging here as distributed framework are not designed for RDF processing nor for evolution management. Distributed data management systems present a promising direction for providing scalability and parallel processing of large volume of RDF data. The development of distributed RDF system is based on the following key principles: (i) the input data is partitioned across multiple nodes such that each node is responsible of a distinct set of triples, (ii) Answering queries typically involve processing of local data at each node with data exchange among nodes. Theses two principles are closely connected as the way we answer a query depends on the way the data is partitioned. Equally, the efficiency of a partitioning strategy depends on the shape of used query. For example, subject-based hash partitioning is efficient with Star-pattern queries while its efficiency drops significantly with more complex query shapes.

Beside the subject, object and property attributes used in RDF, the partitioning of RDF archives has to take into consideration the timestamp/attribute indicating to which version it belongs. How can we partition the data in order to efficiently respond to time-traversing, single version or cross-version queries. Equally, we have to take into consideration the archiving strategy to be used [5,11,15]: Independent Copies, Change-Based and Temporal strategies. The first one is a naive approach since it manages each version of a dataset as an isolated one. While the use of deltas reduces space storage, the computation of full version on-the-fly may cause overhead at query time. Using a distributed framework would give advantage to the Independent Copies approach as delta-based approach may induce the computing of one or more versions on the fly.

In this paper, we use the in-memory cluster computing framework SPARK for managing and querying RDF data archive. We study and compare commonly used RDF archiving techniques and querying strategies. We propose a formal mapping of versioning queries defined with SPARQL into SQL SPARK. Evaluation was performed in cloud environment 'Amazon Web services' using EMR (Elastic Map reduce) as a platform. Commonly used versioning queries are implemented with detailed experimentation.

The paper is organized as follows. Section 2 presents existing approaches for the design and evaluation of RDF archiving and versioning systems. Section 3 presents our approach for managing and querying RDF dataset archives with SPARK. A mapping of SPARQL into SPARK SQL an5d a discussion of the cost

---

of versionning RDF queries are presented in Sect. 4. Finally, an evaluation of RDF versioning queries is presented in Sect. 5.

2   Related Works

Over the last decade, the published data is continuously growing leading to the explosion of the data on the Web and the associated Linked Open Data (LOD) in various domains. This evolution naturally happens without pre-defined policy hence the need to track data changes and thus the requirement to build their own infrastructures in order to preserve and query data over time. RDF archiving systems are not only used to store and provide access to different versions, but should allow different types of queries [5,11,15]. We note version materialization which is a basic query where a full version is retrieved. Delta materialization which is a type of query performed on two versions to detect changes occurring at a given moment. Single and cross-version are SPARQL queries performed respectively on a single or different versions.

The emergent need for efficient web data archiving leads to recently developed Benchmarking RDF archiving systems such as BEAR (BEnchmark of RDF ARchives) [5,6] EvoGen [9] and SPBv [12]. The authors of the BEAR system propose a theoretical formalization of an RDF archive and conceive a benchmark focusing on a set of general and abstract queries with respect to the different categories of queries as defined before. More recently, the EU H2020 HOBBIT project is focusing on the problem of Benchmarking Big Linked Data. In this context, EvoGen is proposed as a configurable and adaptive data and query load generator [9]. EvoGen extends the LUBM ontology and is configurable in terms of archiving strategies and the number of versions or changes. Recently, new Benchmark SPBv was developed with some preliminary experimental results [12]. Similar to EvoGen, SPBv proposes a configurable and adaptive data and query load generator.

Moreover, these archiving systems and Benchmarks adopt different versionning approaches: (a) Independent Copies (IC), (b) Change Based copies (CB) or Deltas and (c) Timestamp-based approaches (TB) [5,11]. We talk about hybrid approaches when the above techniques are combined [15]. The IC approach manages each version of a dataset as an isolated one while the CB approach stores only the changes that should be kept between versions also known as delta. The advantage beyond the use of IC or CB approaches depends on the ratio of changes occurring between consecutive versions. If only few changes are kept, CB approach reduces space overhead compared to the IC one. Nevertheless, if frequent changes are made between consecutive versions, IC approach becomes more storage-efficient than CB. Equally, the computation of full version on-the-fly with CB approach may cause overhead at query time. To resolve this issue, authors in [15] propose hybrid archiving policies to take advantage of both the IC and CB approaches. In fact, a cost model is conceived to determine what to materialize at a given time: a version or a delta.

Many efforts have been done to process RDF linked data with existing Big data processing infrastructure (MapReduce, Hadoop or Spark) [10,14]. An RDF

dataset is stored in one or more files in HDFS and the input dataset is partitioned among nodes such as each node is responsible of its own set of triples
[1]. Using MapReduce, for example, a SPARQL query is executed as a sequence
of iterations - an iteration for each subquery. The final result is obtained by
joining the results obtained in each iteration. The main challenge in developing
distributed RDF systems is how to adequately partition the RDF data in a way
that minimize the number of intermediate result transfers between nodes.

Hash based partitioning is considered as the foundation of parallel processing in database community and it has been applied in several RDF systems
[1,2,10]. Subject hash partitioning has proven its efficiency with queries having
only subject-subject joins (Star query pattern) [2,10]. In fact, triple patterns
having the same subject are stored in the same node and no transfer is needed
between nodes [10]. Nevertheless, the efficiency of subject hash partitioning drops
significantly with queries requiring object-subject/object-object joins. To overcome this problem, a cost based query model is proposed in [10] to reduce the
number of transfer between nodes. CliqueSquare [7] partitions each triple pattern
on the subject, predicate and object. Vertical/relational partitioning is adopted
in [14]. Based on a pre-evaluation of the data, many RDF triple patterns are used
to partition the data into partition tables (a partition for each triple pattern)
[14]. That is, a triple query pattern can be retrieved by only accessing the partition table that bounds the query leading to a reduction of the execution time.

3   RDF Dataset Archiving on Apache Spark

In this section, we present the main features of Apache SPARK cluster computing
framework. We show how we can use it for a distributed storage of RDF datasets
with Independent Copies and Change-based Approaches.

3.1   Apache Spark

Apache Spark [17] is a main-memory extension of the MapReduce model for
parallel computing that brings improvements through the data-sharing abstraction called Resilient Distributed Dataset (RDD) [16] and Data frames offering a
subset of relational operators (*project*, *join* and *filter*) not supported in Hadoop.

Spark also offers two higher-level data accessing models, an API for graphs
and graph-parallel computation called GraphX [8] and Spark SQL, a Spark module for processing semi-structured data. As the RDF data model is interpreted
as a graph and processing SPARQL can be seen as a subgraph query pattern
matching, GraphX seems to offer a natural way for querying RDF data [13].
Nevertheless, GraphX is optimized to distribute the workload of highly-parallel
graph algorithms, such as PageRank, that are performed on the whole graph.
However, this process is not adapted for querying RDF datasets where queries
define a small subgraph pattern leading to highly unbalanced workloads [10,13].

3.2   RDF Dataset Storage and Change Detection

SPARK SQL offers the users the possibility to extract data from heterogeneous data sources and can automatically infer their schema and data types from the language type system (e.g. Scala, Java or Python). In our approach, we use SPARK SQL for querying and managing the evolution of RDF datasets. An RDF dataset stored in HDFS or as a table in Hive or any external database system is mapped into a SPARK dataframes (equivalent to tables in a relational database) with columns corresponding respectively to the subject, property, object, named graph and eventually a tag of the corresponding version.

In order to obtain a view of a dataframe named "table", for example, we execute the following SPARK SQL query:

SELECT * FROM table

Figure 1 shows a view of a SPARK dataframe containing two triples patterns and the values of their attributes in two versions V_1 and V_2.

IRI	Subject	Predicate	Object	Version
g1	toto	hasJob	analyst	v1
g2	mimi	hasJob	develop	v1
g1	toto	hasJob	dataSc	v2
g3	mimi	hasJob	develop	v2

Fig. 1. Example of a dataframe with RDF dataset attributes.

When we want to materialize a given version, V_1 for example, the following SPARK SQL query is used:

SELECT Subject,Object,Predicate FROM table WHERE version ='V$_1$'

Another advantage beyond the use of SPARK SQL for the RDF dataset archiving is the scalability of RDF change detection issue. Many approaches implement change detection algorithms on the MapReduce framework [2]. Using SQL SPARK, we can easily detect the change between two different versions by executing a simple SQL SPARK query:

SELECT Subject,Predicate,Object FROM table WHERE Version='V$_i$'
MINUS
SELECT Subject,Predicate,Object FROM table WHERE Version='V$_j$'

3.3   RDF Dataset Partitioning

In this section, we present the principle that we adopt for the partitioning of RDF dataset archives for efficiently executing single version and cross-versions queries (Fig. 2). Concerning version and delta materialization queries, all the data (version or delta) will be loaded and no partition is needed.

- First of all, we load RDF datasets in a N-triple format from HDFS as input.
- Then, a mapping is realized from RDF files into dataframes with corresponding columns: subject, object, predicate and a tag of the version.
- We adopt a hash partitioning by RDF subject for each version.
- The SPARK SQL engine processes and the query result is returned.

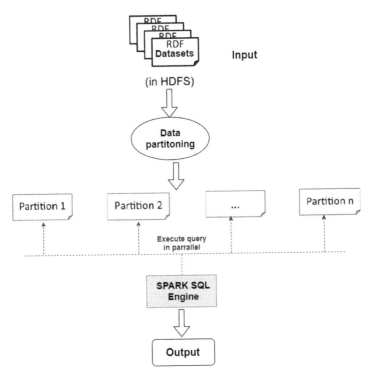

Fig. 2. Query execution with data partition of single version and cross-version queries.

4   Querying RDF Dataset Archives with SPARK SQL

SPARK SQL [4] is a Spark module that performs relational operations via a DataFrame API offering users the advantage of relational processing, namely declarative queries and optimized storage. SPARK SQL supports relational processing both on native RDDs or on external data sources using any of the programming language supported by Spark, e.g., Java, Scala or Python [4]. SPARK SQL can automatically infer their schema and data types from the language type system. SPARK SQL is used in [10,14] for querying large RDF datasets where a query compiler from SPARQL to SPARK SQL is provided. That is, a FILTER expression can be mapped into a condition in Spark SQL while UNION,

OFFSET, LIMIT, ORDER BY and DISTINCT are mapped into their equivalent clauses in the SPARK SQL syntax. Theses mapping rules are used without considering SPARQL query shapes.

In this section, we define basic RDF archiving queries (version/delta materialization, single/cross version query) with SPARK SQL. We propose then a formal mapping of SPARQL into SPARK SQL based on SPARQL query shape patterns.

4.1 Querying RDF Dataset Archives with SPARK SQL

Using SPARK SQL, we can define RDF dataset archiving queries as follows:

- **Version materialization:** $Mat(V_i)$.

  SELECT Subject,Object,Predicate FROM table WHERE Version ='Vi'

- **Delta materialization:** $Delta(V_i, V_j)$.

  SELECT Subject,Predicate,Object FROM table WHERE Version='Vi'
  MINUS
  SELECT Subject,Predicate,Object FROM table WHERE Version='Vj'
  UNION
  SELECT Subject,Predicate,Object FROM table WHERE Version='Vj'
  MINUS
  SELECT Subject,Predicate,Object FROM table WHERE Version='Vi'

- **Single-version query:** $[[Q]]_{V_i}$. We suppose here a simple query Q which asks for all the subject in the RDF dataset.

  SELECT Subject FROM table WHERE Version=Vi

- **Cross-version structured query:** $Join(Q_1, V_i, Q_2, V_j)$. What we need here is a join between the two query results. We define two dataframe $table_i$ and $table_j$ containing respectively the version V_i and V_j. The cross-version query is defined as follows:

  SELECT * FROM df_i
  INNER JOIN df_j
  ON df_i.Subject = df_j.Subject

We note that, for more clarity, we have supposed in this section the use of simple single-version and cross-version queries. Nevertheless, in real world applications, complex SPARQL query are used and a mapping from SPARQL query to SPARK SQL is needed.

4.2   From SPARQL to SPARK SQL

SPARQL graph pattern can have different shapes which can influence query performance. Depending on the position of variables in the triple patterns, SPARQL query pattern may be classified into three shapes:

1. Star pattern: this query pattern is commonly used in SPARQL. A star pattern has diameter (longest path in a pattern) one and is characterized by a subject-subject joins between triple patterns.
2. Chain pattern: this query pattern is characterized by object-subject (or subject-object) joins. The diameter of this query corresponds to the number of triple patterns.
3. Snowflake pattern: this query pattern results from the combination of many star patterns connected by short paths.

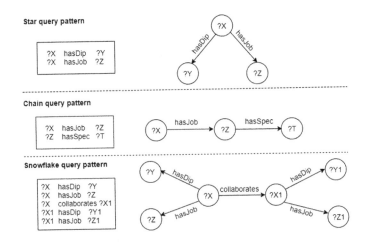

Fig. 3. SPARQL graph pattern shapes.

When we query RDF dataset archives, we have to deal with SPARQL query shapes only in single version and cross-version queries. We propose in the following a mapping from SPARQL to SPARK SQL based on query shapes (Fig. 3):

– Star pattern: a Star SPARQL query with n triple patterns P_i is mapped into a SPARK SQL query with n-1 joins on the subject attribute. If we consider a SPARQL query with two triple patterns P_1 and P_2 of the form $(?x_1,p_1,?y_1)$ and $(?x_1,p_2,?z_2)$, the dataframes df_1 and df_2 corresponding respectively to the query patterns P_1 and P_2 are defined with SPARK SQL as follows:

df_1= "SELECT Subject, Object FROM table
WHERE Predicate = 'p₁'"
df_2= "SELECT Subject, Object FROM table
WHERE Predicate = 'p₂'"

For example, given a SPARQL query pattern (?X, hasDip ?Y, ?X hasJob ?Z), we need to create two dataframes df_1 and df_2 as follows:

> df_1= "SELECT Subject, Object FROM table
> WHERE Predicate = 'hasDip'"
> df_2= "SELECT Subject, Object FROM table
> WHERE Predicate = 'hasJob'"

We give in the following the obtained SPARK SQL query:

> SELECT * FROM df_1
> INNER JOIN
> df_2 ON df_1.Subject = df_2.Subject

- Chain pattern: a chain SPARQL query with n triple patterns t_i is mapped into a SPARK SQL query with n-1 joins object-subject (or subject-object):

$$join(join(join(join(df_1, df_2), df_3), df_4), ..., df_n)$$

If we consider a SPARQL query with two triple patterns P_1 and P_2 of the form (?x$_1$,p$_1$,?z$_1$) and (?z$_1$,p$_2$,?t$_2$), the dataframes df_1 and df_2 corresponding respectively to the query patterns P_1 and P_2 are defined with SPARK SQL as follows:

> df_1= "SELECT Subject, Object FROM table
> WHERE Predicate = 'p$_1$'"
> df_2= "SELECT Subject, Object FROM table
> WHERE Predicate = 'p$_2$'"

For example, given a SPARQL query with two triples (?X, hasJob ?Z, ?Z hasSpec ?Z), we need to create a dataframe for each triple:

> df_1= "SELECT Subject, Object FROM table
> WHERE Predicate = 'hasJob'"
> df_2= "SELECT Subject, Object FROM table
> WHERE Predicate = 'hasSpec'"

The query result is obtained as a join between dataframes df_1 and df_2:

> SELECT * FROM df_1
> INNER JOIN
> df_2 ON df_1.Object = df_2.Subject

- Snowflake pattern: the rewritten of snowflake queries follows the same principle and may need more join operations depending equally on the number of triples used in the query.

For single version query $[[Q]]_{V_i}$, we need to add a condition on the version for which we want to execute the query Q. Nevertheless, the problem becomes more complex for cross-version join query $Join(Q_1, V_i, Q_2, V_j)$ as other join operations are needed between different versions of the dataset. Two cases may occur:

1. Cross-version query $type_1$: this type of cross-version queries concerns the case where we have one query Q on two or more different versions. For example, to follow the evolution of a given person career, we need to execute (?x,hasJob,?z) on different versions. Given a query Q and n versions, we denote $T_1,...,T_n$ the results obtained by executing Q on versions $V_1,...,V_n$ respectively. The final result is obtained by realizing the union of the T_i. What we can conclude here is that the number of versions does not increase the number of joins which only depends on the shape of the query. Given a SPARQL query with a triple pattern P of the form $(?x_1,p,?y_1)$ defined on different versions V_1 and V_2, the SPARK SQL query is defined as follows:

> SELECT Subject, Object FROM table
> WHERE Predicate = 'p' and Version = 'V_1'
> UNION
> SELECT Subject, Object FROM table
> WHERE Predicate = 'p' and Version = 'V_2'

2. Cross-version query $type_2$: the second case occurs when we have two or more different queries $Q_1, Q_2,...,Q_m$ on different versions. For example, we may need to know if the diploma of a person $?x$ has any equivalence in RDF dataset archive:

> Q_1 :?x hasDip ?y on version V_1
> Q_2 :?y hasEqui ?z on versions $V_2, ..., V_n$

Given a SPARQL patterns P_1 and P_2 of the form $(?x_1,p_1,?z_1)$ and $(?z_1,p_2,?t_2)$ defined on different versions V_1 and V_2, the dataframes df_1 and df_2 corresponding respectively to the query patterns P_1 and P_2 are defined with SPARK SQL as follows:

> df_1= "SELECT Subject, Object FROM table
> WHERE Predicate = 'p_1' and Version = 'V_1'
> df_2= "SELECT Subject, Object FROM table
> WHERE Predicate = 'p_2' Version = 'V_2'

The query result is obtained as a join between dataframes df_1 and df_2:

> SELECT * FROM df_1
> INNER JOIN
> df_2 ON df_1.Object = df_2.Subject

Given $df_1,...,df_n$ the different dataframes obtained by executing $Q_1, Q_2,...,Q_n$, respectively, on versions $V_1,...,V_n$, the final result is obtained with a combination of join and/or union operations between the df_i. In the worst case we may need to compute n-1 joins:

$$join(join(join(join(df_1, df_2), df_3), df_4), ..., df_n)$$

That is, for cross-version query $type_2$, the number of joins depends on the shape of the query as well as the number of versions.

5   Experimental Evaluation

Evaluation was performed in cloud environment 'Amazon Web services' using EMR (Elastic Map reduce) as a platform. The data input files were saved on S3 Amazon. The experiments were done in a cluster with three nodes (one master and 2 core nodes) using m3.xlarge as an instance type. We use the BEAR dataset Benchmark which monitors more than 650 different domains across time and is composed of 58 snapshots. A description of the dataset is given in Table 1.

Table 1. RDF dataset description

Versions	Triples	Added triples	Deleted triples
Version 1	30,035,245	-	-
Version 5	27,377,065	6,922,375	9,598,805
Version 10	28,910,781	9,752,568	11,092,386
Version 15	33,253,221	14,110,358	11,150,069
Version 20	35,161,469	18,233,113	13,164,710
Version 25	31,510,558	16,901,310	15,493,857
Version 30	44,025,238	30,697,869	16,797,313
Version 35	32,606,132	19,210,291	16,645,753
Version 40	32,923,367	18,125,524	15,312,146

In the following we present the evaluation[2] of versioning queries on top of SPARK framework. The evaluation concerns four query types: version and delta materialization, single version and cross-version queries respectively.

5.1   Version and Delta Materialization

The content of the entire version (resp. Delta) is materialized. For each version, the average execution time of the queries was computed. Based on the plots shown in Fig. 4, we observe that the execution times obtained with IC strategy are approximately constant and show better results compared to the ones obtained with CB approach. In fact, versions in CB approach are not already stored and need to be computed each time we want to query a given version (resp. delta).

5.2   Single-Version Queries

We use for this series of experimentation the Independent Copies archiving approach. We realize different experimentations with queries where the object and/or predicate is given whereas the subject corresponds to what we ask for.

---

[2] https://github.com/meriemlaajimi/Archiving.

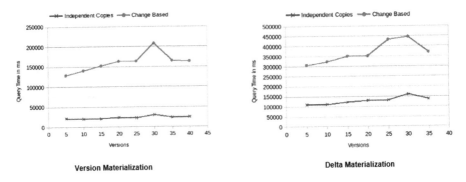

Fig. 4. Version and delta materialization IC and CB approaches

The analysis of the obtained plots (Fig. 5 shows that the use of subject-hash partitioning ameliorates query execution times. Nevertheless, using query with individual triple pattern does not need an important number of I/O operations. That is, the real advantage beyond the use of partitioning is not highlighted for this kind of queries.

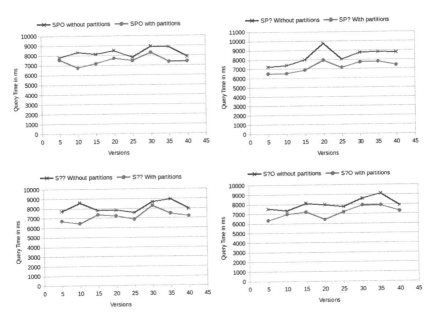

Fig. 5. Single version queries (Subject)

5.3   Cross-Version Queries

In this section, we focus on Cross-version queries with IC archiving approach. The first series of tests are realized with cross-version STAR query shape of the form (?X, p, ?Y) and (?X, q, ?Z). The obtained execution times are shown in Table 2. We note that the advantage beyond the use of partitioning is highlighted for this kind of queries compared to the result obtained with single triple queries. As we can see in Fig. 6, the use of subject-hash partitioning ameliorates execution times. In fact, Star query invokes triple patterns having the same subject which are loaded in the same partition.

Table 2. Query time evaluation of Star query (SQ)

Versions	Triples	SQ without partitions (ms)	SQ with partitions (ms)
V_1 and V_5	57,412,310	15005.226	12431.357
V_5 and V_{10}	56,287,846	15808.009	13531.05
V_{10} and V_{15}	62,164,002	16482.251	13223.434
V_{15} and V_{20}	68,414,690	16563.959	14165.733
V_{20} and V_{25}	66,672,027	15839.788	14532.462
V_{25} and V_{30}	75,535,796	16158.124	15053.127

We realize a second series of tests using cross-version Chain queries with two triples patterns of the form (?X, p, ?Y) and (?Y, q, ?Z). As we can see in Table 3 the use of partitioning ameliorates execution times. Eventhough we have

Table 3. Runtime evaluation of Chain query (CQ)

Versions	Triples	CQ without partitions (ms)	CQ with partitions (ms)
V_1 and V_5	57,412,310	15002.811	13630.838
V_5 and V_{10}	56,287,846	16072.282	14029,593
V_{10} and V_{15}	62,164,002	16939.459	14395.548
V_{15} and V_{20}	68,414,690	17670.103	14247.463
V_{20} and V_{25}	66,672,027	16999.656	14681.513
V_{25} and V_{30}	75,535,796	19044.695	16257.424

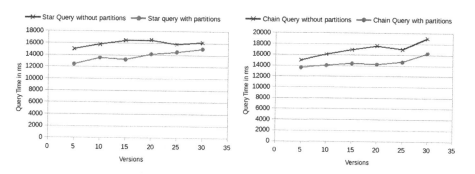

Fig. 6. Cross-version queries: Star and Chain query shapes

used queries with only two triple patterns and two versions, the execution times obtained with Chain queries are superior to the ones obtained with Star queries. In fact, for executing Chain queries, object-subject joins are needed and data transfer between nodes is necessary. That is, the performance of cross-version Chain query depends on the number of triple patterns as well as the number of versions.

6   Conclusion

In this paper, we study and compare main versioning queries and RDF archiving techniques with Spark. We propose a formal mapping of versioning queries defined with SPARQL into SQL SPARK. We make a series of experimentation of these queries to study the effects of RDF archives partitioning. Different performance tests have been realized based on: versioning approaches (Change Based or Independent Copies), the types of RDF archiving queries, the size of versions, the shape of SPARQL queries and finally the data partitioning strategy.

Experimentations are realized with IC and CB versioning approaches. The use of IC approach in distributed environment is more efficient than the use of CB one. Equally, the advantage beyond the use of subject-hash partitioning is shown with SPARQL Star queries. This is not the case of cross-version Chain queries where join between triple patterns belonging to different nodes is needed. In the future works we project to use different partitioning strategies and to define execution plan by taking into consideration, the size of a version, the number of versions and the shape of SPARQL queries.

References

1. Abdelaziz, I., Harbi, R., Khayyat, Z., Kalnis, P.: A survey and experimental comparison of distributed SPARQL engines for very large RDF data. In: Proceedings of the VLDB Endowment - Proceedings of the 43rd International Conference on Very Large Data Bases, Munich, Germany, vol. 10 issue 13, pp. 2049–2060 September 2017
2. Ahn, J., Im, D.-H., Eom, J.-H., Zong, N., Kim, H.-G.: G-Diff: a grouping algorithm for RDF change detection on MapReduce. In: Supnithi, T., Yamaguchi, T., Pan, J.Z., Wuwongse, V., Buranarach, M. (eds.) JIST 2014. LNCS, vol. 8943, pp. 230–235. Springer, Cham (2015). https://doi.org/10.1007/978-3-319-15615-6_17
3. Abele, A., McCrae, J.P., Buitelaar, P., Jentzsch, A., Cyganiak, R.: Linking Open Data cloud diagram 2018 (2018). http://lod-cloud.net/. Accessed Apr 2018
4. Armbrust, M., Xin, R.S., Lian, C., Huai, Y., Liu, D., Bradley, J.K., Meng, X., Kaftan, T., Franklin, M.J., Ghodsi, A., Zaharia, M.: Spark SQL: relational data processing in spark. In: Proceedings of the SIGMOD International Conference on Management of Data, Melbourne, Victoria, Australia, pp. 1383–1394, 31 May–4 June 2015
5. Fernández, J.D., Umbrich, J., Polleres, A., Knuth, M.: Evaluating query and storage strategies for RDF archives. In: Proceedings of the 12th International Conference on Semantic Systems, pp. 41–48. ACM, New York (2016)

6. Fernandez, J.D., Umbrich, J., Polleres, A., Knuth, M.: Evaluating query and storage strategies for RDF archives. Semantic Web – Interoperability, Usability, Applicability (Semantic Web Journal) (2018, to appear). (accepted for publication)
7. Goasdoué, F., Kaoudi, Z., Manolescu, I., Quiané-Ruiz, J.A., Zampetakis, S.: CliqueSquare in action: flat plans for massively parallel RDF queries, October 2014
8. Graube, M., Hensel, S., Urbas, L.: R43ples: revisions for triples - an approach for version control in the semantic web. In: Proceedings of the 1st Workshop on Linked Data Quality co-located with 10th International Conference on Semantic Systems, Leipzig, Germany, 2 September 2014
9. Meimaris, M., Papastefanatos, G.: The EvoGen benchmark suite for evolving RDF data. In: MEPDaW Workshop, Extended Semantic Web Conference (2016)
10. Naacke, H., Curé, O., Amann, B.: SPARQL query processing with apache spark. CoRR (2016)
11. Papakonstantinou, V., Flouris, G., Fundulaki, I., Stefanidis, K., Roussakis, G.: Versioning for linked data: archiving systems and benchmarks. In: Proceedings of the Workshop on Benchmarking Linked Data, Kobe, Japan, 18 October 2016
12. Papakonstantinou, V., Flouris, G., Fundulaki, I., Stefanidis, K., Roussakis, Y.: SPBv: benchmarking linked data archiving systems. In: 2nd International Workshop on Benchmarking Linked Data co-located with 16th International Semantic Web Conference (ISWC 2017), Vienna, Austria, 21-22 October 2017
13. Schätzle, A., Przyjaciel-Zablocki, M., Berberich, T., Lausen, G.: S2X: graph-parallel querying of RDF with GraphX. In: Wang, F., Luo, G., Weng, C., Khan, A., Mitra, P., Yu, C. (eds.) Big-O(Q)/DMAH -2015. LNCS, vol. 9579, pp. 155–168. Springer, Cham (2016). https://doi.org/10.1007/978-3-319-41576-5_12
14. Schätzle, A., Przyjaciel-Zablocki, M., Skilevic, S., Lausen, G.: S2RDF: RDF querying with SPARQL on spark. PVLDB 9(10), 804–815 (2016)
15. Stefanidis, K., Chrysakis, I., Flouris, G.: On designing archiving policies for evolving RDF datasets on the Web. In: Yu, E., Dobbie, G., Jarke, M., Purao, S. (eds.) ER 2014. LNCS, vol. 8824, pp. 43–56. Springer, Cham (2014). https://doi.org/10.1007/978-3-319-12206-9_4
16. Zaharia, M., Chowdhury, M., Das, T., Dave, A., Ma, J., McCauly, M., Franklin, M.J., Shenker, S., Stoica, I.: Resilient distributed datasets: a fault-tolerant abstraction for in-memory cluster computing. In: Proceedings of the 9th USENIX Symposium on Networked Systems Design and Implementation, San Jose, CA, USA, pp. 15–28, 25–27 April2012
17. Zaharia, M., Xin, R.S., Wendell, P., Das, T., Armbrust, M., Dave, A., Meng, X., Rosen, J., Venkataraman, S., Franklin, M.J., Ghodsi, A., Gonzalez, J., Shenker, S., Stoica, I.: Apache Spark: a unified engine for big data processing. Commun. ACM 59(11), 56–65 (2016)

1st Workshop on Deep Learning for Knowledge Graphs and Semantic Technologies

Assessing FAIR Data Principles Against the 5-Star Open Data Principles

Ali Hasnain[✉] and Dietrich Rebholz-Schuhmann

Insight Centre for Data Analytics, National University of Ireland, Galway, Ireland
{ali.hasnain,dietrich.rebholz-schuhmann}@insight-centre.org

Abstract. Access to biomedical data is increasingly important to enable data driven science in the research community. The Linked Open Data (LOD) principles (by Tim Berner-Lee) have been suggested to judge the quality of data by its accessibility (open data access), by its format and structures, and by its interoperability with other data sources. The objective is to use interoperable data sources across the Web with ease.

The FAIR (findable, accessible, interoperable, reusable) data principles have been introduced for similar reasons with a stronger emphasis on achieving reusability. In this manuscript we assess the FAIR principles against the LOD principles to determine, to which degree, the FAIR principles reuse LOD principles, and to which degree they extend the LOD principles. This assessment helps to clarify the relationship between both schemes and gives a better understanding, what extension FAIR represents in comparison to LOD.

We conclude, that LOD gives a clear mandate to the openness of data, whereas FAIR asks for a stated license for access and thus includes the concept of reusability under consideration of the license agreement. Furthermore, FAIR makes strong reference to the contextual information required to improve reuse of the data, e.g., provenance information. According to the LOD principles, such meta-data would be considered interoperable data as well, however, the requirement of extending of data with meta-data does indicate that FAIR is an extension of the LOD (in contrast to the inverse).

Keywords: Linked Open Data (LOD) · Linked Open Data 5-star
FAIR data principles

1 Introduction

The advent of the World Wide Web [2] has enabled public publishing and consumption of information on a unique scale in terms of cost, accessibility and size. In the past few years, the linked open data cloud has earned a fair amount of attention and it is becoming the standard for publishing data on the Web [5,8,11].

One of the ambitions behind the linked data effort is the ability to create a Web of interlinked data which can be queried using a unified query language and

© Springer Nature Switzerland AG 2018
A. Gangemi et al. (Eds.): ESWC 2018 Satellite Events, LNCS 11155, pp. 469–477, 2018.
https://doi.org/10.1007/978-3-319-98192-5_60

protocol, regardless of where the data is stored [7,9]. Core to this achievement is the adoption of the resource description framework (RDF) as the knowledge representation formalism as well as the SPARQL protocol for the retrieval of data. Ideally, all data is openly available and accessible through a maintained IT infrastructure [12].

Since the idea of linked data is in place, different schemes, proposals and recommendations (with guiding principles) have emerged from researchers and practitioners to make it open and easy to use by others [13]. One such scheme is proposed by Tim Berners-Lee in year 2010 known as "Linked Open Data 5-star [1]". Under the star scheme, one star can be get if the information has been made public under an open licence. More stars denote the quality of data leading to better structure and interoperability for reuse.

While LOD has had some uptake across the web, the number of datasets using this protocol compared to the other technologies is not up to the mark and significantly modest [9]. But whether or not one uses LOD, one does need to ensure that the datasets are designed specifically for the web and for reuse by humans and machines. To provide guidance for creating such data content independent of the technology used, recently the FAIR principles were issued through the Future of Research Communications and e-Scholarship (FORCE11) [3]. The FAIR principles provided by Wilkinson et al. [17] put forth characteristics that contemporary data resources, tools, vocabularies and infrastructures should exhibit to assist discovery and reuse by third-parties through the web. FAIR stands for: Findable, Accessible, Interoperable and Re-usable.

In this paper we want to highlight the overlapping aspects proposed by Linked Open Data 5-star and FAIR principles and present our position on how these two are related.

2   Related Work

Cox et al. [4] presented a rating system known as the 5* OzNome Data tool[1] which allows users to carry out a self-assessment by classifying the 14 facets into data quality guidelines. These data quality guidelines are provided and derived by FAIR principles (Findable, Accessible, Interoperable, Reusable) along with an additional dimension called Trustable or being Trusted. In doing the self-assessment, one can explore ways in which they are able to improve their data collection and how it is accessed by others. This gives data providers targets to improve their data collection and publishing process.

Related work can also be taken into account from the perspective of quality analysis of datasets. Although this paper doesn't provide insights or comparative quality analysis of existing approaches, but both the FAIR and 5-star principles targets the quality aspects of data.

Yamaguchi et al. presented YummyData [18] which is designed to improve the findability and reusability of Life Science Linked Open Data (LS-LOD) by monitoring the states of their Linked Data implementations and content.

---

[1] (http://oznome.csiro.au/5star/) la:20-03-2018.

SPARQLES[2] [15] monitors SPARQL endpoints registered in DataHub to determine their availability, performance, interoperability, and discoverability.

Hasnain et al. [9,10] presented SPORTAL (SPARQL portal) that provides the analysis in terms of discoverability, findability and accessibility aspects of Linked Open Data publish as public SPARQL endpoints.

3   LOD 5-Star

Tim Berners-Lee proposed 5-star scheme for Linked Open Data that provide guidelines for data providers and publishers in order to make data more accessible, available and reusable over the Web.

> ★ make your stuff available on the Web (whatever format) under an open license
>
> ★★ make it available as structured data (e.g., Excel instead of image scan of a table)
>
> ★ ★ ★ make it available in a non-proprietary open format (e.g., CSV instead of Excel)
>
> ★ ★ ★★ use URIs to denote things, so that people can point at your stuff
>
> ★ ★ ★ ★ ★ link your data to other data to provide context

In the following subsection we look into the importance of achieving these stars from user and publisher perspective

- **One** ★: Achieving *one star* means that the user can be able to (1) access the data, (2) consume the data, (3) store it locally, (4) manipulate the data and 5 share the data. Whereas being publisher (1) it is easy and simple to publish the data.
- **Two** ★★: Achieving *two stars* the user can be able to (1) process the data, (2) aggregate the data, (3) perform calculations, (4) visualise the data and can be exported into another (structured) format. Whereas being data publisher it is still simple to publish.
- **Three** ★ ★ ★: Achieving *three stars* helps data user to do all what can be done using *two stars* Web data and additionally one can manipulate the data without any proprietary software package. Similarly as data publisher a converter may be needed to export the data from the proprietary format.
- **Four** ★ ★ ★★: Achieving *four stars* helps data user to do all what can be done using *three stars* Web data and additionally (1) data can be linked using URI's, (2) data can be partly accessed and (3) existing tools and libraries can be reused. On the other hand as data publisher (1) using RDF "Graph" of data can be more effort than tabular (Excel/CSV) or tree (XML/JSON) data, data can be combined safely with other data, (2) data can be merged and combined safely, (3) data can be presented using URIs which is a global scheme for representing data. Being publisher (1) one has fine-granular control

---

[2] http://sparqles.ai.wu.ac.at/ l.a (10-04-2018).

over the data items and can optimise their access (load balancing, caching, etc.), (2) data can easily be sliced and diced, (3) URIs must be assigned to data.

- **Five** ★ ★ ★ ★ ★: Achieving *five stars* helps data user to do all what can be done using *four stars* Web data and additionally (1) More data can be discovered while consuming the data, (2) data schema can directly be learned, (3) consumers have to deal with broken data links, and (4) One have to be cautious for linking new data with existing for trust and provenance related issues. On the other hand being data provider or publisher one (1) must have to make data discover-able, (2) can increase the value of the data, (3) can gain the same benefits from the links as the consumers, (4) need to invest resources to link data to existing data over the Web and (5) may face some overhead to repair broken or incorrect links.

From the first star to the last star, the openness of the data is supported by better structure, better interoperability, and thus better reuse through open access, openness of data standards and the interlinking of data as a World Wide Web (WWW) data resource.

4   Fair Data

As proposed by Wilkinson et al. [17] the FAIR principles provide guidelines so that any resource over the Web including data resources, tools, vocabularies and infrastructures should exhibit certain characteristics to ensure the discovery and reuse by anyone. These principles also provide guidelines for data publishing, exploration, sharing, and reuse in both manual as well as automated settings. There have been a number of recent domain specific practices and guidelines for data publishing and management [6,14,16], FAIR guiding principles stand unique in number of ways as these are domain-independent and high-level that can be applied to both metadata as well as data.

In the following we present the elements of FAIR Principles directly taken from Wilkinson et al. [17]. It is worth noting that these elements are related but independent of each other.

The FAIR Guiding Principles [17]:

To be Findable:

- F1. (meta)data are assigned a globally unique and persistent identifier
  => corresponds to the usage of URIs (i.e. **Four** ★ ★ ★★).
- F2. data are described with rich metadata (defined by R1 below)
  => this certainly requires structured representation (i.e. **Two** ★★) and at best would relate to linkage to other data for context (i.e. **Five** ★ ★ ★ ★ ★).
- F3. metadata clearly and explicitly include the identifier of the data it describes
  => corresponds to the usage of URIs (i.e. **Four** ★ ★ ★★).
- F4. (meta)data are registered or indexed in a searchable resource
  => this is a statement about technologies making use of the data, which is the consequence of data access over the Web (i.e. **One** ★)

To be Accessible:

- A1. (meta)data are retrievable by their identifier using a standardised communications protocol
  => corresponds to the usage of URIs (i.e. **Four** ★ ★ ★★), although other identifiers could be used as well.
- A1.1 the protocol is open, free, and universally implementable
  => corresponds again to URIs and related open data standards (i.e. **Four** ★ ★ ★★).
- A1.2 the protocol allows for an authentication and authorisation procedure, where necessary
  => the LOD only covers the open access part as the primary requirement (i.e. **One** ★).
- A2. metadata are accessible, even when the data are no longer available
  => At best, this corresponds to the URIs, but long-term acquisition is not a matter of data standards but relates to IT infrastructures.

To be Interoperable:

- I1. (meta)data use a formal, accessible, shared, and broadly applicable language for knowledge representation
  => this corresponds to the use of "non-proprietary open formats" (i.e. **Three** ★ ★ ★).
- I2. (meta)data use vocabularies that follow FAIR principles
  => this statement is self-referential and refers to contextual standardised data (i.e. **Five** ★ ★ ★ ★ ★).
- I3. (meta)data include qualified references to other (meta)data
  => again this refers to contextual standardised data (i.e. **Five** ★ ★ ★ ★ ★).

To be Reusable:

- R1. meta(data) are richly described with a plurality of accurate and relevant attributes
  => this refers to the structured data, but makes a stronger reference to contextual information (i.e. **Three** ★ ★ ★).
- R1.1. (meta)data are released with a clear and accessible data usage license
  => a statement about the delivery of (meta)data, which is meant to be open according to LOD (i.e. **One** ★).
- R1.2. (meta)data are associated with detailed provenance
  => provenance is part of the contextual data (i.e. **Five** ★ ★ ★ ★ ★).
- R1.3. (meta)data meet domain-relevant community standards
  => again, community standards are part of the contextual data and should be openly available (according to LOD, i.e. **Five** ★ ★ ★ ★ ★).

Like LOD five stars these principles are incremental and can be considered in any combination result in achieving the higher degrees of 'FAIRness'. In other words, the better the adoption of FAIR guidelines the higher is the degree of 'FAIRness' claimed.

For each FAIR principle, we give a judgement, which LOD star is best aligned with the FAIR principle, if any applies. As can be seen from the Table 1, more than one LOD principle could be linked to a FAIR principle, but we only give a judgement to the highest LOD 5-star principle.

Table 1. FAIR principles mapping to LOD 5-star scheme.

	★	★★	★ ★ ★	★ ★ ★★	★ ★ ★ ★ ★
F1				X	
F2					X
F3				X	
F4	X				
A1		X	X	X	
A1.1	X	X	X	X	
A1.2	X				
A2					
I1	X	X	X		
I2	X	X			X
I3				X	X
R1			X		X
R1.1	X				
R1.2				X	X
R1.3	X	X			X

5 Distinctions and Overlaps

5.1 LOD and Non-data Assets

The LOD 5 stars scheme is for the Open Data. This scheme provides the guidelines for data providers and publishers in order to make data more accessible, available and reusable. Whereas the FAIR principles can equally be applied to any non-data assets in the same manner as data.

FAIR does not impose any constraint that the data must be openly available and requires that access to the license agreement is made available. The concern can be raised that restricted data will also limit reusability only by the limitation that access is not openly available.

Furthermore, FAIR asks for meta-data to be provided with the data to improve interoperability, which relates to the contextual information from the LOD principles through interoperable data linked as one or several interoperable open data sources. Here, the FAIR data principles envision data about data to improve reusability.

Next, FAIR sees access to the FAIR data as a task which would have to be achieved through a supported IT infrastructure. This is certainly a requirement which would play a more important role on data that is not openly available (non open access data), since the data cannot be openly replicated without license agreement.

Finally, the LOD principles reside on URIs as the key element to achieve openness, interoperability and reuse, whereas FAIR would allow for a wider range of identifiers that would achieve the same purpose. This principle certainly – again – applies mainly to data sources that are more restricted in comparison to Linked Open Data.

5.2   Tool and Technology Independent

The high-level FAIR Guiding Principles are independent of implementation choices, and do not suggest any specific technology, standard, or implementation-solution. On the other hand, these principles are not, themselves, a standard or a specification. They act as a guide to data publishers as well as consumers to assist them in evaluating whether any specific implementation choices are able to support their digital research artefacts Findable, Accessible, Interoperable, and Reusable [17]. Same is the case with LOD 5-star scheme, which are not themselves a standard or a specification but provides the guideline for choosing the tools and technologies to make linked open data more available, searchable and open.

6   Discussion and Conclusion

The LOD 5-star scheme has been developed under the assumption that linked and open data will lead to reusability, shared benefits and other advantages. This could lead to the conclusion that the LOD scheme has been defined for a more narrowly defined set of data, i.e. data that is openly available, in contrast to the larger range of data, i.e. data that has to used in compliance with license restrictions. It is straight forward to assume that data will be openly accessibly in the future, however, in recent periods this state did not necessarily come about.

On the other side, the FAIR data principles have been defined to drive re-usability of data. The used approach for the definition of FAIR data makes strong reference to the existence of meta-data for the reusable data, in particular to cover license agreements, however, the FAIR approach did not (seem to) capitalise on the LOD data principles. A priori, we can argue that FAIR data would cover a broader scope and would include precious data that is not given in the open space, e.g. data being provided by publishing companies, and still we could take the opposite position pointing out that even data under license agreements would be best served in the linked open data space.

Another point of distinction is related to the requirements of accessibility as an essential element of reusability. As pointed out in our reasoning, this aspect is directly depending on IT infrastructures that serve the data. In this sense, the FAIR principles are more driven by implementation considerations than the

LOD principles are. To some degree, we can reason that the FAIR principles cover a wider scope (e.g., including the licensed data), but - by contrary - also have to realise the burden to deliver the data to the users without making strong assumptions on the openness of the data.

As an overall conclusion, the FAIR principles are focused to user needs around a wide range of existing data, whereas the LOD principles form an idealistic approach to a world using open data. LOD principles appear to be more stringent in its own principles, whereas the FAIR data principles can be seen as reusing the LOD principles without making explicit reference and with added aspects of separating data into the core data as well as the meta-data, including license considerations. The future will tell, whether the FAIR data principles lead to the reusability of data under the consideration that the access to meta-data and to license agreements open the avenues of reusabiltiy, or whether the LOD principles are the gatekeepers to reusability, since – a priori – the data should be openly available anyways.

Acknowledgement. This publication has emanated from research conducted with the financial support of Science Foundation Ireland (SFI) under Grant Number SFI/12/RC/2289, co-funded by the European Regional Development Fund.

References

1. Berners-Lee, T.: Is your linked open data 5 star. Repéré à (2010). https://www.w3.org/DesignIssues/LinkedData.html
2. Berners-Lee, T., Fischetti, M., Foreword By-Dertouzos, M.L.: Weaving the web: the original design and ultimate destiny of the World Wide Web by its inventor. HarperInformation (2000)
3. Bourne, P.E., et al.: Improving The future of research communications and e-Scholarship (Dagstuhl Perspectives Workshop 11331). Dagstuhl Manifestos 1(1), 41–60 (2012). http://drops.dagstuhl.de/opus/volltexte/2012/3445
4. Cox, S., Yu, J.: Oznome 5-star tool: a rating system for making data fair and trustable. In: Proceedings of the 2018 eResearch Australasia Conference (2017)
5. Hasnain, A., Fox, R., Decker, S., Deus, H.F.: Cataloguing and linking life sciences LOD Cloud. In: 1st International Workshop on Ontology Engineering in a Data-Driven World Collocated with EKAW 2012 (2012)
6. Hasnain, A., et al.: Linked biomedical dataspace: lessons learned integrating data for drug discovery. In: Mika, P., et al. (eds.) ISWC 2014. LNCS, vol. 8796, pp. 114–130. Springer, Cham (2014). https://doi.org/10.1007/978-3-319-11964-9_8
7. Hasnain, A., et al.: BioFed: federated query processing over life sciences linked open data. JBMS 8(1), 13 (2017)
8. Hasnain, A., Mehmood, Q., Sana e Zainab, S., Decker, S.: A provenance assisted roadmap for life sciences linked open data cloud. In: Klinov, P., Mouromtsev, D. (eds.) KESW 2015. CCIS, vol. 518, pp. 72–86. Springer, Cham (2015). https://doi.org/10.1007/978-3-319-24543-0_6
9. Hasnain, A., Mehmood, Q., e Zainab, S.S., Hogan, A.: SPORTAL: profiling the content of public SPARQL endpoints. Int. J. Semant. Web Inf. Syst. (IJSWIS) 12(3), 134–163 (2016). http://www.igi-global.com/article/sportal/160175

10. Hasnain, A., Mehmood, Q., e Zainab, S.S., Hogan, A.: SPORTAL: Searching for public SPARQL endpoints. In: International Semantic Web Conference (Posters & Demos) (2016)
11. Hasnain, A., et al.: A roadmap for navigating the life sciences linked open data cloud. In: Supnithi, T., Yamaguchi, T., Pan, J.Z., Wuwongse, V., Buranarach, M. (eds.) JIST 2014. LNCS, vol. 8943, pp. 97–112. Springer, Cham (2015). https:// doi.org/10.1007/978-3-319-15615-6_8
12. Hasnain, S.M.A.: Cataloguing and linking publicly available biomedical SPARQL endpoints for federation-addressing aPosteriori data integration. Ph.D. thesis (2017)
13. Saleem, M., Hasnain, A., Ngomo, A.C.N.: LargeRDFBench: a billion triples benchmark for SPARQL endpoint federation. J. Web Semant. 48, 85–125 (2018)
14. Sandve, G.K., Nekrutenko, A., Taylor, J., Hovig, E.: Ten simple rules for reproducible computational research. PLoS Comput. Biol. 9(10), e1003285 (2013)
15. Vandenbussche, P.Y., Umbrich, J., Matteis, L., Hogan, A., Buil-Aranda, C.: SPARQLES: monitoring public SPARQL endpoints. Semant. Web 8(6), 1049–1065 (2017)
16. White, E.P., Baldridge, E., Brym, Z.T., Locey, K.J., McGlinn, D.J., Supp, S.R.: Nine simple ways to make it easier to (re) use your data. PeerJ PrePrints (2013)
17. Wilkinson, M.D., et al.: The fair guiding principles for scientific data management and stewardship. Sci. Data 3, 160018 (2016)
18. Yamamoto, Y., Yamaguchi, A., Splendiani, A.: YummyData: providing high-quality open life science data. In: Database 2018 (2018)

Translational Models
for Item Recommendation

Enrico Palumbo[1,2,3(✉)], Giuseppe Rizzo[1], Raphaël Troncy[2], Elena Baralis[3],
Michele Osella[1], and Enrico Ferro[1]

[1] ISMB, Turin, Italy
{palumbo,giuseppe.rizzo,osella,ferro}@ismb.it
[2] EURECOM, Biot, France
raphael.troncy@eurecom.fr
[3] Politecnico di Torino, Turin, Italy
elena.baralis@polito.it

Abstract. Translational models have proven to be accurate and efficient at learning entity and relation representations from knowledge graphs for machine learning tasks such as knowledge graph completion. In the past years, knowledge graphs have shown to be beneficial for recommender systems, efficiently addressing paramount issues such as new items and data sparsity. In this paper, we show that the item recommendation problem can be seen as a specific case of knowledge graph completion problem, where the "feedback" property, which connects users to items that they like, has to be predicted. We empirically compare a set of state-of-the-art knowledge graph embeddings algorithms on the task of item recommendation on the Movielens 1M and on the LibraryThing dataset. The results show that translational models outperform typical baseline approaches based on collaborative filtering and popularity and that the dimension of the embedding vector influences the accuracy of the recommendations.

Keywords: Knowledge graphs · Recommender systems · Embedding
Translational models

1 Introduction

Recommender systems are traditionally divided in two families: content-based and collaborative filtering algorithms. Content-based algorithms recommend items similar to the set of items that a user has liked in the past, considering the item content, i.e. its metadata. On the other hand, collaborative filtering algorithms look for users that are similar in terms of item preferences and suggest to a user items that similar users have liked. Hybrid systems attempt to put together the best of both worlds, by combining content-based filtering and collaborative filtering [1]. Knowledge graphs provide an ideal data structure for such systems, as a consequence of their ability of encompassing heterogeneous information, such as user-item interactions and items' relation with other entities, at

© Springer Nature Switzerland AG 2018
A. Gangemi et al. (Eds.): ESWC 2018 Satellite Events, LNCS 11155, pp. 478–490, 2018.
https://doi.org/10.1007/978-3-319-98192-5_61

the same time. Recommender systems leveraging knowledge graphs have shown to be competitive with state-of-the-art collaborative filtering and to efficiently address issues such as new items and data sparsity [6, 16–18, 24]. In recent years, a great deal of attention has been given to machine learning algorithms able to learn entity and relation vector representations ('embeddings') from knowledge graphs for prediction tasks, such as knowledge graph completion, triple classification, entity resolution [22]. More in detail, translational models, which model relations between entities as translations in a vector space, have shown to be quite accurate at these prediction tasks, while being computationally efficient and scalable to large graphs [3, 13, 23].

In this paper, we show how translational models can be used to create hybrid recommender systems leveraging knowledge graphs, we evaluate their accuracy and we compare them empirically. More in detail, we address the following research questions:

1. How can translational models for knowledge graph embeddings be used for item recommendation?
2. How do they perform on two standard benchmark datasets and how do they compare with collaborative filtering baselines?
3. How much is the performance affected by the hyper-parameters, such as the embedding size?

We show that, when modelling users and items as entities of a knowledge graph, the item recommendation problem can be seen as a specific case of knowledge graph completion problem, where the "feedback" property has to be predicted. Thus, we compare three popular translational models for knowledge graph embeddings (TransE [3], TransH [23], TransR [13]) on the problem of item recommendation. The evaluation on the Movielens 1M and the Library-Thing dataset shows that: (1) knowledge graph embeddings methods outperform SVD, a matrix factorization collaborative filtering baseline, and the "Most Popular" baseline (2) models such as TransE and TransH obtain better performance with respect to TransR (3) the embedding size affects the accuracy of the recommendations, but TransE performs better than competing methods on the Movielens1M dataset for almost all metrics and dimensions d.

2   Related Work

Knowledge Graph Embeddings: the term knowledge graph embeddings refer to vector representations of entities and/or relations that attempt to preserve the structure and the semantics of the knowledge graph. Comprehensive surveys of machine learning algorithms used to learn features from knowledge graphs are [14, 22]. All methods attempt to describe the existing triples in the knowledge graph by learning latent features according to some modeling assumption. RESCAL [15] is a tensor factorization method that explains triples via pairwise interactions of vector representations of entities; NTN (Neural Tensor Network) is an expressive non-linear model that learns representations using neural networks [20]; distance based models, such as the Structured Embeddings (SE) [4], explain triples using a distance in the vector space. Translational models are a special case of distance-based models that model relations as translations in the vector space and score triples according to a distance function. These models have shown to be computationally efficient and accurate at the same time and are described more in detail Sect. 3, as they are the object the paper. **Recommendations Using Knowledge Graphs**: in the past years, several works have shown the effectiveness of external knowledge resources to enhance the performance of recommender systems. In [6,24] the authors start from a graph-based data model including user feedback and item properties to generate personalized entity recommendations. In [16,17] a hybrid graph-based data model is used leveraging Linked Open Data to extract metapath-based feature that are fed into a learning to rank framework. In [19] the authors propose a content-based recommender system that automatically learns item representations using a feature learning algorithm on a knowledge graph and show the effectiveness of the learned representations in an Item-based K-Nearest Neighbor method. In [18], the authors use property-specific knowledge graph embeddings based on node2vec [10] and learning to rank to provide item recommendations. In [25], the authors use knowledge graph embeddings considering structural knowledge (e.g. triples), textual knowledge (e.g. abstract) and visual knowledge (e.g. poster) to derive semantic representation of items for item recommendation.

3   Approach

In this paper, we introduce the definition of knowledge graph, we describe translational models, we show how the problem of item recommendation can be interpreted as a knowledge graph completion problem and how a ranking function for item recommendation can be derived from translational models (Fig. 1).

3.1   Knowledge Graph

We use the definition of knowledge graph given in [18]. A knowledge graph is defined as a set $K = (E, R, O)$ where E is the set of entities, $R \subset ExΓxE$ is a set of typed relations among entities, and O is an ontology, which defines the set of relation types ('properties') $Γ$. Entities include users $u \in U \subset E$ and items $i \in I \subset E \setminus U$. An observed positive feedback between a user and an item[1] is described by a special property, which we name 'feedback'. In this work, the ontology O is represented by the DBpedia ontology [2].

3.2   Translational Models

In order to predict missing relations in a knowledge graph, most algorithms rely on feature learning approaches that are able to map entities and relations into a

---

[1] Movie ratings are given by users on a 1–5 scale, we assume $r \geq 4$ to be a positive rating.

vector space, generating knowledge graph embeddings. In this work, we compare the following models (known as "translational models"):

- **TransE** [3]: learns representations of entities and relations so that $h + l \approx t$ where $(h, l, t) \in R$ is a triple. h is the 'head' entity, l is the relation and t is the 'tail' entity. The score function for a triple is thus $f(h, l, t) = D(h + l, t)$ where D is a distance function such as the L_1 or the L_2 norm.
- **TransH** [23]: first extension of TransE, enables entities to have different representations when involved in different relations by projecting entities on a hyperplane identified by the normal vector w_l. The score function becomes: $f(h, l, t) = D(h_\perp + l, t_\perp)$, where $h_\perp = h - w_l^T h w_l$ and $t_\perp = t - w_l^T t w_l$ and D is a distance function such as the L_1 or the L_2 norm.
- **TransR** [13]: enables entities and relations to be embedded in a separate vector space through a matrix M_l associated to any relation l that performs projections of vectors from entity to relation space. The score function is: $f(h, l, t) = D(h_l + l, t_l)$ where $h_l = h M_l$ and $t_l = t M_l$ and D is a distance function such as the L_1 or the L_2 norm.

The models are trained through the minimization of a pairwise ranking loss function L that measures the total difference between the scores of 'positive triples' D^+ and 'negative triples' D^-, plus regularization terms such as the margin γ and other constraints:

$$L = \sum_{(h,l,t)\in D^+} \sum_{(h',l,t')\in D^-} max(0, \gamma + f_l(h, t) - f_l(h', t')) \tag{1}$$

Positive triples D^+ are triples of the knowledge graph K, whereas negative triples D^- are obtained by 'corrupting' positive triples replacing the head or tail entities with other entities. Notice that this strategy can produce false negatives, as knowledge graphs are known to be incomplete and missing triples can still be valid facts. In order to reduce this risk, we adopt the strategy described in [23], which considers non-uniform sampling probabilities depending on the type of relation.

3.3 Item Recommendation

The problem of item recommendation is that of ranking a set of N candidate items $I_{candidates} \subset I$ according to what a user may like. More formally, the problem consists in defining a ranking function $\rho(u, i)$ that assigns a score to any user-item pair $(u, i) \in U x I_{candidates}$ and then sorting the items according to $\rho(u, i)$:

$$L(u) = \{i_1, i_2, ..., i_N\} \tag{2}$$

where $\rho(u, i) > \rho(u, i+1)$ for any $i = 1..N - 1$. The core idea of using knowledge graph embeddings for item recommendation is that of using the negative score assigned to a triple $f(u, feedback, i)$ as the ranking function $\rho(u, i)$ (Fig. 2). Thus, the approach can be summarized as:

– **Data splitting:** define the set of users' feedback X as a set of triples $(u, feedback, i)$. We split the set of triples X into a X_{train} and X_{test} so that $X = X_{train} \bigcup X_{test}$.

– **Training:** learn the knowledge graph embeddings from K, which includes all the triples in X_{train} as well as other triples describing item content (see how the knowledge graph is built in Sect. 4.1), obtaining vector representations of each $e \in E$ and $r \in R$ (including the 'feedback' property)

– **Testing:** for every $u \in U$, sort every $i \in I_{candidates}$ according to the score assigned to the triple $(u, feedback, i)$ by the trained translational model $\rho(u, i) = -f(u, feedback, i)$

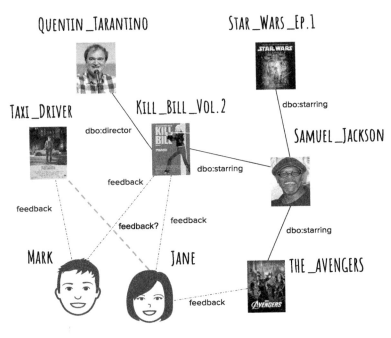

Fig. 1. Recommending items as a knowledge graph completion problem

4   Experimental Setup

4.1   Knowledge Graph Construction

The first dataset used for the comparison of the knowledge graph embeddings methods is MovieLens 1M[2]. MovieLens 1M [11] is a well known dataset for the evaluation of recommender systems and it contains 1,000,209 anonymous ratings of approximately 3,900 movies made by 6,040 MovieLens users. MovieLens 1M items have been mapped to the corresponding DBpedia entities [17] and we

---

[2] https://grouplens.org/datasets/movielens/1m/.

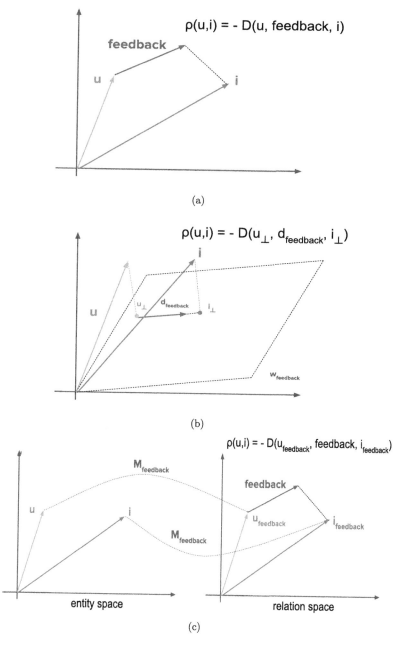

Fig. 2. (a): in TransE, user, items and relations are embedded in the same space and the ranking function is defined through the distance between the $u + feedback$ and i (b): in TransH, translations are performed on the hyperplane $w_{feedback}$ and thus the ranking function is defined through the distance between $u_\perp + d_{feedback}$ and $i_\perp$ (c): in TransR, entities and relations are embedded in different vector spaces and thus the ranking function is defined through the distance between $u_{feedback} + feedback$ and $i_{feedback}$

leverage these publicly available mappings to create the knowledge graph K using DBpedia data. Since not every item in the Movielens data has a corresponding DBpedia entity, after this mapping we have 948978 ratings, from 6040 users on 3226 items. We split the data into a training X_{train}, validation X_{val} and test set X_{test}, containing, per each user, respectively 70%, 10% and 20% of the ratings. In order to select the most relevant properties for the knowledge graph construction, we count what are the most frequent properties used in DBpedia to describe the items in the Movielens1M dataset and we sort them according to their frequency. We select a subset of properties of the DBpedia Ontology[3] to create the knowledge graph by sorting them according to their frequency of occurrence and selecting the first K so that the frequency of the K+1 property is less than 50% of the previous one. We obtain: ["dbo:director", "dbo:starring", "dbo:distributor", "dbo:writer", "dbo:musicComposer", "dbo:producer", "dbo:cinematography", "dbo:editing"]. In this way, we avoid to select a fixed number of properties and we rely on the actual frequency of occurrence to determine the cut-off. We also add "dct:subject" to the set of properties, as it provides an extremely rich categorization of items. For each item property p, we include in K all the triples (i, p, e) where $i \in I$ and $e \in E$, e.g. (dbr:Pulp_Fiction, dbo:director, dbr:Quentin_Tarantino). We finally add the 'feedback' property, modeling all movie ratings that are $r \geq 4$ in X_{train} as triples $(u, feedback, i)$. The second dataset used for the comparison is LibraryThing[4], which contains book ratings on a 1–10 scale. By using the same mappings [17] used for Movielens1M, we obtain 410199 ratings, given by 6789 users to 9926 items linked to DBpedia. The selected properties according to the strategy described above are: ["dbo:author", "dbo:publisher", "dbo:literaryGenre", "dbo:mediaType", "dbo:subsequentWork", "dbo:previousWork", "dbo:series", "dbo:country", "dbo:language", "dbo:coverArtist", "dct:subject"]. We convert ratings into the 'feedback' property when $r \geq 8$ and we apply the same data splitting procedure as for the Movielens1M dataset. Datasets statistics are summarized in Table 1. The sparsity of the ratings matrix ρ_r is defined as the ratio between the actual ratings and the number of possible existing user-item interactions:

$$\rho_r = \frac{T}{|U||I|} \tag{3}$$

where T is the number of ratings, $|U|$ is the number of users and $|I|$ is the number of items in the dataset. The sparsity of the knowledge graph ρ_k is defined as the ratio between the number of existing edges and the number of possible existing edges:

$$\rho_k = \frac{M}{N(N-1)} \tag{4}$$

where $M = |E x \Gamma x E|$ is the number of edges and $N = |E|$ is the number of entities in the graph.

---

[3] https://wiki.dbpedia.org/services-resources/ontology.
[4] https://www.librarything.com.

Table 1. Datasets stats. ρ_r represents the sparsity of the ratings matrix, P the number of distinct properties in the knowledge graph, N the number of nodes in the graph, M the number of edges in the graph, ρ_k is the sparsity of the graph.

Dataset	Type	Ratings	Users	Items	ρ_r	P	N	M	ρ_k
Movielens1M	Film	948976	6040	3226	95.130	10	29166	465338	99.945
LibraryThing	Book	410199	6789	9926	99.391	12	35768	283967	99.978

4.2 Evaluation

We use the evaluation protocol known as AllUnratedItems [21], i.e. for each user we select as possible candidate items all the items either in the training or in the test set that he or she has not rated before in the training set. Items that are not appearing in test set are considered as negative examples, which is a pessimistic assumption, as users may actually like items that they have not seen yet. Scores are thus to be considered as a worst-case estimate of the real recommendation quality that would derive from an online recommendation scenario. We measure standard information retrieval metrics such as P@5, P@10, Mean Average Precision (MAP), NDCG (Normalized Discounted Cumulative Gain) to assess the quality of the ranking function. In addition to these precision-focused metrics, we also measure the serendipity of the recommendations. Serendipity can be defined as the capability of identifying items that are both attractive and unexpected [9]. Ge *et al.* proposed to measure it by considering the precision of the recommended items after having discarded the ones that are too obvious [8]. Equation 5 details how we compute this metric. The value of *hit* is 1 if the recommended item i is relevant to user u, otherwise it is 0. Differently from the metric of precision, we consider the top-k most popular items always as non-relevant, even if they are included in the test set of user u. Popular items can be regarded as obvious because they are well-known by many users.

$$\text{SER}(k) = \frac{1}{|U| \times k} \sum_{u \in U} \sum_{j=1}^{k} \text{hit}(i_j, u) \tag{5}$$

As baselines, we use state-of-the-art collaborative filtering algorithms based on Singular Value Decomposition [12] and the Most Popular Items recommendation strategy, which simply ranks items based on their popularity (i.e. number of positive ratings). All the baselines have been trained on the user ratings contained in X_{train} in the original matrix format and tested on X_{test}. The baselines are implemented using the *surprise* python library[5]. The implementation of the translational based embeddings[6] and the script used to compare them[7] are publicly available on Github. The models are compared using default hyper-parameters: $d = 100$, $k = 100$ (TransR), *learning_rate* $= 0.001$, $\gamma = 1$, *epochs* $= 1000$.

---

[5] http://surprise.readthedocs.io/en/v1.0.2/matrix_factorization.html.
[6] https://github.com/thunlp/KB2E.
[7] https://github.com/D2KLab/entity2rec/blob/dev/entity2rec/trans_recommender.py.

5 Results

5.1 Empirical Comparison of Translational Models

In this section, we empirically compare translational models for item recommendation. The results of the evaluation on the Movielens 1M are reported in Table 2. The results show that all knowledge graph embeddings algorithms significantly outperform baselines such as SVD, MostPop and Random. At the same time, we observe that the MostPop baseline, although trivial, is able to achieve very good results, outperforming the SVD method. Note that the MostPop is known to be quite effective on MovieLens due to the power-law distribution of user feedback data, i.e. to the fact that most user ratings tend to be concentrated on few very popular items [7]. TransE and TransH obtain the best scores for item recommendations on the Movielens1M dataset. In particular, TransE is the best performing method among translational models, showing that, for the case of Movielens 1M, a simple model with fewer parameters to learn is more effective than more complex ones such as TransR and even TransH. For LibraryThing (Table 3), where the graph and ratings are sparser, TransH obtains the best scores, but TransE still outperforms TransR. We also observe that the MostPop and SVD are much less effective on LibraryThing, which is significantly sparser than Movielens1M in terms of ρ_r (Table 1).

Table 2. Comparison of knowledge graph embeddings and collaborative filtering algorithms on the Movielens1M dataset

System	P@5	P@10	MAP	R@5	R@10	NDCG	SER@5	SER@10
TransE	**0.201424**	**0.175066**	**0.13912**	**0.079105**	**0.130375**	**0.466307**	**0.195099**	**0.163758**
TransH	0.200132	0.173493	0.136114	0.077194	0.12898	0.463236	0.191987	0.159172
TransR	0.186424	0.161325	0.127131	0.073067	0.123122	0.454165	0.182185	0.151258
MostPop	0.144603	0.129156	0.092103	0.049231	0.084936	0.406294	0.064669	0.053692
SVD	0.067814	0.0624	0.04267	0.02021	0.037233	0.328776	0.059238	0.047202
Random	0.005762	0.005861	0.008381	0.001456	0.003241	0.245982	0.005629	0.005579

Table 3. Comparison of knowledge graph embeddings and collaborative filtering algorithms on the LibraryThing dataset

System	P@5	P@10	MAP	R@5	R@10	NDCG	SER@5	SER@10
TransH	**0.10411**	**0.082781**	**0.071303**	**0.063403**	**0.095078**	**0.335357**	**0.101576**	**0.07873**
TransE	0.097187	0.079054	0.067255	0.059799	0.09194	0.329329	0.094388	0.075357
TransR	0.07739	0.06484	0.054964	0.04585	0.072106	0.312535	0.074768	0.061246
MostPop	0.034261	0.029872	0.028128	0.025619	0.04302	0.237088	0.006982	0.005583
SVD	0.012019	0.010149	0.01085	0.010236	0.016683	0.188468	0.009368	0.006864
Random	0.000648	0.000604	0.001665	0.000354	0.000791	0.155435	0.000619	0.000574

5.2 Embedding Dimension

In this section, we study how the quality of the recommendations varies as we vary the dimension of the embedding vector d. For TransR, we keep the dimension of the relation space $k = d$, as in the default configuration. We conduct the experiment on the Movielens 1M dataset. As we can see from Table 4, the best performance is achieved by TransE when $d = 50$, which is slightly better than the default configuration $d = 100$ for all metrics under consideration except for $SER@10$. In general, TransE appears to perform better than the other approaches for all values of d, except for $d = 20$ where all the models have very similar performance and where for some metrics (e.g. R@5 and R@10) TransR seems to perform slightly better. To better compare the models, in Fig. 3 we depict the evolution of the NDCG as a function of d for the translational models. We observe that when $d = 20$ the models have very similar performance, but in general TransE performs better than TransH and TransR for most values of d. It is also interesting to notice that there is large gap between TransE and the other two methods when $d = 10$, showing that a simpler model can obtain significantly better results when the number of features is small. The peak performance varies: TransE has its peak when $d = 50$, whereas TransH and TransR when $d = 100$. For all models, it seems a good strategy to not increase d over 100. In general, the default configuration of $d = 100$ appears to be justified and sensible, but the picture shows that tuning the embedding dimension parameter to generate item recommendations can still improve the performance in some cases.

Table 4. Translational models performance on the Movielens 1M dataset as a function of the embedding dimension d.

Model	d	P@5	P@10	MAP	R@5	R@10	NDCG	SER@5	SER@10
TransE	10	0.093444	0.08904	0.068161	0.020198	0.039709	0.366541	0.091556	0.085083
TransH	10	0.002649	0.003874	0.029036	0.000473	0.001633	0.303868	0.002649	0.003825
TransR	10	0.018212	0.021589	0.024472	0.005329	0.013912	0.297924	0.018212	0.021589
TransE	20	0.159172	0.144917	0.110341	0.050229	0.091037	0.429045	0.151854	0.132103
TransH	20	0.151854	0.139007	0.106262	0.050553	0.090665	0.425542	0.14394	0.125728
TransR	20	0.15149	0.138808	0.108588	0.052173	0.093729	0.428234	0.148841	0.132815
TransE	30	0.188609	0.168245	0.128919	0.06693	0.117108	0.452667	0.176689	0.150414
TransH	30	0.185728	0.165877	0.126865	0.06692	0.115647	0.4504	0.173377	0.148709
TransR	30	0.175728	0.154272	0.120587	0.062922	0.109542	0.44422	0.169272	0.142616
TransE	**50**	**0.207053**	**0.179834**	**0.143832**	**0.081219**	**0.134856**	**0.471388**	**0.195828**	0.163411
TransH	50	0.192715	0.168891	0.13259	0.072662	0.122104	0.458386	0.183808	0.155298
TransR	50	0.173709	0.152384	0.118384	0.066293	0.113591	0.442525	0.166589	0.14149
TransE	100	0.201424	0.175066	0.13912	0.079105	0.130375	0.466307	0.195099	**0.163758**
TransH	100	0.200132	0.173493	0.136114	0.077194	0.12898	0.463236	0.191987	0.159172
TransR	100	0.186424	0.161325	0.127131	0.073067	0.123122	0.454165	0.182185	0.151258
TransE	200	0.174272	0.152616	0.118552	0.067019	0.108311	0.443624	0.170861	0.143262
TransH	200	0.169768	0.146722	0.11241	0.062785	0.100185	0.436909	0.161689	0.133858
TransR	200	0.145232	0.10856	0.107458	0.062646	0.098634	0.430513	0.143311	0.102401

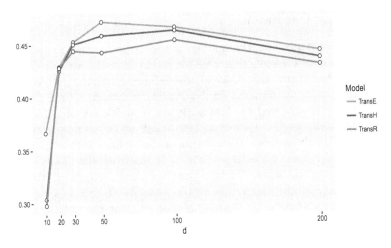

Fig. 3. NDCG of translational models on the Movielens 1M dataset as a function of the embedding dimension d

We leave as future work the study of the importance of other hyper-parameters such as the learning rate or the margin γ of the loss function.

6   Conclusions

In this work, we have described the application of translational models for item recommendation, addressing the following research questions:

(1) How can translational models for knowledge graph embeddings be used for item recommendation?
     Item recommendation can be interpreted as a knowledge graph completion problem, where a special property called 'feedback', modeling users preferences for items, has to be predicted. More precisely, translational models can be used to learn knowledge graph embeddings and to score triples to 'complete' the knowledge graph by predicting the feedback property. The score assigned to triples $(u, feedback, i)$ defines a ranking function to perform item recommendation.
(2) How do they perform on two standard benchmark datasets and how do they compare with collaborative filtering baselines?
     We have evaluated the translational models on the Movielens 1M and the LibraryThing datasets, comparing them to SVD and MostPop observing that: (1) knowledge graph embeddings algorithms outperform traditional collaborative filtering algorithms such as SVD for item recommendation (2) TransE performs better for Movielens1M, whereas TransH has a better accuracy for LibraryThing. TransR, albeit being more complex, has in general a worse performance, except for some specific configurations of the embeddings size and some metrics in which it performs slightly better than the others ($d = 20$ and recall metrics).

(3) How much is the performance affected by the hyper-parameters, such as the embedding size?

The embedding size affects the accuracy of the recommendations, but TransE seems better than the other approaches consistently for almost all values of d under consideration and to preserve its quality even with very small sizes such as $d = 10$.

In a future work, we plan to extend this evaluation to other datasets using implicit feedback such as LastFM [5], to include in the evaluation other existing recommender systems based on knowledge graphs such as Sprank [17], RDF2Vec [19] or entity2rec [18], to take into account specific collaborative filtering issues such as new items and data sparsity, perform exhaustive search and optimization of the hyper-parameters of the models and to account for multiple possible interactions between users and items.

References

1. Adomavicius, G., Tuzhilin, A.: Toward the next generation of recommender systems: a survey of the state-of-the-art and possible extensions. IEEE Trans. Knowl. Data Eng. **17**(6), 734–749 (2005)
2. Auer, S., Bizer, C., Kobilarov, G., Lehmann, J., Cyganiak, R., Ives, Z.: DBpedia: a nucleus for a web of open data. In: Aberer, K., et al. (eds.) ASWC/ISWC -2007. LNCS, vol. 4825, pp. 722–735. Springer, Heidelberg (2007). https://doi.org/10.1007/978-3-540-76298-0_52
3. Bordes, A., Usunier, N., Garcia-Duran, A., Weston, J., Yakhnenko, O.: Translating embeddings for modeling multi-relational data. In: Advances in Neural Information Processing Systems, pp. 2787–2795 (2013)
4. Bordes, A., Weston, J., Collobert, R., Bengio, Y., et al.: Learning structured embeddings of knowledge bases. In: AAAI, vol. 6, p. 6 (2011)
5. Cantador, I., Brusilovsky, P., Kuflik, T.: 2nd workshop on information heterogeneity and fusion in recommender systems (HetRec 2011). In: Proceedings of the 5th ACM Conference on Recommender Systems, RecSys 2011. ACM, New York (2011)
6. Catherine, R., Cohen, W.: Personalized recommendations using knowledge graphs: a probabilistic logic programming approach. In: Proceedings of the 10th ACM Conference on Recommender Systems, pp. 325–332. ACM (2016)
7. Cremonesi, P., Koren, Y., Turrin, R.: Performance of recommender algorithms on top-n recommendation tasks. In: Proceedings of the Fourth ACM Conference on Recommender Systems, pp. 39–46. ACM (2010)
8. Ge, M., Delgado-Battenfeld, C., Jannach, D.: Beyond accuracy: evaluating recommender systems by coverage and serendipity. In: Proceedings of the Fourth ACM Conference on Recommender Systems, pp. 257–260. ACM Press (2010)
9. de Gemmis, M., Lops, P., Semeraro, G., Musto, C.: An investigation on the serendipity problem in recommender systems. Inf. Process. Manag. **51**(5), 695–717 (2015)
10. Grover, A., Leskovec, J.: node2vec: scalable feature learning for networks. In: Proceedings of the 22nd ACM SIGKDD International Conference on Knowledge Discovery and Data Mining, pp. 855–864. ACM (2016)
11. Harper, F.M., Konstan, J.A.: The movielens datasets: history and context. ACM Trans. Interact. Intell. Syst. (TiiS) **5**(4), 19 (2016)

12. Koren, Y., Bell, R., Volinsky, C.: Matrix factorization techniques for recommender systems. Computer **42**(8), 30–37 (2009)
13. Lin, Y., Liu, Z., Sun, M., Liu, Y., Zhu, X.: Learning entity and relation embeddings for knowledge graph completion. In: AAAI, vol. 15, pp. 2181–2187 (2015)
14. Nickel, M., Murphy, K., Tresp, V., Gabrilovich, E.: A review of relational machine learning for knowledge graphs. Proc. IEEE **104**(1), 11–33 (2016)
15. Nickel, M., Tresp, V., Kriegel, H.P.: A three-way model for collective learning on multi-relational data. In: ICML, vol. 11, pp. 809–816 (2011)
16. Noia, T.D., Ostuni, V.C., Tomeo, P., Sciascio, E.D.: Sprank: semantic path-based ranking for top-n recommendations using linked open data. ACM Trans. Intell. Syst. Technol. (TIST) **8**(1), 9 (2016)
17. Ostuni, V.C., Di Noia, T., Di Sciascio, E., Mirizzi, R.: Top-n recommendations from implicit feedback leveraging linked open data. In: Proceedings of the 7th ACM Conference on Recommender Systems, pp. 85–92. ACM (2013)
18. Palumbo, E., Rizzo, G., Troncy, R.: entity2rec: learning user-item relatedness from knowledge graphs for top-n item recommendation. In: Proceedings of the Eleventh ACM Conference on Recommender Systems, pp. 32–36. ACM (2017)
19. Rosati, J., Ristoski, P., Di Noia, T., Leone, R.d., Paulheim, H.: RDF graph embeddings for content-based recommender systems. In: CEUR Workshop Proceedings, vol. 1673, pp. 23–30. RWTH (2016)
20. Socher, R., Chen, D., Manning, C.D., Ng, A.: Reasoning with neural tensor networks for knowledge base completion. In: Advances in Neural Information Processing Systems, pp. 926–934 (2013)
21. Steck, H.: Evaluation of recommendations: rating-prediction and ranking. In: Proceedings of the 7th ACM Conference on Recommender Systems, pp. 213–220. ACM (2013)
22. Wang, Q., Mao, Z., Wang, B., Guo, L.: Knowledge graph embedding: a survey of approaches and applications. IEEE Trans. Knowl. Data Eng. **29**(12), 2724–2743 (2017)
23. Wang, Z., Zhang, J., Feng, J., Chen, Z.: Knowledge graph embedding by translating on hyperplanes. In: AAAI, vol. 14, pp. 1112–1119 (2014)
24. Yu, X., et al.: Personalized entity recommendation: a heterogeneous information network approach. In: Proceedings of the 7th ACM International Conference on Web Search and Data Mining, pp. 283–292. ACM (2014)
25. Zhang, F., Yuan, N.J., Lian, D., Xie, X., Ma, W.Y.: Collaborative knowledge base embedding for recommender systems. In: Proceedings of the 22nd ACM SIGKDD International Conference on Knowledge Discovery and Data Mining, pp. 353–362. ACM (2016)

Correction to: Ontology ABox Comparison

Jan Martin Keil

Correction to:
Chapter "Ontology ABox Comparison" in: A. Gangemi et al.
(Eds.): *The Semantic Web: ESWC 2018 Satellite Events*,
LNCS 11155, https://doi.org/10.1007/978-3-319-98192-5_43

Chapter, ["Ontology ABox Comparison"] was previously published non-open access. It has now been changed to open access under a CC BY 4.0 license and the copyright holder updated to 'The Author(s)'. The book has also been updated with this change.

The updated original version of this chapter can be found at
https://doi.org/10.1007/978-3-319-98192-5_43

A. Gangemi et al. (Eds.): ESWC 2018 Satellite Events, LNCS 11155, p. C1, 2023.
https://doi.org/10.1007/978-3-319-98192-5_62

Author Index

Printed in the United States
by Baker & Taylor Publisher Services